PERSONAL GENOME MEDICINE

In the years following FDA approval of direct-to-consumer, genetic-health-risk/ DTCGHR testing, millions of people in the US have sent their DNA to companies to receive personal genome health risk information without physician or other learned medical professional involvement. In *Personal Genome Medicine*, Michael J. Malinowski examines the ethical, legal, and social implications of this development. Drawing from the past and present of medicine in the US, Malinowski applies law, policy, public and private sector practices, and governing norms to analyze the commercial personal genome sequencing and testing sectors and to assess their impact on the future of US medicine. Written in relatable and accessible language, the book also proposes regulatory reforms for government and medical professionals that will enable technological advancements while maintaining personal and public health standards.

Michael J. Malinowski is the Ernest R. and Iris M. Eldred Endowed Professor of Law and the Lawrence B. Sandoz Jr. Endowed Professor of Law at the Paul M. Hebert Law Center, Louisiana State University. He has published extensively on biotechnology research and development/R&D, health care, and bioethics.

Personal Genome Medicine

THE LEGAL AND REGULATORY TRANSFORMATION OF US MEDICINE

MICHAEL J. MALINOWSKI
Louisiana State University

Shaftesbury Road, Cambridge CB2 8EA, United Kingdom

One Liberty Plaza, 20th Floor, New York, NY 10006, USA

477 Williamstown Road, Port Melbourne, VIC 3207, Australia

314–321, 3rd Floor, Plot 3, Splendor Forum, Jasola District Centre, New Delhi – 110025, India

103 Penang Road, #05–06/07, Visioncrest Commercial, Singapore 238467

Cambridge University Press is part of Cambridge University Press & Assessment,
a department of the University of Cambridge.

We share the University's mission to contribute to society through the pursuit of
education, learning and research at the highest international levels of excellence.

www.cambridge.org
Information on this title: www.cambridge.org/9781009293327

DOI: 10.1017/9781009293341

First published 2023

A catalogue record for this publication is available from the British Library

A Cataloging-in-Publication data record for this book is available from the Library of Congress

ISBN 978-1-009-29332-7 Hardback
ISBN 978-1-009-29336-5 Paperback

This book is dedicated to the real-time pursuit of evidentiary science-based truth in patient clinical care – to the practice of responsible medicine, including personal genome medicine.

Contents

Reader's Note

The overarching focus of this book is US medicine. For clarity, given the mixed science research and clinical care content, the use of the title "Dr." is generally limited throughout to distinguish persons with medical doctorates/MDs. This book went into production in fall 2022, and the manuscript was updated throughout 2022. Changes thereafter are not necessarily reflected.

Acknowledgments

This project was built from myriad sources drawn from multiple disciplines. The authors and originators of the sources I reference enabled my effort – literally made this book possible, as evident in the citations to them. Thank you. I humbly hope to pay it forward with *Personal Genome Medicine*.

Throughout my career, from my first serious scholarly study of US health care some three decades ago, Paul Starr's *Social Transformation of American Medicine* (1984) has been my professional Bible. Often, when grappling with contemporary US health-care issues, understanding the past, so beautifully and scholarly chronicled in *Social Transformation*, has provided understanding and triggered epiphanies for the present and future. Paul Starr, my sincere, career-encompassing appreciation to you.

This undertaking has been life *all-consuming* for over three years. Dr. Grant G. Gautreaux, thank you for reading every page of the first full working draft as each chapter came to fruition. Your input was invaluable. Your support and patience were even more invaluable. You renewed my determination many times when I was completely spent and beyond discouraged. *We* researched, wrote, endlessly self-edited, and endured this undertaking because I could not have done it without you.

Professor Darlene Goring and Interim Dean Lee Ann Lockridge, my LSU Law Center colleagues, you recognized the scholarly importance of this project without pause and my personal commitment to it. You supported both. Thank you.

My appreciation also to the Cambridge University Press/CUP editorial and production team, Matt Gallaway, Jessica Norman, Jadyn Fauconier-Herry, and Snadha Sureshbabu. When fully consumed and overwhelmed by this project, my unmet expectations were unrealistic – bordering on best-selling author expectations for a major popular press. Instead, you gave me academic and intellectual freedom, trusted me with the content, and showed deference to my writing. You gave me *a lot*. Also, Grace Annie Chintoh, thank you for being my research assistant during your year of studies at LSU when your time was so precious.

Prologue

Revolution, Transition, and Transformation

On May 31, 2007, at a ceremony in Houston, Texas, biotechnology scientist and entrepreneur Jonathan Rothberg handed a hard drive tied with a simple red ribbon to James Watson – a Nobel Laureate for co-discovering the double-helix structure of DNA, and the chief architect of the Human Genome Project/HGP.[1] When Watson accepted that hard drive in the palm of his hand, he became "the first of the rest of us" to receive the DNA sequence of his entire personal genome.[2]

Rothberg's company, 454 Life Sciences, sequenced Watson's genome in collaboration with Dr. Richard Gibbs, Director of the Human Genome Sequencing Center at the Baylor College of Medicine. They used the first "next-generation sequencing"/NGS technology – DNA speed-reading technology with the potential to impact genome analysis the way microprocessors enabled computing beginning in the 1960s.[3] A handful of scientists accomplished this feat in four months and at a cost of less than $1.5 million.[4] In comparison, the draft human genome sequence completed in 2003 through HGP – our genetic common denominator drawn from several individuals' genomes – was a global undertaking compiled through the concerted efforts of more than a thousand researchers across six nations, took approximately thirteen years to complete, and consumed $2.7 billion (FY1991 dollars) in US government funding alone.[5]

Genomic sequencing capacity has continued to soar and its cost to plummet by multiples in the years since Dr. Watson was handed his personal genome sequence. Rothberg predicted then that "sequencing throughput would grow at least fivefold over the coming years ...."[6] His prediction was realized, as graphed by the National Human Genome Research Institute/NHGRI:[7]

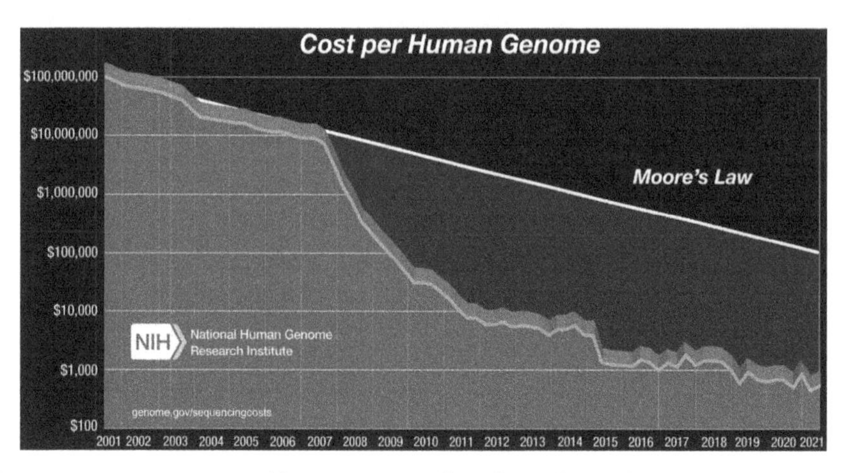

Source: www.genome.gov/about-genomics/fact-sheets/DNA-Sequencing-Costs-Data

Moreover, "Innovation in genome-sequencing technologies and strategies does not appear to be slowing."[8] The National Academies of Science, Engineering, and Medicine/NASEM recognized the same in 2017 after comprehensively surveying the biotechnology landscape spanning into a ten-year horizon.[9]

At the time the Houston ceremony took place (2007), leaders in the field gauged the threshold price for critical mass consumer consumption of whole genome sequencing at $1,000. "[T]he figure emerged as a mythic technological totem in the world of genetics, sending a generation of DNA geeks chasing after it for the better part of the 21st century."[10] Illumina, Inc. and Veritas Genetics reached that $1,000 price point in 2014, Veritas began selling consumers their full personal genome sequences for $999 in 2016, and other companies followed.[11] By 2018, more than a million people had purchased their whole genome sequences.[12] Subsequently, the science community's quest shifted from realizing the $1,000 personal genome to realizing the $100.00 or less personal genome, sequenced within minutes with extreme precision through dozens of proofing runs, and by standalone computer hardware that fits comfortably on the corner of a desk – "in the not-too-distant future."[13]

The ability to generate medical meaning from sequenced DNA – the overarching, long-term mission of HGP, Watson, Rothberg, their science contemporaries and progeny, and now millions in the biopharmaceutical ("biopharma"), medical, and patient communities – is amassing along with the advancement of sequencing technologies.[14] With completion of a draft sequence of the human genome came the epiphany that, not only are we are 99.9 percent the same genetically (all of our genetic variation is attributable to one-tenth of one percent of human DNA), but our genetic variation is attributable to a currently estimated 20,500 active (protein-coding) genes.[15] Yet, the scope of tangible, observable human variation – from physical differences to the occurrence of diseases, to responsiveness to prescription biopharmaceuticals, and well beyond – remains very real. Genes multi-task exponentially more than anticipated prior to HGP, and perspective about gene function has shifted. Scientists have a significantly heightened appreciation for the dynamism of genetics, the intricacies of genetic expression, and ongoing, pervasive interactions among genes, proteins, and environmental influences, as well as gene interactions with each other.[16] Genes multitask – often dizzyingly so. Throughout our lives, each of us is a simmering, swirling pot of genomic gumbo, with constantly changing conditions and ingredients (environmental influences) added continuously.

Given this level of genetic intricacy, complexity, and dynamism, DNA samples and accompanying medical information – typically, voluminous amounts of both – are the means to make medical and clinical sense out of the human genome. As explained by Eric Lander, a trailblazer in the DNA sequencing world who joined forces with Dr. Francis Collins in the US government effort to map the human genome, "You have to compare genomes to learn anything … maybe between dozens or hundreds or of people with a disease or without a disease."[17] In fact, gathering accurate, reliable personal health and lifestyle data is the primary challenge for human health application. As Anne Wojcicki, co-founder and CEO of 23andMe, the seminal direct-to-consumer/DTC personal genome health services/PGHS company, relayed to researchers during an event on the company's campus in May 2019, "Anyone can go get genomes. What's really hard is phenotypic [observable characteristics resulting from interaction between one's genotype and environment] data."[18] Managing voluminous phenotypic data poses another daunting challenge. According to Sean Harper, Amgen's executive vice president for research and development/R&D, Amgen invested more than a billion dollars over nearly two decades to develop the capability to routinely extract data necessary to validate and invalidate drug targets, but "The hard part is to get all these medical records and lab tests curated in a computer system where they are query-able and to perfect the analytics."[19]

As you read this sentence, legions of scientists around the world are translating the human genome's three billion nucleotide base pairs (the "As, Cs, Gs, and Ts" for the compounds adenine, cytosine, guanine, and thymine) into the medical meaning necessary for precision medicine (treatments tailored to a person's genome) and personalized medicine (treatments derived from a person's genome). They are working at an ever-quickening pace.[20] For example, the ongoing Personal Genome Project/PGP, initiated in 2005, embodies a "coalition of projects across the world dedicated to creating public genome, health, and trait data."[21] The PGP global network of participants includes Harvard PGP, PGP Canada, PGP UK, Genom Austria, and PGP China.[22]

Governments, industry, and academia have been gathering the DNA samples and related health information needed for translation for some time, on a constantly widening scale and with increasing intensity. The business of biobanking – the organized, typically large-scale ("population genetics" and "population genomics") collection of DNA samples and associated medical information – has matured into a multifaceted, diverse, and global endeavor.[23]

The US government is an ambitious biobanker.[24] The Department of Veteran Affairs has been building the Million Veteran Program/MVP since 2011 and, as of 2019, had recruited 650,000 veterans and collected years of their medical records, including physician prescription data.[25] The US also launched the Precision Medicine Initiative/PMI in 2015, renamed the All of Us Research Program ("AllUs") in 2016, with $130 million allocated to NIH to build a national cohort of research participants, and $70 million allocated to the National Cancer Institute for genomics (the study of gene function in the context of a genome, which is an organism's complete set of genes) in oncology through the Center for Cancer Genomics/CCG. AllUs is a NIH undertaking to recruit a cohort of a million or more residents in the US representative of the nation's population diversity.[26] AllUs participants agree to give blood samples, to have their genomes sequenced, to provide medical and lifestyle information and, potentially, to wear devices to continuously track their vital signs and monitor their physical activity. The goal of the program is that, "[b]y taking into account individual differences in lifestyle, environment, and biology, researchers will uncover paths toward delivering precision medicine."[27] Congress budgeted $230 million for AllUs in 2017 and, on a scale somewhat comparable with HGP ($3 billion spread over fifteen years) given the advancement of related technologies (notably, next-generation sequencing/NGS) and genomics since HGP was launched in 1990, authorized $1.455 billion over ten years. Reminiscent of HGP and the Manhattan Project during WWII, AllUs "has contracted with scientists at just about every leading university, as well as with companies like Verily, a subsidiary of Alphabet Inc. – the conglomerate parent of Google."[28]

Several US-based for-profit companies also are major biobankers, including Amgen Inc. – a 1980 California start-up that ranked 129 on the 2019 (prior to the COVID-19 pandemic declaration) Fortune 500 List.[29] In 2012, Amgen purchased deCODE Genetics, Inc., the holder of a biobank of DNA samples and substantial medical information inclusive of approximately 160,000 Icelanders – nearly half of the island nation's entire population – for $415 million.[30] Regeneron Pharmaceuticals, Inc., another leading US biotech company, established The Regeneron Genetics Center®/RGC, which is a genomics "big data" enabling technology provider engaged in multiple biobanking efforts, both public and private. For example, RGC is the catalyst for a consortium among AbbVie, Alnylam Pharmaceuticals, AstraZeneca, Biogen, and Pfizer to accelerate drug R&D by mining genomic sequence data and medical information from the UK Biobank's 500,000 participants.[31] Kaiser Permanente and Geisinger Health Systems/GHS, two large US health care providers with direct access to vast cohorts of patients and their medical information, also are engaged in large-scale biobanking.[32]

The fusion of genomic sequencing technologies and the phenotypic riches of biobank data generates genetic testing capabilities with predictive health implications, which is commonly referred to as "genetic wellness" and "genetic health risk/GHR" testing.[33] The commercial sector providing consumers with these personal genome testing services is burgeoning economically and transforming culture, medicine, and health care.[34] Even with DNA sequencing costs plummeting as capacity soars (more testing potentially available to consumers at declining prices from the same DNA sample), the global genetic testing and consumer wellness genomic market, valued at $2.24 billion in 2015, has been projected to double by 2025.[35]

On April 6, 2017, the US Food and Drug Administration/FDA granted an application submitted by 23andMe to market a portfolio of direct-to-consumer, genetic-health risk/DTCGHR testing services, which included genetic markers for Alzheimer's Disease and Parkinson's Disease.[36] 23andMe's DTCGHR testing is offered to consumers through its Personal Genome Health Service/PGHS, which makes physician and other learned medical professional involvement wholly consumer optional.[37] Under the 23andMe business model for DTCGHR testing, individuals purchase kits, send their DNA to the company through the mail, and access their personal GHR information through an internet portal without any requisite physician or other learned medical professional involvement. Subsequently, millions of consumers have embraced the opportunity to take genome science and its medical interpretation into their own hands – to delve into their personal genomes for health decision-making – and demand is on the rise.[38] Consumers, investors, the FDA, and biopharma collaborators have proven responsive to 23andMe. As of July 2018 (less than fifteen months after the FDA approved the company's first physician-free DTCGHR tests), some five million people had purchased kits from and submitted their saliva to 23andMe for GHR testing.[39] 23andMe became a flagship company in a robustly emerging DTC personal genome testing global sector:

> Equity firms are pouring fortunes into these companies, not just because of the testing kits they sell but the personal information they collect, which can be shared and monetized. It's all happening amid a patchwork of laws and regulations that predate the growth of direct-to-consumer DNA testing.[40]

On June 17, 2021, through a merger, 23andMe was renamed 23andMe Holding Co. and became publicly traded on NASDAQ.[41] On November 1, 2021, 23andMe Holding acquired Lemonaid Health, a national telemedicine and digital pharmacy company, to overcome physician skepticism and uncertainty about its PGHS reports and, on August 9, 2022, the company declared "expan[sion] beyond its core consumer genetic testing into a new business line called its genomic health service."[42]

The FDA's market approval of DTCGHR testing without requisite medical professional involvement, beyond a milestone for 23andMe and its investors, was a rite of passage in an ongoing transition in the practice of US medicine – a transition to personal genome medicine/PGM that predates and will transcend the FDA's 2017 DTCGHR decision by decades.[43] Revolutions triggered by scientific advancements, such as the biotech revolution that began in the 1980s and the information and communication technology/ICT revolution that began in the 1990s (merger of the two and the advancement of DNA sequencing technologies seeded a genomic revolution and advanced personal genome testing and genomic medicine), cause seismic change with momentum to continue over time.[44] US enactment of technology transfer law and policy/TTLP in 1980 incentivized collaboration and responsiveness to biotech R&D among government, academia, industry, and investors.[45] In fact, TTLP motivated a genomic revolution that rages on and into clinical medicine.[46] The creation of vaccines to protect against COVID-19 and the development of CRISPR technologies – a gene editing toolbox of technologies that already includes some that are surprisingly user-friendly – are the latest phase in this innovation revolution and mark the beginning of the next one.[47] The ICT revolution of the 1990s was triggered by the convergence of explosive scientific advances in digital computing and telecommunications.[48] ICT technologies/ICTs fundamentally changed how people, businesses, and governments communicate, interact, and work.[49] Human health transitions brought about by the application of scientific innovation, such as doubling the average human lifespan between 1920 and 2020, are the culmination of incremental changes over time.[50] The net effect of both revolutions and transitions brought about by scientific innovation is transformation with ethical, legal, and social implications. The architects of HGP recognized as much and complemented mapping the human genome with an Ethical, Legal, and Social Implications/ELSI Research Program counterpart to HGP.[51]

The US medical profession and the practice of medicine have undergone several defining transitions during their evolution since the late nineteenth century, which have proven transformative.[52] At the turn of the twentieth century, an apprenticeship-based profession formalized itself through requisite, standardized medical education with a clinical component, licensure, and credentialing, and became recognized and esteemed as a learned profession.[53] The medical profession assumed the role of sentinel over the science and evidence base of US medicine, earned deference and trust in that role, and became a self-regulating profession devoted to protecting and promoting the practice of medicine and individualized patient care.[54] The sanctity of the doctor–patient relationship became recognized and respected, with medical provider commitment to individualized patient care.

The infusion of medical science advancements during the twentieth century that improved human health substantially fortified the medical profession's influence and sovereignty; the profession became the trusted conduit for responsible clinical uptake of science innovation.[55] The doctor–patient relationship became a sanctified domain for individualized patient care dominated by learned and licensed medical professionals.[56] Beginning in the 1980s, the proliferation of managed care and the biotech revolution integrated government, academia, and industry in both science and medicine.[57] The reach of the World Wide Web and the consumer availability of personal computers enabled internet communication and networking during the 1990s, which fueled a global ICT revolution that permeated government, business, society, and culture.[58] By the end of the millennium, a social media movement was amassing and drawing in generations from Millennials (born from 1981 to 1996) to Baby Boomers (born from 1946 to 1964).[59] Generation Z ("Zoomers" born from the mid-1990s into this millennium) gained awareness with ICT and social media – information and communication readily accessible through the strokes of computer keys and mobile phone keypads – as norms. Medical professional filters no longer restrained the flow of science and medical information. The culmination of these forces inspired a participatory health movement fueled by DTC biopharma marketing and internet access to science and medical information, which gained momentum in this millennium and now embraces DTC personal genome testing, personal genome autonomy, and patient self-determination.[60]

Extensive media coverage of the HGP and DNA in the years leading to the project's completion of a draft human genome sequence in 2003 and the subsequent infusion of tangible clinical applications of genomic medicine, such as elevated precision medicine and personalized medicine including life-saving oncology immunotherapies, have changed public perception of genetic testing.[61] Apprehension about commercial DTC genetic testing services for BRCA1 and BRCA2 (genetic variations, or alleles, associated with breast and other cancers) introduced in 1996 inspired forty-four states to enact legislation addressing genetic privacy, genetic discrimination, or some combination of the two by early 1999.[62] By 2010, US law and policy established federal medical privacy rights and barred genetic discrimination and health insurers from considering preexisting conditions, which quelled anxieties about genetic information prevalent in the 1990s.[63] Familiarity with DNA conceptually and experientially made DTC genetic testing much more comfortable. Recreational genetics for ancestry was socially and culturally popular early in this millennium, which incentivized US corporate and consumer citizens to undertake DTCGHR testing.[64] As observed by James Watson, "DNA has moved from being an esoteric molecule of interest to only a handful of specialists to being the heart of a technology that is transforming many aspects of the way we all live."[65] "It's in my DNA" is an often-used colloquialism, DNA ancestry kits have been one of the "it" gifts for years (Christmas, Mother's Day, Father's Day, and just because), and now there is the option of adding GHR information.[66] Media coverage of science responsiveness to the COVID-19 pandemic has further familiarized and normalized DNA and genomics in US perception and culture.

23andMe's Anne Wojcicki envisions that personal genome technology will transform health care. In her words, "The mission of 23andMe is not just about genetics. We have research, and again, all of that which is already a big mission, but we really want to transform health care."[67] 23andMe's mission is to empower individuals to exert unprecedented control over their health care through DTCGHR testing, and to realize consumer-centric personal genome medicine/PGM. Wojcicki, Watson, and numerous other influencers in genomics anticipate a health care system in which individuals bring their personal genome data to physicians and other medical professionals at their discretion to enable them to make their own health care decisions.[68] Our entire personal genome sequences already are available for purchase at a price point manageable for many millions of consumers.[69] It is inevitable that we each will have increasing access to our personal genomes and related health information – to insights pulled from the pages of our present and "future medical diaries."[70] James Watson predicts that "The future will surely be one of ubiquitous genomics and real-time information that will transform public health and individual medical treatment."[71]

Expansion of the genetic health testing portfolio available to individuals – whether the testing is clinically and medically decisive, interpretive, or speculative – is opportunity for each of us to learn more about our personal genomes, to increase our medical autonomy, and to take more control over our health and health care. PGM *will* transform US medicine and our health care system. The core question is not whether, but *how* we make this transition and realize the PGM transformation. The sentiment of Watson, shared by Wojcicki and many now working at the forefront of PGM, is that "It cannot come too soon."[72] In fact, it can if clinically sound, responsible science and evidence-based medicine is undermined during the transition to PGM to the detriment of patient health and the practice of medicine.

Law is a discipline that defers to, protects, and builds upon precedent, and deference to the past is readily apparent in US regulation of the practice of medicine. The US federal government, including the FDA, restrains from intruding on the practice of medicine and doctor-patient decision-making – as recognized under US law for over a century. In 1925, the Supreme Court held that, "[o]bviously, direct control of medical practice in the States is beyond the power of the Federal Government."[73] The medical profession's sovereignty is illustrated vividly in physician discretion to prescribe FDA-approved drugs off-label, meaning independent of the clinical data relied upon by the FDA to put them on the market, and the extent to which US physicians exercise that discretion.[74] Consider physician opioid prescribing practices well beyond the scope of the FDA's approved use and the conditions the agency imposed through labeling, product inserts, guidance documents, and warnings during the approximately fifteen-year escalation of the nation's opioid addiction problem into an undeniable public health emergency.[75] The US' learned physicians proved extraordinarily susceptible to fraudulent industry marketing.[76] They wrote prescriptions for opioids that enabled the epidemic as they directly witnessed it build well over a decade, patient-by-patient, within the sanctity of their doctor–patient relationships and individualized patient care.[77]

Twentieth-century reliance on the medical profession, physician–patient decision-making, and the FDA to protect patients and to ensure sound science and evidence-based medicine is misplaced in twenty-first-century US health care. While most of the medical profession's midcentury predecessors were independent solo practitioners whom patients often compensated out of their pockets, today's physicians are accountable to businesses and health care networks under pressure to be cost-effective and profitable.[78] Patients, "informed" through DTC biopharma marketing, their internet searches, and social media are often demanding consumers of physician services.[79] US law remains deferential to the sanctity of the doctor–patient relationship and individualized patient care, but the learned professionals in those relationships, unlike their last-century predecessors, are subject to the demands of "self-learned" patient consumers.[80]

US medical profession adherence to science and evidence-based clinical practice as the epicenter of good medicine, which became the primary catalyst for the evolution of both the medical profession and the practice of medicine during the twentieth century, is even more essential in PGM.[81] The scope of PGM spans the human genome and is all-inclusive of human health, and genomics is an ongoing deluge of dynamic science innovation in real time with dimensions of complexity.[82] "[T]aken together, the relations of genes, organisms, and environments are reciprocal relations in which all three elements are both causes and effects."[83] Genomics with adherence to evidentiary science-based medicine has been the means to counter the ongoing global COVID-19 pandemic – the deadliest pandemic in over a century, and the cause of global social and economic disruption, including the largest global recession since the Great Depression.[84] The unabashed politicization of science by the Trump Administration during the COVID-19 pandemic made the vulnerability of the science and evidence base of medicine all too vivid.[85]

Today's medical profession has far less control over the evidentiary-science base of medicine and industry has much more.[86] The primary mechanisms relied upon by the medical profession to protect the base of medicine are ongoing, rigorous scrutiny and uptake of medical science innovation through peer-reviewed medical journals (the "medical journal establishment/MJE") and control of the content and quality of ongoing medical education by the profession's most preeminent.[87] Although the overwhelming complexity of contemporary medical science has increased dependency on the MJE and esteemed medical profession influencers, these mechanisms have lost much of their reliable objectivity.[88] The biopharma industry finances and controls clinical research, which is the content fodder for the MJE.[89] Today's MJE is financially dependent on biopharma advertising, sponsorship, and reprint purchases for distribution to those who provide clinical care to incentivize use, including off label uses.[90] At the outset of this millennium, the MJE self-acknowledged its unreliability on its own pages:

> In September 2001 an unprecedented alarm was sounded. The editors of 12 of the world's most influential medical journals, including the *Journal of the American Medical Association*, the *New England Journal of Medicine*, *The Lancet*, and the *Annals of Internal Medicine*, issued an extraordinary joint statement in their publications. In words that should have shaken the medical profession to its core, the statement told of "draconian" terms being imposed on medical researchers by corporate sponsors. And it warned that the "precious objectivity" of the clinical studies that were being published in their journals was being threatened by the transformation of clinical research into a commercial activity.
>
> The editors said that the use of commercially sponsored clinical trials "primarily for marketing ... makes a mockery of clinical investigation and is misuse of a

powerful tool." Medical scientists working on corporate-sponsored research, the editors warned, "may have little or no input into trial design, no access to the raw data, and limited participation in data interpretation."[91]

The integration of academia, industry, and government through TTLP introduced in 1980, which enabled the genomic revolution and development of novel mRNA COVID-19 vaccines in a year, is prevalent in both clinical research and clinical care. Interactions between industry and renowned influencers in science and medicine are commonplace, and the biopharma sector is a generous sponsor of research studies, consulting agreements, speaking engagement honoraria, and continuing medical education/CME.[92] The biopharma sector also invests heavily in direct-to-physician/DTP marketing – a practice welcomed under US law and policy, which recognizes biopharma DTP and DTC marketing as corporate free speech and continues to entrust the medical profession to protect and promote the evidentiary-science base of medicine with adherence to objective truth as it did throughout the twentieth century.[93]

The FDA, a government entity with all the associated political and budgeting vulnerabilities, must endure the full R&D impact of the genomic revolution by its regulatory charge and very existence. The agency, which is the *recipient* of corporate citizen-sponsored applications and associated data, has become financially dependent on the biopharma industry to accomplish its mission since the introduction of user fees under the Prescription Drug User Fee Act/PDUFA of 1992.[94] The agency has actively collaborated with industry since enactment of the Food and Drug Administration Modernization Act/FDAMA and PDUFA renewal/PDUFA II in 1997, as it was mandated to do.[95] FDAMA and PDUFA II imposed heightened regulatory transparency and accountability on the FDA and changed the agency's culture by expanding its mission to include efficiency, along with product safety and efficacy, to be accomplished through heightened responsiveness to industry, patient, and provider ("stakeholder") concerns about its timeliness.[96] Prohibited from interfering with the practice of medicine, the FDA is under a constant barrage of criticism from multiple industry sectors, patient advocates, the medical profession, influencers in academia (the disciplines of medicine, public health, science, business, and beyond), the media, and the public for allegedly impeding the availability of innovative new products with life, death, and overall human health consequences.[97]

Traditional US reliance on its medical profession to ensure science and evidence-based, responsible medicine without more federal government involvement is antiquated and misplaced in consumer-centric PGM.[98] The advent of FDA-approved DTCGHR testing with any learned medical professional involvement wholly consumer optional is a tangible indicator of the need to question the reliability of US regulation of medicine during this phase of the genomic revolution and into the foreseeable future. Overall, GHR tests are distinguishable clinically from other categories of medical device diagnostics due to the information they relay about susceptibility to non-onset medical conditions and the complexity and dynamism of genetic influences on human health.[99] The intricacies of genomics make for extraordinarily complicated medical science, amassed in probabilities and possibilities subject to the dynamism of expansive, ongoing research across the human genome.

Genomics, given its reach into human health, is just coming into being in responsible clinical care.[100] The clinically sound personal genome testing already available is an extraordinarily varied, dynamic, and rapidly building portfolio of testing capabilities, which overall are far less definitive and tangible than traditional medical testing – for both patients and medical providers.[101] Genomics imposes a tremendous burden on clinicians to size up each personal genome test from a research perspective for each patient, especially given research inconsistencies among them and the ongoing, real-time data nature of genomics.[102] The burden on clinicians to then communicate (translate) the same to individual patients who are not learned in science and medicine but who are often "internet self-learned" is daunting.[103] Moreover, any personal genome test result is only as reliable as the test itself and how it is performed, and the US has no reliable oversight of the vast, varied commercial landscape populated by DTC personal genome testing providers.[104] The potential personal genome testing universe beyond the filter of established clinical standards for predictability, validity, and utility is infinite. Imagine the burden and risk of potential liability when patients present US medical professionals with their entire personal genome sequence.[105]

The dawn of wholly DTCGHR testing services, the proliferation of DTC genetic and proteomic (protein function in the context of an entire set of proteins within a genome at a given time, known as a proteome) testing, and increasing realization of PGM demand reflection and evaluation of the reliability of traditional good medicine norms and mechanisms to protect patients and medicine. The foundation of good medicine, its evidentiary-science base, must be reinforced to position the US to embrace the infusion of genomics in a manner aligned with contemporary culture, medicine, and health care. Only then may the US undergo the health care transformation Ms. Wojcicki envisions in tandem with twenty-first-century assurances of science and evidence-based, responsible clinical practice, patient protection, and the advancement of human health. Adherence to science and evidence-based medicine is synonymous with fully realizing the health care autonomy and human health potential gifted through the progress of genomic science and the evolution of PGM.

NOTES

1 *See generally* James D. Watson, The Double Helix: A Personal Account of the Discovery of the Structure of DNA (2001).

2 Meredith Wadman, *James Watson's Genome Sequenced at High Speed: New-generation Technology Takes Just Four Months and Costs a Fraction of Old Method*, 452 Nature 788, 788 (Apr. 16, 2008) (quoting Jonathan Rothberg), www.nature.com/news/2008/080416/full/452788b.html. *See* James D. Watson, DNA: The Story of the Genetic Revolution 195–202 (2nd ed., 2017) (with Andrew Berry, Kevin Davies) (updated commemoration of the fiftieth anniversary of the discovery of the double helix). *See also* National Human Genome Research Institute/NHGRI, *Human Genome Research Project*

FAQ (updated Nov. 12, 2018), www.genome.gov/human-genome-project/Completion-FAQ; Nicholas Wade, *Genome of DNA Pioneer Is Deciphered*, N.Y. TIMES (May 31, 2007), www.nytimes.com/2007/05/31/science/31cnd-gene.html.

3 *See generally* PAUL E. CERUZZI, COMPUTING: A CONCISE HISTORY (2012) (The MIT Press Essential Knowledge series).

4 *See generally* Wadman, *Watson's Genome*, *supra* note 2.

5 *See* KEVIN DAVIES, $1,000 GENOME: THE REVOLUTION IN DNA SEQUENCING AND THE NEW ERA OF PERSONALIZED MEDICINE 15–29 (2010); President William Jefferson Clinton, *Remarks on the Completion of the First Survey of the Entire Human Genome Project* (June 26, 2000), www.genome.gov/10001356; Wadman, *Watson's Genome*, *supra* note 2, at 788. The US government HGP team and a competing privately funded effort jointly announced completion of a *preliminary* rough draft of the HGP sequence in 2000, which they released in 2001. *See generally* 291 SCIENCE 1145 (Feb. 16, 2001) (issue entitled "The Human Genome"); 409 NATURE 745 (Feb. 15, 2001) (issue entitled "Information about the Human Genome Project" dedicated to the release of a preliminary draft of the human genome sequence). *See generally also* GEORGINA FERRY, JOHN SULSTON, THE COMMON THREAD: A STORY OF SCIENCE, POLITICS, ETHICS AND THE HUMAN GENOME (2002). HGP and its commercial competitor released a draft map of the human genome in April 2003. *See* Byjon Heggie, *Genomics: A Revolution in Health Care? Drugs Affect People Differently and We're Increasingly Understanding Why. For Many of Us, It's Down to Our Genes*, NAT'L GEO. (Feb. 20, 2019), www.nationalgeographic.com/science/article/partner-content-genomics-health-care. Subsequently, researchers worked to make corrections and to complete gaps in the draft sequence. *See infra* note 15. The National Human Genome Research Institute/NHGRI announced the first *complete* sequence of the human genome on March 31, 2022. *See* NHGRI, Prabarna Ganguly, Rachael Zisk, *Press Release, Researchers Generate the First Complete, Gapless Sequence of a Human Genome* (Mar. 31, 2022), www.genome.gov/news/news-release/researchers-generate-the-first-complete-gapless-sequence-of-a-human-genome.

6 DAVIES, $1,000 GENOME, *supra* note 5, at 29 ("The same way you saw your computers at WalMart for less than $1,000, you'll see the $1,000 genome.").

7 NIH, NHGRI, *Cost per Human Genome* (updated Nov. 1, 2021), www.genome.gov/about-genomics/fact-sheets/DNA-Sequencing-Costs-Data.

8 NIH, NHGRI, *The Cost of Sequencing a Human Genome* (last updated Dec. 7, 2020), www.genome.gov/about-genomics/fact-sheets/Sequencing-Human-Genome-cost. The dramatic 2008–2010 genome sequencing milestone vivid in NHGRI's graph reflects a fundamental, jolting technology advancement from Sanger sequencing, introduced in 1977 and the primary DNA sequencing method for 40 years, to next generation sequencing/NGS platforms. Rothberg and his colleagues used the first NGS platform to produce Dr. Watson's genome. *See id.*; WATSON, THE STORY, *supra* note 2, at 195–96. Kevin Davies, the founding editor of *Nature Genetics*, recognized the accomplishment and sequencing potential in 2010:

> [T]he cost of sequencing a human genome has plummeted from billions of dollars for the HGP to a couple of thousand dollars in 2010. That's a remarkable drop of a million-fold, or a factor of 10 every year, far outstripping Moore's law (Intel cofounder Gordon Moore's 1965 maxim that the density of transistors on a computer chip doubles every 18–24 months). And that's before a new wave of third-generation sequencing technologies emerge—machines and possibly even portable battery powered Tricorder-like devices that can sequence a human genome in fifteen minutes for $100.

DAVIES, $1,000 GENOME, *supra* note 5, at 13. *See also* Meg Tirrell, CNBC, *Genome Sequencing: A Glimpse of the Future* (Dec. 10, 2015), www.cnbc.com/2015/12/10/unlocking-my-genome-was-it-worth-it.html.

9 *See* US NATIONAL ACADEMIES OF SCIENCE, ENGINEERING, AND MEDICINE/NASEM, PREPARING FOR THE FUTURE PRODUCTS OF BIOTECHNOLOGY 28 (2017) (surveying the present and approaching wave of genomic innovation in medicine and commerce), www.nap.edu/catalog/24605/preparing-for-future-products-of-biotechnology.

10 Megan Molteni, *Now You Can Sequence Your Whole Genome for Just $200*, WIRED (Nov. 19, 2018), www.wired.com/story/whole-genome-sequencing-cost-200-dollars/. "[A] new movement was taking root committed to democratizing genomics and empowering consumers by providing them with personal genetic information, all for less than $1,000 – and a small sample of spit." DAVIES, $1,000.00 GENOME, *supra* note 5, at 29.

11 *See* DAVIES, $1,000.00 GENOME, *supra* note 5, at 29; WATSON, THE STORY, *supra* note 2, at 218, 224. Veritas offers consumers genome sequencing through its Whole Genome Sequencing/WGS and myGenome technologies. *See generally* Veritas, *Press Release, Veritas Genetics Launches Two New Whole Genome Sequencing Products*, CISION PR NEWSWIRE (Nov. 1, 2018), www.prnewswire.com/news-releases/veritas-genetics-launches-two-new-whole-genome-sequencing-products-300741689.html. Veritas began providing this service to consumers in 2016, though with their access conditioned on physician endorsement. *See* Molteni, *Whole Genome, supra* note 10. However, in the event of physician resistance, Veritas identified responsive physicians. *See id.* Trends and company business plans have shifted with advances in the relevant technologies since Dr. Watson was handed his DNA. *See generally* NIH, NHGRI, *Cost of Sequencing, supra* note 8; NHGRI, *Cost per Genome, supra* note 7. In February 2020, Nebula Genomics launched DTC whole genome sequencing for $299. *See* Laura Lovett, *Nebula Genomics launches $299 direct-to-consumer whole genome sequencing*, MOBIHEALTHNEWS (Feb. 18, 2020), www.mobihealthnews.com/news/nebula-genomics-launches-299-direct-consumer-whole-genome-sequencing.

12 *See* Molteni, *Whole Genome, supra* note 10. In comparison, at that time, an estimated 17 million consumers had purchased limited personal genome sequencing through 23andMe and Ancestry DTC genetic testing services. *See id.*

13 GATTACA (Sony Pictures, 1997) (depicting a society that has embraced genetic technology in human reproduction to control genetic variations and strengthen the human species). "In January 2017, Illumina's new CEO, Francis deSouza, unveiled his company's latest sequencer, the Nova Seq, which might deliver the $100 genome within a few years." WATSON, THE STORY, *supra* note 2, at 224. Biopharma business and science development plans vary from becoming a centralized sequencing service provider (like Google's role in IT) to creating portable hardware with the sequencing capabilities inclusive as depicted in the text, and combinations of the two. *See* DAVIES, $1,000 GENOME, *supra* note 5, at 79–101; WATSON, THE STORY, *supra* note 2, at 194–225.

14 *See generally* NHGRI, 2020 NHGRI STRATEGIC VISION: STRATEGIC VISION FOR IMPROVING HUMAN HEALTH AT THE FOREFRONT OF GENOMICS (2020), www.genome.gov/2020SV; WATSON, THE STORY, *supra* note 2; *Chapter 4, infra. See also* Francis S. Collins et al., *New Goals for the US Human Genome Project: 1998–2003*, 282 SCIENCE 682, 683 (1998) (addressing the HGP mission to improve the treatment and prevention of diseases through the development of effective genetic tests and therapies); Eric S. Lander, *Scientific Commentary: The Scientific Foundations and Medical and Social Prospects of the Human Genome Project*, 26 J.L. MED. & ETHICS 184, 184 (1998) (explaining HGP and the possibilities that arise with assembling the "human periodic table"). When handing Watson his digital personal genome sequence, Rothberg declared:

> This is the end of one quest—the dream to sequence a genome—and the beginning of another quest—to develop and perfect the methods to routinely sequence an individual's genome for $1,000 or less, and to learn precisely what the sequence of those billions of base pairs means for one's health behavior, and sense of self.

DAVIES, $1,000 GENOME, *supra* note 5, at 29.

15 *See* US Department of Energy Office of Science, Office of Biological and Environmental Research, *About the Human Genome Project* (last modified Mar. 26, 2019) ("The current consensus predicts about 20,500 genes, but this number has fluctuated a great deal since the project began."), https://web.ornl.gov/sci/techresources/Human_Genome/project/index.shtml. As relayed by James Watson in 2017, the NIH and its international counterparts, such as the international consortium GENCODE, continuously analyze and revise the human genome gene tally. "Their latest predictions for protein-coding genes range from 19,800 to 22,700 and average out at 21,035." WATSON, THE STORY, *supra* note 2, at 229. *See* Tirrell, *Glimpse*, *supra* note 8 ("It's in that last one-tenth of 1 percent where we find all of human variation – those things that make us special: athletic abilities (not so much in my case), frizzy hair (unfortunately for me) … and in some cases, a predisposition to disease."). *See also* J. Michael McGinnis, *Population Health and the Influence of Medical and Scientific Advances*, 66 LA L. REV. 9, 10 (2006). Once a draft genome sequence was in hand in 2003, scientists focused on finding and correcting errors in the sequence, often attributed to the "shot-gunning" methodology employed by Human Genome Sciences – the commercial competitor to the US government-led effort, which was founded in 1992 by science maverick Craig Venter. *See* Martti T. Tammi, Erik Arner, Ellen Kindlund, BjoÈrn Andersson, *Correcting Errors in Shotgun Sequences*, 31(15) NUCLEIC ACIDS RES. 4663–72 (Aug. 1, 2003), www.ncbi.nlm.nih.gov/pmc/articles/PMC169956/pdf/gkg653.pdf; Laurie Goodman, *Random Shotgun Fire*, 8 GENOME RES. 567–68 (1998), https://genome.cshlp.org/content/8/6/567.full. *See generally* FERRY, SULSTON, THE COMMON THREAD, *supra* note 5. Scientists also have found medical meaning in human genome DNA perceived in 2003 as inactive and dismissed as "junk DNA." *See* Stephen S. Hall, *Hidden Treasures in Junk DNA*, 307 SCI. AM., No. 4 (2012); Carl Zimmer, *Darwin's Junkyard*, N. Y. TIMES MAG. (Mar. 8, 2015), at 60–63, 69. For example, Yale researchers identified "jumping genes" in so-called junk DNA that may advance understanding of the origins of neurodegenerative disease. *See* Bill Hathaway, *'Jumping' Genes Yield New Clues to Origins of Neurodegenerative Disease*, YALENEWS (Sept. 6, 2022) ("Massive, repetitive stretches of DNA in the human genome may harbor hints about the onset of a rare, inherited neurodegenerative disorder called ataxia-telangiectasia as well as other related diseases, a new Yale School of Medicine study finds."), https://news.yale.edu/2022/09/06/jumping-genes-yield-new-clues-origins-neurodegenerative-disease?utm_source=YaleToday&utm_medium=Email&utm_campaign=YT_Yale%20Today%20Alum%20no%20Parents_9-8-2022. Beyond the currently estimated 20,500 protein-coding genes, "there are another 30,000 to 40,000 genes that produce RNA [ribonucleic acid] transcripts but do not code for proteins." WATSON, THE STORY, *supra* note 2, at 223 (includes a genes tally comparison table). Consequently, scientists worked on filling gaps left in the 2003 draft human genome sequence. The NHGRI announced completion of the first *complete* sequence of the human genome on March 31, 2022. *See* Ganguly, Zisk, *Gapless Sequence, supra* note 5. "According to researchers, having a complete, gap-free sequence of the roughly 3 billion bases (or "letters") in our DNA is critical for understanding the full spectrum of human genomic variation and for understanding the genetic contributions to certain diseases." *Id.* The difference has been analogized to introducing a new pair of

glasses for scientists that enables markedly clearer vision. *Id*. Also, the UK Biobank has undertaken a project to assemble a proteomics (genes make proteins, and proteins turn genes on and off) counterpart to the HGP sequence. *See* Adam Bonislawski, *UK Biobank Proteomics Project Produces Large-Scale Map of Human Gene-Protein Linkages*, GenomeWeb (July 29, 2022), www.genomeweb.com/proteomics-protein-research/uk-biobank-proteomics-project-produces-large-scale-map-human-gene?utm_source=Sailthru&utm_medium=email&utm_campaign=GWDN%20Wed%20PM%202022-06-29&utm_term=GW%20Daily%20News%20Bulletin#.YrywoXbMK3A.

16 *See generally* Oscar J. Wambuguh, Examining the Causal Relationship between Genes, Epigenetics, and Human Health (2019). Epigenetics is the study of changes in organisms caused by modifications of gene *expression*, rather than genes themselves – such as by environmental exposures – and includes inheritance by mechanisms other than genes. *Id. See also* Michael J. Malinowski, Handbook on Biotechnology Law, Business, and Policy xvii (2016). *Cf.* Secretary's Advisory Committee on Genetic Testing/SACGT, Enhancing the Oversight of Genetic Tests: Recommendations of the SACGT 15–19 (July 2000) (addressing the clinical complexities of human genetics), https://osp.od.nih.gov/sagct_document_archi/enhancing-the-oversight-of-genetic-tests-recommendations-of-the-sacgt/. *See also Chapter 6, infra*, at notes 43–98, and accompanying text ("The Complexities of Personal Genome Medical Decision-Making").

17 Tirrell, *Genome Sequencing, supra* note 8. *See generally*, Philip Elmer-DeWitt, *The 2004 Time 100: Our List of the 100 Most Influential People in the World Today*, Time Mag. (Apr. 26, 2004). *See* Yourgenome.org, *Giants in Genomics: Francis Collins* (updated June 13, 2016) (a website produced by the Wellcome Genome Campus, Wellcome Trust Sanger Institute, and the European Bioinformatics Institute), www.yourgenome.org/stories/giants-in-genomics-francis-collins; Sarah Zhang, *Big Pharma Would Like Your DNA: 23andMe's $300 Million Deal with GlaxoSmithKline is Just the Tip of the Iceberg*, The Atlantic (July 27, 2018). Post completion of the HGP draft human genome sequence, Dr. Lander became the founding director of the Eli and Edythe L. Broad Institute, which is jointly affiliated with Harvard University and the Massachusetts Institute of Technology/MIT. *Visit* The Eli and Edythe L. Broad Institute, official site, https://broadfoundation.org/grantees/the-broad-institute/. *See also* Tirrell, *Genome Sequencing, supra* note 8.

18 Megan Molteni, *23andMe's Pharma Deals Have Been the Plan All Along*, Wired (Aug. 3, 2018), www.wired.com/story/23andme-glaxosmithkline-pharma-deal/. A 23andMe cornerstone business plan strategy has been to circumvent medical privacy complications, such as those imposed by the Health Insurance Portability and Accountability Act/HIPAA, Pub. L. 104–91 (1996), by offering services at a price-point that enables consumers to directly purchase, to self-report medical information to the company, to directly receive reports from the company, and to disclose company-generated personal genome information to medical providers wholly at their discretion. *See id.*

19 Gina Kolata, *The Struggle to Build a Massive 'Biobank' of Patient Data*, N.Y. TIMES (Mar. 19, 2018), at D1, www.nytimes.com/2018/03/19/health/nih-biobank-genes.html.

20 *See* NIH, NHGRI, *DNA Sequencing Fact Sheet* (updated Aug. 16, 2020), www.genome.gov/about-genomics/fact-sheets/DNA-Sequencing-Fact-Sheet. Once genes (defined bits of DNA compiled from base pairs) are identified, comparisons can be made among individuals to identify variations and to assess their function and impact on human health. *See* Ctr. for Genetics Ed., *The Human Genetic Code – The Human Genome Project and Beyond* (2007) (noting diagnostic and predictive testing for genetic conditions), https://web.ornl.gov/sci/techresources/Human_Genome/publicat/primer2001/primer2pager.pdf. By 1995,

some 5,000 genes and genetic variations ("alleles") had been associated with medical conditions, and similar data began amassing rapidly. *See* Michael J. Malinowski, Robin J.R. Blatt, *Commercialization of Genetic Testing Services: The FDA, Market Forces, and Biological Tarot Cards* (1997), 71 TULANE L. REV. 1212, 1217–18 (1997); Ellie McCormack, *Sought-After Counselors Find It's All in the Genes*, BOSTON BUS. J. (Apr. 26-May 2, 1996), at 3, 23. Completion of a draft of the human genome sequence in 2003, advancement of sequencing technologies and human genome science, biobank enablers, and the prescription drug R&D shift in focus to genetics, genomics, and proteomics have brought the rising number of identified genotype-phenotype connections (notably variations in single nucleotide bases, commonly referred to as single nucleotide polymorphisms/SNPs) well into the millions. With an occurrence rate of 1 in 1,000 genes, there are an estimated 4–5 million SNPs, many of which multitask in phenotypic expression. *See generally* NIH, GENETICS HOME REFERENCE, *What Are Single Nucleotide Polymorphisms (SNPs)?* (July 16, 2019), https://ghr.nlm.nih.gov/primer/genomicresearch/snp.

21 *Visit* Personal Genome Project/PGP, official site (visited July 5, 2022), www.personalgenomes.org/.

22 *Visit id.* (providing guidelines and links to global PGP network participants).

23 *See generally* MINE S. CICEK, *BIOBANKING FOR THE 21ST CENTURY*, *in* THE AMERICAN ASSOCIATION FOR CLINICAL CHEMISTRY/AACC (Dec. 1, 2017), www.aacc.org/publications/cln/articles/2017/december/biobanking-for-the-21st-century; Judita Kinkorová, *Biobanks in the Era of Personalized Medicine: Objectives, Challenges, and Innovation*, 7 EPMA 4 (2016), www.ncbi.nlm.nih.gov/pmc/articles/PMC4762166/. *See also* Kolata, *Build Biobank*, *supra* note 19, at D1. deCODE Genetics, Inc. launched an initiative in the late 1990s to collect samples and medical information from the entire population of Iceland (270,000 people at the time) to enable discovery of genetic risk factors for common diseases. *See* Donna M. Gitter, *The Ethics of Big Data in Genomics: The Instructive Icelandic Saga of the Incidentalome*, 18 WASH. U. GLOBAL STUD. L. REV. 351, 358–67 (2019). *See generally* Michael J. Malinowski, *Technology Transfer in Biobanking: Credits, Debits, and Population Health Futures*, 33 J.L. MED. & ETHICS 54 (2005). *See also* Stuart Leavenworth, *This Nation Faces a DNA Dilemma: Whether to Notify People Carrying Cancer Genes*, MCCLATCHY (June 14, 2018), www.mcclatchydc.com/news/nation-world/article213014904.html. Subsequently, population-wide biobanks have been initiated in many countries, including Canada, Denmark, Estonia, Japan, Latvia, Singapore, South Korea, Sweden, the UK, and the US. *See* Yvonne G. De Souza, John S. Greenspan, *Biobanking Past, Present and Future: Responsibilities and Benefits*, 27 AIDS 303–312 (2013), www.ncbi.nlm.nih.gov/pmc/articles/PMC3894636/.

The UK Biobank, with primary funding from the Medical Research Council/MRC and the Wellcome Trust, recruited 500,000 people during 2006–2010 between the ages of 40 and 69 from across the country, along with their complete medical records and additional data, and subsequently has followed their health and well-being in an ongoing manner. *See* MRC, *UK Biobank*, https://mrc.ukri.org/research/facilities-and-resources-for-researchers/biobank/. The UK Biobank enters into collaborations and shares data with qualifying researchers inside and outside of the country, whether based in universities, charities, government agencies, or industry. *See generally* UK Biobank, official site, www.ukbiobank.ac.uk/. Its objective is "to improve the prevention, diagnosis and treatment of a wide range of serious and life-threatening illnesses–including cancer, heart diseases, stroke, diabetes, arthritis, osteoporosis, eye disorders, depression and forms of dementia." *Id. See generally U.K. Biobank*, NATURE.COM (Oct. 11, 2018) (compilation of UK Biobank publications and additional information), www.nature.com/collections/bpthhnywqk.

24 Genome era biobanking is preceded by a US government legacy of population sample collection and studies, including the Framingham Heart Study/FHS, which tracked over 14,000 people from three generations to study how cardiovascular health affects the rest of the body. *See generally* NIH, National Heart, Lung, and Blood Institute, *Framingham Heart Study (FHS)* (visited Apr. 16, 2022), www.nhlbi.nih.gov/science/framingham-heart-study-fhs.

25 *See* US Dep. Veterans Affairs, Office of Research & Development, *Million Veteran Program (MVP)* (reviewed Mar. 14, 2022), www.research.va.gov/mvp/. The MVP was budgeted $250 million over its first seven years, and "[i]nvestigators expect to sequence the DNA of 100,000 participants in the next two years, at a cost of $1,000 for each person's entire genome. The data will be available to approved researchers." Kolata, *Build Biobank, supra* note 19, at D1.

26 *See* Kolata, *Build Biobank, supra* note 19, at D1. Congress also budgeted $230 million to AllUs for fiscal year 2017, of which $40 million came from the 21st Century Cures Act. *See* An Act to Accelerate the Discovery, Development, and Delivery of twenty-first Century Cures, and for Other Purposes ("21st Century Cures Act"), Pub. L. 114–255 (Dec. 13, 2016). *See generally* NIH, All of Us Research Program, official site (reviewed Nov. 2, 2021), https://allofus.nih.gov/. AllUs is doing much recruiting through collaborators. Representation of US population diversity is a priority. For example, AllUs awarded the San Francisco General Hospital Foundation a grant to recruit bisexual, gay, lesbian, and transgender participants. *See* Kolata, *Build Biobank, supra* note 19, at D1. NIH also awarded 23andMe a $1.7-million grant to sequence the genomes of hundreds of thousands of its African American customers. *See* Erika Check Hayden, *The Rise and Fall and Rise Again of 23andMe*, 550 NATURE 174–77 (Oct. 11, 2017), www.nature.com/articles/550174a. Data presented at the 2022 annual conference of the American Society of Human Genetics/ASHG underscored the importance of diversity in study populations. *See* Forest Ray, *Value of Diversity in Study Populations Highlighted at ASHG*, GENOMEWEB (Oct. 31, 2022), www.genomeweb.com/genetic-research/value-diversity-study-populations-highlighted-ashg#.Y2aZoXbMK3A. "The lack of diversity in study populations, ranging from basic research on cell lines to clinical trials, biases the benefits of scientific findings to people of largely European descent. Results presented at the conference provided evidence for the biomedical relevance of greater diversity." *Id. But see* DOROTHY ROBERTS, FATAL INVENTION: HOW SCIENCE, POLITICS, AND BIG BUSINESS RE-CREATE RACE IN THE TWENTY-FIRST CENTURY (2012) (rejecting "hard"/natural evidentiary-science data that establishes and underscores the importance of ancestry diversity in genome study populations based on social science arguments – potentially to the exclusion and significant health care detriment of groups she purports to protect).

27 NIH, AllUs, *supra* note 26, at *The Future of Health Begins with You*, https://allofus.nih.gov/. A major logistics obstacle for the AllUs effort is that, reflective of the US' privatized, decentralized, and fragmented health care system, "Americans tend to have medical records stored slapdash all over the place, and they change insurers and medical plans frequently. There is little uniformity in the country's electronic health systems." Kolata, *Build Biobank, supra* note 19, at D1.

28 Kolata, *Build Biobank, supra* note 19, at D1. *See* Michael J. Malinowski, *The US Science and Technology "Triple Threat": A Regulatory Treatment Plan for the Nation's Addiction to Prescription Opioids*, 48 U. MEM. L. REV. 1028, 1058–64 (2018) (discussing the US government-academia-industry triple threat legacy in technology innovation). *See generally Chapter 2, infra.*

29 *See Fortune 500 Companies*, FORTUNE, (2019), http://fortune.com/fortune500/list/filtered?searchByName=Amgen; Amgen Inc., official site, www.amgen.com/.

30 *See* Amgen, Inc., *Press Release, Amgen to Acquire deCODE Genetics, a Global Leader in Human Genetics* (Dec. 10, 2012), http://investors.amgen.com/phoenix.zhtml?c=61656&p=irol-newsArticle&ID=1765710. The following year, Amgen spun off some of the deCODE technology to a new company, NextCODE Health, which was purchased by WuXi PharmaTech, a Chinese company, in 2015 for $65 million. *See Press Release, WuXi PharmaTech Acquires NextCODE Health to Create Global Leader in Genomic Medicine*, PR NEWSWIRE (Jan. 9, 2015), www.prnewswire.com/news-releases/wuxi-pharmatech-acquires-nextcode-health-to-create-global-leader-in-genomic-medicine-300018311.html; Allison Proffit, *NextCODE Health Launches deCODE's Clinical Genomics Platform*, BIO IT WORLD (Oct. 21, 2013), www.bio-itworld.com/news/2013/10/24/nextcode-health-launches-decodes-clinical-genomics-platform.

31 *See* Regeneron Pharmaceuticals, official site (visited Apr. 16, 2022), www.regeneron.com/about; Regeneron Pharmaceuticals, *Press Release, Regeneron Forms Consortium of Leading Life Sciences Companies to Accelerate Largest Widely-Available 'Big Data' Human Sequencing Resource with UK Biobank* (Jan. 8, 2018), https://investor.regeneron.com/news-releases/news-release-details/regeneron-forms-consortium-leading-life-sciences-companies.

32 Geisinger has enrolled more than 190,000 participants in MyCode, a system-wide biobank, through its Community Health Initiative. *Visit* Geisinger, official site, *What is MyCode?*, www.geisinger.org/precision-health/mycode. Kaiser, with more than 12.2 million plan members in 2018, established the Kaiser Permanente Research Bank. *Visit* Kaiser Permanente, official site, *at* https://researchbank.kaiserpermanente.org/.

33 *See generally Chapter 4, infra.*

34 *See generally Chapter 6, infra.*

35 *See generally* THE PEW CHARITABLE TRUSTS, REPORT, THE ROLE OF LAB-DEVELOPED TESTS IN THE IN VITRO DIAGNOSTICS MARKET (Oct. 2021) (lab tests run with blood and other bodily samples, including noninvasive prenatal tests/NIPTs), www.pewtrusts.org/-/media/assets/2021/10/understanding-the-role-of-lab-developed-tests-in-vitro-diagnostics.pdf. *See* Carmel Shachar, I Glen Cohen, Nita A. Farahany, Henry T. Greely, *Introduction, in* CONSUMER GENETIC TECHNOLOGIES 1 (J. Glenn Cohen, Nita A. Farahany, Henry T. Greely, and Carmel Schachar eds., 2021), *citing* GRAND VIEW RESEARCH, PREDICTIVE GENETIC TESTING AND CONSUMER GENETICS MARKET SIZE, SHARE & TRENDS ANALYSIS REPORT BY TEST TYPE (POPULATION SCREENING, SUSCEPTIBILITY), BY APPLICATION, BY SETTING TYPE, AND SEGMENT FORECASTS, 2019-2025 (2019).

36 *See* US Food & Drug Admin., DEN160026, Evaluation of Automatic Class III Designation for the 23andMe Personal Genome Service (PGS) Genetic Health Risk Test for Hereditary Thrombophilia, Alpha-1 Antitryspin Deficiency, Alzheimer's Disease, Parkinson's Disease, Gaucher Disease Type 1, Factor XI Deficiency, Celiac Disease, G6PD Deficiency, Hereditary Hemochromatosis and Early-Onset Primary Dystonia: Decision Summary (2017), www.accessdata.fda.gov/cdrh_docs/reviews/DEN160026.pdf; WATSON, THE STORY, *supra* note 2, at 207; Catherine M. Sharkey, *Direct-to-Consumer Genetic Testing: The FDA's Dual Role As Safety and Health Information Regulator*, 68 DEPAUL L. REV. 343, 355–57 (2019). In 2015, the FDA had approved a 23andMe wholly DTC *carrier screening* test for Bloom Syndrome – a rare genetic disorder associated with, among other characteristics, increased susceptibility to leukemia, lymphoma, gastrointestinal tract tumors, and other cancers. *See* FDA, Evaluation of Automatic Class III Designation for the 23andMe Personal Genome Service Carrier Screening Test for Bloom Syndrome: Decision Summary (Feb. 2015), www.accessdata.fda.gov/cdrh_docs/reviews/DEN140044.pdf.

37 *See Chapter 4, infra*, at notes 116-83, and accompanying text ("23andMe: The Seminal Direct-t-Consumer, Genetic-Health Risk/DTCGHR Testing Services Company").

38 *See supra* note 35, and accompanying text. As observed by Watson in 2017 (original publication date of THE STORY), "[W]ith more than 1 million DNA records at its disposal, 23andMe has finally reached critical mass for usefulness to big pharma and has signed several lucrative deals as well as hiring a distinguished former Genentech R&D chief to spearhead its own drug discovery program." WATSON, THE STORY, *supra* note 2, at 21. In July 2018, 23andMe announced a data-sharing deal with GlaxoSmithkline (separate from a preexisting 23-GSK research collaboration) for four years, with a GSK year five option. *See* Molteni, *Plan All Along, supra* note 18. *See also* Jamie Ducharme, *A Major Drug Company Now Has Access to 23andMe's Genetic Data. Should You Be Concerned?*, TIME (July 26, 2018), https://time.com/5349896/23andme-glaxo-smith-kline); Nick Paul Taylor, *GlaxoSmithKline Makes $300M Investment in 23andMe, Forms 50–50 R&D*, FIERCEBIOTECH (Jul. 25, 2018), www.fiercebiotech.com/biotech/glaxosmithkline-makes-300m-investment-23andme-forms-50-50-r-d-pact.

39 *See* Molteni, *Plan All Along, supra* note 18 ("23andMe has convinced more than 5 million people to fill a plastic tube with half a teaspoon of saliva"); Ducharme, *Concerned?, supra* note 38.

40 Stuart Leavenworth, *DNA Testing Is Like the 'Wild West'; Should It Be More Tightly Regulated?*, MCCLATCHY (June 1, 2018), www.mcclatchydc.com/news/nation-world/article212256094.html. *See NBC Nightly News with Lester Holt, High-Tech Heritage* (July 14, 2018) (addressing how, with some 5 million consumers, purchasing 23andMe services has become relatively normal); 23andMe, *Press Release, 23andMe to Merge with Virgin Group's VG Acquisition Corp to Become Publicly-Traded Company Set to Revolutionize Personalized Healthcare and Therapeutic Development through Human Genetics* (Feb. 4, 2021), https://mediacenter.23andme.com/press-releases/23andme-merges-with-vgac/. *See generally* James W. Hazel, *Privacy Best Practices for Direct-to-Consumer Genetic Testing Services: Are Industry Efforts at Self-Regulation Sufficient?*, *in* CONSUMER GENETIC TECHNOLOGIES, *supra* note 35, at 260, 274-75. *See also Chapter 4, infra*, at notes 116-83, and accompanying text ("23andMe: The Seminal Direct-to-Consumer, Genetic-Health-Risk/DTCGHR Testing Services Company").

41 *See* Natalie Clarkson, *23andMe and Virgin Group's VG Acquisition Corp. Successfully Close Business Combination*, VIRGIN (June 16, 2021) (Virgin journalist reporting), www.virgin.com/about-virgin/virgin-group/news/23andme-and-virgin-groups-vg-acquisition-corp-successfully-close-business.

42 Neil Versel, *23andMe Pins Future on 'Genomic Health Service,' Therapeutic Development*, GENOMEWEB (Aug. 9, 2022), www.genomeweb.com/business-news/23andme-pins-future-genomic-health-service-therapeutic-development#.Y1MLmnbMK3A. *See* 23andMe Holding Co., *Current Report (Form 8-K)* (Nov. 1, 2021), https://investors.23andme.com/static-files/8a43d3a5-2529-422c-937b-db40a7eeb875. *See also* 23andMe, *A Letter from Anne: Making Personalized Healthcare a Reality* (Oct. 22, 2021), https://you.23andme.com/p/28ba69b793a2c6ff/article/a-letter-from-anne-making-personalized-healthcare-a-reality-3ebee7dfb59a/. On October 12, 2022, 23andMe relayed the following to me and its other PGHS customers via an email (on file with the author):

> Together, we're setting off on a mission to change the future of healthcare for you. We want to transform the primary care experience and make personalized healthcare, powered by genetic and non-genetic data, a reality.
>
> In addition to the personalized genetic insights 23andMe offers about your health, we also want to introduce you to Lemonaid Health's telehealth services. You can connect online with their licensed medical team and pharmacy to get affordable, accessible healthcare when and where you need it.

43 *See generally* NHGRI, 2020 NHGRI STRATEGIC VISION: STRATEGIC VISION FOR IMPROVING HUMAN HEALTH AT THE FOREFRONT OF GENOMICS (2020), www.genome.gov/2020SV; SACGT, RECOMMENDATIONS, *supra* note 16; WATSON, THE STORY, *supra* note 2; *Chapter 4, infra*.
44 *See* MANUEL CASTELLS, THE RISE OF THE NETWORK SOCIETY xxv (2nd ed., 2009); *Chapter 2, infra*, at notes 164–237, and accompanying text (addressing the biotech revolution, the genomic revolution, and the personal genome medicine future).
45 *See Chapter 2, infra*, at notes 164–98, and accompanying text (addressing TTLP and the biotech revolution). *See generally* Michael J. Malinowski, Bartha Maria Knoppers, Claude Bouchard, *Symposium: Proceedings of "The Genomics Revolution? Science, Law and Policy,"* 66 LA. L. REV. 1 (2005) (centennial issue). The US enacted and expanded TTLP during the 1980s and 1990s, commencing in 1980 with enactment of complementary legislation: Bayh-Dole Act, Patent Rights in Inventions Made with Federal Assistance, Pub. L. No. 96–517, 94 Stat. 3020 (1980), *codified at* 35 U.S.C. §§ 200–21 (focused on academic research with federal funding); Stevenson-Wydler Technology Innovation Act, Pub. L. No. 96-480, 94 Stat. 2311 (1980), *codified at* 15 U.S.C. §§ 3701–3717 (centered on government agencies, researchers, and laboratories). *See* MALINOWSKI, HANDBOOK, *supra* note 16, at 69–77.
46 *See Chapter 2, infra*, at notes 199–230, and accompanying text ("The Genomic Revolution").
47 *See generally* WALTER ISAACSON, THE CODE BREAKER (2021). "Nature and nature's God, in their infinite wisdom, have evolved a species that is able to modify its own genome, and that species happens to be ours." *Id.* at 481. *Cf. generally* SIDDHARTHA MUKHERJEE, THE SONG OF THE CELL (2022). Jennifer Anne Doudna and Emmanuelle Charpentier were awarded the 2020 Nobel Prize in Chemistry for their pioneering work in CRISPR gene editing. *See* Heidi Ledford, Ewen Callaway, *Pioneers of Revolutionary CRISPR Gene Editing Win Chemistry Nobel*, 586 NATURE 346–347 (Oct. 7, 2020), www.nature.com/articles/d41586-020-02765-9#:~:text=Emmanuelle%20Charpentier%20and%20Jennifer%20Doudna,the%20precise%20genome%2Dediting%20technology.&text=It's%20CRISPR.,year's%20Nobel%20Prize%20in%20Chemistry. *See Chapter 2, infra*, at notes 1–27, and accompanying text (discussing CRISPR technologies).
48 *See generally* CASTELLS, NETWORK SOCIETY, *supra* note 44.
49 *See id. See also* Jennifer Earl, Jayson Hunt, R. Kelly Garrett, *Chapter 16: Social movements and the ICT revolution, in* HANDBOOK OF POLITICAL CITIZENSHIP AND SOCIAL MOVEMENTS (Hein-Anton van der Heijden ed., 2014).
50 *See generally* STEVEN JOHNSON. EXTRA LIFE: A SHORT HISTORY OF LIVING LONGER (2021). Although critical scientific breakthroughs such as vaccines, germ theory, and antibiotics made this transformation in longevity possible, the work of political activists, intellectuals, and legal reformers brought their benefits to the masses. "Important breakthroughs in health don't just have to be discovered; they also have to be argued for, championed, defended." *Id.* at 51.
51 *See* NIH, NHGRI, *Ethical, Legal and Social Implications Research Program*, www.genome.gov/Funded-Programs-Projects/ELSI-Research-Program-ethical-legal-social-implications.
52 *See generally* PAUL STARR, THE SOCIAL TRANSFORMATION OF AMERICAN MEDICINE: THE RISE OF A SOVEREIGN PROFESSION AND THE MAKING OF A VAST INDUSTRY (1984) (awarded the Pulitzer Prize).
53 For the medical profession, "[s]tandardization of training and licensing became the means for realizing both the search for authority and control of the market." *Id.* at 22. *See generally Chapter 1, infra*.

54 *See Chapter 1, infra*, at notes 35-45, and accompanying text ("US Law-Policy Recognition of Clinical Medicine as the Medical Profession's Domain").
55 *See* JOHNSON, EXTRA LIFE, *supra* note 50 (attributes doubling the average human life span between 1920 and 2020 to scientific advances *accompanied by* the work of activists, legal reformers, and other enablers).
56 *See generally* JAY KATZ, THE SILENT WORLD OF DOCTOR AND PATIENT (rev. ed., 2002) (addressing paternalism in twentieth century US medicine).
57 *See generally Chapter 5, infra. See also* Michael J. Malinowski, *Capitation, Advances in Medical Technology, and the Advent of a New Era in Medical Ethics*, 22 AM. J. L. & MED. 335, 337-39 (1996 symposium), *reprinted in* TAKING SIDES: CLASHING VIEWS ON CONTROVERSIAL BIOETHICAL Issues (Carol Levine ed., 7th ed., 1997).
58 "Computer networking, open-source software (including Internet protocols), and fast development of digital switching and transmission capacity in the telecommunications networks led to the expansion of the Internet after privatization in the 1990s and to the generalization of its use in all domains of activity." CASTELLS, NETWORK SOCIETY, *supra* note 44, at xxv.
59 *See generally* History Cooperative, Matthew Jones, *The Complete History of Social Media: A Timeline of the Invention of Online Networking* (June 16, 2015), https://historycooperative.org/the-history-of-social-media/. *Cf.* DAVID KIRKPATRICK, THE FACEBOOK EFFECT: THE INSIDE STORY OF THE COMPANY THAT IS CONNECTING (2011).
60 *See Chapter 5, infra*, at notes 113-77, and accompanying text ("Today's US Physician-Patient Relationship, and the State of Physician Decision Making"). *See also* Sharkey, *FDA's Dual Role, supra* note 36, at 346; Anna B. Laakmann, *The New Genomic Semicommons*, 5 UC IRVINE L. REV. 1001, 1033 (2015).
61 *Visit* NHGRI, *Genomics and Medicine* (visited Sept. 22, 2021), www.genome.gov/health/Genomics-and-Medicine. *See generally* Heggie, *Genomics, supra* note 5; FRANCIS S. COLLINS, THE LANGUAGE OF LIFE: DNA AND THE REVOLUTION IN PERSONALIZED MEDICINE (illustrated ed., 2011); MISHA ANGRIST, HERE IS A HUMAN BEING: AT THE DAWN OF PERSONAL GENOMICS (2010); DAVIES, $1,000 GENOME, *supra* note 5.
62 *See generally* William F. Mulholland, II, Ami S. Jaeger, *Genetic Privacy and Discrimination: A Survey of State Legislation*, 39 JURIMETRICS J. 317, 318 (1999). *See* Michael J. Malinowski, *Separating Predictive Genetic Testing from Snake Oil: Regulation, Liabilities, and Lost Opportunities*, 41 JURIMETIRCS 23, 28–29 (2001) (live and published symposium contribution).
63 Although the US enacted the Health Insurance Portability and Accountability Act/HIPAA in 1996, the Department of Health and Human Services/HHS did not issue a Final Rule for HIPAA enforcement until February 16, 2006, and it did not become effective until March 16, 2006. *See* HIPAA, Pub. L. 104–91 (1996). *See also* Rob Stein, *Medical Privacy Law Nets No Fines*, WASH. POST (June 5, 2006), www.washingtonpost.com/wp-dyn/content/article/2006/06/04/AR2006060400672.html. The medical privacy rights and protections realized through HIPAA implementation and enforcement were complemented by a national prohibition on genetic discrimination for some health insurers and employers under the Genetics Information and Nondiscrimination Act of 2008/GINA, Pub. L. 110–233, 122 Stat. 881 (2008). Enactment of the Patient Protection and Affordable Care Act/ACA of 2010 pushed some residual consumer caution about genetic testing to the side by prohibiting health insurers from denying coverage based on preexisting conditions. *See* ACA, Pub. L. No. 111-148, H.R. 3590, 124 Stat. 119 (2010), *amended by* Health Care and Education Reconciliation Act of 2010, Pub. L. No. 111-152, 124 Stat. 1029 (2010). *See Chapter 4, infra*, at notes 7-10, and accompanying text (addressing enactment of HIPAA, GINA, and the ACA, and their impact on genetic privacy concerns).

64 *See Chapter 4, infra*, at notes 15-16, and accompanying text.
65 WATSON, THE STORY, *supra* note 2, at ix.
66 *See* Maren Estrada, *DNA Tests are the Hottest Christmas Gifts of the Season, and There's Still Time to Get One on Sale*, BRG [Boy Genius Rep.] (Dec. 22, 2018) ("As was the case during last year's big holiday shopping season, DNA tests are among the hottest gifts of Christmas 2018."), https://bgr.com/2018/12/22/dna-test-deals-last-minute-christmas-sale/; *NBC Nightly News with Lester Holt* (aired Dec. 23, 2019) (reporting that home DNA testing kits that help trace a person's ancestry or flag potential vulnerability to disease were one of the year's hottest Xmas gifts). Purchaser-multiplication marketing has proven highly effective in the social media consumer demographic. For example, consumers gift 23andMe kits to their family members and friends, for which 23andMe runs successful sale campaigns during holiday seasons, and then offers a "plus one" discount after delivering results to build sales around each purchaser's family and social circles. *See* Estrada, *supra*.
67 Recode, *Full Transcript: 23andMe CEO Anne Wojcicki Answers Genetics and Privacy Questions on Too Embarrassed to Ask*, VOX.COM (Sept. 29, 2017), www.vox.com/2017/9/29/16385320/transcript-23andme-ceo-anne-wojcicki-genetics-privacy-health-questions-too-embarrassed-to-ask.
68 *See, e.g.*, WATSON, THE STORY, *supra* note 2, at 208-09 ("I for one wholeheartedly endorse consumers' right to know their person genetic information and to take what measures seem appropriate."); Anne Wojcicki, *23andMe Receives FDA Clearance for Genetic Health Risk Report that Looks at a Hereditary Colorectal Cancer Syndrome*, 23ANDME-BLOG (Jan. 22, 2019) ("We are committed to giving people affordable and direct access to important health information that can impact their lives …."), https://blog.23andme.com/health-traits/23andme-receives-fda-clearance-for-genetic-health-risk-report-that-looks-at-a-hereditary-colorectal-cancer-syndrome/.
69 *See generally* NIH, NHGRI, *Cost of Sequencing, supra* note 8; NHGRI, *Cost per Genome, supra* note 7. In February 2020, Nebula Genomics began offering DTC whole genome sequencing for $299. *See* Molteni, *Whole Genome, supra* note 10.
70 George J. Annas, *Genetic Privacy: There Ought to Be a Law*, 4 TEX. REV. L. & POL. 9, 11 (1999).
71 WATSON, THE STORY, *supra* note 2, at 224.
72 *Id.*
73 *Linder v. United States*, 268 US 5, 18 (1925). The Court unanimously overturned the conviction of a physician for prescribing drugs to addicts in violation of the Harrison Act, a predecessor of the Controlled Substances Act. *See* Comprehensive Drug Abuse Prevention and Control Act, Pub. L. 91-513, 84 Stat. 1236 (1970), *codified as amended*, 21 U.S.C. §§ 801-971 (2012) (regulating the manufacture, importation, possession, use and distribution of defined and scheduled substances); Harrison Narcotics Tax Act, ch. 1, 38 Stat. 785 (1914), *codified as amended*, 26 U.S.C. §§ 4702-4900 (2012) (imposing a tax on drugs such as cocaine and morphine that effectively became a prohibition on them). Although *Linder* has been mostly overruled or superseded, the Court relied on its rationale in 2006 when it upheld physician discretion to prescribe FDA-approved drugs to end life in compliance with Oregon's Death With Dignity Act. *See generally Gonzales v. Oregon*, 546 US 243 (2006). *See also Chapter 1, infra*, at notes 160–83, and accompanying text ("Deference to and Reliance on the Medical Profession").
74 *See Chapter 3, infra*, at notes 56, 63–66, and accompanying text (discussing discretion to prescribe off label post *Washington Legal*).
75 *See generally* Malinowski, *Triple Threat, supra* note 28. *See also Chapter 3, infra*, at notes 146-47, and accompanying text (addressing the medical profession's role in the US opioid addiction crisis).

76 See PATRICK RADDEN KEEFE, EMPIRE OF PAIN: THE SECRET HISTORY OF THE SACKLER FAMILY 205–219 (2021) (by 2021, five years after the FDA granted Purdue market approval for Oxycontin, the company was paying its sales representatives *average* annual bonuses of nearly $250,000).

77 *See* Malinowski, *"Triple Threat," supra* note 28, at 1030-34. Due to the highly addictive nature of opioids, legitimate prescription use has been the beginning of long-term addiction for an astounding number of people. *See* NAT'L CTR. FOR INJURY PREVENTION & CONTROL, CTRS. FOR DISEASE CONTROL & PREVENTION, ANNUAL SURVEILLANCE REPORT OF DRUG-RELATED RISKS AND OUTCOMES: UNITED STATES, 2017, 13 (2017), www.cdc.gov/drugoverdose/pdf/pubs/2017-cdc-drug-surveillance-report.pdf. According to the President's National Commission on Combating Drug Addiction and the Opioid Crisis in 2017, four out of every five new heroin users first used prescription opioids. THE PRESIDENT'S COMM'N ON COMBATING DRUG ADDICTION AND THE OPIOID CRISIS, FINAL REPORT 28, 117 (2017), https://trumpwhitehouse.archives.gov/sites/whitehouse.gov/files/images/Final_Report_Draft_11-15-2017.pd.

78 The proliferation of managed care and commercialization of medicine in the 1980s and 1990s impacted the practice of medicine, medical ethos, and patient trust. *See* John ABRAMSON, OVERDOSED AMERICA: THE BROKEN PROMISE OF AMERICAN MEDICINE 81–82 (2005). The coupling of technology and time constraints has fundamentally changed the physician-patient relationship and the practice of medicine:

> A paper published a decade ago in the *American Journal of Public Health* estimated that it would take over four hours a day for a general internist to provide just the preventive care – scheduling mammograms, arranging screening colonoscopies, and so on – that is currently recommended for an average-size panel of adult patients (this on top of the regular workday managing acute problems and emergencies).

SANDEEP JUAHAR, DOCTORED: THE DISILLUSIONMENT OF AN AMERICAN PHYSICIAN 11 (2015). As experienced by Dr. Otis Webb Brawley, who served as Chief Medical and Scientific Officer and Executive Vice President of the American Cancer Society from 2007 to 2018, "We doctors are paid for services we provide, a variant of 'piecework' that guarantees that we will err on the side of selling more, sometimes believing that we are helping, sometimes knowing that we are not, and sometimes simply not giving a shit." OTIS WEBB BRAWLEY, HOW WE DO HARM: A DOCTOR BREAKS RANKS ABOUT BEING SICK IN AMERICA 24 (2011).

79 As experienced by Dr. Abramson,

> Largely freed of concerns about out-of-pocket costs, enticed by advertising and media coverage of developments in medicine, and emboldened by a sense of autonomy, patients began requesting, and then demanding, specific tests, drugs, and procedures. Indeed, it became nearly impossible to convince many patients that more medical care was not necessarily better.... To exactly the same extent that a person is seduced by the false hopes and dreams offered by the medical industry's marketing efforts, the ability to trust his or her doctor, especially a primary care doctor, is eroded.

ABRAMSON, *supra* note 78, at 80. Patient self-determination initiatives are part of US history, but the ongoing patient autonomy and self-determination movement is a distinguishable break from our twentieth century experience. *See Chapter* 5, *infra*, at notes 58-61, and accompanying text. *See generally* KATZ, SILENT WORLD, *supra* note 56 (addressing paternalism in twentieth century US medicine). *But see generally* LEWIS A. GROSSMAN, CHOOSE YOUR MEDICINE: FREEDOM OF THERAPEUTIC CHOICE IN AMERICA (2021) (arguing patient self-determination in US history beyond outsider movements).

80 *See Chapter 5, infra*, at notes 113–77, and accompanying text ("Today's US Physician-Patient Relationship, and the State of Physician Decision Making").
81 *See Chapter 6, infra*, at notes 43-98, and accompanying text ("The Complexities of Personal Genome Medical Decision-Making").
82 *See generally* SACGT, RECOMMENDATIONS, *supra* note 16, at 15–19 (a report issued in 2000 surveying and addressing the clinical complexities of human genetics), https://osp.od.nih.gov/sagct_document_archi/enhancing-the-oversight-of-genetic-tests-recommendations-of-the-sacgt/.
83 ABRAMSON, *supra* note 78, at 206.
84 *See* David C. Wheelock, *Comparing the COVID-19 Recession with the Great Depression*, ECON. SYNOPSES (Aug. 12, 2020) (Economic Research Division, Federal Reserve Bank of St. Louis), https://research.stlouisfed.org/publications/economic-synopses/2020/08/12/comparing-the-covid-19-recession-with-the-great-depression.
85 *See generally* MICHAEL GOUGH, POLITICIZING SCIENCE: THE ALCHEMY OF POLICY-MAKING (2003) (addressing the dangers of manipulating science for political gain). In July 2020, Tom Frieden, Jeffrey Koplan, David Satcher and Richard Besser, who collectively headed the CDC for over fifteen years, jointly challenged the Trump Administration's mandate to open the nation's schools in conflict with CDC guidelines and warned that "Trying to fight this pandemic while subverting scientific expertise is like fighting blindfolded." Tom Frieden, Jeffrey Koplan, David Satcher, Richard Besser, *We Ran the CDC. No President Ever Politicized its Science the Way Trump Has*, WASH. POST (July 14, 2020), www.washingtonpost.com/outlook/2020/07/14/cdc-directors-trump-politics/. *See generally* MICHAEL LEWIS, THE PREMONITION (2021) (addressing how scientific expertise within the US government was ignored prior to and during the onset of the COVID-19 pandemic, and how a group of doctors nicknamed "the Wolverines" worked from inside the US government to challenge the Trump Administration's official response). The politicization of science in the context of vaccines predated the pandemic, which made COVID-19 vaccines highly susceptible at a time when the public health stakes were at a premium. *See generally* HEIDI J. LARSON, STUCK: HOW VACCINE RUMORS START – AND WHY THEY DON'T GO AWAY (2020) ("Today's anti-vaccine positions find audiences where they've never existed previously.").
86 *See generally* ABRAMSON, OVERDOSED, *supra* note 78; BRAWLEY, HARM, *supra* note 78; BEN GOLDACRE, BAD PHARMA: HOW DRUG COMPANIES MISLEAD DOCTORS AND HARM PATIENTS (2012); RAY MOYNIHAN, ALAN CASSELS, SELLING SICKNESS: HOW THE WORLD'S BIGGEST PHARMACEUTICAL COMPANIES ARE TURNING US ALL INTO PATIENTS (2005); ELISABETH ROSENTHAL, AN AMERICAN SICKNESS: HOW HEALTHCARE BECAME BIG BUSINESS AND HOW YOU CAN TAKE IT BACK (2017). *See generally Chapter 5, infra*.
87 *See generally Chapter 5, infra*.
88 Corporate sponsorship of medical journals, research studies, patient groups, and physician authors through myriad interactions – past, present, and future – and the conflicts of interest these interactions weave throughout the fabric of the profession jeopardize science objectivity, reliability, and integrity. *See* ABRAMSON, OVERDOSED, *supra* note 78, at xvii, 111, 241–2; *id.* at ch.7 (*Commercial Takeover of Medical Knowledge*), pp. 93-110; GOLDACRE, BAD PHARMA, *supra* note 86, at ix, 241–42, 287–311 (2012). *See generally Chapter 5, infra* (discussing TTLP, PDUFA, FDAMA, and resulting industry influence).
89 *See* SETON HALL SCHOOL OF LAW, THE CENTER FOR HEALTH & PHARMACEUTICAL LAW & POLICY, CONFLICTS OF INTEREST IN CLINICAL TRIAL RECRUITMENT & ENROLLMENT: A CALL FOR INCREASED OVERSIGHT 5 ((Nov. 2009) (White Paper). *See also* ISAACSON, CODE BREAKER, *supra* note 47, at 97. *Visit* Association of Clinical Research Organizations/ACRO, official site (visited Dec. 2, 2015), www.acrohealth.org/

90 *See Chapter* 5, *infra*, at notes 207–320, and accompanying text (industry influence over the MJE and medical education). Following WWII and through the 1970s, the NIH was a generous financier of clinical as well as basic research. "An article published in the journal Science in 1982 describes medical scientists thumbing 'their academic noses at industrial money.'" ABRAMSON, OVERDOSED, *supra* note 78, at 94. Enactment and implementation of TTLP in the 1980s created a chasm between basic research funding and clinical research funding, with government on one side and industry on the other:

> As drug and biotech industries assumed an ever-larger role in funding clinical trials (reaching 80 percent by 2002), they increasingly exercised the power of their purse. Control over clinical research changed – quietly at first, but very quickly, and with profound effects on medical practice. The role of academic medical centers in clinical research diminished precipitously during the 1990s as the drug industry turned increasingly to new independent, for-profit medical research companies [contract research organizations/CROs] emerged in response to commercial funding opportunities.... [Industry] could now call the shots on most of the studies that were evaluating its own products without having to accept input from academics who were grounded in traditional standards of medical science. And the increasing competition for commercial research dollars put academic centers under even more pressure to accept the terms offered by the commercial sponsors of research, threatening the independence and scientific integrity that had been the hallmark of the academic environment.

Id. at 95. *See generally* SETON HALL LAW, WHITE PAPER: CONFLICTS, *supra* note 89; *Chapter* 2, *infra*. In addition to financing clinical research and sponsoring studies that publications are based upon, industry directly finances academic journals. GOLDACRE, BAD PHARMA, *supra* note 86, at 244–45, 304–307. Today, the biopharmaceutical industry "buys a lot of advertising space in academic journals, often representing the greatest single component of a journal's income stream, as editors very well know." GOLDACRE, *supra*, at 304-05.

91 ABRAMSON, OVERDOSED, *supra* note 78, at 96. *See generally* Frank Davidoff, Catherine DeAngelis, Jeffrey Drazen et al., *Sponsorship, Authorship, and Accountability*, 286 JAMA 1232–1234 (2001), www.nejm.org/doi/10.1056/NEJMed010093?url_ver=Z39.88-2003&rfr_id=ori:rid:crossref.org&rfr_dat=cr_pub%20%20www.ncbi.nlm.nih.gov.

92 *See generally Chapter* 5, *infra*.

93 *See generally* TAMARA R. PIETY, BRANDISHING THE FIRST AMENDMENT (2012); Tamara R. Piety, *The First Amendment and the Corporate Civil Rights Movement*, 11 J. BUS. & TECH. L. 1, 2–24 (2016); Wayne L. Pines, A *History and Perspective on Direct-to-Consumer Promotion*, 54 FOOD AND DRUG L.J. 489 (1999). *See Chapter* 3, *infra*, at notes 31–70, and accompanying text ("Recognition of Biopharma Marketing as Protected Commercial Speech").

94 PDUFA, Pub. L. No. 102–571, 106 Stat. 4491 (1992) (codified as amended at 21 U.S.C. §§ 379g–h). *See* MALINOWSKI, HANDBOOK, *supra* note 15, at 14–15.

95 *See* FDAMA, Pub. L. No. 105–115, 111 Stat. 2296 (1997) (codified primarily in sections throughout 21 U.S.C., including §§ 352, 355, 356, 356(b), 360aaa–1–3, 379r). *See* MALINOWSKI, HANDBOOK, *supra* note 16, at 14–15.

96 *See Chapter* 7, *infra*, at notes 159–60, and accompanying text.

97 The right-to-try movement to remove FDA oversight of access to investigational drugs and government responsiveness through enactment of state legislation and the federal Right to Try Act of 2017, 21 U.S.C. § 360bbb-0a (2018), underscores this point. *Cf.* Rebecca Dresser, *Informed Consent in Right-to-Try-A Dubious Assumption*, 11 WAKE FOREST J.L. & POL'Y 1 (2020). Intellectual influencers who have promoted and drawn

much multidisciplinary and public attention to the premise that the post-FDAMA FDA overregulates biopharmaceutical R&D to the serious detriment of the practice of medicine and patient care include Dr. David Gratzer, Dr. Henry Miller, and law professor Richard Epstein. *See generally* Richard A. Epstein, Overdose: How Excessive Government Regulation Stifles Pharmaceutical Innovation (2006); David Gratzer, The Cure: How Capitalism Can Save American Health Care (2008); Henry Miller, *Correspondence, FDA Not NIH Can Speed New Drugs*, 472 Nature 169 (Apr. 14, 2011). *See Chapter 7, infra*, at notes 142-65, and accompanying text (addressing and rebutting this categorical attack on the FDA post FDAMA, PDUFA, the Food and Drug Administration Safety and Innovation Act/FDASIA of 2012, and the Cures Act).

98 *See also Chapter 6, infra*, at notes 43–98, and accompanying text ("The Complexities of Personal Genome Medical Decision-Making").

99 *See generally* SACGT, Recommendations, *supra* note 16. *See also* Malinowski, *Snake Oil*, *supra* note 62, at 38–39. *See generally* Martina Cornel, Carla van El, Pascal Borry, *The Challenge of Implementing Genetic Tests With Clinical Utility while Avoiding Unsound Applications*, 5 J. Community Genet. 7 (2014), https://pubmed.ncbi.nlm.nih.gov/23055102/. *Cf.* Carl Zimmer, She Has Her Mother's Laugh: The Powers, Perversions, and Potential of Heredity (2019).

100 *See Chapter 6, infra*, at notes 43-98, and accompanying text ("The Complexities of Personal Genome Medical Decision-Making"). *Cf. generally* Mukherjee, Song, *supra* note 47.

101 *See generally* Pew, Report, *supra* note 35; SACGT, Recommendations, *supra* note 16; *Chapter 4, infra* (addressing DTC personal genome testing, including genetic health risk testing that does not meet established clinical standards). *See also Chapter 6, infra*, at notes 63–75, and accompanying text (addressing lab tests run with blood and other bodily samples, including noninvasive prenatal tests/NIPTs).

102 *See generally* SACGT, Recommendations, *supra* note 16.

103 *See generally* Cornel, *Challenge*, *supra* note 99; David J. Hunter, Muin J. Khoury, Jeffrey M. Drazen, *Letting the Genome Out of the Bottle – Will We Get Our Wish?*, 358 N. Eng. J. Med. 105 (Jan. 10, 2008), www.nejm.org/doi/10.1056/NEJMp0708162. *See also NEJM Editorial Warns of Downside to 'Premature' Consumer Genomics Market*, GenomeWeb (Jan. 11, 2008), www.genomeweb.com/archive/nejm-editorial-warns-downside-%25E2%2580%2598premature%25E2%2580%2599-consumer-genomics-market#.XSNiUuhKjBQ.

104 *See generally* Pew, Report, *supra* note 35 (addressing laboratory performed in vitro diagnostic tests/IVDs available on the US market). *See also Chapter 6, infra*, at notes 63-75, and accompanying text (addressing the market availability and uptake of noninvasive prenatal tests/NIPTs and *New York Times* investigation of NIPTs); *Chapter 7, infra*, at notes 166-89, and accompanying text ("Proposals to Enhance CLIA Regulation of Personal Genome Testing").

105 *See* Gary E. Marchant, Mark Barnes, Ellen W. Clayton, Susan M. Wolf, *Liability Implications of Direct-to-Consumer Genetic Testing*, *in* Consumer Genetic Technologies 21–24 (J. Glenn Cohen, Nita A. Farahany, Henry T. Greely, Carmel Schachar eds., 2021). *See also* Royal College of Physicians, British Pharmacological Society, Personalised prescribing: using pharmacogenomics to improve patient outcomes 40–41 (2022) (addressing the realization of genetic testing liability in the US), www.rcp.ac.uk/projects/outputs/personalised-prescribing-using-pharmacogenomics-improve-patient-outcomes.

1

Medical Profession Sovereignty to Protect and Promote the Science and Evidence Base of US Medicine

The American Medical Association/AMA entered this millennium with 240,000 physician and medical student members, and with one of the largest annual political lobbying budgets of any US organization.[1] The AMA has an elaborate, hierarchical governance infrastructure and system for policymaking, with expansive grassroots reach through more than 190 state and specialty medical societies.[2] Domestically, the AMA augments its influence, resources, and involvement in law and policy through strategic collaborations, alliances, and partnerships with other influential stakeholders.[3] The organization self-identifies as representing US physicians "with a unified voice in courts and legislative bodies across the nation, removing obstacles that interfere with patient care, leading the charge to prevent chronic disease and confront public health crises, and driving the future of medicine to tackle the biggest challenges in health care and training the leaders of tomorrow."[4] The AMA also engages robustly in international strategy and advocacy, often in collaboration with the World Medical Association/WMA and other global organizations.[5]

The AMA was founded in 1847 – a time when "Many people thought of medicine as an inferior profession, or at least as a career with inferior prospects."[6] In 1869, the *Medical Record*, a professional journal, commented that "In all of our American colleges medicine has ever been and is now, the most despised of all the professions which liberally-educated men are expected to enter."[7] A doctor's social status then was a reflection of family background and the status of one's patients given that "The role of doctor did not confer a clear and unequivocal class position in American Society."[8] As explained by sociologist, professor, and Pulitzer Prize recipient Paul Starr,

> From the perspective of democratic thought in the early nineteenth century, the seeming complexity of medicine was artificial; if properly understood, medicine could be brought within reach of "common sense." The development of science broke that confidence. It helped establish the cultural authority of medicine by restoring a sense of *legitimate complexity*.[9]

The AMA was established to elevate both the medical profession and the practice of medicine – "to promote the art and science of medicine and the betterment of public health."[10] It succeeded. By the 1950s, the AMA had become the epicenter of a learned, organized, vocal, and esteemed professional discipline – a national physician professional association with reach through fifty-three state and territorial societies – that had "attained a position of undeniable authority and influence over medical affairs."[11]

The following discussion begins by profiling the mutually inclusive advancement of the US medical profession and medical science during the twentieth century. The medical profession's devotion to science and evidence-based medicine stimulated robust progress in clinical care and trust in the learned medical professionals providing it. US law and policy recognized clinical medicine as the medical profession's domain.

The discussion then addresses how the US, prompted by national crises, introduced federal regulation of medicinal products to protect patients and did so in a manner that shored up the medical profession's role as a sentinel over their clinical use. The result was a symbiotic relationship between the Food and Drug Administration/FDA and the medical profession, each committed to protecting and promoting the evidentiary-science base of US medicine. The discussion concludes by addressing how the US increased its reliance on the medical profession to protect the patient consumers of FDA-regulated medical products at the end of the twentieth century – reliance that has continued to increase in this millennium, and with the advent of personal genome medicine/PGM.

A PROFESSION BUILT ON THE EVIDENTIARY-SCIENCE BASE OF MEDICINE

Sound science and evidence-based medicine are verifiable, repeatable, and centered on the pursuit of objective truth. "We tend to think of science as providing a single, definitive answer, but that isn't really how it works. Science is, above all, a method of inquiry, a process of posing questions and rigorously testing these hypotheses. With new and better data, we arrive at new and better conclusions."[12] The nexus between medicine and sound, objective, verifiable science in matters of life and death distinguishes the medical profession. "Unlike the law and the clergy, [the medical profession] enjoys close bonds with modern science, and at least for most of the last century, scientific knowledge has held a privileged status in the hierarchy of belief."[13] The first half of the twentieth century was a remarkably simpler time in both science and medicine.[14] While major medical science advances – notably in fighting infection, vaccination, hygiene, and public health in general – validated and inspired, fluid integration of medicine and science was evolving at a pace that allowed for deliberative uptake and absorption. "As recently as the 1950s, remember, medicine was driven almost entirely by anecdote and eminence."[15]

Increased faith in both medicine and science enabled the US medical profession to achieve sovereign status over the practice of medicine.[16] Formal, standardized, university-affiliated medical education with a strong clinical component and physician licensing under state medical practice acts implemented by medical boards emerged in the late nineteenth century.[17] The AMA made them established norms during the twentieth century. Once the AMA had secured its footing as a national organization, it made medical education, training, and licensing priorities:

> In 1904, the AMA established a Council on Medical Education, composed of five medical professors from major universities, with a permanent secretary, a regular budget, and mandate to elevate and standardize the requirements for medical education. As one of its first acts, the council formulated a minimum standard for physicians calling for four years of high school, an equal period of medical training, and passage of a licensing test; its "ideal" standard stipulated five years of medical school (including one year of basic sciences, later pushed into the "premedical" curriculum in college) and a sixth of hospital internship.[18]

For the medical profession, "[s]tandardization of training and licensing became the means for realizing both the search for authority and control of the market."[19] As the medical profession amassed control, it campaigned mightily against commercial influences, and most vehemently against private industry influence through patent medicines.[20]

Medicine transformed from an apprenticeship-based trade into a formally learned and credentialed profession entrusted to self-regulate. Medicine also became extremely hierarchical.[21] The most learned and credentialed assumed the role of influencers – educators and science contributors who engaged in ongoing, rigorous scrutiny of medical science through peer-reviewed journals. Influencers chose their successors. Medical knowledge and education relied on these acclaimed individuals within the profession, the clinical data they generated, their publications, and the peer review they provided – as did the medical profession as a whole, and the practice of medicine. Esteemed medical journals, collectively "the medical journal establishment"/MJE, became the tangible evidentiary-science authority cynosure of medicine and created enormous physician reliance, which continues today.[22]

The footings for self-regulation the medical profession poured in the early twentieth century were solid and, by mid-century, "physicians were the pillars of any community."[23] Reliance on the learned profession increased with the progress of science and its ongoing infusion into medicine, which was seismic during the latter half of the twentieth century.[24] World War II science research and development/"R&D" necessity was inspirational and transformative. The US government–academia–industry "triple threat" methodology for science R&D that made the atomic bomb to end World War II also mass-produced penicillin to treat the millions engaged in it:

> Aided by the advanced production techniques of the drug companies, the United States was soon mass-producing a stable penicillin in quantities sufficient to be distributed to military hospitals around the world. When the Allied troops landed on the Normandy beaches on June 6, 1944, they were carrying penicillin along with their weapons.[25]

Nearly every strain of penicillin used today is a descendant of the bacterial colony developed by Allied scientists during the war.[26] Some twentieth-century "miracle drugs" predated penicillin (notably Salvarsan introduced in 1910 to treat syphilis, insulin introduced in the 1920s to treat diabetes, and sulfa drugs introduced in the 1930s as the first broadly effective antibacterial drugs), but mass-produced penicillin gave rise to an antibiotics revolution that meaningfully elongated the human lifespan and categorically elevated the practice of medicine.[27] Routine treatments were freed from association with life-threatening infections, new treatments including then radical surgical procedures became possible and mainstreamed, and hospitals transitioned from sanitoriums for patient isolation and death to desired destinations for disease treatment and cures.

The WWII science R&D experience, the medical innovation it produced, the medicines R&D and manufacturing infrastructure it established, and the US employer-provided group health insurance it incentivized drew industry and investors to pharmaceuticals.[28] "The development of penicillin by eleven US pharmaceutical companies under the oversight of the War Production Board gave US firms a leading position after WWII. In the late 1940s, they produced over half of the world's pharmaceuticals and accounted for one-third of international trade in medicines."[29] Industry undertook mass production of drugs previously manufactured by individual pharmacies or prepared by practicing physicians, and "[p]harmaceutical firms in the U.S., Europe, and Japan expanded rapidly following the war with strong investments in research, development, and marketing. In this period of rapid growth in pharmaceutical research, companies expanded in-house R&D while continuing collaborations and consulting relationships with academic researchers."[30] Industry profits from the mass production of antibiotics and other medicine market successes financed the establishment of sophisticated pharmaceutical research campuses:

> Within a short time, firms shifted their research focus from natural products to modified natural products to synthetic chemistry. Associated with this shift, new analytical techniques and instrumentation entered the research laboratory to aid in the determination of the molecular structures of antibiotics, steroids, and other potential medicines. X-ray crystallography, as well as ultraviolet and infrared spectroscopy, initiated a gradual shift from wet chemistry of solutions in beakers and test tubes to dry chemistry of minute samples and molecular models. As a result, chemists began to develop a good working knowledge of the relationships between molecular structure and bioactivity, making possible the first effective antipsychotics, tranquilizers, antidepressants, and antihistamines.[31]

Industry's pharmaceutical research campuses infused sound science exploration and innovation into medicine. "The R&D labs created by Big Pharma in the twentieth century gave medicine a comparable exploratory power: experimenting with thousands of intriguing compounds, looking for magic bullets in the mix."[32] Randomized controlled trials/RCTs were introduced in the late 1940s – a profound statistical breakthrough that enabled researchers to test experimental treatments to determine their efficacy and to detect associated health risks with scientific methodology.[33] Overall, drug R&D evolved from the serendipitous discovery and intuition utilized by the Allied scientists to create mass-produced penicillin to an endeavor undertaken with calculated, science-driven methodology from laboratory bench research to medicinal products on pharmacy shelves.[34]

US LAW-POLICY RECOGNITION OF CLINICAL MEDICINE AS THE MEDICAL PROFESSION'S DOMAIN

The US medical profession's accomplishments in establishing medicine as science and evidence-based and itself as the learned sentinel of clinical care was codified in US law and policy. Beginning early in the twentieth century, influenced by an organized medical profession, states enacted increasingly restrictive licensing laws – medical practice acts – that made licensure a prerequisite for practicing medicine within their jurisdictions.[35] States created medical boards for licensure and discipline, and they bestowed the medical profession with control over them and over the privilege of practicing medicine within their borders.

Restrictive licensure was a means for the medical profession to distinguish itself "from business and trade by claiming to be above the market and pure commercialism."[36] Courts recognized and many state legislatures codified the Corporate Practice of Medicine Doctrine/CPMD to prohibit corporate citizens and laypersons from practicing medicine that requires state licensure.[37] As managed care began to proliferate rapidly in the 1980s and consolidation gained momentum in US health care, commerce and medicine comingled, and medical malpractice became a national crisis.[38] In response, Congress enacted the Health Care Quality Improvement Act/HCQIA of 1986.[39] The HCQIA ensures that the practice of medicine within hospitals and other health care institutions is governed by medical staff bylaws controlled by the medical profession, with confidential peer review by licensed medical professionals who are shielded from liability to promote rigor.[40] The HCQIA protects the independence of medical staff bylaws and physician peer review from hospital corporate bylaws and decision-making even when physicians are their employees. Congress enacted the Antikickback Statute (1972) and Stark Law (beginning in 1988) to shield the judgment of physicians and the practice of medicine from being undermined by the undue influence of personal financial gain.[41]

The Supreme Court held in 1925 that, "[o]bviously, direct control of medical practice in the States is beyond the power of the Federal Government."[42] The Court has continued to recognize and protect physician discretion to practice medicine in this millennium.[43] For example, in *Buckman Co. v. Plaintiffs' Legal Committee*, the Court found that "fraud-on-the-Food and Drug Administration/FDA" claims to challenge the off-label promotion of prescription drugs (commonly referred to as "Rx drugs" and new chemical entities/NCEs) were implicitly preempted. The Court reasoned that giving credence to such claims would discourage physicians from engaging in discretionary off-label clinical uses and undermine the FDA's obligation to self-restrain from interfering with the medical profession's judgment in the practice of medicine.[44] In *Gonzales v. Oregon*, the Court upheld physicians' discretion to prescribe FDA-approved pain medications in a manner that *intentionally ends life* when permitted under state law.[45]

NATIONAL REGULATION FOR MARKET SAFETY

At the outset of the twentieth century, while physicians were coming into being as an organized medical profession and before the medical profession achieved the recognition that clinical care is its domain under US law and policy, medicine was a "free market" in a vacuum of national regulatory controls.[46] People were dependent on the governments where they lived to protect them from the sellers of snake oil, but those local and state authorities relied heavily on members of the medical profession to assess the curative value of medicines. They also were limited in their ability to investigate the sources of problematic medicines, especially as the peddlers of "miracle cures" and the sellers of patent medicines became increasingly mobile and interstate.[47] Nostrum peddlers "mimicked, distorted, derided and undercut the authority of the profession. While they often claimed to be doctors themselves, or to operate institutes or medical colleges, or to have the endorsement of eminent physicians, they also frequently insinuated that the profession was jealously conspiring to suppress their discoveries."[48] Patent medicine makers, in direct competition with physician practitioners who prepared their own medicines, offered courses of therapy and advice to sell their products. For instance, they "distributed guides to health and invited the puzzled and the sick to write them for advice about their medical problems."[49] The practice of medicine, dependent on sound medical science, was stymied by patent medicine manufacturers until WWII:

> Just eighty years ago, before the outbreak of WWII, the overwhelming majority of medicine on the market was useless, if it wasn't actively harmful. There is something strangely asynchronous about medicine's sorry state in the first half of the twentieth century. What was holding back the science of medicine when so many other fields were climbing the ladder of progress?
>
> Several important factors explain medicine's late arrival. But one of the most critical has to be that there was no legal prohibition on selling junk medicine. In fact, the entire pharmaceutical industry was almost entirely unregulated for the first decades of the twentieth century.[50]

The AMA welcomed national government intervention foremost to overcome the patent medicines business. By the beginning of the twentieth century, patent medicine manufacturers, not nostrum peddlers, were the medical profession's most formidable challenger for control over the practice of medicine. "From its founding, the AMA was at odds with the patent medicine business. It divided drugs into 'ethical' preparations of known composition advertised only to the profession, and patent medicines of secret composition sold directly to the public."[51] The medical profession's demand for medicine transparency and quest for control over the delivery of medical information to patients were strong influences at the origin of the contemporary FDA:

> Between 1900 and 1910, three changes enabled the medical profession to wrestle control of the flow of pharmaceutical information. First, and perhaps most important, muckraking journalists and other Progressives joined physicians in a crusade for regulation of patent medicines as part of a more general assault on deceptive business practices. Second, as a result of its growing membership, the AMA finally acquired the financial resources to create its own regulatory apparatus and to mount a major effort against the nostrum makers. And, third, the drug makers were forced to recognize that they depended increasingly on doctors to market their drugs because of the public's increased reliance on professional opinion in decisions about medication.[52]

The first major US national medicines legislation, the Biologics Control Act/BCA of 1902, was enacted when twenty-two children died from tetanus after receiving a biologic (medicinal products derived from living organisms, such as vaccines and blood products) in the fall of 1901.[53] Tetanus is a bacterial infection, commonly referred to as lockjaw because it affects the nervous system and causes muscles to contract, often in the jaw and neck.[54] Thirteen of the deaths occurred in St. Louis, Missouri when patients, mostly children, were inoculated with a contaminated antitoxin produced to treat and prevent diphtheria – a bacterial infection of the nose and throat which may cause severe difficulty breathing, paralysis, heart failure, and even death.[55] The public sought diphtheria treatment and prevention; the disease was a very present and tangible danger – the cause of some 15,000 US deaths annually, and the leading cause of death among teenagers.[56] The diphtheria antitoxin was manufactured from the blood of horses, typically in local establishments with no central, uniform controls. Such was the case in St. Louis:

> The St. Louis Health Department ran a low-budget operation in which a part-time bacteriologist assisted by a janitor from the City Chemist's office used horses stabled on the grounds of the poor house to produce diphtheria antitoxin. One of the horses[, a retired milk horse named Jim,] developed tetanus a few days after it had been bled for serum, but instead of being discarded, the serum was labeled with the date of an earlier bleeding and distributed without having been tested in guinea pigs because the supply of antitoxin from previous bleedings had been exhausted.[57]

An investigation during the crisis determined that "Almost no serum was in fact tested, laboratory bottles were improperly identified and mislabeled, and, even more startling, those in charge of serum production were fully aware of having distributed diphtheria antitoxin that was contaminated."[58]

At about the same time, over 100 children in Camden, New Jersey contracted tetanus after being inoculated with a vaccine (another biologic) for smallpox.[59] Nine children died. There was an ongoing national smallpox epidemic, which created a surge in public demand for smallpox vaccine prevention. Although smallpox vaccination through exposure to the relatively mild cowpox virus had been discovered in 1796 and smallpox vaccination was familiar, the nation relied heavily on a single Philadelphia manufacturer, H.K. Mulford and Co. Reliance on industry over state and local governments for the production of biologics was supposed to make them safer and more reliable:

> The production of biologics had begun in the public sector, but once commercial manufacturers learned how to make them, the companies wanted government out of the business. Their main arguments were that the production facilities of local governments were inadequate—an argument with some validity because funding depended on elected officials—and that governments should not compete against private enterprise. For several years there had been a campaign in the pharmaceutical and medical press, probably generated by biologics manufacturers, against "municipal socialism" and alleged unsanitary conditions in governmental facilities. Mulford sued several times attempting to stop governmental production. A petition circulated by the trade publication *Druggists' Circular* and signed by over four thousand doctors and druggists asked New York City to stop producing biologics.[60]

The press, public, and many in the medical and public health professions attributed the crisis to vaccine contamination, especially after a Philadelphia College of Physicians investigatory committee suggested the same.[61]

These crises involving the deaths of children drew national media attention and generated fear, outrage, and support for immediate government regulation and direct government production to ensure vaccine safety:

> In speaking to the New York Academy of Medicine in February 1902, Milton Rosenau, the director of the Service's [referring to the US Public Health and Marine Hospital Service, renamed the US Public Health Service/USPHS in 1912] Hygienic Laboratory, reported on his laboratory's tests of vaccine produced by various manufacturers: there was substantial contamination—"immense numbers of bacteria" present in the vaccines, in the words of a journal news report. "Dr. Rosenau said that his opinion, based on the results of this investigation, was that governmental control should be exercised." Some medical publications also called for governmental inspection and licensing of biologics manufacturers. The *Journal of the American Medical Association* editorialized that "If necessary, legislation should be had forbidding the sale or use of any antitoxin not … tested and

> certified by some competent authority." *The New York Times* called for more intensive inspection and supervision of commercial biologics producers. In October 1902, the Conference of State and Provincial Boards of Health of North America recommended that vaccine should be produced either by governments or by private producers "under the closest supervision of qualified government officials."[62]

Congress had been contemplating legislation for years without success, but the BCA was rushed through Congress – entirely drafted and enacted in only a few months – in response to the realized danger of biologics contamination. The Medical Society of the District of Columbia already had proposed template legislation in response to the crises, and the established biologics industry actively supported the BCA:

> The biologics industry sought passage of the 1902 Act primarily because it feared that the contamination incidents would cause additional state and local health departments to make their own vaccines and antitoxins, wiping out the commercial biologics business.... [A]fter the 1901 incidents, discussion focused on the alternatives of governmental production or governmental regulation. Governmental manufacturing had been a threat to the industry since its inception, and the St. Louis and Camden incidents increased the odds of a wholesale takeover of biologics production by health departments.[63]

The biologics industry wanted to instill public and medical profession faith in their products, and "may also have been motivated by a desire of the large manufacturers to reduce competition by establishing strict governmental standards that small producers would have difficulty meeting."[64]

The BCA granted the USPHS regulatory control over biologics with a focus on preventing contamination in *on-the-market* products.[65] The act authorized the USPHS to introduce licensing requirements for all entities to engage in preparing and selling biologic products applicable to human disease in interstate and foreign commerce and to inspect all licensed establishments. The BCA required all products covered by the act to carry an expiration date and to be accurately labeled with the name of the product and the address and license number of the manufacturer. Sparsity in the Act's statutory text left the USPHS to develop policies for meaningful implementation, such as potency standards and acceptable manufacturing practices.[66] Medicines made without living organisms (not biologics) remained beyond the scope of the federal regulatory control established under the BCA. The Federal Bureau of Chemistry ("Federal Bureau") within the US Department of Agriculture/USDA had been regulating medicines since 1901, but its responsibility was limited to ensuring accuracy in commerce – namely, that medicines contained the chemical ingredients manufacturers listed on their labels.[67] The BCA, with its scope restricted to biologics and without a requirement to establish clinical safety as a condition for market approval, did not significantly augment the Federal Bureau's regulatory oversight. The 1901 crises and passage of the BCA did, however, generate momentum for more national regulation of medicines – by both the medical profession and government.

The AMA established a Council on Pharmacy and Chemistry ("AMA Council") in 1905 with a laboratory to evaluate medicines.[68] The AMA Council, in communication and cooperation with the Federal Bureau (which became the FDA in 1930), set standards for medicines and challenged medicine manufacturers.[69] Congress did not introduce substantive oversight of medicines beyond biologics until the Pure Food and Drug Act of 1906 ("1906 Act"), and then only with support from the AMA.[70] The 1906 Act is referred to often as "the Wiley Act" in reference to its chief advocate, Dr. Harvey Washington Wiley – a medical doctor, chemist, and the first commissioner of the FDA who championed regulation of food adulteration and the purity of drugs.[71] Wiley, generally recognized by historians as "the Father of the Pure Food and Drug Act," had been appointed the USDA's Chief Chemist in 1882, and the Federal Bureau was strengthened immensely under his leadership. Wiley brought national science-based scrutiny and challenges to commercial manufacturers' use of food additives, mobilized consumer protection coalitions and other advocacy groups during the Progressive Era of legislation (1896–1916) to build political persuasion on the local, state, and national levels, and his work established national government science scrutiny of both food and drugs.[72]

Consistent with the work of the AMA Council, "The logic of the 1906 law was to improve the functioning of the market by making consumer information more accurate."[73] The intent of the 1906 Act was to expand federal regulation of drugs beyond biologics to police the reliability of drug composition and quality *with deference to physician discretion to choose them*.[74] To protect physicians and pharmacists as well as patients, the 1906 Act required manufacturers to identify the inclusion of substances known as highly addictive; manufacturers were required to "bear a statement on the label of the quantity or proportion of any alcohol, morphine, opium, cocaine, heroin," and derivates of those substances.[75] Violators were subject to fines and, for subsequent offenses, potential imprisonment of up to one year. The federal government was authorized to seize and destroy adulterated goods.

The AMA and the American Pharmacists Association/APhA were delighted with the labeling provisions that mandated the identification of drug content, and especially the imposition of information requirements on over-the-counter/OTC medications.[76] Physicians and pharmacists shared an interest in protecting patients and limiting liability, as well as economic interest. "Their economic interest was clear: patent medicines and nostrums, sold directly to the consumer by traveling medicine men and in other ways, competed with their services."[77] However, all non-narcotic drugs still could be sold legally without a prescription, and many manufacturers of those products directed their advertising at consumers. Also, the 1906 law was enacted with the medical profession's expectation that physicians would have full discretion over clinical use including efficacy assessment, and the Supreme Court agreed. When the Federal Bureau attempted to implement the 1906 Act more expansively by prosecuting manufacturer labels that stated products could cure cancer, the Supreme Court ruled in 1911 that the misbranding provisions of the

1906 Act prohibited false statements about drug *identity*, not false statements about their therapeutic effectiveness.[78] Congress responded the following year by enacting the Sherley Amendment to prohibit false therapeutic claims on labels *intended to defraud* consumers.[79] Although false and misleading claims about curative value became actionable, the government shouldered the burden of establishing intent. The government found it difficult to prove intent to defraud before the judiciary at the time, and the 1906 Act also was ineffective in protecting patients in other fundamental ways:

> As it turned out, establishing that the manufacturer knew ahead of time that the product wouldn't deliver the claimed cure, i.e., that the claim was false and there was intent to defraud, proved difficult to establish in a court of law. A further shortcoming was that the ingredients of the medicine didn't have to be displayed anywhere on the container. This was clearly a boon to the manufacturer of the "wonder drug" who wanted to keep the formula secret and mysterious. But this led to many serious problems for the unsuspecting sick individual, including death.... It wasn't until the Gould Amendment of 1913 that the manufacturer was required to display the contents plainly and conspicuously on the outside of the package.[80]

The 1906 Act, fully implemented, did not prevent the sale of a radioactive beverage, "cures" for diabetes and tuberculosis that did not cure, and a portfolio of similar products.

NATIONAL REGULATION TO REQUIRE *PREMARKET* PROOF OF SAFETY

By the 1930s, journalists, consumer protection groups, federal regulators, members of Congress, and medical professionals – pharmacists (APhA) as well as physicians (AMA) – had become orchestrated, agitated, and vocal advocates for increasing federal regulation of medicinal products. "The election of Franklin Roosevelt in 1932 led the FDA to make a determined effort to strengthen its enforcement powers beyond those provided in the 1906 act."[81] Some FDA officials supported completely repealing and replacing the 1906 Act, and drug manufacturers were concerned that they would be regulated out of business. Industry pushback with free market sentiment stalled legislation until another national medicine crisis in 1937: More than 100 people died from Elixir Sulfanilamide, and many of them were children.[82]

Sulfanilamide had been used safely in tablet and powder forms to treat streptococcal infections beginning in the mid-1930s.[83] The drug, one of the first anti-infective agents to be prepared synthetically, was highly regarded for its powerful antibacterial curative effects.[84] Elixir Sulfanilamide was manufactured by The S. E. Massengill Company of Bristol, Tennessee, which was directed by Dr. Samuel Evans Massengill and was regarded as a producer of high-quality pharmaceuticals. Harold Cole Watkins, Massengill's chief chemist and pharmacist, responded to the demand for sulfanilamide in a more palatable liquid form easier to administer to young children. Watkins dissolved sulfanilamide in diethylene glycol – a chemical used as an antifreeze.[85] The company developed the more palatable elixir – diethylene glycol sweetened with a raspberry-like flavor – and shipped it throughout the country, primarily to treat children for sore throats.[86] There were no regulations requiring premarket clinical safety testing of drugs (just assurance of safety for drugs on the market, and satisfaction of manufacturing requirements), and the company did not perform any. Physicians trusted the new formulation of a familiar drug, some with dire consequences:

> But to realize that six human beings, all of them my patients, one of them my best friend, are dead because they took medicine that I prescribed for them innocently, and to realize that that medicine which I had used for years in such cases suddenly had become a deadly poison in its newest and most modern form, as recommended by a great and reputable pharmaceutical firm in Tennessee: well, that realization has given me such days and nights of mental and spiritual agony as I did not believe a human being could undergo and survive. I have known hours when death for me would be a welcome relief from this agony. (Letter by Dr. A. S. Calhoun, October 22, 1937)[87]

Patients experienced excruciating pain, convulsions, and kidney failure, and there was no known treatment for diethylene glycol poisoning at the time.

Massengill had elected not to inform the AMA Council about the composition of its drug and had not sent a product sample. AMA officials in Chicago were notified about deaths in Tulsa, Oklahoma, immediately requested samples from Tulsa, and isolated the diethylene glycol. The AMA launched a national warning campaign through newspapers and radio. The FDA was not notified until three days after the AMA, and then by a New York physician associated with another pharmaceutical company. Massengill telegraphed more than a thousand salesmen, druggists, and doctors with requests to return any of its product immediately, but the company neglected to mention the risk of death. The FDA urged Massengill to send a follow-up telegram with the caution "Product may be dangerous to life" and, utilizing nearly its entire field force of inspectors and chemists, undertook an expansive drug tracking and retrieval initiative with state and local officials.[88] Ultimately, 107 patients died and many of them were children. The FDA brought criminal charges against S. E. Massengill. The company paid the federal government $24,600 – the largest fine ever assessed under the 1906 Act – and over $500,000 in wrongful death claims.[89] Watkins, the chemist creator of the Elixir Sulfanilamide, committed suicide while litigation was pending.

Medicine manufacturers, confronted with the potential losses that could be incurred from marketing such drugs, realized the potential commercial value of reasonable government safety regulation.[90] The AMA, the APhA, the national press, and a strong coalition of advocacy groups demanded a new FDA bill, and FDA leadership utilized its podium:

> The FDA found a number of allies in its campaign for increased powers in the national women's organizations, whose support once again was to prove crucial in eventual passage of a new law. The American Association of University Women, the American Home Economics Association, the National Congress of Parents and Teachers, the National Women's Trade Union League, and the National Board of the YWCA, among others, together with the same constellation of groups that had worked so tirelessly for the 1906 law, all endorsed the [revised after the Elixir Sulfanilamide tragedy] Copeland bill.[91]

Public outrage compelled Congress to enact the Federal Food, Drug, and Cosmetic Act/FDCA of 1938.[92] The FDCA drew from the Elixir Sulfanilamide experience to establish a new system of drug control and consumer protection with *premarket* safety (toxicity) testing requirements.

Congress increased federal regulatory authority substantially.[93] The manufacturers of new drugs now were required to investigate and report their safety to the FDA *before* selling them and to obtain a premarket approval.[94] The FDCA prohibited interstate and foreign commerce in new drugs unless they were safe under the conditions of use identified on their labels, and explicitly required drug labels to include adequate directions for use.[95] The FDA was authorized to remove any drug from the market that proved to be unsafe.[96] The act banned manufacturers from making false therapeutic claims on their labels, and the FDA no longer was required to prove fraudulent intent.[97] The FDCA expanded FDA authority to inspect manufacturing facilities, and also to undertake some regulation of therapeutic devices and cosmetics.[98] The act granted the Federal Trade Commission/FTC power to oversee advertising for all FDA-regulated products, with the exception of prescription/Rx drug advertising under concurrent FDA-FTC jurisdiction. The FDA, which holds primary regulatory responsibility for Rx drugs pursuant to a long-standing memorandum of understanding between the two agencies, defers heavily to learned physician discretion over clinical use and patient access to market-approved medicines.[99]

Congress introduced the FDCA under the scrutiny of an established medical profession that was still organizing, amassing power, increasingly self-regulating, and suspicious of national government intrusion into the practice of medicine. However, the medical profession was more concerned about industry intrusion through consumer marketing and threats to safety that undermined US medicine and the public's trust in it.[100] Ultimately, the AMA welcomed some additional government involvement, but the FDCA of 1938, centered on safety, simply did not grant the FDA enough authority to keep the drug supply safe:

> The FDA had only sixty days to approve or reject a new medicine; if the medical reviewers failed to make a determination during that time, the manufacturer was free to bring it to market. Most astonishingly, the manufacturer had no obligation to submit proof that the new drug actually *worked*. If the FDA was satisfied that a

> new drug wasn't dangerous, the agency would allow its pharma company to bring it to market. The manufacturers could stir together a random cocktail of ingredients and call it a cure for arthritis, and as long as it didn't contain any known toxins, they could sell it by the barrel to unwitting customers.[101]

Before and after the FDCA of 1938, the AMA regulated medicine manufacturers beyond the US government through its AMA Council – though that was by wielding its physician influence over market consumption to generate manufacturer voluntary participation, not under the rule of law. Favorable public opinion enhanced the medical profession's authority, individual physicians became more authoritative with patient consumers, and manufacturers of medicines voluntarily sought the profession's approval to realize market demand.

THE MEDICAL PROFESSION'S ROLE AS SENTINEL OVER CLINICAL USE

The AMA Council's evaluation of medicines, introduced in 1905, evolved into a professional regulatory system with market control. The base methodology of the AMA's medicines regulatory system was to block manufacturer information to consumers and to direct consumer medicine purchasing through physicians. "The shift meant a structural change in the market rather than simply an improvement in functioning, and it gave physicians a larger share of the purchasing power of their patients."[102] The AMA Council required manufacturers to comply with requirements and rules that extended well beyond disclosing drug composition and abstaining from false advertising claims:

> The council also would not approve any drug that was directly advertised to the public, or whose "label package or circular" listed the diseases for which the drug was to be used. Companies would have a choice of markets: If they wished to advertise a drug to doctors, they could not advertise it to the public or instruct laymen in its use. For such drugs, the public would have to turn to physicians.[103]

The AMA's power of public persuasion enabled it to extend its authority into markets related to health, such as infant food preparations. "The shift to dependence on physicians in infant feeding followed the same pattern as in the use of drugs. Increasingly, the child-care literature counseled parents to consult a physician about their baby's diet."[104]

The FDA supported the medical profession's role as sentinel over clinical use of prescription medicines. In its 1939 Annual Report, the FDA relayed that "Many drugs of great value to the physician are dangerous in the hands of those unskilled in the use of drugs. The statute obviously was not intended to deprive the medical profession of potent but valuable medicaments."[105] The FDA began to designate drugs as safe for use *only* under medical professional supervision, that category of drugs amassed quickly, and the AMA was delighted. In the fall of 1940, the FDA

Commissioner instructed firms selling drugs it deemed prescription-only to remove any information from their labels that might guide layperson users. The AMA, which had been making manufacturers choose to communicate with physicians or the public for some time through its AMA Council, continued lobbying for regulation to further limit consumer self-medication.[106]

In 1951, Congress officially codified a prescription-only category of drugs into law under the Durham-Humphrey Amendment, which identified two drug categories – legend (prescription, or Rx only) and OTC.[107] By 1954, the FDA was devoting at least a third of its budget earmarked for drug regulation to ensuring physician control over restricted drugs.[108] The FDA had shifted focus and resources from guaranteeing the safety of medicines on the market and preventing drug manufacturer fraud to supervising the direct sale of medicines to consumers, which channeled consumers into physician decision making about prescription drug use.

NATIONAL REGULATION TO REQUIRE *PREMARKET* PROOF OF EFFICACY

Publication of the first randomized controlled trial/RCT in medicine in 1948 enabled sound clinical efficacy assessment for R&D, by the medical profession, and potentially by government regulators.[109] The uptake of RCTs escalated the jolting evolution of pharmaceutical science that originated from the WWII triple-threat methodology.[110] Democratic society had been saved through science during the war, technological advancement was a mantra for the future after it, and pharmaceutical industry R&D – an endeavor to create medicinal weaponry in the war against disease and preventable death – was hailed as part of the US science progress movement.[111] Industry-produced drugs after the war was a global phenomenon among developed-economy countries.[112] According to the FDA's 1956 Annual Report, at least ninety percent of drug prescriptions were for medications not commercially available when the FDCA was enacted in 1938.[113]

In the US, FDA regulation for drug safety before and when medicines were on the market raised the public trust level of physicians, pharmacists, and patients, and "A cozy symbiotic relation developed between the pharmaceutical industry and the FDA …"[114] FDA regulation of safety with deference to industry regarding what products they developed, the uses of those products, and the prices they charged for them was good for pharma business. Actual use in clinical care after FDA approval was largely between the medical profession and the pharmaceutical industry. Years of doing business under the AMA Council's heavy market influence had made industry accustomed to direct marketing to physicians.[115] Clinical efficacy assessment of prescription medicines – meaning evaluation of the extent to which they helped individual patients as manufacturers represented to the FDA and beyond – was left largely to physician discretion, which the medical profession continued to protect as part of its practice-of-medicine domain. The public had faith in the doctor–patient relationship, and pharma manufacturers were responsive to it – cooperating with and marketing to the medical profession for prescription drug use, and separately marketing directly to consumers for uptake of nonprescription drugs.

Then, in the mid-1950s, a symbiotic relationship developed between the medical profession and the FDA to the detriment of the FDA's relationship with the pharmaceutical industry. Beginning in 1954, the FDA augmented its official reliance on physicians and pharmacists for clinical safety assessment by engaging them in a voluntary drug reaction reporting program.[116] The following year, the US launched a long-anticipated mass polio vaccination campaign, only to quickly suspend it when children contracted polio through bad batches of vaccine.[117] The crisis renewed suspicion about industry and doubts about the FDA's consumer protection reliability.[118] The FDA, with limited resources, had only six personnel assigned to oversee vaccine manufacturing.[119] In May 1955, NIH and the Public Health Service/PHS established a Technical Committee on Poliomyelitis Vaccine to test and review all polio vaccine lots before releasing them for public use, but the public's confidence in polio vaccines was shaken – to be overcome only by fear of contracting polio.[120]

Next came AMA and FDA joint criticism of pharmaceutical pricing, which was much more threatening to industry than voluntary medical professional drug reaction reporting. In 1959, the US Senate's Subcommittee (of the Judiciary Committee) on Antitrust and Monopoly began hearings to investigate the pharmaceutical industry for allegedly charging exorbitant prices in the US for drugs of questionable value.[121] These hearings complemented a campaign, jointly engaged in by the FDA and AMA, against medicinal quackery targeted at consumers. The campaign culminated in a Congress on Medical Quackery held in Washington, DC, in 1961 under dual FDA-AMA sponsorship.[122] Still, Congress did not expand the FDA's review and approval of prescription medicines to include premarket efficacy assessment until another medicinal catastrophe – thalidomide.

Sedatives were widely accepted in Western medicine and culture during the 1930s and 1940s, barbiturates were popular prescription "wonder drugs" leading into World War II, and the US Military generously issued barbiturates ("goofballs") to enlisted personnel during the war to raise tolerance for war conditions.[123] The government's issuance of barbiturates during the war reinforced acceptance by the medical profession and in popular culture, and soldiers returned from the war with barbiturate addictions. When soldiers brought their barbiturate addictions home, physicians readily prescribed to them and others:

> Tranquilizers and sleeping pills played a large role in the uncertain [Cold War] Utopia of the 1950s. One doctor testified in Congress that "the people of this nation are being steadily educated by doctors and the drug industry to take a drug whenever they felt anxious about anything." For many people, another testified, "drugs were used as a panacea to solve personal problems." .... In 1955, the United States produced almost 4 billion barbiturates, or twenty-six pills for every man, woman, and child in the country.[124]

In 1957, the German drug manufacturer Chemie Grünenthal ("Chemie") began to market thalidomide as a sedative alternative for pregnant women suffering from insomnia and morning sickness.[125] Chemie premised its marketing on thalidomide having no side effects and being completely safe. The company alleged that no lethal dose could be established, and continued to make that assertion when removing the drug from markets and defending itself after. "'If Marilyn Monroe had taken thalidomide', the company argued, 'she would still be alive'."[126] Thalidomide quickly became extremely popular with pregnant women and was widely prescribed in Australia, Britain, Canada, and Germany. At times, it was made OTC available outside the US. The drug was licensed "in 79 countries under no fewer than 49 different brand names" before it was withdrawn from markets in November 1961.[127]

In 1960, Chemie applied to the FDA to distribute thalidomide in the US, the application was deemed incomplete, and some quantities of the drug were distributed in the US for controlled testing purposes (randomized controlled trials/RCTs) to obtain FDA approval.[128] While that application was pending, an Australian gynecologist reported his suspicions that thalidomide was responsible for severe limb and bowel malformations in three children he was treating. Evidence amassed quickly that thalidomide was responsible for severe birth disorders, and Chemie withdrew the drug from markets and its pending FDA application.[129] Thalidomide caused some 2,000 reported deaths (the number of additional in utero deaths is uncertain) and 10,000 reported incidents of congenital disorders primarily in Australia, Canada, and Europe.[130] In the UK alone, during the three to four years thalidomide was licensed for use beginning in 1958, approximately 2,000 "thalidomide babies" were born with missing limbs, blindness, deafness, and other disorders.[131] The assigned FDA reviewer, Dr. Frances Oldham Kelsey, had delayed the application out of concern about its completeness and the safety data Chemie had submitted. The US drug review process was credited with being more rigorous than its UK and other industrialized economy counterparts, and President Kennedy awarded Dr. Kelsey the President's Award for Distinguished Federal Civilian Service in 1962.[132] She was the second woman to receive the honor.

The international thalidomide experience and media coverage of how heightened FDA diligence had spared US children and their families from sharing in it generated global admiration of FDA review standards and solidified domestic political and public support for stronger US medicine laws.[133] The US law-policy response came in 1962 – the Kefauver–Harris/K–H Amendments to the FDCA, which required drug manufacturers to establish efficacy as well as safety for FDA market approval.[134] The K–H amendments bestowed substantially expanded authority upon the FDA and imposed counterpart burdens on pharmaceutical manufacturers. In sum, provisions:

- [R]equired that manufacturers prove the effectiveness of drug products before they go on the market, and afterward report any serious side effects.

- [R]equired that evidence of effectiveness be based on adequate and well-controlled clinical studies conducted by qualified experts. Study subjects would be required to give their informed consent.
- [G]ave FDA 180 days to approve a new drug application, and required FDA approval before the drug could be marketed in the United States.
- [M]andated that FDA conduct a retrospective evaluation of the effectiveness of drugs approved for safety – but not for effectiveness – between 1938 and 1962.
- [A]llowed FDA to set good manufacturing practices for industry and mandated regular inspections of production facilities.
- [T]ransferred to FDA control of prescription drug advertising, which would have to include accurate information about side effects.
- [C]ontrolled the marketing of generic drugs to keep them from being sold as expensive medications under new trade names.[135]

The FDA faced the immediate challenge of dealing with the nearly 4,000 prescription drugs within the scope of the FDCA that had been introduced to the market between 1938 (enactment of the FDCA) and 1962 – with requisite premarket proof of safety, but before premarket proof of effectiveness was required.[136] Short of fraud, efficacy assessment had been the domain of the medical profession during this era, though the federal government did have some legacy of attempting to prohibit commerce in ineffective medicines as fraud dating back to the nineteenth century.[137] Congress required this review in the 1962 amendments without specifying how to do it, and the FDA responded by reaching outside of the agency to independent medical science expertise – consistent with adhering to the evidentiary-science base of medicine.

The FDA contracted with the National Research Council/NRC of the National Academy of Sciences/NAS to obtain external medical science advice.[138] This methodology of drawing advice from independent medical science experts evolved to make independent science advisory committee input fundamental in FDA medicinal product decision-making.[139] In fact, when Congress amended the FDCA in 1976 to also categorically regulate medical devices for safety and efficacy, it *mandated* independent science advisory committee input for both device risk classification (the core methodology for FDA regulation of medical devices) and product evaluation.[140] The FDA is not bound to accept independent advisory committee recommendations, but an examination of recommendations addressing safety and efficacy from 2008 to 2015 and FDA actions taken within one year concluded that it typically did during that timeframe. "According to the findings of this analysis, the FDA agrees with the recommendations of its advisory committees nearly eighty percent of the time. In cases of disagreement, the FDA is less likely to approve new products or supplemental indications or authorize safety changes compared to its advisory committee."[141]

However, there have been some significant differences in more recent years, with FDA decisions in favor of market approval contrary to advisory committee recommendations. One of the most contentious was the FDA's June 2021 decision to approve Biogen Inc.'s extremely expensive drug aducanumab (trade name Aduhelm) to treat patients with Alzheimer's contrary to the extremely deliberative recommendation of a prestigious advisory panel.[142] Three esteemed advisors on the panel of eleven members resigned within days. On July 9, 2021, the FDA requested the Office of Inspector General to conduct an independent federal probe into its representatives' interactions with Biogen that led to the approval of aducanumab.[143] On May 3, 2022, Biogen announced that the company would "replace its CEO and largely abandon marketing of its controversial Alzheimer's drug Aduhelm less than a year after the medication's launch triggered a backlash from experts, doctors and insurers."[144]

THE "US DRUG LAG"

Expansion of the regulatory authority of the FDA in 1962 began a lengthy era of intense tension between the FDA and the pharmaceutical industry, which culminated in the passage of the Prescription Drug User Fee Act/PDUFA in 1992 and the Food and Drug Administration Modernization Act/FDAMA with PDUFA renewal ("PDUFA II") in 1997.[145] Pharma R&D progressed explosively during that time (1962–1992), but the number of new Rx medicine approvals (also referred to as new chemical entities/NCEs) dropped, the cost of drug development soared, and the FDA was often slower in conducting reviews than its industrialized economy counterparts. As summarized in 1980 by Milton and Rose Friedman in *Free to Choose*,

> [T]he number of "new chemical entities" introduced each year has fallen by more than 50 percent since 1962. Equally important, it now takes much longer for a new drug to be approved and, partly as a result, the cost of developing a new drug has been multiplied manyfold. According to one estimate for the 1950s and early 1960s, it then cost about half a million dollars and took about twenty-five months to develop a new drug and bring it to market. Allowing for inflation since then would raise the cost to a little over $1 milllion. By 1978, 'it [was] costing $54 million and about eight years of effort to bring a drug to market"—a hundredfold increase in cost and quadrupling of time, compared with a doubling of prices in general.[146]

By the mid-1970s, thirteen of the fourteen drugs the FDA identified as most important to approve were already on the market in other industrialized economy countries.[147] A 1978 highly regarded empirical study by William Wardell of the Center for the Study of Drug Development at the University of Rochester documented what he coined a "US drug lag." Comparing new drug availability between the US and Great Britain, the study concluded that Britain approved new drugs sooner and more of them.[148]

The additional clinical trials imposed on drug manufacturers to establish efficacy delayed approvals, which effectively decreased the market patent life of products.

Congress addressed this issue and the cost of prescription drugs in the Drug Price Competition and Patent Term Restoration Act of 1984, commonly known as "Hatch-Waxman" – a compromise between the "pioneer" or "innovator" pharmaceutical manufacturers and generic drug manufacturers.[149] To address drug pricing and access concerns, Hatch-Waxman created an accelerated track to market – an Abbreviated New Drug Application/ANDA for generic drugs. ANDA sponsors do not have to repeat the clinical trial research of their drug innovator predecessors, provided they establish that their drug is the bioequivalent of a predecessor drug. Bioequivalence means that, based on active ingredients, dosage forms, and other key variables, for all intents and purposes, two drugs would be expected to be the same clinically.[150] Hatch–Waxman granted pharmaceutical innovators patent protection measures – notably, patent term extensions to offset regulatory delays, such as those caused by FDA-imposed clinical trials, and an automatic stay of ANDAs until the resolution of any patent disputes.[151]

The medical profession and patient advocacy groups joined forces with industry during the HIV/AIDS activism era (1980s into the 1990s) to demand quicker FDA decision-making about new drug candidates. In 1990, the year the US commenced the Human Genome Project/HGP during an ongoing biotech revolution, Dr. Louis Lasagna, chairman of a presidential advisory panel on drug approval, estimated that FDA delays were causing the deaths of thousands of cancer and AIDS patients annually.[152] The FDA issued new rules to expedite the approval of drugs for life-threatening diseases and increased patient access to experimental treatments.[153] Congress and the FDA eliminated the overall US drug lag in the 1990s through the enactment of PDUFA in 1992 and FDAMA and PDUFA II in 1997.[154] PDUFA introduced user fee revenue for the FDA to be allocated to increase agency resources to accelerate the review of innovator NCEs. PDUFA was enacted with a five-year sunset provision – user fee payer (industry) leverage to ensure ongoing industry–government negotiations – as have PDUFA renewals. Government and industry negotiations for FDAMA took place with amassing FDA dependence on substantial user fee funding, which now is nearly half of the agency's overall budget.[155] FDAMA and PDUFA II expanded the FDA's mission to include *efficiency* along with product safety and efficacy, to be accomplished through heightened responsiveness to stakeholder concerns about timeliness.[156] FDAMA imposed enhanced accountability and regulatory transparency on the FDA and changed the agency's culture to be much more collaborative with application sponsors to achieve efficiency. According to Dr. Marcia Angell, a renowned physician who served as Interim Editor-in-Chief of *The New England Journal of Medicine* (the first woman to hold that position in any capacity), PDUFA user fees combined with FDAMA created an imbalance within the FDA and infused too much industry influence:

> Since the lion's share [of user fee revenue] can go only to expedited approvals, that area of the agency has grown while staffing and resources in other parts of the FDA have been relatively starved. As drugs enter the market faster, it becomes

> increasingly difficult for the FDA to perform its other functions—including monitoring drug safety, ensuring manufacturing standards, and regulating marketing. The agency also has a direct interest in satisfying the industry, because that is what Congress expects of it.[157]

Congress expanded FDA authority to collect user fees under the Food and Drug Administration Safety and Innovation Act/FDASIA of 2012 and shifted authority away from the FDA and to industry further through enactment of the 21st Century Cures Act in 2016.[158]

When Congress overhauled the FDA through enactment of FDAMA, it expressly reaffirmed and reinforced physician control over the practice of medicine, including discretionary use of FDA-approved medicinal products in the delivery of care. The accompanying House Report was unequivocal: "FDA has no authority to regulate how physicians prescribe approved drugs in the context of their medical practice. Physicians prescribing off-label uses of approved drugs is not within the jurisdiction of the FDA."[159]

DEFERENCE TO AND RELIANCE ON THE MEDICAL PROFESSION

The legacy of physician discretion to prescribe has been honored by Congress, the judiciary, HHS, and the FDA faithfully and repeatedly.[160] The FDA's efficacy standard for market approval reflects the twentieth-century experience in 1962 when the proof of efficacy requirement was introduced. In the US, with our largely privatized, decentralized, and fragmented free-market health care system, entrusting actual clinical use determinations for prescription medications to the medical profession theoretically negates the need for substantive national government regulation even with an efficacy regulatory prerequisite for market use. New drug sponsors may satisfy the FDA's efficacy requirement with evidence that a drug is more effective than a placebo, "meaning more effective than doing nothing at all."[161] FDA approvals put medicinal products on the market for physicians to utilize in the delivery of health care at their professional discretion provided they do not use them in a manner that a duly licensed, competent, and reasonable medical professional would know to cause harm.[162]

FDA acquiescence to physician discretion in the domain of clinical care includes at times expansive off-label uses wholly removed from the clinical data relied upon by the agency to put them on the market. "A physician may prescribe an approved drug for any medical condition, irrespective of whether FDA has determined that the drug is safe and effective with respect to that illness...."[163] It also includes prescribing new drugs "in place of older, established, and usually less expensive treatments."[164] The absence of efficacy and price comparisons with already available prescription and OTC drugs and other medicinal treatments – a staple in the universal health care systems of industrialized economy peers known as health technology assessment/HTA – has "led to both a plethora of expensive me-too drugs and a dearth of trials and published efficacy studies."[165]

The FDA regulates medical devices with *yet more* reliance on the medical profession to sort out clinical uses and delivery of care problems. The FDA did not even begin to comprehensively regulate medical devices, including diagnostic testing, until 1976 with the enactment of the Medical Device Amendments to the FDCA.[166] Congress passed this legislation in response to more than a decade of myriad clinical problems and demands from both patients and providers for consumer protection.[167] The FDA adopted its safety and effectiveness criteria for medicines to regulate devices, but then applied them with much less clinical invasiveness. Largely because medical devices typically are not intended to be metabolized by patients, new devices are able to propel onto the market by literally piggybacking on previous FDA approvals ("510(k) application devices"), and over seventy percent of new medical devices reach the market this way.[168] Moreover, the FDA now makes these decisions in advance for whole categories of device products, including genetic health risk/GHR tests marketed and sold directly to consumers without any requisite medical professional involvement.[169]

This level of federal government deference to and reliance on the medical profession in the regulation of medicinal products from the end of the last century into this one has resulted in FDA approval and later removal of numerous biopharmaceuticals. These market removals have been due to significant safety concerns typically coupled with questionable efficacy, and only after expensive delivery-of-care use detrimental to patient health.[170] The problem was significant enough at the outset of this millennium to generate reports from the Institute of Medicine/IOM and Government Accountability Office/GAO critical of the FDA's watch over the market and to incentivize Congress to enact the Food and Drug Administration Amendments Act/FDAAA of 2007.[171]

US physician clinical discretion enabled opioid prescribing practices, influenced by aggressive, often fraudulent manufacturer direct-to-physician/DTP marketing, that fed a voracious national addiction for well over a decade as it amassed into a devastating epidemic, a national public health crisis, before the medical profession was meaningfully confronted.[172] The opioid epidemic, exacerbated during the COVID-19 pandemic and now fed by synthetic fentanyl, rages on. "Provisional data from CDC's National Center for Health Statistics indicate that there were an estimated 100,306 drug overdose deaths in the United States during 12-month period ending in April 2021, an increase of 28.5% from the 78,056 deaths during the same period the year before."[173]

US doctors, again exercising broad clinical discretion, engage in expansive and questionable prescribing of antidepressants and other psychotropic drugs, as they have for decades.[174] Antidepressants, the class of drugs prescribed most frequently in the US after cholesterol-lowering statins, are extremely profitable; manufacturers market them aggressively and directly to consumers.[175] Compared with physiologically symptomatic diseases such as cancer and coronary artery disease, depression is challenging to diagnose clinically with precision; it is diagnosed based largely upon how a patient self-reports feeling emotionally.[176] According to the published medical literature, the clinical benefits of antidepressants beyond a placebo is questionable despite the extraordinarily heavy use of them over considerable time:

> A growing body of research suggests that antidepressants aren't as effective as many people believe. An analysis of all FDA clinical trials for four SSRI [selective serotonin reuptake inhibitor] antidepressants found that the drugs didn't perform significantly better than placebos in treating mild or moderate depression, and the benefits of the drugs were "relatively small even for severely depressed patients" (*PLoS Medicine*, 2008).[177]

Moreover, antidepressants are commonly prescribed by primary care and other physicians not fully trained in them or in cognitive therapy treatment alternatives, and they are prescribed heavily to vulnerable patient groups, including nursing home patients and children.[178]

The COVID-19 pandemic provided another vivid illustration of the extent to which US physicians have discretion to prescribe and autonomy in the practice of medicine – prescription use of hydroxychloroquine and chloroquine for the treatment and prevention of COVID-19.[179] Deference to physicians' power to prescribe enabled them to write a surge of off-label prescriptions for hydroxychloroquine and chloroquine for COVID-19 after President Trump promoted the drugs ("Why not take it?") in March 2020 daily press briefings as possible preventative and therapeutic interventions for COVID-19. People dependent on hydroxychloroquine to treat autoimmune diseases such as lupus and rheumatoid arthritis in accordance with established evidentiary science-based medicine experienced a national supply shortage.[180] President Trump, in conjunction with his press briefings to the American people, directed his Secretary of HHS, Alex Azar, to order the FDA to approve hydroxychloroquine and chloroquine to treat COVID-19 regardless of the absence of supportive clinical data. Azar, an attorney and former lobbyist and pharmaceutical executive (president of the US division of Eli Lilly and Company prior to his Secretary of HHS appointment) with no formal medical provider or medical science education, no medical provider professional training, and no medical provider credentials, nearly did:

> About fifteen minutes into the meeting [with health officials, including Dr. Fauci], Azar, who hadn't been invited, stormed in, breathless. He told the president he had conferred with his lawyers and could order the FDA to approve the drugs. The authority of the FDA commissioner was vested in the HHS secretary. Or, if [FDA Commissioner] Hahn did not want to approve the drugs, Azar said he could do so on his own. .... The other health officials were stunned that Azar would even entertain the idea and pushed back fiercely. Trump eventually backed down. But it helped set off the mad scramble to try to appease his insatiable appetite for hydroxychloroquine within the bounds of the law.[181]

The FDA granted emergency use authorization/EUA, which permitted the drugs to be used to combat COVID-19 outside the scope of approved clinical trials, but then reversed its position when sound and damning evidentiary-science data was gathered in real time. In mid-June, when research studies concluded the drugs offered no meaningful benefits for COVID-19 responsiveness and could do serious harm, the FDA revoked its EUA.[182] Nevertheless, the President and his son, Donald Jr., continued to promote the use of hydroxychloroquine for COVID-19 – including in a July 28, 2020, tweet, which Twitter took down for violating its COVID-19 misinformation policy.[183]

THE RESULTING MEDICAL PROFESSION–FDA SYMBIOTIC RELATIONSHIP

The science and evidence base of US medicine was promoted and protected last century through a symbiotic relationship between the medical profession and the FDA. The FDA, throughout its existence, has relied upon the medical profession to determine the actual clinical use of the medicinal products it allows on the market – a policy as strong today as it was last century, if not stronger through litigation tests, legislative codification, and overall reinforcement in US law-policy over time.[184] This symbiotic relationship is anchored by US medical profession self-regulation autonomy and sovereignty over the practice of medicine: The FDA protects and promotes the base of medicine by controlling what medicinal products within its purview are on the US market, with a shift in that responsibility to the medical profession when those products enter the market and the medical profession's domain of clinical use.[185] The medical profession supported the establishment of the FDA and the augmentation of the agency's regulatory powers during the twentieth century in sync with the advancement of medical science and its commercial application.[186] Doing so enabled advancing the base of medicine with reliability, while the medical profession retained its self-regulation autonomy and sovereignty over the practice of medicine.

This symbiotic relationship between the medical profession and the FDA, developed through mutual reliance and shared commitment to the evidentiary-science base of medicine and patient health, still exists. However, at least since the progress of the genomic (the study of gene function in the context of genomes – an organism's complete set of genes) revolution that began in the 1990s, the FDA's regulatory powers have not been augmented in sync with the progress of medical science innovation and its commercialization. Consequently, the US has increased its reliance on the medical profession. In fact, the enactment of PDUFA and FDAMA in the 1990s intentionally checked the FDA's regulatory prowess and increased industry influence over the agency – consistent with the US technology transfer law and policy/TTLP introduced in the 1980s.[187] TTLP, a potent catalyst for the biotech and genomic revolutions, has incentivized intense industry involvement in medical science R&D for several decades, and industry influence has accompanied the clinical evolution (clinical trials research) and commercialization of resulting medical science innovation, which have permeated US medicine together.[188]

The genomic revolution and journey toward PGM rage onward.[189] Reliance on the medical profession to protect and to promote the evidentiary-science base of US medicine, with a legacy dating back to the establishment of clinical medicine as a learned, science and evidence-driven discipline, is remarkably greater.

NOTES

1 *See generally* Editors, *American Medical Association*, ENCYCLOPEDIA BRITANNICA (updated 2019), www.britannica.com/topic/American-Medical-Association. *Visit* AMA, official site, *About* (visited Apr. 18, 2022), www.ama-assn.org/about. The AMA reported spending $20,910,000 on lobbying in 2019, $19,275,000 in 2020 (a COVID-19 pandemic year), $19,490,000 in 2021 (a COVID-19 pandemic year), and $11,360,000 in 2022 as of July 22, 2022. *See Client Profile: American Medical Assn.*, OPENSECRETS (visited Oct. 23, 2022) (calculations based on data from the Senate Office of Public Records), www.opensecrets.org/federal-lobbying/clients/summary?cycle=2019&id=D000000068.

2 *See generally* Editors, AMA, BRITANNICA, *supra* note 1. "The AMA's system of governance and policy making include the board of trustees, House of Delegates, executive vice president, councils and committees, special sections, and AMA senior leadership and staff." AMA, *About, supra* note 1. The AMA's House of Delegates/HOD envelopes the nation:

> The House of Delegates (HOD) includes well over 600 voting delegates (and a corresponding number of alternate delegates), all of whom are members of the AMA and who have been selected by the organization they represent, such as state or territorial medical associations, national medical specialty organizations, professional interest medical associations, the federal services and the AMA's member sections. Some organizations are also allowed to officially observe the proceedings of the HOD, although they are not able to vote.

AMA, *Delegates & Federation Societies* (visited Apr. 18, 2022), www.ama-assn.org/house-delegates/hod-organization/delegates-federation-societies.

3 *Visit* AMA, *Health Care Advocacy* (visited Apr. 18, 2022), www.ama-assn.org/health-care-advocacy. *Cf.* AMA, *Federal Advocacy, What's on the Physician Advocacy Action List for 2021* (Mar. 5, 2021), www.ama-assn.org/health-care-advocacy/federal-advocacy/what-s-physician-advocacy-action-list-2021.

4 AMA, *About, supra* note 1.

5 *See* AMA, Office of International Relations, *AMA's International Involvement* (visited Apr. 18, 2022), www.ama-assn.org/about/office-international-relations/ama-s-international-involvement.

6 PAUL STARR, THE SOCIAL TRANSFORMATION OF AMERICAN MEDICINE: THE RISE OF A SOVEREIGN PROFESSION AND THE MAKING OF A VAST INDUSTRY 82 (1984) (winner of the 1984 Pulitzer Prize for general nonfiction). *See also* EZEKIEL J. EMANUEL, WHICH COUNTRY HAS THE WORLD'S BEST HEALTH CARE? 18–19 (2020).

7 STARR, TRANSFORMATION, *supra* note 6, at 7, *citing American versus European Medical Science*, 4 MED. REC. 133 (May 15, 1869).

8 STARR, TRANSFORMATION, *supra* note 6, at 81.

9 *Id.* at 58–59.

10 AMA, *About*, *supra* note 1.
11 Note, *The American Medical Association: Power, Purpose, and Politics in Organized Medicine*, 63 YALE L.J. 937, 938 (1954). *See* STARR, TRANSFORMATION, *supra* note 6, at 199–232.
12 FAREED ZAKARIA, TEN LESSONS FOR A POST-PANDEMIC WORLD 79 (2020).
13 STARR, TRANSFORMATION, *supra* note 6, at 4.
14 *See* BEN GOLDACRE, BAD PHARMA: HOW DRUG COMPANIES MISLEAD DOCTORS AND HARM PATIENTS 241 (2012); E. Ashworth Underwood, *History of Medicine: Medicine in the 20th Century*, ENCYCLOPEDIA BRITANNICA, www.britannica.com/science/history-of-medicine/Medicine-in-the-20th-century.
15 GOLDACRE, BAD PHARMA, *supra* note 14, at 241.
16 *See generally* STARR, TRANSFORMATION, *supra* note 6 (chronicles the medical profession's organization, formalization of education and credentialing, and attainment of self-regulation and professional autonomy in US medicine).
17 *See id.* at 79–144 ("The Consolidation of Professional Authority 1850–1930").
18 *Id.* at 117–18. In conjunction with establishing standards for medical education, the AMA undertook doing the same for medical schools. *See id.* at 118. In 1910, a national report critical of medical education, the *Flexner Report*, influenced the closure of many proprietary medical schools, and instruction in medical education shifted from part-time community practitioners to full-time academic professors. *See* EMANUEL, WHICH COUNTRY?, *supra* note 6, at 19.
19 STARR, TRANSFORMATION, *supra* note 6, at 22.
20 *See id.* at 127–34, 198–232.
21 The internal governance of the AMA, extremely well established by the 1950s, reflects a profession built upon reinforcing hierarchy. Those in positions of power have much input in the selection of those appointed and leadership successors, and a Board of Trustees wields considerable power over all – internally, and in the practice of medicine. *See generally* Note, *Organized Medicine*, *supra* note 11.
22 "[M]ost doctors still hold fast to the basic tenet of their training: that the scientific evidence reported in respected peer-reviewed medical journals is to be trusted and serve as the basis of good medical care." JOHN ABRAMSON, OVERDOSED AMERICA: THE BROKEN PROMISE OF AMERICAN MEDICINE 96–97 (2005). The judiciary holds the MJE in similar regard. For example, "In establishing the standard of care in medical malpractice actions against physicians for off-label use, peer-reviewed medical journals, introduced by expert testimony, 'are generally considered the only reliable source of sound scientific and medical opinion.'" Lisa E. Smilan, *The Off-Label Loophole in the Psychopharmacologic Setting: Prescription of Antipsychotic Drugs in the Nonpsychotic Patient Population*, 30 HEALTH MATRIX 233, 264 (2020), *quoting* Katherine A. Helm, *Protecting Public Health from Outside the Physician's Office: A Century of FDA Regulation from Drug Safety Labeling to Off-Label Drug Promotion*, 18 FORDHAM INTEL. PROP., MEDIA & ENT. L. J. 116, 170 (2007).
23 SANDEEP JUAHAR, DOCTORED: THE DISILLUSIONMENT OF AN AMERICAN PHYSICIAN 6 (2015) (director of the Heart Failure Program at Long Island Jewish Medical Center).
24 *See* ABRAMSON, OVERDOSED, *supra* note 22, at 42–44. Longevity in the US increased by thirty years during the twentieth century. Even more astonishing, "as a species we have doubled our life expectancy in just one century, and we have reduced the odds of that most devastating of human experiences – the death of a child – by more than a factor of ten." STEVEN JOHNSON, EXTRA LIFE: A SHORT HISTORY OF LIVING LONGER xxv (2021).
25 JOHNSON, EXTRA LIFE, *supra* note 24, at 161. "What made the penicillin revolution so different was how quickly the insight from the cluttered laboratory was able to make it to

mass production, thanks largely to the scaling powers of the United States military and the private drug companies." *Id.* at 162.

26 *See* Johnson, Extra Life, *supra* note 24, at 161. *See also* Steven Johnson, *Between 1920 and 2020, the Average Human Life Span Doubled. How Did We Do It? Science Mattered – But so Did Activism.*, N.Y. Times Mag. (Apr. 27, 2021, updated June 4, 2021), at 54, www.nytimes.com/2021/04/27/magazine/global-life-span.html. For historical discussion of the triple threat R&D methodology, which was utilized to produce the COVID-19 vaccines with unprecedented speed, *see* Michael J. Malinowski, *The US Science and Technology "Triple Threat": A Regulatory Treatment Plan for the Nation's Addiction to Prescription Opioids*, 48 U. Mem. L. Rev. 1027, 1058–65 (2018). *See also* Michael J. Malinowski, *Government Rx – Back to the Future in Science Funding? The Next Era in Drug Development*, 51 U. Louisville L. Rev. 101, 113–14 (2012). *See generally Chapter 2, infra* (addressing TTLP, the triple threat methodology, and its application in Operation Warp Speed/OWS, which orchestrated R&D for COVID-19 responsiveness).

27 *See* Johnson, extra Life, *supra* note 24, at 162–63.

28 *See generally The Pharmaceutical Golden Era: 1930–60*, 83(24) Chem. & Eng. News (June 20, 2005) (no author identified, no page numbers provided), http://pubsapp.acs.org/cen/coverstory/83/8325/8325golden.html. US employer-provided health insurance existed prior to WWII (a Dallas teachers' association is credited with the advent of group health insurance in the 1930s, Blue Cross for hospital care, followed by Blue Shield for provider care), but US law and policy implemented during the war and in the decade after it incentivized dramatic employer uptake:

> First, in 1943 the US government enacted wage and price controls but exempted health insurance, allowing employers to provide coverage valued up to 5% of workers' wages without violating the wage controls. Then in 1954, to encourage the further dissemination of employer-sponsored insurance, Congress enacted the tax exclusion, excluding an employer's contribution toward health insurance premiums from an employee's income and payroll taxes. This made a nontaxed dollar in cash wages.

Emanuel, Which Country?, *supra* note 6, at 20–21. *See generally*, David Blumenthal, *Employer-Sponsored Health Insurance in the United States – Origins and Implications*, 35 N. Eng. J. Med. 82–88 (2006). Presently, approximately half of US citizens get health insurance through their employers, with employers paying most of the premium as a pretax benefit. Emanuel, Which Country?, *supra* note 6, at 2.

29 *Pharmaceutical Golden Era*, *supra* note 28.

30 *Id.*

31 *Id.*

32 Johnson, Extra Life, *supra* note 24, at 225.

33 *See id.* at 162–63. *See also infra* notes 109–10 (addressing introduction of RCTs).

34 Mary Hunt, a bacteriologist on the Allies research team based in Peoria, Illinois, discovered the mold that enabled mass production of penicillin through what might be called "science guided intuition" and sheer determination:

> During the summer months of 1942, shoppers in local grocery stores began to notice a strange presence in the fresh produce aisles: a young woman intently examining the fruit on display, picking out and purchasing the ones with visible rot .... (Her unusual shopping habits ultimately earned her the nickname Moldy Mary.) One of Hunt's molds—growing in a particularly unappetizing cantaloupe—turned out to be far more productive ....

JOHNSON, EXTRA LIFE, *supra* note 24, at 160–61.

35 *See* STARR, TRANSFORMATION, *supra* note 6, at 22–23. *See supra* note 17, and accompanying text (addressing consolidation of power through formalization of medical education and physician licensing).

36 STARR, TRANSFORMATION, *supra* note 6, at 23 ("The contradiction between professionalism and the rule of the market is long-standing and unavoidable."). *See id.* at 199–232 ("Escape from the Corporation 1900–1930").

37 As the AMA consolidated power and control over the practice of medicine during the early part of the twentieth century, the organization was able to persuade state legislatures to codify the CPMD and courts to show deference to the doctrine. *See* John D. Blum, *Feng Shui and the Restructuring of the Hospital Corporation: A Call for Change in the Face of the Medical Error Epidemic*, 14 HEALTH MATRIX 5, 8 (2004). *See also* Maxwell J. Mehlman, *Professional Power and the Standard of Care in Medicine*, 44 ARIZ. ST. L.J. 1165, 1235 (2012); Nicole Huberfeld, *Be Not Afraid of Change: Time to Eliminate the Corporate Practice of Medicine Doctrine*, 14 HEALTH MATRIX 243, 251–53 (2004). For a summary of the state of this law as of 2015, see AMA, Advocacy Resource Center, *Issue brief: Corporate Practice of Medicine* (2015), file:///C:/Users/mjmalin/Downloads/corporate-practice-of-medicine-issue-brief_1.pdf.

38 The first generally recognized US medical malpractice crisis, during which professional liability insurance became too costly and *categorically unavailable*, occurred in the 1970s. "In part due to broader societal shifts that encouraged consumers to challenge authority to a greater extent, the late 1960s and early 1970s witnessed a significant increase in malpractice litigation against physicians." Paul J. Barringer, III, *A New Prescription for America's Medical Liability System*, 9 J. HEALTH CARE L. & POL'Y 235, 237 (2006). The second US malpractice crisis occurred in the mid-1980s:

> The primary characteristic of this "crisis of affordability" was a substantial increase in the cost of malpractice insurance premiums, associated with increased claiming and a difficult investment climate for insurers. Physicians essentially resolved this crisis by passing along their increased malpractice premium costs in the reimbursement rates they charged to public and private payors.

Id. at 238.

39 42 U.S.C. § 11101–15. *See* Craig W. Dallon, *Understanding Judicial Review of Hospitals' Physician Credentialing and Peer Review Decisions*, 73 TEMP. L. REV. 597, 679 (2000).

40 The Joint Commission on Accreditation of Healthcare Organizations ("Joint Commission," previously recognized as JCAHO) issues standards to implement HCQIA. The Joint Commission emphasized from the outset of HCQIA implementation that medical bylaws are intended to "create a framework within which medical staff members can act with a reasonable degree of freedom and confidence." JOINT COMMISSION ON ACCREDITATION OF HOSPITALS, ACCREDITATION MANUAL FOR HOSPITALS 103 (1986). *Visit* Joint Commission, official site, *at* www.jointcommission.org/. The AMA lobbied for legal immunity and confidentiality in the health care peer review process during enactment of the HCQIA to protect physicians performing peer review and, subsequently, those protections have been extended to some non-physician medical professionals/appraisers. *See generally* Dallon, *Peer Review*, *supra* note 39.

41 *See* Medicare and Medicaid Patient Protection Act/PPA of 1987, 42 U.S.C. §1320a–7b ("the Anti-kickback Statute"); "Stark Law," 42 U.S.C. 1395nn (1988 and amendments). *See also* Michael J. Malinowski, *Capitation, Advances in Medical Technology, and the Advent of a New Era in Medical Ethics*, 22 AM. J.L. & MED. 335, 335–60 (1996), *reprinted*

in TAKING SIDES: CLASHING VIEWS ON CONTROVERSIAL BIOETHICAL ISSUES (Carol Levine ed., 7th ed., 1997).

42 *Linder v. United States*, 268 US 5, 18 (1925). The Court unanimously overturned the conviction of a physician for prescribing drugs to addicts in violation of the Harrison Act, a predecessor of the Controlled Substances Act. *See* Comprehensive Drug Abuse Prevention and Control Act, Pub. L. 91–513, 84 Stat. 1236 (1970) (codified as amended at 21 U.S.C. §§ 801–971 (2012)) (regulating the manufacture, importation, possession, use and distribution of defined and scheduled substances); Harrison Narcotics Tax Act, ch. 1, 38 Stat. 785 (1914) (codified as amended at 26 U.S.C. §§ 4702–4900 (2012)) (taxing drugs such as cocaine and morphine to effectively prohibit them). Although *Linder* has been mostly overruled or superseded, the Court relied on its rationale in 2006 when it upheld physician discretion to prescribe FDA-approved drugs to end life in compliance with the Oregon Death With Dignity Act. *See generally Gonzales v. Oregon*, 546 US 243 (2006).

43 There have been some exceptions, such as in the abortion context where, beginning in 1992, state legislatures were able to reach into doctor-patient decision making provided they did not impose an undue burden. *See generally Planned Parenthood v. Casey*, 505 US 833 (1992). *See Chapter* 5, *infra*, at notes 147–77, and accompanying text (addressing state legislatures reaching into the practice of clinical medicine, breaking from the traditional norm of deference to the medical profession, such as in the abortion context). The Court upheld a Congressional ban on a medical procedure, the Partial-Birth Abortion Ban Act of 2003, with the rationale that conflicting expert medical testimony created scientific uncertainty over whether the procedure is ever medically needed, which the Court determined warranted deference to government discretion. *See generally Gonzales v. Carhart*, 540 US 124 (2007). The appointment of Justice Amy Coney Barrett in 2020 to the Supreme Court seat that was occupied by Justice Ruth Bader Ginsburg, which created a conservative majority on the Court, inspired states to enact abortion legislation to test the Court's *Roe* and *Casey* precedents. *See* Caroline Kelly, *More States are Expected to Pass Anti-abortion Bills Challenging* Roe v. Wade *Ahead of Monumental Supreme Court Case*, CNN (May 18, 2021) (reporting on the Court's decision to consider Mississippi's 15-week ban), www.cnn.com/2021/05/18/politics/mississippi-abortion-case-impact-supreme-court-abortion-bans-activists/index.html. On June 24, 2022, the Supreme Court issued its opinion in *Dobbs*, in which the Court overturned *Roe* and *Casey*, holding that the Constitution does not confer a right to abortion and "the authority to regulate abortion is returned to the people and their elected representatives." *Dobbs v. Jackson Women's Health Org. et al.*, No. 19–1392, 2022 WL 2276808 (US June 24, 2022). For discussion of the implication of *Dobbs* regarding government's reach into the practice of medicine, see *Chapter* 5, *infra*, at notes 170–77, and accompanying text.

44 *See* 531 US 341, 350–51 (2001).

45 *See Gonzales v. Oregon*, 46 US 243 (2006).

46 *See* JOHNSON, EXTRA LIFE, *supra* note 24, at 127.

47 *See* Nathan A. Brown, Eli Tomar, *Could State Regulations Be the Next Frontier for Preemption Jurisprudence? Drug Compounding as A Case Study*, 71 FOOD & DRUG L.J. 271, 273 (2016).

48 STARR, TRANSFORMATION, *supra* note 6, at 129.

49 *Id.*

50 JOHNSON, EXTRA LIFE, *supra* note 24, at 127.

51 STARR, TRANSFORMATION, *supra* note 6, at 128.

52 *Id.* at 129.

53 *See* Biologics Control Act/BCA, ch. 1378, 32 Stat. 728 (1902) (repealed), *current version at* 42 U.S.C. §262 (2006). *See* Efthimios Parasidis, *Recalibrating Vaccination Laws*, 97 B.U.

L. REV. 2153, 2201–02 (2017); Ross E. DeHovitz, *The 1901 St. Louis Incident: The First Modern Medical Disaster*, 133 PEDIATRICS 964, 965 (2014). *See also* RONALD HAMOWY, MEDICAL DISASTERS AND GROWTH OF THE FDA, INDEP. POL'Y REP. (Feb. 2010), www.independent.org/pdf/policy_reports/2010-02-10-fda.pdf. The one arguable exception was the Vaccine Act of 1813, ch. 37, 2. Stat. 806, 806–07 (Feb. 27, 1813) (repealed 1822). This law was enacted to encourage vaccination against smallpox, but its life was brief: The Act was repealed less than a decade after it was enacted. For discussion of both the St. Louis and Camden events, see David E. Lillienfeld, *The First Pharmacoepidemiologic Investigations: National Drug Safety Policy in the United States, 1901–1903*, 51 PERSP.'S IN POL. AND MED. 188–98 (2008).

54 *See* Mayo Clinic, official site, *Tetanus* (undated), www.mayoclinic.org/diseases-conditions/tetanus/symptoms-causes/syc-20351625.

55 *See* CDC, official site, *Diphtheria* (reviewed January 19, 2021), www.cdc.gov/diphtheria/index.html.

56 *See* HAMOWY, MEDICAL DISASTERS, *supra* note 53, at 3.

57 Terry S. Coleman, *Early Developments in the Regulation of Biologics*, 71 FOOD & DRUG L.J. 544, 548–49 (2016).

58 HAMOWY, MEDICAL DISASTERS, *supra* note 53, at 3.

59 *See* MICHAEL WILLRICH, POX: AN AMERICAN HISTORY 180–81 (2011); Coleman, *Early Developments*, *supra* note 57, at 549–50. Other cities also experienced tetanus fatalities at the time related to smallpox vaccine, including Atlantic City, New Jersey; Bristol, Pennsylvania; Cleveland, Ohio; and Philadelphia, Pennsylvania. *See id.* at 550.

60 Coleman, *Early Developments*, *supra* note 57, at 551–52.

61 A later investigation by the Camden Board of Health suggested vaccine contamination was not responsible for the Camden post-vaccination tetanus crisis. *See* HAMOWY, MEDICAL DISASTERS, *supra* note 53, at 4. However, the integrity of the board's investigation has been questioned. It has been proposed that public health officials and medical societies, such as the Medical Society of the District of Columbia, strongly supported the 1902 legislation and may have downplayed vaccine contamination because the established biologics industry was supportive of the BCA and collaborating with national public health officials. "The Camden deaths represented a much larger potential public health problem than those in St. Louis, but if the [Camden Board of Health and medical societies] had cited vaccine contamination [as *definitively* causative and *the*] reason for legislation, it would have indiscreetly disparaged the products of the companies enabling its enactment." Coleman, *Early Developments*, *supra* note 57, at 556.

62 Coleman, *Early Developments*, *supra* note 57, at 550, *citing Conference of State and Provincial Boards of Health of North America*, 62 MED. REC. 788, 790 (1902); William Robert Inge Dalton, *The Responsibility for the Recent Deaths from the Use of Impure Antitoxins and Vaccine Virus*, 40 MED. TIMES & REG. 3 (1902) (arguing that boards of health should cease production of their own biologics, stop buying from the lowest bidder, and, instead, enforce regulations leading to reliable products); *Governmental Control of Therapeutic Serums, Vaccine, Etc.*, 61 MED. REC. 495 (1902) (stating "Government control of [biologics] … [is] absolutely imperative."); *Society Reports: New York Academy of Medicine*, 61 MED. REC. 391 (1902); *Unjustifiable Distrust in Diphtheria Antitoxin*, 37 J. AM. MED. ASS'N 1396 (1901); *Vaccination Before the Academy of Medicine*, 75 N. Y. MED. J. 375 (1902); Editorial, *Commercial Virus and Antitoxin*, N.Y. TIMES (Nov. 18, 1901), at 6, https://timesmachine.nytimes.com/timesmachine/1901/11/18/102432344.html?pageNumber=6. *See also* RAMUNAS A. KONDRATAS, BIOLOGICS CONTROL ACT OF 1902, IN THE EARLY YEARS OF FEDERAL FOOD AND DRUG CONTROL 8, 11 (1982); DeHovitz, *First Disaster*, *supra* note 53, at 965; Parasidis, *Recalibrating*, *supra* note 53, at 2241.

63 *Coleman, Early Developments, supra* note 57, at 551. "Although the archives have been purged of [the USPHS] documents related to the legislation, the circumstantial evidence that the bill was a joint undertaking of the industry and PHS is overwhelming." *Id.* at 554.

64 *Id.* at 553.

65 *See* Biologics Control Act/BCA, ch. 1378, 32 Stat. 728 (1902) (repealed), *current version at* 42 U.S.C. §262 (2006). The BCA was incorporated into the PHS Act of 1944, and the USPHS regulated biologics until that responsibility was transferred to the FDA in 1972. *See* Coleman, *Early Developments, supra* note 57, at 544. *See also* HAMOWY, MEDICAL DISASTERS, *supra* note 53, at 3–4.

66 *See* Coleman, *Early Developments, supra* note 57, at 559, 606.

67 The USDA, created in 1862, established a Division of Chemistry, which was redesignated Bureau of Chemistry in 1901 – the predecessor of the FDA. *See* Department of Agriculture Act, Sess. 2, ch. 72, 12 Stat. 387 (May 15 1862); Agricultural Appropriate Act, 31 Stat. 930 (Mar. 2, 1901).

68 *See* Jeffrey Bishop, *Drug Evaluation Programs of the AMA 1905–1966*, 196(6) JAMA 496–98 (May 9, 1966), https://jamanetwork.com/journals/jama/article-abstract/659482. The AMA Council, with its clinical laboratory, culled authority from hard (natural) evidentiary science:

> In its early years, the efforts of the Council were directed to the suppression of advertisements for quack medicines and nostrums, the analysis of secret remedies, and the publication of their formulae. The principle of absolute impartiality to all manufacturers and all products was enunciated and rigidly adhered to. Certain rules and standards concerning the origin, composition, and availability of tests for the identification of proprietary drugs were established with the object[ive] of protecting the medical profession and the public against fraud, undesirable secrecy, and objectionable advertising.

Id. at 496.

69 The Bureau of Chemistry's name was changed to the Food, Drug, and Insecticide Administration in July 1927, and then was shortened to the FDA in 1930. *See* John P. Swann, *FDA's Origin* (current Feb. 1, 2018), www.fda.gov/about-fda/changes-science-law-and-regulatory-authorities/fdas-origin. The FDA remained in the USDA until it was moved to the Federal Security Agency/FSA when that was created in 1940, and then was transferred to the Department of Health, Education, and Welfare/HEW in 1953. *See id.* The FDA became part of the USPHS within HEW in 1968. HEW's education function was removed in 1979 to create the Department of Education/ED (which became operational in 1980 as a cabinet-level department), and HEW was recast as the Department of Health and Human Services/HHS– where the FDA has remained. *See id.*

70 At the turn of the twentieth century, state borders were ineffective fences against the manufacturers of adulterated and mislabeled products and the flow of medicine misinformation. *See* STARR, TRANSFORMATION, *supra* note 6, at 127–29. In response to consumer demand and support from states, the medical profession, the pharmacist profession, and industry, Congress passed the Pure Food and Drug Act of 1906 ("the Wiley Act"), 34 Stat. 768, Chapter 3915. *See* ELISABETH ROSENTHAL, AN AMERICAN SICKNESS: HOW HEALTHCARE BECAME BIG BUSINESS AND HOW YOU CAN TAKE IT BACK 91–2 (2017). *See generally* Ilyse D. Barkan, *Industry Invites Regulation: The Passage of the Pure Food and Drug Act of 1906*, 75, AM. J. PUB. H. 18–26 (1985). *See also* STARR, TRANSFORMATION, *supra* note 6, at 127–29. The Wiley Act required manufacturers to identify active ingredients on drug labels, required that drugs meet purity levels established by the US Pharmacopeia or the

National Formulary, and directed the Bureau of Chemistry to monitor and regulate drug safety and to refer offenders to prosecutors. *See* ROSENTHAL, AMERICAN SICKNESS, at 91.

71 *See generally* DEBORAH BLUM, THE POISON SQUAD: ONE CHEMIST'S SINGLE-MINDED CRUSADE FOR FOOD SAFETY AT THE TURN OF THE TWENTIETH CENTURY (2019); *The Poison Squad*, AMERICAN EXPERIENCE, season 32, episode 2 (PBS, first aired Jan. 28, 2020), www.pbs.org/video/the-poison-squad-5sf93j/.

72 *See* JOHN D. BUENKER, JOHN C. BOOSHAM, ROBERT M. CRUNDEN, PROGRESSIVISM 3–21 (1986). The Progressive Era inspired social activism and political reform that swept the nation and spanned into the 1920s. *See id.* The Progressive Movement addressed problems caused by industrialization, urbanization, immigration, and political corruption, and its members were primarily middle-class citizens. *See id. See also* BACK IN TIME (PBS 2016) (documentary on the life and work of Dr. Harvey Washington Wiley), www.pbs.org/video/back-time-wiley-post/.

73 STARR, TRANSFORMATION, *supra* note 6, at 133.

74 *See* Coleman, *Early Developments*, *supra* note 57, at 593.

75 *See* 35 US Stats. 768 (1906); HAMOWY, MEDICAL DISASTERS, *supra* note 53, at 5.

76 *See* HAMOWY, MEDICAL DISASTERS, *supra* note 53, at 5.

77 MILTON FRIEDMAN, ROSE FRIEDMAN, FREE TO CHOOSE: A PERSONAL STATEMENT 204 (1979).

78 *See United States v. Johnson*, 221 U.S.C. 488; 31 S. Ct. 627 (1911).

79 *See* Act of Aug. 23, 1912, ch. 352, 37 Stat. 416 (1912), 21 U. S. C. § 10 (1934), *overriding US v. Johnson*, 221 US 488, 31 S. Ct. 627, 55 L. Ed. 823 (1911).

80 John Kille, *Regulatory Toxicology, Diethylene Glycol (Elixir Sulfanilamide)*, *in* A COMPREHENSIVE GUIDE TO TOXICOLOGY IN NONCLINICAL DRUG DEVELOPMENT 29 (Ali Said Faqi ed., 2nd ed. 2017). *See also* Oscar Anderson, *Pioneer Statute: The Pure Food and Drugs Act of 1906*, 13 J. PUB. L. 189, 194 (1964).

81 HAMOWY, MEDICAL DISASTERS, *supra* note 53, at 8.

82 *See generally* Carol Ballantine, *Taste of Raspberries, Taste of Death: The 1937 Elixir Sulfanilamide Incident*, FDA CONSUMER MAG. (June 1981), www.fda.gov/about-fda/histories-product-regulation/sulfanilamide-disaster. Most sources place the number of deaths at 107, but Steven Johnson, in his 2021 book, states the catastrophe caused the reported deaths of 71 adults, 34 children, and many near-death hospitalizations. *See* JOHNSON, EXTRA LIFE, *supra* note 24, at 129. Johnson's account is enriched with asides and intriguing details that make the event relatable – as is true throughout his book. *See id.* at 127–29.

83 *See* HAMOWY, MEDICAL DISASTERS, *supra* note 53, at 5.

84 *See id.*

85 Harold Watkins, the creator of Elixir Sulfanimide, committed suicide while awaiting trial. *See* Daniel Duan, *Elixir Sulfanilamide – A Drug that Kills*, LABROOTS.COM (Jan. 24, 2018), www.labroots.com/trending/chemistry-and-physics/7892/elixir-sulfanilamide-drug-kills.

86 *See generally* Ballantine, *Taste of Raspberries*, *supra* note 82.

87 *Id.* at 1.

88 *See id.* at 2. *See* HAMOWY, MEDICAL DISASTERS, *supra* note 53, at 6–7.

89 *See* HAMOWY, MEDICAL DISASTERS, *supra* note 53, at 7.

90 *See* FRIEDMAN, FREE TO CHOOSE, *supra* note 77, at 204; WILLIAM M. WARDELL, LOUIS LASAGNA, REGULATION AND DRUG DEVELOPMENT 8 (1975) (American Enterprise Institute for Public Policy Research).

91 HAMOWY, MEDICAL DISASTERS, *supra* note 53, at 9. US Senator Copeland, a New York Democrat, a homeopathic physician, and a former president of the New York City Board of Health, was a strong advocate for the FDA during the Senate Committee

hearing inquiry. Some in the press referred to him as "counsel for the defense." *See* Charles O. Jackson, Food and Drug Legislation in the New Deal 15 (1970).

92 *See* 21 U.S.C.S. §§ 301, *et seq*. *See also* 21 CFR Part 5 ("Food and Drug Administration, Department of Health and Human Services – Organization").

93 As summarized by the FDA, the FDCA was enacted with provisions:

- Extending control to therapeutic devices and cosmetics.
- Requiring new drugs to be shown safe before marketing, which started a new system of drug regulation.
- Eliminating the Sherley Amendment requirement to prove *intent* to defraud in drug misbranding cases.
- Providing that safe tolerances be set for unavoidable poisonous substances.
- Authorizing standards of identity, quality, and fill-of-container for foods.
- Authorizing factory inspections.
- Adding the remedy of court injunctions to the previous penalties of seizures and prosecutions.

FDA, *Milestones in US Food and Drug Law* (current Jan. 31, 2018), www.fda.gov/about-fda/fda-history/milestones-us-food-and-drug-law.

94 However, the FDA had to make safety determinations (either grant or withhold market approval with reason) within sixty days, and failure to act allowed manufacturers to proceed and engage in commerce. *See* FDA, *Kefauver-Harris Amendments Revolutionized Drug Development* 2 (Oct. 2012) (retrospective provided by former FDA Commissioner Margaret Hamburg), www.gvsu.edu/cms4/asset/F51281F0-00AF-E25A-5BF632E8D4A243C7/kefauver-harris_amendments.fda.thalidomide.pdf. *See also* Friedman, Free to Choose, *supra* note 77, at 204. Prior to the 1938 amendments, the FDA had no authority to enforce good manufacturing practices. *See id*. Even after the 1962 legislation, the FDA *had* to grant or withhold approval within 180 days. *See id*.

95 In 1948, the Supreme Court ruled that the FDA's jurisdiction over illegal drug sales extends to retail stores regardless of when the drug was first sold or how many local sales intervened (addressing distribution chains), and that the FDA could stop illegal drug sales by pharmacies. *See generally US v. Sullivan*, 332 US 689 (1948).

96 The Act authorized:

> multiple seizures in misbranding cases where the Secretary, "without hearings by him or any other officer or employee of the Department," determined that an article was "dangerous to health" or where the label was "fraudulent or, in a material respect misleading." Finally, to the existing penalties of seizure and prosecution, the act added the use of court injunctions.

Hamowy, Medical Disasters, *supra* note 53, at 10.

97 In 1950, the US Court of Appeals for the Ninth Circuit held that drug manufacturers may not evade the Act's prohibition of making false therapeutic claims under 21 U.S.C.A. § 352(f) (1) by omitting the intended use of a drug from its label. *See Alberty Food Products Co. v. United States*, 185 F.2d 321 (9th Cir. 1950).

98 Modern standards for good manufacturing practices/GMPs are rooted in a 1941 incident in which sulfathiazole (an antibiotic) tablets were adulterated with the sedative phenobarbital, which and caused hundreds of deaths and injuries. *See* John Swann, *The 1941 Sulfathiazole Disaster and the Birth of Good Manufacturing Practices*, 53 J. Pharm. Sci. Tech. 148, 148–53 (May–June 1999). The FDA's investigation of the manufacturer, Winthrop Chemical Company, revealed serious quality control deficiencies and

recall irregularities. *See id.* Consequently, the FDA required detailed control standards throughout the industry. *See id.*

99 *See* Memorandum of Understanding Between FTC and the FDA, 36 FED. REG. 18,539 (Sept. 15, 1971), https://fda.report/media/99834/Memorandum-of-Understanding-Between-Federal-Trade-Commission-and-the-Food-and-Drug-Administration.pdf. *See Chapter* 3, *infra*, at note 76, and accompanying text (discussing the memorandum of understanding).

100 *See generally* STARR, TRANSFORMATION, *supra* note 6 (examining how the roles of doctors, hospitals, health plans, and government programs in patient care have evolved over the last two-and-a-half centuries).

101 JOHNSON, EXTRA LIFE, *supra* note 24, at 133.

102 STARR, TRANSFORMATION, *supra* note 6, at 133.

103 *Id.* at 132.

104 *Id.* at 134.

105 FDA, FEDERAL FOOD, DRUG, AND COSMETIC LAW: ADMINISTRATIVE REPORTS, 1907–1949 (1951), *quoted in* HAMOWY, MEDICAL DISASTERS, *supra* note 53, at 10.

106 *See* James G. Burrow, *The Prescription-Drug Policies of the American Medical Association in* THE PROGRESSIVE ERA, *in* SAFEGUARDING THE PUBLIC: HISTORICAL ASPECTS OF MEDICINAL DRUG CONTROL 112, 112–22 (John B. Blake ed., 1970).

107 *See* Pub. L. No. 82–215, § 1, 65 Stat. 648 (1951), *codified as amended*, 21 U.S.C. § 353(b). *See also* Lars Noah, *Reversal of Fortune: Moving Pharmaceuticals from over-the-Counter to Prescription Status?*, 63 VILL. L. REV. 355, 393 (2018).

108 *See* PETER TEMIN, TAKING YOUR MEDICINE: DRUG REGULATION IN THE UNITED STATES 121 (1980).

109 *See* JOHNSON, EXTRA LIFE, *supra* note 24, at 138–39. *See supra* note 33, and accompanying text (addressing introduction of RCTs).

110 *See Chapter* 2, *infra*, at notes 115–27, and accompanying text ("The Origin of US Science R&D Triple-Threat Methodology: WWII Necessity").

111 *See generally* Johnson, *Between 1920 and 2020*, *supra* note 26.

112 *See Pharmaceutical Golden Era*, *supra* note 28.

113 *See* JOHNSON, EXTRA LIFE, *supra* note 24, at 138–39. "Today, of course, we think of medicine as one of the pillars of modern progress, but until quite recently, drug development was a scattershot and largely unscientific endeavor." Johnson, *Between 1920 and 2020*, *supra* note 26, at 21.

114 FRIEDMAN, FREE TO CHOOSE, *supra* note 77, at 204. The New Deal and World War II pivoted the US economy from a market free-for-all to an aggressive capitalist system but with government regulatory controls and interventions:

> Taxes were high, in some cases as high as 92 percent; a third of the nation's workers were union members; vigilant antitrust policy tried to limit monopoly power. And the government, following the ideas developed by Britain's John Maynard Keyes, took an active role in trying to fight recessions and maintain full employment.

Paul Krugman, *Market Watch: The Two Economists Who Fought over How Free the Market Should be*, N.Y. TIMES (Aug. 22, 2021), at 10, www.nytimes.com/2021/08/03/books/the-two-economists-who-fought-over-how-free-the-free-market-should-be.h. The University of Chicago's Milton Friedman sought to replace government "fences" (Congress's legislative and other law-policy interventions) with deft Federal Reserve management of monetary policy. The Massachusetts Institute of Technology's Paul Samuelson, a contemporary of Friedman who adhered to Keynesian economic theory that government spending and taxes were effective means to manage the economy, countered that capitalism and markets work when government intervenes strategically to protect market integrity and the public's interests. *See generally* NICHOLAS WAPSHOTT, SAMUELSON FRIEDMAN, THE BATTLE OVER THE FREE MARKET (2021).

115 *See supra* notes 68–69, 102–03, and accompanying text (addressing the AMA Council's regulation of industry behavior and elevation of medical profession control).

116 The inspiration for this reporting program collaboration was another national safety issue – this one involving chloramphenicol, an antibiotic used to treat serious bacterial infections. A nationwide FDA investigation in 1952 concluded that chloramphenicol caused nearly 180 cases of often deadly blood diseases. *See* FDA, *A Brief History of the Center for Drug Evaluation and Research* (current as of Jan. 31, 2018), www.fda.gov/about-fda/fda-history-exhibits/brief-history-center-drug-evaluation-and-research. A few years later, the FDA engaged the American Society of Hospital Pharmacists, the American Association of Medical Record Librarians, and the AMA in a voluntary program of drug reaction reporting. *See id.* The program blossomed and, by 1963, some 200 hospitals were participating. *See id.*

117 *See* Michael Fitzpatrick, *Review: The Cutter Incident: How America's First Polio Vaccine Led to a Growing Vaccine Crisis*, 99(3) J. ROYAL SOC. MED. 156 (Mar. 2006), www.ncbi.nlm.nih.gov/pmc/articles/PMC1383764/. *See generally* DAVID M. OSHINSKY, POLIO: AN AMERICAN STORY (2006).

118 *See generally The Polio Crusade*, AMERICAN EXPERIENCE (PBS, first aired Feb. 2, 2009).

119 *See generally id.*

120 *See* Justin E. Juskewitch, Carmen J. Tapia, Anthony J. Windebank, *Lessons from the Salk Polio Vaccine: Methods for and Risks of Rapid Translation*, 3(4) CLIN TRANSL SCI. 182–85 (Aug. 2010), www.ncbi.nlm.nih.gov/pmc/articles/PMC2928990/.

121 *See* REPORT OF THE COMMITTEE ON THE JUDICIARY, US SENATE, MADE BY THE SUBCOMMITTEE ON ANTITRUST AND MONOPOLY, ADMINISTERED PRICES: DRUGS, 87th Cong., 1st sess., Report No. 448 (1961), *reprinted in* LEGISLATIVE HISTORY OF THE FOOD, DRUG, AND COSMETIC ACT, vol. 17, at 178–374 (1961); HEARINGS BEFORE THE SUBCOMMITTEE ON ANTITRUST AND MONOPOLY OF THE COMMITTEE ON THE JUDICIARY, US SENATE, DRUG INDUSTRY ANTITRUST ACT, 87th Cong., 1st sess., S. 1552 (1961), *reprinted in* LEGISLATIVE HISTORY OF THE FOOD, DRUG, AND COSMETIC ACT, vol. 17, at 566 (1961).

122 *See* CONGRESS ON MEDICAL QUACKERY: CONFERENCE REPORT, 77 PUB. H. REPS. 453–55 (1962), www.jstor.org/stable/4591517. The Department of Health, Education, and Welfare/DHEW, which would be renamed the Department of Health and Human Services/HHS in 1980, had appointed a Citizen Advisory Committee to investigate quackery in America in 1955. The FDA organized a Division of Public Information in 1958, in part to implement recommendations from the Citizen Advisory Committee. *See* HAMOWY, MEDICAL DISASTERS, *supra* note 53, at 12.

123 US culture embraced pharmaceuticals during the twentieth century including Rx psychoactive drugs, from addictive "pep pills" to their sedating counterparts, all reinforced by the US government during World War II and the Vietnam War. "Amphetamines actually increased in popularity after World War II due to its widespread use (and abuse) in the military. And by the 1960s, it was a full-fledged epidemic, with so-called 'rainbow diet pills' (potent cocktails of sedatives and stimulants) commonly prescribed by doctors." Erin Blakemore, *Golden Age Hollywood Had a Dirty Little Secret: Drugs*, HISTORY.COM (Mar. 1, 2018, updated Nov. 6, 2018), www.history.com/news/judy-garland-barbiturates-hollywood-studio-drugs. "Between the 1920s and the mid-1950s, practically the only drugs used as sedatives and hypnotics were

barbiturates." Francisco López-Muñoz, Ronaldo Ucha-Udabe, Cecilio Alamo, *The History of Barbiturates a Century after Their Clinical Introduction*, 1 NEUROPSYCH. DIS. TRTMNT. 329, 329–43 (2005), www.ncbi.nlm.nih.gov/pmc/articles/PMC2424120/. *See generally* Editors, *Barbiturate*, ENCYCLOPEDIA BRITANNICA (visited Apr. 6, 2023), www.britannica.com/science/barbiturate.

124 TRENT STEPHENS, ROCK BRYNER, DARK REMEDY: THE IMPACT OF THALIDOMIDE AND ITS REVIVAL AS A VITAL MEDICINE 5 (2001). *See generally* Blakemore, *Golden Age*, *supra* note 123.

125 *See generally* MARTIN JOHNSON, RAYMOND G. STOKES, TOBIAS ARNDT, THE THALIDOMIDE CATASTROPHE: HOW IT HAPPENED, WHO WAS RESPONSIBLE AND WHY THE SEARCH FOR JUSTICE CONTINUES AFTER MORE THAN SIX DECADES (2018); ATTACKING THE DEVIL: HAROLD EVANS AND THE LAST NAZI WAR CRIME (Netflix 2016) (documentary). *See* JOHNSON, EXTRA LIFE, *supra* note 24, at 133–37. In the UK, after years of thalidomide litigation that exposed domestic law hostile to plaintiffs and that silenced the press, a settlement was reached, and a trust established for the UK thalidomide victims. *Visit* The Thalidomide Trust, official site, www.thalidomidetrust.org/attacking-devil/.

126 JOHNSON, EXTRA LIFE, *supra* note 24, at 134.

127 *See* JOHNSON, STOKES, ARNDT, THALIDOMIDE CATASTROPHE, *supra* note 125, at 7.

128 *See* JOHNSON, EXTRA LIFE, *supra* note 24, at 134–35.

129 *See generally* STEPHENS, BRYNER, DARK REMEDY, *supra* note 124. However, thalidomide has powerful anti-inflammatory properties, which brought it back to market. Utilizing sound contemporary RCT methodology, thalidomide was reintroduced to world markets over subsequent years to treat millions of people with a range of debilitating diseases, including AIDS, arthritis, brain tumors, other cancers, Crohn's disease, leprosy, lupus, multiple myeloma, multiple sclerosis, and tuberculosis. *See generally id.*

130 *See id.* at 5.

131 *Visit* The Thalidomide Trust, official site, www.thalidomidetrust.org/attacking-devil/.

132 According to a critic of the expansion of FDA regulation under the *Kefauver-Harris* Amendments (*see supra* note 94, and accompanying text), the FDA exploited its institutional delay to build a global perception of FDA delay attributable to elevated regulatory scrutiny and reliability:

> The truth is that thalidomide was not distributed throughout the United States because the agency's approval process was mired in red tape and because a bureaucrat had determined that it really didn't matter how long it took her to approve a drug that might have relieved hundreds of thousands of pregnant women from serious discomfort.

HAMOWY, MEDICAL DISASTERS, *supra* note 53, at 11–12.

133 *See id.*

134 *See* Pub. Law 87–781, 76 Stat. 780, *amendments to* 1 U.S.C. ch. 9 § 301, *et seq*. *See generally* Sam Peltzman, *An Evaluation of Consumer Protection Legislation: The 1962 Drug Amendments*, 81 J. OF POL. ECON. 1051 (1973); FDA, *Kefauver-Harris*, *supra* note 94. *See also* FDA, *Milestones*, *supra* note 93.

135 FDA, *Kefauver-Harris*, *supra* note 94, at 2. The United States Supreme Court upheld the 1962 efficacy requirement and FDA discretion to control entire classes of products in *Weinberger v. Hynson, Wescott & Dunning, Inc.*, 412 US 609 (1973).

136 *See* Committee to Study the Use of Advisory Committees, Institute of Medicine/IOM, *Chapter: 2 Historical Evolution of FDA Advisory Committees*, *in* FOOD AND DRUG ADMINISTRATION ADVISORY COMMITTEES 48 (1992) (Richard A. Rettig, Laurence E. Earley, Richard A. Merrill eds.), www.nap.edu/read/2073/chapter/4. The FDA

estimated that there were 3,000 medicinal products on the market based on applications filed 1938–1962, and another 1,000 marketed without applications. *See id.* at 50, *citing* Memorandum from James L Goddard, M.D., Commissioner of Food and Drugs, to Dr. Keith Cannan, Division of Medical Science, National Academy of Sciences-National Research Council/NAS-NRC, "Efficacy Review of Pre-1962 Drugs" (Mar. 31,1966).

137 *See* JOHN SWANN, SURE CURE: PUBLIC POLICY ON DRUG EFFICACY BEFORE 1962 (1977).

138 *See* Committee to Study, *Historical Evolution, supra* note 136, at 48. In a memorandum to the director of the NAS-NRC Division of Medical Science, the FDA Commissioner wrote:

> Although this is a one-time task requiring evaluation of material somewhat different from that now obtained in current drug approval procedures, its long range significance exceeds that of all other drug activity currently pursued by the Food and Drug Administration. Recommendations from the most expert sources are essential if *this* Administration is to suppress flagrant claims, eliminate worthless products and at the same time protect the physician's therapeutic resources.

Committee to Study, *Historical Evolution*, at 50, *quoting* Memorandum *from* James L Goddard, M.D., Commissioner of Food and Drugs, to Dr. Keith Cannan, Division of Medical Science, National Academy of Sciences-National Research Council/NAS-NRC, *Efficacy Review of Pre-1962 Drugs* (Mar. 31,1966). The study began in 1966 and concluded in 1969. *See id.*

139 *See generally* SHEILA JASANOFF, THE FIFTH BRANCH: SCIENCE ADVISERS AS POLICYMAKERS (1990); BRUCE L. R. SMITH, THE ADVISERS. SCIENTIST IN THE POLICY PROCESS (1992). *The* FDA established review committees for OTC drugs, and then extended the approach to new prescription/RX drugs and other medicinal products. Committee to Study, *Historical Evolution, supra*, at 48. According to FDA specifications,

> An advisory committee ordinarily has a fixed membership, a defined purpose of providing advice to the agency on a particular subject, regular or periodic meetings, and an organizational structure, for example, a chairman and staff, and serves as a source of independent expertise and advice rather than as a representative of or advocate for any particular interest.

21 CFR 14.1(b)(5) (1991). *See* Committee to Study, *Historical Evolution, supra* note 136, at 46.

140 *See* Committee to Study, *Historical Evolution, supra* note 136, at 49, 67. For discussion of the FDA's regulation of medical devices, see JUDITH JOHNSON, FDA REGULATION OF MEDICAL DEVICES, CONG. RES. SERV. (2016), http://med.a51.nl/sites/default/files/pdf/R42130.pdf. *Visit* FDA, *Medical Devices*, www.fda.gov/medical-device. For a very brief, user-friendly summary, see MICHAEL J. MALINOWSKI, HANDBOOK ON BIOTECHNOLOGY LAW, BUSINESS, AND POLICY 138–43 (2016).

141 Cassandra Pardini, *How Often Does the FDA Disagree With Its Advisory Committees' Recommendations?*, MED. PROF. REF. (MPR) (July 23, 2019), www.empr.com/home/news/how-often-does-the-fda-disagree-with-its-advisory-committees-recommendations/. As of 2022, "The FDA ha[d] 31 standing independent advisory committees spanning a range of medical disciplines; these committees usually comprise about a dozen subject matter experts plus patients, consumers, and a (nonvoting) industry representative." C. Joseph Ross Daval, Aaron S. Kesselheim, Ameet Sarpatwari, *Improving the Use of FDA Advisory Committees*, 387(8) N. ENG. J. MED. 675–77, 675 (Aug. 25, 2022) (asserting that "Advisory committees cannot support public trust in FDA decisions if the agency uses them inconsistently" and proposing reforms to improve accountability, transparency, and trust), www.nejm.org/doi/full/10.1056/NEJMp2206492.

142 The FDA advisory panel concluded in November 2020 that a pivotal study failed to show sufficient evidence of efficacy, and it identified multiple problems in Biogen's supportive data analysis. *See* Pam Belluck, Rebecca Robbins, *Medicine for Alzheimer's Poses a Dilemma for US Regulators*, NY TIMES (June 6, 2021), at 1, 15, www.nytimes.com/2021/06/05/health/alzheimers-aducanumab-fda.html; Berkeley Lovelace Jr., *Third Member of Prestigious FDA Panel Resigns over Approval of Biogen's Alzheimer's Drug*, CNBC (June 10, 2015), www.cnbc.com/2021/06/10/third-member-of-prestigious-fda-panel-resigns-over-approval-of-biogens-alzheimers-drug.html.

143 *See* Manas Mishra, *FDA Seeks Probe into its Talks with Biogen before Alzheimer's Drug Approval*, REUTER'S (July 9, 2021), www.reuters.com/business/healthcare-pharmaceuticals/fda-calls-federal-investigation-into-approval-biogens-alzheimers-drug-2021-07-09/.

144 Matthew Perrone, Tom Murphy, *Change at the Top for Biogen after Alzheimer's Drug Flops* ASSOC. PRESS (AP) NEWS (May 3, 2022), https://apnews.com/article/science-business-health-medication-4c25d5aef459f6fff380ff14e354c84b.

145 *See* FDAMA, Pub. L. No. 105–115, 111 Stat. 2296 (1997) (codified primarily in sections throughout 21 U.S.C., including §§ 352, 355, 356, 356(b), 360aaa–1–3, 379r); PDUFA, Pub. L. No. 102–571, 106 Stat. 4491 (1992) (codified as amended at 21 U.S.C. §§ 379g–h). *See* MALINOWSKI, HANDBOOK, *supra* note 140, at 14–15.

146 FRIEDMAN, FREE TO CHOOSE, *supra* note 77, at 206 (internal citation omitted).

147 *See* DAVID FRUM, HOW WE GOT HERE: THE '70S 180 (2000).

148 *See* FRIEDMAN, FREE TO CHOOSE, *supra* note 77, at 206–07.

149 *See* Drug Price Competition and Patent Term Restoration Act of 1984 ("Hatch-Waxman"), Pub. L. No. 98–417, § 202, 98 Stat. 1585, 1603 (1984) (codified as amended at 35 U.S.C. §271(e)(1)); Medicare Prescription Drug, Improvement, and Modernization ACT/Medicare Modernization Act/MMA of 2003, Pub. L. No. 108–173, 117 Stat. 2066 (2003) (amending the Hatch-Waxman Act). *See* MALINOWSKI, BIOTECH HANDBOOK, *supra* note 140, at 160–64. (Figure 6.6., *Hatch-Waxman "Balance Sheet"*). *See generally* FDA, *Abbreviated New Drug Application/ANDA* (current May 22, 2019), www.fda.gov/drugs/types-applications/abbreviated-new-drug-application-anda.

150 *See* Shein Chung Chow. *Bioavailability and Bioequivalence in Drug Development*, 6 WILEY INTERD. REV. COMP. STAT. 304–12 (2014), www.ncbi.nlm.nih.gov/pmc/articles/PMC4157693/.

151 For a timely discussion of patent term restoration under Hatch-Waxman, see Erika Lietzan, Kristina M.L. Acri née Lybecker, *Distorted Drug Patents*, 95 WASH. L. REV. 1317 (2020). For timely discussion of the Hatch-Waxman automatic stay provision and the associated risk of patent holders gaming the patent system to elongate patent life, a practice commonly referred to as "evergreening," see Uri Y. Hacohen, *Evergreening at Risk*, 33 HARV. J.L. & TECH. 479, 531 (2020). Congress has taken measures to counter innovator actions to block generic competition, such as through the CREATES Act, which was enacted in December 2019 as part of the Further Consolidated Appropriations Act of 2020. *See* FDA, *Access to Product Samples: The CREATES Act* (current Mar. 13, 2020), www.fda.gov/drugs/guidance-compliance-regulatory-information/access-product-samples-creates-act. CREATES established a private cause of action for developers to sue brand (innovator) companies that refuse to sell them product samples needed to establish equivalence and to support their ANDA applications. *See generally id.*

152 *See* Robert Pear, *Faster Approval of AIDS Drugs Is Urged*, N.Y. TIMES (Aug. 16, 1990), at B12, www.nytimes.com/1990/08/16/us/faster-approval-of-aids-drugs-is-urged.html.

153 *See* FDA, *Milestones*, *supra* note 93. The accelerated approval rules were expanded and codified in 1992. *See* Vivian I. Orlando, *The FDA's Accelerated Approval Process: Does the Pharmaceutical Industry Have Adequate Incentives for Self-Regulation?*. 25 AM. J. L. & MED. 543, 547 (1999). A treatment Investigational New Drug/IND rule, also referred to as "the IND exemption rule", allows sponsors to make their experimental drugs undergoing clinical trials available to patients with life-threatening and seriously debilitating diseases when new drug candidates constitute a potentially improved alternative to treatments currently available. Another new rule established a parallel track policy to allow new drug developers to provide access to patients for compassionate uses outside of ongoing clinical trials. The FDA has retained and modified these rules to welcome both compassionate uses (a single patient) and treatment INDs (a category of patients). *See generally* FDA, *Expanded Access (Compassionate Use) Submission Data: CDER, CBER and CDRH Expanded Access INDs and Protocols* (2015–2019) (current March 16, 2020), www.fda.gov/news-events/expanded-access/expanded-access-compassionate-use-submission-data.

154 *See* FDAMA, Pub. L. No. 105–115, 111 Stat. 2296 (1997) (codified primarily in sections throughout 21 U.S.C., including §§ 352, 355, 356, 356(b), 360aaa–1–3, 379r); PDUFA, Pub. L. No. 102–571, 106 Stat. 4491 (1992) (codified as amended at 21 U.S.C. §§ 379g–h). *See* MALINOWSKI, HANDBOOK, *supra* note 140, at 14–15.

155 As reported by the FDA in 2020, "About 55 percent, or $3.2 billion, of FDA's budget is provided by federal budget authorization. The remaining 45 percent, or $2.7 billion, is paid for by industry user fees." FDA, *Fact Sheet: FDA At a Glance* (Nov. 2020), www.fda.gov/about-fda/fda-basics/fact-sheet-fda-glance (Nov. 2020). FDA dependence on user fees has raised capture theory and conflicts of interest criticisms. As stated by Dr. Marcia Angell, "The practice puts the FDA on the industry's payroll, drug by drug. The more drugs the agency reviews, the more money it gets from industry.... The arrangement creates a powerful conflict of interest for the FDA." MARCIA ANGELL, THE TRUTH ABOUT DRUG COMPANIES: HOW THEY DECEIVE US AND WHAT TO DO ABOUT IT 243 (2004). Dr. Abramson shares this sentiment, and he considers FDA dependence on user fees just one aspect of pervasive industry influence and a conflicts of interest dilemma:

> How absurd to have more than half the budget of the FDA division that approves new drugs (the Center for Drug Evaluation and Research, CDER) paid directly by the drug companies' user fees because the federal government is unwilling to provide adequate funding. Completely invisible to the public, officials at the National Institutes of Health are allowed to participate in lucrative consulting contracts with the drug companies. Experts with financial ties to the drug companies dominate the FDA's Advisory Committees and the panels that write the clinical guidelines that define the standards of care for practicing doctors. The medical industry even funds the majority of doctors' continuing education.

ABRAMSON, OVERDOSED, *supra* note 22, at 249–50. For discussion of industry influence over the primary mechanisms relied upon by the US medical profession and other stakeholders to protect and promote evidentiary science in medicine, see generally *Chapter 5, infra*.

156 Technically, the FDA's central mission was directly changed under PDUFA II with complementary provisions in FDAMA. While the FDA mission to ensure safety and efficacy was affirmed in both FDAMA and PDUFA II, section 406 of PDUFA II expanded the agency's mission to include efficiency and required the agency to balance safety and efficacy with timeliness. Specifically, section 406 requires the FDA to "promote the

public health by promptly and efficiently reviewing clinical research and taking appropriate action … in a timely manner." 21 U.S.C. § 393(b)(1), *as amended*.

157 *See* ANGELL, TRUTH, *supra* note 155, at 209–10.

158 *See* Food and Drug Administration Safety and Innovation Act/FDASIA of 2012, P.L. 107–250; 21st Century Cures Act, Pub. L. No. 114–255 (Dec. 2016). *See also infra* note 171 (addressing the Cures Act). For discussion of FDASIA and the Cures Act in relation to TTLP, PDUFA, FDAMA, and the FDAAA, see *Chapter 7, infra*, at notes 46–47, 215, and accompanying text. President Biden signed the FDA User Fee Reauthorization Act of 2022 – PDUFA VII, which is the sixth PDUFA reauthorization – into law on September 30, 2022. *See generally* FDA, *PDUFA VII: Fiscal Years 2023–2027* (current Oct. 3, 2022), www.fda.gov/industry/prescription-drug-user-fee-amendments/pdufa-vii-fiscal-years-2023-2027. Overall user fees for FY2023, the benchmark year for PDUFA VII, were adjusted upward significantly based upon anticipated user applications and the revenue they will generate. *See generally* Ferdous Al-Faruque, *FDA posts FY2023 user fee tables*, REG. NEWS (Oct. 6, 2022), www.raps.org/news-and-articles/news-articles/2022/10/fda-posts-fy2023-user-fee-tables. The Cures Act, supported by large biopharma manufacturers and opposed by many consumer organizations, introduced measures to further accelerate medical product discovery, development, and delivery beyond FDAMA – such as by codifying opportunities for companies to provide "data summaries" and "real world evidence" such as observational studies and insurance claims data rather than full clinical trial results. *Id.* (contains three primary titles that address acceleration of medical product discovery, development, and delivery). *See generally* Sheila Kaplan, *Winners and Losers of the 21st Century Cures Act*, STAT News (Dec. 5, 2016), www.statnews.com/2016/12/05/21st-century-cures-act-winners-losers/.

159 H.R. REP. NO. 105–310, at 60 (1997). Former FDA Commissioner David A. Kessler, who ran the agency when PDUFA was enacted and while FDAMA was being negotiated, acknowledged this limitation of FDA authority:

> I need to acknowledge the limits of FDA's authority. It is our job to review drug applications for the indications suggested by the manufacturer. We do not have the authority to require manufacturers to seek approval for indications which they have not studied. Thus, as a matter of law, if an application contains indications only for adults, we're stuck.

David Kessler, *Speech of FDA Commissioner to the American Academy of Pediatrics* (Oct. 14, 1992), *quoted in Ass'n of Am. Physicians & Surgeons, Inc. v. FDA*, 226 F. Supp. 2d 204, 218 (D.D.C. 2002).

160 The FDA and its representatives have restated this policy on numerous occasions, as has HHS. For instance, HHS recognized in 1994 that, "Over a decade ago, the FDA Drug Bulletin informed the medical community that 'once a [drug] product has been approved for marketing, a physician may prescribe it for uses or in treatment regimens of patient populations that are not included in approved labeling ….'" HHS, *Citizen Petition Regarding the Food and Drug Administration's Policy on Promotion of Unapproved Uses of Approved Drugs and Devices; Request for Comments*, 59 FED. REG. 59820, 59821 (1994) (internal footnotes with supportive citations omitted). This deference to the medical profession in delivery of clinical care is shared throughout the federal government. "Congress repeatedly has announced its intention that federal officials take care not to interfere with the practice of medicine." Lars Noah, *Ambivalent Commitments to Federalism in Controlling the Practice of Medicine*, 53 U. KAN. L. REV. 149, 154–55 (2004) (also providing judiciary/case law examples).

161 Rosenthal, American Sickness, *supra* note 70, at 93. *See also* Abramson, Overdosed, *supra* note 22, at 102 ("Evidence of being significantly more effective than no treatment is sufficient for the FDA to approve new drugs and for doctors to prescribe them in place of older, established, and usually less expensive treatments."). In 2022, the Supreme Court heard and decided *Xiulu Ruan v. United States*, 597 US (2022) (No. 20–1410), consolidated cases in which pain management physicians appealed their convictions for wrongfully prescribing controlled substances. Consistent with an abundance of other cases in the wake of the US opioid addiction crises, the physicians were prosecuted for allegedly prescribing medicines, including Schedule II drugs (many of which are opioids), for their own financial gain rather than for the benefit of their patients, and outside the standard of care for their practices. Under 21 CFR §1306.04(a), registered physicians are authorized to dispense controlled substances via prescription, but only if the prescription is "issued for a legitimate medical purpose by an individual practitioner acting in the usual course of his professional practice." In jury trials, each physician argued that they were registered and authorized to prescribe the controlled substances at issue, and that they dispensed them pursuant to valid prescriptions. Each physician was convicted of running a racketeering enterprise in violation of several federal statutes, including provisions of the Controlled Substances Act, and US Courts of Appeals affirmed their convictions. The Supreme Court held that if a defendant produces evidence that their conduct was authorized, the Government must prove *beyond a reasonable doubt* that the defendant *knowingly or intentionally acted in an unauthorized manner*, vacated the judgments of the Courts of Appeals, and remanded the cases for further proceedings. *See generally id.*

162 As observed by Dr. Otis Webb Brawley, who served as Chief Medical and Scientific Officer and Executive Vice President of the American Cancer Society from 2007 to 2018, physician sovereignty limits FDA authority:

> It's important to remember what the FDA does and what it doesn't do. The agency approves the indications—the use of drugs. It manages the package insert—the label. It can tell you that a drug can be used to treat a specific disease. It can make sure that advertised claims are consistent with the language of the label. It can issue safety warnings, institute restrictions, revoke indications. However, the agency is not permitted to regulate the practice of medicine. If doctors want to use a drug in a way that goes beyond the indication on the label, they can do so unimpeded.

Otis Webb Brawley, How We Do Harm: A Doctor Breaks Ranks About Being Sick in America 83–84 (2011).

163 *Washington Legal Foundation v. Friedman*, 13 F. Supp. 2d. 51, 55 (D.D.C. 1998), *amended*, 36 F. Supp. 2d 16 (D.D.C. 1999), *appeal dismissed, judgment vacated in part sub nom., Washington Legal Found. v. Henney*, 202 F.3d 331 (D.C. Cir. 2000), *amended*, 36 F. Supp. 2d 418 (D.D.C. 1999), *appeal dismissed, judgment vacated in part sub nom., Washington Legal Found. v. Henney*, 202 F.3d 331 (D.C. Cir. 2000). *See* Michael J. Malinowski, *Doctors, Patients, and Pills-A System Popping Under Too Much Physician Discretion? A Law-Policy Prescription to Make Drug Approval More Meaningful in the Delivery of Health Care*, 33 Cardozo L. Rev. 1085, 1104–05 (2012). *See also* Malinowski, *"Triple Threat," supra* note 26, at 1047–48 (2018); Michael J. Malinowski, *Throwing Dirt on Doctor Frankenstein's Grave: Access to Experimental Treatments at the End of Life*, 65 Hastings L.J. 615, 636 (2014).

164 Abramson, Overdosed, *supra* note 22, at 102. *See also* Rosenthal, American Sickness, *supra* note 70, at 307 ("[T]he FDA yardstick for approval did not include any consideration of price or measure of cost-effectiveness – a metric that virtually all

other countries now use as they consider admitting new drugs to their formulary."). As explained by Dr. Goldacre, "new drugs are often not a good idea: they're the drugs we know least about. ... [T]hey've often been shown only to be better than nothing, rather than [better than] the best treatments we already have; and last, even if they're equally effective when compared with older drugs, they will be more expensive." GOLDACRE, BAD PHARMA, *supra* note 14, at 249.

165 ROSENTHAL, AMERICAN SICKNESS, *supra* note 70, at 304. Such comparisons are health technology assessment/HTA staples in universal health care systems. *See Chapter 5, infra.*, at notes 384–403, and accompanying text ("The Absence of Centralized, Objective, Reliable Health Technology Assessment/HTA in US Health Care"). As observed by Dr. Rosenthal, "our system has no mechanism whatsoever to control the price of new wonder drugs, or independently estimate their true value for pricing. So they come onto the US market costing two times more than anywhere else in the world, and then rise in price, rather than fall, as they age." ROSENTHAL, AMERICAN SICKNESS, at 307. According to Dr. Angell, "me-too" drugs, which are versions of old drugs marketed as innovative new drugs, are the main business of the biopharma industry. *See* ANGELL, TRUTH, *supra* note 155, at 74–93. Universal health care systems in our industrialized economy counterparts engage in efficacy evaluation beyond market approval. They assess clinical value in the context of cost evaluation to determine actual system uptake and, if so, at what acceptable price. *See* EMMANUEL, WHICH COUNTRY?, supra note 6, at 381–84. *See generally* W. John Thomas, *The Vioxx Story: Would It Have Ended Differently in the European Union?*, 32 AM. J.L. & MED. 365 (2006). According to Dr. Rosenthal, "Doctors abroad are dumbstruck when they hear the prices we pay for pharmaceuticals." ROSENTHAL, AMERICAN SICKNESS, at 307.

166 *See* Medical Device Amendments to the Food, Drug, and Cosmetics Act of 1976, 21. U.S.C. § 301, Pub. L. 94–295, 90 Stat. 539. *See generally* JOHNSON, MEDICAL DEVICES, *supra* note 140. Diagnostic testing performed in-house by clinical laboratories are recognized as clinical laboratory services and are regulated to meet administrative requirements and for proficiency, not clinical use under the Clinical Laboratory Improvement Amendments of 1988/CLIA, Pub. L. No. 100–578, 102 Stat. 2903, *codified as amended*, 42 U.S.C. § 263a (2000). *See Chapter 4, infra*, at notes 34–37, and accompanying text (addressing CLIA regulation in the context of DTC personal genome testing); *Chapter 7, infra*, at notes 166–89, and accompanying text ("Proposals to Enhance CLIA Regulation of Personal Genome Testing").

167 *See* FDA, *A History of Medical Device Regulation & Oversight in the United States* (updated June 24, 2019), www.fda.gov/medical-devices/overview-device-regulation/history-medical-device-regulation-oversight-united-states.

168 *Visit* FDA, *Medical Devices*, www.fda.gov/medical-device. For a very brief, user-friendly summary, see MALINOWSKI, HANDBOOK, *supra* note 140, at 138–43. *See generally* JOHNSON, MEDICAL DEVICES, *supra* note 140.

169 In April 2018, a year after the FDA granted 23andMe approval for an initial portfolio of ten GHR tests that included tests for Alzheimer's and Parkinson's, the FDA announced a GHR tests *category*. *See Chapter 4, infra*, at notes 124–29, and accompanying text. GHR testing service providers are eligible for exemption from premarket review and even premarket notification/PMN once a manufacturer has submitted an approved PMN for their first GHR test:

> The genetic health risk assessment system device, when it has previously received a first-time FDA marketing authorization (e.g., 510(k) clearance) for the genetic health risk assessment system (a "one-time FDA reviewed genetic health risk assessment system"), is exempt from the premarket notification procedures in part

> 807, subpart E, of this chapter subject to the limitations in 866.9. The device must comply with the following special controls ....

21 CFR 866.5950 (revised Apr. 1, 2018, updated Sept, 4, 2018), www.accessdata.fda.gov/scripts/cdrh/cfdocs/cfcfr/cfrsearch.cfm?fr=866.5950.

170 As summarized by Dr. Abramson,

> [T]he number of drugs approved by the FDA but later withdrawn from the market for safety reasons increased from 1.6 percent of drugs approved between 1993 and 1996 to 5.3 percent between 1997 and 2000. Seven drugs that had been approved by the FDA after 1993 were withdrawn from the market because of serious health risks.

ABRAMSON, OVERDOSED, *supra* note 22, at 86. *See also* Malinowski, *"Triple Threat,"* *supra* note 26, at 1079.

171 *See generally* Food and Drug Administration Amendments Act/FDAAA, Pub. L. No. 110–85, 121 Stat. 823 (2007) (codified as amended, 21 U.S.C. §§ 301–399i (2012); INST. OF MED./IOM, THE FUTURE OF DRUG SAFETY: ACTION STEPS FOR CONGRESS (2006), www.nap.edu/resource/11750/futureofdrugsafety_reportbrief.pdf; US GOV'T ACCOUNTABILITY OFFICE/GAO, GAO-06-402, DRUG SAFETY: IMPROVEMENT NEEDED IN FDA'S POSTMARKET DECISION – MAKING AND OVERSIGHT PROCESSES (2006), www.gao.gov/new.items/d06402.pdf. *See also* Michael J. Malinowski, Grant G. Gautreaux, *All That Is Gold Does Not Glitter in Human Clinical Research: A Law-Policy Proposal to Brighten the Global "Gold Standard" for Drug Research and Development*, 45 CORNELL INT'L L.J. 185, 188 (2012) ("Recent market controversies ... have raised concerns regarding the FDA's performance and trustworthiness in overseeing the nation's pharmaceutical market."). Law Professor Barbara Evans has described the FDAAA as "the most momentous shift in drug regulation in half a century." Barbara J. Evans, *Seven Pillars of a New Evidentiary Paradigm: The Food, Drug, and Cosmetic Act Enters the Genomics Era*, 85 NOTRE DAME L. REV. 419, 423 (2010). As enacted, it is. "This sweeping legislation, among other measures, called for the FDA to augment premarket clinical studies, enhance its evidentiary standard, and greatly increase post-market communication and observational studies through Sentinel, a national 2 electronic system for medical product safety surveillance." Malinowski, *"Triple Threat," supra* note 26, at 1052. *See also infra* note 185 (discussing Sentinel). However, overall, the FDAAA embodies much ambiguity, implementation was not adequately budgeted and has been soft, and the FDAAA was followed by the FDASIA (2012), which increased FDA dependence on user fees and reinforced FDAMA. *See Chapter* 7, *infra*, at notes 46–47, and accompanying text. Moreover, within approximately a decade after passing the FDAAA (2007) to instill more FDA scrutiny and reliability, Congress reversed course and passed the 21st Century Cures Act *to accelerate* medical product discovery, development, and delivery beyond FDAMA. *See generally* Pub. L. No. 114–255 (Dec. 2016) (contains three primary titles that address acceleration of medical product discovery, development, and delivery). *See also supra* note 158, and accompanying text (addressing the Cures Act).

172 *See generally* PATRICK RADDEN KEEFE, EMPIRE OF PAIN: THE SECRET HISTORY OF THE SACKLER DYNASTY (2021). "According to the CDC, although from 1999 to 2014 there was no reported change in pain, US sales of prescription opioids almost quadrupled. Moreover, as the FDA recognizes, physicians have been prescribing opioids without a sound knowledge base about them and addiction and, for children, without clinical data." Malinowski, *"Triple Threat," supra* note 26, at 1032. *See also Chapter* 7, *infra*, at notes 207–09, and accompanying text (also addressing physician discretion to prescribe Rx drugs in the context of the US opioid crisis).

173 CDC, *Press Release, Drug Overdose Deaths in the US Top 100,000 Annually* (Nov. 17, 2021), www.cdc.gov/nchs/pressroom/nchs_press_releases/2021/20211117.htm. "Over 81,000 drug overdose deaths occurred in the United States in the 12 months ending in May 2020, the highest number of overdose deaths ever recorded in a 12-month period, according to recent provisional data from the Centers for Disease Control and Prevention (CDC)." CDC, *Press Release, Overdose Deaths Accelerating During COVID-19: Expanded Prevention Efforts Needed* (Dec. 17, 2020), www.cdc.gov/media/releases/2020/p1218-overdose-deaths-covid-19.html. *See generally* Josh Bloom, *It's The Fentanyl Epidemic, Stupid*, AM. COUNCIL ON SCI. AND HEALTH (Dec. 6, 2021), www.acsh.org/news/2021/12/06/its-fentanyl-epidemic-stupid-15965.

174 Award-winning science and history writer Robert Whitaker has questioned why, given the introduction and consumption of psychiatric medications marketed aggressively as innovative and effective in the US for decades, has the number of people in the US diagnosed with mental illness that necessitates *chronic* Rx interventions climbed to epidemic proportions? *See generally* ROBERT WHITAKER, ANATOMY OF AN EPIDEMIC: MAGIC BULLETS, PSYCHIATRIC DRUGS, AND THE ASTONISHING RISE OF MENTAL ILLNESS IN AMERICA (2010) (awarded best investigative journalism book of 2010 by Investigative Reporters and Editors, Inc./IRE). The COVID-19 pandemic imposed global *situational* anxiety and depression. Consistent with prescribing patterns in the US over decades, prescriptions for mental health medications spiked during the pandemic, and especially for children. *See generally* Casey Schwartz, *The Age of Distrati-pression*, N.Y. TIMES (July 10, 2022) (tracking US consumption patterns from the mid-twentieth century to the pandemic present, with commentary on Rx prescribing by therapists), www.nytimes.com/2022/07/09/style/medication-depression-anxiety-adhd.html. "The pandemic's true toll on mental health won't be known for a long time, but data from the past two years indicates a rise – some of it sharp – in prescription drugs for conditions like A.D.H.D. and depression." *Id.*

175 *See* Brendan Smith, *Inappropriate Prescribing*, 43 AMER. PSYCHOL. ASSOC. (APA) 36 (June 2012), www.apa.org/monitor/2012/06/prescribing.

176 Reflective of the nature of mental health, most prescription medications approved by the FDA for mental health treatment are not comfortably understood. Nevertheless, psychiatrists prescribe them off-label rambunctiously – which includes prescribing antipsychotic drugs to nonpsychotic patients. *See generally* Lisa E. Smilan, *The Off-Label Loophole in the Psychopharmacologic Setting: Prescription of Antipsychotic Drugs in the Nonpsychotic Patient Population*, 30 HEALTH MATRIX 233 (2020).

177 Smith, *Inappropriate Prescribing, supra* note 175. *See generally* WHITAKER, MAGIC BULLETS, *supra* note 174.

178 *See* Smith, *Inappropriate Prescribing, supra* note 175; Schwartz, *Distrati-pression, supra* note 174, at 7 (reporting that, in the US, antidepressants are typically prescribed in a primary care setting, by a family doctor or internist, and unaccompanied by talk therapy). "A 2013 study found that more than 79 percent of antidepressant prescriptions were written by primary care physicians." *Id.*

179 *See Chapter 5, infra*, at notes 83–84, 178–86, and accompanying text (addressing Trump administration promotion of hydroxychloroquine and chloroquine during the pandemic without evidentiary-science support and contrary to medical science experts, including top government officials).

180 *See* Michael Erman, *Potential Coronavirus Treatment Touted by Trump Already in Shortage, Pharmacists Say*, REUTERS (Mar. 19, 2020), https://news.yahoo.com/exlcusive-potential-coronavirus-treatment-touted-184603785.html; Blake Ellis, Melanie Hicken,

Sales of Drug Touted by Trump have been Soaring, CNN (May 22, 2020), www.cnn.com/2020/05/22/health/hydroxychloroquine-sales-covid-19-trump-invs/index.html. Almost half-million more prescriptions for hydroxychloroquine and chloroquine were filled between mid-February and late April 2020 than in the same period in 2019. *See generally*, Bella Mehta, Jane Salmon et al., *Potential Shortages of Hydroxychloroquine for Patients with Lupus During the Coronavirus Disease 2019 Pandemic*, 1(4) JAMA (Apr. 10, 2020), https://jamanetwork.com/channels/health-forum/fullarticle/2764607; Anahad O'Connor, *Coronavirus Continues to Disrupt Prescription Drug Supplies*, N.Y. TIMES (June 16, 2020), www.nytimes.com/2020/05/28/well/live/coronavirus-lupus-arthritis-prescription-drugs.html.

181 YASMEEN ABUTALEB, DAMIAN PALETTA, NIGHTMARE SCENARIO: INSIDE THE TRUMP ADMINISTRATION'S RESPONSE TO THE PANDEMIC THAT CHANGED HISTORY 221 (2021). *See generally* DEBORAH BIRX, SILENT INVASION: THE UNTOLD STORY OF THE TRUMP ADMINISTRATION, COVID-19, AND PREVENTING THE NEXT PANDEMIC BEFORE IT'S TOO LATE (2022). Mr. Azar was not the only high-level government health official pressured by President Trump. Dr. Rick Bright, an internationally renowned virologist, filed a whistleblower complaint against the Trump Administration and testified before Congress on May 14, 2020. Dr. Bright alleged that he was ousted from his post as director of the Biomedical Advanced Research and Development Authority/BARDA, which orchestrated Operation Warp Speed/OWS R&D responsive to the COVID-19 pandemic, primarily in retaliation for his opposition to the Trump administration's promotion of unproven drugs such as hydroxychloroquine. *See generally* Matt Naham, *Vaccine Expert Files Whistleblower Complaint, Claims Trump Admin Illegally Retaliated Against Him*, LAW & CRIME (May 5, 2020), https://lawandcrime.com/high-profile/vaccine-expert-files-whistleblower-complaint-claims-trump-admin-illegally-retaliated-against-him/; Dan Mangan, *Coronavirus Whistleblower Rick Bright's Complaint Shows High Likelihood of 'Wrongdoing'*, CNBC (May 14, 2020), www.cnbc.com/2020/05/14/coronavirus-rick-bright-testifies-as-trump-criticizes-him.html.

182 *See generally* FDA, *Fact Sheet for Health Care Providers Emergency Use Authorization/EUA of Hydroxychloroquine Sulfate Supplied from the Strategic National Stockpile for Treatment of Covid-19 in Certain Hospitalized Patients* (alert dated June 15, 2020), www.bop.gov/foia/docs//fda_eua_fact_sheet_hydroxychloroquine_with_revoked_language.pdf. On June 3, 2020, *The New England Journal of Medicine* published a study of 821 asymptomatic participants which concluded that, after high-risk or moderate-risk exposure to COVID-19, hydroxychloroquine did not prevent the illness. *See generally* David R. Boulware, Matthew F. Pullen et al., *A Randomized Trial of Hydroxychloroquine as Postexposure Prophylaxis for Covid-19*, 383 NEW. ENG. J. MED. 517–25 (Aug. 6, 2020), www.nejm.org/doi/full/10.1056/nejmoa2016638.

183 *See* Ben Gittleson, Will Steakin, *Twitter Temporarily Limits Donald Trump Jr.'s Account for COVID-19 Misinformation*, ABC NEWS (July 28, 2020), https://abcnews.go.com/Politics/twitter-temporarily-limits-donald-trump-jrs-account-covid/story?id=72028764. On July 23, 2020, five days prior to the President and his son's tweet to the contrary, *The New England Journal of Medicine* published the results of a randomized study of 667 patients hospitalized with mild-to-moderate COVID-19, which concluded that the use of hydroxychloroquine did not improve clinical status at 15 days as compared with standard care. *See generally* Alexandre Cavalcanti, Fernando Zampieri, Regis Rosa et al., *Hydroxychloroquine With or Without Azithromycin in Mild-to-Moderate Covid-19*, 383 N. ENG. J. MED. 2041–52 (Nov. 19, 2020), www.nejm.org/doi/pdf/10.1056/NEJMoa2019014?articleTools=true.

184 *See* Evans, *Seven Pillars*, *supra* note 171, at 509; *Chapter* 5, *supra*, at notes 113–77, and accompanying text ("Today's US Physician-Patient Relationship, and the State of Physician Decision-Making"). *See also* Noah, *Commitments to Federalism*, *supra* note 160, at 154–55; Anny Huang, *FDA Regulation of Genetic Testing: Institutional Reluctance and Public Guardianship*, 53 FOOD & DRUG L.J. 555, 579 (1998) ("Although there are dependable grounds for asserting statutory jurisdiction, FDA must be wary of encroaching on medical practice.").

185 The FDA's charged responsibility for the products it allows onto the market is ongoing after market approval, so it is cumulative and increases with every additional market approval. The FDA is responsible for monitoring, issuing warnings, and removing products when necessary. Consistent with US deference to the practice of medicine, however, the FDA depends on the medical profession to *voluntarily* report to enable the agency to monitor reliably. *Visit* MedWatch: The FDA Safety Information and Adverse Event Reporting Program (visited July 18, 2022), www.fda.gov/safety/medwatch-fda-safety-information-and-adverse-event-reporting-program; Vaccine Adverse Event Reporting System/VAERS (visited July 18, 2022), https://vaers.hhs.gov/. The FDAAA calls for significantly increasing post-market communication and observational studies through Sentinel, a national electronic system for medical product safety surveillance. *See generally* FDA, *CDER Conversation: The FDA's Sentinel Initiative* (Nov. 21, 2017), www.fda.gov/drugs/news-events-human-drugs/cder-conversation-fdas-sentinel-initiative. *See also supra* note 171 (discussing Sentinel). While needed and arguably profound conceptually and theoretically, the FDAAA did not provide specifics for Sentinel to be sufficiently financed, built, and administered in a timely, reliable manner, nor did it address myriad regulatory issues regarding medical privacy, consent, and the limits of existing law. *See generally* Evans, *Seven Pillars*, *supra* note 171. *See also* Malinowski, *"Triple Threat," supra* note 26, at 1051–52.

186 *See supra* notes 91, 116–22, and accompanying text.

187 *See supra* notes 154–58, and accompanying text (addressing PDUFA and FDAMA, and further enhancement of industry influence through enactment of FDASIA in 2012 and the Cures Act in 2016). The US enacted complementary ("fraternal twin") foundational legislation for TTLP in 1980, Bayh-Dole and Stevenson-Wydler. *See* Bayh-Dole University and Small Business Patent Procedures Act of 1980 ("Bayh-Dole"), Pub. L. No. 96–517, 94 Stat. 3015 (opportunity for academic institutions and researchers to commercialize government-funded invention), *codified as amended*, 35 U.S.C. §§ 200–212, *implemented by* 37 C.F.R. 401 (federal funding agreements with contractors), 37 C.F.R. 404 (licensing inventions owned by the federal government); Stevenson-Wydler Technology Innovation Act of 1980 ("Stevenson-Wydler"), Pub. L. No. 96–480, 94 Stat. 2311, *codified as amended*, 15 U.S.C. §§ 3701–24 (2012) (requires federal agencies and laboratories to actively participate in and budget for technology transfer activities).

188 *See generally Chapter* 2, *infra* (addressing TTLP and associated "triple threat" R&D methodology); *Chapter* 5, *infra* (addressing industry influence post TTLP implementation in medical science, on the medical profession, and on the practice of medicine).

189 *See generally* US NATIONAL ACADEMIES OF SCIENCE, ENGINEERING, AND MEDICINE/NASEM, PREPARING FOR THE FUTURE PRODUCTS OF BIOTECHNOLOGY (2017) (study surveying the approaching wave of biotech/genome science innovation in medicine and commerce), www.nap.edu/catalog/24605/preparing-for-future-products-of-biotechnology; CONSUMER GENETIC TECHNOLOGIES: ETHICAL AND LEGAL CONSIDERATIONS (J. Glenn Cohen, Nita A. Farahany, Henry T. Greely, Carmel Shachar eds., 2021). *See also Chapter* 7, *infra*, at notes 297–320, and accompanying text ("Transformation: Personal Genome Autonomy and Responsible PGM").

2

US Integration of Government, Academia, and Industry

A Catalyst for Science-Technology Revolutions

The 2020 Nobel Prize in Chemistry was awarded to Emmanuelle Charpentier and Jennifer Anne Doudna for their contribution to CRISPR (clustered regularly interspaced short palindromic repeats) technologies – "genetic scissors" that enable editing deoxyribonucleic acid/DNA with precision and "rewriting the code of life."[1] In July 2019, Victoria Gray, a Black mother of four in central Mississippi afflicted with sickle cell disease/SCD, became the first person in the US to be treated with a CRISPR gene-editing tool.[2]

SCD is caused by a genetic variation, an allele, in a *single nucleotide base* among the three billion base pairs in a person's DNA – their personal genome.[3] Whole genes vary in size from a few hundred DNA bases to more than two million, and single nucleotide base variations packing such a potent impact on human health are rare.[4] Single genetic variations that are inheritable and cause diseases such as SCD, Tay–Sachs disease, and Huntington's chorea, are referred to as "Mendelian traits."[5] Worldwide, some 400 million people have been diagnosed with one of about 7,000 Mendelian diseases, and approximately (based on available data compiled by the Centers for Disease Control and Prevention/CDC) 100,000 people in the US have sickle cell disease.[6] Consider that the world population approached eight billion in November 2022.[7] The very defined, powerful genetic lever that causes SCD made it a strong research candidate for a genomic treatment milestone, as is true for other Mendelian trait diseases. However, focusing limited commercial research and development/R&D resources on Mendelian diseases, given the limited patient populations and markets directly associated with them, imposes opportunity costs – at least initially, before any significant off-label use, and with potentially comparable opportunity for clinical success with products associated with much larger markets.[8]

Ms. Gray participated in a clinical trial by CRISPR Therapeutics, a Swiss-American biotech company co-founded by Nobel Laureate Charpentier.[9] The medical team extracted stem cells from Ms. Gray, edited her set of DNA instructions in those cells to remove the allele that causes SCD, and then injected the cells with edited instructions back into Ms. Gray after she underwent a round of chemotherapy.[10] A year later, Ms. Gray was doing well, and her medical team was planning to treat another forty-five people in their clinical trial.[11] "It was an amazing milestone: CRISPR has apparently cured a genetic disease in humans."[12]

Prescription ("Rx") drugs and clinical treatments often turn debilitating and at times life-threatening conditions into chronic ones by masking symptoms rather than curing diseases.[13] Extraordinary efforts and resources have been expended on attempts to cure diseases through gene therapies (biologic infusions) since the 1990s, with disappointment and controversy until the advent of some profound immunotherapies, notably for cancers, in recent years. Messenger ribonucleic acid/mRNA technologies are proving to be gene therapy enablers. Notably, in November 2022, the Food and Drug Administration/FDA approved the first gene therapy for eligible adults with hemophilia B (congenital factor IX deficiency), Hemgenix®, "a one-off [intravenous/IV] infusion that frees patients from regular treatments but costs $3.5 million a dose, making it the most expensive medicine in the world."[14] The potential for next-generation (the present forefront) mRNA and CRISPR clinical applications to treat diseases in the future, to actually *cure* patients through genetic editing precision, is constrained only by imagination. Advanced CRISPR clinical trials already are underway to treat lung cancer and a form of congenital blindness, and scientists are utilizing CRISPR to battle COVID-19 and to build armament through an expanding, varied portfolio of methodologies to fend off future viruses.[15] Before a shift in CRISPR resources in 2020 to respond to the COVID-19 pandemic, some two dozen additional clinical trials utilizing CRISPR were underway or planned for conditions ranging from male pattern baldness to acute myeloid leukemia.[16] As observed by professor and acclaimed author Walter Isaacson in his book *The Code Breaker*, "Like bacteria, we need a system that can be easily adapted to destroy each new virus. CRISPR could provide that to us, as it does [in nature] for bacteria. It could also someday be used to fix genetic problems, defeat cancers, enhance our children, and allow us to hack evolution so that we can steer the future of the human race."[17]

CRISPR is a vast, seemingly infinite science platform frontier in genomics – a field of biology focused on the mapping, structure, function, evolution, and editing of genomes.[18] A genomic revolution was enabled by the advancement of biotechnology in the 1980s – the beginning of a biotech revolution – and by the Human Genome Project/HG throughout the 1990s into this millennium.[19] HGP scientists compiled a draft map of the human genome DNA sequence, the common denominator in our species' genetic instructions (we are 99.9 percent the same genetically), and created a core research resource in biology often analogized to the periodic table of elements in chemistry.[20] The US government launched HGP as a collaborative international science endeavor in 1990.[21] HGP and a commercial competitor released a draft human genome sequence in 2003 – approximately two years ahead of the project's schedule and $300 million under budget:

> In April 2003, the Human Genome Project announced that it had sequenced around 20,000 genes of those that make up the blueprint of our bodies. For 15 years,

> this medical breakthrough has been informing and transforming health care. Genomics, the study of genes [in the interactive community context of whole genomes], is making it possible to predict, diagnose, and treat diseases more precisely and personally than ever.[22]

A surge in genome sequencing capabilities and a plunge in its cost, which accompanied and enabled HGP, is the means for researchers to readily sequence complete genomes.[23] For example, the COVID-19 outbreak in China was first publicly reported on December 31, 2019.[24] The DNA sequence of the coronavirus that causes COVID-19, SARS-CoV-2, was published on January 11, 2020 – in a matter of weeks, even in the midst of international political turbulence over the shared need to identify the origin (the source of the first human infection, referred to as "patient zero") of the virus after it was traced to an initial outbreak in Wuhan, China, secrecy by the government of China that impeded (and is still impeding) the investigation, and travel moratoriums among nations.[25] Bioinformatics (the coupling of biotechnology and information technology) and DNA sequencing technologies stimulated the genomic revolution that now is making precision medicine (treatments tailored to a person's genome) and personalized medicine (treatments derived from a person's genome) – both are applied in personal genome medicine/PGM – increasingly present in the delivery of clinical care.[26] In sum, a genomic revolution emerged from a biotech revolution that began in the 1980s, and it continues to build – presently culminating in CRISPR:

> The invention of CRISPR and the plague of COVID will hasten our transition to the third great revolution of modern times. These revolutions arose from the discovery, beginning just over a century ago, of the three fundamental kernels of our existence: the atom, the bit, and the gene.
>
> The first half of the twentieth century, beginning with Albert Einstein's 1905 papers on relativity and quantum theory, featured a revolution driven by physics. In the five decades following his miracle year, his theories led to atom bombs and nuclear power, transistors and spaceships, lasers and radar.
>
> The second half of the twentieth century was an information-technology era, based on the idea that all information could be encoded by binary digits—known as bits—and all logical processes could be performed by circuits with on-off switches. In the 1950s, this led to the development of the microchip, the computer, and the internet. When these three innovations were combined, the digital revolution was born.
>
> Now we have entered a third and even more momentous era, a life science revolution. Children who study digital coding will be joined by those who study genetic code.[27]

The biotech revolution, HGP, the genomic revolution, vaccines and other countermeasures responsive to COVID-19, and CRISPR share origins in a triple-threat science R&D methodology: intense collaboration among government, academia, and industry focused on applying science-technology to accomplish aspirational objectives. The following discussion profiles the latest US application of its triple-threat methodology – Operation Warp Speed/OWS to produce and disseminate COVID-19 vaccines and other pandemic countermeasures.[28] The discussion then addresses the US science R&D legacy that made OWS possible. First, WWII urgency inspired the integration of government, academia, and industry to undertake the Manhattan Project/MP – a mission to produce nuclear weapons in a wartime race against rival German scientists.[29] Second, the biotech revolution, driven by the promise of recombining DNA from multiple sources, was launched through US federal technology transfer law and policy/TTLP. The TTLP cornerstone legislation was signed into law by President Carter with apprehension at the very end of his administration (he contemplated a pocket veto), and implemented with conviction from the outset of the Reagan Administration to break from the economic misery of the 1970s.[30] Third, the ongoing genomic revolution, which evolved from the success of the biotech revolution and HGP, a government initiative reminiscent of the MP, provided the science platform for OWS and now is advancing personal genome medicine.[31]

THE LATEST US APPLICATION OF TRIPLE-THREAT SCIENCE R&D METHODOLOGY: OPERATION WARP SPEED/OWS

The US launched OWS with an initial budget of approximately $10 billion "to deliver 300 million doses of a safe, effective vaccine for COVID-19 by January 2021, as part of a broader strategy to accelerate the development, manufacturing, and distribution of COVID-19 vaccines, therapeutics, and diagnostics (collectively known as countermeasures)."[32] The resulting vaccine R&D was unprecedented in many ways – most notably in science and speed. The first COVID-19 vaccines, also the first vaccines ever developed using mRNA technology, came to fruition in an extraordinarily expedited manner by immediately decoding the virus's genome, dedicated and masterfully orchestrated collaboration among governments, biopharma companies, and medical researchers, and profound global science sharing:

> After the COVID-19 virus was identified and its genetic material sequenced, scientific and medical communities earnestly started to study it and share the research results. The collaborative effort within the global scientific community helped disseminate invaluable knowledge about the virus, such as how it causes illness and potential vaccination and treatment methods.[33]

The US declared OWS on March 30, 2020, and officially launched the initiative in May 2020.[34] The progression from laboratory bench research to a vaccine licensed for market use traditionally consumes at least ten years, with the daunting risk of failure throughout:

> Traditional vaccines are biological products consisting of defanged bacteria or viruses. Since these vaccines [made with living organisms] contain complex biological molecules which are inherently unstable and prone to degradation, their

manufacturing process is laborious and slow. Vaccine shots through traditional technologies typically take more than a decade to develop.[35]

According to industry self-reported data, just one in fifty new prescription drug candidates reaches human clinical trials, and just one in ten of those is approved by the Food and Drug Administration/FDA for market use – at a cost of approximately $1 billion.[36] "Do the math and that means that a drug has less than a 0.02% to 0.01% chance of making it to market."[37] Historically, vaccine R&D has been even more prone to failure than prescription drugs in preclinical testing and early-stage ("phase 1") clinical trials designed to test primarily for safety.[38]

Vaccine R&D, consistent with prescription medicine R&D in general, encompasses: demands for materials and proprietary enabling technologies; preclinical testing (primarily testing for toxicity); multiphase and multi-site clinical research conducted under regulatory scrutiny, with requisite milestones for each stage of progression; ongoing, real-time regulatory review for sufficient assurance of safety and efficacy; the costs and complexity of building reliable, regulatorily compliant market manufacturing capacity, which includes staffing with requisite professional expertise for operation and oversight; the establishment of distribution and delivery infrastructure, including medical professionals sufficiently trained in product competency; and oversight of market uptake and use.[39] Accomplishing this necessitates immense coordination, cooperation, and communication among myriad individuals and institutions drawn from the public and private sectors and varied professional disciplines.[40]

Vaccine candidates introduce distinguishable clinical research challenges, many of which were exacerbated during the COVID-19 pandemic by specificities of the virus that causes it (the particular type of coronavirus at issue had been observed in other species, but not humans), and by the novel science applications utilized.[41] The very premise of vaccines – dose populations of healthy people, often children, to *reduce the risk of contracting* a virus that they *could* be exposed to and *could* make them ill – raises the standard for safety.[42] Vaccines routinely cause side effects ranging from discomfort at the injection site to influenza-like symptoms of varied severity, to severe (at times life-threatening) adverse events.[43] Research subjects need time after being dosed to produce antibodies, exposure to test efficacy under actual life conditions consumes time, and measuring the durability of vaccine efficacy also necessitates time.[44] Even with data sufficient for regulatory approval and beyond, manufacturers must overcome the public's vaccine hesitancy.[45]

Despite admirable research efforts to produce vaccines against some particularly health-threatening coronaviruses, such as severe acute respiratory syndrome/SARS and Middle East respiratory syndrome/MERS, no vaccine existed prior to the COVID-19 vaccines to prevent *any* coronavirus infection.[46] The preexisting record for the fastest new vaccine R&D, Merck's mumps vaccine licensed in 1967 (Mumpsvax), was four years.[47] Consider that researchers identified the human immunodeficiency virus/HIV as the cause of acquired immunodeficiency syndrome/AIDS in 1984, the National Institutes of Health/NIH commenced the first HIV clinical trial in 1987, and there still is no HIV vaccine on the market even though there are antiretroviral therapies/ARTs to make HIV undetectable in many patients and to significantly reduce the risk of transmission.[48] In March 2022, the International Maternal Pediatric Adolescent AIDS Clinical Trial Network/ IMPAACT even reported (in an observational study) the first case of HIV cure in a woman living with HIV who underwent a dual stem cell transplant.[49]

The COVID-19 vaccines produced by Moderna, Inc. and Pfizer-BioNTech SE utilizing mRNA technology was a novel application of emerging clinical science. As explained by Walter Isaacson, a participant in a Pfizer-BioNTech clinical trial:

> The vaccine that was tested in my clinical trial makes use of the most basic function that RNA performs in the central dogma of biology: serving as a messenger RNA (mRNA) that carries genetic instructions from DNA, which is bunkered inside a cell's nucleus, to the manufacturing region of the cell [the cytoplasm], where it directs what protein to make. In the case of the COVID vaccine, the mRNA instructs cells to make part of the spike protein that is on the surface of the coronavirus.
>
> * * *
>
> An RNA vaccine has certain advantages over a DNA vaccine. Most notably, the RNA does not need to get into the nucleus of the cell, where DNA is headquartered. The RNA does its work in the outer region of cells, the cytoplasm, which is where proteins are constructed. So an RNA vaccine simply needs to deliver its payload into this outer region.
>
> * * *
>
> Now scientists had found a way to enlist RNA's most basic biological function in order to turn our cells into manufacturing plants for the spike protein that would stimulate our immunity to the coronavirus.[50]

A foremost consideration for patients, medical providers, and manufacturers is that, "[a]fter the cells finish making the virus mimicking spike proteins, the injected mRNA gets destroyed and never alters DNA."[51]

Novel clinical technology necessitates added explanation and understanding to attain medical provider competency, provider and research subject/patient trust, use, and reliable regulatory oversight. In addition, the Pfizer-BioNTech vaccine posed potentially overwhelming cold storage challenges when launched.[52] Nevertheless, researchers compiled data that, in accordance with established FDA standards, demonstrated sufficient safety and efficacy approaching ninety-five percent.[53] Many of our most familiar vaccines, such as annual flu vaccines, are efficacious in reducing the risk of illness by 50–60 percent in the general population, which is the base standard for regulatory approval.[54] The FDA issued Emergency Use Authorizations/ EAUs for the Pfizer-BioNTech and Moderna mRNA vaccines in December 2020.[55]

Sandra Lindsay, the director of critical care nursing at Long Island Jewish Medical Center in New York, was vaccinated against COVID-19 on December 14, 2020.[56] She became the first person in the US to receive a COVID-19 vaccine outside of a clinical trial – just nine months after the pandemic forced the nation into quarantine. As of August 2021, approximately seventeen months after the US first declared OWS (March 2020) and fifteen months after its launch (May 2020), more than 192 million people in the US had received some 348 million COVID-19 vaccination doses, and more than 4.25 billion doses had been administered across 180 countries.[57]

OWS IMPLEMENTATION OF TRIPLE-THREAT R&D METHODOLOGY

OWS required coordination, cooperation, and partnership within the US government on an unprecedented scale to produce and disseminate the first COVID-19 vaccines in record time. Spearheaded jointly by the Department of Health and Human Services/HHS and the Department of Defense/DoD, OWS was a partnership among the CDC, FDA, NIH, and HHS's Biomedical Advanced Research and Development Authority/BARDA – all of which prioritized and focused resources on COVID-19 vaccine R&D.[58] OWS also engaged other federal agencies, including the Department of Veterans Affairs/VA. Moreover, OWS coordinated with the NIH's Accelerating COVID-19 Therapeutic Interventions and Vaccines/ACTIV partnership and NIH's Rapid Acceleration of Diagnostics/RADx initiative.[59]

The US government and academia finance and conduct the vast majority of basic (also referred to as "primary," "laboratory bench," and just "bench") research to produce potential new drug candidates, while industry does the same in translational clinical research to turn bench research invention into therapies (therapeutic innovations) that enhance human health.[60] Expedited COVID-19 vaccine R&D necessitated a full partnership between the US government and the private sector, both of which draw from academia. OWS mitigated the overall risk of vaccine development failure by carefully selecting a portfolio of industry collaborators and vaccine candidates using varied mechanisms (distinguishable platform technologies) to stimulate an immune response.[61]

"Coronavirus" represents a group of RNA viruses that cause a gamut of respiratory, gastrointestinal, and neurological diseases ranging from the common cold to SARS.[62] Research labs throughout the world had been working diligently to understand and produce vaccines against them for years prior to the COVID-19 pandemic.[63] Experts at NIH's Vaccine Research Center/VRC had strategically selected a coronavirus and worked to develop a vaccine prototype adaptable to fight a variety of coronaviruses.[64] VRC had that prototype in hand before the spread of COVID-19 escalated into a pandemic.[65] This anticipatory step was crucial for the OWS COVID-19 vaccine R&D accomplishments. Scientists decoded the underlying gene that produces the SARS-CoV-2 spike protein, and the VRC worked with

Moderna, Inc., a then small biotech company based in Cambridge, MA, to customize their prototype.[66] With VRC's data, Moderna was able to design a COVID-19 vaccine candidate, mRNA-1273, by January 13, 2020 – just two days after China released the DNA sequence for COVID-19.[67] The first batch was ready for clinical testing on February 7, 2020, and mRNA-1273 entered clinical trials on March 16, 2020 – two weeks before the initial OWS declaration and two months before its official launch.[68] The Pfizer-BioNTech vaccine candidate, also an mRNA vaccine, followed soon after, along with other COVID-19 vaccine candidates.[69]

Biopharma manufacturers necessarily scale up production to meet clinical trial demands as research advances from phase 1 trials (typically tens of healthy volunteers to test safety), to phase 2 trials (typically hundreds of patient subjects in each trial, with multiple trials), to phase 3 trials (typically thousands of patient subjects at multiple sites, who are dosed in alignment with the intended full market use).[70] Full market-scale manufacturing of novel medicinal products encompasses enormous expense and risk; manufacturing facilities are built in accordance with regulatorily compliant plans and inspected rigorously for assurance of regulatory compliance.[71] According to the FDA, sixty-seven percent of *new drug* candidates do not progress from phase 2 trials to phase 3 trials, and greater than seventy percent do not progress from phase 3 trials to market approval.[72] "Industry benchmarks for *traditional vaccine* development paradigms cite attrition rates for licensed vaccines of more than 90%."[73] The cost, risk, and failure rate of clinical research make market scale-up not economically feasible without the assurance of sound clinical data supporting full market approval – data available towards the end of the clinical trial process. Through OWS, the US government assumed the commercial risk of failure – another unprecedented aspect of the initiative:

> The crucial piece of OWS, beyond allocating hefty funds for vaccine research and development, was that it fundamentally changed how pharmaceutical and biotechnology companies assess the risk of conducting large-scale clinical trials on a brand-new vaccine. This was achieved through the HHS building the requisite infrastructure and guaranteeing the manufacturing of any successful vaccine candidates. They also purchased allotments of the vaccines prior to knowing whether any of the OWS-funded companies would be successful.
>
> Since putting a large number of resources into the manufacturing of millions—if not billions—of doses of a vaccine that is still in the infancy of its development would be a non-starter for any viable pharmaceutical company, the HHS making the decision to substantially de-risk this process in order to expedite the development of candidate vaccines proved to be a game-changer.[74]

HHS's BARDA, an established and experienced intermediary between government and industry in science-technology R&D with mindset and expertise analogous to venture capital firms in the private sector, acted as the financial interface with the biopharma industry.[75] DoD's Defense Advanced Research Projects Agency/DARPA, which has engaged in government-academia-industry R&D projects to advance the forefront of science and technology (often spanning well beyond defined military needs) since 1958, also had industry-interface experience and established relationships, and too contributed immensely to OWS.[76]

The US awarded Moderna $955 million to advance its clinical trials and, while that research highly susceptible to failure was ongoing, contracted to purchase 100 million vaccine doses for $1.5 billion with the option to purchase 400 million more.[77] Although Pfizer declined OWS's offer of clinical research funding (Pfizer accepted financial support from the German government indirectly through BioNTech, but not from the US government), the US contracted with Pfizer to advance purchase 100 million vaccine doses of its potential vaccine for $1.95 billion with the option to purchase an additional 500 million doses.[78] The US also funded clinical-trial research by AstraZeneca, Johnson & Johnson/J&J, and Sanofi-GlaxoSmithKline (a partnership), and advance-purchased 100 million vaccine doses each from AstraZeneca, J&J, Novavax, and Sanofi-GlaxoSmithKline while their clinical research was ongoing with the risk of failure.[79]

These advance purchases provided guaranteed market returns that offset the vaccine R&D risk, and the direct US investments in that R&D "circumvented the financial hurdle, eliminating the need to raise funds, and enabled the pharmaceutical companies to conduct the necessary vaccine research and clinical trials effectually."[80] Resources being limited and zero-sum (any corporate decision to undertake a major R&D initiative is at the opportunity cost of forgoing others), the US softened the investment, risk, and opportunity cost of COVID-19 vaccine clinical R&D. The impact of US vaccine pre-orders and guaranteed purchases on industry behavior was augmented by the same from other governments worldwide.[81]

OWS also worked with the biopharma companies to mitigate manufacturing capacity challenges, such as by facilitating partnerships with additional manufacturers and engaging the Army Corps of Engineers to oversee the expansion and refitting of existing manufacturing facilities.[82] Demand for needed medical materials, such as needles, syringes, and vials, far exceeded supply. The global pandemic disrupted and strained established vaccine manufacturing supply chains in their entirety and unpredictably:

> For example, representatives from one facility manufacturing COVID-19 vaccines stated that they experienced challenges obtaining materials, including reagents and certain chemicals. They also said that due to global demand, they waited 4 to 12 weeks for items that before the pandemic were typically available for shipment within one week.[83]

OWS heavily utilized the DoD's global logistics and coordination capabilities.[84] Through OWS, DoD and HHS expedited procurement, importation, and delivery of essential manufacturing equipment and supplies.[85] They developed a list of critical supplies common among the six OWS vaccine candidates.[86] By December 2020, OWS officials had placed priority ratings on eighteen supply contracts under the

Defense Production Act/DPA, which required contractors to prioritize COVID-19 vaccine production supplies.[87] OWS officials also worked with the Department of State to expedite visa approvals for key technical personnel and to authorize DoD personnel to serve as quality control staff until manufacturers could hire requisite personnel.[88]

Overall, OWS dramatically expedited clinical R&D without compromising FDA standards for safety and efficacy by infusing vast resources and ingenuity into the regulatory process.[89] The US learned from the Ford Administration to not compromise clinical evidentiary-science standards. In 1976, a swine flu vaccine mass immunization campaign was launched during a presidential election, rushed for an anticipated pandemic that did not materialize, and resulted in dozens of vaccine recipients diagnosed with Guillain–Barré syndrome – a rare neurological disorder that causes muscle weakness, tingling in the extremities, and paralysis.[90] Beyond funding clinical trials, OWS assigned a team to each vaccine manufacturer comprised of clinical trial specialists, epidemiologists, and budget experts. "Weekly check-ins not only went through the particulars of the trials but also detailed plans for distribution and manufacturing."[91] National databases were established to find research subjects, to achieve sufficient diversity, and for ongoing oversight and communication with trial participants.[92] Clinical trials were combined or run concurrently and,

> [t]o meet OWS timelines, some vaccine companies relied on data from other vaccines using the same platforms, where available, or conducted certain animal studies at the same time as clinical trials. However, as is done in a non-pandemic environment, all vaccine companies gathered initial safety and antibody response data with a small number of participants before proceeding into large-scale human studies (e.g., [advanced phase 2 and] phase 3 clinical trials).[93]

OWS efforts were complemented globally. "Regulatory agencies worldwide prioritized [COVID-19] studies, committee hearings, and data reviews; [they] instituted rolling reviews, which allowed pharmaceutical companies to submit data on an ongoing basis throughout the trials rather than waiting until the end of the trials."[94] The novel application of mRNA science to vaccine R&D ultimately contributed to the ability to accelerate clinical research:

> Unlike traditional lengthy, cumbersome vaccine development and manufacturing processes, mRNA vaccines are more manageable, cheaper, and faster to manufacture. mRNA molecules for vaccines are manufactured by chemicals rather than by biological synthesis. Hence the mRNA vaccines can be redesigned, scaled up, and mass-produced more efficiently than the conventional vaccines.[95]

The global scale and severity of the pandemic, which triggered an orchestrated symphony of government responsiveness, contributed to the ability to accelerate the vaccine R&D. In addition to science and regulatory focus, efforts, and collaboration, the pandemic generated substantial real-time clinical data and understanding about COVID-19 reflective of the global expanse of its infestation.

The number of subjects in the COVID-19 vaccine trials was aligned with other FDA vaccine trials. "The pervasiveness of the virus made infectious subjects readily available, making the enrollment and studies from the trials adequate and speedy."[96] The three staple phases of clinical research are separated by "clinical endpoints" – outcome measures that refer to the occurrence of disease, symptoms, laboratory results, or other indicators that constitute data targets necessary for completion. The pandemic's impact on human health and the novelty of the COVID-19 virus necessitated flexibility:

> It is important to maintain some flexibility in the clinical end point definition in a pandemic situation involving a novel pathogen because there is limited knowledge of pathogen-specific disease presentation and underlying pathophysiology. This flexibility enables the collection of clinical case data in early-stage clinical trials[, typically conducted with focus contained to safety], with vaccine efficacy being established in later-stage trials using an evolved case definition based on emerging knowledge. Infection or disease end points not included to address an efficacy trial primary objective should, however, be assessed as secondary end points.[97]

The FDA applied this flexibility and, rather than full approvals, vaccine sponsors applied for Emergency Use Authorizations/EUAs and the FDA granted them while additional clinical trial and actual use data were collected in real time.[98] The FDA may issue an EUA when there is good scientific reason to believe that a vaccine is safe and likely to prevent disease without definitive proof of efficacy over time under established standards – especially for diseases that are highly contagious and cause significant mortality:

> Under section 564 of the Federal Food, Drug, and Cosmetic Act (FD&C Act), when the Secretary of HHS declares that an emergency use authorization is appropriate, FDA may authorize unapproved medical products or unapproved uses of approved medical products to be used in an emergency to diagnose, treat, or prevent serious or life-threatening diseases or conditions caused by CBRN[/chemical, biological, radiological, and nuclear] threat agents when certain criteria are met, including there are no adequate, approved, and available alternatives.[99]

As explained by Dr. Helene Gayle, who co-chaired a committee for the National Academies of Sciences, Engineering, and Medicine/NASEM that established a framework for equitable distribution of the vaccine, "Emergency use says you weigh the risks of the moment – the COVID-19 crisis – against the minimal increase in the knowledge you might gain by following the trials longer. It does not mean approval without normal safeguards in place."[100] When the FDA exercises its delegated authority to grant an EUA responsive to public health and military emergencies, the agency also must consult, "to the extent feasible and appropriate given the circumstances of the emergency, with the directors of the National Institutes of Health (NIH) and CDC ...."[101]

The FDA granted EUAs for the Moderna and Pfizer-BioNTech SE vaccines in December 2020 based on analyses that included assessments of safety and efficacy after individuals were given two doses of vaccine and were monitored for about two months for adverse events.[102] The analysis showed sufficient safety and roughly ninety-five percent efficacy for each vaccine.[103] Both vaccine sponsors continued to collect clinical and general population use data for their full approvals, which the FDA granted on August 23, 2021, to the Pfizer-BionNTech (COMIRNATY) vaccine for use in people sixteen years and older and on January 31, 2022, to the Moderna (Spikevax) vaccine for individuals eighteen years and older.[104] The manufacturers agreed, beyond these market approvals, to continue to track individuals who participated in their trials to monitor antibody levels and any related reactions, and to track their phase 3 trial participants for two years to assess long-term protection and safety.[105]

CDC and FDA surveillance of actual use, complemented by and orchestrated with global surveillance, has been extraordinary. For example, this surveillance enabled quickly identifying, defining, and placing (in the context of all COVID-19 vaccines use) the risk of a very rare but also very dangerous clotting condition in people after receiving (within a two-week window, according to May 2022 data) the J&J COVID-19 vaccine, which does not utilize next-generation mRNA technology.[106] On May 5, 2022, the FDA strictly limited its EUA for the J&J vaccine to people eighteen years and older and not candidates for other COVID-19 vaccines, or who would not get vaccinated otherwise.[107] The availability of vaccine alternatives and substantial comparative data about them is reflected in this FDA decision. Given the overall safety and efficacy of the J&J vaccine and the ongoing COVID-19 health risk, the vaccine alternatives and accompanying data made the FDA decision possible and practicable. In sum, "These vaccines have undergone and will continue to undergo the most intensive monitoring in US history, which includes using both established and new safety monitoring systems to ensure that COVID-19 vaccines are both efficacious and safe."[108]

OWS, primarily through DoD logistics expertise and resources, orchestrated the establishment of infrastructure to distribute the vaccines throughout the US immediately upon FDA authorization, and with the capability to track every vaccine vial and the injection schedule for each American receiving a vaccination.[109] HHS and DoD collaborated with private companies to build the necessary information technology/IT system.[110] Through a CDC's pre-existing partnership with McKesson Corporation, the nation's largest distributor of flu shots, OWS contracted with McKesson for distribution, supported by major companies such as UPS and FedEx.[111] OWS fully utilized CDC's public health network – states, some large cities, and beyond – to orchestrate distribution planning.[112]

Through the OWS R&D-stage investments and contract negotiations, the US negotiated vaccine prices on par with flu shots for the doses bought in advance.[113] To maximize public uptake and the effectiveness of OWS, the US government made the COVID-19 vaccines available to people free of charge.[114]

THE ORIGIN OF US SCIENCE R&D TRIPLE-THREAT METHODOLOGY: WWII NECESSITY

Although much of what OWS accomplished was unprecedented, *how* it accomplished was through science R&D methodology with a profound US legacy. Just as CRISPR is the science progeny of the genomic and biotech revolutions, OWS is the latest application of a triple-threat R&D methodology inspired by necessity during World War II.[115] The US entered WWII with no armaments industry, without much of a standing army, and in dire competition with the German government's scientists to be the first to develop the atomic bomb:

> On October 11, 1939, Alexander Sachs, Wall Street economist and longtime friend and unofficial advisor to President Franklin Delano Roosevelt, met with the President to discuss a letter written by Albert Einstein the previous August. Einstein had written to inform Roosevelt that recent research on chain reactions utilizing uranium made it probable that large amounts of power could be produced by a chain reaction and that, by harnessing this power, the construction of "extremely powerful bombs…" was conceivable. Einstein believed that the German government was actively supporting research in this area and urged the United States government to do likewise.[116]

The US, isolated by oceans and a late entrant into the war, proved itself the nation most capable of transferring the discovery of fission science from the laboratory to the battlefield.[117] The US ended the war with an atomic monopoly, albeit a brief one.

President Roosevelt's overall response to Einstein's letter was the Manhattan Project/MP – a massive, hands-on R&D undertaking under extraordinary time pressure to produce the first nuclear weapons, which was led by the US with support from the UK and Canada.[118] Through the MP, the US directly confronted the extraordinary challenge of saving democratic society from potential nuclear weapon annihilation and a German government victory by intervening aggressively to advance science and technology.[119] The MP grew to employ over 130,000 people and cost nearly $2 billion (approximately $23 billion FY2019) – over ninety percent of that spent to build factories and to produce materials capable of sustaining a nuclear fission chain reaction.[120] Research and production drew from government, academia, and industry, and took place at more than thirty sites across the US, UK, and Canada.[121] The US orchestrated the establishment of MP laboratories across the nation and coordinated an army of researchers with industry involvement – most notably Dupont and the Kellog Company – for intense application focus and direction, resources, and overall expertise in product realization and production.[122]

War effort necessity created myriad public-private partnerships, many transformative and profoundly significant after the war. For example, Allied scientists created a strain of penicillin stable enough for mass production under the oversight of the War Productions Board, which elevated the US pharmaceutical industry commercially. "In the late 1940s, [the eleven US companies involved] produced over half of the world's pharmaceuticals and accounted for one-third of international trade in medicines."[123] The penicillin public-private partnership also transformed and elevated pharmaceutical R&D from serendipity to research-driven discovery.[124] The companies drew from their commercial profits to finance sophisticated pharmaceutical research campuses, and "[t]he R&D labs created by Big Pharma in the twentieth century gave medicine a comparable exploratory power: experimenting with thousands of intriguing compounds, looking for magic bullets in the mix."[125]

There was a multiplication effect. The penicillin public-private partnership experience influenced an impressive progeny of others in medicine over the following years. For example, "The public-private partnership that led to the availability of the polio vaccine became an inspiration."[126] In sum, the MP's seamless integration of government, academia, and industry to accomplish an overwhelming science R&D application mission became the seminal R&D precedent for jolting science and technology innovation forward on a transformative scale.[127]

THE US GOVERNMENT'S CENTRALIST ROLE IN SCIENCE-TECHNOLOGY R&D

The US emerged from WWII to plunge directly into the Cold War – a war fought largely with science-technology R&D and the US public's faith that technological progress was synonymous with safety in the present and prosperity in the future.[128] The Cold War powered a science-based technology revolution, which inspired a culture fixated on the progress of science.[129] The US federal government continued its financial investment in science-technology R&D and relationships with industry and academia, but the government-academia-industry triple threat largely fractured into two – government-industry, and government-academia.[130] Academia and industry interacted much more than prior to the war, but each shifted back into their pre-war science-technology domain and culture – albeit changed, and with ongoing and substantial US government interface.[131]

The US made enormous annual science-technology expenditures post WWII, much of that investment in the military-industrial complex/MIC – a term dubbed and made popular by President Eisenhower, who was suspicious of it.[132] Over time, aggressive federal government science-technology funding became normalized. The US government substantially expanded infrastructure for its own direct research capabilities and undertakings (for example, establishment of the National Aeronautics and Space Administration/NASA in 1958), channeled funding into industry through the MIC, and into academia through federal grants allocated with peer review.[133] However, unless US agencies allowed research partners to retain title to invention or chose to license or assign property rights to invention resulting from research the US government paid for and patented, the US government held property rights with discretion to make invention available for the benefit of all:

> Nobody could exploit such research without tedious negotiations with the federal agency concerned. Worse, companies found it nigh impossible to acquire exclusive rights to a government-owned patent. And, without that, few firms were willing to invest millions more of their own money to turn a raw research idea into a marketable product.[134]

Nevertheless, industry and academia partners applied and enhanced their research capabilities through these government-financed engagements, and the US government did allow some collaborators to retain title to resulting inventions and granted some licenses to its patented inventions.[135] This substantial, ongoing, and reliable federal investment in science-technology funding brought strong returns for decades, most notably military strength and Cold War competitiveness, global economic competitiveness, space program success, and the advancement of science-technology innovation.[136]

The centralist role in overall US science-technology R&D the US government assumed under the pressure of WWII necessity became fixed during the science-based technological revolution that followed. WWII and the Cold War elevated the importance of science-technology R&D—foremost in national security, but also in domestic productivity, global market competitiveness, and culture. The nation consumed technology innovation and embraced the future with intoxicating optimism, energy, and imagination:

> THE BITH OF UTOPIA IN THE 1950s proclaimed an era of new dreams. Optimism and energy were everywhere in 1957, as WWII receded into memory and the post war baby boom reached its crest. "Utopian" was the byword in advertising that year, providing a vision shared by millions thanks to television; by then, one out of ten families already had color TVs, many with remote "Channel Commanders." Science offered a wide array of innovations for everyday life, along with the illusion that Tomorrowland had already arrived. Housewives could serve TV dinners in twenty minutes. At shoe stores, kids spent hours pressed up against X-ray machines, watching the bones of their toes wiggle. And it seemed as if DDT was on the verge of eliminating insects once and for all.
>
> In a series of articles unashamedly entitled "New Man's World," the editors of *Life* magazine featured jet-engine cars, plastic houses shaped like mushrooms, and foam-rubber furniture. The intrepid futurists predicted that "personalized flying machines .... will open up hitherto inaccessible rural lands for daily communication" and anticipated that disposable clothes and "dehydrofrozen" meals would be common features of modern life by 1977.
>
> This was dawn of the jet-age. Soon Boeing 707s would be crossing continents and oceans in just a few hours. People could drive coast to coast in record time on Eisenhower's new turnpike system, in the biggest gas guzzlers ever built or in the new German imports, Volkswagens, which could drive thirty miles on a gallon of gas.

There were marvels in every field of human endeavor. Univac, the biggest, fastest computer ever built, had just completed a Bible concordance, 2,000 pages in less than 1,300 hours. Anything and everything could be made from plastic. Infectious diseases, it seemed, had been all but eliminated with universal vaccinations for smallpox, polio, and most of all with accessible antibiotics. Tuberculosis, pneumonia, and other scourges were no longer among the top ten killers, thanks to breakthroughs in drug therapy. And the average life span had increased ten years just since 1935.

"The power and the pace of technology [has] ... brought man to the brink of his greatest technology accomplishment," crowed *Life* magazine. "He [is] ... now ready to rocket himself into the endless emptiness of outer space." Werner Van Braun, the top US rocket scientist, predicted that "we should be able to send men to the moon and back within twenty-five years." In fact, it took half that time. "Whether we know it or not, whether we like it or not," wrote the editors of *Life* in 1957, "the daily life of each of us is being changed—and is destined to be changed far more—by events taking place in laboratories and factories across the land."[137]

Dwight D. Eisenhower, before serving as President of the US during an intense scale-up of the Cold War (1953–61), had served as Supreme Commander of the Allied Expeditionary Force in Europe and achieved the rare five-star rank of General of the Army during WWII.[138] He experienced transformation in the US government's science-technology R&D role – to a centralist force directly reaching into, guiding, giving financially, and receiving from both industry and academia – firsthand, especially as it solidified during his presidency. When he spoke to the American people for the last time as President of the United States through radio and television (prevalent and the dominant political communication venue at the time, though black-and-white for most until the mid-60s) on January 17, 1961, he reflected thoughtfully on the US government centralist role in science-technology R&D under the triple threat methodology, and its implications:

Akin to, and largely responsible for the sweeping changes in our industrial-military posture, has been the technological revolution during recent decades.

In this revolution, research has become central; it also becomes more formalized, complex, and costly. A steadily increasing share is conducted for, by, or at the direction of, the Federal government.

Today, the solitary inventor, tinkering in his shop, has been overshadowed by task forces of scientists in laboratories and testing fields. In the same fashion, the free university, historically the fountainhead of free ideas and scientific discovery, has experienced a revolution in the conduct of research. Partly because of the huge costs involved, a government contract becomes virtually a substitute for intellectual curiosity. For every old blackboard there are now hundreds of new electronic computers.

The prospect of domination of the nation's scholars by Federal employment, project allocations, and the power of money is ever present--and is gravely to be regarded.

Yet, in holding scientific research and discovery in respect, as we should, we must also be alert to the equal and opposite danger that public policy could itself become the captive of a scientific-technological elite.

It is the task of statesmanship to mold, to balance, and to integrate these and other forces, new and old, within the principles of our democratic system—ever aiming toward the supreme goals of our free society.[139]

During the following decade, the nation came to share many of President Eisenhower's reservations about the US government's centralist role in science-technology R&D and its enormous expenditure on it. The 1970s was the only decade since the 1930s during which Americans became poorer than they were at its start:

[T]he mass upward economic mobility of American society ended, perhaps forever. Average weekly earnings, adjusted for inflation, peaked in 1973. Productivity—that is, economic output per man-hour—abruptly stopped growing. The nearly universal assumption in the post-World War II United States was that children would do better than their parents. Upward mobility wasn't just a characteristic of the national culture; it was the defining characteristic. As it slowly began to sink in that everybody wasn't going to be moving forward together anymore, the country became more fragmented, more internally rivalrous, and less sure of its mythology.[140]

The 1970s was a decade of pushback against both big government and big business. "The notion of the virtuous citizen locked in a battle against big government, big business, and a decadent elite was the single most compelling theme of the 1970s."[141] Especially after the US military defeat in the chronic (1955–1975) Vietnam War, the MIC was a blood-red target representing both big government and big business.[142]

By the end of the 1960s, the US had become frustrated with the failure of academic recipients of federal funds to produce tangible science-technology economic returns. "The annus horribilis, 1968, brought an end to the expansion of academic research and anguish over the role that the university had assumed."[143] The constant, gushing flow of precious federal funds, taxpayer dollars, into prestigious university campuses, many private and with gluttonous endowments, so that academic elites could pursue "research for the sake of research" was a target representing big government and the decadent elite. Universities, though recipients of generous federal government funding over decades, had become ungrateful bastions for anti-government protests. Government and public sentiment towards universities soured throughout the 1970s, which was reflected in federal funding decreases.[144] An overall public sense of pessimism squelched the cultural fixation on science-technology progress that had driven support for expansive government funding since WWII.[145] People's priorities and the nation's focus shifted from investment in the future to "ME" – to meeting *my* immediate needs:

One of the things that made the 1970s different from both the 1960s and the 1980s was that for the first time in more than a generation, ordinary Americans genuinely doubted that tomorrow would be better than today. They were not used to feeling

> so pessimistic—which is one reason why people who lived through the 1970s often shudder to recall them.
>
> In their shock and disappointment at the apparent overthrow of their ambitions, many Americans turned inward, to introspection and self-doubt.[146]

Americans sought individualism ("me-ism") in religion, popular culture, and sexuality, and they supported personal liberation and rebellion against authority.[147]

The US entered the 1970s with escalating global competition from the emergence of newly industrialized countries, and domestic tension between cost-cutting manufacturers and their unionized employees.[148] The situation threatened established, staple US sectors that always dominated globally and could be relied upon – notably the steel and automotive industries. The US' automotive industry was losing a significant share of its *domestic* market to smaller, inexpensive, imported vehicles – the opposite of Detroit automobile manufacturing, Cadillac prosperity, over decades.[149] In 1973, the Organization of Arab Petroleum Exporting Countries/OPEC proclaimed an oil embargo against the US and several other nations, though targeted primarily at the US.[150] Oil shortages created a crisis that struck hard in 1974, lingered, and then struck hard again in 1979 when Iran imploded into a revolution and fifty-two US diplomats and citizens were held hostage.[151] Periodic severe oil shortages necessitated harsh rationing. People's access to gasoline, which they had taken for granted over generations, was periodically limited to odd and even-numbered license plate days. Prices at the pump skyrocketed, which put even more pressure on American auto makers. Rather than rising to the challenge, the US automotive industry stumbled into a "malaise era" (1973–1983) of poor performance.[152] The nation experienced a stock market crash in 1973–1974.[153] Decades of post-WWII economic expansion and prosperity derailed into a recession with stagflation, meaning a stagnant economy with simultaneously high unemployment and inflation – inflation during a recession.[154]

The 1970s also was marred by a series of devastating political scandals that shook faith in the US government domestically and abroad. On Sunday, June 13, 1970, *The New York Times* published excerpts from the classified *Report of the Office of the Secretary of Defense Vietnam Task Force*, better known as the *Pentagon Papers* – a DoD history of the US' political and military involvement in Vietnam from 1945 to 1967.[155] Within forty-eight hours, President Nixon claimed executive authority to force the *Times* to suspend publication, asserting publication would cause irreparable injury to US defense interests.[156] Nevertheless, *The Washington Post* published more excerpts that Friday, June 18, 1971. The legal saga that ensued captivated the public's attention, stoked intrigue, and heightened anticipation as it advanced to the nation's highest court. The Supreme Court issued a landmark decision on June 30, 1971, *New York Times Co. v. United States*, in which Justice Hugo Black, writing for the majority with six Justices concurring and three dissenting, elaborated on the absolute superiority of the First Amendment over the government's need for secrecy.[157] A flow of more excerpts appeared on the pages of *the Washington Post* and *The New York Times*, from which the American people learned that the Johnson Administration had systematically lied to them and to Congress about the scope of its actions in the Vietnam War.[158] The Watergate scandal soon followed, 1972–1974, from which the American people learned that members of President Nixon's Committee to Re-Elect the President/CREEP had broken into the Democratic National Committee's Watergate headquarters, stole copies of top-secret documents, and bugged the office's phones.[159] President Nixon resigned in disgrace in 1974, and the US withdrew from the Vietnam War in defeat the following year.

Skepticism of and pushback against the federal government united myriad fronts and conjured political hurricane forces for change.[160] Religious conservatives (notably Jerry Falwell's Moral Majority) organized to challenge access to abortion and social excesses, anti-feminists (notably Phyllis Schlafly and her Stop Taking Our Privileges/STOP followers) did the same to oppose the Equal Rights Amendment/ERA, other social conservatives united to oppose Affirmative Action and racial busing, economic conservatives rallied against taxes, and war hawks disillusioned with the outcome of the Vietnam War and détente united in neoconservatism and advocated for a foreign policy sighted on US international power and aggression towards the Soviet Union.[161] These forces joined to elect Ronald Reagan President in a landslide victory over incumbent Jimmy Carty in 1980.[162] Republicans also took control of the Senate for the first time since the 1950s, though Democrats did retain control of the House of Representatives.[163]

THE BIOTECH REVOLUTION

President Reagan ran a campaign for the 1980 presidential election with a baseline focus on the abysmal economy of the 1970s.[164] During his first year in office, the US undertook a grand science-technology economic development experiment.[165] This experiment was derivative of the US triple threat experience during WWII, with full integration of government, academia, and industry, and a departure from the decades of separation between industry and academia that followed WII.[166] The post-WWII policy was that invention from research funded by the US was owned by the US for everyone's benefit.[167] The reality was that, overall, government-owned invention remained trapped in universities and government bureaucracy, removed from commercial application, and essentially benefited no one:

> Despite the perceived success of federal efforts to support R&D, by the late 1970s there was a growing dissatisfaction with federal policies related to the patenting of scientific knowledge resulting from the research. Many officials, for example, believed that the federal laboratories harbored information that was not being disseminated to those who could make use of it. Similarly, there was a concern that advances attributed to university-based research were not being pursued because

> there was little incentive to seek practical uses for inventions to which the federal government retained title. Those seeking to use government-owned technology found a maze of rules and regulations set out by the agencies in question because there was no uniform federal policy on patents for government-sponsored inventions or on the transfer of technology from the government to the private sector.[168]

In the life sciences and medicine, the opportunity cost was improving human health, saving lives from preventable suffering and death, as well as the economy. "At the time, fewer than 5 percent of the 28,000 patents being held by federal agencies had been licensed, compared with 25 percent to 30 percent of the small number of federal patents for which the government had allowed companies to retain title to the invention."[169]

The US enacted complementary legislation in 1980 that is the foundation for TTLP – the Bayh–Dole Act (academic institutions and researchers) and the Stevenson–Wydler Act (federal government agencies, laboratories, and researchers).[170] Although TTLP has fundamentally changed academic research and institutions, federal government research and researchers, and US medicine over the last several decades, economic development through commercialization of innovation was the driving legislative intent:

> Bayh-Dole's inspiration was not a perceived need to transform the conduct of research but the economic doldrums of the 1970s. Oil embargoes and the resulting energy crisis, combined with the eroding US automobile, steel, and household-appliance industries, deflated the stock market. Pundits predicted that Japan and Germany would soon rule the world's economy. Adding to this malaise was the fallout of Watergate, the custodial presidency of Gerald Ford, and the Iran hostage crisis.[171]

This legislation reformed patent law-policy to enable and encourage the commercial application of invention resulting from federally funded research, albeit with US government retention of a nontransferable, irrevocable, paid-up, nonexclusive license for government purposes worldwide.[172] In other words, there would be a give-away of invention resulting from federally funded research in exchange for its commercial application, but the US government would retain the possibility of government use of the invention for government work, should that need arise. Universities, other not-for-profit organizations, and small businesses now could opt to patent and commercialize invention created with federal funding – with reversion of the same opportunity to researchers who created the inventions when their institutions declined.[173] TTLP also established that federal agencies could grant businesses exclusive licenses for their technology.[174] As stated by NIH, the collective goal of these acts was "to promote economic development, enhance US competitiveness, and benefit the public by encouraging the commercialization of technologies that would otherwise not be developed into products due to lack of incentives."[175] Although the reach of TTLP later was expanded to include large businesses, the US originally sought to stimulate the economy and to increase US science-technology competitiveness by incentivizing the creation of entrepreneurial small businesses – the embodiment of beloved and believed-in American ingenuity ideals, and an alternative to the stale, risk-averse, bureaucratic big businesses America had lost faith in.[176] Congress subsequently enacted the Federal Technology Transfer Act of 1986, which authorizes federal agencies to enter into cooperative research and development agreements/CRADAs with non-federal government partners to conduct research – a government-wide complement to DoD's long-standing DARPA program with choice elements of the MIC.[177]

The fundamental legislative intent of TTLP was fiscal alchemy: to incentivize and turn federal funding of basic (bench) research into invention, commercial application of that invention to develop tangible product innovation, and economic returns on the federal, state, and local levels through the advancement of technology sectors driven by entrepreneurial small businesses not as intimidated by risk as the swollen, bureaucratic, big business establishment.[178] Federal and state governments shored up the TTLP small business model through complementary incentive programs – most notably the federal Small Business Innovation Research/SBIR and Small Business Technology Transfer/STTR programs, with grant application and other assistance from states.[179] In biotechnology, if the science produced, TTLP could move medicine to the molecular level with infinite potential to improve human health.[180] Scientists had developed laboratory methods to create recombinant DNA/rDNA in 1972.[181] These are sequences of DNA deliberately created by recombining genetic material from multiple sources.[182] The resulting capability to alter DNA, change genetic composition, and to produce targeted proteins (genes produce proteins, and proteins turn genes on and off) transported science into a universe of application possibilities in medicine, agriculture, manufacturing, and beyond.[183]

The 1980s began and ended with commercial biotech proof-of-principle milestones. On October 14, 1980, a few months before enactment of Bayh–Dole and Stevenson–Wydler, Genentech, Inc. (producer of the first synthetic human insulin in 1978 using rDNA) made an initial public offering/IPO on NASDAQ of 1.1 million shares and raised the company's value to $532 million[184] Shares opened at $35, skyrocketed to $80 within a minute, and reached $88 within the hour – the fastest first-day gain in Wall Street history by the first biotech company to make an IPO.[185] Genentech's success inspired the creation of a fleet of entrepreneurial biopharma companies in 1980–1981, including Amgen, Calgene, Chiron, Integrated Genetics, and Molecular Genetics. At the end of the decade (1989), Amgen launched Epogen – an anemia-fighting biotech ("big molecule") drug, a red blood cell stimulant, that soon dominated the US renal disease market and generated billions of dollars in revenue annually.[186]

Between these Genentech and Amgen commercial milestones, TTLP proved a potent R&D catalyst and stirred a seismic biotechnology revolution. In just one decade, less time than it takes to make a single innovative new drug (ten to fifteen years according to industry self-reported data), an entire entrepreneurial US biotech sector formed, and the biotech revolution began to produce innovative medicinal products and to reach into the delivery of clinical care.[187] As the first TTLP-generation of biotech invention evolved from laboratory bench science to human health products, the US complemented TTLP by enacting law-policy responsive to the biotech industry's emerging regulatory needs.[188] For example, rare diseases caused by single genetic variants (alleles) with defined patient groups were potentially "low-hanging fruit" for early medicinal product R&D.[189] The US enacted the Orphan Drug Act of 1983 to facilitate the development of "orphan drugs" – drugs for rare diseases, defined as diseases with US patient populations under 200,000 – that it would not be fiscally feasible to develop otherwise.[190]

In 1986, the US issued the Coordinated Framework for Regulation of Biotechnology ("Coordinated Framework"), which assured researchers, manufacturers, and investors that the US would take a product, not a process, approach to regulating biotech innovation.[191] The Coordinated Framework provided assurance that utilizing biotechnology for product development would not necessarily impose an additional layer of regulatory invasiveness on resulting products simply because biotech was used to make them.[192] The Coordinated Framework also imposed an obligation on regulatory agencies to coordinate rather than stack or duplicate their regulatory oversight of biotech products.[193] The National Academies of Science, Engineering, and Medicine/NASEM undertook an exhaustive survey of the biotech product landscape in 2015.[194] NASEM issued a report in 2017 that advised continued regulatory commitment to the Coordinated Framework.[195]

When evaluated based on the core legislative intent of Bayh–Dole and Stevenson–Wydler, US TTLP has proven remarkably successful. *The New England Journal of Medicine* published a favorable assessment in 2013:

> The law certainly contributed substantially to the increase in patents awarded to universities over the past three decades — from 380 in 1980 to 3088 in 2009. More difficult to confirm is industry's estimate that between 1996 and 2007, university-based research-licensing agreements contributed $47 billion to $187 billion to the gross domestic product.[196]

The Government Accountability Office/GAO had evaluated TTLP and reached a similar conclusion in a 1998 report, and NIH did the same in 2001.[197] In 2002, the *Economist* declared, "Possibly the most inspired piece of legislation to be enacted in America over the past half-century was the Bayh-Dole act of 1980."[198]

THE GENOMIC REVOLUTION

A genomic revolution evolved from and with the advancement of the biotech revolution. A genome is a living organism's entire set of DNA instructions – an organism's full portfolio of genes, and its complete genetics operating manual.[199] Genomics is the study of genomes, with focus on the interactive and dynamic community of genes and proteins in them – in contrast with genetics, which is the study of individual genes.[200] As explained by the World Health Organization/WHO,

> Genomics is distinct from genetics. While genetics is the study of heredity, genomics is defined as the study of genes and their functions, and related techniques. The main difference between genomics and genetics is that genetics scrutinizes the functioning and composition of the single gene whereas genomics addresses all genes and their inter relationships in order to identify their combined influence on the growth and development of the organism.[201]

The fact that we are 99.9 percent the same genetically means that all human variation is attributable to approximately 20,500 active genes and environmental influences on them – a testament to the significance of environmental influences and the extent to which genes interface and multitask.[202] Genomics is a means for researchers to understand genetic influences on human health in the context of intersecting layers of complexity:

> Genome-wide association studies are powerful because they combine state-of-the-art genomic technologies with traditional epidemiologic research approaches, such as those that identified smoking and high blood pressure as risk factors for heart disease half a century ago. Early findings from genome-wide studies have identified genetic variants contributing to prostate cancer, breast cancer, diabetes, obesity, eye diseases and a host of other conditions. In the future, physicians and scientists could use such tools to give patients individualized information about their risks of developing certain diseases and potentially, a tailored prevention plan to reduce these risks.[203]

High-throughput next-generation DNA sequencing/NGS with the capacity to sequence entire genomes rapidly and affordably and the bioinformatics capabilities to process, assemble, and analyze the function of specific alleles within the community structure of entire genomes are essential enabling technologies for contemporary genomics.[204] DNA sequencing and bioinformatics technologies were prerequisites for HGP as well, but that enormous undertaking was launched without them; HGP was a proverbial "white elephant" at its start. The project commenced in 1990 – well before James Watson was ceremoniously handed his personal genome sequence in 2007.[205] The NGS and bioinformatics capabilities presently available are a welcomed by-product of HGP.[206]

James Watson and fellow renowned scientists conceptualized HGP at workshops in 1985–1986, and they proposed the project to NIH and DOE even though the sequencing technology means to map the human genome did not exist and would not for some time.[207] The US government's decision to undertake HGP and to intervene in the direction of science research to such a degree in terms of time, money, scope, and speculation was beyond its twentieth-century centrist role in science-technology R&D.[208] HGP was a speculative government reach into the future of science research, not action to respond to an immediate threat to democracy or to fight the Cold War. HGP was a much more aggressive US government intervention in science research than the MP and even the Cold War space program.[209] Rather than the immediacy of war, the premise for undertaking HGP was educated speculation about what science-technology R&D *might* accomplish over fifteen years, coupled with more speculation about its impact on medicine and human health in the possibly very distant future. HGP also carried an opportunity cost in related, ongoing medical science research. Additional funding could have accelerated incremental, focused genetics research already underway – ongoing in real time – with the potential for tangible and much more immediate clinical returns. The US was grappling with pressing and daunting health care needs at the time, most notably HIV/AIDS.[210] Such a substantial commitment over so much time in the zero-sum reality of government grant funding would change the course of science and directly impact the science community by shifting priorities and the career paths of a generation, probably generations, of young scientists.[211]

Many in both science and medicine pushed back against the HGP proposal. Beginning in 1986 as the proposal gained traction, biologists seriously "debated the wisdom of beginning an Apollo moon shot-style program of biomedicine to chart the largely unknown new world of human genes, a scientific adventure that could take a decade or more to complete, consume $3 billion of precious federal government funding, and absorb the lives of hundreds of researchers."[212] Even some esteemed generals in the biotech revolution actively resisted HGP. Vocal opponents included: David Baltimore, a Nobel laureate and director of the Whitehead Institute of Molecular Biology; Dr. David Botstein of the Massachusetts Institute of Technology/MIT; Leroy Hood, a faculty member of the California Institute of Technology/Caltech and the University of Washington who made ground-breaking scientific instruments that enabled significant advances early in the biotech revolution; and Dr. Maxine Singer, a genetics expert and staff scientist at the National Cancer Institute/NCI.[213]

Scientists were concerned that HGP was the latest trend influencing a profession highly susceptible to them. As observed by Dr. Arthur Kornberg, a co-recipient of the 1959 Nobel Prize in Medicine for laboratory synthesis of DNA, "[f]ashions prevail in research as in all other departments of human behavior; tides erode one beach as they create another .... Fertile fields are left fallow as scientists cluster in fashionable areas for the security of being a part of a popular movement."[214] In 1988, Frank Press, then President of the National Academy of Sciences/NAS, advocated putting "big ticket" science projects such as HGP and the Superconducting Super Collider on hold to focus on more urgent and immediate needs, such as HIV/AIDS research – a sentiment shared by other leading scientists in and outside of the federal government.[215] Even after HGP was launched, many biologists continued to challenge its funding on the grounds that its blitzkrieg approach to mechanically decode the entire human genome would siphon funds and steer a generation of research scientists away from core basic science areas and smaller projects of much more immediate value, such as ongoing research on individual disease-causing genes.[216]

Influential members of the medical profession and related disciplines more focused on clinical care immediacy than biology bench research shared these concerns. Critics perceived HGP as the latest example of a basic "hard" (natural) science community difference in priorities – a difference relayed in an often-told parable:

> A surgeon, while jogging around a lake, spotted a man drowning. He dove in, dragged the victim ashore, and resuscitated him. His duty done, he wearily resumed his jogging, only to see two more people drowning. He also saw a colleague, a professor of biochemistry, standing nearby, apparently absorbed in thought. He called to him to go after one while he went after the other. When the biochemist was slow to respond, the surgeon shouted, "Why don't you do something?" The biochemist said, "I *am* doing something. I'm trying to figure out who's throwing all these people in the lake."[217]

The trends of escalating health care costs and the commercialization of medicine under managed care, which had taken hold in the early 1980s, continued to gain momentum.[218] Overwhelmed by these systemic changes and the realities of uninsured Americans and health care rationing, many in the clinical medicine and public health communities balked at the nascent biotech revolution and highly speculative genomic revolution as a science-hyped and Wall Street-driven distraction from real, immediate, and immense health care needs at the opportunity cost of human life in real time.[219] Among these professionals, "biotech often was shrugged off as the most recent fetish in basic science, a field driven by laboratory bench academics removed from the pressing realities of health care and too prone to get caught up in trends."[220] There was genuine concern that the enthusiasm and financial motives of biotech scientists who had "gone commercial" were exaggerating clinical expectations and skewing the allocation of limited biomedical research funding to speculative areas such as gene therapy.[221]

HGP was a success: A completed draft map of the human genome sequence was released in 2003.[222] The enabling technologies (notably sequencing and bioinformatics technologies) essential for HGP were created during it, though doing so consumed most of the project's budget and allocated time. By 1997, approximately halfway through HGP's slated duration, ninety percent of the project's budget had been spent to accurately sequence just 2.68 percent of the human genome.[223] Yet, through government and industry collaboration and competition with substantial academia engagement (the triple-threat methodology), researchers completed HGP ahead of schedule and under budget – somewhat of a phenomenon in "government work."[224]

The sequencing, bioinformatics, and other technologies created to complete HGP proved more immediately important than the map of the human genome. As observed by Walter Isaacson,

> Having a map of DNA did not, it turned out, lead to most of the grand medical breakthroughs that had been predicted. More than four thousand disease-causing

> DNA mutations were found. But no cure sprang forth for even the most simple of single-gene disorders, such as Tay-Sachs, sickle cell, or Huntington's. The men who had sequenced DNA taught us how to read the code of life, but the more important step would be learning how to write that code.[225]

HGP "spurred technological progress that was unprecedented in the life sciences, including the development of high-throughput technologies to detect genetic variation and gene expression. The study of genetics has become 'big data science'."[226] The multinational pharmaceutical sector shifted its R&D focus from traditional chemistry and biochemistry to biotech, genomics, and big data science in the mid-late 1990s when "Big Pharma" realized that its portfolio of enormously profitable drug products was falling off patent protection and that its traditional R&D pipeline was running dry.[227] The pharmaceutical sector made biotech acquisitions, entered into collaborations, and internalized biotech science prowess. The pharma and biotech sectors morphed into biopharma with a shared biotech R&D focus. The FDA acknowledged as much in 2004 when it centralized review of *all* new drugs, including biologic drugs, within the Center for Drug Evaluation and Research/CDER.[228] Industry did the same in 2016 when the biotech sector's trade association, the Biotechnology Industry Organization/BIO, changed its name to the Biotechnology *Innovation* Organization to relay commitment to biotech R&D rather than to a distinct biotech commercial sector.[229]

In sum, the HGP enabling technologies, coupled with the global focus in science that HGP created, stirred a genomic revolution that thunders on and builds, with CRISPR and other technologies emerging from it. Genomics and the underlying triple-threat R&D methodology produced the COVID-19 vaccines – a tangible, real time, twenty-first-century demonstration of their potential to improve human health. The practice of medicine and personal genome medicine/PGM will become synonymous. It is just a matter of human genome science progress and time.[230]

THE US TRIPLE-THREAT PAST, PRESENT, AND PERSONAL GENOME MEDICINE/PGM FUTURE

OWS was the culmination of government-academia-industry integration in science-technology R&D that arose out of WWII necessity, became embedded during the duration of the twentieth century, and made OWS possible.[231] The US embraced and applied its triple-threat R&D infrastructure, which was as essential for OWS as the science-technology in hand at its start – namely DNA next-generation sequencing/NGS technology and genomics.[232]

The success of OWS has reinforced US commitment to its triple-threat methodology, strengthened government-academic-industry relationships, and advanced genomics in addition to orchestrating the creation and dissemination of vaccines, therapeutics, and diagnostics responsive to COVID-19. Scientists are anticipating the next pandemic and utilizing CRISPR to build a defense against it.[233] For example, DARPA has launched a Safe Genes program to develop defense responsiveness with gene editing technologies and, with an investment of $65 million as of 2019, DARPA is the largest single source of funding for CRISPR research as this book goes into production.[234]

The genomic revolution is raging forward on triple-threat infrastructure generations beyond proof of principle. The cost of whole genome sequencing continues to drop while capacity soars, and scientists are utilizing that technology globally to decipher the intricacies of human genetics.[235] Government, academia, and industry are all engaged in biobanking to advance population genetics and genomics. For example, the US government has undertaken the All of Us Research Program to sequence the genomes of a million people representative of the diversity in the US population.[236]

Yes, much about OWS was unprecedented – most notably the mRNA COVID-19 vaccines it produced and the speed with which they were developed and disseminated. However, OWS applied methodology that had been tried and tested over many decades. The underlying R&D triple-threat methodology has a profound US legacy and is the means to an extraordinarily promising health care future – one with PGM as a standard of care in US medicine.[237]

NOTES

1 Walter Isaacson, The Code Breaker 73 (2021). *See* The Royal Swedish Academy of Sciences, *Press Release, The Nobel Prize in Chemistry 2020* (Oct. 7, 2020), www.nobelprize.org/prizes/chemistry/2020/press-release/.

2 *See* Isaacson, Code, *supra* note 1, at 245–47. The Cure Sickle Cell Initiative, a partnership between the Gates Foundation and the National Institutes of Health/NIH with $200 million in funding (FY2020), is working to advance this technology and treatment:

> The primary scientific goal of the initiative is to find a method to edit the sickle-cell mutation inside of a patient without needing to extract bone marrow. One possibility is to inject into the patient's blood a gene-editing molecule with an address label that directs it right to the cells in the bone marrow. The difficult part will be to find the right delivery mechanism, such as a virus-like particle, that won't trigger the patient's immune system.

Id. at 248. *See infra* note 8 (discussing Dr. Francis Collin's work, and a gene therapy cure for SCD through his research).

3 *See* NIH, Nat. Heart, Lung, and Blood Inst., *Sickle Cell Disease* (updated Sept. 1, 2020), www.nhlbi.nih.gov/health-topics/sickle-cell-disease. SCD is a group of inherited red blood cell disorders (sickle cell anemia is the most common) that cause red blood cells to assume a crescent or sickle shape, which blocks blood flow. *See id.* The condition may result in eye problems, infections, extreme pain, and stroke, and SCD increases susceptibility to other severe illnesses such as extreme reactions to COVID-19. *See id.* Standard of care (established in evidentiary science-based clinical care) treatment includes iron infusions, which subject patients to the risk of iron overload, and the only *potential* standard of care cure is a blood and bone marrow transplant. *See id.*

4 *See* Medline Plus, *What Is a Gene?*, Genetics Home Ref. (updated Mar. 22, 2021), https://medlineplus.gov/genetics/understanding/basics/gene/. *See also infra* notes 200–201, and accompanying text (distinguishing genomics from genetics).

5 *Visit* National Human Genome Research Institute/NHGRI, Centers for Mendelian Genomics (visited May 2, 2022), www.genome.gov/Funded-Programs-Projects/NHGRI-Genome-Sequencing-Program/Centers-for-Mendelian-Genomics-CMG. For discussion of the distinction between Mendelian and common diseases in *genetic testing*, see *Chapter 7, infra*, at notes 6–9, and accompanying text.

6 *See generally* NHGRI, *NIH Funds New Effort to Discover Genetic Causes of Single-Gene Disorders* (July 15, 2021), www.genome.gov/news/news-release/NIH-funds-new-effort-to-discover-genetic-causes-of-single-gene-disorders; CDC, *Sickle Cell Disease (SCD)* (reviewed Mar. 30, 2022) (SCD home page, with links to resources), www.cdc.gov/ncbddd/sicklecell/index.html; Matthew Zajac, *How Common Is Sickle Cell Disease?*, SICKLE-CELL.COM (reviewed Jan. 2021) (applying CDC data), https://sickle-cell.com/statistics; NIH, *Sickle Cell Disease, supra* note 3.

7 *See Current World Population*, WOLDOMETER (provides a running tabulation in real time; visited Nov. 25, 2022), www.worldometers.info/world-population/#:~:text=The%20current%20world%20population%20is,currently%20living)%20of%20the%20world.population.

8 Dr Francis Collins, who headed the Human Genome Project/HGP and then was Director of NIH from August 2009 to December 2021, has not been dissuaded by commercial opportunity costs and, to the contrary, has embraced the challenge of overcoming them. He has engaged in fruitful research to identify genes that cause cystic fibrosis and to develop a gene therapy for SCD, and he is an architect of US government initiatives to address rare diseases. *See* Reuters, *Research Group Reports Success in Finding Gene for Cystic Fibrosis*, N.Y. TIMES (Aug. 23, 1989), at A15, www.nytimes.com/1989/08/23/us/research-group-reports-success-in-finding-gene-for-cystic-fibrosis.html. Dr. Collins' work may have produced a cure for SCD. *See* Jon LaPook, *Could Gene Therapy Cure Sickle Cell Anemia?* (Oct. 11, 2020), www.cbsnews.com/news/could-gene-therapy-cure-sickle-cell-anemia-60-minutes-2020-10-11/. In 2021, NIH established the Mendelian Genomics Research Consortium to advance research on Mendelian rare diseases. *See* NHGRI, *Single-Gene Disorders, supra* note 6. For discussion of Ceredase, Genzyme's seminal orphan drug approved by the FDA in 1991, and measures the FDA is currently exploring to lower commercial feasibility barriers, see *infra* note 190.

It should be noted that, since the mid-1980s, the US has attempted to offset the "commercial feasibility factor" and the "shareholder wealth maximization norm" (discussed in *Chapter 5, infra*, at notes 215–18, and in the accompanying text), which dissuade commercial R&D for rare diseases, through the Orphan Drug Act of 1983/ODA, Pub. L. No. 97–414, 96 Stat. 2049, *codified as amended*, 21 U.S.C. §§ 360aa-360ee; 26 U.S.C. § 45C (1994); 42 U.S.C. § 236 (1994). *See infra* note 189–90, and accompanying text. "Orphan drug" designation triggers commercial sponsor benefits – most notably seven years of market exclusivity for orphan products. *See* MICHAEL J. MALINOWSKI, HANDBOOK ON BIOTECHNOLOGY LAW, BUSINESS, AND POLICY 11–12 (2016) (other incentives include tax credits for clinical research and grants to defray the cost of clinical testing). The US has expanded the "orphan" product designation approach well beyond prescription ("Rx") drug products. "The FDA Office of Orphan Products Development/OOPD mission is to advance the evaluation and development of products (drugs, biologics, devices, or medical foods) that demonstrate promise for the diagnosis and/or treatment of rare diseases or conditions." FDA, *Developing Products for Rare Diseases & Conditions* (Dec. 20, 2018), www.fda.gov/industry/developing-products-rare-diseases-conditions. The program has been used increasingly by large biopharma companies as well as by small and medium ones, and other nations have replicated variations of the ODA – which attest to its overall success. *See* Michael J. Malinowski, *Doctors, Patients, and Pills: A System Popping under Too Much Physician Discretion? A Law-Policy Prescription to Make Drug Approval More Meaningful in the Delivery of Health Care*, 33 CARDOZO L. REV. 1085, 1125 (2012). However, critics point to the ODA's susceptibility to industry gaming. Especially in an age of genomic and proteomic (protein function, as discussed *Infra* at Chapter 5, note 47 and in the accompanying text, and at Chapter 7, note 4) precision, biopharma companies have an opportunity to develop drugs and other medicinal products that target a subset of a common disease patient population and qualify for orphan status, though the products reach a much broader patient population once on the market through US physician off-label use. Biopharm has much opportunity to encourage off-label prescribing under US law and policy. *See* Sam F. Halabi, *The Drug Repurposing Ecosystem: Intellectual Property Incentives, Market Exclusivity, and the Future of "New" Medicines*, 20 YALE J. L. & TECH. 1, 28 (2018) (the ODA has "encouraged some firms to intentionally position drugs for orphan indications and then rely on off-label prescribing for non-orphan indications" and "allowed some firms to obtain orphan designation for known drugs already widely prescribed but unapproved for an orphan designation"). *See Chapter 3, infra*, at notes 56, 63–66, and accompanying text (discussing *Washington Legal* and subsequent off-label prescribing).

9 *Visit* CRISPR Therapeutics, official site (visited Apr. 28, 2022), http://crisprtx.com/.

10 *See* ISAACSON, CODE, *supra* note 1, at 245–48.

11 *See* Roz Plater, *First Person Treated for Sickle Cell Disease with CRISPR Is Doing Well*, HEALTHLINE (July 6, 2020), www.healthline.com/health-news/first-person-treated-for-sickle-cell-disease-with-crispr-is-doing-well.

12 ISAACSON, CODE, *supra* note 1, at 247.

13 *See* J. Michael McGinnis, *Population Health and the Influence of Medical and Scientific Advances*, 66 LA. L. REV. (Centennial Issue with proceedings of "The Genomics Revolution?: Science, Law and Policy" – a live and published symposium), 9, 19–20, (2005) (explaining that the application of genomic technologies to medical care has the potential to lessen our dependence on "halfway technologies" that turn diseases into chronic conditions rather than eliminating them, and thereby both improve human health and reduce health care costs).

14 Michelle Fay Cortez, *World's Most Expensive Drug Approved to Treat Hemophilia at $3.5 Million a Dose*, BLOOMBERG (Nov. 23, 2022), www.bloomberg.com/news/articles/2022-11-23/world-s-most-expensive-drug-csl-hemgenix-hemophilia-approved-by-fda?leadSource=uverify%20wall. *See also* Brian Park. *FDA Approval*, MPR (Nov. 23, 2022), www.empr.com/home/news/first-gene-therapy-for-hemophilia-b-gets-fda-approval/. For discussion of immunotherapies to treat cancers, see Ezra Cohen, *What Is Cancer Immunotherapy?*, CANCER RES. INST. (undated), www.cancerresearch.org/en-us/immunotherapy/what-is-immunotherapy; NIH, News Release, *NCI Study Identifies Essential Genes for Cancer Immunotherapy* (Aug.7, 2017), www.nih.gov/news-events/news-releases/nci-study-identifies-essential-genes-cancer-immunotherapy. For example, immunotherapy treatments for non-small cell lung cancer/NSCLC have demonstrated notable clinical success. *See* Sun Min Lim, Min Hee Hong, Hye Ryun Kim, *Immunotherapy for Non-small Cell Lung Cancer: Current Landscape and Future Perspectives*, 20 IMMUNE NET. e10 (Jan. 27, 2020), www.ncbi.nlm.nih.gov/pmc/articles/PMC7049584/. As of May 25, 2020, the FDA had approved four immunotherapies known as immune checkpoint inhibitors/ICI to treat NSCLC, the first in 2015. *See* Emma Shtvivelman, *What's New in Immunotherapy for Non-Small Cell Lung Cancer?*, CANCER COMMONS (May 25, 2020), https://cancercommons.org/latest-insights/new-immunotherapy-non-small-cell-lung-cancer/#:~:text=The%20first%20FDA%2Dapproved%20immunotherapy,four%20ICI%20drugs%20for%20NSCLC. These clinical accomplishments emerged after years of stagnation caused by controversy. The entire field of gene therapy stalled in 1999 due to the death of research participant Jesse Gelsinger during a gene therapy clinical trial run by the University of Pennsylvania, and largely remained so for years. *See* ISAACSON, CODE, *supra* note 1, at 279. According to CRISPR Noble Jennifer Doudna, "That made

the whole field of gene therapy go away, mostly, for at least a decade." *Id. See generally* Robin Fretwell Wilson, *The Death of Jesse Gelsinger: New Evidence of the Influence of Money and Prestige in Human Research*, 36 AM. J.L. & MED. 295, 295 (2010). The principal investigators neglected to inform Jesse, an eighteen-year-old at the time with a mild version of the disease under study, that primates had died in preclinical studies due to a violent immune response to the virus used to deliver the therapeutic gene. Jesse's immune system reacted similarly. The FDA investigated and concluded that the scientists involved in the trial, including co-investigator James Wilson who was Director of the Institute for Human Gene Therapy, violated several rules of conduct. Wilson had sought and received bioethics input for the trial from the University of Pennsylvania's highly regarded Center for Bioethics, then headed by Arthur Caplan – a renowned bioethics expert and frequent media commentator. Jesse's death "came to signify the corrosive influence of financial interests in human subjects research." *Id.* at 295. Jolting advances in stem cell research, beginning with a milestone discovery by James Thomson (University of Wisconsin) and John Gearhart (Johns Hopkins) in 1998, which enabled isolating and culturing stem cells from human embryos and aborted fetuses, and follow-on advances inspired President Obama to allow US federal funding of human embryonic stem cell research/HESCR through an executive order. *See* Exec. Order (Mar. 9, 2009), www.youtube.com/watch?v=2Gs39koIxZo. A researcher who worked with adult stem cells and was the recipient of considerable federal funding that also drew private funding brought a prolonged litigation challenge to block US federal funding of HESCR; HESCR funding was likely to shift federal funding and, consequentially, private investment away from his research. The case was resolved in 2011. *See generally Sherley v. Sebelius (HHS & NIH)*, 644 F.3d 388 (D.C. Cir. Apr. 2011). This litigation rekindled arguments raised regarding the Dickey-Wicker Amendment – an appropriations bill rider, introduced in 1995 (P.L. 104–99) and included each year subsequently, which prohibits federal funding of research that involves the destruction of human embryos. The DC Circuit concluded that stem cell lines cannot develop into a human embryo, so procurement of HESC lines already established for research use is distinguishable from creating them with federal funding through the destruction of embryos. *See generally id.*

15 *See* ISAACSON, CODE, *supra* note 1, at 249–51, 401–57. CRISPR evolved in bacteria as a means to fight viruses. In 2020, Doudna and her team shifted the focus of their work to explore how CRISPR might be deployed to detect and destroy the coronavirus. *See id.* at xviii.

16 *See* Fyodor D Urnov, *Prime Time for Genome Editing?*, 382 N. ENG. J. MED., 481–84 (Jan. 30, 2020), www.nejm.org/doi/full/10.1056/NEJMcibr1914271; Matthew Porteus, *A New Class of Medicines through DNA Editing*, 380 NEW ENG. J. MED. 947–59 (Mar. 7, 2019), www.nejm.org/doi/full/10.1056/NEJMra1800729. *See also* ISAACSON, CODE, *supra* note 1, at 250–51 (with the caption "Coming Soon"). According to UC Berkeley Professor Fyodor Urnov, who is cofounder of Tune Therapeutics, a biotech company focused on epigenome (the multitude of chemicals that tell a genome what to do) editing, progress in CRISPR clinical applications has been profound globally:

> In the United States and in Europe, progress has also been formidable. The biotechnology companies CRISPR Therapeutics and Vertex have cured 31 people with sickle cell disease who no longer experience the debilitating episodes of pain that characterize their condition. Another biotechnology company, Intellia Therapeutics, teamed up with Regeneron and used CRISPR to inactivate a typo-laden toxic gene in the livers of 15 people. A month after this injection, 93 percent of the toxin was gone from the bloodstreams of patients who received the highest dose of CRISPR medicine. Verve Therapeutics is developing a CRISPR treatment for

heart disease, with an initial focus on a severe genetic form. Should Verve meet its goal of expanding this approach to patients with the common type of heart disease, one gene edit could replace daily medications such as statins. Physicians elsewhere are using CRISPR to test a treatment for people who carry H.I.V. by cutting out the virus DNA from their immune system. If they succeed, it's possible that about 40 million people could benefit.

Fyodor Urnov, *We Can Edit a Person's DNA. So Why Don't We?*, N.Y. TIMES (Dec. 11, 2022), www.nytimes.com/2022/12/09/opinion/crispr-gene-editing-cures.html.

17 ISAACSON, CODE, *supra* note 1, at 477. For discussion of ethical, legal, social, and US medicine implications, see *Chapter 6*, *infra*, at notes 153–58, and accompanying text ("Consumer Genetics and Genomics Ethical, Legal, and Social Issues"). *See generally* CONSUMER GENETIC TECHNOLOGIES: ETHICAL AND LEGAL CONSIDERATIONS (J. Glenn Cohen, Nita A. Farahany, Henry T. Greely, Carmel Shachar eds., 2021).

18 *See generally* Ritika Luthra, Simran Kaur, Kriti Bhandari, *Applications of CRISPR as a Potential Therapeutic*, 284 LIFE SCI. 119908 (Nov. 1, 2021), https://pubmed.ncbi.nlm.nih.gov/34453943/ (identifying similar sources); Bridget Balch, *The future of CRISPR is now*, ASSOC. OF AM. MED. COLLEGES/AAMC (Dec. 2, 2021), www.aamc.org/news-insights/future-crispr-now. Ribonucleic acid/RNA editing technologies (RNA is single-stranded, while DNA, with its double-helix structure, is double-stranded and less able to permeate the double-layer nuclear membrane/envelope) is another science technology platform with enormous therapeutic potential – and the two platform technologies are being combined. *See* Sara Reardon, *News Feature, Step aside CRISPR, RNA Editing Is Taking Off*, 578 NATURE 24–27 (Feb. 4, 2020) ("Making changes to the molecular messengers that create proteins might offer flexible therapies for cancer, pain or high cholesterol, in addition to genetic disorders.") (citing similar sources), www.nature.com/articles/d41586-020-00272-5.

19 *See* NHGRI, *Human Genome Project FAQ* (updated Feb. 24, 2020), www.genome.gov/human-genome-project/Completion-FAQ. *See generally Proceedings of "The Genomics Revolution?: Science, Law and Policy,"* 66 LA L. REV. 1–143 (2005) (Centennial Issue for live and published symposium). *See also infra* notes 199–230, and accompanying text ("The Genomic Revolution").

20 *Visit* NHGRI, *The Human Genome Project* (visited Sept. 22, 2021), www.genome.gov/human-genome-project. *See Prologue*, *supra*, at notes 5, 14–15, and accompanying text.

21 The project, launched in 1990 with a target timeline of fifteen years and a budget of $3 billion, was completed in 2003 at a cost of $2.7 billion (FY1991). *See* HGRI, *FAQ*, *supra* note 19. *See also Prologue*, *supra*, at notes 5, 14, and accompanying text.

22 Byjon Heggie, *Genomics: A Revolution in Health Care? Drugs Affect People Differently and We're Increasingly Understanding Why. For Many of Us, It's Down to Our Genes*, NAT'L GEO. (Feb. 20, 2019), www.nationalgeographic.com/science/article/partner-content-genomics-health-care. *See* ISAACSON, CODE, *supra* note 1, at ch. 5, 37–41 ("The Human Genome"). The map of the human was compiled by sequencing and comparing the genomes of several individuals to find our species' DNA common denominator. *See generally* HGRI, *FAQ*, *supra* note 19. A *preliminary* draft was announced in 2000 (the millennia transition year) at a White House Ceremony, during which President Clinton proclaimed, "Today we are learning the language in which God created life," and *The New York Times* reported, "In an achievement that represents a pinnacle of human self-knowledge, two rival groups of scientists said today that they had deciphered the hereditary script, the set of instructions that defines the human organism." Nicholas Wade, *Genetic Code of Human Life Is Cracked by Scientists*, N.Y. TIMES (June 27, 2000),

https://archive.nytimes.com/www.nytimes.com/library/national/science/062700sci-genome.html. A *preliminary* rough draft was released in 2001. *See generally* 409 NATURE 745 (2001) (issue dedicated to the release of a preliminary draft map of the human genome); 291 SCIENCE 1145 (2001) (issue entitled "The Human Genome"). The White House ceremony in 2000 featured James Watson, chief architect of HGP, Dr. Francis Collins who headed the US government HGP effort, and John Craig Venter who headed a commercial rival in the race to complete a map of the human genome sequence. *See generally* GEORGINA FERRY, JOHN SULSTON, THE COMMON THREAD: A STORY OF SCIENCE, POLITICS, ETHICS AND THE HUMAN GENOME (2002); Michael A. Fortun, *Celera Genomics: The Race for the Human Genome Projects, in* ENCYCLOPEDIA OF THE HUMAN GENOME (2006). Venter used a "shotgun sequencing" method for speed, which was questioned and rejected by many HGP scientists as not accurate enough for sequencing a genome as complicated as the human genome. *See generally* Philip Green, *Against a Whole-Genome Shotgun*, 7 GENOME RES. 410–17 (1997), https://genome.cshlp.org/content/7/5/410.full. A completed draft sequence (distinguished from the preliminary draft released in 2001) was released in 2003. *See* NHGRI, *Press Release, International Consortium Completes Human Genome Project* (Apr. 14, 2003), www.genome.gov/11006929. Subsequently, researchers worked to correct mistakes and to fill gaps. The NHGRI released the first *complete* sequence of the human genome on March 31, 2022. *See* NHGRI, Prabarna Ganguly, *Researchers Generate the First Complete, Gapless Sequence of a Human Genome* (Mar. 31, 2022), www.genome.gov/news/news-release/researchers-generate-the-first-complete-gapless-sequence-of-a-human-genome.

23 *See Prologue, supra,* at notes 1–13, and accompanying text.

24 *See* World Health Organization/WHO, *Archived: WHO Timeline – COVID-19* (Apr. 27, 2020), www.who.int/news/item/27-04-2020-who-timeline-covid-19.

25 *See* NIH, *COVID-19 Vaccine Development: Behind the Scenes: Years of Research Enable a COVID-19 Vaccine to Be Developed in Record Time* (visited Aug. 7, 2021), https://covid19.nih.gov/news-and-stories/vaccine-development. *See also* Ayana Byrd, *How the COVID-19 Vaccines Were Made So Quickly – From the Lab to Clinical Trials to FDA Authorization*, HEALTH LIVING (Apr. 15, 2021), www.health.com/condition/infectious-diseases/coronavirus/how-covid-19-vaccine-was-made-quickly; Will Brothers, *A Timeline of COVID-19 Vaccine Development*, BIOSPACE (Dec 03, 2020), www.biospace.com/article/a-timeline-of-covid-19-vaccine-development/. *See also* Jim Geraghty, *Covid Origin Destined to Be a Forever Secret*, NAT'L REV. (Sept. 7, 2022) (addressing the "lab break" and other theories of origin, China government secrecy, and the assessment "that the lack of cooperation from China and incomplete data make it impossible to rule out any point of origin"), www.nationalreview.com/the-morning-jolt/covid-origin-destined-to-be-a-forever-secret/; Michael Worobey, *Dissecting the Early COVID-19 Cases in Wuhan*, 374(6572) SCIENCE 1202–04 (Nov. 18, 2021) ("Elucidating the origin of the pandemic requires understanding of the Wuhan outbreak."), www.science.org/doi/10.1126/science.abm4454; Donna Lu, *The Hunt to Find the Coronavirus Pandemic's Patient Zero*, 245(3276) NEW SCI. 9 (Apr. 4, 2020) ("identifying the source of the outbreak is crucial, given that three coronaviruses – the SARS, MERS and Covid-19 viruses – have all emerged since 2002"), www.ncbi.nlm.nih.gov/pmc/articles/PMC7194960/. President Trump and many others referred to COVID-19 in the media as the "Wuhan Virus," "China Virus," and "Asian Virus," which exacerbated volatility in domestic and international politics and contributed to a domestic spike in hate crimes. *See* Marietta Vazquez, *Calling COVID-19 the "Wuhan Virus" or "China Virus" is Inaccurate and Xenophobic*, YALE SCH. OF MED. NEWSLETTER (Mar. 12, 2020), https://medicine.yale.edu/news-article/calling-covid-19-the-wuhan-virus-or-china-virus-is-inaccurate-and-xenophobic/.

26 *Visit* NHGRI, *Genomics and Medicine* (visited Sept. 22, 2021), www.genome.gov/health/Genomics-and-Medicine. *See also* Heggie, *Genomics*, *supra* note 22. *See generally* FRANCIS S. COLLINS, THE LANGUAGE OF LIFE: DNA AND THE REVOLUTION IN PERSONALIZED MEDICINE (illustrated ed. 2011); MISHA ANGRIST, HERE IS A HUMAN BEING: AT THE DAWN OF PERSONAL GENOMICS (2010); KEVIN DAVIES, THE $1,000 GENOME: THE REVOLUTION IN DNA SEQUENCING AND THE NEW ERA OF PERSONALIZED MEDICINE (2010).

27 ISAACSON, CODE, *supra* note 1, at xvii.

28 *See infra* notes 32–114, and accompanying text ("Latest US Application" and "OWS Implementation").

29 *See infra* notes 115–27, and accompanying text ("WWII Necessity").

30 *See* Howard Markel, *Patents, Profits, and the American People – The Bayh–Dole Act of 1980*, 369 N. ENGL. J. MED. 794–96, 795 (Aug. 29, 2013), www.nejm.org/doi/full/10.1056/nejmp1306553. This legislation and US TTLP are discussed *infra* at notes 164–79, and in the accompanying text.

31 *See infra* notes 199–230, and accompanying text ("The Genomic Revolution").

32 Domestic Preparedness.com, *Fact Sheet: Explaining Operation Warp Speed*, DOM. PREPAREDNESS J. (Aug. 17, 2020), www.domesticpreparedness.com/updates/fact-sheet-explaining-operation-warp-speed/. Congress appropriated most of the budget during spring 2020, but the Trump Administration also supplemented with funds siphoned from other public health programs – including $6 billion from the Strategic National Stockpile and $1 billion from the CDC. *See id*; Aria Bendix, *Operation Warp Speed Bought 100 Million Doses of Pfizer's and Moderna's Vaccines Before Results Came in. That $3.5 billion bet is paying off*, BUS. INSIDER (Nov 19, 2020), www.businessinsider.com/operation-warp-speed-us-coronavirus-vaccine-program-pfizer-moderna-2020-11. Congress also supplemented OWS initial funding with approximately $10 billion, including through the Coronavirus Aid, Relief, and Economic Security Act/CARES Act, Pub. L. 116–36 (Mar. 27, 2020) – a $2.2 trillion economic stimulus bill passed in response to the US domestic economic fallout from the pandemic. Designated funding included $3 billion for NIH research and more than $6.5 billion for countermeasure development. Some of the additional funds were allocated through HHS's BARDA, which interfaces and coordinates with the biopharma industry to advance R&D objectives on an ongoing basis. *See infra* note 75, and accompanying text. Total OWS official funding reached a whopping $18 Billion by October 2020. *See* Stephanie Baker, Cynthia Koons, *Inside Operation Warp Speed's $18 Billion Sprint for a Vaccine*, BLOOMBERG BUSINESSWEEK (Oct. 29, 2020), www.bloomberg.com/news/features/2020-10-29/inside-operation-warp-speed-s-18-billion-sprint-for-a-vaccine. OWS met its Herculean vaccine development objective, and production towards 300 million doses was well underway by January 2021. *See generally* GOVERNMENT ACCOUNTABILITY OFFICE/GAO, OPERATION WARP SPEED: ACCELERATED COVID-19 VACCINE DEVELOPMENT STATUS AND EFFORTS TO ADDRESS MANUFACTURING CHALLENGES, GAO-21-319 (Feb. 11, 2021), www.gao.gov/products/gao-21-319. In addition to the COVID-19 vaccine R&D accomplishments, OWS contracted with Regeneron Pharmaceuticals, Inc. for the development and delivery of a monoclonal antibody therapeutic to treat COVID-19, which was realized and administered to President Trump in October 2020 when he contracted the virus. *See generally* Berkeley Lovelace, Jr., *FDA Authorizes Regeneron's COVID Treatment, Taken by Trump, for Emergency Use*, CNBC (Nov. 21, 2020), www.cnbc.com/2020/11/21/covid-treatment-fda-authorizes-regeneron-drug-used-by-trump.html; Manojna Maddipatla, *US Signs $450 Million Contract with Regeneron for COVID-19 Therapy*, REUTERS (July 7, 2020), www.reuters.com/article/us-health-coronavirus-regeneron-pharms/u-s-signs-450-million-contract-with-regeneron-for-covid-19-therapy-idUSKBN2481GK.

33 Roy Khan, *COVID-19 Vaccine A Monumental Scientific and Collaborative Feat: These Vaccines Save Lives*, FORBES (Aug 5, 2021), www.forbes.com/sites/roomykhan/2021/08/05/covid-19-vaccine-a-monumental-scientific-and-collaborative-feat-these-vaccines-save-lives/?sh=386022a5201b. *See* Tung Thanh Le, Jakob P Cramer, Robert Chen, Stephen Mayhew, *Evolution of the COVID-19 Vaccine Development Landscape*. 19 NAT. REV. DRUG DISC. 667–68 (Oct. 2020), www.nature.com/articles/d41573-020-00151-8. Although the science response to COVID-19 was as shared and as global as the pandemic itself, the US government opted to launch OWS and declined to join COVAX – a global alliance to develop, manufacture, and distribute COVID-19 vaccines formed by the World Health Organization/WHO, the European Commission, and the government of France. *Visit* WHO, COVAX (visited Sept. 2, 2021), www.who.int/initiatives/act-accelerator/covax. *See* Bendix, *Warp Speed, supra* note 32. Also, collaboration among commercial competitors in response to the pandemic gave way to commercial reality in August 2022. Moderna brought a legal action against Pfizer and BioNTech alleging that they infringed on patents filed between 2010 and 2016. *See* Jenny Gross, Rebecca Robbins, *Moderna Sues Pfizer and BioNTech Over Covid Vaccine*, N.Y. TIMES (Aug. 26, 2022) ("The lawsuit, filed Friday, claims that the companies' Covid vaccine violated Moderna's mRNA patents."), www.nytimes.com/2022/08/26/business/moderna-covid-vaccine-lawsuit.html. Pfizer sales for its COVID-19 vaccine reached $36.8 billion in 2021. Moderna too is facing a patent infringement lawsuit over its COVID-19 vaccine. *See* Blake Brittain, *Moderna, Not US Gov't, Must Defend COVID-19 Vaccine Patent Case for Now*, REUTERS (Nov. 2, 2022), www.reuters.com/legal/litigation/moderna-not-us-govt-must-defend-covid-19-vaccine-patent-case-now-2022-11-02/. However, "US District Judge Mitchell Goldberg said he was not yet convinced that the lawsuit by Arbutus Biopharma Corp and Genevant Sciences GmbH should have been brought against the government instead of Cambridge, Massachusetts-based Moderna." *Id.*

34 *See* Bendix, *Warp Speed, supra* note 32. *See generally* GAO, OWS, *supra* note 32.

35 Khan, *Monumental, supra* note 33. *See* NIH, *Behind the Scenes, supra* note 25; Brothers, *Timeline, supra* note 25 ("Vaccine development is an arduous process, taking about 10–15 years on average to accomplish."), www.biospace.com/article/a-timeline-of-covid-19-vaccine-development.

36 *See generally* Olivier J. Wouters, Martin McKee, Jeroen Luyten, *Estimated Research and Development Investment Needed to Bring a New Medicine to Market*, 2009–2018, 323 *JAMA* 844, 844–53 (Mar. 3, 2020), https://jamanetwork.com/journals/jama/fullarticle/2762311. This early 2020 analysis of cost, "which accounts for projects that failed in clinical development, confirms similar numbers that have been published in the past [also based largely on industry self-reported data], although it rebuts a more recent finding putting the costs as high as nearly $3 billion, which used confidential data provided by drugmakers." Jonathan Gardner, *New Estimate Puts Cost to Develop a New Drug at $1B, Adding to Long-Running Debate*, BIOPHARMA DIVE (Mar. 3, 2020), www.biopharmadive.com/news/new-drug-cost-research-development-market-jama-study/573381/. Drug makers voluntarily self-report data to the Tufts Center for the Study of Drug Development ("Tufts CSDD"), which generates reports that are heavily referenced; this has been an industry and Tufts CSDD practice for decades (faithfully throughout the three decades I have been working in the field). *Visit* Tufts CSDD, official site (undated; visited May 1, 2022), http://csdd.tufts.edu/.

37 N. Nicole Stakleff, *A Drug Life: The Chemistry of Patent and Regulatory Exclusivity for Pharmaceuticals*, 16 FL. COASTAL L. REV. 27, 28 (2014).

38 *See* Mark M. Struck, *Vaccine R&D Success Rates and Development Times*, 14 NAT. BIOTECH 591–93 (May 1996), www.nature.com/articles/nbt0596-591.pdf?origin=ppub

(reporting that 1983–1994 data indicated that, in comparison with biopharmaceuticals, only half as many *preclinical* vaccine candidates endured the clinical trial process).

39 *See generally* MALINOWSKI, HANDBOOK, *supra* note 8.

40 *See generally id.*

41 *See generally* Michael Diamond, Theodore Pierson, *The Challenges of Vaccine Development against a New Virus during a Pandemic*, 27 CELL HOST AND MICROBE 699–703 (May 13, 2020), www.cell.com/cell-host-microbe/pdf/S1931-3128(20)30248-1.pdf.

42 The base US regulations to protect human subjects in research, referred to as the Common Rule, recognize children as a protected class under subpart D. 46 C.F.R. Subpart D, §§46.101, et seq. *Cf.* Henry T. Greely, *Crispr'd Babies: Human Germline Genome Editing in the "He Jiankui Affair*", 6 J. L. & BIOSCIENCES 111 (2019) (addressing live births in China following the use of CRISPR for genetic engineering in human reproduction to the dismay of the global science ethics community).

43 *See* Diamond, Pierson, *Challenges, supra* note 41. *See also* Khan, *Monumental, supra* note 33; Max Nisen, *Operation Warp Speed Needs to Waste Money on Vaccines*, BLOOMBERG NEWS (Apr. 30, 2020), www.bloomberg.com/opinion/articles/2020-04-30/operation-warp-speed-needs-to-waste-money-on-covid-vaccines; David Sanger, *Trump Seeks Push to Speed Vaccine, Despite Safety Concerns*, N.Y. TIMES (Apr. 29, 2020), www.nytimes .com/2020/04/29/us/politics/trump-coronavirus-vaccine-operation-warp-speed.html.

44 *See id. See also* Khan, *Monumental, supra* note 33; Nisen, *Needs, supra* note 43; Sanger, *Trump Seeks, supra* note 43.

45 *See generally* HEIDI J. LARSON, STUCK: HOW VACCINE RUMORS START – AND WHY THEY DON'T GO AWAY (2020) (addressing the heightened importance of adhering to sound, evidentiary science with vaccines given vaccine hesitancy and susceptibility to rumors and conspiracy theories not grounded in evidentiary science). *See also Chapter* 5, *infra*, at notes 85–89, and accompanying text. Women protecting their pregnancies have an understandably elevated vaccine hesitancy though, to protect their pregnancies and themselves, they should more aggressively seek out and follow sound evidentiary science-based clinical guidance from learned and licensed physicians – which, unfortunately, many are not doing regarding COVID-19 and beyond. *See generally* Apoorva Mandavilli, *The Covid Pandemic's Hidden Casualties: Pregnant Women*, N.Y. TIMES (Dec. 8, 2022), www.nytimes.com/2022/12/08/health/pregnant-women-covid-flu-vaccine.html. *See also Chapter* 5, *infra*, at note 93, and accompanying text. Only thirty-seven percent of pregnant women had been vaccinated against the flu as of October 2022, as the nation grapples with a viral tripledemic – a synchronized rage of flu, respiratory syncytial virus/RSV, and COVID-19 – that is filling the nation's hospitals. *See id.* Regarding vaccine hesitancy overall, generations removed from the vaccine accomplishments of the twentieth century do not have experiential appreciation for the disease suffering that vaccination has prevented. Without the presence of diseases prevented and associated fear, the public tends to take vaccines for granted. *See* generally *id.* Healthy people, and especially parents protective of their children, when asked to be dosed with a vaccine to contain disease risk, are highly susceptible to misrepresentations contrary to sound evidentiary-science, allegations of industry fraud-for-profit, and other conspiracy theories. Also, human nature is to want explanations for sudden illness (answers to "What caused this?") and, if possible, to place blame. Deliberately fraudulent research published by the *Lancet* in 1998, which suggested that the measles, mumps, and rubella/MMR vaccine might predispose children to autism spectrum disorder/ASD, fired up a global anti-vaccination movement that, despite sound, abundant, and persuasive evidentiary-science data to the contrary, still smolders. *See Retracted Article*: Andrew Wakefield et al. (twelve additional

coauthors), *Ileal-Lymphoid-nodular Hyperplasia, Non-specific Colitis, and Pervasive Developmental Disorder in Children*, 351(9103) LANCET 637–41 (Feb. 28, 1998), www.sciencedirect.com/science/article/pii/S0140673697110960. PubMed provides links for the *Lancet* retraction, responses, and related information at https://pubmed.ncbi.nlm.nih.gov/9500320/. *See generally* T. S. Sathyanarayana Rao, Chittaranjan Andrade, *The MMR Vaccine and Autism: Sensation, Refutation, Retraction, and Fraud*, 53(2) INDIAN J. PSYCH. 95–6 (Apr. 2011), www.ncbi.nlm.nih.gov/pmc/articles/PMC3136032/. *See also Chapter 5, infra*, at notes 86–96, and accompanying text (addressing COVID-19 vaccine hesitancy).

46 *See* Diamond, Pierson, *Challenges*, *supra* note 41.

47 *See* Dave Roos, *History Stories: How a New Vaccine Was Developed in Record Time in the 1960s*, HISTORY.COM (June 22, 2020), www.history.com/news/mumps-vaccine-world-war-ii; Brothers, *Timeline*, *supra* note 25.

48 *See* NIH, *HIV Overview, FDA-Approved HIV Medicines* (last reviewed Feb. 8, 2021), https://hivinfo.nih.gov/understanding-hiv/fact-sheets/fda-approved-hiv-medicines. *See generally* NIH, *History of HIV Vaccine Research* (last reviewed Oct. 22, 2018), www.niaid.nih.gov/diseases-conditions/hiv-vaccine-research-history.

49 *See* World Health Organization/WHO, *HIV Cure: First Case of HIV Cure in a Woman after Stem Cell Transplantation reported at CROI-2022* (Mar. 24, 2022), www.who.int/news/item/24-03-2022-first-case-of-hiv-cure-in-a-woman-after-stem-cell-transplantation-reported-at-croi-2022.

50 ISAACSON, CODE, *supra* note 1, at 440–41. mRNA delivers the blueprint for the COVID-19 spike protein to the protein-making machinery in the nuclei of cells, cells make only the spike protein which is harmless on its own, and the individual's immune system responds by producing antibodies that attack the virus. *See id.* at 446. As observed by Professor Isaacson, "thanks to the new RNA vaccine technology, our defenses against most future viruses are likely to be immensely faster and more effective.... There was a sudden shift in the evolutionary balance between what human technology can do and what viruses can do. We may never have a pandemic again." *Id.* at 447. Beyond vaccinating people against viruses, teams of scientists are competing to utilize CRISPR technologies to genetically modify viruses to neutralize them and make vaccination unnecessary. *See id.* at 449–50. For example, Excision BioTherapeutics, a San Francisco-based biotech company, is conducting clinical trials to test whether a CRISPR infusion can stop HIV from replicating. *Visit* Excision BioTherapeutics, official site (visited Apr. 7, 2023), www.excision.bio/.

51 Khan, *Monumental*, *supra* note 33.

52 *See* Bendix, *Warp Speed*, *supra* note 32. The Pfizer-BioNTech vaccine, as originally released, had to be shipped and stored at -94 degrees Fahrenheit; it spoiled in approximately five days under standard refrigeration. *See id.* The Moderna vaccine, as originally released, had to be kept at −4 degrees Fahrenheit. *See id.* It survived thirty days under standard refrigeration, and twelve hours at room temperature. *See id.*

53 *See* GAO, OWS, *supra* note 32, at "GAO Highlights." ("The two EUAs issued in December 2020 were based on analyses of clinical trial participants and showed about 95 percent efficacy for each vaccine.")

54 *See* CDC, *Q&A: Vaccine Effectiveness: How Well Do Flu Vaccines Work?* (reviewed Aug. 26, 2021), www.cdc.gov/flu/vaccines-work/vaccineeffect.htm.

55 *See* GAO, OWS, *supra* note 32, at "GAO Highlights." The FDA granted full market approval of the Pfizer-BioNTech vaccine, marketed as Comirnaty, for the prevention of COVID-19 disease in individuals sixteen years of age and older on August 23, 2021. *See* FDA, *News Release, FDA Approves First COVID-19 Vaccine* (Aug. 23, 2021), www.fda.gov/news-events/press-announcements/fda-approves-first-covid-19-vaccine. Although

an abundance of global real-world data/RWD was compiled in real time from when the FDA issued EUAs that made the vaccines broadly available to when the FDA granted full market approvals, vaccines necessitate time for research subjects to build responsive immunity, to assess the sustainability of immunity in subjects over time, for assurance of safety over time, and to fully (experientially) assess manufacturing and distribution. *See supra* notes 42–45, and accompanying text (discussing fundamental vaccine R&D challenges). *Cf.* FDA, *Emergency Use Authorization for Vaccines Explained* (current Nov. 20, 2020), www.fda.gov/vaccines-blood-biologics/vaccines/emergency-use-authorization-vaccines-explained. Incidentally, The 21st Century Cures Act, Pub. L. 114–255 (2016), pressures the FDA to consider "real-world evidence" in its regulation of the safety and efficacy of drugs and devices. *See generally* Elizabeth Hall-Lipsy, Leila Barraza, Christopher Robertson, *Practice-Based Research Networks and the Mandate for Real-World Evidence*, 44 AM. J. L. MED. 219–36 (2018), https://pubmed.ncbi.nlm.nih.gov/30106651/. In advance of the pandemic, the FDA established a real-world evidence/RWE framework in 2018, which it has supplemented with guidance documents that address issues such as data standards and registries. *See generally* FDA, FRAMEWORK FOR FDA'S REAL-WORLD EVIDENCE PROGRAM (Dec. 2018), www.fda.gov/media/120060/download. The FDA also established a program, RCT Duplicate, to evaluate whether randomized controlled trials/RCTs relied on for product market approval can be emulated with real-world evidence/RWE across a range of therapeutic areas. *Visit* FDA, RCT Duplicate, official site (undated; visited June 14, 2022), www.rctduplicate.org/. *See* Zachary Brennan, *Real World Evidence: Lessons Learned from an FDA Pilot Show the Limits of Emulating RCTs*, ENDPOINTSNEWS (May 16, 2022), https://endpts.com/real-world-evidence-lessons-learned-from-an-fda-pilot-show-the-limits-of-emulating-rcts/.

56 *See* Byrd, *Quickly*, *supra* note 25.

57 *See* Baker, Koons, *Inside*, *supra* note 32; Khan, *Monumental*, *supra* note 33; NIH, *Behind the Scenes*, *supra* note 25.

58 *See generally* GAO, OWS, *supra* note 32. *See* Bendix, *Warp Speed*, *supra* note 32; Domestic Preparedness.com, *Fact Sheet*, *supra* note 32; Khan, *Monumental*, *supra* note 33; NIH, *Behind the Scenes*, *supra* note 25.

59 *See* Khan, *Monumental*, *supra* note 33; NIH, *Behind the Scenes*, *supra* note 25; Baker, Koons, *Inside*, *supra* note 32; Bendix, *Warp Speed*, *supra* note 32; Domestic Preparedness.com, *Fact Sheet*, *supra* note 32.

60 *See* MALINOWSKI, HANDBOOK, *supra* note 8, at xxvi; SETON HALL SCHOOL OF LAW, THE CENTER FOR HEALTH & PHARMACEUTICAL LAW & POLICY, CONFLICTS OF INTEREST IN CLINICAL TRIAL RECRUITMENT & ENROLLMENT: A CALL FOR INCREASED OVERSIGHT 5 (Nov. 2009) (White Paper), https://law.shu.edu/health-law/upload/health_center_whitepaper_nov2009.pdf. *See also* ISAACSON, CODE, *supra* note 1, at 97.

61 *See generally* GAO, OWS, *supra* note 32. OWS entered into agreements with AstraZeneca, Johnson & Johnson, Moderna, Novavax, Pfizer, and Sanofi-GlaxoSmithKline (a vaccine R&D partnership). *See infra* notes 77–81, and accompanying text.

62 *See* Byrd, *Quickly*, *supra* note 25. "Corona" means crown, which is the shape the top of a coronaviruses resembles when viewed under a microscope. *See* John Hopkins Medicine, *What Is Coronavirus?* (undated; visited Apr. 30, 2022) (includes link to informative video), www.hopkinsmedicine.org/health/conditions-and-diseases/coronavirus.

63 *See* Byrd, *Quickly*, *supra* note 25.

64 *See* NIH, *Behind the Scenes*, *supra* note 25.

65 *See id.*

66 Moderna, with just 800 employees at the time, was utilizing mRNA to develop personal cancer treatments and had begun applying the technology to make vaccines against viruses. *See* Isaacson, Code, *supra* note 1, at 442; Byrd, *Quickly, supra* note 25.

67 *See* Isaacson, Code, *supra* note 1, at 442; Byrd, *Quickly, supra* note 25.

68 *See* NIH, *Behind the Scenes, supra* note 25; Byrd, *Quickly, supra* note 25.

69 *See* Brothers, *Timeline, supra* note 25. In April 2020, the Coalition for Epidemic Preparedness Innovations/CEPI assessed all COVID-19 vaccine candidates in development. *See generally Development Landscape, supra* note 17.

70 *See* FDA, *The Drug Development Process* (current Jan. 4, 2018), www.fda.gov/patients/learn-about-drug-and-device-approvals/drug-development-process.

71 *Cf.* FDA, *Current Good Manufacturing Practice (CGMP) Regulations* (Sept. 21, 2020), www.fda.gov/drugs/pharmaceutical-quality-resources/current-good-manufacturing-practice-cgmp-regulations; Kate Coleman, *Engineering Angles: Optimizing the Facility Design Phase*, Pharma Manuf. Mag. (Nov. 17, 2021), www.pharmamanufacturing.com/articles/2021/engineering-angles-optimizing-the-facility-design-phase/.

72 *See id.* Failure to progress may be due to sponsor business decision making beyond clinical data. According to analysis by MIT authors of data on drugs and vaccines from January 1, 2000, to October 31, 2015, the probabilities for candidates overall (not distinguished by therapeutic areas), are that 48.6 percent fail to progress from phase 2 to phase 3 trials, and 49 percent of the remaining full market candidates from phase 3 trials to market approval. *See* Chi Heem Wong, Kien Wei Siah, Andrew W Lo, *Estimation of Clinical Trial Success Rates and Related Parameters*, 20 Biostatistics 273–86 (Apr. 2019), https://academic.oup.com/biostatistics/article/20/2/273/4817524; Alex Berezow, *Clinical Trial Success Rates by Phase and Therapeutic Area*, Amer. Council on Sci. and Health (June 11, 2020), www.acsh.org/news/2020/06/11/clinical-trial-success-rates-phase-and-therapeutic-area-14845. This analysis of probabilities concluded that vaccines fare relatively well in phases 2 and 3, with 58.2 percent progressing from phase 2 to 3 (after the sorting out during phase 1), and 85.4 progressing from phase 3 to approval. *See id.*

73 *Development Landscape, supra* note 17 (a study by the Coalition for Epidemic Preparedness Innovations/CEPI.

74 Brothers, *Timeline, supra* note 25. *See also* Bendix, *Warp Speed, supra* note 32; Khan, *Monumental, supra* note 33.

75 *Visit* Office of the Assistant Secretary for Preparedness & Response/ASPR, Biomedical Advanced Research and Development Authority/BARDA, official site (visited May 3, 2022), https://aspr.hhs.gov/AboutASPR/ProgramOffices/BARDA/Pages/default.aspx.

76 *Visit* DARPA, official site, www.darpa.mil/.

77 *See generally* GAO, OWS, *supra* note 32. *See also* Baker, Koons, *Inside*, supra note 32; Bendix, *Warp Speed, supra* note 32; Domestic Preparedness.com, *Fact Sheet, supra* note 32; Khan, *Monumental, supra* note 33; NIH, *Behind the Scenes, supra* note 25.

78 *See* Khan, *Monumental, supra* note 33; Riley Griffin, Drew Armstrong, *Pfizer Vaccine's Funding Came From Berlin, Not Washington*, Bloomberg (Nov. 9, 2020), www.bloomberg.com/news/articles/2020-11-09/pfizer-vaccine-s-funding-came-from-berlin-not-washington. *Cf.* James G. Hodge, Jr., *National Legal Paradigms for Public Health Emergency Responses*, 71 Am. U. L. Rev. 65, 109 (2021).

79 *See* Bendix, *Warp Speed, supra* note 32.

80 *Id.*

81 *See id.*

82 *See* GAO, OWS, *supra* note 32, at 31 ("Highlights"). *See also* Alex Azar, *HHS Secretary Azar: Why Operation Warp Speed Is a Made-in-America Story*, Fox Bus. (Oct. 22, 2020), www.foxbusiness.com/healthcare/hhs-azar-operation-warp-speed ("Not only has

manufacturing work begun, it's begun on an industrial scale for all six OWS-supported vaccines. More than 23 manufacturing facilities across the US have already been augmented and scaled up with support from OWS.").

83 GAO, OWS, *supra* note 32.

84 *See* Azar, *Why*, *supra* note 82.

85 *See* GAO, OWS, *supra* note 32 at "Highlights" (page nos. not provided).

86 *See id.*

87 *See id.*

88 *See id.*

89 *See generally* Byrd, *Quickly*, *supra* note 25. Standing fundamental weaknesses in FDA regulatory oversight were COVID-19 vaccine R&D inclusive, rather than COVID-19 exclusive or exceptions to. Perhaps most notably, FDA's "grossly inadequate" oversight of clinical trial sites is a chronic and unacceptable shortcoming, as HHS's Office of Inspector General/OIG recognized in 2007. "A report in 2007 by the Department of Health and Human Services' Office of the Inspector General found the FDA audited less than 1% of the nation's clinical trial sites between 2000 and 2005 and was highly critical of the agency because it did not have a database of operational clinical trial sites," and that regulatory Shortcoming Continues. Maryanne Demasi, *BMJ Investigation, FDA Oversight of Clinical trials is "grossly inadequate," say experts*, 379 Brit. Med. J./BMJ 2628 (Nov. 16, 2022), www.bmj.com/content/bmj/379/bmj.o2628.full.pdf; Shawn Radcliffe, *FDA Oversight of Clinical Trials was 'Grossly Inadequate,' Report Claims*, Healthline (Nov. 18, 2022), www.healthline.com/health-news/fda-oversight-of-clinical-trials-was-grossly-inadequate-report-claims. Fortunately, COVID-19 vaccine R&D was a global initiative with clinical and regulatory sharing, and many of the US' universal health care system counterparts oversee clinical trial sites much more reliably with fewer resources. *Cf.* Demasi, *BMJ Investigation, supra;* Radcliffe, *FDA Oversight, supra* (sources do not recognize the universal health care system information and oversight advantages, which enable more reliable regulatory oversight with fewer resources). Nevertheless, "Regulatory documents show that only nine out of 153 Pfizer trial sites1 were subject to FDA inspection before licensing the mRNA vaccine. Similarly, only 10 out of 99 Moderna trial sites and five of 73 remdesivir trial sites were inspected." Demasi, *BMJ Investigation, supra*, at 2628.

90 *See* Christopher Klein, *History Stories: When the US Government Tried to Fast-Track a Flu Vaccine*, History.com (Sept. 2, 2020), www.history.com/news/swine-flu-rush-vaccine-election-year-1976.

91 Byrd, *Quickly*, *supra* note 25.

92 *See id.*

93 GAO, OWS, *supra* note 32, at "Highlights" (page nos. not provided). *See also* Khan, *Monumental*, *supra* note 33 ("During the pandemic, many of these timelines were accelerated and done in parallel to shorten development.").

94 Khan, *Monumental*, *supra* note 33 (page numbers not provided).

95 *Id.*

96 *Id.*

97 Tung Thanh Le, *Evolution*, *supra* note 33, at 668. *See generally* Joanne S. Eglovitch, *FDA Finalizes Multiple Endpoints Guidance*, Reg. News (Oct. 20, 2022), www.raps.org/news-and-articles/news-articles/2022/10/fda-finalizes-multiple-endpoints-guidance. For discussion of use of surrogate endpoints in clinical trials, see *Chapter 5, infra*, at notes 99–102, and accompanying text.

98 *See* GAO, OWS, *supra* note 32, at 7.

99 FDA, *Emergency Use*, *supra* note 55 (page nos. not provided).

100 Byrd, *Quickly*, *supra* note 25 (page nos. not provided).
101 Stuart L. Nightingale, Joanna M. Prasher, Stewart Simonson, *Emergency Use Authorization (EUA) to Enable Use of Needed Products in Civilian and Military Emergencies, United States*, 13 Emerging Infectious Diseases 1046, 1048 (July 2007), file:///C:/Users/mjmalin/Downloads/06-1188%20(2).pdf.
102 *See* GAO, OWS, *supra* note 32, at "Highlights," 21.
103 *See id*. at "Highlights," 1–2, 7, 21, 32.
104 *See* FDA, News Release, *FDA Approves First COVID-19 Vaccine* (Aug. 23, 2021), www.fda.gov/news-events/press-announcements/fda-approves-first-covid-19-vaccine; FDA, News Release, *Coronavirus (COVID-19) Update: FDA Takes Key Action by Approving Second COVID-19 Vaccine* (Jan. 31, 2022), www.fda.gov/news-events/press-announcements/coronavirus-covid-19-update-fda-takes-key-action-approving-second-covid-19-vaccine. *See also* CDC, *Developing COVID-19 Vaccines* (updated Feb. 4, 2022), www.cdc.gov/coronavirus/2019-ncov/vaccines/distributing/steps-ensure-safety.html?s_cid=11700:fda%20covid%20vaccine:sem.ga:p:RG:GM:gen:PTN:FY22; Johns Hopkins, Coronavirus Research Center, *Vaccine Research & Development: How Can COVID-19 Vaccine Development by Done Quickly and Safely?* (undated; visited Aug. 7, 2021), https://coronavirus.jhu.edu/vaccines/timeline.
105 *See* CDC, *Developing, supra note* 104.; Johns Hopkins, *How Can?*, *supra* note 104.
106 *See* Katherine Dillinger, *FDA Puts Strict Limits on Johnson & Johnson COVID-19 Vaccine* (May 5, 2022), www.cnn.com/2022/05/05/health/fda-johnson-johnson-vaccine-eua/index.html.
107 *See* FDA, News Release, *Coronavirus (COVID-19) Update: FDA Limits Use of Janssen COVID-19 Vaccine to Certain Individuals* (May 5, 2022), www.fda.gov/news-events/press-announcements/coronavirus-covid-19-update-fda-limits-use-janssen-covid-19-vaccine-certain-individuals.
108 Khan, *Monumental*, *supra* note 33 (page nos. not provided).
109 *See generally* HHS, DoD, From the Factory to the Frontlines: The Operation Warp Speed Strategy for Distributing a COVID-19 Vaccine (undated), www.hhs.gov/sites/default/files/strategy-for-distributing-covid-19-vaccine.pdf; C. Todd Lopez, *In Warp Speed Effort, Knowing Where Vaccines Are Is Key to Distribution Strategy*, Dep. of Def. (Oct. 28, 2020), www.defense.gov/Explore/News/Article/Article/2395789/in-warp-speed-effort-knowing-where-vaccines-are-is-key-to-distribution-strategy/. *See also* Azar, *Why*, *supra* note 82; Bendix, *Warp Speed*, *supra* note 32.
110 *See generally* HHS, DoD, From the Factory, *supra* note 109.
111 *See* Bendix, *Warp Speed*, *supra* note 32. Pfizer opted to use its delivery system centered in Michigan and Wisconsin. *Id*.
112 *See generally* HHS, DoD, From the Factory, *supra* note 109.
113 *See* Karyn Schwartz, Meredith Freed, Juliette Cubanski et al., *Issue Brief: Vaccine Coverage, Pricing, and Reimbursement in the U.S.*, Kaiser Family Found./KFF (Nov. 18, 2020), www.kff.org/coronavirus-covid-19/issue-brief/vaccine-coverage-pricing-and-reimbursement-in-the-u-s/. *See also* Susan E. Martonosi, Banafsheh Behzad, Kayla Cummings, *Pricing the COVID-19 Vaccine: A Mathematical Approach*, 103 Omega 102451 (Sept. 2021) (proposing an approach to calculate future pricing as R&D agreements and pre-purchases are negotiated, and before resulting products go commercial in the US), www.ncbi.nlm.nih.gov/pmc/articles/PMC7992367/. Pfizer set the initial price at $19.50 a dose ($39 per patient) and Moderna at $25 per dose ($50 per patient). *See id.*
114 *See* CDC, *COVID-19 Vaccines Are Free to the Public* (updated Nov. 3, 2021), www.cdc.gov/coronavirus/2019-ncov/vaccines/no-cost.html?s_cid=10473:free%20covid%20vaccine:sem.ga:p:RG:GM:gen:PTN:FY21.

115 *See* Michael J. Malinowski, *The US Science and Technology "Triple Threat": A Regulatory Treatment Plan for the Nation's Addiction to Prescription Opioids*, 48 U. Mem. L. Rev. 1027, 1028–79 (2018). *See generally* Michael J. Malinowski, *Government Rx – Back to the Future in Science Funding? The Next Era in Drug Development*, 51 U. Louisv. L. Rev. 101 (2012).

116 F. G. Gosling, The Manhattan Project: Making the Atomic Bomb vii (US Dep't of Energy, revised 2010), www.energy.gov/management/downloads/gosling-manhattan-project-making-atomic-bomb. As stated by President Eisenhower in his farewell address on the evening of January 17, 1961:

> Until the latest of our world conflicts, the United States had no armaments industry. American makers of plowshares could, with time and as required, make swords as well. But now we can no longer risk emergency improvisation of national defense; we have been compelled to create a permanent armaments industry of vast proportions. Added to this, three and a half million men and women are directly engaged in the defense establishment. We annually spend on military security more than the net income of all United States corporations.

President Dwight D. Eisenhower, *Farewell Radio and Television Address to the American People*, The Am. Pres. Proj. (Jan. 17, 1961), www.presidency.ucsb.edu/documents/farewell-radio-and-television-address-the-american-people.

117 *See generally* Gosling, Manhattan Project, *supra* note 116.

118 Gosling, Manhattan Project, *supra* note 116, at vii; Atomic Heritage Found, *The Manhattan Project* (May 12, 2017), www.atomicheritage.org/history/manhattan-project. *See generally* Bruce Cameron Reed, Manhattan Project: The Story of the Century (2020). *See also* The Manhattan Project: The Birth of the Atomic Bomb in the Words of its Creators, Eyewitnesses, and Historians 294–313 (Cynthia C. Kelly ed., 2007).

119 *See generally* Gosling, Manhattan Project, *supra* note 116; Richard Rhodes, The Making of the Atomic Bomb (1986). *See also* Malinowski, *Gov. Rx*, *supra* note 115, at 101–02.

120 *See* Brookings Institution, *The Cost of the Manhattan Project* (2002), www.brookings.edu/the-costs-of-the-manhattan-project/.

121 *See generally* Reed, Story, *supra* note 118; Gosling, Manhattan Project, *supra* note 116; Rhodes, Making Atomic, *supra* note 119.

122 *See* Rhodes, Making Atomic, *supra* note 119, at 431. *See generally* Gosling, Manhattan Project, *supra* note 116. "Given the absolute priority of the war effort, the usual academic tasks of universities were largely displaced for the duration." Roger L. Geiger, Research & Relevant Knowledge 7 (2nd. ed. 2004). Consequently, the MP also established seminal precedent for federal research grant funding with the addition of "administrative overhead" compensation (a percentage, perhaps forty percent or more for especially prestigious institutions, of grant budgets that becomes non-designated institution funding staple in present times under TTLP), to institutions:

> The basic relationship between the federal government and universities for conducting wartime research was governed by contracts negotiated according to the principle of no-loss and no-gain. Universities were reimbursed for the direct costs they incurred and also given some allowance for overhead.

Id. at 6.

123 *The Pharmaceutical Golden Era: 1930–60*, 83 Chem. & Eng. News no. 25 (June 20, 2005) (part of a special issue, "The Top Pharmaceuticals that Changed the World"),

http://pubsapp.acs.org/cen/coverstory/83/8325/8325golden.html (no author identified; page nos. unavailable).

124 *See Chapter 1, supra*, at note 34 (the "Moldy Mary" cantaloupe story).

125 Steven Johnson, Extra Life: A Short History of Living Longer 225 (2021). *See also Chapter 1, supra*, at notes 28–34, and accompanying text (the transformational impact of the WWII experience on the US pharmaceutical industry).

126 Isaacson, Code, *supra* note 1, at 248.

127 *See* Malinowski, *"Triple Threat," supra* note 115, at 1028–79.

128 *See generally* Naomi Oreskes, John Krige, Angela N. H. Creager et al., Science and Technology in the Global Cold War (2014) (includes "Transformations: Studies in the History of Science and Technology"); Audra J. Wolfe, Competing with the Soviets: Science, Technology, and the State in Cold War America (2013) (Johns Hopkins Introductory Studies in the History of Science). The Defense Advanced Research Projects Agency/DARPA embodies the lasting impact of the Cold War on US science-technology R&D. President Eisenhower created this agency within DoD, originally the Advanced Research Projects Agency/ARPA, on February 7, 1958, in response to the Soviet launch of Sputnik 1 in 1957. *Visit* DARPA, *About DARPA* (undated; visited May 4, 2022), www.darpa.mil/about-us/about-darpa. DARPA engages in R&D projects to advance science-technology, often beyond immediate US military needs, and its science-technology accomplishments have inspired other nations to attempt to create their own versions of the agency. *See A Growing Number of Governments Hope to Clone America's DARPA*, Economist (June 5, 2021), at 67–68, www.economist.com/science-and-technology/2021/06/03/a-growing-number-of-governments-hope-to-clone-americas-darpa.

129 *See generally* World's Fairs in the Cold War: Science, Technology, and the Culture of Progress (Arthur P. Molella, Scott Gabriel Knowles eds., 2019) (chronicling the Cold War culture of progress through the lens of world's fairs). *See infra* note 137, and accompanying text (quotation in text that captures mid-twentieth century culture that embraced science-technology progress).

130 *See* GAO, OWS, *supra* note 32, at 2–4 ("Background").

131 *See* Geiger, Research, *supra* note 122, at 30–146. *See infra* note 139, and accompanying text (President Eisenhower's *Farewell Address* acknowledgement of the pre-to-post WWII change).

132 *See generally* Michael Swanson, The War State: The Cold War Origins of the Military-Industrial Complex and the Power Elite, 1945–1963 (2013). *See also* Malinowski, *Gov. Rx, supra* note 115, at 105–07.

133 *See* Government Accountability Office/GAO, Report to Congressional Committees, Technology Transfer – Admin. of the Bayh-Dole Act by Res. Universities 2–4 (1998) ("Background"), GAO/RCED 98–126, www.gao.gov/products/rced-98-126. *See generally* Swanson, Military-Industrial Complex, *supra* note 132; Geiger, Knowledge, *supra* note 122.

134 *Op. Ed., Innovation's Golden Goose*, 365 Economist 3 (Dec.14, 2002), www.economist.com/technology-quarterly/2002/12/14/innovations-golden-goose. *See infra* notes 167–69, and accompanying text (addressing US patent policy prior to TTLP).

135 *See* GAO, Technology Transfer, *supra* note 133, at 3; Chester Morore, *Killing the Bayh-Dole Act's Golden Goose*, 8 Tul. J. Tech. & Intel. Prop. 151, 151 (2006).

136 *See generally* Swanson, Military-Industrial Complex, *supra* note 132. *See* Geiger, Knowledge, *supra* note 122, at 157–217.

137 Trent Stephens, Rock Bryner, Dark Remedy: The Impact of Thalidomide and Its Revival as a Vital Medicine 2–3 (2001).

138 *See generally* JEAN EDWARD SMITH, EISENHOWER IN WAR AND PEACE 290–317 (2013).
139 President Dwight D. Eisenhower, *Farewell Radio and Television Address to the American People*, THE AM. PRES. PROJECT (Jan. 17, 1961), www.presidency.ucsb.edu/documents/farewell-radio-and-television-address-the-american-people.
140 Nicholas Lemmon, *How the Seventies Changed America*, 42(4) AM. HERITAGE (July/Aug. 1991) (online; page nos. unavailable), www.americanheritage.com/how-seventies-changed-america#2.
141 DOMINIC SANDBROOK, MAD AS HELL: THE CRISIS OF THE 1970S AND THE RISE OF THE POPULIST RIGHT xiii (2012). *See generally* BRUCE J. SCHULMAN, THE SEVENTIES: THE GREAT SHIFT IN AMERICAN CULTURE, SOCIETY, AND POLITICS (2002).
142 *See generally* Alan Rhon, *How Much Did the Vietnam War Cost?*, VIETNAM WAR (updated Apr. 5, 2016) (page nos. unavailable online), https://thevietnamwar.info/how-much-vietnam-war-cost/. In addition to the mental anguish of soldiers, their friends and family, and the nation, the human cost of the Vietnam War included 58,220 Americans dead, 153,303 wounded, 1,643 missing, and the more than 23,214 soldiers who returned home with physical disabilities, many severe disabilities. *See id.* According to DoD, the direct monetary cost was approximately $168 billion ($1.4 trillion FY2020). *See id.*
143 GEIGER, KNOWLEDGE, *supra* note 122, at xv. *See* Malinowski, *Gov. Rx*, *supra* note 115, at 106–07.
144 *See* Malinowski, *Gov. Rx*, *supra* note 115, at 106–07.
145 *See supra* notes 132–36, and accompanying text (US post-WWII science-technology funding), 137 (US Utopia culture).
146 SANDBROOK, *supra* note 141, at xii. Renowned author Tom Wolfe introduced the term "the Me Decade" to capture the 1970s, and it became a label for 70s culture. *See id.*
147 *See generally* SCHULMAN, SEVENTIES, *supra* note 141.
148 *See generally* JUDITH STEIN, PIVOTAL DECADE: HOW THE UNITED STATES TRADED FACTORIES FOR FINANCE IN THE SEVENTIES (2011).
149 American automobile industry executives, living in the norms of their sumptuously profitable past, were in denial, oblivious, or a combination of the two. The US was wholly dependent upon and took for granted a flow of cheap oil imports – which the nation woke to realize when the spigot was closed. Within the US, there was social and cultural disconnect:

> The intelligentsia of America, much given to driving small, fuel-efficient, rather cramped foreign cars, often mocked Detroit for the grossness and gaudiness of its product. To many liberal intellectuals Detroit symbolized all that was excessive in the materialism of American life (just as to many small-town American conservatives, the companies' partner, the United Auto Workers, symbolized everything that was excessive about the post-New Deal liberal society). None of this carping bothered Detroit.

DAVID HALBERSTAM, *Chapter 1: Maxwell's Warning*, *in* THE RECKONING (2012).
150 *See generally* MEG JACOBS, PANIC AT THE PUMP: THE ENERGY CRISIS AND THE TRANSFORMATION OF AMERICAN POLITICS IN THE 1970S (2017). OPEC targeted their embargo at nations distinguished as supporting Israel during the Yom Kippur War. *See id.* at 54–64. As relayed by Pulitzer Prize-winning journalist David Halberstam:

> [O]n October 6, 1973 on the eve of Yom Kippur, the holiest of Jewish holidays, Egypt tried a military strike on Israel. Eventually Israel struck back and once again, for the third time since World War II, defeated the Egyptians. To the Arab world this humiliation was one more demonstration of its powerlessness. The Arabs blamed Israel's existence on its American sponsorship. Thwarted both militarily

> and politically, the Arabs now turned at last to their real strength, their economic leverage. They began an oil embargo on the West. Before it was over, the price of oil had rocketed from $3 a barrel to $12 a barrel.

HALBERSTAM, *Warning*, *supra* note 149, at *Chapter 1: Maxwell's Warning*.

151 *See generally* HALBERSTAM, *Warning*, *supra* note 149; MARK BOWDEN, GUESTS OF THE AYATOLLAH: THE FIRST BATTLE IN AMERICA'S WAR WITH MILITANT ISLAM (2006).

152 The Pinto, the first subcompact vehicle produced by Ford in North America, captures the era. The Pinto became an often-referenced case study in business ethics and tort reform after rear-end collisions caused its fuel tank to rupture, resulting in dozens of deadly fires, litigation, media attention, and government scrutiny. The Pinto is a case study staple for ethics analysis in multiple disciplines. *See, e.g.*, Max H. Bazerman, Ann E. Tenbrunsel, *Ethical Breakdowns*, 89 HARV. BUS. REV. 58–65, 137 (2011), https://hbr.org/2011/04/ethical-breakdowns.

153 *See The 1973–1974 Bear Market*, CAPITALGROUP.COM (no author identified and undated; visited May 6, 2022), www.capitalgroup.com/advisor/tools/guide-to-market-volatility/mountain-chart/1974-recession.html.

154 *See* MANCUR OLSON, THE RISE AND DECLINE OF NATIONS: ECONOMIC GROWTH, STAGFLATION AND SOCIAL RIGIDITIES 181–238 (1982).

155 *See generally* NEIL SHEEHAN, THE PENTAGON PAPERS: THE SECRET HISTORY OF THE VIETNAM WAR (2017).

156 *See id.* at *Foreword* (by James L. Greenfield, a *Pentagon Papers* reporter and project editor).

157 *See generally New York Times Co. v. United States*, 403 US 713 (1971).

158 On the 40th anniversary of the original leak to the press, the National Archives, in conjunction with the Kennedy, Johnson, and Nixon Presidential Libraries, released the complete report. *See Pentagon Papers*, National Archives (July 29, 2019), www.archives.gov/research/pentagon-papers.

159 *See generally* GARRETT M. GRAFF, SUMMARY WATERGATE: A NEW HISTORY (2022); Editors, *Watergate Scandal*, HISTORY.COM (updated June 16, 2021), www.history.com/topics/1970s/watergate.

160 *See generally* SCHULMAN, SEVENTIES, *supra* note 141.

161 *See generally* ANDREW E. BUSCH, REAGAN'S VICTORY: THE PRESIDENTIAL ELECTION OF 1980 AND THE RISE OF THE RIGHT (2005). *See* SCHULMAN, SEVENTIES, *supra* note 141, at 218–52.

162 *See generally* BUSCH, REAGAN'S VICTORY, *supra* note 161.

163 *See* SCHULMAN, SEVENTIES, *supra* note 141, at 218–52.

164 *See generally id.*

165 *See generally* Markel, *Patents, Profits*, *supra* note 30.

166 *See generally* Malinowski, *Gov. Rx*, *supra* note 115, at 104–07.

167 *See supra* note 134, and accompanying text (patents held by the government allegedly to benefit all).

168 GAO, TECHNOLOGY TRANSFER, *supra* note 133, at 3.

169 *Id. See generally* Morore, *Golden Goose*, *supra* note 135. *See also* Nightengale, *Emergency Use*, *supra* note 101, at 1033–34.

170 *See* Bayh-Dole University and Small Business Patent Procedures Act of 1980/"Bayh-Dole," Pub. L. No. 96–517, 94 Stat. 3015, *codified as amended*, 35 U.S.C. §§ 200–212, *implemented by* 37 C.F.R. 401 ("Rights to Inventions Made by Nonprofit Organizations and Small Business Firms Under Government Grants, Contracts, and Cooperative Agreements") and 37 C.F.R. 404 ("Licensing of Government-Owned Inventions"); Stevenson-Wydler Technology

Innovation Act of 1980, Pub. L. No. 96–480/"Stevenson-Wydler," 94 Stat. 2311, *codified as amended*, 15 U.S.C. §§ 3701–3724 (2012) (requires federal agencies/laboratories to actively participate in and budget for technology transfer activities). *See generally* Markel, *Patents, Profits, supra* note 30 (discussing the political landscape and activity resulting in this legislation). In 1987, the Department of Commerce issued regulations, codified at 37 C.F.R. 401 (2012), to more fully implement Bayh-Dole. The Reagan Administration and Congress added to these acts to expand R&D opportunities, to make opportunities for federal agencies, laboratories, and researchers more on par with those of their academic counterparts, and for administrative support and infrastructure to implement their full intent. *See, e.g.*, Exec. Order No. 12591, 52 Fed. Reg. 13,414 (Apr. 22, 1987); American Technology Preeminence Act of 1991, Pub. L. No. 102–245, 106 Stat. 7 (codified in scattered sections of 15 U.S.C. and 42 U.S.C.); National Technology Transfer and Advancement Act of 1995, Pub. L. No. 104–113, 110 Stat. 775 (codified in scattered sections of 15 U.S.C.).

171 Markel, *Patents, Profits, supra* note 30, at 794. *See generally Chapter 5, infra* (addressing TTLP's impact on mechanisms to protect the evidentiary-science base of US medicine); *Chapter 6, infra* (addressing TTLP's impact on US medicine, with focus on emerging PGM).

172 "With the passage of the Act, universities could file, at their own expense, patent applications on inventions they elected to own, with the Government retaining rights to enforce diligent commercial development of inventions, and the Government would also have a royalty-free, nonexclusive license to practice the invention worldwide for government purposes." The Bayh-Dole Act, Federal Grant Practice § 51:22 (2021 ed.). *See generally* Markel, *Patents, Profits, supra* note 30. *See also* Malinowski, Handbook, *supra* note 8, at 69–77 (*Chapter 3. Technology Transfer Law and Policy*).

173 *See generally* Matthew Herder, *Asking for Money Back – Chilling Commercialization or Recouping Public Trust in the Context of Stem Cell Research?*, 9 Colum. Sci. & Tech. L. Rev. 203 (2008) (providing a detailed discussion of the proposed recoupment provisions and associated testimony).

174 The Stevenson-Wydler Act, Bayh-Dole's "fraternal twin" legislation, bestowed federal agencies, laboratories, and researchers with TTLP opportunities analogous to those allotted to academic research institutions and researchers under Bayh-Dole. *See supra* note 170 and citations therein (relevant legislation, regulations, and other primary law).

175 NIH, Office of Tech. Transfer, NIH Response to the Conference Report Request for a Plan to Ensure Taxpayer Interests Are Protected 4 (2001), www.ott.nih.gov/sites/default/files/documents/policy/wydenrpt.pdf.

176 *See* GAO, OWS, *supra* note 32, at 2–3.

177 *See* Federal Technology Transfer Act of 1986, 15 U.S.C. § 3710(a) (2006). For discussion of DARPA, *see supra* note 128, and accompanying text.

178 *See* GAO, Tech. Trans., *supra* note 133, at 2–4 (*Background*); NIH, Taxpayer, *supra* note 175, at 4–12 ("*Background*"); Malinowski, Handbook, *supra* note 8, at 69–77 (*Chapter 3. Technology Transfer Law and Policy*).

179 *Visit* SBIR/STTR (official site), www.sbir.gov/about/about-sbir (last visited Dec. 26, 2014). *See* Malinowski, Handbook, *supra* note 8, at 11721 (*Chapter 5. Finance Overview*, at subsection "B.2. Federal and State Small Business Support").

180 *See generally* Bernard R. Glick, Cheryl L. Patten, Molecular Biotechnology: Principles and Applications of Recombinant DNA (5th ed. 2021).

181 *See generally* NHGRI, *1972: First Recombinant DNA* (updated Apr. 26, 2013), www.genome.gov/25520302/online-education-kit-1972-first-recombinant-dna.

182 *See* NHGRI, *Recombinant DNA Technology* (updated May 6, 2022) (page nos. unavailable), www.genome.gov/genetics-glossary/Recombinant-DNA-Technology.

183 *See generally* McKinsey & Company, Report, The Bio Revolution: Innovations transforming economies, societies, and our lives (May 13, 2020) (relaying the scope of biotech innovation), www.mckinsey.com/industries/life-sciences/our-insights/the-bio-revolution-innovations-transforming-economies-societies-and-our-lives; US National Academies of Science, Engineering, and Medicine/NASEM, Preparing for the Future Products of Biotechnology 28 (2017) (study surveying the present and approaching wave of genomic innovation in medicine and commerce), www.nap.edu/catalog/24605/preparing-for-future-products-of-biotechnology.

184 *See* Sally Smith Hughes, Genentech: The Beginnings of Biotech 158–59 (2011). Genentech, with a name derived from "genetic engineering technology," was a 1976 Northern California high-risk start-up founded with faith that recombinant DNA technology – DNA formed by combining constituents from different organisms – could be utilized to make genetically engineered blockbuster drugs. Just two years later, the company "blasted into hypergrowth when it won a bet-the-company race to make a synthetic version of insulin to treat diabetes." Isaacson, Code, *supra* note 1, at 99.

185 *See* Hughes, Genentech, *supra* note 184, at 158–59; Isaacson, Code, *supra* note 1, at 100.

186 Amgen, like Genentech, began as a high-risk San Francisco Bay-area start-up with belief in the drug-making potential of recombinant DNA technology. *See generally* David Ewing Duncan, Amgen Story: 25 Years of Visionary Science and Powerful Medicine (2005). In 2003, Epogen became the first molecule to generate $10 billion annually. *See* Krishon Maggon, *The Ten Billion Dollar Molecule*, Pharm. Exec. (Nov. 1, 2003), www.pharmexec.com/ten-billion-dollar-molecule (last visited Jan. 5, 2019). By 2007, Epogen was being administered to virtually every dialysis patient in the US, and it had become the most successful biotech drug in history. *See id*; *Editorial, Sacrificing the Cash Cow*, 25 Nat. Biotech 363 (2007), www.nature.com/articles/nbt0407-363 (last visited Jan. 5, 2019).

187 *See generally* Michael J. Malinowski, Maureen A. O'Rourke, A *False Start? The Impact of Federal Policy on the Genotechnology Industry*, 13 Yale J. on Reg. 163 (1996).

188 Major US law-policy enacted lockstep with the development and needs of the biotech industry includes the Orphan Drug Act/ODA of 1983, Pub. L. No. 97–414, 96 Stat. 2049, *codified as amended*, 21 U.S.C. §§ 360aa-360ee; 26 U.S.C. § 45C (1994); 42 U.S.C. § 236 (1994); Coordinated Framework for Regulation of Biotechnology, 51 Fed. Reg. 23,302 (June 26, 1986) (issued by the Office of Science and Technology Policy/OTP under the Reagan Administration); Food and Drug Administration Modernization Act/FDAMA of 1997, Pub. L. No. 105–115, 111 Stat. 2296 (codified in scattered sections of 21 U.S.C.); and enactment and reauthorizations (every 5 years since 1992) of the Prescription Drug User Fee Act of 1992/PDUFA, Pub. L. No. 102–571, 106 Stat. 4491 (codified in scattered sections of 21 U.S.C.). For a clear summary of the requirements set forth in these regulations, see GAO, Tech. Trans., *supra* note 133, at 4–19. The orchestration of this law-policy and its effectiveness is addressed in GAO, Tech. Trans., *supra* note 133; NIH, Taxpayer, *supra* note 175; Malinowski, Handbook, *supra* note 8, at 1–20 (*Chapter 1. Introduction: The US Success Story in Biotechnology*).

189 *See supra* notes 5–8, and accompanying text (addressing Mendelian traits with the Sickle Cell Disease/SCD application, and the Orphan Drug Act/ODA).

190 *See supra* note 8 (discussing the ODA). A notable orphan drug example is Ceredase to treat Gaucher's disease. The disease, most common in Jewish people of Eastern and Central European (Ashkenazi) descent, causes fatty substances to amass in the spleen, liver, and other organs and affects their function. *See* Mayo Clinic, *Gaucher disease* (visited Sept. 18, 2021), www.mayoclinic.org/diseases-conditions/gauchers-disease/symptoms-causes/syc-20355546. Symptoms, which vary significantly, include abdominal

complaints, skeletal abnormalities (weakened and porous bones due to lack of blood supply, potentially leading to fractures and bone death), and blood disorders such as anemia and poor clotting. The latter may impact the brain and cause abnormal eye movements, muscle rigidity, swallowing difficulties, and seizures. An especially rare subtype of the disease causes the onset of symptoms during infancy with a prognosis of death. Genzyme Corporation (Sanofi Genzyme since Sanofi acquired the company in 2011 as a wholly owned subsidiary) developed and launched Ceredase in 1991 to treat Gaucher's disease, only afflicting approximately 20,000 patients worldwide at the time, with tremendous global commercial success. *See* Genzyme Corp., *The Early 1990s: Product Breakthroughs, Corporate Strategies*, ENCYCLOPEDIA.COM (visited Sept. 18, 2001), www.encyclopedia.com/social-sciences-and-law/economics-business-and-labor/businesses-and-occupations/genzyme-corp. Ceredase (followed by Cerezyme, which is easier to manufacture and administer) became a model for drug development under the ODA, but also an often-referenced example of associated drug pricing and alleged ODA abuses. Ceredase, which treated and alleviated symptoms but did not cure and therefore had to be taken chronically, cost on average $150,000 per patient annually – the most expensive drug ever sold as we entered this millennium. *Id.* Uncommon diseases remain potentially low-hanging fruit for clinical R&D given the degree of causative genetic expression, and the organization of and communication among patients and providers in our social medial age. The advancement of human genome science, especially with CRISPR and mRNA technologies, has seeded potentially bountiful orchards. However, even with the ODA and enactment of the Food and Drug Administration Safety and Innovation Act/FDASIA of 2012, P.L. 107–250, which created a breakthrough therapy designation program and made rare pediatric diseases eligible for a priority review voucher program, commercial viability remains a significant barrier. Peter Marks, Director of the FDA's Center for Biologics Evaluation and Research/CBER, addressed this problem in November 2022 at "Meeting on the Mesa," a conference attended by many in the cell and gene therapy field. *See generally* Ned Pagliarulo, *'We have to find a way': FDA Seeks Solutions to Aid Bespoke Gene Therapy*, BIOPHARMA DIVE (Oct. 13, 2022), www.biopharmadive.com/news/marks-fda-gene-therapy-commercial-viability-ultra-rare/634041/. "[C]ommercial viability for a gene therapy means administering roughly 100 to 200 treatments a year, a threshold that could be difficult to clear in a single country for rare conditions like severe combined immunodeficiencies or adrenoleukodystrophies." *Id.* According to Director Marks, the FDA is exploring additional measures to lower commercial feasibility barriers:

- "The agency is currently putting together a 'cookbook' for developing and manufacturing of bespoke gene therapies, which could help academic groups more easily transfer treatments they're working on to industry. It's also looking into how to use non-clinical and manufacturing data from one application to speed the review of others that share similar technology."
- "Automated manufacturing could be another solution to help lower the costs of production, which are significantly higher for cell and gene therapies than for other more established drug types."
- "The FDA is also hoping to get on the same page with other regulators so that developers could be more confident a product they gain approval for in one country would have a good chance of success in others."

Id.

191 *See* Coordinated Framework for Regulation of Biotechnology, 51 Fed. Reg. 23,302 (June 26, 1986).

192 *See* Barbara J. Evans, *Programming Our Genomes, Programming Ourselves: The Moral and Regulatory Challenge of Regulating Do-It-Yourself Gene Editing*, *in* Consumer Genetic Technologies, *supra* note 17, at 130–31.
193 The Coordinated Framework charged agencies with coordination and cooperation to avoid duplicative regulation among the Environmental Protection Agency/EPA, FDA, NIH, Occupational and Safety Health Administration/OSHA, National Science Foundation/NSF, and US Department of Agriculture/USDA. *See* Coordinated Framework, *supra* note 191. Disputes over regulatory responsibility "were resolved when executive oversight pushed the agencies to sign an agreement that divided tasks among the agencies, thus setting new expectations about which agencies should perform which tasks." Jason Marisam, *Duplicative Delegations*, 63 Admin. L. Rev. 181, 217 (2011) www.administrativelawreview.org/wp-content/uploads/2014/04/Duplicative-Delegations.pdf.
194 *See* Evans, *Regulatory Challenge*, *supra* note 192, at 129.
195 *See* NASEM, Preparing, *supra* note 183, at 28. *See Chapter 7*, *infra*, at notes 64–71, and accompanying text (discussing NASEM's charge, responsive effort, and conclusions).
196 Markel, *Patents, Profits*, *supra* note 30, at 794.
197 *See generally* Nih Response, *supra* note 175; Gao, Tech. Trans., *supra* note 133.
198 Op. Ed., *Golden Goose*, *supra* note 134 (page nos. unavailable online).
199 As explained by NHGRI,

> Your genome is the operating manual containing all the instructions that helped you develop from a single cell into the person you are today. It guides your growth, helps your organs to do their jobs, and repairs itself when it becomes damaged. And it's unique to you. The more you know about your genome and how it works, the more you'll understand your own health and make informed health decisions.

NHGRI, *Introduction to Genomics, What's a Genome?* (updated Oct. 11, 2019), www.genome.gov/About-Genomics/Introduction-to-Genomics.
200 *See* NHGRI, *Genetics vs. Genomics Fact Sheet* (updated Sept. 7, 2018), www.genome.gov/about-genomics/fact-sheets/Genetics-vs-Genomics.
201 WHO, *What Is Genomics?* (Nov. 12, 2020), www.who.int/news-room/q-a-detail/genomics. Genomics encompasses epigenetics – the study of changes in organisms caused by modification of gene expression rather than alteration of the genetic code itself, such as changes caused by environmental influences that may become heritable without altering an organism's DNA sequence. *See generally* Nessa Carey, The Epigenetics Revolution: How Modern Biology Is Rewriting Our Understanding of Genetics, Disease, and Inheritance (2013). The scope of genomics to improve human health is not limited to the human genome:

> The human genome interacts with those of a myriad other organisms, including plants, vectors and pathogens. Genomics is considered across all organisms, as relevant to public health in human populations. In addition to genomics knowledge, we also consider technologies that make use of genomics knowledge.

WHO, *Genomics?*, *supra* (online; page nos. unavailable).
202 *See supra* notes 20–22, and accompanying text (map of the human genome sequence). *See Prologue*, *supra*, at notes 14–16, and accompanying text (addressing the extent to which genes multitask, and the shift in perspective with completion of a map of the human genome sequence).
203 NHGRI, *Bringing the Genomic Revolution to the Public* (reviewed Feb. 26, 2012), www.genome.gov/26524162/bringing-the-genomic-revolution-to-the-public.

204 *See Prologue*, *supra*, at notes 6–13, and accompanying text.

205 *See id*. at notes 1–5, and accompanying text. *See generally* Meredith Wadman, *James Watson's Genome Sequenced at High Speed: New-generation Technology Takes Just Four Months and Costs a Fraction of Old Method*, 452 NATURE 788 (Apr. 16, 2008) (*quoting* Jonathan Rothberg), www.nature.com/news/2008/080416/full/452788b.html (last visited May 21, 2019). *See also* JAMES D. WATSON, DNA: THE STORY OF THE GENETIC REVOLUTION 195–202 (2nd ed. 2017) (with Andrew Berry, Kevin Davies) (updated to commemorate the fiftieth anniversary of the discovery of the double helix); HGRI, *FAQ*, *supra* note 19; Nicholas Wade, *Genome of DNA Pioneer Is Deciphered*, N.Y. TIMES (May 31, 2007), www.nytimes.com/2007/05/31/science/31cnd-gene.html.

206 *See supra* notes 19–22, and accompanying text (US' HGP undertaking).

207 *See* Larry Thompson, *Science under Fire behind the Clash between Congress and Nobel Laureate David Baltimore*, WASH. POST (May 9, 1989), www.washingtonpost.com/archive/lifestyle/wellness/1989/05/09/science-under-fire-behind-the-clash-between-congress-and-nobel-laureate-david-baltimore/3068efef-b614-4a89-84f8-6ac721f5d187/; Larry Thompson, *Genes, Politics and Money Biology's Most Ambitious Project Will Cost a Fortune, But Its Value Could Be Beyond Measure*, WASH. POST (Feb. 24, 1987), www.washingtonpost.com/archive/lifestyle/wellness/1987/02/24/genes-politics-and-money-biologys-most-ambitious-project-will-cost-a-fortune-but-its-value-could-be-beyond-measure/ac8dafaf-b55a-4773-934f-6b20a1db4f94/.

208 *See supra* notes 128–63, and accompanying text ("The US Government's Centralist Role in Science-Technology R&D").

209 *See generally* ORESKES ET AL., GLOBAL COLD WAR, *supra* note 128; WOLFE, COMPETING WITH THE SOVIETS, *supra* note 128. *See supra* note 128, and accompanying text.

210 *See generally* RANDY SHILTZ, AND THE BAND PLAYED ON: POLITICS, PEOPLE, AND THE AIDS EPIDEMIC (20th Anniversary ed. 2007).

211 *See* ARTHUR KORNBERG, THE GOLDEN HELIX: INSIDE BIOTECH VENTURES 5–7 (1995).

212 Larry Thompson, *Genes, Politics and Money Biology's Most Ambitious Project Will Cost a Fortune, But Its Value Could Be Beyond Measure*, WASH. POST (Feb. 24, 1987), www.washingtonpost.com/archive/lifestyle/wellness/1987/02/24/genes-politics-and-money-biologys-most-ambitious-project-will-cost-a-fortune-but-its-value-could-be-beyond-measure/ac8dafaf-b55a-4773-934f-6b20a1db4f94/.

213 *See id*. *See also* Thompson, *Science under Fire*, *supra* note 207; Juan Enriquez, Ray Goldberg, *Transforming Life, Transforming Business: The Life-Science Revolution*, HARV. BUS. REV. (Mar.-Apr. 2000), at 95 ("Advances in genetic research are setting off an industrial convergence."), https://hbr.org/2000/03/transforming-life-transforming-business-the-life-science-revolution. *See also* Michael J. Malinowski, *Separating Predictive Genetic Testing from Snake Oil: Regulation, Liabilities, and Lost Opportunities*, 41 JURIMETRICS 23, 23–26 (2001) (live and published symposium). Ironically, Dr. Hood and his labs made sequencing technology that proved crucial to enable completion of a map of the human genome ahead of schedule and under budget. Specifically, they are attributed with creating instrumentation for DNA sequencing and synthesis fundamental for high-throughput biological data and the era of big data in biology and medicine. The accomplishments include automated DNA sequencers, DNA synthesizers, protein sequencers, peptide synthesizers, the ink jet printer for constructing DNA arrays and large-scale synthesis of DNA, and the nanostring instrument for the single molecule analysis of RNA and DNA. *See generally* LUKE TIMMERMAN, HOOD: TRAILBLAZER OF THE GENOMICS AGE (2016).

214 KORNBERG, GOLDEN HELIX, *supra* note 211, at 5–7.

215 *See* Thompson, *Science under Fire*, *supra* note 207.
216 *See* Robert Cooke, *The Genome Project: Will It Be Allowed to Survive?*, NEWSDAY (May 19, 1992), at sec. Disc., p. 61; *Academy President Recommends Priorities for Federal R&D Support*, INSIDE ENERGY WITH FED. LANDS (May 2, 1988), 1988 WLNR 588507; *Scientists Say Basic Research Is Hurt by Cut in New Grants; Fewer Promising Young People Will Enter Field, Scholar Predicts*, WASH. POST (Apr. 3, 1990), at Sec. A. *See also* Michael Kirby, *The Human Genome Project – Promise and Problems*, 11 J. CONTEMP. HEALTH L. & POL'Y 1, 8 (1994) ("Some critics assess[ed] that it would be preferable to spend the limited funds available to determine the complete structure and function of individual genes of medical importance.").
217 KORNBERG, GOLDEN HELIX, *supra* note 211, at 7. *See also* Malinowski, *Snake Oil*, *supra* note 213, at 24–25.
218 *See* PAUL STARR, THE SOCIAL TRANSFORMATION OF AMERICAN MEDICINE: THE RISE OF A SOVEREIGN PROFESSION AND THE MAKING OF A VAST INDUSTRY 420–49 (1984).
219 *See Snake Oil*, *supra* note 213, at 24–25.
220 *Id.* at 24.
221 *See* Christine Gorman, *Has Gene Therapy Stalled?*, TIME (Oct. 9, 1995), at 62–3; Malinowski, O'Rourke, *False Start?*, *supra* note 187, at 163, 168 ("Critics allege that scientific judgment is being sacrificed for quick profits."); Malinowski, *Snake Oil*, *supra* note 213, at 24.
222 *See supra* notes 19–22, and accompanying text (the US' HGP undertaking).
223 *See* Enriquez, *Transforming Life*, *supra* note 213, at 95 (noting that advances in genetic research are setting off an industrial convergence), https://hbr.org/2000/03/transforming-life-transforming-business-the-life-science-revolution.
224 *See supra* note 22, and accompanying text (addressing completion of the draft sequence of the human genome in 2003).
225 ISAACSON, CODE, *supra* note 1, at 41.
226 Marten H. Hofker, Jingyuan Fu, Cisca Wijmenga, *The Genome Revolution and Its Role in Understanding Complex Diseases*, 1842 SCIENCEDIRECT 1889, 1889–95 (Oct. 10, 2014), www.sciencedirect.com/science/article/pii/S0925443914001306.
227 *See* Michael J. Malinowski, *Law, Policy, and Market Implications of Genetic Profiling in Drug Development*, 2 HOUS. J. HEALTH L. & POL'Y 31, 34–35 (2002).
228 *See id.*; Malinowski, "Triple Threat," *supra* note 115, at 1079; Michael J. Malinowski, Grant G. Gautreaux, *Drug Development: Stuck in a State of Puberty?: Regulatory Reform of Human Clinical Research to Raise Responsiveness to the Reality of Human Variability*, 56 ST. LOUIS U. L.J. 363, 389 (2012). *See also* FDA, *Press Release, FDA Completes Final Phase of Planning for Consolidation of Certain Products from CBER to CDER* (Mar. 17, 2003), www3.scienceblog.com/community/older/archives/M/2/fda1387.htm.
229 *Visit* Biotechnology Innovation Organization/BIO, official site, www.bio.org.
230 *See generally* ANGRIST, DAWN, *supra* note 26; COLLINS, LANGUAGE OF LIFE, *supra* note 26; DAVIES, $1,000 GENOME, *supra* note 26. *Cf. generally* ISAACSON, CODE BREAKER, *supra* note 1; SIDDHARTHA MUKHERJEE, THE SONG OF THE CELL (2022).
231 *See supra* notes 115–27, and accompanying text ("The Origin of US Science R&D Triple-Threat Methodology: WWII Necessity").
232 *See id.* at notes 32–114, and accompanying text ("The Latest US Application … OWS" and "OWS Implementation").
233 *See* ISAACSON, CODE, *supra* note 1, at 437–45. As Dr. Anthony Fauci shared when reflecting upon his dual positions at the National Institute of Allergy and Infectious Diseases/NIAID, where he served as a physician-scientist for fifty-four years and director for thirty-eight years, "when it comes to emerging infectious diseases, it's never over. As

infectious-disease specialists, we must be perpetually prepared and able to respond to the perpetual challenge." Anthony S. Fauci, *Perspectives, It Ain't Over Till It's Over ... but It's Never Over– Emerging and Reemerging Infectious Diseases*, 387(22) N. Eng. J. Med. 2009–11, 2009 (Dec. 1, 2022), www.nejm.org/doi/pdf/10.1056/NEJMp2213814?articleTools=true.

234 *See* ISAACSON, CODE, *supra* note 1, at 260; Antonio Regalado, *The Search for the Kryptonite That Can Stop CRISPR*, MIT TECH. REV. (May 2, 2019), www.technologyreview.com/2019/05/02/65813/the-search-for-the-kryptonite-that-can-stop-crispr/. *See* Dr. Anne Cheever, *Safe Genes*, DARPA (visited Sept. 19, 2021), www.darpa.mil/program/safe-genes.

235 *See* Xu Xun, *We Are Witnessing a Revolution in Genomics – And it's only Just Begun*, WORLD ECON. FORUM (June 24, 2019), www.weforum.org/agenda/2019/06/today-you-can-have-your-genome-sequenced-at-the-supermarket/. For discussion of potential uptake of whole-genome sequencing in clinical care, see *Chapter 6*, *infra*, at note 29, and accompanying text (discussing how whole genome sequencing was addressed at the National Society of Genetic Counselors/NSGC 2022 annual meeting, and a UK study to sequence the whole genomes of 100,000 newborns).

236 *See generally* NIH, All of Us Research Program, official site, https://allofus.nih.gov/. *See also Prologue*, *supra*, at notes 26–28, and accompanying text. AllUs is applying triple-threat methodology. For example, AllUs awarded the San Francisco General Hospital Foundation a grant to recruit lesbian, bisexual, gay, and transgender participants. *See* Gina Kolata, *The Struggle to Build a Massive 'Biobank' of Patient Data*, N.Y. TIMES (Mar. 19, 2018), at D1, www.nytimes.com/2018/03/19/health/nih-biobank-genes.html. NIH also awarded 23andMe a $1.7-million grant to sequence the genomes of hundreds of thousands of its African American customers. *See* Erika Check Hayden, *The Rise and Fall and Rise Again of 23andMe*, 550 NATURE 174–77 (Oct. 11, 2017), www.nature.com/articles/550174a.

237 *Visit* NHGRI, *Genomics and Medicine* (visited Sept. 22, 2021), www.genome.gov/health/Genomics-and-Medicine. *See, e.g.*, Heggie, *Genomics*, *supra* note 22. *See also supra* note 26, and accompanying text (addressing and distinguishing precision medicine and personalized medicine through genomics). *Cf. generally* ISAACSON, CODE BREAKER, *supra* note 1; MUKHERJEE, CELL, *supra* note 230.

3

Direct-to-Consumer/DTC and Direct-to-Physician/ DTP Biopharma Marketing in the US

Many of my law students, generally in their mid-20s, are surprised to learn that the US Food and Drug Administration/FDA prohibited prescription drug television advertising until 1997.[1] In fact, the FDA limited prescription ("Rx") drug marketing to physicians until the mid-1980s.[2]

The US medical profession, not the US government, originally established a physician-only marketing limitation for prescription medicines. "From its founding, the AMA was at odds with the patent medicines business. It divided drugs into 'ethical' preparations of known composition advertised only to the profession, and patent medicines of secret composition sold directly to the public."[3] As the AMA consolidated its power and elevated the practice of medicine during the first half of the twentieth century, the association accrued control over the flow of pharmaceutical information to consumers and overcame its most formidable challenger – patent medicine manufacturers.[4] The AMA utilized physician influence over patients – the public's increasing trust in the medical profession and reliance on learned physician opinion in decisions about their medications – to stifle medicine manufacturers' direct communication with consumers. The organization established a Council on Pharmacy and Chemistry ("AMA Council") in 1905 with a laboratory to evaluate medicines.[5] The AMA Council evolved into a professional regulatory system centered on objective evidentiary science that amassed physician control over the medicines market well before the establishment of a US government regulatory system capable of accomplishing and maintaining the same.[6]

With AMA *support*, Congress and the FDA introduced a government regulatory system in the mid-twentieth century that enhanced physician control over pharmaceutical information and elevated the medical profession's role as sentinel over the clinical use of prescription medicines.[7] Beginning in 1940, the FDA instructed firms selling prescription-only drugs to remove any information from their labels that might guide layperson users.[8] In 1951, Congress codified a prescription-only category of drugs, and the FDA subsequently devoted much of its budget to ensure physician control over restricted drugs and to stop consumer self-medication through direct interaction with manufacturers.[9] Over the past three decades, however, the

US has broken from its twentieth-century past to *normalize* aggressive biopharma DTC marketing – an abnormality among industrialized-economy nations. The US is distinguishable in not having a health care system that meaningfully contains DTP biopharma marketing and prohibits DTC prescription drug marketing.[10]

The following discussion begins by profiling US DTP and DTC biopharma marketing. Next, it addresses the US judiciary's recognition of biopharma marketing as commercial speech protected under the First Amendment of the US Constitution. The discussion then focuses on the FDA's regulation of biopharma marketing in this millennium. The final section addresses the impact of biopharma DTP and DTC marketing on US medicine during the ongoing transition to personal genome medicine. The discussion concludes that, by resurrecting early twentieth-century DTC medicines marketing norms, the US has elevated reliance on its medical profession to protect the evidentiary-science base of medicine during a genomic revolution.

US DTC AND DTP BIOPHARMA MARKETING

1997 was the beginning of a new era for the biopharma sectors and the FDA. *Not coincidentally*, the FDA changed its rules to allow biopharma television advertising the same year the US enacted the Food and Drug Modernization Act of 1997/FDAMA and reauthorized the Prescription Drug User Fee Act of 1992/PDUFA; the reauthorization is referred to as PDUFA II.[11] Through FDAMA and PDUFA II, Congress expanded the FDA's very mission from ensuring product safety and efficacy to include efficiency – to be accomplished through increased agency responsiveness to biopharma, patient, and provider (collectively "stakeholder") concerns about the agency's timeliness.[12] FDAMA and PDUFA II imposed heightened regulatory transparency and accountability on the agency (time-keeping with self-reporting) and changed its culture. The intense, chronic negotiations between industry and government that produced FDAMA and PDUFA II were an extension of negotiations that produced PDUFA I in 1992.[13] PDUFA I vested biopharma with leverage. While the FDAMA negotiations were ongoing with PDUFA user fee implementation, the FDA became increasingly accustomed to and dependent on a substantial user fee cash flow from new drug sponsors. PDUFA I was enacted with a five-year sunset provision – biopharma assurance that the FDA would comply with its terms and spirit and that government-industry negotiations would continue, including over the agency's allocation of user fee revenue and resources.[14] PDUFA I and its sunset provision have been reincarnated through a chain of reauthorizations; PDUFA VI governed through FY2022, with a shift to PDUFA VII for FY2023-FY2027.[15]

The FDA rule change in 1997 to allow biopharma prescription drug television and radio advertising was transformational for biopharma DTC marketing and, ultimately, for US medicine. Prescription drug makers now could run television and radio ads about their drugs and the conditions they were approved to treat, provided they sufficiently identified major side effects and contraindications.[16] Moreover, they could accomplish the latter in part by directing consumers to other sources, such as websites and medical providers, for more complete information. The impact on biopharma marketing behavior was immediate and immense. "By 1999, the average American was exposed to nine prescription drug advertisements on television every day. The number of television ads [overall, meaning to promote specific prescription drugs in addition to brand and disease recognition,] increased 40-fold between 1994 and 2000."[17] Biopharma increased spending on US DTC ads 58-fold between 1991 and 2003, to reach $3.2 billion per year.[18] The largest biopharma companies augmented their annual US marketing budgets by more than thirty-two percent between 1998 and 2001, while they decreased their budgets in England and France by four percent annually.[19] European nations welcomed this shift. In 2003, the European Union/EU voted to continue its ban on DTC prescription drug ads, which limits biopharma dissemination of medical information about Rx drugs to independent national sources and licensed medical professionals.[20]

In 2007, *The New England Journal of Medicine/NEJM* published the results of a study that assessed biopharma DTC marketing during the decade following the FDA law-policy events of 1997. The study determined that, "Since 2000, direct-to-consumer advertising of prescription drugs has continued to grow both in absolute dollars and relative to other forms of promotion."[21] This biopharma marketing trend continued subsequently, into the present. In 2017–2018, biopharma spent nearly $5.9 billion on product promotion – $4.5 billion of that allocated to Rx drug television ads.[22] Biopharma increased marketing budgets again in 2019 and 2020, reaching into the onset of the COVID-19 pandemic:

> On average, pharma companies allocated more than 12 million US dollars to their marketing budgets in 2020, representing a growth of roughly 30 percent over the preceding year. Compared to other types of health care companies, pharmaceutical manufacturers had the largest marketing budgets and the majority of pharma executives also indicated that their marketing allowances were set to increase.[23]

Although allocation between DTC and DTP in marketing budgets may oscillate going forward (for example, from DTC television advertising to physician "education," or vice versa), overall product promotion expenditure is likely to continue to increase in the foreseeable future because it has proven effective and profitable. Otherwise, sophisticated for-profit companies would not have continued and increased DTC and DTP marketing consistently over such a span of years. For more than a decade, "Some have estimated that the pharmaceutical industry overall spends about twice as much on marketing and promotion as it does on research and development."[24]

US Rx drug consumption and prices have increased along with DTP and DTC marketing to promote them – an indication that both physicians and the public are responsive to it. Biopharma R&D continues to draw substantial investment as well as market consumption of resulting product innovation. "Drug spending in the

United States jumped by 76% between 2000 and 2017, and the costs are expected to increase faster than other areas of health care spending over the next decade as new, expensive specialty drugs are approved."[25] Biologics, gifted by the progress of the genomic revolution, are the most expensive Rx therapeutics and among the most heavily advertised on television.[26]

The Pharmaceutical Research and Manufacturers of America/PhRMA, the trade organization that represents the largest biopharma companies, introduced a *voluntary* code of ethics in 2002 that applies to company interactions with US health care professionals, which it updated in 2009, 2019, and 2022.[27] The mantra of the PhRMA Code is that biopharma should engage in DTP marketing through physician *education based on data*, and it provides guidance for doing so ethically and responsibly – as self-determined by PhRMA. The PhRMA Code is implemented through voluntary company participation with PhRMA oversight and reporting:

> Companies that publicly announce their commitment to abide by the Code and that complete an annual certification that they have policies and procedures in place to foster compliance with the Code will be identified by PhRMA on a public web site. The certification must be signed by the company's Chief Executive Officer and Chief Compliance Officer. The web site will identify the companies that commit to abide by the Code; provide contact information for their Chief Compliance Officers; and, at the appropriate time, publish the status of each company's annual certification.[28]

The actual impact of the PhRMA Code on biopharma DTP marketing practices, the evidentiary-science base of medicine, and US health care is subject to much speculation. Voluntary, nonbinding industry guidelines often are ineffective, as has been the situation thus far regarding an effort among leading DTC personal genome testing companies to develop and implement privacy best practices.[29] Biopharma DTP marketing activity over the last few decades is a much more tangible and definitive indicator of corporate behavior.[30]

RECOGNITION OF BIOPHARMA MARKETING AS PROTECTED COMMERCIAL SPEECH

Over the last half-century and particularly in the last quarter-century, US federal courts, Congress and, consequently, the FDA have been responsive to a corporate civil rights movement that recognizes the commercial speech doctrine.[31] "In the United States the rights of commercial speech are given far greater priority than in the other countries – a balance that is tipping ever more in favor of commercial activity."[32]

In 1976, the Supreme Court held in *Va. State Bd. of Pharmacy v. Va. Citizens Consumer Council, Inc.* ("*Virginia Pharmacy*") that, with exceptions, commercial Rx drug advertising is protected by the First Amendment under the commercial speech doctrine.[33] In that case, a consumer group challenged a Virginia law that prohibited pharmacists from advertising drug prices on the grounds that it violated consumers' First Amendment right to hear truthful price information.[34] The Court ruled in favor of First Amendment protection for this commercial advertising, concluding:

> Advertising, however tasteless and excessive it sometimes may seem, is nonetheless dissemination of information as to who is producing and selling what product, for what reason, and at what price. So long as we preserve a predominantly free enterprise economy, the allocation of our resources in large measure will be made through numerous private economic decisions. It is a matter of public interest that those decisions, in the aggregate, be intelligent and well informed. To this end, the free flow of commercial information is indispensable.[35]

However, the Court also recognized the government's right to regulate in some ways.[36] For clarity, the Court provided examples of types of permissible regulation – such as for truthfulness, and time, place, and manner restrictions.[37]

Four years later, in *Central Hudson Gas Co. & Electric Corp. v. Public Service Commission of New York* ("*Hudson*"), the Supreme Court introduced a four-part test for determining when restrictions on commercial speech violate the First Amendment, commonly referred to as "the *Hudson* four-part test."[38] In that case, an electric company challenged a ban on any language in marketing materials that promoted the use of electricity. A public utility company had issued the ban to promote energy conservation. The Court ruled that the ban violated the First and Fourteenth Amendments, and held that, to be protected under the First Amendment, commercial speech (1) must involve a lawful activity and not be misleading. When a plaintiff satisfies this requirement, the burden shifts to the defendant. For a regulation intruding on commercial speech to then be upheld, it (2) must involve a "substantial government interest," (3) must directly advance that interest, and (4) must do so in a manner "not more extensive than is necessary."[39]

Although the *Hudson* Court declared this to be an "intermediate scrutiny" test, government defendants had an increasingly difficult time satisfying it:

> Indeed, almost nothing ever did. Case after case was brought and in each the regulation was struck down, even regulation of tobacco advertising, a product increasing subject to regulation. At the century's close, some academics, and some advocacy groups, were arguing that commercial speech (and then later, corporate speakers generally) shouldn't be treated as a "second-class" level of speech and that it should receive full First Amendment protection. This view had even gained an adherent on the Court. Somehow the intermediate scrutiny test had morphed into a de facto strict scrutiny test without anyone being quite sure how it had happened.[40]

The Supreme Court directly addressed "commercial speech *discrimination*" in 1993.[41] Cincinnati had banned distribution of commercial material in news racks to reduce litter and urban blight, but not newspapers. The Court struck the ban on the grounds that it was not content-neutral. The Court determined that the distinction between commercial and non-commercial had no bearing on the issue Cincinnati had enacted the ban to address – litter reduction.[42] "This introduced into the commercial speech jurisprudence something which had not been there before, the notion that subjecting commercial speech to additional regulation for no reason other than that it was commercial might be suspect."[43]

Commercial speech was strengthened further by the judiciary at the end of the millennium – in the prescription drug context, and with direct impact on FDA regulation of biopharma DTP marketing. FDAMA, although the product of extensive government-industry negotiations, did not quell ongoing disputes between industry and the FDA over DTP marketing to promote off-label uses through dissemination of article reprints from medical and scientific journals and textbook excerpts, and by involvement in continuing medical education/CME and "enduring materials" – non-live CME activity that "endures" over time. According to the Accreditation Counsel for Continuing Medical Education/ACCME,

> An enduring material is an on-demand activity that does not have a specific time or location designated for participation; rather, the participant determines whether and when to complete the activity. The content can be accessed at any point during the lifespan of the activity and there is no specific time designated for participation. Examples include online interactive educational modules, recorded presentations, printed materials, and podcasts.[44]

After FDAMA was enacted in 1997, biopharma asserted that DTP marketing through dissemination of medical journal article reprints and other authoritative medical literature and involvement in medical education through the medical profession establishment constitutes protected commercial speech between drug makers and physicians, which resulted in *Washington Legal Foundation v. Friedman*.[45] The FDA had issued Guidances, also referred to as "Guidance documents," with policies that heightened its regulation of industry influence over CME events and enduring materials and through dissemination of medical literature to physicians that promotes off-label uses of a company's FDA-approved products.[46] As explained by the FDA,

> Guidance documents represent FDA's current thinking on a topic. They do not create or confer any rights for or on any person and do not operate to bind FDA or the public. You can use an alternative approach if the approach satisfies the requirements of the applicable statutes and regulations.
>
> Guidance documents describe FDA's interpretation of our policy on a regulatory issue (21 CFR 10.115(b)). These documents usually discuss more specific products or issues that relate to the design, production, labeling, promotion, manufacturing, and testing of regulated products. Guidance documents may also relate to the processing, content, and evaluation or approval of submissions as well as to inspection and enforcement policies.[47]

The legacy of physician discretion to prescribe FDA-approved drugs in any arguably reasonable manner not known to cause harm has been honored by Congress, the courts, and even the FDA faithfully and repeatedly for decades.[48] As recognized by the US Department of Health and Human Services/HHS in 1994,

> Over a decade ago, the FDA Drug Bulletin informed the medical community that "once a [drug] product has been approved for marketing, a physician may prescribe it for uses or in treatment regimens of patient populations that are not included in approved labeling...." The agency and its representatives have restated this policy on numerous occasions.[49]

Given that "[a] physician may prescribe an approved drug for any medical condition, irrespective of whether FDA has determined that the drug is safe and effective with respect to that illness[,]"[50] physicians are heavily dependent upon the medical literature, CMEs, and enduring materials to grapple with the overwhelming complexities of medical innovation and patient demands.[51]

In *Washington Legal*, the D.C. Federal District Court rejected the FDA's attempt to distinguish *Hudson* on the grounds that: (1) its Guidances were regulation of conduct, not speech and, (2) given the off-label clinical use context, the commercial speech in dispute was in an exceptionally regulated area subject to distinguishable regulatory discretion.[52] The Court concluded, first, that "There may certainly be a 'line' between education and promotion as regards a drug manufacturer's marketing activities, but that is the line between pure speech and commercial speech, not between speech and conduct."[53] Second, according to the Court, "[T]he argument that a certain subset of speech may be considered completely outside of the First Amendment framework because the speech occurs in an area of extensive government regulation is a proposition whose continuing validity is at best questionable."[54]

The *Washington Legal* Court then applied the *Hudson* test, and it determined that the plaintiff had satisfied the truthfulness first prong:

> [The] FDA exaggerates its overall place in the universe.... [T]he conclusions reached by a laboratory scientist or university academic and presented in a peer-reviewed journal or textbook, or the findings presented by a physician at a CME seminar are not "untruthful" or "inherently misleading" merely because the FDA has not yet had the opportunity to evaluate the claim.[55]

In addition to the presumed soundness of the information at issue given that it emanated from peer review in a scientific discipline, the Court emphasized that the recipients of the information were learned and licensed physicians who might rely upon it to prescribe off label *based on their medical judgment*.[56] The Court underscored the point by acknowledging that the FDA had no problem with the same exchange of information when *requested* by physicians.[57] Burden under the *Hudson* test then shifted to the FDA. The Court agreed that the FDA has a substantial interest in requiring manufacturers to get new uses for previously approved drugs on-label (through FDA review and approval) given Congress's mandate that *all* uses of a drug must be proven safe and effective by the agency, which was reaffirmed in FDAMA.[58] The Court also found that the FDA directly advanced that interest, but it concluded that the agency had done so in a manner that was excessive and unduly burdened important speech.[59]

The *Washington Legal* Court issued a permanent injunction to stop the FDA from enforcing its Guidances:

1. Defendants SHALL NOT in any way prohibit, restrict, sanction or otherwise seek to limit any pharmaceutical or medical device manufacturer or any other person:
    a) from disseminating or redistributing to physicians or other medical professionals any article concerning prescription drugs or medical devices previously published in a bona fide peer-reviewed professional journal, regardless of whether such article includes a significant or exclusive focus on uses of drugs or medical devices other than those approved by FDA and regardless of whether such article reports the original study on which FDA approval of the drug or device in question was based;
    b) from disseminating or redistributing to physicians or other medical professionals any reference textbook (including any medical textbook or compendium) or any portion thereof published by a bona fide independent publisher and otherwise generally available for sale in bookstores or other distribution channels where similar books are normally available, regardless of whether such reference textbook or portion thereof includes a significant or exclusive focus on uses of drugs or medical devices other than those approved by FDA; or
    c) from suggesting content or speakers to an independent program provider in connection with a continuing medical education seminar program or other symposium, regardless of whether uses of drugs and medical devices other than those approved by FDA are to be discussed.
2. For purposes of this injunction, a "bona fide peer-reviewed journal" is a journal that uses experts to objectively review and select, reject, or provide comments about proposed articles. Such experts should have demonstrated expertise in the subject of the article under review, and be independent from the journal.
3. For purposes of this injunction, a "bona fide independent publisher" is a publisher that has no common ownership or other corporate affiliation with a pharmaceutical or medical device manufacturer and whose principal business is the publication and distribution of books through normal distribution channels.
4. For purposes of this injunction, an "independent program provider" is an entity that has no common ownership or other corporate affiliation with a pharmaceutical or medical device manufacturer, that engages in the business

of creating and producing continuing medical education seminars, programs or other symposia and that is accredited by a national accrediting organization pertinent to the topic of such seminars, programs or symposia.

5. Nothing herein shall be construed to limit Defendants' application or enforcement of any rules, regulations, guidances, statutes or other provisions of law that sanction the dissemination or redistribution of any material that is false or misleading. In addition, Defendants may require any pharmaceutical or medical device manufacturer that sponsors or provides financial support for the dissemination or redistribution of articles or reference textbooks or for seminars or symposia that include references to uses of drugs or medical devices other than those approved by FDA to disclose (i) its interest in such drugs or devices, and (ii) the fact that the use discussed has not been approved by FDA.[60]

This permanent injunction was lifted in 2000 after the FDA adopted a highly refined and much restrained position, which it presented in an oral argument finale on the matter.[61] The FDA emphasized that the Guidances at issue predated FDAMA. The agency assured that it would implement them in accordance with FDAMA-imposed criteria, and *only to establish a safe harbor* for manufacturers.[62]

The *Washington Legal* reasoning is premised on faith, embedded since the early-to-mid twentieth century, that learned and licensed physicians have the capability to sort out information relayed by biopharma manufacturers – at least information within the scope of the published materials and medical education involvement at issue in the case.[63] Given the extent to which the US defers to physician medical judgment for off-label use, *Washington Legal* incentivized DTP marketing in general.[64] For example, the decision encouraged biopharma "to fund journals and sponsor research to generate favorable publications and to disseminate resulting articles to doctors to encourage unapproved uses of their drugs."[65] The decision pushed back the reach of FDA regulation and widened biopharma manufacturers' latitude to publicize non-FDA-approved uses of biopharmaceuticals to medical providers, so long as they include disclaimers.[66]

In an interesting twist on biopharma commercial free speech, the Trump Administration's first attempt to implement its May 2018 "Blueprint to Lower Drug Prices" to curtail the cost of Rx drugs was to require biopharma companies to disclose list prices in television ads – referred to as the "Price Rule."[67] In other words, the Trump Administration attempted to force biopharma commercial speech about pricing. Merck & Co Inc., Eli Lilly and Co, and Amgen Inc. filed an action in the Federal District Court for the District of Columbia to challenge the Price Rule on the grounds that list and wholesale prices are not consumer prices, and well beyond factual, non-controversial information the government is permitted to require at times.[68] On July 8, 2019, the day before the Price Rule was set to take effect, the Court held that HHS lacked authority from Congress to compel drug manufacturers to disclose list prices as proposed and that the rule violated drug makers' free-speech rights under the First Amendment.[69] The Court set aside the entire Price Rule as invalid.[70]

FDA REGULATION OF DTC BIOPHARMA MARKETING

The nation relies immensely on the FDA to control and oversee the biopharma medicinal products on the US market.[71] The FDA is charged to ensure that the medicinal products under its watch are safe and efficacious for use in clinical care *and also* to promote the nation's health at the juncture between biopharma innovation and medicinal product availability – and with minimum delay post-FDAMA and PDUFA II.[72] The FDA has been demonstrating efficiency since FDAMA and PDUFA II were enacted in 1997. According to the Congressional Budget Office/ CBO in a 2021 report, "The number of new drugs approved each year has … grown over the past decade. On average, the Food and Drug Administration (FDA) approved 38 new drugs per year from 2010 through 2019 (with a peak of 59 in 2018), which is 60 percent more than the yearly average over the previous decade."[73]

The medical profession, the public, and the evidentiary-science base of medicine have depended on the FDA to fulfill its charged roles since Congress granted the agency the authority to restrict distribution of Rx drugs through physicians in 1951, and the authority to demand that manufacturers establish product efficacy before granting market approval in 1962.[74] To meet these expectations extending into clinical (physician–patient) use of the products under its watch, the FDA, beyond its own means, efforts, and authority, relies on the medical profession – as do the nation's patients. This reliance never has been greater.[75]

The FDA and the Federal Trade Commission/FTC share concurrent jurisdiction to regulate the marketing of prescription drugs, but that responsibility is allocated primarily to the FDA under a long-standing Memorandum of Understanding/ MOU between the two agencies.[76] Following *Washington Legal*, the FDA assumed a restrained stance in regulating biopharma marketing. Despite a robust rise in biopharma marketing activity following enactment of FDAMA, reauthorization of PDUFA, and the FDA television advertising rule change in 1997, FDA letters to biopharma companies for advertising violations dropped. The number of FDA letters fell from ninety-five in 1999 to twenty-seven in 2002, and then to twenty-three in 2003.[77] In 2007, *The New England Journal of Medicine /NEJM* published a comprehensive, rigorous, and heavily referenced study ("the *NEJM* study") of industry-wide Rx drug DTC trends over the decade following the FDA's allowance of television advertising for Rx drugs in 1997.[78] According to the study:

- Total biopharma spending on Rx drug promotion increased from $11.4 billion in 1996 to $29.9 billion in 2005 (an average annual growth rate of 10.6 percent);
- Spending on advertising slowed briefly 2000–2001, then grew at an average annual rate of 14.3 percent from 2002 to 2005;

- During that time, biopharma spending on DTC Rx advertising increased by 330 percent, and constituted fourteen percent of the total 2005 biopharma marketing expenditure;
- DTC campaigns generally begin within a year after FDA approval – typically well before many adverse events, on and off label, are ascertained;
- In spite of pressure on manufacturers to curtail spending on DTC and DTP advertising, including criticism documented in reports issued by the Government Accountability Office/GAO, Institute of Medicine/IOM, and others, industry continued to increase spending in both absolute terms and as a percentage of pharmaceutical sales, with promotion to physicians the dominant marketing strategy, and possibly passed the cost on to consumers; and
- In spite of these increases, the number of letters issued by the FDA to biopharma manufacturers for drug advertising violations dropped from 142 in 1997 to twenty-one in 2006.[79]

The significant reduction of FDA enforcement actions against biopharma manufacturers engaged in DTC advertising reflects a serious depletion of FDA capacity that began some fifteen years before the Trump Administration imposed a deregulation wave across the executive branch.[80] The *NEJM* study includes stunning observations of HHS-imposed bureaucracy coupled with insufficient FDA personnel charged to regulate biopharma advertising:

- "First, in 2002 the Secretary of Health and Human Services began requiring that all draft FDA regulatory letters, including letters related to advertising violations, be reviewed and approved by the FDA's Office of Chief Counsel before they are issued. A GAO report found that this legal review has led to a reduction in the number of letters issued, as well as to delays such that FDA warning letters are frequently sent out long after the false or misleading advertising campaign has run its course. Notably, the number of regulatory letters sent by the FDA in 2002 was less than half that in 2001 (28 vs. 68)."[81]
- "A second indication of weakening FDA oversight of direct-to-consumer advertising in recent years is that the number of staff members who are dedicated to reviewing advertisements has remained relatively stable, whereas the use of such advertising has grown substantially. In 2002, three FDA staff members were dedicated to reviewing direct-to-consumer advertisements. In 2004, four staffers were reviewing such advertisements, even though spending on this form of advertising (and probably the volume of ads to review) had increased by 45%, from $2.9 billion to $4.2 billion (Table 1)."[82]
- "Finally, consistent with the hypothesis that staffing has not kept pace with the number of prescription-drug advertisements, the proportion of broadcast advertisements that underwent FDA review before airing declined from 64% in 1999 to only 32% in 2004."[83]

Biopharma has much control over the allocation of user fees through PDUFA and its reauthorizations, and the FDA simply was not provided the resources necessary to feasibly respond to:

- A surge in DTC advertising;[84]
- A voracious increase in Rx drug consumption with the introduction of Medicare Part D;[85]
- Vioxx[86] and other Rx market controversies, including Avandia prescribed heavily to treat type 2 diabetes,[87] which raised questions about the FDA's effectiveness and reliability;[88]
- Criticisms of FDA effectiveness regulating drugs once approved, as documented in highly credible reports issued by IOM, GAO, and others;[89] and
- Enactment of the Food and Drug Administration Amendments Act/FDAAA of 2007, which was responsive to the FDA Rx controversies and criticisms of the agency that inspired its enactment.[90]

By 2017, a "patient-driven participatory health movement grounded in patient autonomy and empowerment"[91] was robust and building from our internet and social media culture.[92] Human genome science, which had advanced enough to make access to one's personal genome available and affordable for many, raged on.[93] The Trump Administration was rolling back federal regulations across agencies, as President Trump fulfilled his campaign vow to do so to "make America great again."[94] The FDA was without a commissioner during the Trump Administration (from January 20, 2017) until Dr. Scott Gottlieb, who had direct financial and other ties to some twenty biopharma and health care companies, was sworn in on May 11, 2017.[95] Consistent with the Trump Administration's position on regulation, Commissioner Gottlieb was "expected to push the boundaries of FDA reviews and use new authority under the 21st Century Cures Act (2016) to speed up evaluations."[96]

During his term as FDA Commissioner, Dr. Gottlieb extended the mission of efficiency and collaboration with new product sponsors codified in FDAMA and PDUFA II to situate the FDA as a facilitator of laboratory test innovation.[97] One company, 23andMe, Inc., a privately held, personal genomics company, was uniquely positioned to embrace the opportunity to advance realization of personal genome medicine through DTC genetic health risk/DTCGHR testing.[98] It did. On April 6, 2017, 23andMe became the first recipient of FDA approval for DTCGHR testing services.[99] With the FDA approval, 23andMe was free to market the opportunity for individuals to send the company their DNA in a small vial of saliva and receive personal genetic health risk/GHR information without physician or other learned medical professional involvement. Over twelve million people had embraced the opportunity to use 23andMe's health and ancestry personal genome services as of October 2021, demand is on the rise, and a DTCGHR sector is emerging.[100]

Dr. Scott Gotlieb left the FDA on April 5, 2019, was succeeded by Dr. Stephen Michael Hahn on December 17, 2019, and global focus shifted to the COVID-19 pandemic soon after.[101] The Trump Administration was faithful in keeping its deregulation vow to biopharma overall, but with a major exception – a multifaceted, concerted campaign to bring down Rx drug pricing in the US in spite of the nation's long legacy of no prescription drug price controls beyond Veterans Health Administration/VHA negotiations.[102] The Administration's primary strategy was to force biopharma companies to disclose prescription drug list price information.[103] Judicial recognition of corporate civil rights and commercial speech protection under the First Amendment defeated the Trump Administration's campaign; it met the same fate as many of the pre-FDAMA and pre-PDUFA II FDA efforts to regulate biopharma marketing.[104]

THE IMPACT OF US BIOPHARMA MARKETING ON THE PRACTICE OF MEDICINE

The AMA, an organization that passionately protects its members' discretion to practice medicine without federal government intrusion, called for a ban on DTC biopharma advertising in late 2015.[105] It is difficult for the AMA, an enormous professional, hierarchical, and highly political organization – internally as well as externally – to take such a public stance.[106] At least four out of five family doctors did not support DTC advertising at the outset of this millennium, and the medical profession has actively opposed DTC medicinal product marketing for over a century.[107]

Physicians and the AMA oppose biopharma DTC marketing because it is effective and, consequently, it infiltrates doctor–patient decision-making, impacts medical provider–patient relationships, and potentially muddles the practice of science and evidence-based clinical practice. "Advertisers know that their challenge is to evoke emotional responses that are strong enough to override traditional doctor-patient relationships.... [M]ore often than not, doctors accede to patients' requests."[108] Physicians know that, when a patient requests a specific Rx drug, leaving their office with a prescription for it (better yet, manufacturer-provided free samples) or an explanation to their satisfaction that dissuades them will impact the patient's assessment of the success of the visit.[109] Today's physicians are highly conscious of the fact that they practice medicine in a commercially competitive environment. Hospitals and managed care organizations expect physicians to be profitable. For example, "Physicians in private practice – who treat more than three-quarters of cancer patients in the United States – are expected to generate certain revenues, and their take-home pay is usually determined by the amount of medical services and drugs they provide."[110]

Working within tight time constraints, physicians are reluctant to be drawn into difficult, potentially lengthy discussions and often go along with their patients' requests for advertised drugs – especially if the drug and accompanying data are new, the underlying science is novel and complicated, biopharma marketing and "education" supports use, and they are not fully apprised of the drug and related data.[111] The FDA conducted a study of physician responsiveness to patient Rx drug requests that garnered much attention at the outset of this millennium, and both biopharma marketing and patient self-determination have increased substantially since then. According to this study, patients received prescriptions for requested drugs fifty percent of the time.[112] "Even when studies that do not support the use of a sponsor's product are published in medical journals, there is still a chance that well-funded marketing and public relations efforts will be able to protect drug sales."[113]

Effective US biopharma DTC marketing sells new products to the public as the embodiment of innovative medical science. Patients then are inclined to be at least somewhat assertive – from inquiries, to requests, to demands – in discussions with their physicians about them.[114] A change in the twentieth-century doctor–patient relationship and decision-making, a shift in authority from the learned physician to medical science itself, was apparent decades ago. As shared by Dr. John Abramson,

> Often the breakthroughs and sophisticated technology themselves weaken doctors' ability to help their patients by drawing attention away from real encounters between real people working together to arrive at the best approach to each situation. As these relationships become less important, not only are we spending inordinate amounts of money on therapies that don't provide commensurate value, but our health is actually suffering. This was the biggest surprise for me as I began to understand the real truth about the "scientific evidence" upon which I was basing my medical decisions.[115]

Genomics, which is centered on understanding individual genomes and the community of ongoing gene and protein interactions within them, innately makes science personal.[116] Through media coverage of the Human Genome Project/HGP, the biotech revolution, and the emerging genomic revolution during the 1990s, "It's in my DNA" became a colloquialism. Regardless of one's knowledge about or affinity for hard genomic science, the message resonated: Genetics is the means for each of us to learn about ourselves on the molecular level and to personalize medicine. Broadcast news coverage of DNA forensics and case study applications in the "true crime" television genre – there are a *lot* of series and documentaries and there have been for some time, which suggests strong viewer demand – make DNA science tangible, problem-solving, and familiar.

Bioparma DTC marketing has been saturating the US public with accessible and enticing medicinal product profiles that embody DNA science innovation for decades.[117] Public faith in ongoing genomic science has been reinforced by witnessing the development of COVID-19 vaccines in real time with extraordinarily advanced molecular (mRNA) science at unprecedented speed.[118] Biopharma played a primary role and was credited by government officials, renowned scientists, and preeminent physicians for doing so. People's willingness to question some of the US' most renowned scientists, public health officials, and physicians in COVID-19-related medical science matters, from wearing face masks to the personal health importance of getting vaccinated, attests to their faith in themselves and the information they gather directly when making medical decisions. Millions made

COVID-19-related decisions about their health independent from and contrary to learned medical science expert advice based on an abundance of global data, and despite sickness and death rates high enough to shut down economies.[119] US physicians face this dilemma daily when treating patients.[120]

Permissive US biopharma marketing, both DTC and DTP, and disease awareness campaigns, which some European nations also are allowing, penetrate the discipline of medicine to create and define diseases.[121] "Rightly rewarded for saving life and reducing suffering, the global [Rx] drug giants are no longer content selling medicines only to the ill. Because as Wall St. knows well, there's a lot of money to be made telling healthy people they're sick."[122] While advertising about the risks and benefits of medicines is regulated by the FDA, "claims about diseases remain a virtual free-for-all."[123] Natural processes that are familiar facets of ordinary life and aging, such as menopause, high cholesterol, hypertension, anxiety, and situational depression, have been defined as "medical illnesses" in conjunction with the promotion of Rx drugs to treat them:

> This whole process has been bundled up under names like "disease-mongering" and "medicalization": social processes, where the pharmaceutical companies widen the boundaries of diagnosis, to increase their market and sell the idea that a complex social or personal problem is a molecular disease, in order to sell their own molecules, in pills, to fix it.[124]

Consequently, the distinction between risk of disease and disease onset has shifted in the delivery of care for many common conditions, such as high cholesterol and high blood pressure. Both are common and readily modified through prescription drugs.[125] The extent to which these indicators are risk factors for future medical conditions or actual medical conditions suitable for prescription medicine interventions is the subject of much debate, and the same is true for an amassing number of others.[126] Predictive personal genome testing that identifies susceptibilities to diseases and health risks adds another dimension to this debate.[127] Introducing and expanding disease labels in conjunction with biopharmaceuticals to treat them has proven extremely profitable for biopharma, and for some time. Notable examples include statins to treat high cholesterol as a preventative for coronary-artery disease,[128] Activase to treat stroke victims,[129] Fosamax to treat osteoporosis,[130] and Zoloft to treat social anxiety disorder.[131] Responsiveness to this marketing often introduces risks of drug interactions, side effects, adverse events, and even medical conditions directly associated with the medical conditions those Rx drugs are prescribed to treat. For example,

> Long-term hormone replacement therapy increases the risk of heart attacks for women, while antidepressants appear to increase the risk of suicidal thinking among the young. At least one of the blockbuster cholesterol-lowering drugs has been withdrawn from the market because it was implicated in causing deaths. In one of the most horrific cases of all, a drug sold as helping with common bowel problems led to constipation so severe for some people, they simply died.[132]

While perhaps half of all deaths in the US could be attributed to largely preventable behaviors and exposures, nearly all (an estimated ninety-five percent) of US health care spending is directed at biomedically-oriented medical care.[133] The millions of Americans who resisted (many flatly refused) wearing face masks and social distancing during a raging COVID-19 pandemic while the nation (along with the global community) collectively focused on the development and distribution of vaccines and therapeutics attests to this behavior.[134] The overall delivery-of-care danger of disease mongering through biopharma marketing is the creation of serious and even life-threatening human health opportunity costs, as well as financial ones. They include consumption of therapeutics and procedures that distract patients and physicians from much more clinically effective lifestyle choices, forgoing more beneficial "tried and proven true" treatments, clinical uptake of Rx interventions not fully understood that introduce side effects and other serious human health consequences, and an enormous waste of health care dollars.[135]

EARLY TWENTIETH-CENTURY PATENT MEDICINES MARKETING NORMS IN A PERSONAL GENOME MEDICINE/PGM ERA

Historically, states have been the primary protectors of their citizens' health.[136] States bestow the privilege to practice medicine within their borders, protect their citizens as health care consumers, regulate the health insurance markets within their jurisdictions, and possess substantial public health powers under the Tenth Amendment.[137] Physicians, who write prescriptions for patients and oversee clinical use of Rx products, have been the ultimate Rx consumer protectors since US law recognized prescription-only drugs in 1951, and even before through the AMA Council's market control over medicines.[138]

The AMA fended off DTC communication by patent medicine makers through its AMA Council and supported the shift from medical profession regulation to government regulation when the FDA was empowered to accomplish the same.[139] At least since 1962 (well over a half-century) when prescription drug makers were required to establish clinical efficacy for market access, the FDA has been the nation's official Rx products market gatekeeper, Rx market sentinel, and overseer of biopharma marketing.[140] The FDA decides what medicinal products are sound for market access, and then the medical profession decides how it will use them with immense discretion – the two united through the shared mission to protect and promote the evidentiary-science base of US medicine. The FDA continues to shoulder considerable responsibility through its charge to regulate Rx products and biopharma marketing, but the US has become much more dependent on its medical profession to protect and promote the base of medicine over the last quarter-century.

US law has not been supportive of the FDA meeting its awesome responsibilities during the genomic era. Congress has made the agency dependent on biopharma funding through PDUFA I-VII, with sunset provisions that make the agency chronically vulnerable to losing that funding revenue and to industry intrusion over how the revenue is allocated.[141] Congress also "modernized" (fundamentally changed) the FDA in 1997 to be more industry-friendly through FDAMA and PDUFA II – a transformation illustrated in the *Washington Legal* dispute and decision, resolved with FDA assurance of adherence to FDAMA.[142]

The post-FDAMA and post-PDUFA II FDA is shackled by US law-policy that protects biopharma marketing as commercial speech and yet continues to protect the medical profession's sovereignty over the practice of medicine in accordance with mid-twentieth century norms established when science was much simpler and patients much less "informed" and directive.[143] The US medical profession elevated the practice of medicine, amassed its sovereignty over it under US law-policy, and established related norms through pious-like devotion to the evidentiary-science base of medicine.[144] Since *Washington Legal*, physician off-label prescribing has soared along with biopharma marketing.[145] The US opioid epidemic, largely attributed to fraudulent biopharma marketing and other industry (including national pharmacy chains and distributors) bad behavior in litigation and the media, attests to the present vulnerability of the evidentiary-science base of US medicine.[146] Industry behavior was abhorrent, but the nation's opioid addiction amassed over more than a decade under the watch of the post-FDAMA and post-PDUFA II FDA, with its heightened deference to biopharma commercial speech and to the medical profession's sovereignty over the practice of medicine.[147] Physicians witnessed the addiction impact of opioids on their patients firsthand during those many years, patient-by-patient, within their practice-of-medicine domain and cloaked by the sanctity of individualized patient care.

The evidentiary-science base of medicine is increasingly genomics – medicine on the molecular level, often overwhelmingly complicated even for the most learned medical professionals, and centered on the individual's personal genome.[148] Today's patient is "informed" by biopharma marketing and the internet, and much more self-determined in their doctor–patient decision-making – especially when commercialization in US medicine itself has become a norm.[149] Medicine is no longer perceived as an enclave shielded from commercial influences because, in fact, it is not. Today, in our DTC genomics era, biopharma is in direct, robust marketing dialogue with the public – reminiscent of the relationship between the patent medicine manufacturers and the US public at the outset of the twentieth century.[150]

Today's US biopharma industry has regained much of the influence over consumers lost last century by its patent medicines predecessor. Consumers are influencing their physicians, while biopharma influences their physicians too through pervasive and aggressive DTP marketing, and beyond.[151] Overall, through DTC and DTP marketing, biopharma manufacturers have achieved immense influence over patients, physicians, and US medicine. Their patent medicine predecessors would be impressed.

NOTES

1 *See* ELISABETH ROSENTHAL, AN AMERICAN SICKNESS: HOW HEALTHCARE BECAME BIG BUSINESS AND HOW YOU CAN TAKE IT BACK 100 (2017) ("drug advertising is now a constant in our lives"); JOHN ABRAMSON, OVERDOSED AMERICA: THE BROKEN PROMISE OF AMERICAN MEDICINE 150–52 (2005). FDA marketing rules were relaxed in sync with the passage of FDAMA and PDUFA II in 1997, and biopharma increased investment in Rx drug advertising rapidly and substantially. *See* ABRAMSON, *supra*, at 150–52. *See also infra* notes 11–20, and accompanying text (FDA rule change to allow Rx television advertising).

2 *See infra* notes 8–9, and accompanying text (FDA marketing restrictions in the 1940s, followed by Congress codifying a "prescription-only" category of drugs in 1951). In 1981, the drug industry began asserting that the public was being denied access to Rx "knowledge," and the agency agreed to allow some DTC advertising four years later. *See* ABRAMSON, OVERDOSED, *supra* note 1, at 150–51. However, the FDA did so with strict rules:

> Drugs could be mentioned by name, but advertisements that discussed the treatment of specific conditions were required to include a lengthy list of side effects and contraindications (situations in which the drug should not be used). As a result, the ads were vague and unfocused, primarily brand-awareness campaigns designed to smooth the way at the doctor's office.

Id.

3 PAUL STARR, THE SOCIAL TRANSFORMATION OF AMERICAN MEDICINE: THE RISE OF A SOVEREIGN PROFESSION AND THE MAKING OF A VAST INDUSTRY 128 (1984) (awarded the 1984 Pulitzer Prize for general nonfiction).

4 *See* Nathan A. Brown, Eli Tomar, *Could State Regulations Be the Next Frontier for Preemption Jurisprudence? Drug Compounding as A Case Study*, 71 FOOD & DRUG L.J. 271, 273 (2016). Nostrum peddlers "mimicked, distorted, derided and undercut the authority of the profession. While they often claimed to be doctors themselves, or to operate institutes or medical colleges, or to have the endorsement of eminent physicians, they also frequently insinuated that the [medical] profession was jealously conspiring to suppress their discoveries." STARR, SOCIAL TRANSFORMATION, *supra* note 3, at 129. Patent medicine makers used marketing to compete directly with physicians who prepared their own medicines in the delivery of care, a norm at the time. For instance, they "distributed guides to health and invited the puzzled and the sick to write them for advice about their medical problems." *Id.*

5 *See generally* Austin Smith, *The Council on Pharmacy and Chemistry of the American Medical Association: A Historical Review of Its Relation to Medical Therapy and Research*, 1(2) FOOD, DRUG, COSMETIC L. QUART. 186, 186–95 (June 1946), www.jstor.org/stable/26651664.

6 Medicine manufacturers were almost entirely unregulated by government in a meaningful manner for the first decades of the twentieth century. *See* STEVEN JOHNSON, EXTRA LIFE: A SHORT HISTORY OF LIVING Longer 127 (2021). The AMA Council filled this vacuum. Unless evaluated and approved by the AMA Council, physicians withheld manufacturer information and their medicines from patients. Manufactures had to comply with AMA Council requirements and rules, which included not advertising directly to the public and not listing diseases for which a drug was intended to treat on labels or in packaging. *See* STARR, SOCIAL TRANSFORMATION, *supra* note 3, at 132. The AMA Council succeeded in channeling substantial consumer medicine purchasing through physicians. "The shift meant a structural change in the market rather than simply an improvement in functioning, and it gave physicians a larger share of the purchasing power of their patients." *Id.* at 133.

7 *See* James G. Burrow, *The Prescription-Drug Policies of the American Medical Association in the Progressive Era, in* SAFEGUARDING THE PUBLIC: HISTORICAL ASPECTS OF MEDICINAL DRUG CONTROL 112–22 (John B. Blake ed., 1970).

8 In its 1939 Annual Report, the FDA opined that "Many drugs of great value to the physician are dangerous in the hands of those unskilled in the use of drugs. The statute obviously was not intended to deprive the medical profession of potent but valuable medicaments." FDA, FEDERAL FOOD, DRUG, AND COSMETIC LAW: ADMINISTRATIVE REPORTS, 1907–49 (1951), *quoted in* RONALD HAMOWY, MEDICAL DISASTERS AND GROWTH OF THE FDA, INDEP. POL'Y REP. 10 (Feb. 2010), www.independent.org/pdf/policy_reports/2010-02-10-fda.pdf.

9 *See* Durham-Humphrey Amendment, Pub. L. No. 82–215, § 1, 65 Stat. 648 (1951), *codified as amended*, 21 U.S.C. § 353(b). *See* PETER TEMIN, TAKING YOUR MEDICINE: DRUG REGULATION IN THE UNITED STATES 121 (1980); Burrow, *Policies, supra* note 7, at 112–22. *See also* Lars Noah, *Reversal of Fortune: Moving Pharmaceuticals from Over-the-Counter to Prescription Status?*, 63 VILL. L. REV. 355, 393 (2018).

10 *See generally* EZEKIEL J. EMANUEL, WHICH COUNTRY HAS THE WORLD'S BEST HEALTH CARE? (2020). Only the US and New Zealand allow DTC prescription drug marketing, which both nations began to do in the 1980s. Almost all industrialized-economy countries expressly banned DTC Rx drug advertising in the 1940s and continue to do so substantially. *See* BEN GOLDACRE, BAD PHARMA: HOW DRUG COMPANIES MISLEAD DOCTORS AND HARM PATIENTS 247 (2012). Notably, in 2003, the European Union/EU voted to continue its ban on DTC Rx drug ads and to limit dissemination of product information to independent national sources and licensed medical professionals. *See* ABRAMSON, OVERDOSED, *supra* note 1, at 157. However, DTC ads and information on the internet often transcend borders and they are reaching Canadians and Europeans. *See* GOLDACRE, BAD PHARMA, *supra*, at 247; ABRAMSON, OVERDOSED, *supra* note 1, at 157. Also, countries are joining the FDA in allowing biopharma "awareness campaigns" to enlighten the public about a specific medical condition without mentioning a specific drug. *See* GOLDACRE, BAD PHARMA, *supra*, at 247. These campaigns often refer people to their physicians and other sources, such as a website or phone hotline, for more information. *See* GOLDACRE, BAD PHARMA, *supra*, at 247.

11 *See* FDAMA, Pub. L. No. 105–115, 111 Stat. 2296 (1997) (codified primarily in sections throughout 21 U.S.C., including §§ 352, 355, 356, 356(b), 360aaa–1–3, 379r). *Visit* FDA, *Prescription Drug User Fee Amendments* (current Oct. 27, 2021) (links to provision specifics and background information for PDUFA I-VI), www.fda.gov/industry/fda-user-fee-programs/prescription-drug-user-fee-amendments. For detailed discussion of PDUFA I-III, the allocation of FDA resources under their industry-government negotiated provisions, and the impact on FDA review and performance, see generally James L. Zelenay, Jr., *The Prescription Drug User Fee Act: Is a Faster Food and Drug Administration Always a Better Food and Drug Administration?*, 60 FOOD & DRUG L.J. 261 (2005).

12 Technically, the FDA's central mission was directly changed in PDUFA II with complementary provisions in FDAMA. *See also infra* notes 141–42, and accompanying text. While the FDA mission to ensure safety and efficacy was affirmed in FDAMA and PDUFA II, section 406 of PDUFA II expanded the agency's mission to include efficiency and required the agency to balance safety and efficacy with timeliness. Specifically, section 406 requires the FDA to "promote the public health by promptly and efficiently reviewing clinical research and taking appropriate action … in a timely manner." 21 U.S.C. § 393(b)(1), *as amended*. *See* Zelenay, *Faster, supra* note 11, at 295.

13 *See* Prescription Drug User Fee Act/PDUFA, Pub. L. No. 102–571, 106 Stat. 4491 (1992), *codified as amended*, 21 U.S.C. §§ 379g–h. *See* MICHAEL J. MALINOWSKI, HANDBOOK ON BIOTECHNOLOGY LAW, BUSINESS, AND POLICY 14–15 (2016). "Simplified, PDUFA

I allowed FDA to collect 'user fees' from manufacturers or drug sponsors when they submitted a [New Drug Application/NDA] for review, maintained certain drugs on the market, or maintained certain manufacturing facilities. FDA was then to use these fees to hire additional review staff in order to reduce drug review times." Zelenay, *Faster, supra* note 11, at 275 (identifying and summarizing the provisions of PDUFA I-III).

14 PDUFA negotiation for reauthorization is a chronic US government-biopharma staple:

> PDUFA must be renewed every five years, which provides an occasion for other FDA policymaking, as legislators now consider it a must-pass piece of legislation. Discussions about the content of the PDUFA renewal tends to occur anywhere from two to three years prior to the renewal deadline and the framework of the draft legislation is often presented to Congress as a negotiated agreement between FDA and industry.

Aaron S. Kesselheim, Michael S. Sinha, Jerry Avorn, Ameet Sarpatwari, *Pharmaceutical Policy in the United States in 2019: An Overview of the Landscape and Avenues for Improvement*, 30 STAN. L. & POL'Y REV. 421, 438 (2019).

15 The FDA has established user fee programs for prescription drugs, generic drugs, biosimilars and medical devices. PDUFA VI was signed into law on August 18, 2017, under the Food and Drug Administration Reauthorization Act/FDARA of 2017, P.L. 115–52. *See generally* CONG. RES. SERV., FDA REAUTHORIZATION ACT OF 2017 (FDARA, P.L. 115–52) (Sept. 21, 2017), https://sgp.fas.org/crs/misc/R44961.pdf; FDA, *PDUFA VI: Fiscal Years 2018–2022* (current July 7, 2020), www.fda.gov/industry/prescription-drug-user-fee-amendments/pdufa-vi-fiscal-years-2018–2022. President Biden signed the FDA User Fee Reauthorization Act of 2022 – PDUFA VII, which is the sixth PDUFA reauthorization – into law on September 30, 2022. *See generally* FDA, *PDUFA VII: Fiscal Years 2023–2027* (current Oct. 3, 2022), www.fda.gov/industry/prescription-drug-user-fee-amendments/pdufa-vii-fiscal-years-2023-2027. Overall user fees for FY2023, the benchmark year for PDUFA VII, were adjusted upward significantly based upon anticipated user applications and the revenue they will generate. *See generally* Ferdous Al-Faruque, *FDA Posts FY2023 User Fee Tables*, REG. NEWS (Oct. 6, 2022), www.raps.org/news-and-articles/news-articles/2022/10/fda-posts-fy2023-user-fee-tables. *See also* FDA, PDUFA REAUTHORIZATION PERFORMANCE GOALS AND PROCEDURES FISCAL YEARS 2023 THROUGH 2027 (undated; visited May 24, 2022), www.fda.gov/media/151712/download.

16 *See* ABRAMSON, OVERDOSED, *supra* note 1, at 151; GOLDACRE, BAD PHARMA, *supra* note 10, at 247–48.

17 ABRAMSON, OVERDOSED, *supra* note 1, at 151.

18 *See id.* at 159. As summarized by Dr. Abramson,

> [T]he stage could not have been set more perfectly for prescription drug advertising to become a major force in American medicine. And so it did. In 1991, the drug companies spent a paltry $55 million on advertising drugs directly to consumers. Over the next 11 years, this increased more than 50-fold to over $3 billion in 2003. The ads appeal to viewers as independent decision makers – capable of forming their own opinions about which drugs they need – and resonate with the growing concern that HMOs and managed care plans tend to withhold the best care to save money.

Id. at 80.

19 *See id.* at 159.

20 *See id.* at 157. However, both the EU and Canada struggle to block biopharma DTC internet pervasiveness. *See* GOLDACRE, BAD PHARMA, *supra* note 10, at 247.

21 Julie M. Donohue, Marisa Cevasco, Meredith B. Rosenthal, A *Decade of Direct-to-Consumer Advertising of Prescription Drugs*, 357 N. Eng. J. Med. 673, 673–81 (2007), www.nejm.org/doi/full/10.1056/nejmsa070502.

22 Glenn Thrush, Katie Thomas, *Drug Prices Will Soon Appear in Many TV Ads*, N.Y. Times (May 8, 2019) (data attributed to Kantar Media, www.kantarmedia.com, which tracks media spending), www.nytimes.com/2019/05/08/us/politics/drug-prices-tv-advertisements.html.

23 *See* Statista Res. Dep., *Most Advertised Drugs on US TV 2021*, Statista.com (Apr. 6, 2021), www.statista.com/statistics/639356/tv-advertise-drugs-usa/#:~:text=%20Dupixent%2C%20Rybelsus%2C%20and%20Humira%20were%20the%20top,and%20Humira%20spent%2019.9%20and%2019.6%20million%2C%20respectively.

24 Goldacre, Bad Pharma, *supra* note 10, at 245.

25 RAND Corp., *Press Release, Prescription Drug Prices in the United States Are 2.56 Times Those in Other Countries* (Jan. 28, 2021), www.rand.org/news/press/2021/01/28.html. *See generally* Andrew W. Mulcahy, Christopher M. Whaley, Mahlet Gizaw et al., *International Prescription Drug Price Comparisons: Current Empirical Estimates and Comparison with Previous Studies*, RAND (2021) (study sponsored by US HHS), www.rand.org/pubs/research_reports/RR2956.html.

26 *See* RAND, *Prices*, *supra* note 25 (quoting Anndrew W. Mulcahy, Rand Senior Policy Researcher). All industrialized nations are destined to grapple with the exorbitant costs of clinically remarkable and remarkably expensive biologic therapeutics, which have just begun to emerge from the R&D pipeline. *See* Canadian Public Broadcasting/CPB News, *The Real Cost of the World's Most Expensive Drug* (June 24, 2015) (profiling the drug Soliris as a case study in biologics and unavoidable health care system rationing in the clinical genomics era), www.youtube.com/watch?v=0uYCw5EDX8U. *See generally Joint FDA-FTC Statement Regarding Collaboration to Advance Competition in the Biologic Marketplace* (Feb. 3, 2020) ("Public and private insurers in the US spent $125.5 billion on biologics in 2018 alone."), www.ftc.gov/public-statements/2020/02/joint-fda-ftc-statement-regarding-collaboration-advance-competition. On Nov. 22, 2022, the FDA approved Hemgenix, a one-time gene therapy product given as a single dose by IV infusion to effectively cure Hemophilia B, but at a cost of $3.5 million – making it now the world's most expensive drug (with more $ gene therapies to come). *See* Miryam Naddaf, *Researchers Welcome $3.5-million Haemophilia Gene Therapy – but Questions Remain*, NATURE (Dec. 6, 2022), www.nature.com/articles/d41586-022-04327-7. For more discussion of gene therapies coming to fruition, *see Chapter* 2, at notes 1–17, and accompanying text (profiling utilization of mRNA and CRISPR technologies); *Chapter 6, infra*, at note 37, and accompanying text.

27 *See* PhRMA, Code on Interactions with Health Care Professionals (2022) ("PhRMA Code"), www.phrma.org/-/media/Project/PhRMA/PhRMA-Org/PhRMA-Org/PDF/P-R/PhRMA-Code--Final.pdf.

28 *Id.* at 15.1 ("Adherence to the Code").

29 *See* Future of Privacy Forum, Best Practices for Consumer Genetic Testing Services (July 31, 2018), www.geneticdataprotection.com/wp-content/uploads/2019/05/Future-of-Privacy-Forum-Privacy-Best-Practices-July-2018.pdf. According to a recent assessment of this attempt at self-regulation, "not only do the *Best Practices* have several limitations and shortcomings, but none of the eight companies examined appeared to be in full compliance with the guidelines." James W. Hazel, *Privacy Best Practices for Direct-to-Consumer Genetic Testing Services: Are Industry Efforts at Self-Regulation Sufficient?*, *in* Consumer Genetic Technologies 262 (J. Glenn Cohen, Nita A. Farahany, Henry T. Greely, Carmel Schachar eds., 2021).

30 *See supra* notes 16–24, and accompanying text (discussing substantial increase in biopharma marketing since the television advertising rule change and passage of FDAMA and PDUFA II in 1997).

31 *See* ABRAMSON, OVERDOSED, *supra* note 1, at 157. *See generally*, TAMARA R. PIETY, BRANDISHING THE FIRST AMENDMENT (2012); Tamara R. Piety, *The First Amendment and the Corporate Civil Rights Movement*, 11 J. BUS. & TECH. L. 1, 2–24 (2016); Wayne L. Pines, A *History and Perspective on Direct-to-Consumer Promotion*, 54 FOOD AND DRUG L. J. 489 (1999). The corporate civil rights movement achieved influential political and law-policy momentum well before the election of President Trump and his administration's aggressive deregulation agenda. *See* Avery Anapol, *Trump Signs Order Giving Agency Heads More Power to Appoint Regulatory Judges*, 2018 THE HILL 39645 (July 11, 2018), *available at* 2018 WL 3371968 ("Trump has vowed to dramatically roll back federal regulations, one of his campaign promises...."); *infra* note 80, and accompanying text (the Trump Administration inaugural deregulation measures). Notably, the Supreme Court, in a 5–4 decision, struck down limits Congress set on campaign donations by corporations and unions under the First Amendment in *Citizens United v. Federal Election Commission*, 130 S. Ct. 876 (2010). In his last book, former Justice John Paul Stevens, reflecting on his thirty-five years serving on the Court, declared the *Citizens United* decision the Court's "second biggest mistake" after *Bush v. Gore*, 531 US 98, 121 S. Ct. 525, 148 L. Ed. 2d 388 (2000) (ruling that manual recounts of presidential election ballots ordered by the Florida Supreme Court was without specific standards and therefore violated equal protection). *See* JOHN PAUL STEVENS, THE MAKING OF A JUSTICE: REFLECTIONS ON MY FIRST 94 YEARS 360–74, 500–03 (2019). Justice Stevens wrote strong dissenting opinions in both cases. *See* Emily Bazelon, Book Review, *Justice John Paul Stevens Had Some Things to Say Before He Died*, N.Y. TIMES (May 14, 2019) (stating that, according to Gallup, public approval ratings of the Court dropped after both decisions), www.nytimes.com/2019/05/14/books/review/john-paul-stevens-making-of-a-justice.html; Emily Birnbaum, *Retired Justice Stevens: Gun Control Case,* Gore v. Bush *among Three Biggest 'Errors' Supreme Court Made during His Tenure*, THE HILL (Nov. 28, 2018), https://thehill.com/regulation/court-battles/418203-john-paul-stevens-names-three-biggest-errors-supreme-court-made/.

32 ABRAMSON, OVERDOSED, *supra* note 1, at 157.

33 *See Virginia Pharmacy*, 425 US 748, 759 (1976). *See also* Piety, *Corporate Civil Rights*, *supra* note 31, at 4–8.

34 *See Virginia Pharmacy*, *supra* note 33, at 749–50; Piety, *Corporate Civil Rights*, *supra* note 31, at 4–8: Alan Morrison, *How We Got the Commercial Speech Doctrine: An Originalist's Recollections*, 54 Case W. Res. L. Rev. 1189, 1192 (2004). More than for decades after *Virginia Pharmacy* and subsequent jurisprudence increasingly supportive of commercial speech protection, the Trump Administration's primary strategy to contain drug price inflation was to force commercial speech – to require biopharma to disclose drug "sticker prices" to consumers. *See infra* notes 67–70, 103–04, and accompanying text (Trump Administration's Blueprint effort to force biopharma drug pricing disclosure).

35 *Virginia Pharmacy*, *supra* note 33, at 765. As summarized by Professor Piety,

> [B]efore 1976, most scholars, judges and lawyers thought that advertising was not covered by the First Amendment. Indeed, in 1942 the Supreme Court had unequivocally stated that it wasn't. But between 1942 and 1976 the Court decided cases involving ads – political ads, classified ads, ads for abortion services – in which the Court held that the speech in question was protected. But it was not clear if these holdings represented exceptions to the categorical exclusion of advertising from

First Amendment protection, or if they signaled a new attitude toward advertising. Soon, it became apparent that it was the latter.

Piety, *Corporate Civil Rights*, *supra* note 31, at 4.

36 *See Virginia Pharmacy*, *supra* note 33, at 770 ("In concluding that commercial speech … is protected, we of course do not hold that it can never be regulated in any way. Some forms of commercial speech regulation are surely permissible.").

37 *See id.* at 770–72.

38 *Hudson*, 447 US 557 (1980). *See* Piety, *Corporate Civil Rights*, *supra* note 31, at 10.

39 *Hudson*, *supra* note 38, at 566.

40 Piety, *Corporate Civil Rights*, *supra* note 31, at 11–12.

41 *See City of Cincinnati v. Discovery Network, Inc.*, 507 US 410 (1993).

42 *See id.* at 430–31.

43 Piety, *Corporate Civil Rights*, *supra* note 31, at 17.

44 Accreditation Council for Continuing Medical Education/ACCME, *Fact Search: How Is an Enduring Material Activity Defined?* (revised Nov. 16, 2021), www.accme.org/faq/how-enduring-material-activity-defined-0.

45 *See generally Washington Legal Found. v. Friedman*, 13 F. Supp. 2d 51 (D.D.C. 1998), *amended*, 36 F. Supp. 2d 16 (D.D.C. 1999), *appeal dism'd, judgm't vac'd in part sub nom.*, *Washington Legal Found. v. Henney*, 202 F.3d 331 (D.C. Cir. 2000), *amended*, 36 F. Supp. 2d 418 (D.D.C. 1999), *appeal dism'd, judgm't vac'd in part sub nom.*, *Washington Legal Found. v. Henney*, 202 F.3d 331 (D.C. Cir. 2000).

46 *See* FDA, *Final Guidance on Industry-Supported Scientific and Educational Activities*, 62 FED. REG. 64074 (1997); Advertising and Promotion, Guidances, 61 FED. REG. 52800 (1996).

47 FDA, *Guidances* (current Jan. 24, 2022), www.fda.gov/industry/fda-basics-industry/guidances.

48 *See Chapter 1*, *supra*, at notes 42–45, 159–60, and accompanying text (addressing US legacy of recognizing physician discretion to prescribe off label).

49 Dep. Health and Human Serv's, Citizen Petition Regarding the Food and Drug Administration's Policy on Promotion of Unapproved Uses of Approved Drugs and Devices, Request for Comments, 59 FED. REG. 59820, 59821 (1994) (internal footnotes with supportive citations omitted).

50 *Washington Legal*, *supra* note 45, 13 F. Supp. 2d at 55.

51 *See* Michael J. Malinowski, *The US Science and Technology "Triple Threat": A Regulatory Treatment Plan for the Nation's Addiction to Prescription Opioids*, 48 U. Mem. L. Rev. 1027, 1049–50 (2018). *See generally*, Matt Hellman, *Commercial Drug Claims, the FDA, and the First Amendment* (Harv. Univ. Third-Year Paper, 2001), https://dash.harvard.edu/bitstream/handle/1/8852198/Hellman01.pdf. The *Washington Legal* Court recognized the same – and especially so in the context of off-label use which does not have the benefits of a FDA-approved label and product insert. *See Washington Legal*, *supra* note 45, 13 F. Supp. 2d at 56.

52 *See Washington Legal*, *supra* note 45, 13 F. Supp. 2d at 59.

53 *Id.*

54 *Id.* at 60.

55 *Washington Legal*, *supra* note 45, 13 F. Supp. 2d at 67. The Court's conclusion does not necessarily reflect contemporary reality. *See generally Chapter 5*, *infra* (addressing industry influence on the medical journal establishment/MJE, continuing medical education/CME, and individual physicians after decades of US technology transfer law and policy/TTLP implementation).

56 *See Washington Legal, supra* note 45, 13 F. Supp. 2d at 69–70.
57 *See id.*
58 *See id.* at 71.
59 *See id.* at 71–74.
60 *Washington Legal, supra* note 45, 3 F. Supp. 2d at 74–5.
61 *See* ABRAMSON, OVERDOSED, *supra* note 1, at 151–52 (FDA relaxation of rules in sync with the passage of FDAMA and PDUFA II in 1997).
62 *See Washington Legal Foundation, supra* note 45, 128 F. Supp. 2d at 13 (vacating permanent injunction); 202 F.3d at 335–36 (denying Washington Legal's motion to confirm and enforce permanent injunction).
63 *See generally Washington Legal, supra* note 45.
64 *See generally* Michael J. Malinowski, *Doctors, Patients, and Pills – A System Popping Under Too Much Physician Discretion? A Law-Policy Prescription to Make Drug Approval More Meaningful in the Delivery of Health Care*, 33 Cardozo L. Rev. 1085, 1106–09 (2012).
65 *Id.* at 1107.
66 *See generally* Hellman, *Commercial Drug Claims, supra* note 51; Cynthia M. Ho, *A Dangerous Concoction: Pharmaceutical Marketing, Cognitive Biases, and First Amendment Overprotection*, 94 Ind. L. J. 773 (2019).
67 *See* HHS, *Blueprint to Lower Drug Prices and Reduce Out-of-Pocket Costs*, 83 FED. REG. 22,692 (May 16, 2018); HHS, *Notice of Proposed Rulemaking, Medicare and Medicaid Programs; Regulation to Require Drug Pricing Transparency*, 83 FED. REG. 52,789 (Oct. 18, 2018). *See also* HHS, *Centers for Medicare and Medicaid Services, Rule: Medicare and Medicaid Programs; Regulation to Require Drug Pricing Transparency*, 84 FED. REG. 20732, 20732–58, 42 CFR 403 (May 10, 2019) (effective date July 9, 2019). *See supra* note 34 *(Virginia Pharmacy), infra* notes 103–04 (Price Rule struck down), and accompanying text.
68 *See Zauderer v. Office of Disciplinary Counsel of the Supreme Court of Ohio*, 471 US 626 (1985).
69 *See generally Merck & Co. v. United States Dep't of Health & Hum. Servs.*, 385 F. Supp. 3d 81, 90 (D.D.C. 2019), *aff'd*, 962 F.3d 531 (D.C. Cir. 2020).
70 *See* Tina Bellon, Nate Raymond, *US Judge Strikes Down Trump Administration Rule Requiring Drug Prices in TV Ads*, REUTER'S (July 8, 2019), www.reuters.com/article/us-usa-drugpricing-lawsuit/u-s-judge-strikes-down-trump-administration-rule-requiring-drug-prices-in-tv-ads-idUSKCN1U32L2. *See infra* notes 103–04, and accompanying text (Trump Blueprint provision to force drug pricing disclosure struck down).
71 *See Chapter 1, supra*, at notes 184–89, and accompanying text ("Medical Profession-FDA Symbiotic Relationship").
72 *See supra* note 12, and accompanying text (FDAMA and PDUFA II added efficiency to the FDA's mission).
73 CBO, RESEARCH AND DEVELOPMENT IN THE PHARMACEUTICAL INDUSTRY (2021), www.cbo.gov/publication/57126.
74 *See* Kefauver-Harris Amend's, Pub. Law 87–781, 76 Stat. 780, *amend's to* 1 U.S.C. ch. 9 § 301, *et seq.*; Durham-Humphrey Amend't, Pub. L. No. 82–215, § 1, 65 Stat. 648 (1951), *codified as amended*, 21 U.S.C. § 353(b). Pub. Law 87–781, 76 Stat. 780, *amendments to* 1 U.S.C. ch. 9 § 301, *et seq*.
75 *See Chapter 1, supra*, at notes 81–144, and accompanying text (FDA premarket proof of safety and efficacy); notes 184–89, and accompanying text (symbiotic relationship between the FDA and the US medical profession).
76 See Memorandum of Understanding between FTC and the FDA, 36 FED. REG. 18,539 (Sept. 15, 1971), https://fda.report/media/99834/Memorandum-of-Understanding-

Between-Federal-Trade-Commission-and-the-Food-and-Drug-Administration.pdf. The agencies work collaboratively, however. *See, e.g.*, FTC, *Press Release, FTC Staff Provides FDA with Comments on Direct-To-Consumer Prescription Drug Advertising* (Dec. 2, 2003), www.ftc.gov/news-events/press-releases/2003/12/ftc-staff-provides-fda-comments-direct-consumer-prescription-drug; FTC, *Press Release, FTC Testifies on the Internet Sale of Prescription Drugs from Domestic Web Sites* (Mar. 27, 2003), www.ftc.gov/news-events/press-releases/2003/03/ftc-testifies-internet-sale-prescription-drugs-domestic-web-sites. The FTC may assume primary responsibility in matters of significant prescription drug consumer fraud, and especially if conducted through the internet. A notable example is FTC involvement in opioid consumer fraud. *See, e.g.*, FTC, *Press Release, FTC Returns Nearly $60 Million to Those Suffering from Opioid Addiction Who Were Allegedly Overcharged in Suboxone Film Scheme* (May 10, 2021), www.ftc.gov/news-events/press-releases/2021/05/ftc-returns-nearly-60-million-those-suffering-opioid-addiction. Also, the agencies may exercise jurisdiction more concurrently at times, such as in advancing competition in the biologics marketplace due to their exceptional costs. *See Joint FDA-FTC Statement, supra* note 26 ("Public and private insurers in the US spent $125.5 billion on biologics in 2018 alone.").

77 *See* ABRAMSON, OVERDOSED, *supra* note 1, at 158. Beginning in 2001, the HHS Office of Chief Counsel must review and approve all FDA letters to drug companies for marketing violations before they are sent. According to the Government Accountability Office/GAO in a 2002 report, "prior to this change, letters had been issued within several days of identifying a violation, but the additional legal review was taking so long, an average of 41 days and as many as 78, that 'misleading advertisements may have completed their broadcast life cycle before FDA issued the letters.'" *Id.* A US House report concluded that these delays increased from an average of 41 days in 2002 to 177 days for many ads in 2003. *See id.*

78 *See generally* Donohue et al., *Decade of DTC, supra* note 21.

79 *See id.* (all bulleted points paraphrase study findings). *See also* GOVERNMENT ACCOUNTABILITY OFFICE/GAO, PRESCRIPTION DRUGS: IMPROVEMENTS NEEDED IN FDA'S OVERSIGHT OF DIRECT-TO-CONSUMER ADVERTISING (2006) (criticizing the FDA's enforcement of regulations that govern DTC advertising), www.gao.gov/products/gao-07-54; INSTITUTE OF MEDICINE/IOM, COMMITTEE ON THE ASSESSMENT OF THE US DRUG SAFETY SYSTEM, THE FUTURE OF DRUG SAFETY: PROMOTING AND PROTECTING THE HEALTH OF THE PUBLIC (2006) (Alina Baciu, Kathleen Stratton, Sheila P. Burke eds.) (calling on the FDA to place limits on DTC advertising, and particularly for new drugs), https://nap.nationalacademies.org/catalog/11750/the-future-of-drug-safety-promoting-and-protecting-the-health.

80 On January 30, 2017, just ten days after being sworn into office, President Trump signed an executive order that directed federal agencies to repeal two existing regulations for every new regulation. *See* Reducing Regulation and Controlling Regulatory Costs, Exec. Order No. 13771, 82 FED. REG. 9339 (Jan. 30, 2017), https://trumpwhitehouse.archives.gov/presidential-actions/presidential-executive-order-reducing-regulation-controlling-regulatory-costs/. *See also* Nolan D. McCaskill, Matthew Nussbaum, *President Donald Trump Signed an Executive Order Monday Morning Requiring That for Every New Federal Regulation Implemented, Two Must Be Rescinded*, POLITICO (Jan. 30, 2017), www.politico.com/story/2017/01/trump-signs-executive-order-requiring-that-for-every-one-new-regulation-two-must-be-revoked-234365. Six months later (July 2017), he signed another to allow agency heads to directly hire administrative law judges – about 2,000 officials who rule on regulatory legal issues – which made it easier to fire them and added

agency pressure to the job. *See* Avery Anapol, *Trump Signs Order, supra* note 31. *See also supra* note 31 (corporate civil rights), *infra* note 94 (deregulation), and accompanying text.

81 Donohue et al., *Decade of DTC, supra* note 21, at 74–75 (footnotes omitted).

82 *Id.* at 75–76 (footnotes omitted).

83 *Id.* at 76 (footnotes omitted).

84 *See supra* notes 17–24, and accompanying text (discussing substantial increase in biopharma marketing since television advertising rule change and enactment of FDAMA and PDUFA II in 1997).

85 *See* Medicare Prescription Drug Improvement and Modernization Act ("Medicare Part D"), Pub. L. No. 108–73, *codified at* 42 U.S.C.A. §§ 1395w–101, *et seq.* (2003). "Enacted in 2003 and implemented in 2006, Medicare Part D quelled the drug pricing controversy for several years, at least to the point of making it manageable for industry." MALINOWSKI, BIOTECH HANDBOOK, *supra* note 13, at 18. Due to increased consumption at market prices, those who spent $2,319 out of pocket in 2003 without Part D coverage were projected to spend $2,911 in 2007 with it. *See id.* at 245. Incidentally, the Part D enabling legislation prohibited the federal government from using its purchasing power to negotiate lower drug prices, which is referred to as "the noninterference clause." *See* ABRAMSON, OVERDOSED, *supra* note 1, at 244–45. The Inflation Reduction Act of 2022/IRA, Pub. Law 117–169, which was signed into law by President Biden on Aug. 16, 2022, established precedent (however limited) to preempt the noninterference clause. *See infra* note 104 and accompanying text (addressing the IRA).

86 "In the studies that led to Vioxx's being approved for sale, the group treated with Vioxx had a fourfold higher risk for cardiovascular events than those on naproxen [which is available over the counter and extremely affordable under brand names such as Aleve and All Day Pain Relief], 0.4 percent versus 0.1 percent." OTIS WEBB BRAWLEY, HOW WE DO HARM: A DOCTOR BREAKS RANKS ABOUT BEING SICK IN AMERICA 200 (2011). Nevertheless, the FDA, consistent with a presumption in favor of market access with conditional follow-on studies under section 506(B) of FDAMA, decided to put the drug on the market. "Vioxx became a blockbuster. Its 2003 sales were $2.5 billion. It cost $2.50 per pill or $90 per month. While it was on the market [from 1999 to 2004], more than 80 million people were prescribed this drug worldwide." *Id.* at 201.

87 As I co-wrote in 2012,

> The recent Avandia controversy triggered an expansive US Senate Finance Committee inquiry and bipartisan report highly critical of both GlaxoSmithKline ("GSK") and the FDA. This medication, introduced to the market in 1999 and prescribed to hundreds of thousands of patients annually to treat type 2 diabetes, caused 83,000 heart attacks between 1999 and 2007, according to the FDA's own estimates. GSK researchers identified a link between Avandia and serious heart disease in 2004, 2005, and 2006, the FDA issued a warning in 2007, the FDA's top officials in the Office of Surveillance and Epidemiology recommended a full market recall, and internal FDA reports indicated that switching Avandia patients to an alternative drug could prevent about 500 heart attacks and 300 cases of heart failure each month. According to the Senate Report, executives at the pharmaceutical company "attempted to intimidate independent physicians, focused on strategies to minimize or misrepresent findings that Avandia may increase cardiovascular risk, and sought ways to downplay findings that a competing drug might reduce cardiovascular risk.

Michael J. Malinowski, Grant G. Gautreaux, *Drug Development-Stuck in a State of Puberty?: Regulatory Reform of Human Clinical Research to Raise Responsiveness to the Reality of Human Variability*, 56 St. Louis U. L.J. 363, 418 (2012) (internal citations omitted).

88 Some biopharmaceuticals the FDA approved for market use *caused* the serious health conditions they were prescribed to prevent:

> In the fall of 2010, the FDA itself "concluded that in some cases two types of drugs that were supposed to be preventing serious medical problems were, in fact, causing them." These were Avandia, prescribed heavily to treat type-2 diabetes, and bisphosphonates–an active agent in the prescription drugs Fosamax, Actonel, and Boniva – used widely to prevent fractures common in people with osteoporosis. Avandia was associated with an increased risk of heart attacks and strokes, a major problem for its target patient group given two thirds of diabetics die of heart problems, and bisphosphonates was determined to actually cause fractures of the thigh bone and degeneration of the jawbone.

Id. at 394–95 (internal footnotes with citations omitted).

89 *See* Donohue et al., *Decade of DTC, supra* note 21, at 74–76. *See generally* GAO, IMPROVEMENTS NEEDED, *supra* note 79 (criticizing the FDA's enforcement of regulations that govern DTC advertising); IOM, THE FUTURE OF DRUG SAFETY, *supra* note 79 (calling on the FDA to place limits on DTC advertising, and particularly for new drugs). Dr. Marcia Angell, former Editor-in-Chief of *The New England Journal of Medicine* with two decades of *NEJM* experience, was compelled to publish a book (winner of a Polk Award for excellence in journalism) to share her first-hand experiences, both as a practicing physician and with *NEJM*, of increasing biopharma manipulation through DTP and DTC marketing, the Vioxx scandal, and beyond. *See Generally*, MARCIA ANGELL, THE TRUTH ABOUT DRUG COMPANIES (2005).

90 *See generally* Food and Drug Administration Amendments Act/FDAAA, Pub. L. No. 110–85, 121 Stat. 823 (2007), *codified as amended*, 21 U.S.C. §§ 301–399i (2012). Professor Barbara Evans has described the FDAAA as "the most momentous shift in drug regulation in half a century." Barbara J. Evans, *Seven Pillars of a New Evidentiary Paradigm: The Food, Drug, and Cosmetic Act Enters the Genomics Era*, 85 Notre Dame L. Rev. 419, 423 (2010). *See also* Malinowski, *"Triple Threat," supra* note 51, at 1051–52. She was correct based on the letter of the law Congress passed and accompanying legislative history. However, overall, the FDAAA embodies much ambiguity, implementation has been soft, and the FDAAA was followed by enactment of the Food and Drug Administration Safety and Innovation Act/FDASIA of 2012, P.L. 107-250, which increased FDA dependence on user fees and reinforced FDAMA. *See infra* note 96, and accompanying text (Cur.es Act).

91 Catherine M. Sharkey, *Direct-to-Consumer Genetic Testing: The FDA's Dual Role as Safety and Health Information Regulator*, 68 DEPAUL L. REV. 343, 344 (2019). *But see generally* STEPHEN LANDSMAN, MICHAEL J. SACKS, CLOSING DEATH'S DOOR: LEGAL INNOVATIONS TO STEM THE EPIDEMIC OF HEALTHCARE HARM (2020) (proposing that the US medical profession resists uptake of technology that would enable patients to make better medical decisions).

92 *See Chapter 4, infra*, at notes 79–80 (advent of social media), and accompanying text. *See also Chapter 5, infra*, at notes 113–77, and accompanying text ("Today's US Physician-Patient Relationship, and the State of Physician Decision Making"). *Cf.* JAY KATZ, THE SILENT WORLD OF DOCTOR AND PATIENT (1984) (addressing physician paternalism in US health care during the twentieth century). *But see* LEWIS A. GROSSMAN, CHOOSE YOUR MEDICINE: FREEDOM OF THERAPEUTIC CHOICE IN AMERICA 5 (2021) (proposing that the mid-late twentieth century patient deference to the medical profession was an aberration, and that the ongoing patient self-determination movement is consistent with popular movements throughout American history inspired by belief that "people have a right to choose their preferred medical treatments without government interference").

93 *See Chapter 2, supra*, at notes 199–230, and accompanying text ("The Genomic Revolution"). Dr. Watson, reflecting on the progress of DNA sequencing and genomics, wrote in 2017 that "[T]he cost today of sequencing a patient's entire genome – about two to three thousand dollars – is ironically less than some companies charge to sequence a single patented cancer gene, as Myriad Genetics does with its BRCA*Analysis* test." JAMES D. WATSON, DNA: THE STORY OF THE GENETIC REVOLUTION 213 (2nd ed. 2017) (with Andrew Berry, Kevin Davies) (updated commemoration of the fiftieth anniversary of the discovery of the double helix).

94 Avery Anapol, *Trump Signs Order, supra* note 31 ("Trump has vowed to dramatically roll back federal regulations, one of his campaign promises …."). *See supra* note 80, and accompanying text (addressing the Trump Administration mandate to remove two regulations for every one added and measures to make administrative law judges vulnerable to firing by agency heads).

95 *See* Heidi Ledford, *Physician with Drug-Industry Ties Is Trump's FDA Pick: Scott Gottlieb May Face Scrutiny over Potential Conflicts of Interest*, Nature News (Mar. 10, 2017, updated Mar. 13, 2017), www.nature.com/news/physician-with-drug-industry-ties-is-trump-s-fda-pick-1.21619; Katie Thomas, *F.D.A. Nominee, Paid Millions by Industry, Says He'll Recuse Himself if Needed*, N.Y. Times (Mar. 29, 2017), www.nytimes.com/2017/03/29/health/fda-nominee-scott-gottlieb-recuse-conflicts.html?login=smartlock&auth=login-smartlock.

96 Sarah Karlin-Smith, Brent Griffiths, *Gottlieb Confirmed as FDA Chief*, POLITICO (May 9, 2017), www.politico.com/story/2017/05/09/drugs-fda-commmisioner-238172. *See generally* 21st Century Cures Act, Pub. L. 114–255, 103 Stat. 1033 (2016). The Cures Act contains provisions that roll back pharma regulations, and much of its funding is subject to annual appropriations:

> The catch was that while the regulatory rollback that so rankled some Democrats is guaranteed, the research funding is not. It will have to be appropriated each year. Even worse in Democrats' eyes, it will be paid for in part by raiding more than $3 billion from Obamacare's Prevention and Public Health Fund, which pays for anti-smoking campaigns and other preventive health efforts.
>
> Biden and other supporters told concerned Democrats that the Obamacare money would disappear anyway with the repeal of the health law.

Sarah Karlin-Smith et al., *Biden's Farewell Gift: Cancer Moonshot Helps Pass $6.3 Billion Research Bill*, POLITICO (Dec. 7, 2016), www.politico.com/story/2016/12/joe-biden-cancer-moonshot-bill-232342. Congress passed the 21st Century Cures Act in 2016 *to accelerate* medical product discovery, development, and delivery beyond FDAMA *See* Cures Act, Pub. L. No. 114-255 (Dec. 2016) (contains three primary titles that address acceleration of medical product discovery, development, and delivery). This was within a decade from passing the Food and Drug Administration Amendments Act/FDAAA (2007) to instill *more* FDA scrutiny and reliability, See FDAAA, Pub. L. No. 110–85, 121 Stat. 823 (2007), *codified as amended*, 21 U.S.C. §§ 301–399i (2012). *See Chapter 1, supra*, at notes 154–58, 171, and accompanying text (addressing PDUFA and FDAMA, and further enhancement of industry influence through enactment of FDASIA in 2012, P.L. 107–250, and the Cures Act in 2016). For further discussion of FDASIA and the Cures Act in relation to US technology transfer law and policy/TTLP, PDUFA, FDAMA, and the FDAAA, see *Chapter 7, infra*, at notes 46, 215, and accompanying text.

97 *See* Sharkey, *FDA's Dual Role, supra* note 91, at 358. *See supra* note 11, and accompanying text (FDAMA and PDUFA II added efficiency to the FDA's established mission of ensuring safety and efficacy).

98 *See Chapter 4, infra*, at notes 116–83, and accompanying text ("23andMe: The Seminal DTCGHR Testing Services Company").

99 *See* US Food & Drug Admin., DEN160026, Evaluation of Automatic Class III Designation for the 23andMe Personal Genome Service (PGS) Genetic Health Risk Test for Hereditary Thrombophilia, Alpha-1 Antitryspin Deficiency, Alzheimer's Disease, Parkinson's Disease, Gaucher Disease Type 1, Factor XI Deficiency, Celiac Disease, G6PD Deficiency, Hereditary Hemochromatosis and Early-Onset Primary Dystonia: Decision Summary (2017), www.accessdata.fda.gov/cdrh_docs/reviews/DEN160026.pdf. *See also* WATSON, *supra* note 93, at 207; Sharkey, *Dual Role*, *supra* note 91, at 355–57. *See Chapter 4, infra*, at notes 125–29, and accompanying text (FDA 2017 approval of 23andMe's DTCGHR tests provided to consumers through its PGHS, and establishment of a DTCGHR tests category for express approval moving forward).

100 *See* 23andMe, *23andMe for Health Professionals* (visited Oct. 14, 20201), https://medical.23andme.com/. *See also* Carmel Shachar, I Glen Cohen, Nita A. Farahany, Henry T. Greely, *Introduction*, *in* CONSUMER GENETIC TECHNOLOGIES, *supra* note 29, at 1, *citing* GRAND VIEW RESEARCH, PREDICTIVE GENETIC TESTING AND CONSUMER GENETICS MARKET SIZE, SHARE & TRENDS ANALYSIS REPORT BY TEST TYPE (POPULATION SCREENING, SUSCEPTIBILITY), BY APPLICATION, BY SETTING TYPE, AND SEGMENT FORECASTS, 2019–25 (2019). *See generally Chapter 4, infra* (discussing market uptake of DTCGHR testing with consumer and sector information); THE PEW CHARITABLE TRUSTS, REPORT, THE ROLE OF LAB-DEVELOPED TESTS IN THE IN VITRO DIAGNOSTICS MARKET (Oct. 2021), www.pewtrusts.org/-/; FUTURE OF PRIVACY FORUM, BEST PRACTICES FOR CONSUMER GENETIC TESTING SERVICES (July 31, 2018), www.geneticdataprotection.com/wp-content/uploads/2019/05/Future-of-Privacy-Forum-Privacy-Best-Practices-July-2018.pdf. *Cf.* CONGRESSIONAL BUDGET OFFICE/CBO, RESEARCH AND DEVELOPMENT IN THE PHARMACEUTICAL INDUSTRY (2021), www.cbo.gov/publication/57126; US NATIONAL ACADEMIES OF SCIENCE, ENGINEERING, AND MEDICINE/NASEM, PREPARING FOR THE FUTURE PRODUCTS OF BIOTECHNOLOGY (2017), www.nap.edu/catalog/24605/preparing-for-future-products-of-biotechnology.

101 The World Health Organization/WHO declared the spread of COVID-19 a "Public Health Emergency of International Concern" on January 30, 2020, and a pandemic on March 11, 2020. *See* WHO, *WHO Director-General's Opening Remarks at the Media Briefing on COVID-19–11 March 2020* (Mar. 11, 2020), www.who.int/director-general/speeches/detail/who-director-general-s-opening-remarks-at-the-media-briefing-on-covid-19—11-march-2020.

102 *See supra* note 80, and accompanying text (elimination of two regulations for every one added, and direct agency hire of new administrative law judges). A notable chapter in the US Rx drug pricing controversy is the Medicare prescription drug benefit, Medicare Part D, which was enacted as part of the Medicare Modernization Act of 2003 and went into effect on January 1, 2006. *See* Medicare Prescription Drug, Improvement, and Modernization Act of 2003, Pub. L. No. 108–173, § 1860D-4, 117 Stat. 2066, 2081, *codified at* 42 U.S.C. § 1395w-104(e)(6). The Part D enabling legislation bars the federal government from using its purchasing power to negotiate lower drug prices. *See* ABRAMSON, OVERDOSED, supra note 1, at 244–45. However, the Inflation Reduction Act of 2022/IRA, Pub. Law 117-169, which was signed into law by President Biden on Aug. 16, 2022, established precedent (however limited) to trump this "noninterference clause." *See infra* note 104 and accompanying text.

103 *See supra* note 34 (*Virginia Pharmacy*), 67–70 (Price Rule struck down), and accompanying text. *See* HHS, *Blueprint to Lower Drug Prices and Reduce Out-of-Pocket Costs*. 83 FED. REG. 22,692 (May 16, 2018); HHS, *Notice of Proposed Rulemaking, Medicare and*

Medicaid Programs; Regulation to Require Drug Pricing Transparency, 83 FED. REG. 52,789 (Oct. 18, 2018) HHS, *Centers for Medicare and Medicaid Services, Rule: Medicare and Medicaid Programs; Regulation To Require Drug Pricing Transparency*, 84 FED. REG. 20732, 20732–58, 42 CFR 403 (May 10, 2019) (effective date July 9, 2019).

104 *See supra* notes 34, 67–70, and accompanying text (*Virginia Pharmacy* and the Blueprint Price Rule); *supra* notes 45–66 and accompanying test (FDA Guidances disputed in *Washington Legal*). The Biden Administration was able to introduce a precedent for the US government to negotiate and control Rx drug prices through enactment of the Inflation Reduction Act/IRA of 2022, Pub. Law 117–169, which was signed into law on Aug. 16, 2022. *See generally* Juliette Cubanski, Tricia Neuman, Meredith Freed, *Explaining the Prescription Drug Provisions in the Inflation Reduction Act*, KAISER FAMILY FOUNDATION/KFF (Sept. 22, 2022), www.kff.org/medicare/issue-brief/explaining-the-prescription-drug-provisions-in-the-inflation-reduction-act/#:~:text=The%20Inflation%20Reduction%20Act%20limits,and%20no%20deductible%20will%20apply. IRA is a break from the US legacy of no government Rx price controls beyond Veterans Health Administration/VHA drug price negotiations and demanding adherence to the average wholesale price (the average drug price paid by a retailer to buy from a wholesaler) benchmark when determining pricing of prescription drugs for government programs. However, IRA is limited to ten Medicare drugs, and those price controls are slated to be introduced over years, starting with insulin; the cost of insulin for Medicare beneficiaries is capped at $35.00 monthly. *See generally id.*

105 *See* ROSENTHAL, AN AMERICAN SICKNESS, *supra* note 1, at 307.

106 The AMA embraced professional credentialing and hierarchy in its founding, organization, and operations. *See* STARR, SOCIAL TRANSFORMATION, *supra* note 3, at 199–232. *See generally* Note, *The American Medical Association: Power, Purpose, and Politics in Organized Medicine*, 63 Yale L.J. 937 (1954).

107 *See* ABRAMSON, OVERDOSED, *supra* note 1, at 156. Opposition to direct communication between patent medicine manufactures and the public was an organizing force for the AMA. *See supra* notes 3–4, and accompanying text.

108 ABRAMSON, OVERDOSED, *supra* note 1, at 155. Consider Johnson & Johnson's/J&J's marketing to sell Procrit, an anemia-fighting drug, to cancer patients: "You ask twenty-five healthy people if they are tired, and the majority will say yes. And so J&J's Super Bowl advertising was selling a problem as much as a solution. In fact, the company manufactured a medical condition called cancer fatigue." BRAWLEY, BREAKS RANKS, *supra* note 86, at 75. A substantial study published subsequently in the *Journal of the American Medical Association/JAMA* concluded that cancer patients who received Procrit and other erythropoietin-stimulating agents to fight fatigue and avoid transfusions experienced an increased risk of death. *See* Charles Bennett, Samuel Silver, Benjamin Djulbegovic et al., *Venous Thromboembolism and Mortality Associated with Recombinant Erythropoietin and Darbepoetin Administration for the Treatment of Cancer-Associated Anemia.*, 299 JAMA 914–24 (2008), https://jamanetwork.com/journals/jama/article-abstract/181533.

109 *See* ABRAMSON, OVERDOSED, *supra* note 1, at 205. According to a Rand Corporation study published in *The New England Journal of Medicine* in December 2003, "doctors provide appropriate counseling to their patients only 19 percent of the time." *Id. See generally* Elizabeth McGlynn, Steven Asch et al., *The Quality of Health Care Delivered to Adults in the United States*, 384 N. Eng. J. Med. 2635, 2635–264 (2003), www.nejm.org/doi/full/10.1056/nejmsa022615.

110 BRAWLEY, BREAKS RANKS, *supra* note 86, at 85.

111 *See* Sandeep Juahar, Doctored: The Disillusionment of an American Physician 11 (2015). Many physicians are simply overwhelmed and beaten down; they were well before the COVID-19 pandemic. As relayed by Dr. Brawley, "We doctors are paid for services we provide, a variant of 'piecework' that guarantees that we will err on the sale of selling more, sometimes believing that we are helping, sometimes knowing that we are not, and sometimes simply not giving a shit." Brawley, Breaks Ranks, *supra* note 86, at 24.
112 *See* Abramson, Overdosed, *supra* note 1, at 155–56.
113 *Id*. at 107 (illustrating with Cardura, a brand-name blood pressure drug manufactured by Pfizer). *See also*, Goldacre, Bad Pharma, *supra* note 10, at pp. 240–341.
114 *Cf*. Goldacre, Bad Pharma, *supra* note 10, at 247.
115 Abramson, Overdosed, *supra* note 1, at 11 (an experienced American physician and clinical faculty member of Harvard Medical School challenges assumptions that medicine is reliably grounded on a bedrock of sound science, is evidence-based, and is protected dearly by those entrusted to practice it).
116 Genomics is the study of genomes, with focus on the community of genes in them. *See* NHGRI, *Genetics vs. Genomics Fact Sheet* (updated Sept. 7, 2018), www.genome.gov/about-genomics/fact-sheets/Genetics-vs-Genomics. *See Chapter* 2, *supra*, at notes 199–202, and accompanying text.
117 *See supra* notes 11–24, and accompanying text.
118 *See Chapter* 2, *supra*, at notes 32–114, and accompanying text (discussing Operation Warp Speed/OWS in detail).
119 *See Chapter* 5, *infra*, at notes 79–96, and accompanying text (politicization of science and public self-determination contrary to sound evidentiary science-based responsiveness to COVID-19). The World Health Organization/WHO Coronavirus (COVID-19) Dashboard has presented official daily counts of cases and deaths worldwide for some time, and the Centers for Disease Control and Prevention/CDC has done the same domestically throughout the pandemic. *Visit* WHO, WHO Coronavirus (COVID-19) Dashboard (visited May 23, 2020) (522,783,196 cumulative cases, 6,276,210 cumulative deaths), https://covid19.who.int/; CDC, Covid Data Tracker (visited May 23, 2022) (83,145,591 total cases, 999,384 total deaths), https://covid.cdc.gov/covid-data-tracker/#datatracker-home.
120 *See Chapter* 5, *infra*, at notes 79–96, and accompanying text (politicization of science and public self-determination contrary to sound evidentiary science-based responsiveness to COVID-19).
121 *See* Goldacre, Bad Pharma, *supra* note 10, at 247; *supra* note 10, and accompanying text (discussing how US' approach to biopharma marketing is distinguishable among industrialized-economy nations).
122 Rosenthal, An American Sickness, *supra* note 1, at x.
123 *Id*. at 101.
124 Goldacre, Bad Pharma, *supra* note 10, at 59–60. *See id* at 259–66. *See also* Abramson, Overdosed, *supra* note 1, at Part III, 187–240 (addressing disease mongering with examples); Ray Moynihan, Alan Cassels, Selling Sickness: How the World's Biggest Pharmaceutical Companies are Turning Us All into Patients xii, xvii, 178 (2005). As shared by Dr. Goldacre in 2012, "The Reuters Business Insight report is essentially an insider's intelligence assessment. Its chapters cover several of the conditions where huge growth is expected in the sales of 'lifestyle' drugs in the coming years: depression, obesity, smoking cessation, hair loss, skin aging, oral contraception, and sexual dysfunction." Goldacre, Bad Pharma, *supra* note 10, at 247–51. A common biopharma marketing tactic for introducing new medical conditions and stirring demand for

biopharmaceuticals to treat them is to present science data to the public in relative rather than in absolute risk-reduction terms – for example, relaying the percentage of patients *less likely to develop* a given disease by taking a drug, rather than the number of people out of 100 *protected from the disease* by taking the drug. *See* ROSENTHAL, AN AMERICAN SICKNESS, *supra* note 1, at 86; ABRAMSON, OVERDOSED, *supra* note 1, at 257.

125 *See* ROSENTHAL, AN AMERICAN SICKNESS, *supra* note 1, at 81, 83.

126 For example, as explained by authors Ray Moynihan and Alan Cassels, for many people, a raised cholesterol level is an indicator of increased risk of future heart attacks and strokes, but there is medical science uncertainty about what a raised cholesterol level indicates across the general population. *See* MOYNIHAN, CASSELS, SELLING SICKNESS, *supra* note 124, at 1–2. The science is incomplete and, "Contrary to what many might think, cholesterol itself is not a deadly enemy, it is an essential element of the body's makeup, and is vital to life." *Id.* at 1. US medical practice guidelines embrace treatment without evidentiary-science certainty:

> Under recent U.S guidelines, more than 40 million Americans are categorized as having "high blood pressure" and an estimated 90 percent of those over the age of fifty-five will someday have it if they don't already. As with other conditions, the definition of what constitutes high blood pressure is regularly revised, and the notch on the dial that describes "high" seems to creep lower over time.

Id. at 83. *See also infra* note 133 (Dr. Abramson addressing cardiology in the US since the 1980s).

127 *See Chapter 6, infra,* at notes 43–98, and accompanying text ("The Complexities of Personal Genome Medical Decision-Making").

128 *See* ABRAMSON, OVERDOSED, *supra* note 1, at 15–17. *See also supra* note 126 (addressing the medical science uncertainty of "high cholesterol" in the general population); *infra* note 133 (Dr. Abramson addressing cardiology in the US since the 1980s).

129 *See* ABRAMSON, OVERDOSED, *supra* note 1, at 1, 227. According to Dr. Abramson, "The end result is that Activase, a very expensive therapy that can help fewer than 1 out of 25 stroke victims, is getting the majority of our medical attention regarding strokes, while exercise, not smoking, control of blood pressure, and prevention of diabetes are all far more effective ways to decrease the terrible toll of strokes and improve overall health at the same time." *Id.*

130 As summarized by authors Moynihan and Cassels,

> What the campaign propaganda usually leaves out is that the value of these bone density tests is highly controversial, the drugs are often of modest benefit yet carry serious side effects, and whether this is a disease at all is open to question. The loss of bone density is something that occurs in many people as they age; it is a natural, normal process, except in very rare cases.
>
> * * *
>
> There are many ways to try to prevent hip and other fractures, including changes in lifestyle, diet, and household arrangements....
>
> * * *
>
> In 2003 Americans spent $1.7 billion on just one osteoporosis drug to slow the loss of bone density – Fosamax – yet it's highly likely the nation only spent a tiny fraction of that on public awareness campaigns to try to prevent elderly people falling.

MOYNIHAN, CASSELS, SELLING SICKNESS, *supra* note 124, at 140–41.

131 As summarized by Dr. Abramson,

> Social anxiety disorder used to be a rare disease – that is, before public relations firms went into action representing the makers of the new antidepressants. [By 2005], according to an advertisement for Zoloft, this medical condition [was affecting] over 16 million Americans.... This pattern mirrors the study of social anxiety: short-term treatment with an antidepressant medication relieves symptoms but appears to decrease the likelihood of patients making the positive life changes necessary to prevent symptoms from recurring.... To see these "diseases" through this evidence-based lens would turn American medicine on its head. The drug companies have a great deal at stake in persuading doctors and the public to limit their view of social anxiety disorder and depression to the biomedical model of disease.

ABRAMSON, OVERDOSED, *supra* note 1, at 232–34.

132 MOYNIHAN, CASSELS, SELLING SICKNESS, *supra* note 124, at xv. *Id.* at 150 ("For most relatively healthy people at low risk, taking a powerful drug over the long term could do more harm than good."). *See also supra* note 88 (addressing more examples – Avandia and bisphosphonates, which includes Fosamax, Actonel, and Boniva).

133 *See* ABRAMSON, OVERDOSED, *supra* note 1, at 204–05. Cardiology in the US during the last quarter of the twentieth century provides an illustrative example. Clot-busting drugs and angioplasty, introduced in the mid-late 1980s as preventative heart treatments, realized a death rate decline from 3.1 percent per year between 1970 and 1990 to 2.8 percent per year between 1990 and 2000. *Id.* at 220–22. As explained by Dr. Abramson, these medical interventions distracted medicine and the public from the importance of healthy diet and exercise:

> Given the amount or resources committed to educating people about lowering cholesterol compared with helping people eat a healthy diet, one might correctly surmise that drug companies have much more money to spend promoting the "scientific evidence" that supports lowering LDL cholesterol with statins than do the flaxseed, canola, olive, soybean, walnut, and vegetable farmers who would benefit from the widespread promotion of the Mediterranean diet.

ABRAMSON, OVERDOSED, *supra* note 1, at 224–25. *See also supra* note 126 (addressing the medical science uncertainty of proclaimed "high cholesterol" for the general population).

134 *See Chapter* 5, *infra*, at notes 79–96, and accompanying text (politicization of science and public self-determination contrary to sound evidentiary science-based responsiveness to COVID-19).

135 As explained by Dr. Goldacre,

> [T]he evidence shows that ads change behavior, and they change it for the worse .... First, drugs are advertised more when the number of potential patients, rather than current patients, is large. This is an interesting finding, because it means that people are turned into patients, which is good news if they're sick, but bad news if they're not. Second, drugs get advertised more when they are new.... [N]ew drugs are often not a good idea: they're the drugs we know least about.... [T]hey've often been shown only to be better than nothing, rather than the best treatments we already have; and last, even if they're equally effective when compared with older drugs, they will be more expensive.

GOLDACRE, BAD PHARMA, *supra* note 10, at 249.

136 *See generally* STARR, SOCIAL TRANSFORMATION, *supra* note 3. *See* Michael L. Rustad, Thomas H. Koenig, *Reforming Public Interest Tort Law to Redress Public Health Epidemics*, 14 J. HEALTH CARE L. & POL'Y 331, 370 (2011) ("States, rather than Congress, historically have exercised the primary responsibility for protecting the health and welfare of their citizens.").

137 *See generally* STARR, SOCIAL TRANSFORMATION, *supra* note 3. *See Wyeth v. Levine*, 555 US 555, 567, 129 S. Ct. 1187, 1195–96, 173 L. Ed. 2d 51 (2009) ("As it enlarged the FDA's powers to 'protect the public health' and 'assure the safety, effectiveness, and reliability of drugs,' Congress took care to preserve state law. The 1962 amendments added a saving clause, indicating that a provision of state law would only be invalidated upon a 'direct and positive conflict' with the FDCA.") (internal citations omitted); *Hillsborough Cnty., Fla. v. Automated Med. Lab'ys, Inc.*, 471 US 707, 719, 105 S. Ct. 2371, 2378, 85 L. Ed. 2d 714 (1985) ("[T]he regulation of health and safety matters is primarily, and historically, a matter of local concern.").

138 *See supra* note 6 (AMA Council), 9 (Durham-Humphrey Amendment), and accompanying text.

139 *See supra notes* 5–9, and accompanying text.

140 *See Chapter 1, supra*, at notes 133–35, and accompanying text (FDA's regulatory authority and role elevated in response to the thalidomide crisis).

141 *See supra* notes 11–15, and accompanying text (addressing sunset provision in PDUFA and its renewals and change in FDA's mission to include efficiency)

142 *See id.*

143 *See supra* notes 31–70, and accompanying text ("Recognition of Biopharma Marketing as Protected Commercial Speech").

144 *See Chapter 1, supra*, at notes 12–34, and accompanying text ("A Profession Built on the Evidentiary-Science Base of Medicine").

145 *See supra* at notes 45–66, and accompanying text (discussing *Washington Legal*).

146 For discussion of the US opioid crisis, see *Chapter 1, supra*, at notes 172–73, and accompanying text; *Chapter 5, infra*, at notes 375–78, and accompanying text.

147 *See Chapter 1, supra*, at notes 172–73, and accompanying text.

148 *See Chapter 6, infra*, at notes 43–98, and accompanying text ("The Complexities of Personal Genome Medical Decision-Making").

149 *See Chapter 5, infra*, at notes 113–77, and accompanying text ("Today's US Physician-Patient Relationship and the State of Physician Decision-Making"); *Chapter 6, infra*, at notes 43–152, and accompanying text ("The Complexities of Personal Genome Medical Decision-Making" and "US Health Care System and Consumer Genetics and Genomics Market Issues").

150 *See Chapter 1, supra*, at notes 46–52, and accompanying text (discussing the market presence and practices of patent medicine manufacturers as the prelude to the AMA Council and national government regulation for market safety).

151 *See generally Chapter 5, infra* (addressing industry influence on the medical journal establishment/MJE, continuing medical education/CME, and individual physicians after decades of US technology transfer law and policy/TTLP implementation).

4

The Evolution of Consumer Genetic Testing Services from Oncormed, Inc. to 23andMe Holding Co.

The proverbial "What a difference a generation makes" is underscored in US consumer genetic testing. The 1990s was a decade of economic and cultural indulgence in "the DNA mystique" – to the point of intoxication according to many in the medical, public health, and bioethics communities.[1] Wall Street, the media, and the public were captivated by the Human Genome Project/HGP and the science and commercial advancement of biotechnology. Tangible progress was heavily reported in the media and marketed by biopharma. The FDA approved fifty-three new drugs in 1996, many made with biotech and truly innovative.[2] Biopharma and its supporters harnessed this enthusiasm to persuade Congress to overhaul and modernize the FDA with focus on streamlining regulation to promote innovation. Modernization of the agency included establishing a fast track to market for innovative new drugs and biologics to treat life-threatening and seriously debilitating conditions.[3] For innovative new products, the FDA adopted an "approve and watch" approach, and thereby introduced a presumption favoring approval – albeit often with requisite follow-on phase 4 trials.[4] The decade and millennium culminated with the announcement of a preliminary draft map of the human genome of the human genome sequence in 2000.[5]

Yet, people were highly protective of their medical privacy and cautious about predictive genetic testing during the 1990s. An infusion of emerging genetic testing capabilities with varied clinical validity and utility created by the progress of biotech was checked by resonating voices urging caution from a chorus of medical practitioners, bioethicists, and patient advocates.[6] The public embraced the progress of biotech and a surge in information and communication technology/ICT, but with concerns about medical privacy, discrimination, and commercial exploitation. A protective, self-defense mantra inspired enactment of the Health Insurance Portability and Accountability Act/HIPAA of 1996 to protect all medical privacy and myriad state genetics privacy and nondiscrimination legislation.[7]

Implementation of HIPAA and enactment of the Genetic Information and Nondiscrimination Act/GINA in 2008 created a sense of sense of security and control over protected health information/PHI, including *genetic* health information. GINA, though limited to employers with fifteen or more employees and health insurers (non-inclusive of life, long-term care, and other insurances), introduced protections specifically for genetic information.[8] GINA restricts use and prohibits misuse of genetic information by employers and many health insurance providers, and expressly limits their discretion to require genetic testing and to collect genetic information.[9] Enactment of the Affordable Care Act/ACA in 2010 with a prohibition against denying health insurance coverage based on preexisting conditions helped to suppress much residual consumer concern about discrimination from genetic testing:

> The Affordable Care Act (ACA) addressed one glaring limitation of GINA—namely, its lack of protection for people with genetic predispositions for diseases once they show symptoms—by preventing health insurance companies from using pre-existing health conditions to deny coverage. In this way, the ACA is one of the most important legislative responses to concerns about genetic discrimination in healthcare.[10]

This protective federal legislation was complemented by social and cultural change, the culmination of which shifted public perception about predictive genetic health testing from apprehension in the 1990s to consumer demand for access in this millennium.[11] The availability of personal computers and the internet introduced in the 1990s gifted direct access to a universe of information expanding in real time and unprecedented ability to network and communicate with one another:

> Computer networking, open-source software (including Internet protocols), and fast development of digital switching and transmission capacity in the telecommunications networks led to the expansion of the Internet after privatization in the 1990s and to the generalization of its use in all domains of activity.[12]

A global ICT era emerged.[13] Internet access to information about medicine and science was confidence-building for many, and the US public was saturated with it through direct-to-consumer/DTC biopharma marketing on television beginning in 1997.[14] The advent and proliferation of social media shifted cultural norms away from privacy and towards self-discovery and sharing with online "friends" and followers.[15] By the beginning of this century, many thousands of people were mailing their DNA to companies on an ongoing basis, often contributing to public databases later used for genetic genealogy (family tree) services, to plunge into their genetic ancestry – to discover their genetic selves – and then sharing that information with family, friends, and social media followers.[16]

Today's post-HGP internet and social media culture embraces the individual, information gathering, and information sharing.[17] US medicine is much more commercial and consumer driven.[18] A patient participatory health and self-determination movement has considerable momentum.[19] Aggressive DTC biopharma marketing is a norm.[20] Human genome science has burgeoned beyond the clinical application competency of most in the medical profession – certainly the majority of primary care and family medicine physicians whose expansive scope of practice subjects them to its full impact.[21]

Investors and millions of consumers have embraced the health-related genetic testing services offered by 23andMe, Inc. and other companies that interact one-on-one with customers, and offer them opportunities to self-discover on a molecular DNA level with the involvement of medical providers wholly optional. These companies promote medical autonomy and individual control over one's health and health care.[22] The vision of personal genome-enabled, consumer-centric medicine is materializing and, increasingly, the public is embracing it – as made evident by consumer demand for 23andMe's genetic health risk/GHR services and the company's commercial success.[23] Anne Wojcicki, CEO and co-founder of 23andMe, Inc. shares this vision, and she and 23andMe, the seminal DTC genetic health risk/DTCGHR testing company, are on a mission to realize it as soon as possible:

> I think that there's a huge opportunity for the consumer to have a voice. People want to engage. People want to learn about themselves. They want to be healthier. They want to know more [about] what they can do. I feel like I now have this responsibility to tell you, "I told you you're high risk for Alzheimer's, you're high risk for Parkinson's, you're high risk for a stroke. I told you really meaningful information about yourself. Now I need to help you execute on your life." I think that's where, when I think about the potential of raising this capital, ... we want to expand, and I think that there's a real opportunity to think about an affordable consumer-centric health care system.[24]

The following discussion profiles the evolution of US social and cultural responsiveness to, commercialization of, and regulation of genomics-era consumer genetic health testing services. The discussion spans from the predictive genetic testing for BRCA alleles (genetic variations) marketed directly to consumers by three small companies in 1996 to the personal genome testing services offered by 23andMe and other companies today.

ERA OF FDA RESTRAINT

A personal genome testing milestone occurred in 1996: Three small companies broadly marketed genetic testing directly to the public to identify genetic susceptibilities to breast and ovarian cancers.[25] Oncormed, a Bethesda, Maryland company, announced in January 1996 that it was selling a testing service to identify the presence of genetic variations (alleles) of a gene called BRCA1 ("breast cancer 1") linked to breast and ovarian cancers through data collected from targeted populations.[26] Although the company directly marketed its genetic screening service to the public, it required a physician to order the service and for the physician to comply with its consumer intake and use criteria. Oncormed had developed these criteria, which included a thoughtful informed consent protocol, by establishing an independent (not tied to an organization that receives federal funding for research) institutional review board/IRB – a committee of credentialed, accomplished experts, and the primary mechanism relied upon by institutions that receive federal funding to protect participants in research on human subjects.[27] Within a few months, Genetics & IVF Institute ("IVF") of Fairfax, Virginia, offered a variation of the test to any Jewish woman (the alleles in hand at the time were identified primarily through research on an Ashkenazi Jewish population in upper-state New York) willing to pay $295 and simply referred by a physician.[28] In July 1996, Oncormed expanded its genetic screening service to include alleles of a second gene, BRCA2 ("breast cancer 2"), for between $400 and $1,200, depending on the number of alleles screened for.[29] Then, in fall 1996, a third company, Myriad Genetic Laboratories, Inc. ("Myriad"), a Salt Lake City company, began DTC marketing to sell a combined test for several alleles in the two genes for $2,400.[30]

These companies did not submit their genetic tests to the FDA for review and approval before entering the US market. In fact, they declared that they did not have to.[31] The FDA countered by proclaiming "that it has authority, by law, to regulate such tests, but the agency has elected as a matter of enforcement discretion to not exercise that authority, in part because the number of such tests is estimated to exceed the agency's current review capacity."[32] However, a US Task Force on Genetic Testing ("Task Force") acknowledged in 1997 that "developers of genetic tests who do not rely on federal funds are under no legal obligation to submit protocols to the proposed [new national regulating body for genetic health testing] and have not always obtained IRB approval for validation protocols of tests they plan to market as laboratory services."[33]

These early DTC BRCA genetic health risk screening companies tested the reach of established US law and policy. The limits of existing law, policy, and FDA enforcement were drawn – albeit with ambiguity given the FDA's proclamation of authority combined with agency inaction. Provided companies sold their genetic tests as a clinical service they performed in-house, deemed "home brew" testing with lab-developed tests/LDTs, the laboratories that performed them would be subject only to standard clinical laboratory regulations under the Clinical Laboratory Improvement Act/CLIA.[34]

CLIA requires laboratory inspection and certification, and imposes test-specific proficiency rate requirements.[35] To achieve and maintain reliable accuracy and proficiency, CLIA also imposes administrative and procedural requirements, such as sufficiently credentialed personnel, facility and equipment requirements, batch testing, and verification procedures. The objective of CLIA is to ensure that a test to diagnose, prevent, or treat disease will be *highly accurate*; the base for the proficiency scale is eighty percent though, depending on the test, may well exceed ninety percent.[36] In sum, CLIA requires that a test for X will be reliably accurate Y percent of the time, and with administrative and facility assurances. CLIA does not evaluate the clinical utility or efficacy of a test for X, nor the clinical safety of using a test for X beyond complexity assessment and risk classification – contrary to FDA medical device regulations, which impose clinical safety and efficacy standards.[37] In other words, CLIA may be satisfied by testing with requisite accuracy and proficiency even if the test has little clinical value and potentially muddles clinical care. The expectation is that *physicians* and other learned and licensed medical providers, such as certified genetic counselors/CGCs, will make the clinical use evaluation.

The advent of commercial BRCA predictive genetic health testing with DTC marketing triggered the notion of cash-strapped biotech companies exploiting vulnerable consumers and attention, criticism, and concern. A then ongoing HGP science policy debate, which began when the idea of HGP was originally discussed at science conferences in the mid-1980s, intensified with an element of "I told you so."[38] Many in the "hard science" (the natural life sciences) community questioned HGP into the 1990s, including some renowned generals in the biotech revolution such as Dr. Leroy Hood and Nobel Laureate David Baltimore. They "debated the wisdom of beginning an Apollo moon shot-style program of biomedicine to chart the largely unknown new world of human genes, a scientific adventure that could take a decade or more to complete, consume $3 billion and absorb the lives of hundreds of researchers."[39] Similarly, many in the medical profession and public health stakeholders argued that, rather than HGP, funding and research focus should be on immediate health care needs, such as the HIV/AIDS epidemic, or at least on specific genes already determined to be associated with serious health conditions.[40]

Patient advocacy groups such as the National Breast Cancer Coalition/NBCC and the delivery of care disciplines of medicine, public health, and bioethics reacted to the ethical, legal, and social implications of commercial DTC predictive genetic health testing with time-is-of-the-essence passion.[41] With HGP ongoing and overwhelming, they had much support from those in the hard science community highly appreciative of (humbled by) the complexity of genomics and cautious about prematurely commercializing and undermining their work. Given the advancement of genomics scientifically and commercially, BRCA genetic testing marketed DTC made very real the possibility of a deluge of predictive genetic testing in disparate stages of clinical development and with varied predictive value and utility for individual patients.[42]

Small, entrepreneurial biotech companies had amassed into a meaningful commercial sector by the 1990s. By 1997, "In the roughly 25 years since the development of recombinant DNA technologies in research laboratories, over 2,000 firms [had] been founded in the United States alone to explore and take advantage of this new field."[43] These biotech companies were competing aggressively for and burning through capital – driven to overcome daunting obstacles to realize science research and business objectives, to produce innovation prone for commercial application, and to achieve financial gain.[44] Despite the research and development/R&D cost and risk of failure, biotech companies were alluring to investors given the pharmaceutical industry's legacy of success and the potential impact of biotech on human health and beyond. Their commodity was science innovation with the promise of replacing existing, profitable treatments in a distinguishably profitable market and conquering seriously debilitating and life-threatening diseases. Selling predictive genetic testing of suspect clinical value to women – approximately half of the human population – anxious about their susceptibilities to breast and ovarian cancers created a tangible scenario for commercial exploitation, medical confusion, and waste.[45]

The NBCC, its sister organizations, and myriad patient advocacy and protection organizations mobilized.[46] Members of the medical profession and other health care and medical science professionals joined them and warned of the dangers of prematurely mainstreaming clinical science that was just coming into being, scientifically unreliable, difficult if not impossible to interpret on an individual patient level in the context of full clinical practice, and grossly susceptible to misinterpretation – by providers and patients alike.[47] Luminaries in the field of genetics and genomics, including Dr. Francis Collins who was head of HGP, cautioned about the current unreliability of predictive genetic testing clinical capabilities: "The benefits of pre symptomatic testing to determine susceptibility to common cancers such as those of the breast, ovary, colon, and prostate are potentially substantial. Nonetheless, it is critical that we create safeguards to ensure that the benefits of testing exceed the risks."[48]

Internet access to information and the proliferation of DTC biopharma and health care marketing that emerged in the 1990s "informed" patients and elevated their self-confidence in health care decision-making. The nation's practicing physicians were not well versed in the advances in human genome science, let alone genetic counseling.[49] Data compilation was ongoing, clinically dynamic, and overwhelming – as it is today on a vastly more expansive scale and at an exponentially accelerated pace given biobanks (organized collections of DNA profiles and related information) and next-generation sequencing/NGS technologies.[50] In the auspices of HGP and the genomic revolution, early BRCA testing could be the first of an avalanche of genetic and proteomic (genes make proteins, and proteins impact genetic expression) tests for susceptibilities to diseases based on actuarial calculations derived from novel, complex, and changing clinical data, derived from populations far narrower than the general population. Patients would readily comprehend tangible diseases and health conditions associated with predictive genetic tests, especially ones they knew and feared. How would the average patient without science or medical education and training possibly comprehend an incoming blizzard of genetic health tests backed by varying amounts of changing data and the accompanying statistics, probabilities, and possibilities? Most likely, they would oversimplify and equate a positive genetic test with a predictive disease diagnosis, and over rely on a negative test result.[51]

Suspicion of commercial biotech sellers of predictive genetic health testing services was complemented, if not surpassed, by mistrust of the potential discriminatory uses of resulting genetic information in a nation without a universal health care system, with a commerce-driven and employer-based system, which had become the global epicenter for biotech and genomic revolutions.[52] Especially prior to the enactment of national laws to protect medical privacy, to prohibit genetic discrimination, and to prevent denial of health insurance coverage based upon pre-existing conditions, consumers needed to be forewarned of the potential uses of predictive genetic testing results against them.[53] Would individuals in pursuit of embracing genomics to attain a heightened level of control over their health destinies inadvertently subject themselves, and maybe even their biological relatives, to the risks of discrimination from employers, insurers, schools, and beyond?[54] How would this technology actually improve their health, and at what cost to their mental health and lives? At what cost to a financially strapped health care system already not accessible to tens of millions of people?

The US did not enact comprehensive national medical privacy legislation until HIPAA in 1996, and HIPAA's Privacy Rule (standards and requirements for protected health information/PHI) and Security Rule (requisite administrative measures, including for electronic protected health information/e-PHI) were subject to incremental implementation and enforcement, revisions, and updates into 2013.[55] The nation did not realize comprehensive genetic nondiscrimination legislation to protect employees and insureds until the passage of GINA in 2008 and protection from health insurers discriminating based upon preexisting conditions until passage of the Affordable Care Act/ACA in 2010.[56] However, during the interim from the early DTC commercialization of BRCA testing to enactment and implementation of these laws, state legislatures took action.[57] Professor George Annas and his colleagues at the Boston University School of Public Health developed The Genetics Privacy Act in 1995 as a model for legislation, which inspired many national and state legislative initiatives.[58] By early 1999, forty-four states had enacted genetics legislation, much directed to employers and health insurers, and typically addressing genetic privacy, genetic discrimination, or some combination of the two.[59] In 2000, the Department of Health and Human Services/HHS, Secretary's Advisory Committee on Genetic Testing/SACGT concluded that existing US regulatory oversight of genetic testing was not sufficient to assure their clinical use accuracy and effectiveness.[60] SACGT made thoughtful, well-substantiated recommendations by applying long-established clinical standards to the complexities of genetic testing in human health.[61] Unfortunately, SACGT's report was completed and issued at the very end of the Clinton Administration, the Bush Administration took office, and SACGT's recommendations drifted into a government purgatory.

Biopharma lobbied intensely against proposed legislation and regulation that singled out genetic health information from other medical information, which it referred to as "genetic exceptionalism."[62] Although not always successful in each of the fifty states, biopharma's efforts proved successful on the national level – at least until the enactment of GINA in 2008, which was signed into law by a politically conservative president (though moderate by today's standards).[63] The biotech and pharma sectors emphasized that the most useful genetic information typically is family history, genetics factor into all that is health status, and genetic information is medical information. The industry position was that genetic information is destined to permeate throughout health care, including patients' responses to prescription drugs and therapies, and states should wait for enactment and implementation of HIPAA – comprehensive national medical privacy protection. After HIPAA was enacted, the argument shifted to states should wait for its full implementation.

The biotech sector, in collaboration with the pharma sector, monitored and countered state legislative initiatives through its national trade organization, the Biotechnology Industry Organization/BIO. BIO is now the Biotechnology *Innovation* Organization, a name change reflective of biopharma integration and the fact that biotech is the shared forefront of therapeutic medicinal product R&D.[64] BIO had a network of state affiliates covering the nation domestically, and global reach through EuropaBio, its European counterpart. At BIO's founding in 1993, the Pharmaceutical Research and Manufacturers of America/PhRMA, the US traditional pharmaceutical company ("Big Pharma") trade organization, contributed considerably to the creation of BIO – a small, entrepreneurial, innovative company counterpart with a persuasive lobbying voice. PhRMA and BIO collaboration proved very persuasive in Washington, D.C. Nevertheless, states enacted genetic-specific laws and, when HIPAA and GINA were enacted, these national laws did not include provisions to preempt nonconflicting state protections.[65]

After the trilogy of small companies introduced DTC BRCA testing to the US market in 1996, Myriad's competitors dropped out of the market. Myriad, however, amassed intellectual property rights to BRCA genetic tests and worked with the National Institutes of Health/NIH and others to accumulate the general population data needed to develop clinically sound correlations between BRCA alleles and cancers.[66] In 2013, actress, filmmaker, human rights activist, and popular culture icon Angelina Jolie announced that she had undergone a preventative double mastectomy based on Myriad BRCA test results and her family history, and she shared her personal story in an opinion-editorial published in *The New York Times*.[67] Ample general population data had been gathered about the BRCA1 and BRCA2 alleles, which accounted for a range of factors, most notably family history, and enabled development of the positive predictive value/PPV – the probability that a person who receives a positive test result will actually get the disease – of the Myriad test for sound clinical use.[68] Still, as is typical for common diseases, it was predictive genetic health testing that produced probabilities subject to variation among individuals depending on their family histories and other variables – not certainties.[69] Ms. Jolie, with the results from *clinically sound* genetic testing in hand and resources to access the input of preeminent medical experts, was confronted with probabilities, possibilities, and complicated *choices*:

> Jolie, by nearly universal agreement, made the right choice for her. She tested positive for the breast-cancer-related BRCA1 gene, putting the probability that she would develop the disease at a terrifying 87%; after her surgery, her doctors put that number at just 5%. But a lot of experts worry that we may overread the lessons. Genetic screening is a young science, and while we may have detected genes

linked to a host of ills — Alzheimer's disease, prostate cancer, rheumatoid arthritis, diabetes, heart disease — we often do a terrible job of calculating our resulting risks. Just over one-tenth of 1% of all women carry the same BRCA mutation Jolie has, and yet doctors expect a stampede of women requesting the test. In the U.S., 36% of women who test positive opt for preventive mastectomy, but some doctors argue that regular MRIs and other screening tests may be sufficient to detect the disease, and that less radical procedures, like lumpectomies, may be sufficient to treat it if it does occur.[70]

Angelina Jolie had to decide what to do with the genetic health information in her own life, to her own body, and the decision she made coupled with her decision to share it publicly proved inspirational. Her experience boosted the public perception of and trust in predictive genetic health testing categorically – a phenomenon coined "the Angelina effect." The Angelina effect triggered "a cultural and medical earthquake."[71]

That same year (2013), the US Supreme Court decided a chronic patent challenge to Myriad's BRCA tests.[72] The Court took on and answered a question raised in BRCA patent litigation and by gene patenting in general: "Who should benefit from discoveries pertaining to nature or the human body?"[73] The Court held that patent protection does not extend to the isolation of natural forms of DNA, and thereby dramatically reduced the patent protection available for genetic tests – whether used in research or in the delivery of care.[74] As observed by James Watson, "Essentially, the Court was saying: identifying and extracting an important gene from the human genome is valuable, but that doesn't earn you the right to patent the sequence.... Within weeks of the ruling, several diagnostics firms launched their own BRCA1 testing services at much more affordable rates."[75] The Court had invalidated method (process) patents relied upon for the marketing of a diagnostic kit to assist in prescribing medications the year before, holding unanimously that claims directed to adjusting the dosage of a drug based on the measurement of properties naturally produced by patients, such as protein indicators, are not patentable subject matter.[76]

These Supreme Court decisions were a two-edged scythe to a thicket of gene patents that had impeded both research and clinical access to scientifically sound genetic testing for personal genome medicine. The US now is being overwhelmed with genetic health testing of varied clinical soundness and health importance, and potentially at the expense of industry investment to produce more clinically sound and health care significant predictive personal genome tests.[77] The delivery of care impact of these decisions was made evident in DTC television marketing of immunotherapies and personal genome medicine through genetics, genomics, and proteomics by national cancer centers within a few years.[78] The Court's decisions have enabled mainstream clinical uptake of presently developed (clinically sound) personal genome testing by the medical profession and increased clinical access to multiplex (bundles of) health testing capabilities for diagnosis, treatment, and prevention.

ERA OF FDA CONFRONTATION, DELIBERATION, AND NEGOTIATION

Social culture changed immensely during the turn of the millennium, most notably with ICT progress and the advent and evolution of social media from America Online's release of its Instant Messenger – "You've Got Mail" – in 1997, to the launches of Facebook in 2004 and Twitter in 2006. As the US entered the twenty-first century, scientists completed the draft HGP sequence in 2003.[79] The public had become familiar with DNA conceptually and colloquially – "It's in my DNA" – through extensive news and entertainment media coverage, and DNA sequencing technology surged forward.[80] Yet, presumably driven by uncertainty about its authority under US law, the FDA pretty much maintained the ambiguous regulatory stance – a proclamation of regulatory authority paired with inaction – on home brew predictive genetic health testing it took in response to the BRCA DTC testing introduced to the market in 1996. It was as though the agency was just observing – watching and waiting to be challenged enough to respond more definitively.

That challenge emerged in November 2007. Two companies announced their market introductions of wholly DTC personal genome tests for genetic health risk factors based on single nucleotide polymorphisms/SNPs – variations in the six billion single letters (three billion base pairs) in the chain of adenine/A, cytosine/C, guanine/G, and thymine/T nucleic bases that, collectively, are the human genome sequence.[81] Both companies had interacted one-on-one with consumers to provide genetic ancestry testing and DNA genealogy (the DNA version of the family tree) for years. Now they were adding medically relevant information without FDA approval of their tests.[82] Neither marketed their genetic health testing services as "diagnostic" and, to the contrary, both emphasized the diagnostic, predictive, and other clinical limitations of their tests.[83] Both encouraged, though did not require, consultations with physicians and genetic counselors for any of their medically relevant services.[84] This approach and consumer out-of-pocket payment kept the information outside of customer medical records (arguably outside the scope of HIPAA) unless they or their health care providers chose to add it to them.[85] More fundamentally, the founders and CEOs of both companies believed passionately that providing individuals with direct, affordable access to their personal genome information was a means to empower them to take more control over their health destinies.[86]

One of the companies, deCODE Genetics, had been amassing a biobank from the people of Iceland with global attention and publishing gene-association discoveries in esteemed science journals for over a decade.[87] deCODE was a serious 23andMe rival in 2007.[88] However, deCODE went into bankruptcy in 2009 during Iceland's 2008–2010 economic crash. The company then traversed a series of corporate transactions, which culminated in Amgen purchasing it in 2012.[89] deCODE's genetic testing service, deCODEme, was discontinued at the outset of 2013, and the company stopped selling personal genome health testing services altogether.[90]

The other company was California-based 23andMe, Inc., which was founded in 2006 – just the year prior to its 2007 launch of DTCGHR testing services.[91] 23andMe was birthed from Silicon Valley talent, vision, intensity, regulatory-blind drive, connections, and wealth – with Google LLC and Genentech, Inc. among its original investors.[92] The company embodies the internet-accessible information epicenter and individual search enablement essence (customers are given the means to search for their own genetic information) of Google and the "me" psyche of Facebook, Instagram, and Twitter prevalent in social media culture, and deliberately so.[93] CEO Anne Wojcicki cofounded the company to offer individuals direct internet access to their personal genomes through 23andMe's Personal Genome Health Service/PGHS unimpeded by physician permissions, and affordable enough to be accessible out of pocket and avoid medical insurance payers and medical record inclusion.[94] Ms. Wojcicki's vision, at the time she co-founded 23andMe and now, is a full transformation of health care: Individuals who choose to be enlightened about their personal genomes are able to do so affordably, and to utilize that information to take more control of their health and preventive care.[95] It is Ms. Wojcicki's conviction that, with their personal genome profiles in hand, individuals have the means to make more informed and autonomous health care decisions – with the assistance of, rather than through directives from, health care professionals.[96] She also has faith that physicians and other health care providers, pushed by patient demands and expectations, will become more learned about current human genome science and more inclined to fully utilize the potential of personal genome medicine in prescribing and overall patient clinical care.[97]

23andMe collects saliva directly from customers through its kits, which are available for purchase from the company's online store and Amazon.[98] 23andMe runs samples through a DNA microarray made by Illumina, Inc. Illumina scans for specific nucleotide bases (As, Cs, Gs, and Ts) associated with ancestry, genealogy, inherited traits, and SNPs associated with health conditions, and then releases results directly to customers via its secure website.[99] Like Facebook and other social media providers, customers contribute to the company's PGS (which encompasses ancestry) and PGHS by the very act of registering their kits and using them. Consumer consumption builds 23andMe's DNA core data bank of genetic profiles (DNA sequences and related phenotype and other information). Both 23andMe and Facebook sell user data to third parties.[100] Customer use with data contributions thereby creates science and business opportunities for 23andMe and raises its PGHS appeal to new subscribers by improving and expanding the health risk testing portfolio it offers.[101] To maximize these returns, 23andMe asks customers to participate in research to advance overall understanding of the human genome, with assurance that they may withdraw from future – distinguished from past and ongoing – research at any point.[102] This methodology enabled 23andMe to amass more than a million DNA profiles and related health information by 2015 and over 5 million globally by 2018,[103] to enter into collaborations with esteemed research institutions and companies,[104] and to itself become a laboratory bench-to-market biopharmaceutical R&D company.[105]

23andMe originally offered individuals the opportunity to search their DNA for genetic characteristics associated with ancestry, personal traits such as ear wax consistency, some serious medical conditions such as Parkinson's and Alzheimer's, and groups of genetic variants associated with elevated risks of common complex disorders, such as multiple sclerosis, heart disease, and some cancers.[106] Competitors quickly followed,[107] but 23andMe distinguished itself in its early years through Sillicon Valley-style marketing creativity:

> [The company hosted] celebrity "spit parties" attracting rock stars, models and Hollywood A-listers—from Peter Gabriel at Davos to Harvey Weinstein and Rupert Murdoch in Manhattan. A blimp brandishing the 23andMe logo could be seen flying over the Bay Area, and the firm won *Time* magazine's Invention of the Year distinction in 2008 (infuriating their Icelandic [deCODE] competitors).[108]

The November 2007 market introduction of DTCGHR testing services triggered concern from scientists, bioethicists, and other health care professionals reminiscent of the DTC BRCA predictive genetic testing introduced by small, entrepreneurial biotech companies in 1996.[109] In January 2008, *The New England Journal of Medicine/NEJM* published an editorial that expressed some of these strongest sentiments, which was co-authored by its editor-in-chief, a professor in the Departments of Epidemiology and Nutrition at the Harvard School of Public Health who also was a statistical consultant to *NEJM*, and the director of the National Office of Public Health Genomics at the Centers for Disease Control and Prevention/CDC.[110] In the editorial, entitled "Letting the Genome out of the Bottle – Will We Get Our Wish?," the authors expressed serious clinical (delivery of care) concerns about "recreational genetics":

> [S]such premature attempts at popularizing genetic testing seem to neglect key aspects of the established multifaceted evaluation of genetic tests for clinical applications.
>
> * * *
>
> More information is needed on the clinical utility of this information in the light of existing disease-specific opportunities for prevention or early detection and the potential value that genomic profiles can add to that of simpler tools, such as the family health history. Finally, given the risk of commercial exploitation, if patients are determined to proceed, perhaps because they are simply curious, are genetic hobbyists, or are "early adopters" of new technology, it would make sense to encourage them to enroll in formal scientific studies.
>
> ***
>
> Until the genome can be put to useful work, the children of the man [who was gifted personal genome health risk testing] would have been better off spending their money on a gym membership or a personal trainer so that their father could follow a diet and exercise regimen that we know will decrease his risk of heart disease and diabetes.[111]

Nevertheless, people wanted the personal genome information enough for 23andMe to amass a database of more than 650,000 DNA profiles within six years of its founding, most accompanied by customer-volunteered personal health information provided in response to online questionnaires.[112] As 23andMe kits gained popularity, the FDA just observed – until November 2013, the year of the Angelina effect.[113] When 23andMe launched a television campaign to net yet more PGHS consumers and their data, it received a cease-and-desist letter from the FDA that enjoined it from reporting any health-related genetic findings to customers. The FDA was pushed enough to act on its 1996–1997 proclamation of regulatory authority – some seventeen years later. The FDA illustrated the danger of DTCGHR testing with a hypothetical situation in which a woman receives a false-positive BRCA1 test result that confuses her physician and results in unnecessary surgery. As observed by James Watson, "Curiously, however, the FDA did not block customers from downloading their raw genomic data or prevent them from turning around and uploading it to other websites offering interpretation services, such as Prometheus [a party in the 2012 Supreme Court case]."[114] 23andMe continued to provide ancestry reports and raw data to clients, and delved – a collaborative effort among the company's scientists, medical experts, product designers, and legal advisors – into a nearly two-year regulatory interface with the FDA over PGS testing related to health.[115]

23ANDME: THE SEMINAL DIRECT-TO-CONSUMER, GENETIC-HEALTH-RISK/DTCGHR TESTING SERVICES COMPANY

While 23andMe and the FDA were engaged in regulatory interface (negotiations) over PGS health testing, the company crossed another milestone. In February 2015, the FDA approved 23andMe's DTCGHR *carrier* screening test (tests used most often by those who are considering becoming pregnant) for Bloom Syndrome – a rare genetic disorder associated with, among other characteristics, increased susceptibility to leukemia, lymphoma, gastrointestinal tract tumors, and other cancers.[116] 23andMe became the manufacturer of "the first and only genetic service available directly to individuals in the United States that includes reports that meet FDA requirements for being scientifically and clinically valid."[117] Moreover, 23andMe satisfied the FDA's demand for assurance of consumer comprehension.[118] The FDA was more generous in its review than the company initially anticipated. The FDA's Center for Devices and Radiological Health/CDRH utilizes a I-to-III classification system based upon complexity and risks to patients and providers.[119] Within that system, the FDA approved 23andMe's clinically sound carrier screening test as a Class II (moderate risk) device with "special controls" even though the company had submitted for Class III (high risk) approval.[120]

Beyond a milestone for the company, 23andMe created and pushed open a gate in the FDA's medical device regulatory framework to market DTCGHR testing services. "Device" regulations encompass a sweeping expanse of myriad products, ranging from tongue suppressors to the latest imaging technologies and intricate robotic surgery systems.[121] To maximize its limited resources and to minimize delays, the CDRH, in addition to its risk classification for the intake of applications, relies heavily on a product matching system that heavily utilizes review and approval precedents.[122] Sponsors match their new products as closely as possible with those that the agency has already reviewed and approved to lessen regulatory invasiveness, which enables the agency to allocate limited regulatory resources and concentrate them commensurate with risk. Generally, the more exact a new device is matched to one the FDA has reviewed and approved previously, especially if the approved device has acquired clinical familiarity and a history of sound safety, efficacy, and utility, the more the CDRH is willing to rely on its previous analysis. The more exact the match, the quicker new devices pass through the FDA and onto the market.[123] Moreover, the FDA advances matching *categorically* and, provided requirements for the category are satisfied, exempts new devices from review altogether, including its premarket notification/PMN requirement after a sponsor has satisfied that once, and clears them for market use.[124]

Under these standard CDRH operating procedures, 23andMe was well positioned for follow-on applications for its already developed PGHS and GHR test portfolio, and the company took full advantage of the opportunity. In April 2017, the FDA approved 23andMe's DTCGHR tests for ten diseases, including Alzheimer's and Parkinson's – unquestionably seriously debilitating and life-threatening diseases.[125] Moreover, based upon these approvals, the FDA announced a "genetic health risk assessment system devices" *category* eligible for exemption from premarket review and even PMN once a manufacturer has submitted a PMN for their first DTCGHR test(s).[126] The agency's stated purpose was to allow "similar tests to enter the market as quickly as possible and in the least burdensome way, after a one-time FDA review."[127] However, the agency did subject the GHR tests category to special controls aligned with those imposed on 23andMe – notably, establishing sufficient consumer comprehension and a "limiting statement" disclaiming clinical use without physician or other learned and licensed medical provider involvement.[128] The FDA also expressly limited the exemption category to tests intended to provide genetic health risk information to consumers but not to "determine a person's overall risk of developing a disease or condition" given environmental, lifestyle, and other influencing factors – including other genetic influences.[129]

23andMe achieved two additional major regulatory milestones for both the company and DTCGHR testing in 2018. First, in March, the company received the FDA's first authorization for a DTCGHR genetic test for a cancer risk.[130] This authorization allowed 23andMe to provide customers with the results of its DTCGHR test for three alleles found on the BRCA1 and BRCA2 genes associated with increased risks for breast, ovarian, and prostate cancers – thereby positioning the company to take full advantage of the still resonating Angelina effect.[131]

Second, in October 2018, 23andMe accomplished a milestone in the field of pharmacogenetics – the study of the link between an individual's genetic profile and their responsiveness and other reactions to prescription drugs and biologics.[132] Specifically, the FDA approved a 23andMe pharmacogenetic test to detect thirty-three variants for multiple genes associated with a patient's ability to metabolize drugs.[133] However, the Agency did impose six special controls, including a labeling requirement – a warning statement that consumers should not use the test's results to stop or change any medication they are taking.[134] In a press release about its approval, the FDA acknowledged that "consumers are increasingly interested in genetic information to help make decisions about their health care," but emphasized that the test "does not determine whether a medication is appropriate for a patient, does not provide medical advice and does not diagnose any health conditions."[135] The agency also cautioned both consumers and providers that "Any medical decisions should be made only after discussing the results with a licensed health care provider and results have been confirmed using *clinical* pharmacogenetic testing."[136] The FDA released a safety communication warning to patients and physicians to reinforce the same:

> Consumers are increasingly embracing direct-to-consumer genetic testing to better understand their ancestry or individual risk for developing diseases. Health care providers are using genetic testing to help inform decisions about their patients' health, health risks and more.
>
> * * *
>
> [W]e are warning consumers about many such genetic tests being marketed directly to consumers or offered through health care providers that claim to predict how a patient will respond to specific medications. Tests that make such claims that have not been evaluated by the FDA and are not supported by prescribing recommendations in the FDA-approved drug label, may not be supported by scientific and clinical evidence, and may not be accurate.[137]

23andMe complemented these regulatory milestones with a substantial corporate one. In July 2018, the company announced a data-sharing deal with GlaxoSmithKline/GSK – separate from an ongoing 23-GSK research collaboration – for four years, with a GSK year five option.[138] For an investment of $300 million, GSK obtained exclusive rights to mine 23andMe's massive biobank, derived from its then five million customers globally, for drug target discovery.[139] "GSK will receive the same kind of data pharma partners have generally received (summary level statistics that 23andMe scientists gather from analyses on de-identified, aggregate customer information), though it will have four years of exclusive rights to run analyses to discover new drug targets."[140] In comparison, back in 2015 when 23andMe's biobank held data derived from approximately 650,000 customers, the company entered its inaugural data-sharing deal with Genentech, Inc. for $10 million and a conditional $50 million more if its data proved useful for developing Parkinson's treatments,[141] followed by another data-sharing deal with Pfizer.[142] In addition to these disclosed deals, 23andMe is reported to have entered several others.[143] This 2018 GSK deal is distinguishable beyond the amount of the financial investment, its scope, and GSK's exclusivity in that it elevated 23andMe's opportunity to test the extent to which its data could improve drug R&D beyond the traditional medical research model.[144]

In January 2019, 23andMe accomplished yet another regulatory milestone predicated on its 2018 BRCA DTCGHR testing approval. The FDA approved a 23andMe 510(k) application (satisfaction of the FDA's "substantial equivalence" standard) for a second 23andMe DTCGHR cancer test.[145] This DTCGHR cancer test is for the two most common genetic variants that influence a hereditary colorectal cancer syndrome called MUTYH-associated polyposis/MAP.[146] The company relayed the news in the context of its overall personal genome medicine mission:

> This new clearance is part of 23andMe's ongoing efforts to work with the FDA to offer additional Genetic Health Risk reports as part of its Health + Ancestry Service. "We are committed to giving people affordable and direct access to important health information that can impact their lives," said Anne Wojcicki, 23andMe CEO and co-founder.[147]

The FDA's intense collaborative interaction with 23andMe over several years and the resulting approvals of the company's DTCGHR tests are consistent with:

- Non-clinical designation for the 2017 approval and the agency's established methodology for regulating medical devices post FDAMA and PDUFA II;[148]
- The Trump Administration's mandate to roll back regulations;[149]
- Commercial free speech and corporate "civil rights" jurisprudence;[150]
- The human genome science research need for DNA profiles and related health information (biobanking) to translate the human genome into medical meaning and to realize human health benefits through population genetics and genomics;[151]
- The patient participatory health and self-determination (personal genome autonomy) movement, and consumer demand for personal genome information as recognized by the FDA;[152]
- Our ICT and social media culture, in which consumers may wish to share genome insights about themselves with networks of followers, who are sharing reinforcers and potential DTCGHR testing customers;[153] and
- 23andMe's mission to advance consumer-centric medicine through personal genome autonomy, and to transform health care through its PGHS and R&D.[154]

The FDA exercised its discretion under established law in its role as market gatekeeper for medical devices, non-clinical distinguished from clinical, post FDAMA with the PDUFA II mandate to do so efficiently.[155] The agency's decisions are consistent with the nation's law-policy legacy of deference to and reliance on the medical profession in *matters of clinical care*.[156] Professor Sharkey has told her version of the 23andMe story with a focus on the company's interactions with the FDA, from which she has interpreted a change in the FDA's role from reviewer and regulator of the products under its watch to "dual role as safety and health information regulator."[157] My interpretation is that the FDA decidedly did not assume this role in any meaningful way other than by mandating "consumer comprehension" communication and warnings to emphasize when DTCGHR tests *do not meet established science and evidence-based clinical standards.* Rather, the FDA decided to allow DTCGHR testing to go forward as *nonclinical* testing to meet consumer demand, which the agency acknowledged.[158] The FDA left the impact of DTCGHR testing on individual patient clinical care and the practice of medicine to be sorted out by the medical profession. Given consumer demand for DTGHR testing and patient self-determination in medicine, the FDA did increase the burden on the medical profession to adhere to and protect science and evidence-based clinical practice, and that burden will swell with the progress of human genome science.[159]

Consistent with the FDA's overall approvals of diagnostic medical devices, the agency required 23andMe (1) to provide data to establish safety and efficacy under the Food, Drug, and Cosmetic Act/FDCA deemed sufficient *for nonclinical use,* and (2) to satisfy laboratory standards for analytic validity and proficiency – the capacity of a test and the facility performing it to detect the presence of targeted alleles with the high rates of accuracy and reliability required under CLIA.[160] Consistent with CDRH policies, procedures, and methodology, the FDA authorized 23andMe's DTCGHR tests in 2017 with special controls to define and limit approved use – *to exclude clinical use* without the involvement of a licensed medical professional.[161] Through implementation of these special controls, the FDA denounced non-approved uses by emphasizing that the GHR reports produced by 23andMe are not for medical diagnosis, clinical decision making, or prescription medication use decision making, which are the domain of learned and licensed medical professionals.[162] The FDA's decision to introduce a category for similar DTCGHR tests and its approval of 23andMe's 510(k) application for its DTC BRCA testing were consistent with the FDA's matching methodology, policies, and standard practices for medical devices overall – agency policies, practices, and norms established for some time.[163]

23andMe was the sponsor of *all* DTCGHR tests authorized by the FDA as of December 20, 2019, but the accomplishment of major regulatory milestones often draws capital, as it did for 23andMe, and the infusion of capital in commerce inspires competition.[164] It was reported in 2017 that:

> [A] growing crop of genetic-analysis companies are now competing for 23andMe's customers. They include firms offering inexpensive, targeted medical sequencing (Color Genomics in Burlingame, California); ancestry testing (Ancestry DNA, based in Salt Lake City, Utah); whole-genome sequencing, either on its own (Veritas, based in Danvers, Massachusetts) or in combination with medical testing (Craig Venter's Human Longevity in San Diego, California) or with apps for interpreting genomic data (Helix of San Carlos, California).[165]

By 2018, "Equity firms [were] pouring fortunes into these [personal genome service] companies, not just because of the testing kits they sell but the personal information they collect, which can be shared and monetized."[166]

Under the CDRH's matching and precedent-driven methodology, 23andMe's regulatory milestones have created an express lane to market for DTCGHR tests and similar services provided by others. In fact, Ancestry.com LLC, the global leader in family-tree genetic testing (genetic genealogy) with 3.6 million paying subscribers and more than eighteen million people in its DNA network at the time,[167] launched AncestryHealth on October 15, 2019, to offer DTCGHR testing services in direct competition with 23andMe.[168] However, whether due to the COVID-19 pandemic or just an interim stagnation of consumer interest in DTCGHR testing, 2020 proved a difficult year for companies providing DTCGHR testing services. "At the start of [2020], both Ancestry and 23andMe cut approximately 100 jobs, and smaller firms shuttered among sluggish sales."[169] In January 2021, Ancestry.com LLC announced that it was discontinuing AncestryHealth to focus on its core family-tree business.[170]

Nevertheless, 23andMe emerged in 2021 stronger than ever. In February of 2021, 23andMe announced plans to become a publicly traded company.[171] Ms. Wojcicki shared the news in an email to existing customers:

> When we started 23andMe we had dreams of being able to transform the world of healthcare, research and therapeutic discovery by empowering individuals with genetic information. Fifteen years later, we are getting closer and closer to that goal.
>
> Today, I am excited to share that we are taking steps to become a public company....
>
> Our mission is to help people access, understand and benefit from the human genome. We have made incredible progress in both empowering our customers with direct access and helping them to understand their personal genetic information. And we believe the future of our company is in helping customers like you, and the world, benefit from a new, more personalized and proactive approach to healthcare. It will take additional capital and investment to accelerate this innovation and disruption.[172]

True to its word, 23andMe, Inc. merged with VG Acquisition Corp. in a $3.5 billion deal to become 23andMe Holding Co., which was listed on the NASDAQ stock exchange on June 17, 2021.[173] The stock soared twenty-two percent on the day of closing and listing.[174]

Moreover, on October 22, 2021, 23andMe announced its acquisition of Lemonaid Health, a national telemedicine and digital pharmacy company, to overcome physician skepticism and uncertainty about its PGHS reports. The transaction was completed on November 1, 2021.[175] In 2022, 23andMe announced expansion of its business plan to embrace and prioritize becoming a provider of DTC personal genome *clinical care* through a genomic health service business line, which the company shared with its PGS customers in an October 2022 email:

> Together, we're setting off on a mission to change the future of healthcare for you. We want to transform the primary care experience and make personalized healthcare, powered by genetic and non-genetic data, a reality.
>
> In addition to the personalized genetic insights 23andMe offers about your health, we also want to introduce you to Lemonaid Health's telehealth services.

> You can connect online with their licensed medical team and pharmacy to get affordable, accessible healthcare when and where you need it.[176]

Arguably, based upon investor behavior and a decline in the number of truly visionary (not "me-too") startup companies over the last several decades, overall, the US has slipped into an era of relative economic idea stagnation:

> [T]the people with the most experience starting businesses look around at their investment opportunities and see many more start-ups that resemble Theranos [the fraudulent biotech blood testing company] than resemble Amazon, let alone the behemoths of the old economy. And the dearth of corporate investment also means that the steady climb of the stock market has boosted the wealth of a rentier class — basically, already-rich investors getting richer off dividends — rather than reflecting surging prosperity in general.[177]

Recognizing the transformation of US medicine to personal genome medicine and capitalizing on it successfully as accomplished by 23andMe resembles Amazon, not Theranos.[178] Many me-too DTC personal genome testing and service companies have emerged, with many more to follow into the foreseeable future absent a chronic downturn in the US economy or substantial changes in US regulation—whether by government, by the medical profession, or by a combination of the two. Again, consumer DNA testing surged in 2017, and continued to do so until interrupted by the COVID-19 pandemic in 2020.[179] 23andMe's subsequent corporate and regulatory milestones and financial success coupled with the progress of human genome science and its headway into the delivery of clinical care,[180] the US patient-driven participatory health movement encouraged by DTC biopharma marketing,[181] and our social media culture in which DNA is familiar and individuals want to discover their genetic selves[182] suggest a DTC personal genome testing sector poised for enormous growth.[183]

MEDICAL PROFESSION CONCERNS – THEN AND NOW

Many of the medical profession's concerns about DTCGHR testing articulated in *The New England Journal of Medicine's* 2008 editorial echoed concerns raised about the DTC BRCA testing introduced in 1996.[184] Primary among those are:

- Muddling patient care by distracting and confusing patients with personal genome test results from tests not clinically sound—meaning not developed from a base of general population data and without defined, evidentiary science-based clinical validity and utility;
- The risk of misinterpretation given that predictive personal genome test results typically are complicated to interpret by learned and licensed medical professionals, and even more difficult for patients to comprehend—especially when generated by tests not clinically sound; and
- The risk of commercial exploitation of people concerned about their health.[185]

Incidentally, overall, the medical profession embraced Myriad's BRCA testing for responsible clinical use once it was developed to be clinically sound (before the Angelina effect), though many balked at its cost.[186]

The progress of human genome science between the US market availability of Oncormed's DTC BRCA tests in 1996 and 23andMe's DTCGHR tests in 2017 was astonishing.[187] While that accomplishment gifted immense potential to improve human health, it did not reduced the innate complexity of clinical genetics, the significance of environmental influences and other variables when interpreting an individual's personal genome test results, or the enormous range of influence specific genetic variations typically have on any individual's health.[188] The progress of genomics has not reduced the layperson's difficulty comprehending predictive genetic testing results, nor the typical physician's difficulty understanding and explaining them to patients.[189] The progress of genomics has, however, introduced a universe of identified alleles, and that universe is expanding in real time – meaning exponentially more to potentially test for. Patient-consumers deluging the practice of medicine with portfolios of results from DTC personal genome testing services, however "informed" they may be that their DTCGHR tests are distinguishable from clinically sound genetic tests, is becoming much more tangible. The commercial availability of DTC personal genome testing not developed for clinical use and without learned and licensed medical professional involvement has become a reality.

Medical profession concerns about direct patient access to a multitude of personal genome tests (genetic, genomic, and proteomic tests) and services not developed for responsible clinical use – most notably, the potential detriment to individual patient care and the practice of medicine – are much more valid today than they were in 1996 and 2008.[190] The FDA demonstrated restraint after proclaiming to have regulatory authority when BRCA testing was marketed directly to consumers in 1996, but the agency did so with good medicine (science and evidence-based clinical practice) assurance from the *consumer use prerequisite of physician involvement*. In contrast, more than a quarter-century of genomic science progress later, with a robust genomic revolution and prolific discovery ongoing in real time, the FDA approved and then created an express lane to market for DTCGHR testing not clinically sound, with any medical professional involvement *wholly consumer optional*.

NOTES

1 *See generally* DOROTHY NELKIN, M. SUSAN LINDEE, THE DNA MYSTIQUE: THE GENE AS A CULTURAL ICON (1995).

2 *See* Michael J. Malinowski, Grant G. Gautreaux, *Drug Development – Stuck in a State of Puberty? Regulatory Reform of Human Clinical Research to Raise Responsiveness to the Reality of Human Variability*, 56 ST. LOUIS U. L.J. 363, 394 (2012). In contrast, and despite enormous industry and government investment, the US experienced new drug disappointment during the first decade of the new millennium:

> [N]ew drug approvals fell to a twenty-five year low in 2007, just eighteen, followed by a slight bump to twenty-four in 2008 and twenty-six in 2009. In 2010, Pfizer Inc., the world's largest research-based pharmaceutical company, did not produce a single new drug approval. In comparison, new drug approvals peaked in 1996 when the FDA approved fifty-three.

Id. at 393 (internal citations omitted). This disappointment was due largely to the multinational pharmaceutical sector's difficult transition from reliance on traditional biochemistry to biotech and genomics-driven research and development/R&D. *See generally id. See also* Michael J. Malinowski, Grant G. Gautreaux, *All That is Gold Does Not Glitter in Human Clinical Research: A Law-Policy Proposal to Brighten the Global "Gold Standard" for Drug Research and Development*, 45 CORNELL J. INT'L LAW 185 (2012).

3 *See* Food and Drug Administration Modernization Act/FDAMA, Pub. L. No. 105–115, 111 Stat. 2296 (1997) (codified primarily in sections throughout 21 U.S.C., including §§ 352, 355, 356, 356(b), 360aaa–1–3, 379r).

4 The same FDAMA provision (and mission change through the companion PDUFA II legislation, as noted in *Chapter* 3, *supra*, at note 12, and accompanying text) that codified the fast track, 506B, introduced a presumption in favor of market approval with enforcement authority under 21 U.S.C. § 356b (2006) to impose phase 4 clinical trial obligations (follow-on trials after market approval). *See* FDA, REPORTS ON THE STATUS OF POSTMARKETING STUDIES – IMPLEMENTATION OF SECTION 130 OF THE FOOD AND DRUG ADMINISTRATION MODERNIZATION ACT OF 1997 1 (2006), www.fda.gov/regulatory-information/search-fda-guidance-documents/reports-status-postmarketing-study-commitments-implementation-section-130-food-and-drug. The purpose of phase 4 studies is to probe lingering questions and to perfect clinical use. *See* PETER BARTON HUTT ET AL., FOOD AND DRUG LAW, at 734–38 (3d ed. 2007).

5 On the DNA level, we are 99.9 percent the same. *See* US Department of Energy Office of Science, Office of Biological and Environmental Research, *About the Human Genome Project* (modified Mar. 26, 2019) ("The current consensus predicts about 20,500 genes, but this number has fluctuated a great deal since the project began."), https://web.ornl.gov/sci/techresources/Human_Genome/project/index.shtml. The draft map of the human genome sequence released in 2003 was compiled by sequencing and comparing the genomes of several individuals to find our species' DNA common denominator. *See generally* 291 SCIENCE 1145 (Feb. 16, 2001) (issue entitled "The Human Genome"); 409 NATURE 745 (Feb. 15, 2001) (issue entitled "Information about the Human Genome Project" and dedicated to the release of a *preliminary draft* map of the human genome sequence). A preliminary draft of the human genome sequence was announced in 2000 at a White House ceremony featuring James Watson who was the chief architect of HGP, Francis Collins who headed the US government HGP effort, and John Craig Venter who headed a commercial rival in a race to complete the human genome sequence. Venter used a "shotgun sequencing" method for speed, which was questioned and rejected by many scientists as not accurate enough for sequencing a genome as complicated as the human genome. *See* Philip Green, *Against a Whole-Genome Shotgun*, 7 GENOME RES. 410–17 (1997), https://genome.cshlp.org/content/7/5/410.full. During the millennial transition year ceremony, President Clinton proclaimed "Today we are learning the language in which God created life," and *The New York Times* reported "In an achievement that represents a pinnacle of human self-knowledge, two rival groups of scientists said today that they had deciphered the hereditary script, the set of instructions that defines the human organism." Nicholas Wade, *Genetic Code of Human Life Is Cracked by Scientists*, N.Y. TIMES (June 27, 2000), https://archive.nytimes.com/www.nytimes.com/library/national/science/062700sci-genome.html. A *completed draft* map of the human genome sequence

was released in April 2003, with media attention on the potential to improve medicine and human health. *See, e.g.*, Byjon Heggie, *Genomics: A Revolution in Health Care? Drugs Affect People Differently and We're Increasingly Understanding Why. For Many of Us, It's Down to Our Genes*, NAT'L GEO. (Feb. 20, 2019), www.nationalgeographic .com/science/article/partner-content-genomics-health-care. *See also* WALTER ISAACSON, THE CODE BREAKER 37–41 (2021) (*ch.* 5 *The Human Genome*). The project, launched in 1990 with a target timeline of fifteen years and a budget of $3 billion, was completed in 2003 at a cost of $2.7 billion (FY 1991). *See* NHGRI, *Fact Sheet, Human Genome Project* (Aug. 24, 2022), www.genome.gov/about-genomics/educational-resources/fact-sheets/ human-genome-project; NHGRI, *Human Genome Project FAQ* (undated), www.genome .gov/sites/default/files/genome-old/pages/Education/Smithsonian_Exhibition/Human_ Genome_Project_FAQ.pdf. Subsequently, researchers corrected errors and filled gaps in the sequence. The NHGRI released the *first complete sequence* of the human genome on March 31, 2022. *See* Prabarna Ganguly, *Researchers Generate the First Complete, Gapless Sequence of a Human Genome* (Mar. 31, 2022), www.genome.gov/news/news-release/ researchers-generate-the-first-complete-gapless-sequence-of-a-human-genome.

6 *See infra* notes 41–48, and accompanying text.

7 *See* Pub. L. 104–91 (1996); *infra* note 55, and accompanying text (addressing the HIPAA Privacy Rule and Security Rule); William F. Mulholland, II, Ami S. Jaeger, *Genetic Privacy and Discrimination: A Survey of State Legislation*, 39 JURIMETRICS 317–26 (1999). *See also* Michael J. Malinowski, *Doctors, Patients, and Pills – A System Popping under Too Much Physician Discretion? A Law-Policy Prescription to Make Drug Approval More Meaningful in the Delivery of Health Care*, 33 CARDOZO L. REV. 1085, 1087–88 (2012). HIPAA essentially made one's protected health information/PHI their personal property through recognition of rights. *See* US Dep. of Health and Human Services/ HHS, *Summary of the HIPAA Security Rule* (last reviewed July 26, 2013), www.hhs.gov/ hipaa/for-professionals/security/laws-regulations/index.html; HHS, *Health Information Privacy* (links to resources), www.hhs.gov/hipaa/index.html. *See also* HHS *Your Rights under HIPAA* (last reviewed Nov. 2, 2020), www.hhs.gov/hipaa/for-individuals/guidance-materials-for-consumers/index.html; HHS, *Health Information Privacy, Your Medical Records* (last reviewed Nov. 2, 2020), www.hhs.gov/hipaa/for-individuals/medical-records/ index.html (visited Mar. 3, 2021).

8 *See generally* GINA, Pub. L. No. 110–233, 122 Stat. 881 (2008) (codified as amended in scattered sections of 29 U.S.C. and 42 U.S.C.).

9 *See id.* GINA restricts employers from using genetic information in employment decision making (notably hiring, firing, promotion, and compensation), and limits collecting employees' genetic information. *See* 42 U.S.C. §§ 1395ss, 2000ff-1, 2 (2012). Health insurers and plan managers are restricted in using genetic information in base coverage and premium determinations, and from requiring people to undergo genetic testing – though they may be given the option with the possibility of realizing premiums below market rates based on results. *See* 42 U.S.C. § 1395ss(s)(2)(F)(ii). *See also* Yaniv Heled, Liza Vertinsky, *Genetic Paparazzi: Beyond Genetic Privacy*, 82 OHIO ST. L.J., 409, 441–42 (2021).

10 Heled, Vertinsky, *Paparazzi*, *supra* note 9, at 409, 441–42. *See* Patient Protection and Affordable Care Act ("Affordable Care Act/ACA"), Pub. L. No. 111–148, 124 Stat. 119 (2010) (codified as amended in scattered sections of the U.S.C.).

11 23andMe amassed a database of more than 650,000 DNA profiles with related health information within six years of its founding in 2006, more than a million by 2015, and over five million globally by 2018. *See infra* notes 103, 112, and accompanying text.

12 MANUEL CASTELLS, THE RISE OF THE NETWORK SOCIETY xxv (2nd ed. 2009).

13 *See generally id.*
14 *See* ELISABETH ROSENTHAL, AN AMERICAN SICKNESS: HOW HEALTHCARE BECAME BIG BUSINESS AND HOW YOU CAN TAKE IT BACK 100 (2017) ("drug advertising is now a constant in our lives"); JOHN ABRAMSON, OVERDOSED AMERICA: THE BROKEN PROMISE OF AMERICAN MEDICINE 150–52 (2005) (addressing FDA relaxation of rules in sync with the passage of FDAMA and PDUFA II in 1997).
15 *See generally* Matthew Jones, *The Complete History of Social Media: A Timeline of the Invention of Online Networking* (June 16, 2015), https://historycooperative.org/the-history-of-social-media/. *Cf.* DAVID KIRKPATRICK, THE FACEBOOK EFFECT: THE INSIDE STORY OF THE COMPANY THAT IS CONNECTING (2011).
16 Ancestry, founded in 1983 as a publisher of genealogical data in the form of print books and magazines, established Ancestry.com LLC, an online, subscription-based DNA ancestry service, in 1996. *See* Anna Nowogrodzki, *Ancestry Moves Further into Consumer Genetics*, MIT TECH. REV. (July 16, 2015), www.technologyreview.com/2015/07/16/110196/ancestry-moves-further-into-consumer-genetics/. On August 6, 2020, The Blackstone Group announced plans to acquire the company in a deal valued at $4.7 billion. *See* Ortenca Aliaj, Kaye Wiggins, *Blackstone Snaps Up Ancestry.com in $4.7bn Deal*, FIN. TIMES (Aug. 5, 2020), www.ft.com/content/b84613e4-8751-45e6-94ff-a014de6e4c0d. 23andMe, founded in 2006, partnered with Ancestry.Com in 2008 and amassed more than 650,000 DNA profiles within six years. *See* Ancestry.Com, *Press Release, 23andMe and Ancestry.com Partner to Extend Access to Genetic Ancestry Expertise* (Sept. 9, 2008), www.ancestry.com/corporate/newsroom/press-releases/23andme-and-ancestrycom-partner-extend-access-genetic-ancestry-expertise; Erika Check Hayden, *The Rise and Fall and Rise Again of 23andMe*, 550 NATURE 174–77 (Oct. 11, 2017), www.nature.com/news/the-rise-and-fall-and-rise-again-of-23andme-1.22801. Consumers volunteered personal health information in response to 23andMe's online questionnaires and enabled 23andMe to quickly amass an impressive biobank of DNA profiles and related information. *See* JAMES D. WATSON, DNA: THE STORY OF THE GENETIC REVOLUTION 210 (2nd ed. 2017) (with Andrew Berry, Kevin Davies) (updated commemoration of the fiftieth anniversary of the discovery of the double helix).
17 *See generally* Jones, *History of Social Media*, *supra* note 15; KIRKPATRICK, FACEBOOK EFFECT, *supra* note 15.
18 *See generally* ABRAMSON, OVERDOSED, *supra* note 14; OTIS WEBB BRAWLEY, HOW WE DO HARM: A DOCTOR BREAKS RANKS ABOUT BEING SICK IN AMERICA (2011); ROSENTHAL, AN AMERICAN SICKNESS, *supra* note 14. *See* SANDEEP JUAHAR, DOCTORED: THE DISILLUSIONMENT OF AN AMERICAN PHYSICIAN 11 (2015).
19 *See* Catherine M. Sharkey, *Direct-to-Consumer Genetic Testing: The FDA's Dual Role As Safety and Health Information Regulator*, 68 DEPAUL L. REV. 343, 346 (2019); Anna B. Laakmann, *The New Genomic Semicommons*, 5 UC IRVINE L. REV. 1001, 1033 (2015). *See also* CASTELLS, NETWORK SOCIETY, *supra* note 12, at xxv. Bioethics groundwork for the movement was established during the 1970s and 1980s. *See generally* JAY KATZ: THE SILENT WORLD OF DOCTOR AND PATIENT (1984) (pushback against twentieth century physician paternalism in medicine); George J. Annas, *The Patient Rights Advocate: Redefining the Doctor-Patient Relationship in the Hospital Context*, 27 VAND. L. REV. 243 (1974). Consumer demand for 23andMe's DTC genetic testing services for health-related information from its founding in 2006 is addressed in note 11, *supra*, and *infra* at notes 103, 112, and in the accompanying text.
20 *See generally Chapter 3, supra.*

21 *See Chapter 6, infra*, at notes 43–98, and accompanying text ("The Complexities of Personal Genome Medical Decision-Making").

22 In 2021, in a $3.5 billion transaction, 23andMe, Inc. merged with VG Acquisition Corp. – Sir Richard Branson's special-purpose acquisition company. *See* Kristen V. Brown, *23andMe Goes Public as $3.5 Billion Company With Branson Aid*, BLOOMBERG (Feb. 4, 2021), www.bloomberg.com/news/articles/2021-02-04/23andme-to-go-public-as-3-5-billion-company-via-branson-merger. The combined company was renamed 23andMe Holding Co. and became publicly traded on NASDAQ on June 17, 2021. *See* Natalie Clarkson, *23andMe and Virgin Group's VG Acquisition Corp. Successfully Close Business Combination*, VIRGIN (June 16, 2021) (Virgin journalist reporting), www.virgin.com/about-virgin/virgin-group/news/23andme-and-virgin-groups-vg-acquisition-corp-successfully-close-business. The stock soared twenty-two percent on the day of closing and listing. *See* Reporter, *23andMe Stock Soars 22 Percent on Closing of Merger With VG Acquisition Corp.*, GENOMEWEB (June 17, 2021) (anonymous staff reporter), www.genomeweb.com/business-news/23andme-stock-soars-22-percent-closing-merger-vg-acquisition-corp#.Ypp3kKjMK3A. Throughout this chapter, "23andMe" will be used to refer to both 23andMe, Inc. and 23andMe Holding Co. unless distinction is necessary. 23andMe modified and expanded its business plan aspirations to prioritize becoming a clinical (primary care and beyond) genomic services company. *See infra* notes 24, 175–176, and accompanying text.

23 *See infra* notes 116–83, and accompanying text ("23andMe: The Seminal Direct-to-Consumer, Genetic Health Risk/DTCGHR Testing Services Company").

24 Recode, *Full Transcript: 23andMe CEO Anne Wojcicki Answers Genetics and Privacy Questions on Too Embarrased to Ask* (Sept. 29, 2017), www.vox.com/2017/9/29/16385320/transcript-23andme-ceo-anne-wojcicki-genetics-privacy-health-questions-too-embarrassed-to-ask. *See also NBC Nightly News with Lester Holt, High-Tech Heritage*, (NBC television broadcast July 14, 2018) (interview with Anne Wojcicki, in which she explains, "We're big believers in that the more I can educate you earlier in life, the more you're actually going to have information to try to prevent the condition."). On June 17, 2021, through a merger, 23andMe was renamed 23andMe Holding Co. ("23andMe Holding") and became publicly traded on NASDAQ. *See* Clarkson, *Successfully Close, supra* note 22. *See also Prologue, supra*, at notes 41–42, and accompanying text; *infra* notes 173–74, and accompanying text. On November 1, 2021, 23andMe Holding acquired Lemonaid Health, a national telemedicine and digital pharmacy company, to overcome physician skepticism and uncertainty about its Personal Genome Health Service/PGHS. *See* 23andMe Holding Co., *Current Report (Form 8-K)* (Nov. 1, 2021), https://investors.23andme.com/static-files/8a43d3a5-2529-422c-937b-db40a7eeb875; *Prologue, supra*, at note 42, and accompanying text; *infra* notes 175–76, and accompanying text. In 2022, 23andMe Holding modified its business plan aspirations to envelope and prioritize a comprehensive spectrum of clinical health care services. On August 9, 2022, the company declared "expan[sion] beyond its core consumer genetic testing into a new business line called its genomic health service." Neil Versel, *23andMe Pins Future on 'Genomic Health Service,' Therapeutic Development*, GENOMEWEB (Aug. 9, 2022), www.genomeweb.com/business-news/23andme-pins-future-genomic-health-service-therapeutic-development#.Y1MLmnbMK3A. 23andMe Holding's mission is "to transform the primary care experience and make personalized healthcare, powered by genetic and non-genetic data, a reality." *Prologue, supra*, at note 42, and accompanying text (quoting 23andMe communication with its PGHS consumers on Oct. 12, 2022). *See also* 23andMe, *A Letter from Anne: Making Personalized Healthcare a Reality* (October 22, 2021), https://you.23andme.com/p/28ba69b793a2c6ff/article/a-letter-from-anne-making-personalized-healthcare-a-reality-3ebee7dfb59a/.

25 *See* Michael J. Malinowski, Robin J.R. Blatt, *Commercialization of Genetic Testing Services: The FDA, Market Forces, and Biological Tarot Cards*, 71 TULANE L. REV. 1212–13 (1997). For an account of the evolution of genetic testing as a discipline and the genetic counseling profession throughout the twentieth century, see generally ALEXANDRA MINNA STERN, TELLING GENES: THE STORY OF GENETIC COUNSELING IN AMERICA (2012). *See also* Ricki Lewis, *A Brief History of Genetic Testing: What the First Generation of Tests Can Tell Us About the Latest*, SCI. PROGRESS: GENETICS (May 5, 2008), https://scienceprogress.org/2008/05/a-brief-history-of-genetic-testing/.

26 *See* Malinowski, Blatt, *Tarot Cards*, *supra* note 25, at 1213. BRCA1, located on chromosome 17, was found to code for a protein with a tumor-suppressor function. *See* D. Shattuck-Eidens et al., *A Collaborative Study of 80 Mutations in the BRCA1 Breast and Ovarian Cancer Susceptibility Gene*, 273 JAMA 535, 535–41 (1995) (stating that over 100 distinct mutations of BRCA1 have been identified); Yoshio Miki et al., *A Strong Candidate for the Breast and Ovarian Susceptibility Gene BRCA1*, 266 SCIENCE 66, 66–71 (1994); Stephen C. Rubin et al., *Clinical and Pathological Features of Ovarian Cancer in Women with Germ-Line Mutations of BRCA1*, 335 NEW ENG. J. MED. 1413, 1413 (1996) (reporting that this form of inherited cancer is more responsive to clinical treatment).

27 Federal funding in research triggers the Common Rule – the US' law-policy base for the protection of participants in research involving humans. *See* 45 CFR part 46. *See also* HHS, *Federal Policy for the Protection of Human Subjects* ("Common Rule") (last reviewed Mar. 18, 2016), www.hhs.gov/ohrp/regulations-and-policy/regulations/common-rule/index.html.

28 *See* Malinowski, Blatt, *Biological Tarot*, *supra* note 25, at 1255. *See also* Rick Weiss, *Tests' Availability Tangles Ethical and Genetic Codes*, WASH. POST (May 26, 1996), at A2, www.washingtonpost.com/archive/politics/1996/05/26/tests-availability-tangles-ethical-and-genetic-codes/c0698d86-5bca-4aa7-9d9d-57bee556fc7d/. The reliable data available *at the time* estimated one BRCA1 mutation, 185delAG, to occur in one percent of people of Ashkenazi Jewish ancestry. *See* J.P. Struewing et al., *The Carrier Frequency of the BRCA1 185delAG Mutation is Approximately 1 Percent in Ashkenazi Jewish Individuals*, 11 NATURE GEN. 198, 198–200 (1995). However, general population data attributed only five to ten percent of all incidents of breast cancer to inherited genes. *See generally The Scientific Questions*, 18 PERSP. GEN. COUNSELING 4 (1996) (estimating breast cancer incidents attributable to germline mutations). The *Washington Post* reported that one of the first clients of a physician associated with IVF was his wife, who underwent the test at the age of thirty-eight, tested positive, and had both of her breasts removed. *See* Meredith Wadman, *Women Need Not Apply*, WASH. POST (May 5, 1996), at C3. *See also* David S. Hilzenrath, *Md. Firm's Gene Test to Intensify Bioethics Debate*, WASH. POST (July 25, 1996), at D14 (describing a service to detect predisposition to breast and ovarian cancer), www.washingtonpost.com/archive/business/1996/07/25/md-firms-gene-test-to-intensify-bioethics-debate/4e961fbe-ecbe-4943-b6d7-eef099a331cb/. For information about BRCA2 at the time testing was marketed in 1996, see Richard Saltus, *2d Cancer Gene Cited in 1 of 100 Ashkenazi Jewish Women*, BOST. GL. (Oct. 2, 1996), at A18.

29 *See* Ridgely Ochs, *New Test Offered for Cancer Gene*, NEWSDAY (July 24, 1996), at A7 ("Oncormed … plans next week to introduce a new service that will raise the stakes in one of biotechnology's biggest ethical debates …."); Hilzenrath, *Debate*, *supra* note 28, at D14 (describing service to detect predisposition to breast and ovarian cancers).

30 *See* Sean Taytigian et al., *The Complete BRCA2 Gene and Mutations in Chromosome 13q-Linked Kindreds*, 12 NATURE GEN. 333, 333–37 (1996) (publishing full sequence of BRCA2 breast cancer gene by Myriad Genetics). Also, to advance compilation of the data

needed to raise the clinical value of its BRCA testing, Myriad worked with the National Institutes of Health/NIH and established a registry at the Dana-Farber Cancer Institute (Boston, MA) in 1996. *See* Richard Saltus, *Gene Test for Cancer Risk is Offered*, Bost. Gl. (Oct. 25, 1996), at A1. *See infra* note 66, and accompanying text (addressing Myriad collaborations to gather data for its BRCA testing).

31 *See* Malinowski, Blatt, *Biological Tarot*, *supra* note 25, at 1214–15; *Oncormed BRCA1 Testing Service Commercialization Enters Second Phase Through New IRB Protocol*, 39 Blue Sheet 6, 6–7 (1996).

32 Secretary's Advisory Committee on Genetic Testing/SACGT, Enhancing the Oversight of Genetic Tests: Recommendations of the SACGT 10 (July 2000), https://osp.od.nih.gov/sagct_document_archi/enhancing-the-oversight-of-genetic-tests-recommendations-of-the-sacgt/.

33 Proposed Recommendations of the Task Force on Genetic Testing, Meeting Notice, 62 Fed. Reg. 4539, 4544 (1997). The Task Force was assembled in 1994 to comprehensively evaluate genetic testing in the US and to make recommendations to the Secretary of HHS. *See id.* In 1998, the Clinton Administration established the SACGT, which issued a report and recommendations in 2000. *See generally* SACGT, Recommendations, *supra* note 32. *Visit* NIH, Office of Science Policy/OSP, *Secretary's Advisory Committee on Genetic Testing Archives* (Apr. 26, 2017), https://osp.od.nih.gov/scientific-sharing/secretarys-advisory-committee-on-genetic-testing-archives/.

34 These laboratory regulations, collectively referred to as CLIA, encompass the Clinical Laboratory Improvement Act of 1967 ("CLIA67"), 42 U.S.C. § 263(a), and the Clinical Laboratory Improvement Amendments of 1988 ("CLIA88"), Pub. L. No. 100–578, 102 Stat. 2903, *codified as amended*, 42 U.S.C. § 263a (2000). *See* Michael J. Malinowski, Handbook on Biotechnology Law, Business, and Policy 141–43, 171–82 (2016). *See also* Michael J. Malinowski, *Separating Predictive Genetic Testing from Snake Oil: Regulation, Liabilities, and Lost Opportunities*, 41 Jurimetircs 23, 23–52 (2001) (live and published symposium); Malinowski, Blatt, *Biological Tarot*, *supra* note 25, at 1229–33.

35 *Visit* HHS, Clinical Laboratory Improvement Amendments/CLIA, *Guidance for the Clinical Laboratory Improvement Amendments (CLIA) program* (issued Sept. 15, 2020) (providing links to resources), www.hhs.gov/guidance/document/clinical-laboratory-improvement-amendments-clia.

36 *Visit* Centers for Disease Control and Prevention/CDC, *Proficiency Testing Programs* (modified Jan. 15, 2021), www.cms.gov/Regulations-and-Guidance/Legislation/CLIA/Proficiency_Testing_Providers.

37 Though heavily supplemented, the core statutory authority that empowers the FDA's Center for Devices and Radiological Health/CDRH and imposes regulatory responsibility, consists of the 1976 Medical Device Amendments to the FDCA, 21 U.S.C. § 301, Pub. L. 94–295, 90 Stat. 539; the Medical Devices Act of 1990, Pub. L. 101–629; the Medical Device Amendments of 1992, Pub. L. 102–300; and FDAMA, Pub. L. No. 105–115, 111 Stat. 2296 (1997) (codified primarily in sections throughout 21 U.S.C., including §§ 352, 355, 356, 356(b), 360aaa–1–3, 379r). *See generally* FDA, *Overview of Device Regulation*, www.fda.gov/MedicalDevices/DeviceRegulationandGuidance/Overview/ (current as of Sept. 4, 2020). *Visit* CDRH, official site, www.fda.gov/about-fda/fda-organization/center-devices-and-radiological-health.

38 *See Chapter 2*, *supra*, at notes 207–21, and accompanying text (the 1980s and 1990s science community debate over HGP centered on prioritizing immediate clinical care returns from incremental, focused gene research already underway versus undertaking a blitzkrieg approach to genetic research for an "Apollo moon-shot scale" project). *See generally id.*

39 Larry Thompson, *Genes, Politics and Money Biology's Most Ambitious Project Will Cost a Fortune, But Its Value Could Be Beyond Measure*, WASH. POST (Feb. 24, 1987) (page nos. unavailable online), www.washingtonpost.com/archive/lifestyle/wellness/1987/02/24/genes-politics-and-money-biologys-most-ambitious-project-will-cost-a-fortune-but-its-value-could-be-beyond-measure/ac8dafaf-b55a-4773-934f-6b20a1db4f94/.

40 *See Chapter* 2, *supra*, at notes 217–21, and accompanying text (involvement of delivery-of-care stakeholders in the HGP debate).

41 The conditions for such a storm were set decades before. *See* Malinowski, *Snake Oil*, *supra* note 34, at 39–40. In the 1970s, misuse of population testing for sickle cell anemia triggered bioethics debate about the commercialization and health care use of predictive genetic testing. *See* Melinda B. Kaufman, *Genetic Discrimination in the Workplace: An Overview of Existing Protections*, 30 LOY. U. CHI. L.J. 393, 401–03 (1999). With escalation of the biotech revolution during the 1980s, the genetic testing debate broadened and deepened to develop issues of privacy, confidentiality, discrimination, personal autonomy, ownership of samples, and eugenics. It was enriched and further developed during the 1990s with federal government support through the Ethical, Legal, and Social Implications/ELSI program of HGP. *See* David H. Kaye, *Respecting Genetic Privacy: The ASU-SB Conference on Law, Science, and Technology*, 40 JURIMETRICS J. 1, 5 n.22 (1999) (between 1990 and 1997, more than $50 million was expended on ELSI studies and projects). Yet, prior to the DTC commercialization of BRCA testing in 1996, much of the bioethics debate was philosophic and academic or fixated on regulations to protect human subjects, and it overlooked much of the pragmatic, direct application issues (for example, the relevance of FDA regulation of medical devices, FDA authority in general, and federal regulation of commercial testing under CLIA, though the Task Force assembled in 1994, *supra* note 33, directly addressed these issues) raised by the systemic introduction of predictive genetic testing into health care. *See* David Korn, *Genetic Privacy, Medical Information Privacy, and the Use of Human Tissue Specimens in Research*, *in* GENETIC TESTING AND THE USE OF INFORMATION 18–19 (Clarisa Long ed., 1999) (commenting on the resulting scholarship, including its deontological nature and basis in protection of human subjects jurisprudence). The reality of commercial BRCA testing jolted the debate with immediacy and pragmatism. *See generally Snake Oil*, *supra* note 34.

42 *See* Philip J. Boyle, *Shaping Priorities in Genetic Medicine*, HASTINGS CENT. REP. (Supplement, May-June 1995), at 1. *See also* Weiss, *Tests' Availability*, *supra* note 28, at A1 ("New genetic tests are moving rapidly from research laboratories into doctors' offices, where they are being marketed as a way to predict people's chances of getting common diseases such as colon cancer, breast cancer and Alzheimer's disease."). Even as early as 1995, more than 5,000 genes/genetic variants had been associated with medical conditions, and similar data was amassing rapidly – much catalogued and made available on the World Wide Web. *See* Malinowski, Blatt, *Biological Tarot*, *supra* note 25, at notes 13, 18; Ellie McCormack, *Sought-After Counselors Find It's All in the Genes*, BOST. BUS. J. (Apr. 26-May 2, 1996), at 3, 23.

43 US DEP. OF COM., OFFICE OF TECH. POL'Y, MEETING THE CHALLENGE: US INDUSTRY FACES THE 21ST CENTURY, THE US BIOTECHNOLOGY INDUSTRY (July 1997), https://webharvest.gov/peth04/20041017062206/http://www.technology.gov/Reports/biotechnology/cd93a.pdf.

44 *See generally* Michael J. Malinowski, Maureen A. O'Rourke, *A False Start? The Impact of Federal Policy on the Genotechnology Industry*, 13 YALE J. REG. 163 (1996).

45 *See* Malinowski, *Snake Oil*, *supra* note 34, at 24. "At the risk of sounding as paternalistic as the doctors they often fight against, members [of the National Breast Cancer Coalition/

NBCC and other patient advocates] said the test's general[,] ambiguous results may trigger unnecessary panic in many women while reassuring others who should remain vigilant." Malinowski, Blatt, *Biological Tarot, supra* note 25, at note 84. Myriad Labs engaged in aggressive DTC marketing and, when soliciting investors, brashly estimated tremendous market demand. They pointed out that half of the population is concerned about getting breast cancer – despite the limited clinical utility of its test under then-available data. *See* Malinowski, Blatt, *Biological Tarot, supra* note 25, at 35–36.

46 *See* Malinowski, *Snake Oil, supra* note 34, at 35–38. *See also* Weiss, *Tests' Availability, supra* note 28, at A1. Political groups focused on breast cancer formed in the 1980s, and they became extremely active and influential as a coalition in the 1990s. "In 1993, ... they strong-armed Congress to provide $300 million in new funds for breast-cancer research. That more than tripled the $90 million the [National Cancer Institute/]NCI was spending before the coalition's appearance." Brawley, Harm, *supra* note 18, at 265. *Dr. Susan Love's Breast Book,* first published in 1990, was a powerful catalyst. "There were breast cancer books before Love's, but hers did something new: it laid out the science comprehensively, in a dispassionate manner, with the sole purpose of helping women make decisions on treatment." *Id.* at 261–62.

47 *See* Malinowski, *Snake Oil, supra* note 34, at 35–38. *See also* Weiss, *Tests' Availability, supra* note 28, at A1.

48 Frances S. Collins, *BRCA1 – Lots of Mutations, Lots of Dilemmas*, 334 New Eng. J. Med. 186, 187 (1996) (emphasizing the scientific unreliability of current testing capability), www.nejm.org/doi/full/10.1056/NEJM199601183340311. *See generally id.*

49 "[G]enetic counseling is expensive and not necessarily covered by insurance; the United States does not have enough certified, practicing genetic counselors; and health care providers are not knowledgeable enough about genetics to help stretch these limited resources." Malinowski, Blatt, *Biological Tarot, supra* note 25, at 1249–50 (internal citations omitted). *See* Leroy Hood, Lee Rowen, *Genes, Genomes, and Society, in* Genetic Secrets 26 (Mark A. Rothstein ed., 1997) (noting the need for more trained genetic counseling professionals); Michael S. Watson, *The Regulation of Genetic Testing, in* Genetic Testing and the Use of Information 89 (Clarisa Long ed., 1999). *See Chapter 6, infra*, at notes 15–32, and accompanying text (addressing genetic counseling in the delivery of care presently, as well as the US genetic counseling profession's background).

50 *See Prologue, supra*, at notes 1–13, and accompanying text (the advancement of DNA sequencing technologies). *See Chapter 6, infra*, at notes 43–152, and accompanying text ("The Complexities of Personal Genome Medical Decision-Making" and "US Health Care System and Consumer Genetics and Genomics Market Issues").

51 *See generally* SACGT, Recommendations, *supra* note 32.

52 *See generally* Malinowski, *Snake Oil, supra* note 34; Malinowski, Blatt, *Biological Tarot, supra* note 25.

53 *See supra* notes 7–10, and accompanying text (addressing the impact of HIPAA, GINA, and ACA).

54 *See* Deborah Hellman, *What Makes Genetic Discrimination Exceptional?*, 29 Am. J.L. & Med. 77, 77 (2003); Eric Mills Holmes, *Solving the Insurance/Genetic Fair/Unfair Discrimination Dilemma in Light of the Human Genome Project*, 85 Ky. L.J. 503, 527 (1997) (addressing the potential for discrimination based upon misunderstanding genetic data and actuarial analysis).

55 *See* HIPAA, Pub. L. 104–191 (1996). HHS published a final Privacy Rule in December 2000, which was modified in August 2002, and HHS published a final Security Rule in February 2003. *See* HIPAA Privacy Rule, 45 CFR Parts 160, 164 (subparts A, E); HIPAA Security Rule, 45 CFR Parts 160, 162, 164. *Visit* HHS, *HIPAA for Professionals* (Aug. 31,

2023), www.hhs.gov/hipaa/for-professionals/index.html. Compliance with the Privacy Rule was required as of April 14, 2003 (April 14, 2004, for small health plans), and compliance with the Security Rule was required as of April 20, 2005 (April 20, 2006, for small health plans). Nevertheless, HIPAA was not implemented with any meaningful enforcement until 2006. *See* Rob Stein, *Medical Privacy Law Nets No Fines*, Wash. Post (June 5, 2006) (addressing lack of meaningful enforcement until 2006), www.washingtonpost.com/wp-dyn/content/article/2006/06/04/AR2006060400672. Subsequently, the Privacy Rule and Security Rule were subject to updates and revisions responsive to GINA and HITECH, culminating with the Omnibus HIPAA Final Rule. *See* HHS, Modifications to the HIPAA Privacy, Security, Enforcement, and Breach html Notification Rules Under the Health Information Technology for Economic and Clinical Health Act/HITECH and the Genetic Information Nondiscrimination Act/GINA; Other Modifications to the HIPAA Rules, 45 CFR Parts 160, 164 (Jan. 25, 2013) ("Omnibus HIPAA Final Rule"), www.govinfo.gov/content/pkg/FR-2013-01-25/pdf/2013-01073.pdf. The regulatory scope of HIPAA does not encompass deidentified data and, further, "The Privacy Rule relaxes the data-deidentification requirements for circumstances in which having additional patient details might be necessary, such as in research contexts." Sharona Hoffman, *Perspective, Privacy and Security – Protecting Patients' Health Information*, 1056(10) NEW. ENGL. J. MED. 1913–16, 1915 (Nov. 24, 2022), www.nejm.org/doi/pdf/10.1056/NEJMp2201676?articleTools=true. *See* 45 CFR 164.501, 164.508, 164.512(i). *See also* 45 CFR 164.514(e), 164.528, 164.532. As summarized by HHS,

> In the course of conducting research, researchers may obtain, create, use, and/or disclose individually identifiable health information. Under the Privacy Rule, covered entities are permitted to use and disclose protected health information for research with individual authorization, or without individual authorization under limited circumstances set forth in the Privacy Rule.

HHS, HIPAA, *Research* (reviewed June 13, 2018), www.hhs.gov/hipaa/for-professionals/special-topics/research/index.html. For further discussion of the limitations of HIPAA protections for biobanking and other human genome science big data initiatives and resulting privacy and security concerns, see *Chapter 6, infra*, at notes 159–224, and accompanying text ("Privacy and Associated Risks").

56 *See* GINA, Pub. L. 110–233, 122 Stat. 881; Affordable Care Act/ACA, Pub. L. No. 111–148, 124 Stat. 119 (2010). *See supra* notes 8–10 and accompanying text (addressing HIPAA, GINA, and ACA).

57 BRCA testing inspired many state legislatures to establish task forces and committees to explore the need for legislation. *Cf.* Mulholland, Jaeger, *State Legislation, supra* note 7. Massachusetts established a Special Committee on Genetic Information in 1995, on which I served from 1995 to 1997. The Special Committee solicited much stakeholder input, including position statements and public testimony from health care providers, insurers (life and disability, as well as health), patients and their families, and patient advocates.

58 *See* George J. Annas et al., THE GENETIC PRIVACY ACT AND COMMENTARY (1995), https://web.ornl.gov/sci/techresources/Human_Genome/resource/privacyact.pdf; George J. Annas et al., *Drafting of the Genetic Privacy Act: Science, Policy, and Practical Considerations*, 23 J. LAW, MED. & ETHICS 360 (1995); Patricia ("Winnie") Roche, Leonard H. Glantz, George J. Annas, *The Genetic Privacy Act: A Proposal for National Legislation*, 37 JURIMETRICS J. 1 (1996). As Manager of Government Affairs for the Massachusetts Biotechnology Council, Inc./MBC from 1997 to 1998, and while serving on the Massachusetts Special Committee on Genetic Information for two years before, I was directly involved in this debate on the state and national (notably through committee

service and other interaction with the Biotechnology Industry Organization/BIO, now the Biotechnology Innovation Organization) levels.

59 *See generally* Mulholland, Jaeger, *State Legislation, supra* note 7. *See* Malinowski, *Snake Oil, supra* note 34, at 21.

60 *See generally* SACGT, RECOMMENDATIONS, *supra* note 32.

61 *See generally id.*

62 *See generally* Philip R. Reilly, *Genetic Discrimination, in* GENETIC TESTING AND THE USE OF INFORMATION 106, 107 (Clarisa Long ed., 1999). Biopharma and many commentators at the time shared the position that genetic-specific legislation is shortsighted and unwise. *See, e.g.*, Mark A. Rothstein, *Why Treating Genetic Information Separately Is a Bad Idea*, 4 TEX. REV. L. & POL. 33 (1999); Mark Rothstein, *Genetic Secrets: A Policy Framework, in* GENETIC SECRETS 453 (Mark Rothstein ed., 1997); Michael Watson, *Regulation, supra* note 49.

63 I was Manager of Government Affairs for the Massachusetts Biotechnology Council, Inc. /MBC, the Massachusetts' biotech trade organization, from 1997–1998, and I worked closely with the Biotechnology Industry Organization/BIO and Council of State Bioscience Associations/CSBA on genetic and medical privacy during that time. It should be noted that primary issues often fragmented, and there was not always agreement among the state BIO affiliates, or between any given state affiliate and BIO. In fact, on the issue of genetics legislation for Massachusetts, at one point, the MBC adopted a position on state genetics legislation contrary to the position of some of its strongest members, BIO, and the Pharmaceutical Research and Manufacturers of America/PhRMA.

64 *Visit* BIO, official site, www.bio.org. In addition to their affiliations with BIO, which represented the interests of small and medium *biotech* companies, the state biotech trade organizations collaborated through the Council of State Bioscience Associations/CSBA to protect and promote their members' interests contrary to "Big Pharma" interests. *Visit* CSBA, official site, www.bio.org/csba. On January 4, 2016, BIO changed its name to the Biotechnology *Innovation* Organization – a reflection of convergence of the traditional pharmaceutical sector and the biotechnology sector into biopharma, with a shared biotech R&D base. The name change reflects that BIO's primary mission is to protect and promote biotech science and resulting innovation, not an industry sector.

65 *See generally* Mulholland, Jaeger, *Survey, supra* note 7. Also, HIPAA and GINA have limitations. *See, e.g., Chapter 6, infra*, at notes 159–224, and accompanying text ("Privacy and Associated Risks").

66 In addition to sample collection through sales of its testing services, Myriad's BRCA research to develop its clinically sound test "built on previous publicly funded work and was partially supported by the National Institutes of Health." *Howard Markel, Patents, Profits, and the American People – The Bayh–Dole Act of* 1980, 369 N. ENGL. J. MED. 794–96, at 794 (Aug. 29, 2013), www.nejm.org/doi/full/10.1056/nejmp1306553. Myriad directly collaborated with NIH and established a registry at the Dana-Farber Cancer Institute (Boston, MA) in 1996, which drew participation from many breast cancer patients individually and through organizations originally opposed to the tests' commercialization – notably the National Breast Cancer Coalition/NBCC. Breast cancer patients wanted *clinically sound* genetic tests, as did NIH. *See* Richard Saltus, *Gene Test for Cancer Risk is Offered*, BOSTON GLOBE (Oct. 25, 1996), at A1. Myriad's BRCA patent rights became the subject of major litigation, which raised fundamental questions about the ownership of genes. *See generally* JORGE CONTRERAS, THE GENOME DEFENSE: INSIDE THE EPIC LEGAL BATTLE TO DETERMINE WHO OWNS THEIR DNA (2021). The Supreme Court resolved the dispute in 2013 in a decision that significantly reduced the patentability of genetic tests. *See generally Association for Molecular Pathology v. Myriad Genetics, Inc.*, 133 S. Ct. 2107, 569 US

12 (2013). *See infra* notes 72–76, and accompanying text (addressing the *Myriad* decision, and the Court's *Prometheus* decision, 132 S. Ct. at 1289, the year before).

67 *See* Angelina Jolie, *My Medical Choice*, N.Y. TIMES (May 14, 2013), at A25, www.nytimes.com/2013/05/14/opinion/my-medical-choice.html?module=inline. Two years later, in another opinion-editorial published by *The New York Times*, Ms. Jolie shared that she also underwent surgery to remove her ovaries and fallopian tubes, as well as a small, benign tumor, and she shared more about her BRCA testing and decision-making experience. *See* Angelina Jolie Pitt, *Diary of a Surgery*, N. Y. TIMES (Mar. 24, 2015), at A23, www.nytimes.com/2015/03/24/opinion/angelina-jolie-pitt-diary-of-a-surgery.html.

68 *See supra* note 66, and accompanying text (discussing Myriad's acquisition of intellectual property rights and data collection through collaborations).

69 SACGT did an excellent job explaining clinical soundness (evidentiary-science standards for analytical validity, clinical validity, and clinical utility) in the context of genetic testing, and the complexities of clinical genetics. *See generally* SACGT, Recommendations, *supra* note 32.

70 Jeffrey Kluger, Alice Park, *The Angelina Effect*, TIME (May 27, 2013), at 28, http://healthland.time.com/2013/05/15/the-angelina-effect-times-new-cover-image-revealed/.

71 *Id.*

72 *See generally Association for Molecular Pathology v. Myriad Genetics, Inc.*, 133 S. Ct. 2107, 569 US 12 (2013). As explained by James Watson,

> In May 2009, the American Civil Liberties Union (ACLU) filed suit on behalf of two women against the US Patent and Trademark Office and Myriad Genetics, the Salt Lake City diagnostics company that owned the patent to the breast cancer genes BRCA1 and BRCA2. The lawsuit alleged that Myriad's fiercely defended monopoly on breast cancer genetic testing had prevented one of the plaintiffs from obtaining a second opinion on her results, and the other was unable to obtain Medicare coverage for the test.... The case went all the way to the US Supreme Court. At stake was not just the fate of Myriad's BRCA1-related patents but a central tenet to the biotech industry: the idea that human genes, once isolated, are akin to inventions and thus can be patented.

Watson, The Story, *supra* note 16, at 214–15. *See generally* CONTRERAS, DETERMINE WHO, *supra* note 66.

73 *Markel, Patents, Profits, supra note* 66, at 795. *See generally* CONTRERAS, DETERMINE WHO, *supra* note 66.

74 *See generally Assoc'n for Molecular Pathology v. Myriad Genetics, Inc.*, 133 S. Ct. 2107, 569 US 12 (2013).

75 WATSON, THE STORY, *supra* note 16, at 215–16.

76 *See generally Mayo Collaborative Servs. v. Prometheus Labs., Inc.*, 132 S. Ct. 1289, 182 L. Ed. 2d 321 (2012). *See also Gottschalk v. Benson*, 409 US 63, 70 (1972) ("A process is a mode of treatment of certain materials to produce a given result. It is an act, or a series of acts, performed upon the subject-matter to be transformed and reduced to a different state or thing."); In re *Kollar*, 286 F.3d 1326, 1332 (Fed. Cir. 2002) ("[A] process...consists of a series of acts or steps.... It consists of doing something, and therefore has to be carried out or performed.").

77 *See generally* Anna B. Laakmann, *The Meaning of Myriad*, 5 UC IRVINE L. REV. 1001 (2015). *See also* Daniel K. Yarbrough, *After Myriad: Reconsidering the Incentives for Innovation in the Biotech Industry*, 21 MICH. TELECOMM. & TECH. L. REV. 141, 142–67 (2014).

78 As a resident of Louisiana, I witnessed firsthand an onset of these commercials within a few years or so after the *Myriad* decision by the Cancer Treatment Centers of America/

CTCA and the University of Texas's MD Anderson Cancer Center, which have a strong regional presence.

79 *See supra* note 5, and accompanying text (completion of the draft map of the human genome sequence in 2003, and subsequent research to make corrections and fill gaps).

80 *See Prologue, supra*, at notes 1–13, and accompanying text (addressing sequencing technology).

81 *See* WATSON, THE STORY, *supra* note 16, at 207–11. Searching for SNPs is a much cheaper and efficient way to provide personal genetic information to consumers than comprehensive genome sequencing. As explained by James Watson,

> In plain English, rather than reading all 3 billion bases of the genome, this method surveys about 1 million predetermined sites – so-called single nucleotide polymorphisms, or SNPs ("snips"). These are locations where the genetic code varies fairly frequently from individual to individual – where you may have an A, I might have a G.... [T]housands are associated with a host of rare or common diseases, as well as other physical and behavioral traits.

Id. at 206. SNPs are variations in single nucleotide bases identified to impact phenotype (physical/realized characteristics) with a frequency of at least one percent in the human population—the presently governing standard for being deemed significant, though that may be lowered given increasing understanding of genomic complexity. *See generally* NIH, Genetics Home Reference, *What are single nucleotide polymorphisms (SNPs)?* (July 16, 2019), https://ghr.nlm.nih.gov/primer/genomicresearch/snp; Helen M. Berman, Rochelle C. Dreyfuss, *Reflections on the Science and Law of Structural Biology, Genomics, and Drug Development*, 53 UCLA L. REV. 871, 882–83 (2006). The SNP Consortium/TSC was established in 1999 to discover and bank SNPs as a public resource, with the goal of 300,000 SNPs in two years. *See* A. Gudmundur, A. Thorisson, Lincoln D. Stein, *The SNP Consortium Website: Past, Present and Future*, 31 NUCLEIC ACIDS RES. 124–27 (2003), www.ncbi.nlm.nih.gov/pmc/articles/PMC165499/. By the end of 2001 (within just a few years from its start), TSC had achieved 1.4 million SNPs – a tangible indication of the pace of the advancement of DNA sequencing technology and access to human samples and medical information even at that time. *See id. See generally, International SNP Map Working Group, A Map of Human Genome Sequence Variation Containing 1.42 Million Single Nucleotide Polymorphisms*, 409 NATURE 928 (2001), www.nature.com/articles/35057149.

82 *See* WATSON, THE STORY, *supra* note 16, at 207–11.

83 *See id.*

84 *See id.*

85 *See id.* at 207–08. *See also* Megan Molteni, *23andMe's Pharma Deals Have Been the Plan All Along*, WIRED (Aug. 3, 2018) ("The hypothesis of this company was to circumvent medical records and just self-report....") (quoting Ann Wojcicki at a public forum), www.wired.com/story/23andme-glaxosmithkline-pharma-deal/.

86 *See* WATSON, THE STORY, *supra* note 16, at 207–08. *See supra* note 24, and accompanying text (23andMe's mission as relayed colloquially by Ann Wojcicki).

87 "Iceland's geographically isolated population of Norsk and Celtic (Viking) heritage, presently 330,000 people, is a 'living laboratory for DNA testing.'" Stuart Leavenworth, *This Nation Faces a DNA Dilemma: Whether to Notify People Carrying Cancer Genes*, MCCLATCHY NEWSPAPERS (June 14, 2018), www.mcclatchydc.com/news/nation-world/article213014904.html.

88 *See* WATSON, THE STORY, *supra* note 16, at 207–08; Leavenworth, *DNA Dilemma*, *supra* note 87.

89 *See* Amgen, *Press Release, Amgen to Acquire deCODE Genetics, a Global Leader in Human Genetics* (Dec. 10, 2012), www.amgen.com/newsroom/press-releases/2012/12/amgen-to-acquire-decode-genetics-a-global-leader-in-human-genetics; Ben Hirschler, *Amgen Buys Icelandic Gene Hunter Decode for $415 Million*, Reuters (Dec. 10, 2012), www.reuters.com/article/us-amgen-decode/amgen-buys-icelandic-gene-hunter-decode-for-415-million-idUSBRE8B90IU20121210.

90 *See deCODEme Consumer Tests Discontinued, DNAeXplained – Genetic Genealogy* (Sept. 30, 2014) (blog post includes deCODEme letter to customers), https://dna-explained.com/2014/09/30/decodeme-consumer-tests-discontinued/.

91 Law professor Catherine Sharkey recently published her account of 23andMe's story leading up to the FDA's decision to approve the company's DTCGHR tests through its PGHS in 2017, which is inclusive of the essential facts, events, and related US law-policy. *See* Sharkey, *Dual Role, supra* note 19, at 349–58. *See also infra* note 155–59, and accompanying text (my contrasting law-policy interpretation of the FDA's decision to approve 23andMe's DTCGHR tests).

92 *See* Hayden, *Rise and Fall, supra* note 16.

93 *See* Kevin Davies, $1,000 Genome: The Revolution in DNA Sequencing and the New Era of Personalized Medicine 32 (2010) (discussing 23andMe's governing principles and methodology, also addressed *infra* at notes 94–97, and accompanying text). CEO Anne Wojcicki was married to Google co-founder Sergey Brin at the time she co-founded 23andMe. *See* Darah Hansen, *CEO 23andMe on Knowing Your DNA Data (and Being Married to the Boss of Google)*, Yahoo Fin. Canada (Oct 2, 2014), https://ca.finance.yahoo.com/news/5q–anne-wojcicki–ceo-23andme-on-knowing-your-dna-data-and-being-married-to-the-boss-of-google-203324408.html. Mr. Brin announced in 2008 that his personal genome includes a genetic variation (allele) associated with increased risk of Parkinson's disease – which he discovered through 23andMe. *See generally* Thomas Goetz, *Sergey Brin's Search for a Parkinson's Cure*, Wired (June 22, 2010), www.wired.com/2010/06/ff-sergeys-search/. Mr. Brin shares the allele with his mother, who has Parkinson's disease. *See id.* Ms. Wojcicki and Mr. Brin have two biological children who potentially inherited the allele and heightened genetic susceptibility to Parkinson's. *See* Matthew Herper, *Surprise! With $60 Million Genentech Deal, 23andMe Has A Business Plan*, Forbes (Jan 6, 2015), www.forbes.com/sites/matthewherper/2015/01/06/surprise-with-60-million-genentech-deal-23andme-has-a-business-plan/#4f97d5c12be9.

94 *See supra* note 24, and accompanying text (quoting Ms. Wojcicki). *See also* Davies, $1,000 Genome, *supra* note 93, at 32; Recode, *Transcript, supra* note 24; *NBC Nightly News, Heritage, supra* note 24. Although 23andMe's GHR tests are wholly DTC and removed from medical insurance when consumers pay out-of-pocket, the IRS has determined that their cost (paid through tax-advantaged health accounts) constitutes "medical care" for tax purposes and, therefore, is tax deductible. *See* Richard Rubin, Amy Dockser Marcus, *IRS Greenlights Tax Breaks for Buyers of 23andMe Genetic Tests*, Wall St. J. (July 22, 2019), www.wsj.com/articles/irs-greenlights-tax-breaks-for-buyers-of-23andme-genetic-tests-11563800520.

95 23andMe was founded with governing principles that include:

- Individuals should have the right to search for their own genetic information;
- Individuals should control their own information but can share it with others if they so choose;
- The value of a person's genetic information will increase over time; and
- Privacy is paramount.

Davies, $1,000, *supra* note 93, at 32. For discussion of Ms. Wojcicki's driving health care and personal genome medicine influences, see *id.* at 35–37.

96 *See id* at 32, 35–37.

97 *See id.*

98 *See* 23andMe, official site, *Where Can I Buy A 23andMe Kit?* (undated, visited June 4, 2022), https://customercare.23andme.com/hc/en-us/articles/115014501108-Where-Can-I-Buy-a-23andMe-Kit-. According to the same 23andMe source when visited in 2019, kits were available for purchase at Best Buy (select locations), CVS Pharmacy, Sam's Club (select locations), Target, Walgreens, and Walmart. Such a shelf presence was itself DTC marketing. 23andMe may have opted for direct sales because the company no longer needs this shelf exposure given its brand and product recognition, quality control is much more practicable with direct sales, profits are higher with direct sales, liability risk is more controlled with direct sales, or some combination of these – and perhaps other – variables.

99 SNPs are addressed *supra* at note 81, and in the accompanying text. *See* DAVIES, $1,000 GENOME, *supra* note 93, at 32. Illumina launched a complete genome sequencing service in 2010 at a starting price of $50k per genome. Rather than taking the 23andMe's DTC approach and assuming the risk of FDA intervention, Illumina required consumers to obtain physician prescriptions – resulting in the first prescription for a whole person genome sequence. *See* WATSON, THE STORY, *supra* note 16, at 206. As discussed in the *Prologue*, *supra*, at notes 7–13, and in the accompanying text, the cost of whole genome sequencing plummeted to reach a $1,000 price point in 2014.

100 "[J]ust as Facebook sells user data to third parties, 23andMe sells its user 'data' to third parties. 23andMe has made several deals with pharmaceutical companies where it sells access to its genetic database." Sharkey, *Dual Role*, *supra* note 19, at 350 *See generally* Molteni, *Plan All Along*, *supra* note 85 (addressing the company's execution of its long-term plan to sell access to customer data); Sarah Zhang, *Big Pharma Would Like Your DNA: 23andMe's $300 Million Deal with GlaxoSmithKline is Just the Tip of the Iceberg*, THE ATLANTIC (July 27, 2018, updated July 28, 2018) ("23andMe has always planned to sell access to its customers' DNA – a fact it has not exactly kept secret."), www.theatlantic.com/science/archive/2018/07/big-pharma-dna/566240/. 23andMe's role of collector, keeper, and seller of customer data was a fundamental component of its business plan from the start:

> When the company's DNA-testing service launched in 2007, *Wired* touted its quest to amass a "treasure trove of data … to drive research forward" as a "key part of the 23andMe business plan." Co-founders Anne Wojcicki and Linda Avey outright told the *San Francisco Chronicle* that selling kits was only the first step. "The long game here is not to make money selling kits, although the kits are essential to get the base level data," a 23andMe board member said to Fast Company in 2013. "Once you have the data, [the company] does actually become the Google of personalized health care."

Zhang, *Your DNA*, *supra*. For information about 23andMe's primary engagements with other companies (prior to becoming 23andMe Holding and acquisition of Lemonaid, which is addressed *infra* at notes 173–76, and in the accompanying text), *see infra* notes 138–44, and accompanying text.

101 "Since 2007, 23andMe has offered an inexpensive product to consumers (personalized genetic analysis) to generate broader consumer data and then leveraged that data to generate profit and business opportunities, becoming – as board member Patrick Chung put it – 'the Google of personalized health care.'" Kayte Spector-Bagdady, *"The Google of Healthcare": Enabling the Privatization of Genetic Bio/Databanking*, 26 ANNALS OF EPIDEMIOLOGY 515, 515 (2016), www.sciencedirect.com/science/article/abs/pii/S1047279716301545.

102 "23andMe is continually pushing surveys out to its customers. A few questions here, a few questions there; it's kind of like going on a first date every time you log on. *And people love talking about themselves*. 'We specialize in capturing phenotypic data on people longitudinally – on average 300 data points on each customer,' Wojcicki said." Molteni, *Plan All Along*, *supra* note 85 (emphasis added). *See also* WATSON, THE STORY, *supra* note 16, at 210 ("Customers have each answered an average of 300 questions on a huge array of traits, including their medical histories."); Hayden, *Rise and Fall*, *supra* note 16. I became a 23andMe customer, primarily for this book project but also with some curiosity about my personal genome. I also agreed to participate in the company's research – frankly, I felt obligated to do so given my work, but also beyond. I believe in the human health potential of human genome science and personal genome medicine. However, I stopped responding to the company's email request for participation because I found the exchanges dangerously shallow and a threat to genomic research. The adage "garbage in, garbage out" is very applicable to data collection and research with it, and in the uptake of resulting innovation in clinical care. For example, I was questioned about my eyesight. I was asked whether I am nearsighted/farsighted, but there was no opportunity for me to deviate from the options and explain that I had LASIK eye surgery which directly changed my vision and shifted those variables. Beyond 23andMe and its direct research partners, the path to sound science and evidence-based personal genome medicine will become much more winding with this poor quality of data intake potentially polluting the wider body of data – for example, through 23andMe's direct collaborators, or even those who rely on 23andMe's research findings based on such data. Others share my assessment and concerns. *See infra* note 144 (suspicion of self-reported data in depression study). As for the practicalities of withdrawing from research,

> 23andMe customers can withdraw consent at any time, but it may take up to 30 days for their requests to go into effect. And any data shared prior to that date can't be clawed back from any third parties that might be using it. Deleting your data entirely is even harder – nearly impossible, as Bloomberg reporter Kristen Brown reported, because federal laws require clinical laboratories to keep de-identified DNA test results on file for a minimum of 10 years.

Molteni, *Plan All Along*, *supra* note 85.

103 *See generally* Molteni, *Plan All Along*, *supra* note 85 ("23andMe has convinced more than 5 million people to fill a plastic tube with half a teaspoon of saliva"); Jamie Ducharme, *A Major Drug Company Now Has Access to 23andMe's Genetic Data. Should You Be Concerned?*, TIME (July 26, 2018), https://time.com/5349896/23andme-glaxo-smith-kline/; Anne Wojcicki, *Power of One Million*, 23ANDME BLOG (June 18, 2015) (commenting on the significance of the 1 million achievement), https://blog.23andme.com/news/one-in-a-million/.

104 *See infra* notes 138–44, and accompanying text (information about 23andMe's engagements with corporate third parties as of 2018).

105 *See* WATSON, THE STORY, *supra* note 16, at 211 ("[W]ith more than 1 million DNA records at its disposal, 23andMe has finally reached critical mass for usefulness to big pharma and has signed several lucrative deals as well as hiring a distinguished former Genentech R&D chief to spearhead its own drug discovery program."); *infra* notes 138–44, and accompanying text (collaborative deals with the potential to demonstrate 23andMe as a resource for innovative drug R&D as of 2018).

106 *See* DAVIES, $1,000, *supra* note 93, at 32–3; WATSON, THE STORY, *supra* note 16, at 207–08. Prior to 2013 (when the company was stopped by the FDA), 23andMe provided customers with genetic information on hundreds of health conditions. *See* Hayden, *Rise and Fall*, *supra* note 16. The inclusion of Parkinson's was not by chance and, in

fact, the disease inspired founding the company. Anne Wojcicki was married to Google co-founder Sergey Brin at the time she co-founded 23andMe, Google was a primary initial 23andMe investor, Mr. Brin's family history includes Parkinson's disease, and he and Ms. Wojcicki have two biological children. *See supra* note 93 (Mr. Brin's personal story, which he shared with the media). 23andMe was quick to develop a test for the Parkinson's allele in Mr. Brin's family, and Mr. Brin was quick to take it and learn that he has the allele and increased susceptibility to the disease. *See id.*

107 In addition to deCODE Genetics, the competition in 2008 included Navigenics and Knome. *See* David J. Hunter Muin, J. Khoury, Jeffrey M. Drazen, *Letting the Genome out of the Bottle – Will We Get Our Wish?*, 358 N. ENG. J. MED. 105, 105 (Jan. 10, 2008), www.nejm.org/doi/full/10.1056/nejmp0708162.

108 WATSON, THE STORY, *supra* note 16, at 209. 23andMe has marketed its PGHS brilliantly, with social media savvy, and successfully from the start. "The launch was beautifully choreographed with judiciously timed stories in the New York Times and Wired and the rapt attention of a fascinated blogosphere." DAVIES, $1,000 GENOME, *supra* note 93, at 33. The launch was accompanied by a media blitz that included network television – for example, company profile segments on ABC's *Nightline* and NBC's *Today Show*. *See id.* at 33–34.

109 *See supra* notes 46–48, and accompanying text (response to DTC BRCA testing in 1996). *See also* WATSON, THE STORY, *supra* note 16, at 208 ("A little knowledge can seem a dangerous thing, or at least pointless. The arrival of 23andMe released a fusillade of scorn from the medical establishment and jokes about 'recreational genomics.'").

110 *See generally* Hunter et al., *Bottle*, *supra* note 107. *See also* Staff Reporter, *NEJM Editorial Warns of Downside to 'Premature' Consumer Genomics Market*, GENOMEWEB (Jan. 11, 2008), www.genomeweb.com/archive/nejm-editorial-warns-downside-%25E2%2580%2598premature%25E2%2580%2599-consumer-genomics-market#.XSNiUuhKjBQ.

111 Hunter et al., *Bottle*, *supra* note 107. *See Warns of Downside*, *supra* note 110. James Watson, commenting on the editorial, shared that, although he is supportive of personal genome genetic testing, "My good friend Sydney Brenner[, a co-recipient of the 2002 Nobel Prize in Physiology or Medicine,] dismissed recreational genomics as the equivalent of astrology." WATSON, THE STORY, *supra* note 16, at 208–09. The *NEJM* editorial echoes clinical concerns expressed by SACGT in 2000. *See generally* SACGT, RECOMMENDATIONS, *supra* note 32.

112 *See supra* note 16 (discussing the early consumer demand and biobanking success of Ancestry and 23andMe). The company amassed over a million DNA profiles and related health information by 2015. *See* Anne Wojcicki, *Power of One Million*, 23ANDME BLOG (June 18, 2015) (addressing the research and commercial significance of the one million achievement), https://blog.23andme.com/news/one-in-a-million/. 23andMe's biobank of DNA profiles and related health information swelled to over five million globally by the summer of 2018. *See generally* Molteni, *Plan All Along*, *supra* note 85 ("23andMe has convinced more than 5 million people to fill a plastic tube with half a teaspoon of saliva"); Ducharme, *Concerned?*, *supra* note 103.

113 *See* WATSON, THE STORY, *supra* note 16, at 210.

114 *Id.* For discussion of *Prometheus*, 132 S. Ct. at 1289, *see supra* notes 72–76, and accompanying text.

115 *See* WATSON, THE STORY, *supra* note 16, at 210; 23andMe, *23andMe and the FDA* (2019) (communication posted on the company's site), https://customercare.23andme.com/hc/en-us/articles/211831908-23andMe-and-the-FDA.

116 *See* FDA, DEN140044, EVALUATION OF AUTOMATIC CLASS III DESIGNATION FOR The 23andMe Personal Genome Service Carrier Screening Test for Bloom

Syndrome, DECISION SUMMARY (Feb. 2015, subsequently correct), www.accessdata.fda.gov/cdrh_docs/reviews/den140044.pdf. Bloom syndrome is caused by a recessive genetic variation (allele) in the BLM gene, meaning that each carrier without onset of the syndrome has one of the alleles in their two sets of chromosomes. When both parents are carriers, their offspring have a twenty-five percent chance of not inheriting the allele from either parent and a twenty-five percent change of inheriting the allele from both of them and, consequently, developing Bloom Syndrome. Offspring also have a fifty percent chance of inheriting one of the alleles and being a carrier like their parents. "The incidence of Bloom syndrome is unknown, and fewer than 300 affected individuals have been reported. Approximately one-third of people with the disease are of Ashkenazi Jewish descent, making it more common in this population than in others. Roughly 1 in 48,000 Ashkenazi Jews is affected by the disease." Myriad Genetics, *What is Bloom Syndrome?* (visited Jan. 8, 2023), https://myriad.com/womens-health/diseases/bloom-syndrome/. The National Organization for Rare Disorders/NORD maintains a database and provides information for Bloom Syndrome and other rare disorders. *Visit* NORD, Rare Disease Database: Bloom Syndrome, https://rarediseases.org/rare-diseases/bloom-syndrome/.

117 23andMe, *FDA*, *supra* note 115.

118 *See* FDA, EVALUATION, *supra* note 116, at 23–34 (comprehension data submitted indicating overall comprehension rates above ninety percent). For discussion of the FDA's role evaluating consumer comprehension in DTCGHR testing interface and my firsthand experience with and evaluation of 23andMe's consumer comprehension, see *infra* note 128, and accompanying text.

119 *See* MALINOWSKI, BIOTECH HANDBOOK, *supra* note 34, at 139–41. "The core methodology of CDRH is to sort devices upon notice and intake according to risk – to best allocate its resources to be commensurate with complexity and risk." *Id.* at 139.

120 *See generally* FDA, EVALUATION, *supra* note 116. *See id.* at 30 (special controls).

121 The FDA regulates devices (complemented by regulation of laboratories under CLIA, addressed *supra* in notes 34–37, and in the accompanying text) through CDRH with base regulatory authority and responsibility under the 1976 Medical Device Amendments to the FDCA, 21. U.S.C. § 301, Pub. L. 94–295, 90 Stat. 539; the Medical Devices Act of 1990, Pub. L. 101–629; the Medical Device Amendments of 1992, Pub. L. 102–300; and FDAMA, Pub. L. No. 105–115, 111 Stat. 2296 (1997) (codified primarily in sections throughout 21 U.S.C., including §§ 352, 355, 356, 356(b), 360aaa–1–3, 379r). *See generally* FDA, *Overview of Device Regulation* (updated June 26, 2014), www.fda.gov/MedicalDevices/DeviceRegulationandGuidance/Overview/. The FDA defines "device" as:

> [A]n instrument, apparatus, implement, machine … including any component, part, or accessory, which is … intended for use in the diagnosis of disease or other conditions, or in the cure, mitigation, treatment, or prevention of disease, in man … which does not achieve its primary intended purposes through chemical action within or on the body of man [and not] dependent upon *being metabolized* for the achievement of its primary intended purposes.

21 U.S.C. § 321 (2012) (emphasis added).

122 A rationale for this matching system, beyond the scope and volume of products that constitute "medical devices," is that devices typically are not metabolized, while drugs and biologics innately are. *See id. See also* MALINOWSKI, BIOTECH HANDBOOK, *supra* note 34, at 139.

123 Most new devices are approved through this matching process, which is carried out under section 510(k) of the Food, Drug, and Cosmetic Act/FDCA (incorporating medical

device amendments). *See supra* note 121. According to Drugwatch, a patient-protection organization that works with medical and legal experts, "Between 95 and 98 percent of medical devices on sale in the US [in 2020] were cleared by the FDA through the 510(k) process, meaning the vast majority of medical devices used on patients have received little government scrutiny." Elaine Silvestrini, *FDA 510(k) Clearance Process* (last modified Mar. 15, 2021), www.drugwatch.com/fda/510k-clearance/#:~:text=Between%20 95%20and%2098%20percent,have%20received%20little%20government%20scrutiny. The CDRH clears new devices for market use under 510(k) provided their sponsors (1) register with the FDA, (2) establish that the new devices are the substantial equivalents of devices already reviewed and approved for market use and, when necessary, account for any differences, and (3) notify the FDA of their intent to market a medical device at least ninety days in advance, which is known as Premarket Notification/PMN. *See* FDA, *510(k) Clearances* (current as of Aug. 31, 2021), www.fda.gov/medical-devices/device-approvals-denials-and-clearances/510k-clearances.

124 *See* Malinowski, Biotech Handbook, *supra* note 34, at 139. *See infra* notes 126–29, and accompanying text (codification of the DTCGHR tests category).

125 *See* FDA, DEN160026, EVALUATION OF AUTOMATIC CLASS III DESIGNATION FOR The 23andMe Personal Genome Service (PGS) Genetic Health Risk Test for Hereditary Thrombophilia, Alpha-1 Antitrypsin Deficiency, Alzheimer's Disease, Parkinson's Disease, Gaucher Disease Type 1, Factor XI Deficiency, Celiac Disease, G6PD Deficiency, Hereditary Hemochromatosis and Early-Onset Primary Dystonia, DECISION SUMMARY (Apr. 6, 2017, revised May 2, 2017, correction Nov. 2, 2017), www.accessdata.fda.gov/cdrh_docs/reviews/DEN160026.pdf. *See also*, FDA, *Press Release, FDA Allows Marketing of First Direct-to-Consumer Tests That Provide Genetic Risk Information for Certain Conditions* (Apr. 6, 2017), www.fda.gov/NewsEvents/Newsroom/PressAnnouncements/ucm551185.htm.

126 Section 866.5950 (Genetic health risk assessment system) of Title 21 provides, in part:

> The genetic health risk assessment system device, when it has previously received a first-time FDA marketing authorization (e.g., 510(k) clearance) for the genetic health risk assessment system (a "one-time FDA reviewed genetic health risk assessment system"), is exempt from the premarket notification procedures in part 807, subpart E, of this chapter subject to the limitations in 866.9. The device must comply with the following special controls ....

21 CFR 866.5950 (revised Apr. 1, 2020), www.accessdata.fda.gov/scripts/cdrh/cfdocs/cfcfr/cfrsearch.cfm?fr=866.5950.

127 FDA, *Press Release, Genetic Risk Information*, *supra* note 126.

128 23andMe's DTCGHR testing, with no requisite medical provider involvement, pushed the FDA to evaluate the company's communication with users and to assess consumer comprehension. *See* Sharkey, *Dual Role*, *supra* note 19, at notes 40–43, and accompanying text. Consumer comprehension about a *clinically sound* test for *carrier* screening, such as 23andMe's test for Bloom Syndrome, is highly distinguishable from a portfolio of not clinically sound genetic health risk test results for an individual's own health decision making. *See* SACGT, Recommendations, *supra* note 32.

When I began this project, I purchased a 23andMe kit and became a subscriber to its PGHS service. Frankly, when I accessed my DTCGHR test results through the company's internet portal, I was stunned by the base information exchange the FDA deemed to constitute sufficient assurance of consumer comprehension for DTCGHR testing. Years later, I am still dismayed when I think about it. I authored a children's book to introduce young readers (7–10 years of age) to DNA and its meaning in their lives, Why Am I Me? (2019), so I have some appreciation for comprehension among young children. The purpose of the children's book was to communicate perspective about DNA – that it is important but typically not definitive of who a person is; people make choices and have experiences, and their personhood is shaped by those. In the company's and FDA's defense, 23andMe does enable inquisitive customers to access higher tiers of more meaningful information, ultimately including the underlying data tests are based upon. However, in my opinion, there is no meaningful "assurance of consumer comprehension" prerequisite for customer use embodied in 23andMe's PGHS service. I found the requisite information exchange comparable to communication with perhaps a middle school-level child who has average intelligence. The information exchange simply does not achieve perspective about the testing and its results – simply a linear communication that the tests are not, on their own, medically definitive. In my opinion, the message the FDA should have mandated to be communicated and comprehended is "This is *recreational* genetics for entertainment, not for medical use. It is an opportunity for you to preview, to glimpse, into the medical and clinical opportunities that are forthcoming with personal genome medicine." Obviously, this message would not sell DTCGHR testing kits to the public as effectively.

129 *See* FDA, *Press Release, Genetic Risk Information*, *supra* note 126.

130 *See* 23andMe, *23andMe and the FDA*, *supra* note 115.

131 *See* FDA, DEN170046, EVALUATION OF AUTOMATIC CLASS III DESINGATION FOR The 23andMe Personal Genome Service (PGS) Genetic Health Risk Report for BRCA1/BRCA2 (Selected Variants), DECISION SUMMARY (Apr. 2018, contains subsequent corrections), www.accessdata.fda.gov/cdrh_docs/reviews/DEN170046.pdf. *See also supra* notes 70–71, and accompanying text (discussing "the Angelina effect").

132 *See* Liam Drew, *Pharmacogenetics: The Right Drug for You*, 537 NATURE S60–62 (2016), www.nature.com/articles/537S60a (last visited July 19, 2019).

133 *See generally* FDA, DEN180028, EVALUATION OF AUTOMATIC CLASS III DESIGNATION FOR The 23andMe Personal Genome Service (PGS) Pharmacogenetic Reports, DECISION SUMMARY (2018), www.accessdata.fda.gov/cdrh_docs/reviews/DEN180028.pdf (2018). *See also* FDA, *Press Release, FDA Authorizes First Direct-to-Consumer Test for Detecting Genetic Variants That May Be Associated with Medication Metabolism* (Oct. 31, 2018), www.fda.gov/NewsEvents/Newsroom/PressAnnouncements/ucm624753.htm.

134 *See* FDA, DEN180028, *supra* note 133, at 16–18.

135 FDA, *Press Release, Medication Metabolism*, *supra* note 133.

136 *Id.* (emphasis added).

137 Jeffrey Shuren, Janet Woodcock, *Jeffrey Shuren, M.D., J.D., Director of the FDA's* Center *for Devices and Radiological Health, and Janet Woodcock, M.D., Director of the FDA's Center for Drug Evaluation and Research on Agency's Warning to Consumers About Genetic Tests That Claim to Predict Patients' Responses to Specific Medications* (Nov. 1, 2018), www.fda.gov/NewsEvents/Newsroom/PressAnnouncements/ucm624794.htm. *See generally* FDA, *Safety Communication, The FDA Warns Against the Use of Many Genetic Tests with Unapproved Claims to Predict Patient Response to Specific Medications: FDA Safety Communication* (Oct. 31, 2018) (current as of Nov. 1, 2018), www.fda.gov/medical-devices/safety-communications/fda-warns-against-use-many-genetic-tests-unapproved-claims-predict-patient-response-specific.

138 *See* Nick Paul Taylor, *GlaxoSmithKline Makes $300M Investment in 23andMe, Forms 50–50 R&D*, FIERCEBIOTECH (Jul. 25, 2018), www.fiercebiotech.com/biotech/gsk-s-big-r-d-idea-focusing-immune-system-as-new-cso-barron-makes-some-changes. In 2015, 23andMe created an in-house therapeutics division which, as of August 2018, had identified ten drug targets from 23andMe customer data. *See* Molteni, *Plan All Along*, *supra*

note 85. Under their collaboration agreement, 23andMe and GSK jointly make decisions about the advancement of these targets to human clinical trials. *See id*; Taylor, *supra*; Ducharme, *Concerned?*, *supra* note 103.

139 *See* Molteni, *Plan All Along*, *supra* note 85.

140 *Id*. "Its agreement with customers forbids it from sharing their actual data with collaborators, so scientists see only the results of analyses run by the company and never have access to the raw data that inform the studies." Hayden, *Rise and Fall*, *supra* note 16.

141 *See generally* Herper, *Surprise!*, *supra* note 93.

142 *See* Molteni, *Plan All Along*, *supra* note 85.

143 *See id*. (reporting additional deals with Lundbeck, Janssen, Biogen, and Alynlam Pharmaceuticals since 2015).

144 *See id*. The alchemy of churning genotypic and accompanying phenotypic data into medical meaning is in development:

> Several high-profile drugs based on human-genetics research have failed to live up to their potential, or have failed entirely. In May [2017], for instance, pharmaceutical company Amgen, based in Thousand Oaks, California, announced that its genetically targeted osteoporosis drug romosozumab raised the risk of heart disease by as much as 30% in a clinical trial with 4,000 people.

Hayden, *Rise and Fall*, *supra* note 16. Some scientists question the soundness of 23andMe's phenotypic base data – information self-reported in response to the company's questionnaires:

> Neurogeneticist Ashley Winslow, for instance, who led a high-profile collaboration with Pfizer to identify genetic markers associated with depression, says that peer reviewers of the resulting paper were concerned about the veracity of 23andme's customer data. They argued that people who said that they had been diagnosed with clinical depression might just have been feeling low on the day that they took the company's survey.

Id. *See supra* note 102 (author's experience engaging with 23andMe's questionnaires).

145 *See supra* note 123, and accompanying text (discussing the 510(k) approval process); *supra* note 130, and accompanying text (discussing the first 23andMe cancer test approval).

146 *See* FDA, DEN170046, 510(k) SUBSTANTIAL EQUIVALENCE DETERMINATION DECISION SUMMARY (2019), www.accessdata.fda.gov/cdrh_docs/reviews/K182784.pdf. *See also* 23andMe, *23andMe Receives FDA Clearance for Genetic Health Risk Report that Looks at a Hereditary Colorectal Cancer Syndrome*, 23ANDME BLOG (Jan. 22, 2019), https://blog.23andme.com/health-traits/23andme-receives-fda-clearance-for-genetic-health-risk-report-that-looks-at-a-hereditary-colorectal-cancer-syndrome/. *See generally* Maartje Nielsena, Hans Morreau, Hans F.A. Vasenc, Frederik J. Hesa, *MUTYH-associated polyposis (MAP)*, 79 CRIT. REV. ONC./HEM. 1–16 (July 2011), www.sciencedirect.com/science/article/abs/pii/S1040842810001472.

147 23andMe, *Hereditary Colorectal Cancer Syndrome*, *supra* note 146.

148 For discussion of the PDUFA, PDUFA reauthorizations, and FDAMA, see *Chapter* 3, *supra*, at notes 11–15, 72, 141–43, and accompanying text.

149 *See* Avery Anapol, *Trump Signs Order Giving Agency Heads More Power to Appoint Regulatory Judges*, 2018 THE HILL 39645 (July 11, 2018) ("Trump has vowed to dramatically roll back federal regulations, one of his campaign promises...."), https://thehill.com/homenews/administration/396451-trump-signs-order-giving-agency-heads-more-power-to-appoint. In January 2018, President Trump signed an executive order that required agencies to revoke two regulations for every new one. Six months later (July),

he signed another that allows agency heads to directly hire administrative law judges – about 2,000 officials who rule on regulatory legal issues – which makes it easier for agency heads to fire and pressure the judges, whether directly or indirectly. *See id.*

150 *See Chapter 3, supra*, at notes 31–70, and accompanying text ("Recognition of Biopharma Marketing as Protected Commercial Speech").

151 *See Prologue, supra*, at notes 23–32 (discussion of biobanking). *See, e.g.*, NIH, official site, All of Us Research Program, https://allofus.nih.gov/ (addressing the contributions to human health objective of this US biobanking initiative).

152 *See supra* notes 11 (consumer DNA profiles amassed), 137 (FDA acknowledgement of consumer demand), and accompanying text.

153 See *supra* notes 12–16 (public access to personal computers and the internet), 79 (milestones in social media culture, beginning with AOL's Instant Messenger in 1997), and accompanying text.

154 *See supra* notes 24 (Ms. Wojcicki's quote about the mission), 95–96 (Ms. Wojcicki's vision), 176 (23andMe's genomic health service business line), and accompanying text.

155 *See* Food and Drug Administration Modernization Act/FDAMA, Pub. L. No. 105–115, 111 Stat. 2296 (1997) (codified primarily in sections throughout 21 U.S.C., including §§ 352, 355, 356, 356(b), 360aaa–1–3, 379r). Section 406 of PDUFA II expanded the agency's mission to include efficiency and required the agency to balance safety and efficacy with timeliness. Specifically, section 406 requires the FDA to "promote the public health by promptly and efficiently reviewing clinical research and taking appropriate action … in a timely manner." 21 U.S.C. § 393(b)(1), *as amended*.

156 *See Chapter 1, supra*, at notes 35–45, and accompanying text ("US Law-Policy Recognition of Clinical Medicine as the Medical Profession's Domain").

157 Sharkey, *Dual Role, supra* note 19, at 349–58.

158 *See supra* note 137, and accompanying text (FDA safety communication warning).

159 *See generally Chapter 6, infra.*

160 *See* FDA, DEN140044 (carrier screening for Bloom syndrome), *supra* note 116; FDA, DEN160026 (ten diseases, including Alzhemier's and Parkinson's), *supra* note 125; FDA, DEN170046 (MUTYH-associated polyposis heredity colorectal cancer screening, and BRCA1/BRCA2 cancer screening), *supra* note 30–31. *See supra* notes 34–37, and accompanying text (addressing CLIA regulations).

161 *See supra* notes 128 (consumer comprehension assurance and limiting statement), 134 (six special controls), and accompanying text.

162 *See supra* notes 134–37, and accompanying text (six special controls and FDA safety warning communication).

163 *See supra* notes 124 (FDA designation of categories), 126–27 (application to 23andMe's DTCGHR testing), and accompanying text.

164 *See* FDA, *Direct to Consumer Tests* (current as of Dec. 20, 2019) ("List of Direct-to-Consumer Tests with Market Authorization"), www.fda.gov/medical-devices/in-vitro-diagnostics/direct-consumer-tests#list. In September 2017, after the FDA approved 23andMe's DTCGHR tests for alleles associated with ten diseases in April 2017, "the company announced that it had raised US$250 million: more than the total amount of capital raised by the company since its inception." Hayden, *Rise and Fall, supra* note 16. In 2017, prior to the significant regulatory and corporate milestones 23andMe realized subsequently, the DTGHR testing marketing was projected to reach $340 million by 2020. *See id. See also NBC Nightly News, Heritage, supra* note 24 ("The market for DNA testing is booming. Last year [2017] the number of people that had their DNA analyzed with a home kit more than doubled.").

165 Erik Hayden, *Rise and Fall, supra* note 16.

166 Stuart Leavenworth, *DNA Testing is Like the 'Wild West'; Should it be More Tightly Regulated?*, McClatchy Newspapers (June 1, 2018), www.mcclatchydc.com/news/nation-world/article212256094.html.

167 Ancestry self-reported over three million paying customers and more than ten billion digital records (public birth, marriage, death, and other records) as of November 2018. *See* Gina Spatafore, *Ancestry Breaks November Sales Record*, Bus. Wire (Nov. 29, 2018), www.businesswire.com/news/home/20181119005208/en/Ancestry-Breaks-November-Sales-Record. AncestryDNA, a subsidiary of Ancestry that offers consumers DTC genealogical DNA testing services, self-reported that their database contained fifteen million completed consumer DNA kits as of May 2019. *See* Claire Santry, *Ancestry's DNA Network Reaches 15 Million Test Samples*, Irish Genealogy News (May 22, 2019), www.irishgenealogynews.com/2019/05/ancestrys-dna-network-reaches-15.html. *See also* Anna Nowogrodzki *Ancestry Moves Further into Consumer Genetics*, MIT Tech. Rev. (May 11, 2016), www.technologyreview.com/s/539321/ancestry-moves-further-into-consumer-genetics/.

168 *See Ancestry Will Offer Health DNA Tests, Setting its Sights on 23andMe*, Advisory Bd. (Oct. 17, 2019) (no author identified), www.advisory.com/daily-briefing/2019/10/17/ancestry; Herper, *Surprise!*, *supra* note 93. AncestryHealth approached the DTCGHR testing market in a manner distinguishable from 23andMe to enhance clinical soundness and utility, and to minimize regulatory intrusion. AncestryHealth solicited the input of outside bioethics and clinical genetics experts to determine what testing and information to offer, customer tests were ordered through a national network of physicians, customers were shown online educational videos about DNA testing before getting results, and the purchase price included access to professional genetic counselors. *See* Herper, *Surprise!*, *supra* note 93. However, network physicians ordering the tests did not initially see or directly interact with consumers, and genetic counseling was left to consumer discretion. *See id*. Nevertheless, the involvement of medical professionals coupled with input from outside experts in determining what tests to offer was enough to limit federal regulation to CLIA compliance – meaning standard regulation of diagnostic clinical laboratories. *See id*.

169 Kristen V Brown, *Ancestry Pulling Health DNA Test Just Over a Year After Launch*, Bloomberg (Jan. 14, 2021), www.bloomberg.com/news/articles/2021-01-14/ancestry-pulling-health-dna-test-just-over-a-year-after-launch.

170 *See id*.

171 *See* 23andMe, *Press Release, 23andMe to Merge with Virgin Group's VG Acquisition Corp to Become Publicly-Traded Company Set to Revolutionize Personalized Healthcare and Therapeutic Development through Human Genetics* (Feb. 4, 2021), https://mediacenter.23andme.com/press-releases/23andme-merges-with-vgac/.

172 23andMe, email correspondence with subscribers (Feb. 26, 2021) (on file with author).

173 *See supra* note 22, 173–74, and accompanying text (discussing the merger and its execution).

174 *See* Staff Reporter, *Stock Soars*, *supra* note 22.

175 *See* 23andMe Holding Co., *Current Report (Form 8-K)* (Nov. 1, 2021), https://investors.23andme.com/static-files/8a43d3a5-2529-422c-937b-db40a7eeb875. In her Oct. 22, 2021, announcement to the "23andMe Community," Ms. Wojcicki wrote:

> Over the years we have asked you, our customers, what more do you want from 23andMe. We heard from many of you that the genetic information you got from 23andMe can change your life — but when you take it to a physician you may meet skepticism or uncertainty about what to do with the information. We want to change that.

> We are acquiring Lemonaid Health so that we can bring true personalized healthcare to 23andMe customers. Personalized healthcare means healthcare that is based on the combination of your genes, your environment, and your lifestyle — with recommendations and plans that are specific to you.

23andMe, *Letter from Anne, supra* note 24. *See also supra* note 24, and accompanying text (summarzing the related corporate plan progression and purchase).

176 23andMe, email correspondence with PGS customers (Oct. 12, 2022) (on file with the author). *See* Versel, *23andMe Pins Future, supra* note 24; 23andMe, *Letter from Anne, supra* note 24. *See also supra* note 24, and accompanying text (summarzing the related corporate plan progression and purchase).

177 Ross Douthat, *The Age of Decadence*, NY TIMES (Feb. 9, 2020), at 4–5, www.nytimes.com/2020/02/07/opinion/sunday/western-society-decadence.html. *See generally* ROSS DOUTHAT, THE DECADENT SOCIETY: HOW WE BECAME THE VICTIMS OF OUR OWN SUCCESS (2020).

178 Theranos and Elizabeth Holmes, the company's founder and CEO convicted of fraud, are discussed in *Chapter 5, infra*, at notes 6–20, and in the accompanying text.

179 *See* Antonio Regalado, *2017 was the Year Consumer DNA Testing Blew Up*, MIT TECH. REV. (Feb. 12, 2018), www.technologyreview.com/s/610233/2017-was-the-year-consumer-dna-testing-blew-up/. Advisory Board, a health care industry organization with over thirty-five years of experience, a team of 350 health care professionals, and a network of more than 4,400 health care organization members, estimated in 2019 (prior to the COVID-19 pandemic) that the market would triple by 2022. *See Ancestry Will Offer, supra* note 168. *Visit* Advisory Board, official site, www.advisory.com/about-us.

180 "For the quarter ended Sept. 30, [2022, 23andMe] booked $75.7 million in revenues, up from $55.2 million in the same period a year earlier." Versel, *23andMe Pins Future, supra* note 24. *See generally* NHGRI, 2020 NHGRI STRATEGIC VISION: STRATEGIC VISION FOR IMPROVING HUMAN HEALTH AT THE FOREFRONT OF GENOMICS (2020), www.genome.gov/2020SV; WATSON, THE STORY, supra note 16.

181 *See supra* note 19, and accompanying text (patient self-determination, autonomy, and participatory health movement). *See also Chapter 6, infra*, at notes 43–98, and accompanying text ("The Complexities of Personal Genome Medical Decision-Making").

182 DNA and genetics have become familiar to the general population and culturally normalized. Millennials who are the parents of Generation Alpha were born into IT immersion and came of age during the genomic revolution, with biotech and DNA forensics routinely covered in broadcast news and entertainment media. They want to discover their DNA selves. DNA ancestry kits have been one of the "it" gifts for years (Mother's Day, Father's Day, and just because), and now there is the option of adding health risk information. *See NBC Nightly News, Heritage, supra* note 24 ("One of this year's hottest Xmas gifts: home DNA testing kits that help trace a person's ancestry or flag potential vulnerability to disease."); Maren Estrada, *DNA Tests are the Hottest Christmas Gifts of the Season, and There's Still Time to Get One on Sale*, BGR [BOY GENIUS REPORT] (Dec. 22, 2018) ("As was the case during last year's big holiday shopping season, DNA tests are among the hottest gifts of Christmas 2018."), https://bgr.com/2018/12/22/dna-test-deals-last-minute-christmas-sale/. Purchaser multiplication marketing has proven highly effective in the social media consumer demographic. As I have witnessed firsthand as a 23andMe consumer and through monitoring 23andMe's marketing from 2017 to the present, consumers gift 23andMe kits to their family members and friends, for which 23andMe runs successful sales campaigns, and then offers

a "plus one" discount after delivering results to build sales around each purchaser's family and social circles. *See* Estrada, *supra*.

183 *See* Carmel Shachar, I Glen Cohen, Nita A. Farahany, Henry T. Greely, *Introduction*, *in* CONSUMER GENETIC TECHNOLOGIES 1 (J. Glenn Cohen, Nita A. Farahany, Henry T. Greely, Carmel Schachar eds., 2021), *citing* GRAND VIEW RESEARCH, PREDICTIVE GENETIC TESTING AND CONSUMER GENETICS MARKET SIZE, SHARE & TRENDS ANALYSIS REPORT BY TEST TYPE (POPULATION SCREENING, SUSCEPTIBILITY), BY APPLICATION, BY SETTING TYPE, AND SEGMENT FORECASTS, 2019–2025 (2019) (projecting the global genetic testing and consumer wellness genomic market, valued at $2.24 billion in 2015, to double by 2025). *Cf.* THE PEW CHARITABLE TRUSTS, REPORT, THE ROLE OF LAB-DEVELOPED TESTS IN THE IN VITRO DIAGNOSTICS MARKET 1 (Oct. 2021), www.pewtrusts.org/-/; FUTURE OF PRIVACY FORUM, BEST PRACTICES FOR CONSUMER GENETIC TESTING SERVICES (July 31, 2018), www.geneticdataprotection.com/wp-content/uploads/2019/05/Future-of-Privacy-Forum-Privacy-Best-Practices-July-2018.pdf. *See generally* CONGRESSIONAL BUDGET OFFICE/CBO, RESEARCH AND DEVELOPMENT IN THE PHARMACEUTICAL INDUSTRY (2021), www.cbo.gov/publication/57126; US NATIONAL ACADEMIES OF SCIENCE, ENGINEERING, AND MEDICINE/NASEM, PREPARING FOR THE FUTURE PRODUCTS OF BIOTECHNOLOGY (2017), www.nap.edu/catalog/24605/preparing-for-future-products-of-biotechnology.

184 *See generally* Hunter et al., *Bottle*, *supra* note 107. *See also NEJM Editorial Warns of Downside to 'Premature' Consumer Genomics Market*, GENOMEWEB (Jan. 11, 2008), www.genomeweb.com/archive/nejm-editorial-warns-downside-%25E2%2580%2598premature%25E2%2580%2599-consumer-genomics-market#.XSNiUuhKjBQ. *See also supra* notes 41–42, and accompanying text (response to the DTC BRCA testing introduced in 1996).

185 *See generally* Hunter et al., *Bottle*, *supra* note 107. *Cf.* SACGT, RECOMMENDATIONS, *supra* note 32 (explaining the complexity of *clinically-sound* genetic testing in the delivery of care).

186 *See supra* notes 30, 66, and accompanying text (Myriad's collaboration with NIH and reputable entities such as the Dana-Farber Cancer Institute to build the data necessary to make their BRCA testing clinically sound).

187 *See generally Prologue*, *supra*.

188 *See generally* SACGT, RECOMMENDATIONS, *supra* note 32. *See, e.g.*, *supra* note 70, and accompanying text (addressing the information Angelina Jolie had to process, though her family history simplified her decision).

189 *See generally* SACGT, RECOMMENDATIONS, *supra* note 32.

190 *See generally Chapter 6*, *infra*.

5

Vulnerability of the Science and Evidence Base of US Medicine

We want, at times *need*, to believe in medical science and the medical profession. "Technological medicine sometimes seems to promote a view of death as an event that can be deferred indefinitely rather than as a normal, natural part of life."[1] Most Americans are somewhat surprised and made uneasy when they learn that, while over 40,000 people die each year in the US as the result of automobile accidents, more than 250,000 die due to medical error under non-pandemic circumstances.[2] Medical error is the third highest cause of death annually, after heart disease and cancer, and it has been so for years.[3] Confrontation with one's mortality and the mortality of loved ones, especially during a health crisis, whether it be grappling with a potentially terminal cancer or an intensive care unit/ICU hospitalization for COVID-19, heightens awareness and the need to believe in both medicine and science.[4] "[T]he very circumstances of sickness promote acceptance of [physicians'] judgment."[5]

Belief in human genome science innovation and the transformation of clinical care to personal genome medicine shared among distinguishably sophisticated investors, preeminent board members, major biopharmaceutical companies, the media, and the public propelled Theranos, Inc.'s rise in value to $10 billion and fall to less than zero within just four years.[6] Theranos, a Silicon Valley startup, professed to have "transformative" proprietary medical technology on the verge of making precision medicine (clinical intervention tailored by a patient's genome) widely available through extraordinarily high-capacity blood testing.[7] Potential investors and collaborators were told that "the startup could run around 95 percent of all conventional lab tests on its proprietary testing devices, and results were ready in 15 or 20 minutes."[8] In addition to raising $50 million from Walgreen Company, the nation's second-largest pharmacy store chain after CVS Health, Theranos had more than forty testing centers in the company's stores.[9] Theranos courted investors and potential collaborators with an intoxicating portfolio of biopharma agreements. "A [PowerPoint] slide deck listed six deals with five companies that would generate revenues of $120 million to $300 million over the next eighteen months. It listed another fifteen deals under negotiation. If those came to fruition, revenues could eventually reach $1.5 billion, according to the PowerPoint presentation."[10]

Elizabeth Holmes, the founder of Theranos, attended Stanford University as a President's Scholar but dropped out at the age of nineteen to pursue a mission shared with Anne Wojcicki, co-founder and CEO of 23andMe, Inc. – to advance consumer-centric health care and, ultimately, to transform US health care.[11] She also aspired to amass personal wealth:

> Over winter break of her freshman year, Elizabeth returned to Houston to celebrate the holidays .... She'd only been in college for a few months, but she was entertaining thoughts of dropping out. During Christmas dinner, her father floated a paper airplane toward her end of the table with the letters "P.H.D." written on its wings.
>
> Elizabeth's response was blunt, according to a family member in attendance: "No, Dad, I'm not interested in getting a Ph.D., I want to make money."[12]

When questioned by the media about her inspiration for founding Theranos, Ms. Holmes shared her ambition to help create "a world when every person has access to actual health information at a time when it matters; a world in which no one has to say 'goodbye' too soon"[13] Ms. Holmes expressed the belief held by 23andMe's Ms. Wojcicki that access to one's personal health information through laboratory testing is a fundamental right. In her words, "The right to protect the health and well-being of every person, of those we love, is a basic human right."[14] Her often-told story of personal inspiration from losing a beloved uncle to skin cancer that quickly turned into brain and bone cancer was moving and proved to be powerfully persuasive.[15]

Owner of more than half of Theranos's value, Ms. Holmes proudly declared that, through the company's Edison, a portable minilab small enough to fit comfortably on the corner of a desk, Theranos was on the cusp of offering direct-to-consumer/DTC diagnostic blood tests for hundreds of common conditions on demand, divined from a few drops of blood.[16] Also, according to the business plan, biopharma companies would utilize Edison to monitor clinical trial subjects in real time and individually tailor their medication dosages:

> The cartridges and readers would be placed in patients' homes during clinical trials. Patients would prick their fingers several times a day and the readers would beam their blood-test results to the trial's sponsor. If the results indicated a bad reaction to the drug, the drug's maker would be able to lower the dosage immediately rather than wait until the end of the trial. This would reduce pharmaceutical companies' research costs by as much as 30 percent.[17]

Unfortunately, according to federal prosecutors, Edison was the product of Elizabeth Holmes's vision coupled with deception and fraud – not a reality grounded in sound evidentiary science.[18] "Holmes, once hailed as the next Steve Jobs, face[d] a dozen federal fraud charges over allegations that she knowingly misled investors, doctors, and patients about her company's blood testing capabilities in order to take their money."[19] Ms. Holmes, who pleaded not guilty, was convicted of four counts of fraud after four months of proceedings that were international media candy, and she was sentenced to eleven years and three months in prison on November 18, 2022.[20]

US medicine became synonymous with evidence-based science, repeatable and verifiable, during the twentieth century.[21] Faith in both enabled the US medical profession to achieve sovereign status over the practice of medicine.[22] Though a legacy of deference to and reliance on the medical profession is embedded and very present today, times have changed.[23] Patients still bring physicians facts about their health status, family history, and lifestyle – as did their parents, grandparents, and other ancestors before. This information has long enabled physicians to draw from medical science, apply their learned knowledge, and provide patients with responsible medical care. However, now patients also bring medical providers information about medicine and science relayed through television commercials and other biopharma marketing, and culled from the internet and social media, with the expectation of receiving clinically sound knowledge about it and treatment responsiveness.[24] In fact, such information often inspires their appointments.[25]

The dynamism, complexity, pace of progress, and expanse of biotech and genomics are largely attributable to a powerful government-academic-industry "triple threat" methodology.[26] This methodology was the catalyst for the Manhattan Project, armed and launched biotech and genomic revolutions through US technology transfer law and policy/TTLP, produced a draft map of the human genome sequence ahead of schedule and under budget, and was employed in Operation Warp Speed/OWS for the research and development/R&D, manufacture, and distribution of COVID-19 vaccines and therapeutics in remarkably little time.[27] TTLP, the nation's core science R&D methodology, centers on integration of government, industry, and academia to produce innovation with commercial application.[28] More than four decades after the cornerstone TTLP legislation was enacted in 1980, generations of basic research invention have been developed into medicinal products and put to clinical use.[29] While an institution with the resources of Harvard, Yale, and Stanford once could directly meet their faculty's resource needs to engage in research throughout the life sciences, research across the vast forefront of human genome science necessitates access to myriad proprietary enabling technologies.[30] Moreover, proprietary enabling technologies and researcher needs are constantly advancing and changing at a dizzying pace.

The biopharma sector is the financier of a significant majority of clinical research (now more than seventy percent) – a strong trend for some time.[31] According to a study published by *JAMA* in 2015, "Examining data according to the first received date, the number of newly registered trials doubled from 9321 in 2006 to 18,400 in 2014. The number of industry-funded trials increased by 1965 (43%). Concurrently, the number of [National Institutes of Health/NIH]-funded trials decreased by 328 (24%)."[32] Industry still engages with and relies on academic medical centers when conducting its clinical trials to some extent, but biopharma has been decreasing its reliance on them since the 1990s. "By 2004, nearly 75% of the clinical research sites sponsored by industry were physicians in private practice or for-profit research centers. Between 1994 and 2004, academic medical centers fell from 63% to 26% of sites where clinical research is conducted."[33] In fact, biopharma now conducts the bulk of its clinical research through contract research organizations/CROs – commercial professional service providers that hold established, ongoing relationships with health care networks worldwide, at times entire universal health care systems.[34]

While the commercial interests harnessed through TTLP have proven extraordinarily powerful and prolific at medical science innovation, they also have changed norms in government and academia. The very objective of TTLP is to create financial conflicts of interests – to integrate industry and commercial incentives with government and academia – that incentivize invention and innovation with commercial application.[35] In contrast, the medical profession and US law and policy have long recognized that undue financial incentives and conflicts of interest jeopardize physician judgment, the physician–patient fiduciary relationship, and the integrity of clinical research and medicine.[36] The US medical profession made the practice of medicine its domain by pushing the patent medicines business and other commercial interests out of doctor–patient decision-making beginning early in the twentieth century.[37]

As the AMA consolidated power and control over the practice of medicine during that time, the organization was able to persuade many state legislatures to codify the Corporate Practice of Medicine Doctrine/CPMD and courts to show deference to the doctrine.[38] By the midcentury, the AMA and Congress (through the Food and Drug Administration/FDA) had established physician control over communication with consumers about prescription ("Rx") medicines.[39] With the rise of a managed care movement in US medicine in the 1980s, Congress enacted the Healthcare Quality and Improvement Act/HCQIA of 1986, which mandates medical staff bylaws separate from corporate bylaws and medical profession control over the practice of medicine within hospitals and other health care organizations.[40] Congress augmented anti-kickback law the following year and then enacted Stark Law (beginning in 1988) prohibitions to shield the judgment of physicians and the practice of medicine from being undermined by the undue influence of personal financial gain.[41]

Implementation of TTLP over more than four decades and the commercialization of US medicine since the proliferation of managed care and consolidation beginning in the 1980s have changed the practice of medicine and the medical profession. Commercial interests have infiltrated the traditional mechanisms the US medical profession employs to protect science and evidence-based medicine and the integrity of individual patient care in a largely privatized, free-market, and fragmented US health care system.[42] Lucrative interaction with industry spanning from the laboratory bench to the delivery of clinical care has been normalized over the last four decades. The Medical Journal Establishment/MJE, professional medical societies and organizations, medical philanthropies, patient groups, and major hospital organizations often receive substantial funding from industry.[43] So do their leadership and other physician influencers through research sponsorships, consulting engagements, professional speaking fees, and conference honoraria.[44] In fact, in our

TTLP era, medical institutions and professionals pursue and compete for lucrative industry engagements and financial support openly and unabashedly.[45] Professional culture has shifted in medical science and US medicine, and norms have changed – in academia, government, industry, and throughout US health care.

The general public's belief in medical science, direct access to information about it through the internet and social media, a patient-self-determination culture, and distance in the US doctor–patient relationship drive US consumer demand for biopharma products marketed directly to them.[46] US consumer purchase options now include very affordable DTC personal genome testing services, which encompass genetic, genomic, and proteomic testing.[47] Genomic and proteomic science encompass the entire human genome and permeate human health in scope – both actual and predictive health.[48] US medicine is likely to be deluged with voluminous genetic health risk/GHR information generated by company-consumer decision-making through DTC personal genome testing that does not meet sound clinical science standards and does not require medical professional involvement.[49] A barrage of this information threatens to muddle the practice of medicine, to introduce risk to individual patient care, and to undermine the US health care system with added costs and waste.[50] Ironically, infusing DTC personal genome testing not developed for sound clinical use too quickly and too broadly also jeopardizes the health care transformation to evidentiary science-based personal genome medicine – the self-professed driving mission of 23andMe and its CEO.[51]

The following discussion begins by addressing contemporary US health care realities. As observed early in this millennium by Dr. John Abramson, a member of the Harvard Medical School faculty and a renowned physician with decades of family practice experience,

> The most important health care issue in the United States today is whether our current method of creating medical knowledge realizes the full potential of medical science to improve our health, and whether this knowledge is then best applied to clinical practice and communicated effectively to the public. By these standards, American medicine is clearly failing to fulfill its promise.[52]

The scope, complexity, and dynamism of ongoing human genome science, the strength and pervasiveness of commercial influences in US biopharma R&D, medicine, and health care, and patient-consumer demands have made the US medical profession ill-equipped recipients and handlers of emerging human genome science innovation in the delivery of care.[53] In an age of TTLP and emerging personal genome medicine, patients cannot rely on the medical profession to protect and build medicine's evidentiary-science base with objectivity, integrity, and learned knowledge as heavily as they have since the mid-twentieth century because the medical profession no longer may rely so heavily on itself.[54] Yet, under US law and policy protective of physician clinical discretion, last-century reliance lingers on. In fact, given the complexity and explosive advancement of human genome science innovation, it never has been greater.[55]

Consumer demand for and the market supply of DTC personal genome testing without requisite medical professional involvement are a testament to the extent to which the doctor–patient relationship and the assurances of good medicine anchored in decades past no longer are US health care reality.

The discussion then questions the medical profession's ability to steward the evidentiary-science base of medicine in an age of genomics given commercial influences on the core mechanisms the profession relies upon. The medical profession's established, primary means to fulfill that obligation are undermined by the MJE's direct financial dependence on biopharma, the risk of biopharma capture of medical journal content, and biopharma influences on medical education.[56]

Among industrialized-economy nations, the US is uniquely dependent on its medical profession for responsible uptake of clinically sound personal genome medicine. In contrast with the US, other industrialized nations have centralized, formal, and objective health technology assessment/HTA mechanisms, which they heavily utilize – and increasingly so.[57] The chapter concludes that, without a centralized, formal HTA mechanism to objectively evaluate the clinical soundness and utility of human genome science innovation, US health care is ill-equipped for the ongoing genomic revolution, and certainly for the emerging era of personal genome medicine.

MEDICAL SCIENCE, THE PUBLIC, AND THE MEDICAL–INDUSTRIAL COMPLEX

The footings for self-governance and sovereignty over clinical care that the US medical profession established in the early twentieth century were solid and, by mid-century, "physicians were the pillars of any community."[58] US physicians also were distinguishably well compensated relative to their counterparts in other developed-economy nations.[59] Most enjoyed professional independence as solo practitioners or as members of small practice groups of their choosing during the decades before pervasive managed care, consolidation, and health care networks with control over markets.[60] They also enjoyed significant financial independence in setting rates and charging fees:

> When Medicare was created in 1965, the new federal program promised to pay doctors the "usual, customary, and reasonable" rates, as a way of muting the AMA's (at that time) consistent opposition to socialized medicine. Naturally, Medicare spending began to skyrocket, as doctors found that they could charge whatever they wanted, and use the most expensive care they sought, with little-to-no oversight from the government immediately.[61]

However, with the support of and through means provided by the AMA, physician independence in billing for their services was curtailed immensely by systematic adoption of the *Current Procedural Terminology/CPT* – copyrighted property of the AMA, which the organization maintains, updates annually, and sells access to.[62] The *CPT* describes medical, surgical, and diagnostic services and procedures, and produces a code set for billing and reimbursement, known as "the *CPT* code set." The US government mandates adherence to the *CPT* code set when establishing fee schedules for medical procedures and services for US health care programs, as do virtually all health insurance payment and information systems.[63] Each *CPT* code represents a written description of a procedure or service, and all medical procedures and services must fit into the *CPT* codes to receive reimbursement – thereby restraining physicians' interpretive discretion over the clinical procedures and services they provide to their patients.[64]

Since introducing the *CPT* in 1966, the AMA has worked diligently to expand the scope of its coverage and its systematic authority – arguably hypocritical given the premium importance the AMA places on individualized patient care, on the sanctity of physician–patient decision-making, and on learned physician discretion when protecting the medical profession's independence and sovereignty over the practice of medicine.[65] The *CPT* generates substantial, ongoing revenue for the AMA through royalties and license fees, digital use access, and "credentialing products":

> This government-granted monopoly is a windfall to the AMA's D.C. pooh-bahs, who reported $72 million in revenues from "royalties and credentialing products" in 2010[, the year the Affordable Care Act/ACA was enacted]. That hefty sum amounted to a quarter of the AMA's total 2010 revenues; by comparison, the organization received $38 million in members' dues in 2010.[66]

Though the *CPT* now is an entrenched staple, the AMA must keep the US government satisfied to maintain its influence, authority, and its *CPT* market monopoly.[67] The US Centers for Medicare and Medicaid Services/CMS provides significant *CPT* input, and the AMA is receptive.[68]

The contemporary "business of medicine" phenomenon, which began in the 1980s with the sweeping uptake of managed care throughout US health care and became increasingly prevalent in this millennium, consumed much more physician independence.[69] Managed care and the accompanying commercialization of US medicine in the 1980s and 1990s fundamentally impacted the practice of medicine, medical ethos, and patient trust. As explained by Dr. Abramson in 2005,

> Initial cost savings had come fairly easily. Doctors, hospitals, and other health care providers had little choice but to accept discounted fees in order to be included in the newly formed networks of health care providers; otherwise they risked losing access to their patients. These so-called volume discounts controlled prices during the transition to managed care, but the apparent solution was short-lived. Once the discounts had been factored in, this apparently exquisite solution to controlling costs—local health care budgets set by the marketplace instead of the government—became the problem. When there were no more cost savings to be

> squeezed out of the fees paid to health care providers, [health maintenance organizations/]HMOs and managed care companies had only one avenue open: they had to start to really "manage" care, that is, control costs by eliminating unnecessary or wasteful care.... Almost overnight, the hyperbolic hopes for managed care and appreciation of the greater coverage quickly turned into hyperbolic vilification.[70]

Well over a decade before the grueling health care work environment imposed by the COVID-19 pandemic, sentiment within the medical profession had shifted:

> Today medicine is just another profession, and doctors have become like everybody else: insecure, discontented, and anxious about the future.... In a 2008 survey of twelve thousand physicians, only 6 percent described their morale as positive.... American doctors are suffering from a collective malaise.[71]

An indication of this change is "a looming shortage of doctors, especially in primary care, which has the lowest reimbursement of all the medical specialties and probably has the most dissatisfied practitioners."[72]

While still shouldering the immense responsibility for the health and well-being of each of their patients that their professional predecessors carried, today's physicians do not have the same level of control in doctor–patient relationships, in how they practice medicine and, collectively, over the evidentiary-science base of medicine.[73] Medical science and the practice of medicine reached the masses in colloquial form beginning in the 1990s with the rampant advancement of another field of science – information and communications technology/ICT.[74] Through the proliferation of biopharma DTC marketing, the internet, social media, and digital communication, the public gained ready access to an onslaught of information, speculation, and misinformation about medicine and science from a complicated cornucopia of sources.[75] In the hands of the masses, layperson "knowledge" stimulated demand for more patient autonomy and undermined the information exchange sanctity of the traditional learned doctor–patient relationship.[76] During that time, medical science advanced, expanded, and became much more complicated – most recently with the infusion of clinical and DTC genomics.[77]

The advancement and complexity of human genome science have elevated the importance of learned and licensed medical provider knowledge in sound delivery-of-care decision-making. Nevertheless, many in the US have discovered faith in the information they gather themselves and their own capacity to make medical decisions.[78] For many, that faith rivals or even surpasses their faith in learned, credentialed medical professionals when it comes to decisions about their personal health care. The susceptibility of COVID-19-related science to politicization during a deadly global pandemic illustrates the current strength of patient self-determination sentiment in US health care.[79] COVID-19 demanded the undivided attention of many of the world's top medical science experts, public and private. The COVID-19 pandemic presented an extreme situation: emerging medical science information delivered in real time from highly credentialed, renowned – many internationally preeminent – medical science and public health experts. These experts, health care administrators, frontline health care workers, and government health officials delivered COVID-19 information directly and continuously to the US public through mainstream broadcast news media outlets as the federal and state governments responded to a raging, life-taking, global public health pandemic.

The Trump Administration officially declared the US COVID-19 outbreak a public health emergency on January 31, 2020, and the World Health Organization/WHO declared COVID-19 a global pandemic on March 11, 2020.[80] At that time, there was a considerable national consensus that the fate of our collective health depended upon sound medical science innovation. The Trump Administration assured that biopharma science would deliver relief in the event the virus did not just "go away" on its own—as President Trump said he anticipated. The Trump Administration launched Operation Warp Speed/OWS, and anxious Americans and government officials alike monitored the daily progress of medical science R&D in the global mission to develop and distribute effective vaccines and therapeutics as COVID-19 cases and deaths amassed.[81] State governors responded increasingly to the prevalence of COVID-19 in their jurisdictions and in neighboring states, listened to the advisories from preeminent medical scientists and health officials, and ordered mask wearing, social distancing, business and school closures, and in some cases full lockdowns—stay-at-home orders and even curfews. The Trump administration, out of concern that these actions would impede the nation's economy more than it perceived was necessary, challenged and contradicted its own health officials – often publicly.[82] 2020 was a combatively divisive presidential election year. As the COVID-19 pandemic raged on, all got much more political and complicated.

President Trump's promotion and stated personal use of hydroxychloroquine and chloroquine to prevent COVID-19 illness beginning in March 2020 without sound evidence-based science support resulted in immediate and frenzied consumer demand for the drugs.[83] Enough physicians deviated from evidentiary science-based clinical practice and prescribed hydroxychloroquine to cause a supply shortage for patients already dependent on the drug to treat lupus, rheumatoid arthritis, and other serious autoimmune diseases – clinical uses supported by evidence-based science and approved by the FDA.[84] The experience was telling, as were the super-spreader gatherings over the 2020 Memorial Day weekend and during Grand Old Party/GOP campaign rallies and other events for President Trump throughout the national election cycle. A large segment of the US population ignored the ongoing advice and pleas of prominent medical science experts and frontline health care providers, supported by an abundance of global epidemiological data and ominous infection and death rates compounding in real time, and refused to social distance and to wear face masks.[85] They protested against social distancing and wearing masks simultaneously by gathering without masks, and frequently at events held in support of the Trump candidacy.

Vaccine hesitancy among industrialized-economy nations was a familiar phenomenon long before COVID-19.[86] It is somewhat understandable that generations removed from the horrific diseases made absent by the twentieth century vaccination accomplishments would question them, and especially when undermined by false science claims that link familiar vaccines tried and tested over decades to the onset of serious diseases and conditions very present today.[87] The COVID-19 pandemic threat, however, was tangible in real time. People were getting infected, terribly ill, and many dying, with the CDC and broadcast news reporting the US and global rates of infection and death continuously; the escalating numbers and projections were daunting.[88] There was a potential opportunity to punch through the vaccine hesitancy phenomenon for the COVID-19 vaccines, but then discussion of potential vaccine mandates and the viral spread of government and biopharma conspiracy theories through orchestrated internet chatter politicized the situation and undermined the supportive science.[89] In the US, getting vaccinated became a personal political decision as well as a health care decision.

No novel, innovative Rx medication is entirely risk free, and certainly not when projecting well into the future. Prescribing and taking Rx medications is case-by-case, cost–benefit analysis of potential risks and benefits with the sound, evidence-based science available at the time. The risks of spread, infection, illness, hospitalization, and death were made tangible through expansive national and global real-world data/RWD that documented the ongoing public health experience. COVID-19 vaccine opponents raised questions about their safety and efficacy contrary to compelling science and evidence-based data – including immense RWD – compiled through global use under intense multinational medical and regulatory oversight.[90] A hostile anti-vaccine campaign incentivized by conservative, pro-Trump Administration broadcast journalists even threatened the lives of preeminent health science experts and their families.[91]

COVID-19 vaccine hesitancy among industrialized nations was notably extreme in the US throughout 2021.[92] The hesitancy lingered in 2022 even after the FDA modified its emergency use authorizations/EUs to full approvals for the Pfizer (August 2021) and Moderna (January 2022) vaccines.[93] As of May 18, 2022, approximately sixty-six percent of the eligible population had gotten fully vaccinated.[94] Many COVID-19 "anti-vaxxers" perceived the vaccines as the government reaching into personal health care decision-making, rather than receiving them as a medical science innovation solution to a looming and potentially fatal personal and public health threat.[95] Ironically, while rejecting the evidentiary science supportive of the COVID-19 vaccines, many unvaccinated COVID-19 patients in need of hospital care demanded unproven treatments:

> "Folks act as if they can come into the hospital and request any certain therapy they want or conversely decline any therapy that they want with the idea being that somehow they can pick and choose and direct their therapy and it doesn't work," Dr. Jack Lyons, a physician at St. Cloud Hospital in St. Cloud, Minnesota, told CNN.[96]

The general public's belief in themselves and the information they gather about medical science is not restrained by reliable clinical data prerequisites, costs, and other realities that constrain learned and responsible physicians who demand and adhere to scientifically sound evidence – meaning sufficient, verifiable, and repeatable.[97] An antecedent for this consumer self-confidence in medicine, grounded in faith in medical science, predates even the ICT era. Beginning with the FDA approval of AZT in 1987 after a single human clinical trial, human immunodeficiency viruses/HIV and acquired immunodeficiency syndrome/AIDS Rx breakthroughs proved a substantial milestone for patient self-determination.[98] This "invisible enemy" precursor to COVID-19 incentivized a consumer and patient advocacy army during a time of personal and public health anxiety. Even without the armament of the internet to disseminate information and to engage in social media networking, the army was victorious:

> These miracle drugs changed not just the acceptable limits of pricing for new medicines but the approval process as well. There was enormous public pressure to get even potentially useful drugs to patients. With the race to treat HIV, a virus that had infected more than a quarter million Americans by 1991, the FDA relaxed its rules for what constituted proof that a drug was effective, allowing for greater use of what are called "surrogate measures." Drug makers no longer had to show that their product actually cured the symptoms of illness over months or years or extended life. Instead they could measure things like blood markers that were felt to correlate with such benefits.[99]

Use of surrogate endpoints – a relaxation of clinical evidentiary-science standards to accelerate product regulatory approvals – made sense for HIV given it is a virus that attacks specific immune cells subject to measurement.[100] New drug sponsors and the FDA embraced surrogate endpoints subsequently. In fact, "More than half of the novel drugs approved by the FDA in 2020 were supported by a single pivotal trial, and slightly less than half of the pivotal trials supporting novel drug approval used surrogate endpoints as a primary outcome, according to new research published in *JAMA Network Open*."[101] Arguably, surrogate endpoints and the accompanying relaxation of evidentiary-science standards are overused. For example, "An in-depth data investigation by the *Milwaukee Journal Sentinel* and *MedPageToday* in 2014 revealed that, due to reliance on surrogate endpoints, 74 percent of cancer drugs approved by the FDA during the previous decade ultimately did not extend life by even a single day."[102]

The 1990s began with the commencement of HGP, Amgen's market launch of Epogen to treat anemia, a vibrant, populated, and propagating US biotech sector, and intense media coverage of the advancement, expansion, and human health potential of the biotech revolution.[103] The first generation of TTLP-era biotech companies produced, in whole or in part, a bounty of FDA-approved innovative new drugs in the mid 1990s.[104] As the decade advanced, "Medical information was becoming increasingly available on the Internet, and media coverage of the latest 'breakthroughs' in medical science further heightened public enthusiasm about the latest developments."[105] The faith of devout believers in the enormous human health potential of biotech and genomic science deepened during the decade, millions joined them and, overall, the public demanded greater inclusion of science advances in their personal health care:

> Americans' faith in the benefits of the latest medical science was high … Almost half of Americans believed that health insurance or the government should "pay for all new medical technologies." One-third of Americans believed that "modern medicine can cure almost any illness for people who have access to the most advanced technology and treatment." And given their strong interest and faith in medical progress, Americans were overwhelmingly of the opinion that more rather than less money should be spent on "improving and protecting the nation's health," by an 11-to-1 margin.[106]

The US also entered this millennium with robust commercialization of medicine in motion – aggressive DTP and DTC prescription drug marketing; the proliferation of managed care; consolidation of hospitals, providers, and payers into networks that controlled markets; hospital conversions from public to private; a wave of change in physician employment status from independent to health care organization employee; and political and public anxiety about rising and unsustainable health care costs with mounting determination to contain them.[107] In approximately just a quarter-century (the mid-1970s to the end of the twentieth century), US medicine was transformed "from a caring endeavor to the most profitable industry in the United States – what many experts refer to as a medical-industrial complex."[108] While health care costs have been rising in all industrialized-economy health care systems for over a half-century, the US is distinguishable:

> Since 1960, health care's share of the GDP has risen by an average of 2.2 percentage points per decade, as compared with an average increase of 1.1 percentage points per decade in 15 other high-income countries since the early 1970s (when the Organization for Economic Cooperation and Development[/OECD] began tracking these data) …[109]

Completion of a preliminary draft map of the human genome sequence at the outset of this millennium (2001) was received as a genomic proof of principle in popular culture as well as in science.[110] With the draft human genome sequence in hand (2003), the media reported voraciously on the unbridled advancement of genomic science and the amassing universe of identified genotype-phenotype connections – potential leads for biopharma R&D and candidates for personal genome testing. The ongoing, profound progress of the life sciences and dissemination of information about it – by the media and broadcast news, through the internet and social media, by biopharma DTC marketing, and from these combined – affirmed and deepened the public's faith in medical science and confidence demanding access to it. Popular culture consumed the internet and social media ravenously, and ICT was especially appealing to Generation Xers (born between 1965 and 1980) and Millennials (born between 1981 and 1996) less concerned about privacy and more comfortable with science and technology than their seniors.[111] Those born after entered life immersed in ICT and social media norms. In the US, the promise of personal genome medicine through genomics and public awareness that physicians are constrained by costs, profits, and other business considerations inspired a robust patient-driven participatory health care and autonomy movement, which rages on.[112]

TODAY'S US PHYSICIAN–PATIENT RELATIONSHIP AND THE STATE OF PHYSICIAN DECISION-MAKING

Today's US physician–patient relationship is generations removed from the mid-twentieth century staple – substantively, as well as by time.[113] "Insensitivity in patient–doctor interactions has become almost normal."[114] Several contemporary factors – deviations from US medicine in the twentieth century – impact the physician–patient relationship and physician decision-making. First, employers routinely change insurers, insurers and providers routinely change provider networks, and patients routinely change employers, insurers, and providers.[115]

Second, the progress of human genome science is exacerbating a long-recognized medical technology paradox: An infusion of medical innovation enables overcoming fatal conditions, often transforming them into chronic ones that require long-term monitoring and management. Patients then live longer to succumb to more complicated health conditions that require more medical innovation for treatment effectiveness.[116] Especially in the US, rabid uptake of medical technology is a staple, and human genome science will generate bountiful medical innovation – from clinically sound personal genome testing, including predictive testing, that leads to follow-on testing and clinical care, to not clinically sound DTCGHR testing that triggers patient demand for clinical care. Even clinically sound personal genome testing for common diseases is typically complicated and necessitates time-consuming, science-based communication with patients who may not achieve understanding and comprehension, and test interpretation may be subject to change from ongoing and future data collection.[117] The coupling of technology and time constraints already has fundamentally changed the physician–patient relationship and the practice of medicine. As relayed by Dr. Sandeep Juahar, director of the Heart Failure Program at Long Island Jewish Medical Center:

> An unintended consequence of progress is that physicians increasingly say they have inadequate time to spend with patients. Medical advances have transformed once terminal diseases—cancer, AIDS, congestive heart failure—into complex chronic conditions that must be managed long term. Physicians also have more diagnostic and treatment options and must provide a growing array of screenings and other preventative services.... A paper published a decade ago in the *American Journal of Public Health* estimated that it would take over four hours a day for a

> general internist to provide just the preventive care—scheduling mammograms, arranging screening colonoscopies, and so on—that is currently recommended for an average-size panel of adult patients (this on top of the regular workday managing acute problems and emergencies).[118]

Increased uptake of ICT in patient management and the delivery of clinical care has the potential to alleviate some existing physician time constraints. The COVID-19 pandemic forced immersion in remote communication technology in virtually all aspects of life, including clinical care.[119] Pandemic necessity jolted uptake of telemedicine and telehealth, though that already was underway:

> Before the pandemic, nearly thirty states joined an interstate compact that cross-licenses physicians in signatory states. Once the pandemic struck, numerous states allowed out-of-state physicians to treat their residents for the duration of the pandemic, and some have revised their laws going forward. But there are a large number of people from Maine to Alaska who cannot take advantage of telemedicine. The principal obstacle to more widespread use of telemedicine is the state monopoly on physician licensing.[120]

The public is exceedingly more familiar with remote communication in general. Young generations of patients are versed in remote learning given the almost universal use of it in education during the pandemic, from primary to college education. Telehealth is being meaningfully incorporated into medical education curricula.[121] Many, if not most, practicing physicians were immersed in telehealth to some extent during the pandemic. ICT capabilities demonstrated the capacity for providing reliable and uninterrupted communication services with medical privacy safeguards, albeit with enforcement of medical privacy standards relaxed to accommodate pandemic conditions.[122] Notably, the HHS Office of Civil Rights/OCR, which enforces federal medical privacy law under the Health Insurance Portability and Accountability Act/HIPAA, announced on March 17, 2020, "effective immediately, [OCR] will exercise its enforcement discretion and will waive potential penalties for HIPAA violations against health care providers that serve patients through everyday communications technologies during the COVID-19 nationwide public health emergency."[123] Although pandemic conditions may not be representative, some available studies conducted during the pandemic are very positive. According to these studies, many physicians and patients were pleasantly surprised by the remote experience and became acclimated to telehealth.[124] Consequently, telehealth appears poised to proliferate quickly provided states maintain modified/modify licensing laws, telehealth proves cost-effective and profitable under managed care, associated legal liabilities are contained, and payers and health care organizations accommodate.

The impact of telehealth on the physician–patient relationship and physicians' ability to communicate effectively with patients in standard (not pandemic) clinical practice over time is uncertain. Telehealth would increase and ease access and should alleviate some existing physician time constraints, but it also could elevate patient access expectations and their demand for medical provider time. Also, distance medicine through technology with easier access could exacerbate patient fixation on the latest medical science solutions. It could reinforce consumer-centric health care to the detriment of evidentiary science-based clinical practice. More fundamentally, remote physician–patient interaction could increase the existing medical provider challenge of communicating with patients well enough to ground decision-making in sound evidentiary science-based medicine.

Third, patients' faith in medical science, coupled with media coverage of science innovation, DTC biopharma marketing, and the internet availability of information about medical science innovation, has created "unrealistic belief that good health is primarily a product of medical science rather than primarily the natural consequence of a healthy lifestyle and environment."[125] The health care market is distinguishable. "As explored fully in legal literature – especially comparative health law literature – patients are not typical consumers, and health care is not a typical product or commodity."[126] Patients are responsive to DTC biopharma marketing and the medical information they garner outside of physician offices.[127] Their frequently time-constrained engagements with medical providers are directly impacted, potentially to the detriment of health care decision-making and the clinical care they receive:

> Often the breakthroughs and sophisticated technology themselves weaken doctors' ability to help their patients by drawing attention away from real encounters between real people working together to arrive at the best approach to each situation. As these relationships become less important, not only are we spending inordinate amounts of money on therapies that don't provide commensurate value, but our health is actually suffering. This was the biggest surprise for me as I began to understand the real truth about the "scientific evidence" upon which I was basing my medical decisions.[128]

Fourth, advances in medical science and technology, both in quantity and quality, have made it much more difficult for physicians to be truly learned under the profession's mid-twentieth-century standard. For example, "The plummeting cost of DNA sequencing coupled with other technological advances is changing the face of clinical diagnostics."[129] Many physicians are already overwhelmed by the complexity and volume of innovative personal genome medicine tests and treatments.[130] The introduction of "new" conditions and diseases created through biopharma DTP and DTC marketing of prescription drugs to treat them has complicated medicine.[131] Responsible physicians must revisit established treatment options in light of new ones, with "self-informed" patients often demanding the latter. Moreover, they must deliver care under the time and cost constraints imposed by managed care and other business-of-medicine realities.[132] Primary care and family practice physicians are impacted with the full scope of the genomic revolution. Nevertheless, specialists dominate academic medical center influence and are compensated with starting salaries more than double those of primary care physicians.[133] Consequently, over the past several decades, US physicians have shifted away from practicing primary care – a major artery in any health care system:

> Most health policy experts recommend that between 42 percent and 50 percent of doctors in the United States should be primary care doctors. Instead 31 percent of doctors in the United States practice primary care and 69 percent are specialists. In order to correct this imbalance, the Council on Graduate Medical Education (a body established by Congress to make recommendations about the supply and distribution of doctors to the US Department of Health and Human Services) recommended training at least 50 percent of physicians as primary care doctors. In 1998, ... [o]nly 36 percent of US medical students that year reported that primary care was their first choice of specialty.... [O]nly four years later, interest in primary care among US medical students plummeted by 40 percent, so that only about one out of five students (21.5 percent) identified primary care as his or her first choice.[134]

Fifth, collectively, the medical profession no longer may rely as heavily on its symbiotic relationship with the FDA to jointly protect the evidentiary-science base of medicine, which has augmented the burden on individual physicians to assess new medicinal products and has complicated making clinical use determinations.[135] The FDA has been under intense political pressure over decades to not impede (in fact, to accelerate) market access for new medicinal products from biopharma, patient advocacy groups, the medical profession, the public, and Congress, and at times from within its own executive branch. That pressure resulted in FDAMA, and it has continued since through chronic PDUFA negotiations with user fee dependence.[136] Consequently, the FDA has approved new medicinal products more readily with follow-on conditions to address uncertainties, and it has shifted more responsibility for maintaining evidentiary science-based clinical practice to the medical profession.[137] US courts have done the same by taking authority away from the FDA. For example, the US Court of Appeals for the District of Columbia recently limited the FDA's discretion, exercised by the agency for decades, to categorize medical devices as drugs when a product meets both definitions, given definitional overlap under the Federal Food, Drug, and Cosmetic Act/FDCA.[138] This decision:

> comes at the end of a decade of growing challenges to the FDA's authority to regulate. From court decisions in the early 2010s that were sympathetic to arguments that FDA policies regarding off-label drug promotion violate the Constitution's First Amendment, to the political (and legislative) success of right-to-try laws that were intended to allow patients access to certain investigational drugs outside clinical trials without FDA authorization, to people and organizations who oppose mandatory Covid-19 vaccination using increased anti-FDA sentiment as a cudgel, the agency enters the new decade on the defensive.[139]

Congress granted the FDA considerable implementation discretion to categorize products when it enacted the FDCA of 1938 and its amendments – as evident in the plain language of the legislation and the overall lack of Congressional intervention to edit FDA authority during decades of agency implementation. The FDA developed standards and norms for product review and approval to meet the responsibilities Congress imposed while maintaining deference to the medical profession's sovereignty over the practice of medicine and physician discretion to use products on the market off label.[140] Judicial limitations on the FDA's regulatory discretion and flexibility that impede the agency's ability to protect consumers, to promote health care innovation, and to protect and promote the science and evidence base of medicine in product review and approval jeopardize the practice of medicine, the evidentiary-science base of medicine, and the delivery of health care.[141] The COVID-19 pandemic vividly illustrated the importance of FDA regulatory flexibility in matters of medical science innovation and the vulnerability of medical science to politicization in the US.[142] The firehose of medical science innovation now reaching the FDA and clinical care necessitates adherence to agency expertise and flexibility, not deviation from it:

> [O]verly restricting the FDA's flexibility to use its expertise could endanger important public health priorities, especially when there are compelling reasons why Congress permitted flexibility. Congress permitted such flexibility for compelling reasons. For example, in 2017, the FDA announced a comprehensive framework for regulating regenerative medicine, which requires manufacturers to obtain premarketing approval for certain products. The framework is partly aimed at reining in the marketing of unproven, potentially harmful stem-cell interventions, which is important for protecting patients, ensuring robust research on safety and effectiveness, and harnessing the long hoped-for benefits of regenerative medicine. The framework, however, relies on the FDA's legal interpretations regarding the appropriate regulatory pathways for cell-based interventions—interpretations that have been challenged, largely unsuccessfully, in litigation brought by stem-cell clinics.[143]

Sixth, legislative intrusion on the medical profession's clinical care discretion that is inconsistent with evidentiary science-based clinical practice, individualized patient care, and the sanctity of medical provider–patient decision making is another deviation from US medicine in the twentieth century. The US federal government has long recognized states' authority to license and regulate the practice of medicine within their jurisdictions.[144] It also has recognized the practice of medicine as the learned medical profession's domain.[145] In this millennium, however, Congress has relaxed its restraint:

> Notwithstanding its repeated expressions of a commitment against federal interference with the practice of medicine, Congress has not invariably practiced what it preached. In 2003, it banned partial-birth abortions, and a couple of years earlier it had considered withdrawing an abortifacient drug [mifepristone, commonly referred to as RU-486,] approved by the FDA [in 2000]. Moreover, notwithstanding the executive branch's purported commitment to principles of federalism, recent initiatives have

signaled a willingness to interfere in the practice of medicine, as happened in disputes over medical marijuana and physician-assisted suicide.[146]

State legislatures also are reaching into the delivery of clinical care beyond shoring up the parameters of good medicine with medical profession input and support – as they and Congress have done through health insurer coverage requirements that counter managed care limitations and protect patients:

> Anecdotal evidence of specific managed care abuses have led legislatures to enact ad hoc patient protections. For example, managed care policies calling for hospitals to discharge newborn children and their mothers from the hospital within 24 hours after birth led to an outcry against "drive-by" deliveries. A number of state legislatures passed laws mandating that insurance companies pay for no less than 48 hours of hospitalization following childbirth, and Congress soon included that requirement in federal law. Other federal statutes mandate coverage for hospitalization following mastectomies, and prohibit certain restrictions on insurance coverage for mental illness that exceed restrictions on coverage for physical illnesses.[147]

The Supreme Court's 2007 decision to uphold Congress's Partial-Birth Abortion Ban Act of 2003 ("PBA Ban") incentivized state legislatures opposed to abortion to craft legislation that reaches into the medical profession's delivery-of-care domain.[148] In fact, Congress enacted the PBA Ban to resurrect a failed attempt by the Nebraska legislature; the Supreme Court struck down a similar Nebraska statute in 2000.[149] The PBA Ban explicitly prohibits a *specific medical procedure*, referred to in the medical literature as intact dilation and extraction, which the law graphically defines as:

> An abortion in which the person performing the abortion, deliberately and intentionally vaginally delivers a living fetus until, in the case of a head-first presentation, the entire fetal head is outside the body of the mother, or, in the case of breech presentation, any part of the fetal trunk past the navel is outside the body of the mother, for the purpose of performing an overt act that the person knows will kill the partially delivered living fetus; and performs the overt act, other than completion of delivery, that kills the partially delivered living fetus.[150]

The PBA Ban incorporates by reference Congress's *select medical* findings that:

> (1) A moral, medical, and ethical consensus exists that the practice of performing a partial-birth abortion … is a gruesome and inhumane procedure that is never medically necessary and should be prohibited. (2) Rather than being an abortion procedure that is embraced by the medical community, particularly among physicians who routinely perform other abortion procedures, partial-birth abortion remains a disfavored procedure that is not only unnecessary to preserve the health of the mother, but in fact poses serious risks to the long-term health of women and in some circumstances, their lives. As a result, at least 27 States banned the procedure as did the United States Congress which voted to ban the procedure during the 104th, 105th, and 106th Congresses.[151]

Justice Samuel Alito, who was appointed in 2006 to the seat vacated by Justice Sandra Day O'Connor, joined the Court's majority (5–4) in upholding the PBA Ban. The Court's rationale was that the act bans a particular procedure rather than abortion generally, and conflicting expert medical testimony created scientific uncertainty over whether the procedure is ever medically needed, which warranted deference to government (Congress's) discretion.[152]

The Court's decision and increased politically conservative justice composition invigorated a trend among states opposed to abortion to test the limits of the "undue burden" standard that the *Casey* Court established in 1992 and to fundamentally challenge *Casey* and *Roe v. Wade*.[153] Under *Casey*, state legislatures could reach into physician–patient decision-making and clinical practice provided they did not impose an undue burden.[154] Subsequent to *Casey*, state legislatures enacted laws with the stated purposes of improving informed consent and promoting medical safety that conditioned and limited access to abortion.[155] For example, Texas, with the stated purpose of promoting medical practice safety, attempted to force abortion clinics to upgrade to hospital-like standards and to require abortion providers to have admitting privileges at nearby (within thirty miles) hospitals.[156] Louisiana, following Texas's lead, enacted an Unsafe Abortion Protection Act, which also required abortion providers to have admitting privileges at hospitals within thirty miles.[157]

The Court, in a 5–3 decision (with Justices Alito, Roberts, and Thomas dissenting, and a replacement for the vacancy left by Justice Scalia pending), held that key provisions in the Texas law imposed undue burdens.[158] The majority reasoned that courts must weigh burdens versus benefits, the provisions at issue would not improve medical practice safety, and a pointless law cannot be constitutional.[159] Justice Gorsuch was appointed in 2017, and the Court (5–4), following the precedent it set in striking the Texas law, also struck the Louisiana statute as unconstitutional. Justice Roberts joined the majority in concurrence with the judgment on the basis of *stare decisis* (the doctrine of precedent, meaning something previously decided) while adhering to his opinion that *Whole Women's Health v. Hellerstedt*, in which the Court struck Texas's similar statute, was wrongfully decided.[160] Justice Roberts adhered to his rejection of the balance test introduced in *Whole Women's Health* (state interests balanced against resulting burdens). According to Justice Roberts, even a pointless law might be constitutional under *Casey* if it does not unduly burden access to abortion.[161] Nevertheless, he joined the majority – again, on the basis of *stare decisis*.

The 2018 appointment of Justice Brett Kavanaugh to the Supreme Court seat vacated by Justice Kennedy and the 2020 appointment of Justice Amy Coney Barrett to the Supreme Court seat vacated by Justice Ruth Bader Ginsburg established a 6–3 conservative majority on the Court. State legislatures opposed to abortion were inspired to test US jurisprudence and to delve further into the practice of medicine.[162] Several state legislatures imposed much more onerous waiting periods, ultrasound (the procedure used to create images of the unborn) and sonogram (the resulting images) prerequisites ranging from discussing the option of an ultrasound to requiring the procedure, to requiring the procedure with patient sonogram viewing, and a wave of so-called "heart beat laws" – also referred to as "fetal heartbeat legislation."[163] These laws require medical providers to conduct ultrasounds before performing abortions and ban the procedure if a heartbeat is detected; a "fetal heartbeat" arguably is detectable at six weeks into pregnancy – before women may know they are pregnant.[164] In 2021, Arkansas and Oklahoma enacted near-total abortion bans, and Idaho, Oklahoma (the state enacted multiple abortion laws), South Carolina, and Texas enacted legislation to ban abortion at the onset of a fetal heartbeat.[165]

The Supreme Court considered a pre-enforcement challenge (a petition for emergency injunctive relief to block enforcement) to the Texas Heartbeat Act, which took effect on September 1, 2021, but allowed the law to remain in effect while doing so; it was not slated to be implemented until 2022.[166] This law created a cause of action for private citizens, including citizens from other states, to bring civil suits against anyone who assists, or intends to assist, a pregnant woman seeking an abortion in violation of it, and the law rewards successful litigants with minimum liability judgments of $10,000 plus costs and fees.[167] On December 10, 2021, the Court decided that abortion providers could proceed past the motion to dismiss stage and bring actions to stop medical licensing officials from enforcing the statue, but foreclosed such actions against state-court officials and the state attorney general.[168] The Court also identified potential pre-enforcement actions available to test the constitutionality of the statute in federal and state court.[169] Again, the Court left the Texas Heartbeat Act in effect.

The Court issued this decision while deliberating the constitutionality of a Mississippi law, enacted in 2018, which bans most abortions after fifteen weeks of pregnancy and which posed a direct challenge to *Roe v. Wade* and *Casey*.[170] The American College of Obstetricians and Gynecologists/ACOG and a coalition of twenty-four prominent national medical professional organizations, including the AMA, filed an amicus brief "expressing the concrete medical consensus in opposition to the Mississippi law...."[171] The nation anxiously awaited the Supreme Court's decision in this Mississippi case, *Dobbs v. Jackson Women's Health Org.*, following public dissemination of a draft Court opinion leaked in May 2022 that suggested *Roe* and *Casey* would be overturned.[172] Many states worked on and some enacted new anti-abortion legislation, while others prepared to implement and enforce anti-abortion "trigger laws" that potentially would be activated in the event the Court did overturn *Roe* and *Casey*.[173] On June 24, 2022, the Supreme Court issued its opinion in *Dobbs*, in which the Court overturned *Roe* and *Casey*, holding that the US Constitution does not confer a right to abortion and that "the authority to regulate abortion is returned to the people and their elected representatives."[174]

Dobbs established precedent with implications well beyond abortion medical procedures. As observed by Justice Sotomayor in *Whole Women's Health v. Jackson*, "In the months since this Court failed to enjoin the [Texas Heartbeat Act, which created a civil cause of action], legislators in several States have discussed or introduced legislation that replicates its scheme to target *locally disfavored rights*."[175] Abortion, chronically encased in volatile controversy in the US over a half-century, encompasses multiple medical procedures and spills into others such as assisted reproduction technology, prenatal genetic testing, clinical care when pregnancies are nonviable or health-threatening, cell and gene therapies already hampered by commercial and regulatory issues, and FDA US market approval authority for mifepristone and beyond.[176] Abortion could prove a catalyst that promotes federalism and originalist jurisprudence in the context of US medicine. Beyond establishing licensure parameters for the practice of medicine within their jurisdictions with oversight by their segments of the medical profession, state government discretion may now reach into the sanctity of medical provider–patient decision-making, medical profession sovereignty over the practice of medicine, individualized patient care, and medical profession protection of the evidentiary-science base of US medicine.[177]

STEWARDSHIP OF THE EVIDENTIARY-SCIENCE BASE OF MEDICINE

The evidentiary-science base of US medicine is vulnerable, as the unabashed politicization of science during the COVID-19 pandemic illustrated all too vividly.[178] On December 17, 2021, the House Oversight Committee's Select Subcommittee on the Coronavirus Crisis released a report summarizing their exhaustive investigation. Their report identifies with specificity how Trump Administration officials ignored early warnings about the crisis and engaged in a relentless pattern of political interference in the pandemic response, including damning interference in the work of some of the nation's foremost health science experts.[179]

The House Oversight Committee report validates criticisms and allegations by preeminent and responsible health officials that preceded it. For example, in July 2020, Tom Frieden, Jeffrey Koplan, David Satcher, and Richard Besser, who collectively headed the Centers for Disease Control and Prevention/CDC for over fifteen years, jointly challenged the Trump Administration's mandate to open schools in conflict with CDC guidelines. They warned that "Trying to fight this pandemic while subverting scientific expertise is like fighting blindfolded."[180] In May 2020, Dr. Rick Bright, an internationally renowned virologist who brought a whistleblower action against the Trump Administration, testified before Congress that the administration's handling of hydroxychloroquine and chloroquine was illustrative of a pervasive pattern of behavior during the pandemic hostile to medical science and evidence-based clinical practice.[181] Dr. Bright alleged that he was ousted from his post as director of the Biomedical Advanced Research and Development Authority/BARDA, the entity responsible for orchestrating Operation Warp Speed/OWS R&D to produce COVID-19 vaccines and therapeutics,[182] primarily in retaliation for his opposition to the Trump Administration's promotion of unproven drugs like hydroxychloroquine and chloroquine when clinical data indicated they caused life-threatening side effects in some COVID-19 patients.[183] In fact, the Trump Administration pressured the FDA to issue EAUs for hydroxychloroquine and choloroquine to prevent and treat COVID-19 – which the agency hastily retracted when multiple, scientifically sound clinical studies published in some of the world's most prestigious medical journals were completed and concluded that hydroxychloroquine and chloroquine introduced serious health risks for COVID-19 patients rather than any meaningful benefit.[184]

Dr. Francis Collins, during an interview upon leaving his position as Director of the National Institutes of Health/NIH in December 2021, revealed that he experienced a heated exchange with former President Trump when he refused to endorse scientifically disproven remedies for COVID-19 – namely hydroxychloroquine, chloroquine, and blood plasma from recovered COVID-19 patients.[185] Dr. Collins, who was recruited to NIH in 1993, directed the Human Genome Project/HGP to success in 2003, and headed NIH for twelve years, shared, "I have done everything I can to stay out of any kind of political, partisan debates, because it really is not a place where medical research belongs."[186]

Today's medical profession has far less control over the evidentiary-science base of medicine than its twentieth-century self, and industry has much more.[187] The Institute of Medicine/IOM of the National Academies acknowledged the change in 2009:

> Collaborations of physicians and researchers with industry can provide valuable benefits to society, particularly in the translation of basic scientific discoveries to new therapies and products. Recent reports and news stories have, however, documented disturbing examples of relationships and practices that put at risk the integrity of medical research, the objectivity of professional education, the quality of patient care, the soundness of clinical practice guidelines, and the public's trust in medicine.[188]

The impact of human genome science on medicine has merely brushed clinical care given what is to come, but its touch already is overwhelming for many providers due to its complexity, ongoing dynamism, and expansive reach – the entirety of the human genome and its responsiveness to therapeutics and environmental influences, including lifestyle choices.[189] Ongoing, rigorous scrutiny and uptake of medical science through peer-reviewed medical journals and continuing medical education/CME by influencer members of the medical profession are not as assuredly objective and scientifically reliable as they were last century, and the medical profession needs them more given the complexity and explosive presence of genomics.[190]

The Medical Journal Establishment/MJE evolved with the medical profession amassing power, influence, and control over the practice of medicine by protecting and promoting the evidentiary-science base of medicine. By the mid-twentieth century, the MJE was the primary touchstone for the medical profession to advance science and evidence-based clinical practice.[191] Rigorous peer review of the latest clinical research by the profession's most learned, credentialed, and trusted became an invaluable, reliable filter for uptake and dissemination of medical science innovation, and for robust integration of science innovation in medical education.[192] The MJE positioned itself as the medical science authority epicenter in evidence-based clinical practice – a mechanism that enabled the seismic progress of medical science after WWII with reliability and trust.[193] The MJE's authority has been reinforced over time and, in today's human genome science era, "most doctors still hold fast to the basic tenet of their training: that the scientific evidence reported in respected peer-reviewed medical journals is to be trusted and serve as the basis of good medical care."[194] The MJE is a medical science touchstone in both the practice of medicine and medical education:

> From their first day of training, medical students are taught to trust the research published in peer-reviewed medical journals. They learn to take for granted that publication of research findings in these journals ensures that the principles of rigorous science have been followed: that the research has been properly designed to answer the question in a way that can be translated into clinical practice; that the data have been analyzed fairly and completely; that the conclusions drawn are justified by the research findings; and that the scientific evidence that has been published constitutes our best medical knowledge. This medical literature then serves as the source that enables doctors to keep current with new developments in medicine.[195]

However, the MJE was institutionalized in scientifically simpler times and in an era with much more separation between US clinical practice and commercial interests. The innovation riches discovered through TTLP, including the biotech and genomic revolutions, have made legacy reliance on the MJE impractical for individual physicians committed to practicing responsible, evidentiary science-based medicine:

> There are tens of thousands of academic journals, and millions of academic medical papers in existence, with more produced every day. One recent study tried to estimate how long it would take to keep up with all this information. The researchers collected every academic paper published in a single month that was relevant to general practice. Taking just a few minutes for each one, they estimated it would take a doctor six hundred hours to skim through them all. That's about twenty-nine hours each weekday, which is, of course, not possible.[196]

Substantively, the science filter function of the MJE is much less reliable due to corporate influences on medical journals' very existence, and on how and what they publish.[197] These influences undermine the MJE's reliability at a time when physicians, enveloped in ongoing medical science innovation, never have been more in need of a reliable medical science touchstone.[198] Ironically, though the medical profession institutionalized the authority of peer-reviewed medical journals to promote the evidentiary-science base of clinical practice, to protect scientific integrity, and to protect medicine from undue commercial influences, corporations arguably now are a primary beneficiary of the MJE's authority.[199]

Biopharma finances most clinical research and lavishly (albeit selectively and strategically) sponsors research studies, which are the fodder for MJE article submissions.[200] As should be expected given companies' obligations to their shareholders, biopharma commercial sponsorship impacts study outcomes:

> Studies repeatedly document the bias in commercially sponsored research, but the medical journals seem powerless to control the scientific integrity of their own pages. In 2003 [when commercial influence was much less prevalent and normalized in US research and medicine], separate studies were published in *JAMA* and the *British Medical Journal* showing that the odds are 3.6 to 4 times greater that commercially sponsored studies will favor the sponsor's product than studies without commercial funding. And in August of 2003 a study published in *JAMA* found that among the highest-quality clinical trials, the odds that those with commercial sponsorship will recommend the new drug are 5.3 times greater than for studies funded by nonprofit organizations.[201]

Internally, the MJE simply is not structurally sound enough today to support the awesome responsibility bestowed upon it:

> In reality, the systems used by journals to select articles are brittle, and vulnerable to exploitation.... [Peer review] is an imperfect and subjective set of judgement calls, standards vary hugely between journals, and there's also room to stick the knife into competitors and enemies, since most reviewers' comments are anonymized.... So the academic literature is a "buyer beware" environment, where judgement must be deployed by expert readers, and you cannot simply say, "I saw it in a peer reviewed paper, therefore it is true."[202]

The MJE self-acknowledged its unreliability on its own pages at the outset of this millennium:

> In September 2001 an unprecedented alarm was sounded. The editors of 12 of the world's most influential medical journals, including the *Journal of the American Medical Association, [T]he New England Journal of Medicine, The Lancet*, and the *Annals of Internal Medicine*, issued an extraordinary joint statement in their publications. In words that should have shaken the medical profession to its core, the statement told of "draconian" terms being imposed on medical researchers by corporate sponsors. And it warned that the "precious objectivity" of the clinical studies that were being published in their journals was being threatened by the transformation of clinical research into a commercial activity. The editors said that the use of commercially sponsored clinical trials "primarily for marketing ... makes a mockery of clinical investigation and is misuse of a powerful tool." Medical scientists working on corporate-sponsored research, the editors warned, "may have little or no input into trial design, no access to the raw data, and limited participation in data interpretation."[203]

In the words of the MJE editors,

> As editors of general medical journals, we recognize that the publication of clinical-research findings in respected peer-reviewed journals is the ultimate basis for most treatment decisions. Public discourse about this published evidence of efficacy and safety rests on the assumption that clinical-trials data have been gathered and are presented in an objective and dispassionate manner. This discourse is vital to the scientific practice of medicine because it shapes treatment decisions made by physicians and drives public and private health care policy. We are concerned that the current intellectual environment in which some clinical research is conceived, study subjects are recruited, and the data are analyzed and reported (or not reported) may threaten this precious objectivity.[204]

US TTLP, introduced in 1980, was fully implemented decades ago.[205] Commercial influences in medical science (basic and clinical research) and academia were commonplace and normalized before the end of the last millennium.[206] They have not been effectively checked by the medical profession over the last quarter-century, and they have become profound and prevalent in the US' highly privatized, decentralized, and fragmented health care system. It is a system without a reliable, centralized joint government-medical profession sentinel to police truth in medical science and to independently assess clinical value – in other words, to conduct formal, centralized, and evidence-base health technology assessment/HTA to protect the evidentiary-science base of US medicine.

MEDICAL JOURNAL DIRECT FINANCIAL DEPENDENCE ON INDUSTRY

The MJE achieved financial sustainability and growth during the twentieth century primarily through subscription fees and support generated from within the medical profession.[207] Today, the biopharmaceutical industry "buys a lot of advertising space in academic journals, often representing the greatest single component of a journal's income stream, as editors very well know."[208] Biopharma advertising and sponsorship paired with ICT has enabled the founding of many specialty peer review medical journals over the last few decades. The trend was anticipated in 2006, in a series questioning the clinical science and ethical soundness of the MJE, which was published by the *Journal of the Royal Society of Medicine*:

> The growth in scientific and medical journals was exponential until a decade or so ago when the whole venture hit the economic buffers.
>
> Some societies and some commercial publishers have grown rich from their journals, earning profit margins of 40%. They were "must have" journals, quasi-monopolies. New paper journals ceased to appear in such large numbers a decade or so ago because the traditional business model—of selling subscriptions primarily to institutions—would no longer work.
>
> However, the exponential increase in journals looks set to return now that electronic journals can be started with minimal funds.[209]

Biopharma also purchases article reprints for distribution to those who provide clinical care – a practice biopharma utilizes heavily in the US to promote off-label uses of FDA-approved products. Though the FDA prohibits and polices biopharma direct marketing of off-label uses, disseminating journal reprints was deemed legal in *Washington Legal Foundation*.[210] Reprint revenue incentivizes medical journals to be receptive to article submissions based upon biopharma-sponsored research.[211]

There is meaningful empirical evidence of correlation between what medical journals publish and their financial dependence on the industry. For example, as summarized in 2012 by physician, academic, and science writer Ben Goldacre:

> Overall, the pharmaceutical industry spends around half a billion dollars a year on advertising in academic journals. The biggest—*NEJM*, *JAMA*—take $10 or $20 million each, and there is a few million each for the next rank down.... To see whether this income has an impact on content, a 2011 paper looked at all the issues of eleven journals read by [general practitioners/]GPs in Germany—a mix of free and subscription publications—and found 412 articles where drug recommendations were made. The results were stark: free journals, subsidized by advertising, "almost exclusively recommended the use of the specific drugs." Journals financed entirely through subscription fees, meanwhile, "tended to recommend against the use of the same drugs."[212]

Medical journals' dependence on industry for their financial sustainability is reflective of science R&D itself in an age of TTLP.[213] The MJE, an institution the medical profession created, has entrusted, and has depended upon to protect and advance the evidentiary-science base of medicine at least since the mid-twentieth century, no longer is a financially independent, objective, and reliable sentinel.

THE RISK OF INDUSTRY CAPTURE OF MEDICAL JOURNAL CONTENT

Dr. Marcia Angell, a preeminent physician and a former Editor-in-Chief of *The New England Journal of Medicine* with decades of *NEJM* leadership, shared her experience at the outset of this millennium:

> I witnessed firsthand the influence of the industry on medical research during my two decades at *The New England Journal of Medicine*.... I saw companies begin to exercise a level of control over the way research is done that was unheard of when I first came to the journal, and the aim was clearly to load the dice to make sure their drugs looked good. As an example, companies would require researchers to compare a new drug with a placebo (sugar pill) instead of with an older drug. That way, the new drug would look good even though it might actually be worse than the older one.... As I saw industry influence grow, I became increasingly troubled by the possibility that much published research is seriously flawed, leading doctors to believe new drugs are generally more effective and safer than they actually are.[214]

For-profit corporations, including those in the business of life science innovation to improve human health, are legal constructs that exist to serve their shareholders under the "shareholder wealth maximization norm."[215] According to this norm, "A business corporation is organized and carried on primarily for the profit of the stockholders."[216] Profit is a powerful incentive, and unapologetically so in our capitalism-driven US culture. Although the shareholder wealth maximization norm is the subject of ongoing academic (business, law, and beyond) debate, it is an entrenched, albeit not absolute, predictor of corporate behavior – especially in the US' intensely free-market, capitalist culture and economy.[217] Biopharma companies engage in substantial philanthropic activities beyond tax benefits, but their very purpose and obligation under the law that creates them is to provide returns to their shareholders to their fullest capacity while acting in compliance with governing US law.[218]

Improving human health is good biopharma business, but "drug companies have no more responsibility to oversee the public's health than the fast-food industry has to oversee the public's diet."[219] Biopharma companies do have a fiduciary responsibility to their shareholders to control risks and maximize returns, and they have been meeting those obligations exceedingly well for decades. Over several decades, the biopharma industry has been "taking in unheard-of profits – more than three times the average of the other Fortune 500 industries, even after accounting for all its R&D costs."[220] Biopharma's economic success is especially extraordinary given that "[s]cientific truth is innately unpredictable, which is bad for business – especially big business with high financial stakes."[221] A potential drug candidate at the basic (commonly referred to as "bench" or "laboratory bench") research stage has less than a .02–.01 percent chance of reaching the market according to industry data.[222] Phase 3 clinical trials, the culmination of R&D spending and an immensely expensive threshold to cross for market access, have [at least] a fifty percent failure rate.[223] As the Congressional Budget Office/CBO summarized in a 2021 report,

> Developing new drugs is a costly and uncertain process, and many potential drugs never make it to market. Only about 12 percent of drugs entering clinical trials are ultimately approved for introduction by the FDA. In recent studies, estimates of the average R&D cost per new drug range from less than $1 billion to more than $2 billion per drug. Those estimates include the costs of both laboratory research and clinical trials of successful new drugs as well as expenditures on drugs that do not make it past the laboratory-development stage, that enter clinical trials but fail in those trials or are withdrawn by the drugmaker for business reasons, or that are not approved by the FDA. Those estimates also include the company's capital costs—the value of other forgone investments—incurred during the R&D process. Such costs can make up a substantial share of the average total cost of developing a new drug. The development process often takes a decade or more, and during that time the company does not receive a financial return on its investment in developing that drug.[224]

US medicine depends upon a sovereign medical profession that is educated and trained, from their medical studies into the delivery of care, to rely on the MJE for good medicine guidance. Scientific evidence recognized as truth in the medical literature drives physician behavior and biopharmaceutical sales.[225] Arguably, "[i]n this context, the role of drug and medical-device companies has evolved so that their most important products are no longer the things they make. Now their most important product is 'scientific evidence.'"[226] Consistent with corporate organizational documents reflective of the law from which corporations are created (the basis for their corporate citizen existence and activities) and fiduciary obligations to shareholders, "at best, the medical knowledge produced by commercial interests is restricted to the medical problems that are most profitable to study. And at worst, research is manipulated, misrepresented, or withheld, with the goal of maximizing sales."[227]

US TTLP has proven a remarkably effective catalyst for advancing medical science innovation – the biotech and genomic revolutions, and well beyond.[228] Its effectiveness at harnessing potent commercial incentives is well beyond proof of principle. According to the CBO,

> The pharmaceutical industry devoted $83 billion to R&D expenditures in 2019.... That amount is about 10 times what the industry spent per year in the 1980s, after adjusting for the effects of inflation. The share of revenues that drug companies devote to R&D has also grown: On average, pharmaceutical companies spent about one-quarter of their revenues (net of expenses and buyer rebates) on R&D expenses in 2019, which is almost twice as large a share of revenues as they spent in 2000. That revenue share is larger than that for other knowledge-based industries, such as semiconductors, technology hardware, and software.[229]

TTLP also has made twentieth-century reliance on the MJE to protect the evidentiary-science base of medicine frighteningly antiquated. TTLP has intentionally created tremendous commercial influence in basic research, which is substantially funded by federal government grants and through reinvestment of TTLP financial returns – a requirement under TTLP.[230] The CBO reported in 2021 that NIH funding over the past two decades has exceeded $700 billion and, "Between 2010 and 2016, every drug approved by the FDA was in some way based on biomedical research funded by NIH."[231] Through TTLP, biopharma shops for invention resulting from this investment in basic research, and academia competes to be marketable to industry in what they invent. The effectiveness of TTLP at the basic research level – a constant supply of bouquets of invention worthy of biopharma product R&D – has caused clinical research to burgeon, biopharma is financing most of it, and biopharma is conducting clinical research largely through contract research organizations/CROs rather than through academic medical centers.[232] Consequently, TTLP has significantly widened a funding divide between US basic research and clinical research for FDA application submissions, with the federal government primarily funding the former and biopharma primarily funding the latter.[233] Consistent with the success of TTLP, biopharma is present and influential from the laboratory bench to the pharmacy shelf and in the delivery of clinical care.[234]

Biopharma companies that behave like other for-profit corporate citizens in our capitalist, free-market system to meet their fiduciary obligations to shareholders while remaining compliant with US law should not be villainized for their behavior. Their behavior should be expected and respected, and even lauded. It is behavior that has made the US economy distinguishably successful over considerable time and it has advanced medical science innovation profoundly. Nevertheless, uptake of clinical research and resulting products in the practice of medicine must be consistent with protecting and promoting science and evidence-based clinical practice. The US mechanisms to check corporate behavior in clinical research to accomplish that are insufficient in our TTLP era:

> Control over clinical research changed—quietly at first, but very quickly, and with profound effects on medical practice. The role of academic medical centers in clinical research diminished precipitously during the 1990s as the drug industry turned increasingly to new independent, for-profit medical research companies [,contract research organizations/CROs,] that emerged in response to commercial funding opportunities.... [Industry] could now call the shots on most of the studies that were evaluating its own products without having to accept input from academics who were grounded in traditional standards of medical science. And the increasing competition for commercial research dollars put academic centers under even more pressure to accept the terms offered by the commercial sponsors of research, threatening the independence and scientific integrity that had been the hallmark of the academic environment.[235]

The susceptibility of contemporary clinical research to commercial influences and manipulation in our TTLP era underscores the importance of protecting the evidentiary-science base of clinical practice beyond the MJE.[236] "Most of us take for granted that the well-established rules of science ensure the validity of medical research, regardless of the purpose for which the research is undertaken or the context in which it is performed. Nothing could be further from the truth."[237] Decades of TTLP implementation have changed the norms for clinical research and science transparency through the MJE. "Rigging medical studies, misrepresenting research results published in even the most influential medical journals, and withholding the findings of whole studies that don't come out in a sponsor's favor have all become the accepted norm in commercially sponsored medical research."[238]

In sum, industry finances most clinical research for US market R&D, which is the fodder for journal submissions.[239] Biopharma companies, accountable to their shareholders, make *business decisions* to conduct clinical trials and to sponsor research to maximize shareholder wealth – the purpose for their corporate citizen existence and a fiduciary obligation.[240] Beyond satisfying regulators, they are the architect and overseer of their clinical research studies. For-profit biopharma companies are corporate citizens with rights and freedom to contract, not philanthropies, academic medical centers, or other non-profits with mission obligations and restrictions tied to their non-profit status with the Internal Revenue Service/IRS.[241] Within the parameters of governing US law, biopharma corporate citizens decide what research they should sponsor, which researchers they want to work with, and under what contractual terms. Over more than two decades, biopharma has demonstrated an increasing desire to work with CROs rather than with academic medical centers. A substantial increase in clinical research has created insatiable demand for research subjects, much of which is met by CROs' global reach and ongoing relationships with networks of medical institutions and even entire health care systems.[242]

Biopharma also has demonstrated desire to work directly with patient organizations rather than reaching patients through academic medical centers. In our ICT and social media age, patients are networked, in communication, and readily mobilized through patient organizations. Biopharma relationships with these organizations have proven an invaluable resource for subject recruitment, clinical research support, putting political pressure on regulators and other government officials, and for stirring market uptake of resulting medicinal products.[243] It is prudent biopharma business decision-making to fund and work with patient groups, and biopharma companies do. Like medical journals, non-profit patient groups are recipients of substantial industry financial support:

> Partnering with patient groups has become a key element of marketing strategies for every major medical condition, and with virtually every major drug company. A survey from Britain [reported in 2000] estimated that two-thirds of global health charities and patient groups now accept support from drug or device manufacturers, though it is often hard to know exactly how much they receive.[244]

According to Dr. Otis Webb Brawley, who served as Chief Medical and Scientific Officer and Executive Vice President of the American Cancer Society/ACS from 2007 to 2018:

> Patient groups get money from the drug and device companies, and occasionally even hospitals and medical practices, because they push the envelope, making claims so outrageous that even special interests dare not make them. Us TOO, which claims to be the world's largest "grassroots, independent, patient-focused charitable organization" with more than 380 chapters in nine countries, is funded almost completely by the pharmaceutical industry. Despite getting more than 90 percent of its funding from drug and device companies with an interest in prostate-cancer screening, Us TOO claims to be independent and not beholden to any company. Moreover, it claims to provide unbiased information regarding screening and treatment. If the drug maker Abbott Labs had worked up the audacity to say some of the things Us TOO and Zero[, formerly the National Prostate Cancer Coalition, with a budget largely funded by drug companies and treatment device manufacturers,] say about the Abbott PSA test, the FDA would issue a warning letter and, likely, levy a fine.[245]

It is important to recognize and be cognizant of the fact that in our free market, capitalist system, the FDA is the *recipient* of sponsor applications. Biopharma applicants and clinical trial sponsors, as corporate citizens with rights, have tremendous discretion over the scope of the applications for market access they submit to the FDA and, consequently, over whether and what clinical research they undertake.[246] New drug and new biologic applications (NDAs and NBAs) and approvals limited in scope do not limit US market access given physician discretion to venture off label.[247]

The FDA's authority is to objectively "grade" the applications corporate citizens submit regarding whether the agency's established standards for safety and efficacy have been satisfied. For example, the FDA had no authority to require pediatric studies even for drugs intended to treat conditions prevalent in children, such as asthma and pain from major injuries and surgeries, until Congress expressly gave it some authority to do so under the Pediatric Research Equity Act/PREA of 2003, and 2007 amendments to the PREA and to the Best Pharmaceuticals for Children Act/BPCA.[248] Children are a protected class under the regulations to protect human subjects, referred to as the Common Rule, meaning more extensive regulatory requirements are imposed when children are included in research.[249] Medically, "children" is not as definitive a category as "adults" given puberty and overall childhood development factors, including brain development. Clinical research is expensive, and adding a pediatric population imposes significant cost – especially if, given puberty and other significant milestones during childhood development, studies must be completed using appropriate formulations for each of several age groups. Prior to the amended PRE and BRCA, many biopharma sponsors simply did not include pediatric use in their new drug and new biologic applications (NDAs and NBAs), knowing that pediatricians were likely to prescribe them off label. Pediatricians, family practice physicians, and specialists treating children did. Before the PREA and BPCA, more than eighty percent of Rx medications approved for adult use were being used in children even though their safety and effectiveness had not been established in children.[250] The percentage has been cut approximately in half since enactment and implementation of the PREA and BPCA.[251]

The FDA first attempted to confront this chronic dearth of pediatric clinical data with incentives, and then incentives coupled with mandates (the "Pediatric Rule") under the original BPCA.[252] The FDA's Pediatric Rule was challenged in federal court on the grounds that requiring manufacturers to test drugs for unclaimed uses exceeded the FDA's statutory authority and, therefore, was arbitrary and capricious.[253] The FDA was accused of reaching into how drugs are prescribed rather than accepting physician discretion to use them off label. The US District Court for the District of Columbia agreed; the Court concluded that the FDCA did not vest the FDA with authority to promulgate the Pediatric Rule.[254]

Overall, for-profit corporate clinical trial sponsors choose what and whom to study, and "[m]any studies choose a population that is younger and fitter than the target population, and therefore less likely to show side effects."[255] Similarly, older and sicker patients may be included in studies to show stronger efficacy. Obviously, when a study population does not fully and accurately represent the end-user patient population for a disease under study, study results often have limited applicability to actual use in medicine. "[T]he systematic inclusion of unrepresentative patients in clinical studies may be good for the profits of the commercial sponsors of the studies (at least in the short term), but it is not good for the people who will receive care based on the distorted 'science.'"[256]

Sponsors of NDAs and NBAs are legally obligated to share all relevant clinical study data with the FDA, and the FDA is obligated to respect sponsors' application discretion and the proprietary nature of the information they share with the agency. The FDA also works to maintain sponsors' trust for future interactions and submissions. Prudent biopharma applicants obviously do not include unfavorable data in the applications they ultimately submit to the FDA for safety and efficacy "grading" unless the situation compels them to, and they shape the scope of their applications. As with Vioxx and Celebrex, the FDA often is put in a terribly conflicted situation. The FDA approved those drugs – pain-management drugs in a class of drugs known as cox-2 inhibitors – with a focus on the NDAs submitted by their sponsors (Merck for Vioxx and G. D. Searle & Company for Celebrex), but also made negative study data publicly available on its website – if anyone bothered to search.[257] Few did until problems with the drugs were identified through clinical care use over years after approval.[258]

Post enactment of FDAMA, when the data submitted to support an application for market approval is adequately sufficient but raises questions, standard FDA practice is to approve with heightened oversight of actual market use. The FDA may approve a NDA or NBA conditioned on completion of follow-on studies (phase 4 or "pharmacovigilance" trials) conducted during market use to address lingering questions and/or with participation in the Risk Evaluation and Mitigation Strategies/REMS program.[259] In response to the Vioxx, Celebrex, and other new drug controversies at the outset of the millennium, Congress attempted to raise the FDA threshold for market approval and to add more regulatory meaning to phase 4 trials and FDA market surveillance requirements under the FDAAA of 2007, which authorized the REMS program.[260] However, FDA resources are limited, industry has much say on how user fee revenues are allocated under PDUFA, and demand on the agency to satisfy voluminous premarket obligations during a genomic revolution far exceeds its resources.

The FDA regulatory rubric post market approval includes dependence on the medical profession to sort out remaining clinical safety and efficacy issues through clinical use – reflective of US law and policy deference to and reliance on the medical profession in practice-of-medicine matters. The FDA regulatory system includes a presumption that physicians will timely identify and report problems to the FDA and product manufacturers. In other words, the regulatory system works on faith that it will prove effective because the medical profession will provide the ultimate market oversight. However, experience has proven that physicians are not timely, reliable reporters:

> [U]ncertainty innate in the art of individualized medicine invites reporting apprehension and hesitation--"physician think," such as, "Perhaps the cause was just my particular patient's drug interactions, lifestyle choices, medical history, or failure to follow orders ... or perhaps my failure to know as much as I should about this particular drug." Concerns about professional ramifications of not knowing do as well.[261]

Congress attempted to shore up market (clinical practice) use reporting through the FDAAA by introducing Sentinel, a national electronic oversight system for medical product safety surveillance, but it did not do so with the specificity and budgeting necessary to make Sentinel a timely reality.[262]

Other industrialized countries with universal health care systems (whether nationalized as in the UK, socialized as in Germany, or single-payer as in Canada) generally require more information for market approval and actual health care system uptake of new medicinal products.[263] For example, Sweden's FDA counterpart, the Swedish Medical Product Agency/MPA, one of the leading regulatory authorities in the EU based on rather than upon applications submitted under the European Medicines Agency's centralized review procedure, requires that drug and biologic applications include all known studies relevant to the products, whether published or not. [264] However, to receive biopharma proprietary information held and not disclosed by the FDA (declared beyond the scope of sponsor-submitted applications), Sweden's MPA adopted a policy in 2019 of providing a confidentiality commitment to comply with the FDA's proprietary information policy. Pursuant to the confidentiality commitment, "The Commissioner of Food and Drugs has certified MPA as having the authority and demonstrated ability to protect trade secret information from disclosure. FDA therefore may provide MPA with certain types of trade secret information at FDA's discretion and upon request by MPA...."[265] However, with the information in hand, Sweden's MPA may factor it into consideration, such as by raising questions with product sponsors, imposing additional clinical research requirements, and limiting or denying market approvals.

Beyond biopharma corporate citizen behavior in new product application submissions and the FDA's recipient role, medical journal article authorship is not always what it used to and innately professes to be. Like clinical research, authorship of medical science articles often is outsourced to professional service providers compensated by corporations.[266] Even more brazen, "some scientists buy papers from third-party firms to help their career[,]" which has given rise to a "paper mill" industry that churns out fraudulent manuscripts to order.[267] The content of legitimate papers is manipulated for derivative uses, such as by modifying nucleotide sequences or reagents – with the risk of tainting the ongoing medical science enterprise with bad data.[268] An investigation by *Nature* determined that, during the first three months of 2021, journals retracted at least 370 papers publicly linked to paper mills and, collectively, papers flagged as suspect encompassed more than 1,000 studies.[269] *Nature* "tallied 370 articles retracted since January 2020, all from authors at Chinese hospitals, that either publishers or independent sleuths have alleged to come from paper mills" and another forty-five articles with publisher expressions of concern.[270] "Editors are so concerned by the issue that[, in September 2020,] the Committee on Publication Ethics (COPE), a publisher-advisory body in London, held a forum dedicated to discussing 'systematic manipulation of the publishing process via paper mills'[.]"[271]

Some journals are addressing the brazen systematic manipulation of the publication process by paper mills by asking authors to submit raw data and by searching images for duplication in other papers.[272] However, even when such fraud is identified by journals, "Publishers almost never explicitly declare on retraction notices that a particular study is fraudulent or was created by a company to order, because it is difficult to prove."[273] Moreover, those engaging in organized fraud are empowered by the ongoing advancement of ICT, such as artificial intelligence/AI techniques.[274]

When renowned medical professionals declare authorship, ghostwriting is invisible unless exposed by irrefutable proof or admission.[275] The academic careers of very credentialed and accomplished people are made and lost over their demonstrated ability to publish, and the academic reputations of institutions rise and fall with faculty publication productivity. Most academic institutions are not seriously looking for ghosts; they want their faculty to publish. "A survey in 2010 of the top fifty medical schools in the United States found that all but thirteen had no policy at all prohibiting their academics [from] putting their name to ghostwritten articles."[276] According to Dr. Goldberg, even if institutions find ghostwriting, they are not punishing faculty for engaging in it:

> [T]o the best of my knowledge, no academic anywhere in the world has ever been punished for putting their name on a ghostwritten academic paper. This is despite everything we know about the enormous prevalence of this unethical activity, and despite endless specific scandals around the world involving named professors and lecturers, with immaculate legal documentation, and despite the fact that it amounts, in many cases, to something that is certainly comparable to the crime of simple plagiarism by a student.[277]

In its defense, the MJE has at least promoted authenticity in authorship by issuing recommendations on who should be named as an author on a paper.[278] However, in practice, these guidelines are more flashlight than search light – too vague and subject to manipulation:

> For example, a paper could legitimately have the name of an independent academic on it, even if they only contributed 10 per cent of the design, 10 per cent of the analysis, a brief revision of the draft, and agreed on the final contents. Meanwhile, a team of commercial medical writers employed by a drug company [and responsible for the other 90 percent] would not appear in the author list, anywhere at all.[279]

Moreover, authors publish in a manner not necessarily reflective of overall research results. When for-profit corporations make business decisions to invest money in research, their protection of that investment beyond determining at the outset what research is done and by whom, includes controlling the dissemination of results:

> Often the medical researchers who carry out company-sponsored studies are not even allowed to see all of the data from the studies they are working on. These researchers are left in the position of analyzing and including in their articles only the data that the drug or device manufacturers have allowed them to see. If even the researchers who write the articles have access to only the data that the corporate sponsors allow them to see, how can anyone have confidence in the "scientific evidence" published in the medical journals? And how can anyone have confidence in the medical care that is based upon results that have been censored to serve commercial interests?[280]

Journal peer reviewers often rely on the data included in article submissions.[281]

Clinical medicine is evidentiary science-based for good reason – most notably, conquering diseases and improving human health. Antidepressants prescribed to young patients is an illustrative case study on the dangers to patients and good medicine when MJE publications fail to accurately represent existing scientific data:

> Although the six studies involving young patients that had been published in medical journals showed that antidepressants are safe and effective, nine studies showing just the opposite had not been published. Doctors, trusting their medical journals, were being misled. Instead of taking protective action based on a clear and present danger, the FDA asked an independent panel of researchers to review the data. When the outside experts agreed with its own, the FDA belatedly mandated the highest level of caution: a "black box warning"' on the drug label and a patient information sheet to accompany the medication. In other words, the drug companies had maintained sales of largely ineffective drugs by not publishing results from their own studies showing that the new antidepressants increase a suicidal behavior in youngsters, thus leaving doctors uninformed about these negative studies.[282]

Vioxx and Celebrex, cox-2 inhibitors prescribed for pain management, provide another example.[283] The FDA approved these drugs fully aware of research data that raised both safety and efficacy concerns unpublished by the MJE.[284] The agency approved them consistent with its approve-and-watch mindset under section 506(b) of FDAMA, which heightens reliance on the learned medical profession as the ultimate good clinical practice regulatory authority for safety and efficacy.[285] Both the *The New England Journal of Medicine/NEJM* and the *Journal of the American Medical Association/JAMA* published articles with conclusions that encouraged physicians to prescribe Viox and Celebrex, despite data publicly available (on the FDA's own website, if anyone decided to search it) that the drugs caused heart attacks and strokes in many patients and were not more effective in combatting pain than ibuprofen available over-the-counter at a nominal price.[286] Vioxx and

Celebrex were two of the drugs most heavily marketed to physicians and patients at the beginning of this millennium.[287] The *NEJM* and *JAMA* articles and manufacturer marketing, the effectiveness of which was bolstered immensely by the articles, trumped the negative data publicly available on the FDA's website. "By the end of 2001, 57 percent of all the money spent on prescription arthritis medication in the United States was spent on Celebrex and Vioxx, and both were among the top 10 selling drugs in the United States."[288] In fact, American physicians prescribed some $7 billion worth of Vioxx, which is estimated to have caused tens of thousands of heart attacks and deaths.[289] Merck withdrew Vioxx from the market in September of 2004 after twenty million Americans had taken the drug, and announced a $4.85 billion settlement fund to end thousands of lawsuits – believed to be the largest drug settlement ever at the time, though Merck earned $5.3 billion in Vioxx sales the year before.[290] Celebrex, the sixth most frequently prescribed drug for American seniors in 2003, was allowed to remain on the market given reported benefits to some patients with gastrointestinal tract sensitivity, but with a strong warning alerting doctors and patients that it elevates the risk of heart attacks and strokes.[291]

The MJE has attempted to intervene to ensure that journal publications reflect existing evidentiary science through revisions to the guidelines of the International Committee of Medical Journal Editors/ICMJE.[292] The guidelines explicitly recommend that researchers have control over their data, analysis, and publication of their work.[293] However, a follow-up study done a year after the recommendations were introduced to assess whether they were being honored in university-based research contracts determined they had not been implemented. The study concluded that "academic institutions rarely ensure that their investigators have … unimpeded access to trial data.'"[294]

INDUSTRY INFLUENCES ON MEDICAL PROFESSION EDUCATION

As stated by Dr. Marcia Angell, former Editor-in-Chief of *The New England Journal of Medicine* with decades of *NEJM* experience, "No one should rely on a business for impartial evaluation of a product it sells."[295] Physicians are professionally obligated to be knowledgeable about medical procedures and FDA-approved medicinal products consistent with the standard of care. To remain competent and maintain their medical licenses and board certifications, they are required to engage in continuing medical education/CME. "This education is expensive, and the state is unwilling to pay, so it is drug companies that pay for talks, tutorials, teaching materials, conference sessions, and whole conferences, featuring experts who they know prefer their drug."[296] CME creates thousands of venues annually, which are opportunities for biopharma sponsors to disseminate product-supportive scientific evidence and medical journal publications.[297]

CME programs/CMEs are regulated by the Accreditation Council for Continuing Medical Education/ACCME, and biopharma has adopted a voluntary code for CME sponsorship.[298] Nevertheless, the Institute of Medicine/IOM and many other medical professional organizations have concluded that CME has become too dependent on industry funding that "tends to promote a narrow focus on the products and to neglect provisions of a broader education on alternative strategies," such as disease prevention.[299] Under industry's CME sponsorship and its voluntary code, "it remains acceptable for a drug company to fly three hundred supposedly independent doctors to a golf resort, pay them to attend, 'educate' them about the company's latest drug, and then train them to become part of the company's stable of paid speakers."[300]

Industry cultivates relationships with physician "thought leaders," also referred to as "influencers" and "key opinion leaders"/KOLs – highly credentialed and respected members of the medical profession who influence medical decision-making and who make CME presentations.[301] Many of these prominent physician experts serve on medical practice guideline-writing panels, and even on the FDA's Advisory Committees. As explained by Dr. Abramson,

> Because crucial recommendations about drug approval and drug labeling are made at the FDA's Advisory Committee meetings, federal law "generally prohibits" the participation of experts who have financial ties to the products being presented on these committees. An article in USA Today in September 2000 shows, however, that the FDA granted so many waivers—800 between 1998 and 2000—that 54 percent of the experts on these all-important Advisory Committees had "a direct financial interest in the drug or topic they are asked to evaluate." And this 54 percent figure does not take into account that FDA rules do not even require an Advisory Committee member to declare receipt of amounts less than $50,000 per year from a drug company as long as the payment is for work not related to the drug being discussed.[302]

ACCME requires program content to be free of commercial interests, but CME providers routinely pitch topics designed to attract commercial sponsorship, and biopharma companies award grants to programs that support their marketing strategies.[303] In fact, reflective of several decades of TTLP implementation and government-academia-industry integration from the laboratory bench to clinical care,

> Nearly half of the members of the task force that establishes the guidelines for drug industry involvement with CME are directly employed by the drug companies or are their paid consultants. Some drug and medical-device companies actually own their own educational subsidiaries to ensure that the right "educational" message gets communicated.[304]

CME has become a business enterprise. An entire sector of medical education and communication companies/MECCs has emerged to meet the demand for CMEs, and biopharma companies are generous event sponsors.[305] Their "research evidence is discussed and disseminated at more than three hundred thousand scientific meetings, events and conferences sponsored by the industry every year, and often hosted by medical societies like the American Heart Association, themselves partially underwritten by drug companies."[306] Industry's investment in CME over time attests to its effectiveness promoting corporate interests:

> Commercial support for doctors' continuing education courses has been increasing at a rapid clip, doubling between 1996 and 2000. The medical industry (and in particular the drug companies) funded more than three-fifths of doctors' continuing education in 2001. Industry spending on doctors' continuing education then increased by another 30 percent in 2002. By 2003, the drug companies were spending more than $1500 per year on CME for every doctor in the United States.[307]

As members of a learned profession based in evidentiary science, with seven or more years of competitive study, residencies, fellowships, licensing and board examinations, accumulation of enormous debt to finance the former, and career responsibility for life-and-death decision-making, many physicians have a well-earned sense of accomplishment. They should. However, and understandably so, many physicians also are over-confident and have a sense of entitlement that makes them vulnerable to commercial influences:

> Doctors tend to believe that they are immune to drug company influence.... Accepting freebies or financial support from industry sponsors seems like a reasonable reward for their efforts. The practice is so pervasive and looks like such standard operating procedure that may doctors believe that it doesn't adversely affect their patient care.[308]

In fact, industry sponsorship impacts physician behavior as well as CME content:

> [D]rug company-sponsored lectures are two-and-a-half to three times more likely to mention the sponsor's drug in a positive light and the competitors' drugs in a neutral or negative light. Doctors who receive honoraria for speaking and research support from a drug company are four and nine times more likely, respectively, to support the use of that company's drug in their hospital. Meanwhile, doctors prescribing on the front lines of medicine, drilled to believe new information when it comes from sources they've been taught to accept as legitimate, are unwittingly and effectively influenced by the underlying commercial agenda of the majority of their continuing 'education.'[309]

Biopharma sales representatives also "educate" physicians about the latest diseases and medicinal technologies in an ongoing manner, typically one-on-one, in the offices and clinical settings where they treat their patients who expect their physicians to be learned about them. Physician direct contact with biopharma sales representatives is seeded when they are hospital interns and residents, often over free doughnuts and pizza.[310] It flourishes when physicians are in practice. "Drug company spending on sales representatives and their free samples is the biggest component of the roughly $25 billion now outlaid annually [FY2005] in the United States for promotion, and it is the foundation of the global web of financial entanglement between the industry and the profession."[311] As observed by Dr. Abramson early in this millennium,

> The number of reps making sales pitches in doctors' offices has tripled over the past 10 years[, 1994–2004]. There is now one full-time drug rep for every four and a half office-based doctors. In 2001, drug companies spent $4.7 billion "detailing" ("industry speak" for drug reps' sales calls) to the 490,000 office-based doctors in the United States, or about $10,000 for each doctor per year. And that doesn't include the cost of the drug samples the reps left.[312]

As with CMEs, these interactions impact physician prescribing behavior – again, affirmed by biopharma's business decisions to invest over time, and increasingly so. Biopharma companies invest approximately twenty-five percent of their revenue in promotional activity.[313] Physician trust in their learned selves makes them vulnerable to influence from pharma sales representatives even when sales representatives lack relevant medical and science credentials, or any such credentials at all:

> Most doctors firmly believe that their opinions about drugs and scientific evidence are not compromised by these interactions. The research shows otherwise.... For example, more interaction with pharmaceutical company marketing people, as well as having drug samples on hand, increases the likelihood that doctors will prescribe newer, more expensive drugs and fewer generic drugs. But most important, the drug companies purchase from local pharmacies individual doctors' prescribing information, so they know exactly what we prescribe, and can precisely measure the effect of their reps' office calls and enticements.[314]

The US' opioid epidemic is a blindingly vivid illustration of biopharma sales representatives' "education" influence over physicians – though, in fact, probably as much a matter of physician greed mixed with manufacturer "information" enablement given how much some physicians benefited financially and successful prosecutions of them.[315] Regardless, once opioids were introduced and marketed by manufacturers as a non-addictive treatment for pain management in the 1990s, physicians prescribed beyond reason for over a decade until resulting addiction became an ominous national public health epidemic.[316] Four out of every five new heroin users first used prescription opioids according to a 2017 report by the President's National Commission on Combating Drug Addiction.[317] The epidemic is still raging, though now fueled by illegal street fentanyl rather than by the "legal" physician opioid prescriptions that created the first generation of opioid addiction and built the crisis during its foundational years.[318]

The medical profession's overall response to the US opioid epidemic – which amassed, patient-by-patient, physician-patient interaction by physician-patient interaction, for well over a decade under the medical profession's watch before the nation fully acknowledged its existence – was to blame Purdue Pharma and other opioid manufacturers and distributors.[319] The medical profession attributed their ignorance about opioids to manufacturers' fraudulent marketing, primarily through their army of sales representatives.[320] Obviously, the manufacturers who engaged in fraudulent marketing deserve blame. However, the medical profession needs to put even more blame on its learned and licensed members, each professionally committed to the evidentiary-science base of medicine and with a fiduciary obligation to each of their patients, for listening to manufacturer sales representatives when they were witnessing patterns of addiction. The medical profession should put yet even more blame on its collective AMA self, the nation's professional organization cloak over evidentiary science-based clinical practice, for not noticing the problem – or noticing, but not acting. Again, opioid manufacturers deserve blame for the opioid crisis – that is obvious. The US opioid addiction case study makes it just as obvious that the AMA, MJE, and CME cannot be relied on to protect the evidentiary-science base of medicine, and that the US' overall regulatory scheme is antiquated.

SCIENCE, STANDARD OF CARE, AND THE INEFFECTIVENESS OF US PRACTICE GUIDELINES

Science is humbling; progress typically unveils more of what remains to be understood. HGP is a wonderful example. With a draft map of the human genome sequence in hand, scientists realized that a mere 20,500 or so active genes combined with environmental influences are responsible for human health diversity – meaning that genes multitask and interact exponentially more than was anticipated at the outset of HGP.[321] Translating the genome sequence map into human health and vice versa became a dimension more complicated. Moreover, despite the extraordinary progress of medical science, beyond routine procedures, medicine remains as much art as science. As explained by Dr. Goldacre, "We're going to see that the whole edifice of medicine is broken, because the evidence we use to make decisions is hopelessly and systematically distorted; and this is no small thing. Because in medicine, doctors and patients use abstract data to make decisions in the very real world of flesh and blood."[322] Responsible physicians are learned, constantly learning more in the never-ending pursuit of evidentiary-science truth, and grounded by humility and honesty about their limitations.[323]

The advancement of science and medicine has promoted a norm of practice specialties and sub-specialties, and the ongoing deluge of science and information is simply too much to absorb even with specialization.[324] Yet, physicians are expected to represent "learned" to maintain the confidence of patients and colleagues. Evidentiary science is the base of medicine, physicians are trained to believe in it and to welcome medical science innovation, and they do – often to a fault. "The profession doesn't police itself. They tend to think the newer pill or newer treatment must be better because it's new."[325] As explained by Dr. Brawley,

> Medicine is especially susceptible to this kind of jumping the gun in adopting new treatments. Surgeons performed disfiguring radical procedures called the Halsted mastectomies for more than seventy-five years because William Stewart Halsted said it was the "right way to treat breast cancer." The era came to an end when a randomized clinical trial demonstrated that a conservative procedure followed by radiation was the treatment benefit equivalent to radical mastectomy.[326]

Similar examples abound, including in cardiac care:

> If American medicine is really guided by scientific evidence, how has our pattern of cardiac care evolved so that, on a per-person basis, the United States is doing three and half times as many invasive cardiac procedures, but has one of the highest death rates from heart disease of 10 industrialized nations, and is losing ground to most of them?[327]

Another example is high-dose chemotherapy/HDC followed by autologous bone marrow transplants/ABMTs (together "HDC/ABMT") to treat breast cancer patients, which emerged in the late 1980s with robust clinical uptake in the 1990s:

> In the 1990s, HDC/ABMT burst on the oncology scene and was catapulted into widespread use before careful evaluation. The unconfirmed promise of this procedure drove clinical practice, health insurance coverage decisions, court decisions about coverage of individual patients, and federal administrative and state legislative mandates of HDT/ABMT as a covered benefit. Entrepreneurial oncology then exploited a lucrative market.[328]

These HDC/ABMT patients were administered extremely high doses of chemotherapy with the intention of reaching and destroying cancer cells in their bone marrow, the "factories" for producing disease-fighting white blood cells, and then reintroduced to their bone marrow which had been extracted in advance.[329] The extraordinarily toxic and painful procedure itself brought patients close to death. HDC/ABMT required a completely sterile environment that necessitated patient isolation, including from loved ones, so oncology units established special wards and training programs at great expense.[330] In addition to the physical and emotional costs to patients, the financial cost of the procedure was $150,000–$200,000.[331]

A single clinical trial conducted in South Africa, the results of which were published by the *Journal of Clinical Oncology* in 1995 and retracted in 2001, affirmed and inspired clinical uptake of HDC/ABMT.[332] At least until 1995, fewer than 1,500 US women participated in randomized controlled trials of HDC/ABMT because they did not want the risk of receiving conventional treatment and, under pressure from the media and through lawsuits, many health insurers covered HDC/ABMT:

> In parallel to rapid and widespread clinical use, randomized clinical trials were begun in 1990-91 to evaluate whether the HDC/ABMT procedure was better than, worse than, or the same as conventional treatment. But these trials struggled to accrue patients in the face of the widespread availability of the new treatment.[333]

This impediment to subject recruitment caused delay, but randomized controlled trials were completed, notably two conducted in the US and one in Sweden, and they showed that the procedure was not beneficial at best, and clearly detrimental in many cases:

> In 1999, at the annual meeting of the American Society of Clinical Oncology, four clinical trials reported "no benefit" in overall survival between HDC/ABMT and conventional treatment. [The] South African trial, the only one to claim benefit, was audited the following year and found to be fraudulent. An earlier trial by the same investigator was audited subsequently and also found to be fraudulent.[334]

In sum, over approximately a decade, thousands of breast cancer patients succumbed to horrifically toxic chemotherapy in isolation from loved ones and forewent other treatment options, many to have their lives shortened rather than saved. Substantial financial and life opportunity costs—interaction with loved ones and more peaceful deaths, if not treatment alternatives—were imposed on these patients, their loved ones, health care providers, and health care payers.[335] "The numbers of women who were unwittingly, unnecessarily—and, yes, fraudulently—harmed by this procedure is staggering. Between 1989 and 2001, at least twenty-three thousand women underwent the procedure outside clinical trials. Some estimates are much higher—thirty-five thousand to forty thousand."[336]

The medical profession's response to COVID-19 has affirmed and deepened faith in the profession's commitment to saving lives even at personal sacrifice, but also has illustrated physician susceptibility to deviation from solid evidentiary science-based medicine in favor of clinical practice speculation. Physicians wrote prescriptions for hydroxychloroquine (FDA-approved to treat lupus, rheumatoid arthritis, other serious autoimmune diseases, malaria, and other tropical diseases in humans), ivermectin (FDA-approved to deworm large animals), and myriad other medications without supportive clinical data.[337] Some physicians advocated their own concoctions and realized considerable personal profit – reminiscent of nineteenth-century snake oil and miracle cure salesmen.[338] Countless others advised against the COVID-19 vaccinations months after the compilation of bountiful and compelling safety and efficacy clinical data and global real world use data compiled under close regulatory and manufacturer supervision.[339]

Fortunately, there has been some state licensing board responsiveness – but belatedly, and not remotely commensurate with the problem. On August 16, 2021, the Federation of State Medical Boards issued a stark warning against physicians promoting false COVID-19 science and straight misinformation, but the behavior continued along with the pandemic.[340] The US medical system depends too heavily on state physician cohorts – medical licensing and disciplinary boards staffed by members of each state's own segment of the medical profession – to check physician clinical behavior.[341] As stated in an opinion-editorial published May 18, 2022, in *The New England Journal of Medicine*:

> With nearly 1 million Americans dead from Covid, and deaths—some of them clearly preventable—continuing at a rate of more than 200,000 per year, it has become imperative for our profession to empower our institutions to signal clearly who is—and who is not—providing evidence-based information. We physicians need to use the institutions we've created for professional self-regulation to maintain public trust by establishing some recognizable boundaries. There aren't always right answers, but some answers are clearly wrong.[342]

Ideally, an organized and unified medical profession, consistent with its legacy of clinical sovereignty and self-regulation, would intervene during our TTLP era to check contemporary commercial influences, shore up the evidentiary-science base of clinical practice against undue commercial, political, and other influences, and prevent the practice of medicine from being overwhelmed by the infusion of human genome science innovation. Theoretically, medical practice guidelines generated from within the profession through unadulterated scrutiny of the relevant science and evidence-based clinical practice data could prove an effective mechanism to accomplish this ideal.[343] Sound practice guidelines accurately reflect existing evidentiary science-based clinical practice with thorough review and analysis, all of which is made transparent. They embrace, encourage, and even direct relevant ongoing scientific research, and are poised to be responsive to forthcoming evidentiary science. As opposed to imposing a one-treatment-fits-all mandate, they acknowledge and respect the limits of the scientific evidence available, the ongoing dynamism of science research, and patient individuality. Sound clinical practice guidelines establish a best practices (standard of care) common denominator that welcomes modification with the infusion of new scientific evidence, and they are issued to impact and better the practice of medicine.

Many US nonprofit and professional medical organizations, such as the American Cancer Society/ACS and the AMA, issue guidelines. The US Preventive Services Task Force/USPSTF arguably is the most rigorous US medical practice guideline-writing group.[344] Congress introduced the USPSTF, an independent, volunteer advisory panel of national experts in disease prevention and evidence-based medicine, in 1984 to make recommendations on a wide range of clinical preventative services.[345] Reflective of the complexities of science and evidence-based medicine and the US' highly decentralized and largely privatized health care system, the USPSTF takes years to process preventative screening guidelines.[346] Moreover, when the USPSTF does reach conclusions about clinical care, it issues *recommendations* subject to approval and uptake throughout the US health care system.

The US government attempted a direct leadership role in US medical practice guidelines through the Agency for Healthcare Research and Quality/AHRQ, which it established in 1989 as the Agency for Health Care Policy and Research/AHCPR.[347] AHCPR was designated an agency within the Public Health Service/PHS committed to enhance the quality, appropriateness, and effectiveness of health care services and access to care by: conducting and supporting research, demonstration projects, and evaluations; developing guidelines; and disseminating information on health care services and delivery systems.[348] AHCPR undertook large multidisciplinary, multi-institutional projects that focused on patient outcomes to improve clinical practice. Its work addressed a range of pragmatic issues, including basic health information technology, patient safety research on wrong-site surgery, medical teamwork, and hospital-acquired conditions.[349]

AHCPR also generated guidelines, several of which triggered professional and political pushback – for example, a cataract guideline that raised concern from ophthalmologists and pharma that it discouraged use of new Rx drugs.[350] When AHCPR produced a guideline that concluded considerable back pain surgery was unnecessary and potentially harmful, chronic lobbying against the agency from a conglomeration of stakeholders culminated in a campaign aided by members of Congress who had undergone back surgery.[351] The agency scaled back but saved its guidelines program, which it centralized by establishing the US National Guideline Clearinghouse/NGC in 1997.[352] AHCPR was reauthorized on December 6, 1999, but with a name change to the Agency for Healthcare Research and Quality/AHRQ.[353]

Through establishment of NGC at the end of the last millennium, the US federal government affirmed its commitment to the implementation and dissemination of practice guidelines. NGC introduced internet-accessible database mechanisms that made objective, detailed information on clinical practice guidelines available "to provide physicians and other health care professionals, health care providers, health plans, integrated delivery systems, purchasers and others an accessible mechanism for obtaining objective, detailed information on clinical practice guidelines and to further their dissemination, implementation, and use."[354] The NGC was "part of a wider movement to better link the practice of medicine to sound scientific research...."[355] In January 1999, NGC also was made available to the public. The NGC database was updated weekly with revisions and additions, and content was audited annually through an Annual Verification process.[356] The NGC site offered:

- An electronic forum for exchanging information on clinical practice guidelines, their development, implementation, and use;
- A Guideline Comparison function, which enabled users to generate side-by-side comparisons for any combination of two or more guidelines;
- A Guideline Syntheses prepared by NGC staff, which compared guidelines covering similar topics, and identified areas of similarity and difference – often inclusive of guidelines developed outside the US, which provided comparative insight regarding international health practices; and
- An Annotated Bibliography database of both publications and resources, which was searchable and enabled users to research guideline development and methodology, structure, evaluation, and implementation.[357]

In January 2001, the AHRQ also established the publicly available National Quality Measures Clearinghouse/NQMC, a data-driven resource complement to NGC,

> to provide practitioners, health care providers, health plans, integrated delivery systems, purchasers and others an accessible mechanism for obtaining detailed information on quality measures, and to further their dissemination, implementation, and use in order to inform health care decisions. NQMC built on AHRQ's previous initiatives in quality measurement, including the Computerized Needs-Oriented Quality Measurement Evaluation System (CONQUEST), the Expansion of Quality of Care Measures (Q-SPAN) project, the Quality Measurement Network (QMNet) project, and the Performance Measures Inventory (PMI).[358]

The Trump Administration cut funding for AHRQ, and the sites for both NGC and NQMC were taken down on July 16, 2018.[359]

Although theoretically ideal to promote science and evidence-based clinical practice, experiential reality is that practice guidelines in US medicine are generally suspect. A number of studies evaluating them have concluded that they often fail to meet established standards – for example, disclosure of the professionals involved in formulating them, sufficient description of the sources of information used to derive the scientific evidence they are based upon, and evidence grading supportive of their main recommendations.[360] Reality in our TTLP era, in which academia is integrated with industry from the laboratory bench to the pharmacy shelf and in clinical care, is that, overall, "It is estimated that almost 90 percent of those who write guidelines for their peers have conflicts of interest because of financial ties to the pharmaceutical industry."[361] Senior physicians recognized nationally for their expertise and who are sought out by industry for their influence, also are sought out for guideline writing and input.[362] According to a study published in *JAMA* in 2002, four out of five experts who participated in the formulation of good clinical practice guidelines (a standard applied often in medical malpractice cases) had financial relationships with drug companies. They each averaged more than ten such relationships, and fifty-nine percent had these relationships with companies whose drugs were considered in the guidelines they helped to author.[363]

The US NIH's cholesterol guidelines provide an illustrative case study for probable industry influence on medical practice guidelines and their impact on physician prescribing practices. Cholesterol-lowering statins were introduced to the market in the mid-1990s.[364] Exactly how much raised cholesterol levels increase patients' risk for heart disease, the likely severity of any associated heart disease, and when statins are a good medicinal intervention are still muddled with clinical uncertainty and debate today.[365] Nevertheless, the seminal statins introduced in the mid-1990s each generated billions of dollars in revenue annually upon market entry, and "nations everywhere have spent more on cholesterol-lowering drugs in recent years than any other category of prescription medicines."[366] Despite the ongoing uncertainty and debate over the medical meaning of cholesterol levels and statins,

> According to the official US National Institutes of Health's cholesterol guidelines from the 1990s, thirteen million Americans might have warranted treatment with statins. In 2001 a new panel of experts rewrote those guidelines, and effectively raised that number to 36 million.... [F]ive of the fourteen authors of this new expanded definition, including the chair of the panel, had financial ties to statin manufacturers. In 2004, yet another new panel of experts updated those guidelines again, recommending that alongside the value of lifestyle changes more than 40 million Americans could benefit by taking the drugs. This time, the conflicts of interest were even worse.[367]

Moreover, rather than a solid professional mass, the US medical profession is a conglomeration of often competing medical specialties and subspecialties, many with their own professional associations.[368] The trend in medicine, consistent with the intricacies of genomics and personal genome medicine, is increasing specialization and sub-specialization.[369] Nevertheless, most major medical organizations explicitly *exclude* specialties from membership on their guideline-writing panels, which leaves the resulting guidelines subject to broad interpretation in practice.[370] For example, "If you are a urologist and you want to perform a lot of surgery, you can find aggressive guidelines that tell it's just the thing to do. After that, you can proudly say, 'I am following evidence-based practice guidelines.'"[371] As opposed to good clinical practice guidelines, many medical specialties issue their own "evidence-based practice guidelines."[372] They too often deviate from sound disclosure standards. In 2000, *The Lancet* published an examination of the processes used to prepare 431 guidelines produced by specialty organizations. Altogether, sixty-seven percent did not fully disclose who participated in making them, eighty-eight percent did not identify how the "relevant literature" was identified, and eighty-two percent failed to grade the strength of the evidence. Only five percent satisfied the three criteria.[373]

Even when the integrity of guideline content is sound, the effectiveness of practice guidelines in US medicine is questionable. Typically, they are subject to suspicion by the medical profession, their scope is limited, their definitiveness is dulled, or the medical profession is simply nonresponsive.[374] The US medical profession aggressively safeguards physician discretion and individualized patient care, and those tenets are embedded in US medicine and culture – from the sanctity of doctor–patient decision-making in the twentieth century, to patient-driven autonomy and participatory health today, to the personal genome medicine that is emerging.

For example, in 2016, after US physicians egregiously over-prescribed opioids and fed a ravenous national addiction for well over a decade, the medical profession challenged a CDC guideline for prescribing opioids for chronic pain.[375] Before and after the CDC issued this guideline, HHS actively sought collaboration with the national medical profession leadership and biopharma to build a response to the opioid addiction crisis that prioritized the advancement of pain management science and clinical understanding. Within a month of the CDC introducing the proposed guideline, the three top FDA physician leaders, Robert M. Califf, Janet Woodcock, and Stephen Ostroff, published an explanation of the HHS opioid intervention strategy in *The New England Journal of Medicine*, which emphasized deference to the medical profession and individualized patient care sensitivity.[376] They stressed the importance of balancing "two complementary principles: that the United States must deal aggressively with opioid misuse and addiction, and at the same time, that it must protect the well-being of people experiencing the devastating effects of acute or chronic pain."[377] Nevertheless, even with the opioid crisis raging, the AMA and some patient advocacy groups, including the National Cancer Coalition, rebuffed the CDC guideline out of concern that it might encroach on physician discretion to prescribe and individualized patient care. In fact, the CDC 2016 guideline was misapplied (US physicians are sensitive to exposure to legal liability), and the CDC issued a revised voluntary guideline with heightened clarity in November 2022.[378]

The US medical profession's resistance to professional practice guidelines reflects that US medicine is fractured well beyond not having a universal health care system foundation. Fifty states, not the federal government, grant physicians licenses to practice medicine within their borders, and there are considerable disparities among them – as reflected in their Medicaid programs, health insurance markets, health care infrastructure, and myriad state health laws and programs. Beyond the common denominators of physician sovereignty over the practice of medicine, the evidentiary-science base of medicine, and physician discretion to practice individualized patient care, which the AMA and other medical professional organizations protect dutifully, the unified "American medical profession" of the twentieth century is not a present-day reality. Internally, the AMA embodies extensive hierarchy, committee bureaucracy, and politicization, and the organization typically struggles to formulate positions on multi-faceted issues.[379] "By the late 1990s, as the solidarity within the profession – and membership – waned, the AMA was trying on more commercial models."[380] AMA membership dropped from nearly 278,000 to 217,000 between 2002 and 2011, and today only about twenty-five percent of eligible physicians join.[381]

The professional association that organized the US medical profession and pushed corporate influences out of the practice of medicine during the first half of the twentieth century now "is a multiheaded hydra that is, in many respects, as much a diversified corporation as a nonprofit professional group."[382] Notably, "The AMA Foundation is today supported by a Corporate Roundtable, 'a group of key stakeholders,' who meet with the AMA to discuss their shared 'commitment to public health in America.' Its platinum, gold, and silver members are all from the pharmaceutical or healthcare industry."[383]

THE ABSENCE OF CENTRALIZED, OBJECTIVE, RELIABLE HEALTH TECHNOLOGY ASSESSMENT/HTA IN US HEALTH CARE

When Professor Ezekiel Emanuel compared health care systems for his recently (2020) published book, *Which Country Has the World's Best Health Care?*, he concluded that "The American system is an order of magnitude more complex and difficult for patients to navigate than any other health care system I studied."[384] In the US' largely privatized, employment-based, and decentralized health care system, employers, private insurers, and other stakeholders demand freedom to contract, and they are corporate citizens with rights recognized under US law and policy. State health care systems exist within the national system. State and medical specialty professional associations co-exist with the AMA. Patients insist on autonomy and self-determination with access to the latest technology. All is set in a charged political, legislative, and litigious "interest group society" environment.[385]

Other industrialized-economy nations have universal health care systems (whether nationalized as in the UK, socialized as in Germany, or single payer as in Canada) that share the US challenge of containing escalating health care costs against a firehose infusion of health technology innovation. However, the US' industrialized counterparts have health care systems with joint government-medical profession decision-making mechanisms.[386] Increasingly since the 1980s, our industrialized counterparts have implemented and utilized formal, centralized, objective, and generally reliable health technology assessment/HTA dedicated to fully evaluate medical innovation with focus on evidentiary science-based clinical data.[387] Their HTA is not limited by the data new product sponsors submit in their applications for market approval or the pages published by the MJE. Rather, these governments collect, consider, and evaluate data with input from trusted expertise within their medical professions, and with a premium on objective evidentiary science-based clinical data. They harness science and medical expertise to engage in full-bodied assessment and decision-making to assess the clinical effectiveness of health technology *in a comparative fashion* – meaning with consideration of treatment options.[388] They also, reflective of their societal and systematic perspective on health care impact, consider pricing, cost-effectiveness, and other zero-sum health care realities.[389] After uptake, they reassess health technology in clinical use with real-world data/RWD in an ongoing manner.[390]

Moreover, given that these national HTA mechanisms share the objective and burden of full evidentiary science-based clinical merit assessment, they collaborate. They work collectively as well as individually to develop the HTA discipline, tools, and methodologies to maximize utilization and effectiveness. They engage in networking, collegial data sharing, and cross-checking – rather than working in the isolation of one nation's system and its subjective influences.[391] The European Commission even established the Health Technology Assessment Network ("HTA Network") to create a hub for Europe's HTA bodies; the HTA Network facilitates sharing and collaboration with the input of EC experts.[392]

The formation, increased membership, and activity of international HTA networks in addition to the EC's HTA Network reflects the extent to which other nations are utilizing HTA, and increasingly so over time. It also attests to the maturation of the HTA discipline and its effectiveness – especially in an emerging genomic medicine era. Notable examples include: the International Network of Agencies for Health Technology Assessment/INAHTA, a network of fifty HTA agencies that support health system decision-making that impacts over 1 billion people in thirty-one countries; Health Technology Assessment international/HTA*i*, a scientific and professional society that represents eighty-two organizations and over 2,500 individual members from sixty-five countries; and the International Society for Pharmacoeconomics and Outcomes Research/ISPOR, a professional society founded in 1995 with 14,000 individual and chapter members from more than 100 countries worldwide.[393] ISPOR welcomes all health care stakeholders as members, including researchers, academicians, regulators and assessors, public and private payers, health care providers, industry, and patient representatives.[394]

The US actually pioneered government technology assessment in the mid-1960s, implemented the discipline in health care in the mid-1970s, and then abandon it as other developed-economy nations discovered and adopted HTA.[395] The US established the Office of Technology Assessment/OTA, which became operational in 1974, to provide members of Congress and congressional committees with objective, reliable, and authoritative analysis of complex scientific and technical issues.[396] OTA introduced a HTA program the following year (1975), which by the 1990s engaged in analysis of cost effectiveness as well as clinical benefits.[397] Opponents, beginning early in the Reagan Administration, characterized OTA as wasteful and hostile to Grand Old Party/GOP interests.[398] The GOP took control of both chambers of Congress in 1994, and OTA was defunded at the end of 1995 under the Contract with America legislative agenda to downsize the federal government.[399] The US Government Accountability Office/GOA established a technology assessment unit to assume some OTA duties, and the Agency for Healthcare Research and Quality/AHRQ endured, albeit with a limited budget and without the National Guideline Clearinghouse/NGC and the National Quality Measures Clearinghouse/NQMC.[400]

The US government utilizes HTA today but in a piecemeal and contained fashion.[401] For example, the Centers for Medicaid and Medicare Services/CMS, the largest single purchaser of health care services in the US, engages in HTA to manage Medicare, Medicaid, and the Child Health Insurance Program/CHIP with focus on assessment of clinical effectiveness and quality of care – not a full-bodied, combined assessment of both clinical effectiveness and cost effectiveness, and certainty not to control market prices.[402] The US government has essentially disengaged from comprehensive, direct, formalized, centralized, and objective HTA – especially in comparison with its industrialized-economy counterparts. "As the influence of technology assessment programs has grown abroad, the United States has virtually dismantled its own."[403] Rather than formalized, centralized, objective HTA, the US relies heavily on its self-regulating medical profession's clinical decision-making and market forces.

THE COST AND WASTE CONSEQUENCES OF WEAKENING THE EVIDENTIARY-SCIENCE BASE OF US MEDICINE

The US has made the practice of medicine an enclave under the watch of its medical profession at least since the mid-twentieth century, with US law and policy shoring up the medical profession's sovereignty over it.[404] This reign, orchestrated by the AMA as it organized and strengthened itself, is premised on the medical profession serving as a reliable sentinel of medical science, medical knowledge, and evidence-based clinical practice.[405] However, the US medical profession has lost substantial control over the integrity and reliability of both medical science and the clinical practice of medicine since last century, and commercial interests have gained considerable influence over both.[406] Decades of TTLP implementation, biopharma marketing, and an overall "business of medicine" transformation of US health care, from hospital conversions to managed care networks with large market shares, have impacted US medicine:

> The overwhelming power that the drug and other medical industries now wield over American politics, science, and health care has created an imbalance between corporate goals and public interest that is no longer self-correcting. In fact, it has become resistant to correction. If democracy is to be more than a ritual dance choreographed by powerful corporations in the postindustrial "information age," government must actively protect the integrity of the information on which we rely to guide our personal and political choices.[407]

US medicine remains based in evidentiary science, but that base is not shielded from commercial influences as it was when established in the twentieth century. According to some commentators, "There has been a virtual takeover of medical knowledge in the United States, leaving doctors and patients little opportunity to know the truth about good medical care and no safe alternative but to pay up and go along."[408]

The reliability of the US medical profession and the MJE to protect the evidentiary-science base of medicine began to falter with occurrences well underway in the 1980s – most notably, TTLP implementation and the proliferation of managed care and consolidation. Once in motion, these influences swelled into potentially controlling forces in science and medicine by the end of the millennium.[409] Medical science, the practice of medicine, the medical profession, and the MJE have changed systemically, yet US deference to and reliance on its medical profession and the MJE have remained remarkably constant since mid-last century.

The US health care system is unique among industrialized nations. Rather than a universal health care system, the US has a largely decentralized, fragmented, highly privatized and free-market health care system.[410] Biopharma companies engage in aggressive DTP and DTC marketing, physicians prescribe biopharma medicinal products well beyond the FDA approvals and clinical data that put them on the market, and biopharma companies price their products at whatever the US market will bear. US TTLP, which intentionally integrates industry with academia and government in science R&D, has proven an extraordinarily powerful catalyst for producing medical science innovation.[411] Yet, unlike other industrialized nations, the US has no formal, centralized, objective HTA mechanism to fully evaluate medical science innovation, to protect the integrity of medical science, and to promote evidentiary science-based clinical practice.[412] Rather, the US government applies HTA in a piecemeal fashion, and heavily depends on its medical profession and largely unchecked market forces in a capitalism culture to sort all out during clinical use.[413]

The ability of the US medical profession to uptake the innovation churned through TTLP with reliable adherence to science and evidence-based clinical practice has been questionable at best for some time. Such reliance is unquestionably misplaced during the ongoing genomic revolution and emerging era of personal genome medicine:

> Without a formal mechanism of health technology assessment, new medical services can be brought into use without strong scientific evidence of benefits. And without limits on spending, new services can be brought into use without evidence that they provide more health value than the services they would be replacing. The absence of both of these constraints on growth of medical technology allows the US health care system to be uniquely shaped by financial incentives.[414]

Individual physicians in the US committed to science and evidence-based clinical practice, as all are professionally bound to be, are subject to systemic commercial influences in medical science R&D, US medicine, and the US' free-market health care system. For example, reliable physician adherence to objective truth in science and evidence-based medicine should make biopharma marketing incidental, if not irrelevant. Once market approved by the FDA, US physicians control the use of Rx products. However, biopharma marketing, especially to the extent allowed under US law, impacts the practice of medicine substantially – which is why biopharma has continued to invest so much in it over time, and increasingly so.[415]

The US' decentralized and fragmented uptake of health technology with reliance on its medical profession, reflective of the US health care system, imposes cost and waste consequences.[416] Again, in comparative analysis among the health care systems of developed-economy nations, US health care is distinguishable: "Along almost all criteria, the American system is more complex and costlier than any other system. And despite placing a high premium on patient choice, American patients actually have less choice than patients [in] many other countries."[417] Relying solely on mid-twentieth century norms to protect the evidentiary-science base of clinical practice has skewed US health care for some time:

> The American health care system keeps edging ever closer to the breaking point. Many factors are contributing, but in the eye of the storm is a single factor: the transformation of medical knowledge from a public good, measured by its potential to improve our health, into a commodity, measured by its commercial value.

> This transformation is the result of the commercial takeover of the process by which 'scientific evidence' is produced.[418]

The US, home to less than 4.5 percent of the world's population, spends roughly twice as much on health care per capita than other developed-economy countries and accounts for forty percent of all drug expenditures.[419] Nevertheless, "the US health care system is not the best, 2nd best, or even third best in the world."[420] According to the latest ranking by the World Health Organization/WHO, which includes the health care systems of 191 countries, the US ranks 37th.[421]

The US' largely employer-based, privatized health care system is an entanglement of payers, federal and state government programs, provider networks, manage care organizations, pharmacy benefit managers, drug wholesalers and distributors, discounts, rebates, and an array of provider fee arrangements such as capitation (fixed, pre-arranged, and per-patient compensation).[422] Federal, state, and local government authorities, professional and government licensing and certification boards, medical professional associations, and myriad programs, federal and state, are woven through all. Also, "A significant portion of the population moves between insurance programs each year and, thus, might have multiple types of insurance during any given year."[423] All of this is held together through layer upon layer of administration, which imposes administrative costs substantially greater than those of our industrialized counterparts.[424]

US faith in its medical profession – trust earned, developed, and embedded during the twentieth century – accompanies the notion that a highly privatized health care system with health care decision-makers responsive to market forces will minimize waste and maximize good medicine returns. Unfortunately, the numbers simply do not add up.[425] The US spends more than three trillion dollars on health care each year ($3.7 trillion in 2018, before the COVID-19 pandemic) – some eighteen percent of its entire gross domestic product, and an amount comparable to the entire economy of France.[426] According to the Centers for Medicare and Medicaid Services/CMS, under current law, annual growth in US health care spending – including government and private sector outlays – "is expected to average 5.1% … and to reach nearly $6.8 trillion by 2030."[427] That projection was calculated prior to the ongoing (as of April 2023) inflation surge. The Organization for Economic Cooperation and Development/OECD routinely ranks the US as spending more per capita on health care than any other industrialized nation.[428] Unfortunately, US spending on health care does not equate with overall human health value: "The US health system generally delivers worse health outcomes than any other developed country, all of which spend on average about half what we do per person."[429]

The shareholder wealth maximization norm is a tangible predictor of US corporate citizen behavior. "Drug companies earn higher profits when more people use expensive drugs, not when more people achieve better health."[430] Similarly, US medical providers are incentivized to provide more services, to instill and maintain patient and colleague confidence that they are learned about the latest evidence-based science and technology, to meet patient demands to keep them satisfied, and to be profitable for their employers – incentives not necessarily consistent with better patient health and good medicine.[431] When US patients have comprehensive insurance coverage, they tend to demand care without consideration of costs, and many of their providers do as well.[432] According to Dr. Brawley,

> The system is not failing. It's functioning exactly as designed. It's designed to run up health-care costs. It's about the greedy serving the gluttonous. Americans consume more health care per capita than the people of any other country. In 2009, we spent more than $2.53 trillion. That's 2.5 times more than we spent on food. It's not easy to envision a trillion.[433]

In such a disjointed and complicated health care system embodying so many free-market sectors and interests, including commercial free speech, proprietary rights, and secrecy, US physicians and patients have little awareness of the actual costs of the drugs prescribed and the procedures performed.[434] In fact, variation among health insurers and individually negotiated health insurance contracts, rebates, discounts, copays, and other factors often make it difficult to determine what the prices actually are; actual charges vary immensely among individual patients. A frequently referenced estimate is that, "[o]verall, costs of branded drugs in the United States are 70 percent higher than in other industrialized countries."[435]

Deviation from sound evidentiary science-based medicine – what the US medical profession professes medicine to be, and the basis for the uniquely high level of deference and self-governance shown to the medical profession under US law and policy – invites substandard medicine and waste in a largely-privatized health care system unable to contain costs.[436] Illustrative examples abound. "The over-use of Vioxx, Celebrex, and cholesterol-lowering drugs in adults, and antidepressants in children and adolescents all show that at the heart of the crisis in American medicine is a crisis in the quality of our medical knowledge."[437]

In the absence of an independent, objective, centralized, and formalized HTA mechanism, what the MJE publishes substantially influences what the medical profession practices – too often resulting in detriments to patient health, alternative treatment opportunity costs, excessive financial costs, and waste. Consider the MJE's publication of studies associated with five antidepressants approved by the FDA at the end of the last millennium, and the impact on US health care:

> Of the 42 relevant studies, 19 of the positive ones generated 22 positive articles, while only 6 of the 21 studies with negative or inconclusive findings were published. When all of the evidence is considered, it turns out that the new antidepressant drugs are no more effective than older tricyclic antidepressants (the classic being amitriptyline, brand name Elavil). More important, the new antidepressants were found to be not even 10 percent more effective than the placebos.... Those on the newer antidepressants also experienced a 4.6 rate increase in suicides. Based on the best information available, antidepressants (almost exclusively the newer ones) were the best-selling class of drugs in the United States between 1999 and 2001,

> and ranked number three behind cholesterol-lowering statins and acid-suppressing drugs in 2002 and 2003. All told, in 2001, Americans spent a total of $12.5 billion on antidepressants. That amounts to $43.85 for every man, woman, child, and infant.[438]

JAMA *Internal Medicine* published a study in October 2021 that showed US Medicare spent nearly $600 million over a three-year period on four cancer drugs that provided no clinical benefit for FDA-approved uses.[439] Some $170 million of this spending was on products voluntarily withdrawn by their manufacturers after clinical data showed that they did not improve overall survival in patients with several cancers, including breast, lung, liver, and urinary tract cancers.[440]

Even after implementation of the Affordable Care Act/ACA and before the COVID-19 pandemic, the US continued to waste approximately twenty-five percent of what is spent on health care, health care costs continued to rise, and some twenty-seven million Americans still were without health insurance.[441] The COVID-19 pandemic, in addition to afflicting illness and deaths across the nation, caused millions of Americans to at least temporarily lose health insurance tied to their jobs.[442] The US government should be commended for assuming significant patient health care costs incurred for responsiveness to the pandemic, most notably the cost of COVID-19 vaccinations, but they are still very real US health care costs. Consider that substantial segments of the US population chronically refused to be COVID-19 vaccinated and to get boosters even with the Omicron variant raging, and many were influenced by the availability of newly developed and arguably *much more experimental* monoclonal antibody therapy to treat COVID-19 patients.[443] It is common knowledge and common sense that the cost of hospitalization and administering in-patient treatment in the US is always significant, and certainly immensely more expensive than free out-patient, preventative vaccinations.

Adherence to evidentiary science-based clinical practice is a prerequisite for responsible medicine, for prudent expenditure of resources invested in health care, and to maximize health improvement returns on those investments. The US medical profession agrees. Evidentiary science-based medicine is the mantra through which it organized and amassed authority and sovereignty over the delivery of care, and how the medical profession retains sovereignty over clinical care today.[444] Other industrialized nations adhere to the evidentiary-science standard in medicine as well, but they implement it with HTA and without naked reliance on their medical profession and market forces. The US, with its deference to and reliance on its medical profession to realize evidentiary science-based clinical practice, invests exceedingly more in health care than any other nation without commensurate good medicine returns:

> The ugliest truth of all is that these enormous costs do not come close to producing commensurate improvements in our health—the health of Americans is actually losing ground to that of the citizens of other industrialized countries, which are spending far less and at the same time providing health care to all of their citizens.[445]

US adherence to what proved effective in mid-twentieth-century medicine does not position the nation well to advance its health care during the ongoing genomic revolution, and certainly not in the emerging era of personal genome medicine.

NOTES

1 LYNNE ANN DESPELDER, ALBERT LEE STRICKLAND, THE LAST DANCE: ENCOUNTERING DEATH AND DYING 39 (1983). *See* Michael J. Malinowski, *Throwing Dirt on Doctor Frankenstein's Grave: Access to Experimental Treatments at the End of Life*, 65 HASTINGS L.J. 615, 631–35 (2014). *See generally* JOHN ABRAMSON, OVERDOSED AMERICA: THE BROKEN PROMISE OF AMERICAN MEDICINE (2005) (raising challenges to the US public's assumptions that medicine is reliably grounded in evidence-based science and that more clinical intervention with innovation is better medicine).

2 *See* Johns Hopkins Medicine, *Study Suggests Medical Errors Now Third Leading Cause of Death in the US* (May 3, 2016) (page nos. unavailable online), www.hopkinsmedicine.org/news/media/releases/study_suggests_medical_errors_now_third_leading_cause_of_death_in_the_us; Heather Lyu, Michol Cooper, Kavita Patel et al., *Prevalence and Data Transparency of National Clinical Registries in the United States*, 38 J. HEALTHCARE QUAL. (JHQ) 223–34 (2016), https://journals.lww.com/jhqonline/Citation/2016/07000/Prevalence_and_Data_Transparency_of_National.4.aspx. *See also* Ray Sipherd, *The Third-Leading Cause of Death in US Most Doctors Don't Want You to Know About*, CNBC (Feb. 22, 2018, updated Feb. 28, 2018), www.cnbc.com/2018/02/22/medical-errors-third-leading-cause-of-death-in-america.html; National Highway Traffic Safety Administration/ NHTSA, *Traffic Deaths Decreased in 2018, but Still 36,560 People Died* (undated; page nos. unavailable online), www.nhtsa.gov/traffic-deaths-decreased-2018-still-36560-people-died#:~:text=Share%3A,that%20motor%20vehicle%20fatalities%20declined. The COVID-19 pandemic exacerbated error in a health care system unprepared for it and prone to mistakes. *See* Danielle Ofri, *Opinion, The Public Has Been Forgiving. But Hospitals Got Some Things Wrong.*, N.Y. TIMES (May 24, 2020), www.nytimes.com/2020/05/22/opinion/sunday/coronavirus-medical-errors-hospitals.html.

3 "After heart disease and cancer, the third leading cause of death in the United States is iatrogenic injury (avoidable injury or infection caused by a healer). Research suggests that avoidable errors claim several hundred thousand lives every year." STEPHEN LANDSMAN, MICHAEL J. SACKS, CLOSING DEATH'S DOOR: LEGAL INNOVATIONS TO STEM THE EPIDEMIC OF HEALTHCARE HARM (2020) (synopsis). *See generally id.*

4 *See* Malinowski, *Frankenstein's Grave*, *supra* note 1, at 631–35. Treatment variation for the same commonly diagnosed condition attests to the significance of physician and patient individuality and the fact that, beyond its evidentiary-science base, clinical practice is a combination of art and science and influenced by factors such as socio-economic disparities and race. *See* George Hripcsak, Patrick B. Ryan, Jon D. Duke et al., *Characterizing Treatment Pathways at Scale Using the OHDSI Network*, 113(27) PROC. NAT'L ACAD. SCI. 7329–36 (July 2016) (study of treatment for 250 million patients), www.pnas.org/content/113/27/7329.full; Mun Keat Looi, *A New Study of 250 Million Patients Shows Medicine is Still Full of Guesswork*, COLUMBIA UNIV. DATA SCI. INST. (June 10, 2016) (page nos. unavailable online), https://datascience.columbia.edu/news/2016/a-new-study-of-250-million-patients-shows-medicine-is-still-full-of-guesswork/.

5 PAUL STARR, THE SOCIAL TRANSFORMATION OF AMERICAN MEDICINE: THE RISE OF A SOVEREIGN PROFESSION AND THE MAKING OF A VAST INDUSTRY 5 (1984) (winner of the Pulitzer Prize for nonfiction).

6 *See generally* JOHN CARREYROU, BAD BLOOD: SECRETS AND LIES IN A SILICON VALLEY STARTUP (2018); THE INVENTOR: OUT FOR BLOOD IN SILICON VALLEY (HBO 2018). Theranos's board of directors included William Foege, former Director of the US Centers for Disease Control and Prevention/CDC; Henry Kissinger, former US Secretary of State; Richard Kovacevich, former CEO of Wells Fargo; Jim Mattis, then a retired Marine Corps four-star general; William Perry, former US Secretary of Defense; and George Shultz, former US Secretary of State. *See* Sophia Kunthara, *A Closer Look At Theranos' Big-Name Investors, Partners and Board as Elizabeth Holmes' Criminal Trial Begins*, CRUNCHBASE NEWS (Sept. 14, 2021) (page nos. unavailable online), https://news.crunchbase.com/news/theranos-elizabeth-holmes-trial-investors-board/; Pamela Wasley, *The Theranos Crisis: Where Was The Board?*, FORBES (Apr. 27, 2016) (page nos. unavailable online), www.forbes.com/sites/groupthink/2016/04/27/the-theranos-crisis-where-was-the-board/?sh=64225fd1c58e. The company's investors included media mogul Rupert Murdoch, who led a $5.8 million Series A (the first round of financing after seed capital) in February 2005 and is reported to have invested $150 million overall; venture capitalist Tim Draper, who continued to publicly defend the company until 2018; Larry Ellison, the founder and Executive Chairman of Oracle; Fortress Investment Group, a large private equity firm; Partner Fund Management, a highly regarded investment management (venture capital) firm; the Walgreens national retail and pharmacy chain; and the Walton family, which inherited their wealth from the founders of Walmart, Inc. *See* Kunthara, *Closer Look*, *supra*; Reed Abelson, Katie Thomas, *Caught in the Theranos Wreckage: Betsy DeVos, Rupert Murdoch and Walmart's Waltons*, N.Y. TIMES (May 4, 2018), www.nytimes.com/2018/05/04/health/theranos-investors-murdoch-devos-walmart.html. Theranos entered a partnership with the Cleveland Clinic and became the Pennsylvania labwork provider for AmeriHealth Caritas and Capital BlueCross. *See* Kunthara, *Closer Look*, *supra*.

7 *See* CARREYROU, BAD BLOOD, *supra* note 6, at 95–108. *See also* HBO, OUT FOR BLOOD, *supra* note 6.

8 Heather Somerville, *Former Walgreens CFO Describes How Theranos Wooed Him*, WALL. ST. J. (Oct. 13, 2021), www.wsj.com/livecoverage/elizabeth-holmes-trial-theranos/card/7kS65DLYUGkDBNqkDXxp#:~:text=Theranos%20and%20the%20drugstore%20chain,technology%2C%20according%20to%20court%20testimony.

9 *See id.*

10 CARREYROU, BAD BLOOD, *supra* note 6, at 7.

11 *See* HBO, OUT FOR BLOOD, *supra* note 6.

12 CARREYROU, BAD BLOOD, *supra* note 6, at 13.

13 HBO, OUT FOR BLOOD, *supra* note 6.

14 *Id.*

15 *See id.*

16 *See* CARREYROU, BAD BLOOD, *supra* note 6, at 95–108.

17 *Id.* at 7–8.

18 *See generally* HBO, OUT FOR BLOOD, *supra* note 6.

19 Sara Ashley O'Brien, *What We Learned this Week in the Trial of Elizabeth Holmes*, CNN BUS. (Nov. 13, 2021), www.cnn.com/2021/11/13/tech/elizabeth-holmes-trial-recap/index.html.

20 Bobby Allyn, *Elizabeth Holmes Sentenced to 11 Years in Prison for Theranos Fraud*, NPR (Nov. 18, 2022), www.npr.org/2022/11/18/1137606060/elizabeth-holmes-sentenced-11-years-prison. "It is nearly unheard of in Silicon Valley for an executive to face criminal prosecution in the wake of a business collapse. But legal experts said the egregiousness of Holmes' crimes, and the fact that she was operating in the highly-regulated health care world, made the Theranos case exceptional." *Id. See also* Erin Griffith, Erin Woo,

Elizabeth Holmes is Found Guilty of Four Counts of Fraud, N.Y. TIMES (Jan. 3, 2022, updated Mar. 22, 2022), www.nytimes.com/live/2022/01/03/technology/elizabeth-holmes-trial-verdict#elizabeth-holmes-guilty. The jury, after fifty hours of deliberations over seven days, convicted Ms. Holms of three counts of wire fraud and one count of conspiracy to commit wire fraud by lying to investors. She was found not guilty on four other counts related to defrauding patients who had used Theranos's blood tests – patients whose care at issue was overseen by licensed physicians and other medical providers. The jury was unable to reach a verdict on three counts of deceiving investors, which resulted in mistrial with prosecutorial discretion to retry them. *See generally* Erin Griffith, *Elizabeth Holmes Denied New Trial and Is Set to Be Sentenced*, N.Y. TIMES (Nov. 8, 2022), www.nytimes.com/2022/11/08/technology/elizabeth-holmes-denied-new-trial.html. Sunny Bulwani, Theranos's former president, was convicted on all twelve counts brought against him in July 2022, and he was sentenced on December 7, 2022, to twelve years and eleven months in prison and 3 years of probation. *See* Jaclyn Diaz, *Ramesh 'Sunny' Balwani is Sentenced to Nearly 13 Years for his Role in Theranos Fraud*, NPR (Dec. 7, 2022), www.npr.org/2022/12/07/1141278121/theranos-sunny-balwani-sentencing-elizabeth-holmes#:~:text=San%20Jose%2C%20Calif.-,on,7%2C%202022.&text=A%20federal%20judge%20in%20California,sentence%20in%20a%20separate%20trial.

21 *See Chapter 1*, *supra*, at notes 12–34, and accompanying text ("A Profession Built on the Science and Evidence Base of Medicine").

22 *See id.* at notes 35–45, and accompanying text ("Medical Profession's Domain").

23 *See* Michael J. Malinowski, *The US Science and Technology "Triple Threat": A Regulatory Treatment Plan for the Nation's Addiction to Prescription Opioids*, 48 U. MEM. L. REV. 1027, 1046 (2018). *See infra* notes 113–77, and accompanying text ("Physician-Patient Relationship").

24 *See infra* notes 113–18, and accompanying text.

25 DTC Rx marketing has proven effective, as demonstrated by biopharma's substantial and increased investment in it over time, and the FDA expressly requires wholly DTCGHR testing service providers to direct their customers to medical professionals for clinical interpretation and medical use. *See Chapter 3*, *supra*, at notes 17–24, and accompanying text (discussing substantial increase in biopharma marketing since the television advertising rule change, passage of FDAMA, and reauthorization of PDUFA in 1997); *Chapter 4*, *supra*, at notes 160–62, and accompanying text (FDA measures to emphasize approval limited to non-clinical use without the involvement of a licensed, competent medical professional).

26 *See generally Chapter 2*, *supra*.

27 *See generally id. See also* Malinowski, *Triple Threat*, *supra* note 23, at 1058–65; Johns Hopkins University of Medicine, Coronavirus Resource Center, *Typical Timeline* (visited Aug. 2022), https://coronavirus.jhu.edu/vaccines/timeline; Marty Johnson, *Trump Administration's 'Operation Warp Speed' Looking at 14 Potential COVID-19 Vaccines to Fast-Track*, THE HILL (May 2, 2020), https://thehill.com/homenews/administration/495831-trump-administrations-operation-warp-speed-looking-at-14-potential.

28 *See generally Chapter 2*, *supra*. *See also* MICHAEL J. MALINOWSKI, HANDBOOK ON BIOTECHNOLOGY LAW, BUSINESS, AND POLICY 69–77 (2016) ("Technology Transfer Law and Policy"); Malinowski, *Triple Threat*, *supra* note 23, at 1058–65.

29 *See* MALINOWSKI, HANDBOOK, *supra* note 28, at v–vii, xxiii–xxx ("Industry Overview"). Complementary ("fraternal twins") legislation, commonly referred to as "Bayh-Dole" and "Stevenson-Wydler," was enacted in 1980. *See* Bayh-Dole University and Small Business Patent Procedures Act of 1980, Pub. L. No. 96–517, 94 Stat. 3015, *codified as amended*, 35 U.S.C. §§ 200–212, *implemented by* 37 C.F.R. 401 (federal funding agreements with contracting parites), 37 C.F.R. 404 (licensing inventions); Stevenson-Wydler Technology

Innovation Act of 1980, Pub. L. No. 96-480, 94 Stat. 2311, *codified as amended*, 15 U.S.C. §§ 3701–3724 (2012) (requires federal agencies, laboratories, and researchers to actively participate in and budget for technology transfer activities).

30 *Cf.* JAMES D. WATSON, DNA: THE STORY OF THE GENETIC REVOLUTION (2nd ed. 2017) (with Andrew Berry. Kevin Davies) (updated commemoration of the fiftieth anniversary of the discovery of the double helix).

31 *See generally* TECONOMY PARTNERS LLC, BIOPHARMACEUTICAL INDUSTRY-SPONSORED CLINICAL TRIALS: GROWING STATE ECONOMIES (2019), www.phrma.org/-/media/TEConomy_PhRMA-Clinical-Trials-Impacts.pdf%EF%BB%BF. *Cf.* CONGRESSIONAL BUDGET OFFICE/CBO, RESEARCH AND DEVELOPMENT IN THE PHARMACEUTICAL INDUSTRY (2021), www.cbo.gov/publication/57126; US NATIONAL ACADEMIES OF SCIENCE, ENGINEERING, AND MEDICINE/NASEM, PREPARING FOR THE FUTURE PRODUCTS OF BIOTECHNOLOGY (2017), www.nap.edu/catalog/24605/preparing-for-future-products-of-biotechnology.

32 Stephan Ehrhardt, Lawrence J. Appel, Curtis L. Meinert, *Trends in National Institutes of Health Funding for Clinical Trials Registered in ClinicalTrials.gov*, 314(23) JAMA 2566–67 (Dec. 15, 2015) (internal table reference omitted), www.ncbi.nlm.nih.gov/pmc/articles/PMC4919115/. ClinicalTrials.gov, a comprehensive public-accessible registry of clinical trials carried out with FDA oversight, is discussed in *Chapter 7*, *infra*, at notes 248–49, and, and accompanying text. Many have argued, and for some time, that the NIH and FDA should fund more clinical trials, including to parallel or replace industry trials as an assurance of research integrity and fundamental, objective clinical understanding. *See, e.g.*, MARCIA ANGELL, THE TRUTH ABOUT DRUG COMPANIES: HOW THEY DECEIVE US AND WHAT TO DO ABOUT IT 244–46 (2004) (winner of a Polk Award for excellence in journalism) (proposing establishment of an independent Institute for Prescription Drug Trials within NIH to administer clinical trials of prescription drugs). *Cf.* ABRAMSON, OVERDOSED, *supra* note 1, at 95, 209.

33 *See* SETON HALL SCHOOL OF LAW, THE CENTER FOR HEALTH & PHARMACEUTICAL LAW & POLICY, CONFLICTS OF INTEREST IN CLINICAL TRIAL RECRUITMENT & ENROLLMENT: A CALL FOR INCREASED OVERSIGHT 5 (Nov. 2009) (White Paper, internal citations omitted), https://law.shu.edu/health-law/upload/health_center_whitepaper_nov2009.pdf.

34 *See* ABRAMSON, OVERDOSED, *supra* note 1, at 95; SETON HALL, CLINICAL TRIAL RECRUITMENT, *supra* note 33, at 5. *See also* WALTER ISAACSON, THE CODE BREAKER 97 (2021). *Visit* Association of Clinical Research Organizations/ACRO, official site, www.acrohealth.org/ (last visited Dec. 2, 2015).

35 *See* MALINOWSKI, HANDBOOK, *supra* note 28, at 69–77. *See generally* TOM HOCKADAY, UNIVERSITY TECHNOLOGY TRANSFER: WHAT IT IS AND HOW TO DO IT (2020); UNIVERSITY TECHNOLOGY TRANSFER: THE GLOBALIZATION OF ACADEMIC INNOVATION (ROUTLEDGE STUDIES IN GLOBAL COMPETITION) (Shiri M. Breznitz, Henry Etzkowitz eds., 2019).

36 *See* STARR, SOCIAL TRANSFORMATION, *supra* note 5, at 98–232 ("Escape from the Corporation, 1900–1930").

37 *See Chapter 1*, *supra*, at notes 46–50, and accompanying text (patent medicine manufacturers at the outset of the twentieth century).

38 *See* John D. Blum, *Feng Shui and the Restructuring of the Hospital Corporation: A Call for Change in the Face of the Medical Error Epidemic*, 14 HEALTH MATRIX 5, 8 (2004). *See also* Maxwell J. Mehlman, *Professional Power and the Standard of Care in Medicine*, 44 ARIZ. ST. L.J. 1165, 1235 (2012); Nicole Huberfeld, *Be Not Afraid of Change: Time to Eliminate the Corporate Practice of Medicine Doctrine*, 14 HEALTH MATRIX 243, 251–53

(2004). For a summary of the status of CPMD as of 2015, see AMA, Advocacy Resource Center, *Issue Brief: Corporate Practice of Medicine* (2015), www.ama-assn.org/sites/ama-assn.org/files/corp/media-browser/premium/arc/corporate-practice-of-medicine-issue-brief_1.pdf#:~:text=The%20corporate%20practice%20of%20medicine%20doctrine%20prohibits%20corporations,certain%20health%20care%20entities.%20Overview%20of%20state%20laws.

39 *See Chapter 1, supra*, at notes 106–8, and accompanying text (establishment of a Rx only-category of drugs with a prohibition of DTC communication). Opposition to patent medicine manufactures direct communication with the public was an organizing force for the AMA during the first half of the twentieth century. *See id.*

40 *See id.* at notes 38–41, and accompanying text.

41 *See* Medicare and Medicaid Patient Protection Act of 1987, 42 U.S.C. §1320a-7b ("the Anti-kickback Statute"); 42 U.S.C. §1395nn (1988 and amendments) ("Stark Law"). *See also* Michael J. Malinowski, *Capitation, Advances in Medical Technology, and the Advent of a New Era in Medical Ethics*, 22 Am. J.L. & Med. 335, 335–60 (1996), *reprinted in* Taking Sides: Clashing Views on Controversial Bioethical Issues (Carol Levine ed., 7th ed. 1997).

42 *See* Abramson, Overdosed, *supra* note 1, at 155–57 ("Disempowering the Doctor-Patient Relationship"); *infra* notes 384–85, and accompanying text (distinguishing the US health care system). *See generally* Ezekiel J. Emanuel, Which Country Has the World's Best Health Care? (2020). The first COVID-19 pandemic wave in the US demonstrated the extent to which US health care is decentralized and fragmented. *See generally* Sabrina Corlette, Christine H. Monahan, *Perspectives, US Health Insurance Coverage and Financing*, 387 (25) New. Eng. J. Med. 2297–300 (Dec. 2, 2022), www.nejm.org/doi/full/10.1056/NEJMp2206049?af=R&rss=currentIssue. Federal-state distribution problems caused disparity in access to personal protection equipment/PPE and other treatment and disease management essentials such as ventilators, testing, and health care personnel. However, the US then was able to remarkably overcome distribution challenges through Operation Warp Speed/OWS. *See Chapter 2, supra*, at notes 32–114, and accompanying text (addressing OWS).

43 *See* Elisabeth Rosenthal, An American Sickness: How Healthcare Became Big Business and How You can Take it Back 317–18 (2017) (asserting that corporate sponsorship of the National Multiple Sclerosis/MS Society keeps the cost of MS drugs high and providing additional examples). *See infra* notes 243–45, and accompanying text (biopharma relationships with patient organizations). Organizations often are recipients of substantial biopharma funding through associate memberships, event and initiative sponsorships, advertising, subscriptions, reprint purchases, and other financial interactions that influence organizations directly and through their leadership. *See infra* notes 295–320, and accompanying text ("Industry Influences on Medical Professional Education").

44 *See* Rosenthal, American Sickness, *supra* note 43, at 317–18. *See infra* notes 298–99, 301–2, 362–63, and accompanying text (thought leaders/key opinion leaders). For example, "The leaders of many medical societies – the American Academy of Neurology, the American Lung Association, and the American Heart Association, to name a few – are paid as industry consultants and speakers." Rosenthal, American Sickness, *supra*, at 318.

45 *See supra* note 35, and accompanying text. *See generally Chapter 2, supra*.

46 *See infra* notes 113–77, and accompanying text ("Today's US Physician-Patient Relationship").

47 *See generally* The Pew Charitable Trusts, Report, The Role of Lab-Developed Tests in the In Vitro Diagnostics Market 1 (Oct. 2021), www.pewtrusts.org/-/; Future of Privacy Forum, Best Practices for Consumer Genetic Testing Services (July 31, 2018), www.geneticdataprotection.com/wp-content/uploads/2019/05/

Future-of-Privacy-Forum-Privacy-Best-Practices-July-2018.pdf.; *Chapter 4, supra*. Genes make proteins, and proteins impact gene expression and cellular differentiation. *See generally* Sagar Aryal, *Genomics Vs Proteomics- Definition and 10 Major Differences*, THE BIOLOGY NOTES (Feb. 16, 2021), https://thebiologynotes.com/difference-between-genomics-and-proteomics/#:~:text=Genomics%20is%20the%20study%20of%20genomes%20which%20refers%20to%20the,the%20genome%20of%20an%20organism. An organism's genome is the complete set of genes in the nucleus of each of the organism's cells – the organism's set of DNA instructions. An organism's genome is a constant; the organism's cells all carry the same set of genes and DNA instructions. Nevertheless, cells differentiate to become specific cell and tissue types. *See id.* The set of proteins produced through gene expression in each of an organism's cells varies in accordance with cell and tissue type, and it is dynamic. *See id.* A proteome is the complete set of proteins that is or can be expressed by a genome, cell, tissue, or organism at a given time and under defined conditions. *See id.* Proteomics is the study of the proteome. *See generally* NATIONAL RESEARCH COUNCIL/NRC, WORKSHOP REPORT, DEFINING THE MANDATE OF PROTEOMICS IN THE POST-GENOMICS ERA: WORKSHOP REPORT (2002), www.ncbi.nlm.nih.gov/books/NBK95348/pdf/Bookshelf_NBK95348.pdf. Genetics is the study of gene expression and function, and genomics is the study of gene expression, function, and interactions in the context of an organism's entire genome. "The main difference between genomics and genetics is that genetics scrutinizes the functioning and composition of the single gene whereas genomics addresses all genes and their inter relationships in order to identify their combined influence on the growth and development of the organism." World Health Organization/WHO, *Genomics* (Nov. 12, 2020), www.who.int/news-room/questions-andanswers/item/genomics#:~:text=The%20main%20difference%20between%20genomics,and%20development%20of%20the%20organism.

48 *See* note 47, *supra*; *Chapter 6, infra*, at notes 43-98, and accompanying text ("The Complexities of Personal Genome Medical Decision-Making"). *Cf.* SECRETARY'S ADVISORY COMMITTEE ON GENETIC TESTING/SACGT, ENHANCING THE OVERSIGHT OF GENETIC TESTS: RECOMMENDATIONS OF THE SACGT (July 2000) (addressing the clinical complexities of *clinically sound* genetic testing), https://osp.od.nih.gov/sagct_document_archi/enhancing-the-oversight-of-genetic-tests-recommendations-of-the-sacgt/.

49 *See Chapter 6, supra*, at notes 43–98, and accompanying text ("The Complexities of Personal Genome Medical Decision-Making").

50 *See id.* at notes 99–152, and accompanying text ("US Health Care System and Consumer Genetics and Genomics Market Issues").

51 *See Chapter 4, supra*, at notes 95–97, and accompanying text (mission to transform US health care through personal genome autonomy and patient self-determination—consumer-centric personal genome medicine/PGM). *See also* Recode, *Full Transcript: 23andMe CEO Anne Wojcicki Answers Genetics and Privacy Questions on Too Embarrased to Ask* (Sept. 29, 2017), www.vox.com/2017/9/29/16385320/transcript-23andme-ceo-anne-wojcicki-genetics-privacy-health-questions-too-embarrassed-to-ask. *See also NBC Nightly News with Lester Holt, High-Tech Heritage* (July 14, 2018) (interview with Anne Wojcicki, in which she explains, "We're big believers in that the more I can educate you earlier in life, the more you're actually going to have information to try to prevent the condition.").

52 ABRAMSON, OVERDOSED, *supra* note 1, at 249.

53 *See Chapter 6, supra*, at notes 43–98, and accompanying text ("The Complexities of Personal Genome Medical Decision-Making"). *Cf.* SACGT, RECOMMENDATIONS, *supra* note 48.

54 *See infra* notes 113–77, and accompanying text ("State of Physician Decision Making").

55 *See Chapter 6, supra*, at notes 43–98, and accompanying text ("The Complexities of Personal Genome Medical Decision-Making").

56 *See infra* notes 207–320, and accompanying text (industry influence on the MJE and medical education).

57 *See* Christopher Buccafusco, Jonathan S. Masur, *Drugs, Patents, and Well-Being*, 98 WASH. U.L. REV. 1403, 1460 (2021); Corrrina Sorenson, Kalipso Chalkidou, *Reflections on the Evolution of Health Technology Assessment in Europe*, 7 HEALTH ECON. POL'Y & L. 25, 26 (2012) (European HTA mechanisms). *See infra* notes 384–403, and accompanying text ("Reliable Health Technology Assessment").

58 SANDEEP JUAHAR, DOCTORED: THE DISILLUSIONMENT OF AN AMERICAN PHYSICIAN 6 (2015) (director of the Heart Failure Program at Long Island Jewish Medical Center).

59 *See* Avik Roy, *Why the American Medical Association Had 72 Million Reasons to Shrink Doctors' Pay*, FORBES (Nov. 28, 2011) ("[T]he American Medical Association played a key role in establishing the power of doctors in the American health-care system, and thereby in the outsized compensation that American physicians enjoy ...."), www.forbes.com/sites/theapothecary/2011/11/28/why-the-american-medical-association-had-72-million-reasons-to-help-shrink-doctors-pay/?sh=29593faa60d9.

60 *See* STARR, SOCIAL TRANSFORMATION, *supra* note 5, at 420–49 ("The Coming of the Corporation").

61 Roy, *Shrink Doctors' Pay*, *supra* note 59.

62 *Visit* American Academy of Professional Coders, *What is CPT®?* (undated), www.aapc.com/resources/medical-coding/cpt.aspx.

63 *See* Roy, *Shrink Doctors' Pay*, *supra* note 59.

64 *Visit What is CPT®?*, *supra* note 62. "Medical coding and coders like ours essentially don't exist in any other healthcare system. And, like an Uber driver or a solar panel installer, a medical coder really didn't exist as a profession here twenty-five years ago either." ROSENTHAL, AMERICAN SICKNESS, *supra* note 43, at 172. *See id.* at 172–77.

65 *See Chapter 1*, *supra*, at notes 35–45, and accompanying text ("US Law-Policy Recognition of Clinical Medicine as the Medical Profession's Domain.").

66 Roy, *Shrink Doctors' Pay*, *supra* note 59 (page nos. unavailable online).

67 *See id.*

68 *See id.*

69 *See generally* Malinowski, *Capitation*, *supra* note 41, and accompanying text (addressing the business of medicine). Corporations presently are investing heavily in US primary care. Notable recent examples are CVS Health's acquisition of Signify Health on September 5, 2022, for approximately $8 billion, and Amazon's announced (July 21, 2022) plan to acquire One Medical, a primary care practice with some 200 locations serving over 700,000 patients, for $3.9 billion. *See generally* Soleil Shah, Hayden Rooke-Ley, Erin C. Fuse Brown, *Corporate Investors in Primary Care – Profits, Progress, and Pitfalls*, 388 N. ENG. J. MED. 99–101 (Jan. 12, 2023), www.nejm.org/doi/full/10.1056/NEJMp2212841.

70 ABRAMSON, OVERDOSED, *supra* note 1, at 81–82. *See generally* Malinowski, *Capitation*, *supra* note 41. A relentless rise in the cost of health care and bleak future cost projections resulted in enactment of the Patient Protection and Affordable Care Act, now referred to as the Affordable Care Act/ACA, Pub. L. No. 111–148, 124 Stat. 119 (2010) (codified as amended in scattered sections of the U.S.C.). The ACA could prove a baseline for evolution of US health care over time into a system with universal access to some fundamental services, but only time will tell.

71 JUAHAR, DOCTORED, *supra* note 58, at 6 (2015) (director of the Heart Failure Program at Long Island Jewish Medical Center). *See generally* ABRAMSON, OVERDOSED, *supra* note 1; OTIS WEBB BRAWLEY, HOW WE DO HARM: A DOCTOR BREAKS RANK ABOUT BEING SICK IN AMERICA (2011).

72 JUAHAR, DOCTORED, *supra* note 58, at 13. The physician shortage is disproportionately dire in family practice. "The percentage of graduates of American medical schools entering family practice residencies declined by almost half between 1997 and 2004 (from 17.3 to 8.8 percent)." ABRAMSON, OVERDOSED, *supra* note 1, at 256.

73 *See infra notes* 113–77, and accompanying text ("Today's US Physician-Patient Relationship"); *infra* notes 178–206 ("Stewardship of the Science and Evidence Base of US Medicine").

74 *See* MANUEL CASTELLS, THE RISE OF THE NETWORK SOCIETY xxv (2nd ed. 2009). *See also Chapter 4, supra*, at 12–16 (addressing the impact of ICT on society, culture, and US health care).

75 *See generally Chapter 3, supra* (biopharma DTC and DTP marketing); *Chapter 4, supra*, at notes 11–20, and accompanying text (addressing the advent of ICT, internet access, and DNA familiarity, and their social and cultural impact).

76 *See generally* JAY KATZ, THE SILENT WORLD OF DOCTOR AND PATIENT (1984, revised ed. 2002) (addressing and challenging the legacy of physician paternalism prior to the mid-1980s). Fortunately, the US federal government developed, codified, implemented, and enforced adherence to the doctrine of voluntary informed consent for research on human subjects beginning in the 1970s. US codification of regulations to protect human subjects – a movement with traction following media reporting on the infamous Tuskegee research studies in 1972 – centers on voluntary, informed consent. *See* David B. Resnik, *Research Ethics Timeline* (last reviewed Aug. 25, 2020), www.niehs.nih.gov/research/resources/bioethics/timeline/. *See generally* SANDRA JOHNSON ET AL., BIOETHICS AND THE LAW IN A NUTSHELL, 223–69 (*Chapter 8. Regulation of Research With Human Subjects*). Development of the doctrine of informed consent in the research context, coupled with social and cultural changes, carried into clinical care – especially with inspiration for assertion of patient rights from the proliferation of managed care, commercialization of medicine, and the comingling of clinical research and clinical care in the following decades:

> From the 1970s to the present, a health-care-rights movement has questioned the medical profession about informed consent, other human subject protections, patient involvement in therapeutic decision-making, the rights of patients to refuse treatment, the right of patients to see medical records, freedom from genetic discrimination, DNA ownership, and other issues, culminating in a call for comprehensive national health care reform.

Michael J. Malinowski, *Doctors, Patients, and Pills-A System Popping Under Too Much Physician Discretion? A Law-Policy Prescription to Make Drug Approval More Meaningful in the Delivery of Health Care*, 33 CARDOZO L. REV. 1085, 1097 (2012) (internal citations omitted). Ongoing debate questions whether the pervasiveness of informed consent throughout US health care *as an administrative requirement* has essentially undermined the doctrine in clinical care. *See, e.g.*, Timothy C. MacDonnell, *Making An Offer That Can't Be Refused: The Need for Reform in the Rules Governing Informed Consent and Doctor-Patient Agreements*, 67(3) Vill. L. Rev. 509 (2022), https://digitalcommons.law.villanova.edu/vlr/vol67/iss3/2.

77 *See Chapter 6, supra*, at notes 43–98, and accompanying text ("The Complexities of Personal Genome Medical Decision-Making").

78 According to Professor Lewis A. Grossman, "throughout most of American history, a broad swath of the population has believed that people have a right to choose their preferred medical treatments without government interference," and he depicts the mid-twentieth century as "an anomalous moment in our history." LEWIS A. GROSSMAN, CHOOSE YOUR

MEDICINE: FREEDOM OF THERAPEUTIC CHOICE IN AMERICA 5, 7 (2021). Based upon my research, reflected in this book, as well as my own decades of experience and research in health law and policy, I believe that the mid-twentieth century was a period during which faith in medical science and physicians' learned knowledge about it was cemented through the realization of significant advances in clinical medicine and a culture of progress through science and technology following WWII. *See generally* WORLD'S FAIRS IN THE COLD WAR: SCIENCE, TECHNOLOGY, AND THE CULTURE OF PROGRESS (Arthur P. Molella, Scott Gabriel Knowles eds., 2019) (chronicling the Cold War culture of progress through the lens of world's fairs). *See Chapter 1, supra*, at notes 28–34, and accompanying text (realization of heightened evidentiary-science standards in pharmaceutical R&D, reflected in pharma establishment of research campuses drawing from and employing academic research norms and researchers). Exploitation by miracle cure and snake oil salesmen and patent medicine manufacturers, Progressive Era (1896–1918) activism against industrialization, and mass detriment to health through crises caused by commercial medicines in the early-to-mid twentieth century stirred public demand for consumer protection and drew both the US medical profession and the US federal government into biologics and drug regulation. *See Chapter 1, supra*, at notes 46–101, and accompanying text (national medical profession and government regulation). Overall, the public may not have wanted the federal government to interfere in the sanctity of their physician-patient decision making, but they wanted the government to ensure safe and effective medicines – as did the medical and pharmacist professions. I believe that Professor Grossman chronicles and profiles major outlier movements that complement the general public's sentiment, at least during much of the twentieth century until the advent of the ICT era in the 1990s. *See supra* note 74, and accompanying text. Dr. Grossman does recognize that "[m]ost people demanding access to pharmaceuticals earlier in the drug development process [, proponents of the "right to try" without FDA interference,] do not wholly reject the legitimacy of conventional science" and he distinguishes "the medical freedom rhetoric of alternative medicine movements" that typically include "a strain of thoroughgoing hostility to scientists, experts, bureaucrats, elites, and big business – a hostility sometimes fading over into paranoid conspiracy mongering." *Id.* at 5.

79 *See infra* notes 178–86, and accompanying text (addressing the House Oversight Committee report on the Trump Administration's handling of the COVID-19 pandemic and documenting a plethora of instances of politicization of science). *See generally* DEBORAH BIRX, SILENT INVASION: THE UNTOLD STORY OF THE TRUMP ADMINISTRATION, COVID-19, AND PREVENTING THE NEXT PANDEMIC BEFORE IT'S TOO LATE (2022).

80 Allison Aubrey, *Trump Declares Coronavirus A Public Health Emergency And Restricts Travel From China*, NPR (Jan. 21, 2020), www.npr.org/sections/health-shots/2020/01/31/801686524/trump-declares-coronavirus-a-public-health-emergency-and-restricts-travel-from-c; WORLD HEALTH ORGANIZATION/WHO, CORONAVIRUS DISEASE 2019 (COVID-19): SITUATION REPORT – 51 (Mar. 11, 2020), www.who.int/docs/default-source/coronaviruse/situation-reports/20200311-sitrep-51-covid-19.pdf; WHO, *WHO Director-General's Opening Remarks at the Media Briefing on COVID-19* (Mar. 11, 2020), www.who.int/director-general/speeches/detail/who-director-general-s-opening-remarks-at-the-media-briefing-on-covid-19---11-march-2020.

81 *See Chapter 2, supra*, at notes 32–114, and accompanying text (addressing Operation Warp Speed/OWS).

82 *See generally* HOUSE OVERSIGHT COM., SELECT SUB. ON THE CORONAVIRUS CRISIS, YEAR-END STAFF REPORT, MORE EFFECTIVE, MORE EQUITABLE: OVERSEEING AN IMPROVING AND ONGOING PANDEMIC RESPONSE (Dec. 17, 2021),

https://coronavirus.house.gov/sites/democrats.coronavirus.house.gov/files/SSCCInterim ReportDec2021V1.pdf; BIRX, UNTOLD STORY, *supra* note 79.

83 For a timeline that illustrates President Trump's contradiction of health experts alongside evidentiary science and clinical understanding developments regarding hydroxychloroquine during the pandemic, see Libby Cathey, *Timeline: Tracking Trump Alongside Scientific Developments on Hydroxychloroquine*, ABC NEWS (Aug. 8, 2020), https://abcnews.go.com/Health/timeline-tracking-trump-alongside-scientific-developments-hydroxychloroquine/story?id=72170553. *See generally* BIRX, UNTOLD STORY, *supra* note 79.

84 *See* Michael Erman, *Potential Coronavirus Treatment Touted by Trump Already in Shortage, Pharmacists Say*, REUTERS (Mar. 19, 2020), https://news.yahoo.com/exlcusive-potential-coronavirus-treatment-touted-184603785.html; Blake Ellis, Melanie Hicken, *Sales of Drug Touted by Trump have been Soaring*, CNN (May 22, 2020), www.cnnphilippines.com/world/2020/5/22/sales-of-antimalarial-drug-soaring.html.

85 *See Chapter 2, supra*, at notes 94–108, and accompanying text (global evidence-based science data supporting the COVID-19 vaccines). The July 2021 mask mandate community meeting experience of Mr. Jonathan Waddell, a retired Air Force sergeant and city commissioner in Enid, Oklahoma, captures the public's volatile politicization of science during the pandemic. *See generally* Sabrina Tavernise, *A Fight About Masks Reveals a Deep Schism in the Soul of a City*, N.Y. TIMES (Dec. 26, 2021), at 1, 22–23. When Mr. Waddell arrived at the meeting, "The parking lot was full, and people wearing red were getting out of their cars greeting one another, looking a bit like players on a sports team." *Id.* at 1. He had an epiphany driving home:

> At the end of the night, the mask mandate failed, and the audience erupted in cheers. But for Mr. Waddell, who had spent seven years making Enid his home, it was only the beginning. He remembers driving home and watching his mirrors to make sure no one was following him. He called his father, a former police officer, and told him what had happened. He said that people were talking about masks, but that it felt like something else. What, exactly, he did not know.

Id.

86 *See generally* HEIDI J. LARSON, STUCK: HOW VACCINE RUMORS START – AND WHY THEY DON'T GO Away (2020) (addressing the heightened importance of adhering to sound, evidence-based science with vaccines given their susceptibility to rumors and conspiracy theories derived from the contrary).

87 Fraudulent research published in the *Lancet* that suggested a link between autism and the measles, mumps, and rubella/MMR vaccination is a notable contemporary example, as discussed in *Chapter 2, supra*, at note 45. *See Retracted Article*: Andrew Wakefield et al. (12 additional coauthors), *Ileal-lymphoid-nodular hyperplasia, non-specific colitis, and pervasive developmental disorder in children*, 351(9103) LANCET 637–41 (Feb. 28, 1998), www.sciencedirect.com/science/article/pii/S0140673697110960. *See Chapter 2, supra*, at note 45 (vaccine hesitancy among pregnant women in the midst of a tripledemic, at great risk to them and their pregnancies).

88 The US surpassed 1 million known COVID-19 deaths in May 2022. *See* Adeel Hassan, *The US Surpasses 1 Million Covid Deaths, the World's Highest Known Total*, N.Y. TIMES (May 19, 2022), www.nytimes.com/2022/05/19/us/us-covid-deaths.html. As reported in May 2022, "The United States has a higher rate of infection than many other wealthy countries do, and the pathogen has continued to spread in a population afflicted by inequity, political divisions, a sometimes-overwhelmed public health system, and an inconsistent array of policies and responses." *Id.*

89 *See generally* Ed Pertwee, Clarissa Simas, Heidi J. Larson, *An Epidemic of Uncertainty: Rumors, Conspiracy Theories and Vaccine Hesitancy*, 28 NATURE MED. 456–59 (Mar. 10, 2022), www.nature.com/articles/s41591-022-01728-z. ("The huge cascade of viral misinformation that has formed part of the COVID-19 infodemic [COVID-19 vaccine science misinformation ("info") during the pandemic ("demic")] has included conspiracy theories about the origins of the virus as well as suspicions around the motives behind government COVID-19 control measures."). *See also Chapter 2, supra*, at note 45, and accompanying text. Admittedly, the FDA's oversight of clinical trials in general is "grossly inadequate," as was recognized by HHS's Office of Inspector General in 2007, but that chronic problem was inclusive of, not exclusive to, the COVID-19 vaccines. *See generally* Maryanne Demasi, *BMJ Investigation, FDA Oversight of Clinical Trials is "Grossly Inadequate," Say Experts*, 379 BRIT. MED. J./BMJ 2628 (Nov. 16, 2022), www.bmj.com/content/bmj/379/bmj.o2628.full.pdf; Shawn Radcliffe, *FDA Oversight of Clinical Trials was 'Grossly Inadequate,' Report Claims*, HEALTHLINE (Nov. 18, 2022), www.healthline.com/health-news/fda-oversight-of-clinical-trials-was-grossly-inadequate-report-claims. Fortunately, COVID-19 vaccine R&D was a global initiative with clinical and regulatory sharing, and many of the US' counterparts with universal health care systems oversee clinical trial sites much more reliably with fewer resources. *See Chapter 2, supra*, at notes 33 (global collaboration), 89 (oversight of clinical trial sites), and accompanying text. Even with US vaccine hesitancy, according to a study by researchers from the Commonwealth Fund and Yale School of Public health released December 12, 2022, "without Covid-19 vaccines, the nation would have had 1.5 times more infections, 3.8 times more hospitalizations and 4.1 times more deaths than it did between December 2020 and November 2022[,]" and the vaccines saved more than 3 million lives. *See* Jen Christensen, *Covid-19 Vaccines have Saved More than 3 Million Lives in US, Study Says, but the Fight Isn't Over*, CNN (Dec. 13, 2022), www.cnn.com/2022/12/13/health/covid-19-vaccines-study/index.html. "As it stands now, Covid-19 has caused at least 99.2 million cases and more than 1.08 million deaths in the US. Just in the past week, there were 2,981 new deaths and 30,253 new hospital admissions, according to the US Centers for Disease Control and Prevention." *Id.*

90 *See Chapter 2, supra*, at notes 94–108, and accompanying text (discussing the unprecedented global evidence-based science data supporting the COVID-19 vaccines). "Misinformation has run rampant during the Covid-19 public health emergency, challenging the communication and trust-building efforts of public health and medical professionals." Janine Knudsen, Maddie Perlman-Gabel, Isabella Guerra Uccelli et al., *Combating Misinformation as a Core Function of Public Health*, 4(2) NEJM CATALYST (Feb. 2023), https://catalyst.nejm.org/doi/full/10.1056/CAT.22.0198.

91 Popular conservative media hosts with large followings have aggressively challenged, at times demonized, Dr. Anthony Fauci – the world's greatest infectious disease expert according to Dr. Francis Collins, and certainly the nation's top COVID-19 science expert official– and other preeminent scientists throughout the pandemic. By doing so, they incentivized threats. *See, e.g., Staff, Laura Ingraham Calls Dr. Fauci Part of "the Medical Deep State,"* MEDIAMATTERS (June 15, 2020), www.mediamatters.org/laura-ingraham/laura-ingraham-calls-dr-fauci-part-medical-deep-state. For example, on December 20, 2021, Fox host Jesse Watters urged a crowd of young conservatives to "ambush" Dr. Fauci and to "go for a rhetorical 'kill shot.'" *See* Aila Slisco, *Fox News Stands by Jesse Watters After 'Kill Shot' Remark While Fauci Wants Him Fired*, NEWSWEEK (Dec. 21, 2021), www.newsweek.com/fox-news-stands-jesse-watters-after-kill-shot-remark-while-fauci-wants-him-fired-1661939.

92 Dr. Francis Collins, reflecting on his career directing NIH for twelve years, including during the first two years of the COVID-19 pandemic, identified failure to anticipate the severity of US vaccine hesitancy despite compelling evidence as the greatest COVID-19

response shortcoming. *See CBS Sunday Morning, Looking Back: Dr. Francis Collins on a Life in Science* (television broadcast first aired Dec. 19, 2021) (video segment with transcript), www.cbsnews.com/news/nih-director-dr-francis-collins-on-a-life-in-science/. COVID-19 vaccine hesitancy has been primarily a dilemma for high-income countries, with many governments of developing-economy countries vying for vaccine access. *See* Anna Rouw, Adam Wexler, Jennifer Kates, Josh Michaud, *Global COVID-19 Vaccine Access: A Snapshot of Inequality*, KAISER FAM. FOUND/KFF (May 17, 2021), www.kff .org/policy-watch/global-covid-19-vaccine-access-snapshot-of-inequality/. As of June 2021, "High-income countries, representing just a fifth of the global adult population, ha[d] purchased more than half of all vaccine doses, resulting in disparities between adult population share and doses purchased for all other country income groups." *Id.* In 2021, vaccine hesitancy was distinguishably prevalent in the US and in some European populations, and "Critical to the success of COVID-19 vaccination campaigns [was] the development of strategic approach against 'infodemic' or widespread misinformation and conspiracy theories on COVID-19 vaccines." Nicky C. Cardenas, *Europe and United States Vaccine Hesitancy: Leveraging Strategic Policy for 'Infodemic' on COVID-19 Vaccines*, J. PUB. HEALTH (OXF.) (Jun 17, 2021), www.ncbi.nlm.nih.gov/pmc/articles/ PMC8344824/. The US and Germany were notably distinguishable among industrialized nations in their levels of COVID-19 vaccine hesitancy and the politicization of related science. "Like the United States, Germany [had] a thriving anti-vaccination movement" which also "encompassed conspiracy theorists, left-leaning spiritualists, and the far right." Edna Bonhomme, *Germany's Anti-vaccination History Is Riddled With Anti-Semitism*, ATLANTIC (May 2, 2021), www.theatlantic.com/health/archive/2021/05/ anti-vaccination-germany-anti-semitism/618777/.

93 The US made the COVID-19 vaccinations available to the public free of charge when the FDA granted emergency use authorizations/EUAs in December 2020. *See* GOVERNMENT ACCOUNTABILITY OFFICE/GAO, OPERATION WARP SPEED: ACCELERATED COVID-19 VACCINE DEVELOPMENT STATUS AND EFFORTS TO ADDRESS MANUFACTURING CHALLENGES, GAO-21-319 (Feb. 11, 2021), at 21 ("Highlights"), www.gao.gov/products/gao-21-319. The FDA granted full market approval to the Pfizer-BionNTech (COMIRNATY) vaccine for use in people sixteen years and older on Aug. 23, 2021, and full market approval to the Moderna (Spikevax) vaccine for individuals eighteen years and older on January 31, 2022. *See* FDA, *News Release, FDA Approves First COVID-19 Vaccine* (Aug. 23, 2021), www.fda.gov/news-events/press-announcements/fda-approves-first-covid-19-vaccine; FDA, *News Release, Coronavirus (COVID-19) Update: FDA Takes Key Action by Approving Second COVID-19 Vaccine* (Jan. 31, 2022), www.fda.gov/news-events/press-announcements/coronavirus-covid-19-up date-fda-takes-key-action-approving-second-covid-19-vaccine. *Visit* Mayo Clinic, *US COVID-19 Vaccine Tracker: See Your State's Progress* (visited June 9, 2022), www.mayo clinic.org/coronavirus-covid-19/vaccine-tracker (vaccine hesitancy concentrations ascertainable). In addition to the data supporting these full market approvals, a concerted effort was made to collect data regarding pregnant women (research involving pregnant women and fetuses triggers heightened regulatory oversight under the Common Rule to protect human subjects) because COVID-19 danger to pregnancy was evident early in the pandemic. *See* Apoorva Mandavilli, *The Covid Pandemic's Hidden Casualties: Pregnant Women*, N.Y. TIMES (Dec. 8, 2022), www.nytimes.com/2022/12/08/health/preg nant-women-covid-flu-vaccine.html. A June 2020 study determined that, among COVID-19-infected women, pregnant women were fifty percent more likely to be admitted to intensive-care units and seventy percent more likely to need a ventilator. *Id.* Subsequent studies indicate that pregnant women are at risk of developing pre-eclampsia-like

conditions with the risk of dangerously high blood pressure. *Id*. Overall, "Covid can kill pregnant women and can result in miscarriage, preterm births and stillbirths even when the women have asymptomatic illness or mild illness. The infection may also affect the baby's brain development." *Id*. The CDC, based upon evidentiary-science data the agency deemed sufficient, wholeheartedly endorsed vaccination for pregnant women in August-September 2021 – approximately three months before Omicron engulfed the nation. *See* CDC, *Media Statement, New CDC Data: COVID-19 Vaccination Safe for Pregnant People* (Aug. 11, 2021), www.cdc.gov/media/releases/2021/s0811-vaccine-safe-pregnant.html. The American College of Obstetricians and Gynecologists/ACOG and the Society for Maternal-Fetal Medicine/SMFM recommended the same over a month before. *See* ACOG, *ACOG, and SMFM Recommend COVID-19 Vaccination for Pregnant Individuals* (July 30, 2021), www.acog.org/news/news-releases/2021/07/acog-smfm-recommend-covid-19-vaccination-for-pregnant-individuals.

94 *See* Christopher Wolf, Adriana Rezal, *The States With the Best COVID-19 Vaccination Rates*, US News (May 20, 2022) (based on USAFacts and data from the Centers for Disease Control and Prevention/CDC), www.usnews.com/news/best-states/articles/these-states-have-the-best-covid-19-vaccination-rates.

95 This theory is consistent with Professor Grossman's fundamental premise. *See generally* Gossman, Choose, *supra* note 78, and accompanying text.

96 Alaa Elassar, Ed Lavandera, Ashley Killough, *Deflated Health Care Workers and Desperate Patients Clash Over Alternative Covid Treatments*, CNN (Dec. 24, 2021), www.cnn.com/2021/12/24/us/doctors-patients-threats-coronavirus-treatments/index.html; Sarah Al-Arshani, *Healthcare Workers Say some COVID-19 Patients and their Families are Demanding Unapproved Therapies*, Bus. Insider (Dec 25, 2021), www.businessinsider.com/healthcare-workers-say-some-covid-19-patients-demand-unproven-drugs-2021-12.

97 *See Chapter 1, supra*, at note 12–34, and accompanying text ("A Profession Built on the Science and Evidence Base of Medicine").

98 *See* Rosenthal, American Sickness, *supra* note 43, at 98–9. *See also* Grossman, Choose, *supra* note 78, at 162–200.

99 Rosenthal, American Sickness, *supra* note 43, at 98–9. However, political campaigns to force US market access to experimental medicinal products must be questioned and the science scrutinized even more closely, as vividly illustrated by a political campaign in the 1970s that fraudulently promoted laetrile, a compound extracted from the pits of apricots and other fruits, as a miracle cure for cancer. *See* Richard D. Lyons, *Rightists Are Linked to Laetrile's Lobby*, N.Y. Times (July 5, 1977), www.nytimes.com/1977/07/05/archives/rightists-are-linked-to-laetriles-lobby-but-backers-of-purported.html. Although the FDA determined laetrile was clinically worthless for treating cancer, potentially toxic, and banned it, ten states were persuaded by an intense national campaign orchestrated by conservative political groups to enact legislation to permit intrastate use. *See id*.

100 *Cf*. US Dep. Veteran's Affairs, *Laboratory Tests and HIV: Entire Lesson* (last updated Oct. 17, 2019), www.hiv.va.gov/patient/diagnosis/labtests-single-page.asp. Traditional endpoints include decisive events, clinical outcomes, such as death and disease remission over enough time to marginalize the risk of recurrence. Surrogate endpoints replace these with indicators available much more quickly, such as measures that indicate incremental responsiveness to treatment while disease is still present. *See generally* FDA, *Surrogate Endpoint Resources for Drug and Biologic Development* (current July 24, 2018), www.fda.gov/drugs/development-resources/surrogate-endpoint-resources-drug-and-biologic-development. "Between 2010 and 2012, the FDA approved 45 percent of new drugs based on a surrogate endpoint. Sometimes surrogate endpoints can support an accelerated approval with lesser evidentiary support, when they are 'reasonably likely to predict a clinical benefit'...." *Id*.

101 Jeff Craven, *Study: Novel Drug Approvals in 2020 Continue Trend of Fewer Preapproval Pivotal Trials, Surrogate Endpoints*, REG. FOCUS (May 17, 2022) (Reg. Affairs Prof. Soc'y publication), www.raps.org/news-and-articles/news-articles/2022/5/study-novel-drug-approvals-in-2020-continue-trend. "The use of fewer pivotal trials and acceptance of surrogate endpoints is the continuation of a trend with the development of new regulatory pathways and a goal to reduce drug development costs and expedite drug approval…." *Id.* The twenty-first Century Cures Act, signed into law in December 2016, which was supported especially by large biopharma manufacturers and opposed by many consumer organizations, codified opportunities for companies to provide "data summaries" and "real world evidence" such as observational studies and insurance claims data rather than full clinical trial results, along with other measures to accelerate FDA review and approval. *See* Pub. L. No. 114-255 (Dec. 2016) (contains three primary titles that address acceleration of medical product discovery, development, and delivery). *See generally* Sheila Kaplan, *Winners and Losers of the 21st Century Cures Act*, STAT NEWS (Dec. 5, 2016), www.statnews.com/2016/12/05/21st-century-cures-act-winners-losers.

102 ROSENTHAL, AMERICAN SICKNESS, *supra* note 43, at 99. *See also infra* note 439, and accompanying text (Medicare expenditure on four cancer drugs that were fast-tracked to market under FDAMA though later determined to provide no clinical benefit). In a study published in 2020, researchers identified 194 unique drug authorizations for 132 cancer drugs that were based on surrogate end points from 1992 through 2019. *See* Emerson Y. Chen, Alyson Haslam, Vinay Prasad, *FDA Acceptance of Surrogate End Points for Cancer Drug Approval:1992–2019*, 180(6) JAMA Intern Med. 912–914 (Apr. 27, 2020), https://jamanetwork.com/journals/jamainternalmedicine/fullarticle/2764287. In October 2022, the FDA finalized guidance to sponsors on managing multiple endpoints in clinical trials to increase clarity and to decrease the risk of false efficacy conclusions through clarification, such as about the differences between and relationships among primary, secondary, and exploratory endpoints. *See* FDA, *Multiple Endpoints in Clinical Trials Guidance for Industry* (Oct. 2022), www.fda.gov/regulatory-information/search-fda-guidance-documents/multiple-endpoints-clinical-trials-guidance-industry. *See also* Joanne S. Eglovitch, *FDA Finalizes Multiple Endpoints Guidance*, REG NEWS (Oct. 20, 2022), www.raps.org/news-and-articles/news-articles/2022/10/fda-finalizes-multiple-endpoints-guidance.

103 *See* KEVIN DAVIES, $1,000 GENOME: THE REVOLUTION IN DNA SEQUENCING AND THE NEW ERA OF PERSONALIZED MEDICINE 15–29 (2010); *id* at 16 ("The HGP took thirteen years and cost $2.7 billion. The preliminary analysis of Watson's genome took thirteen weeks and a mere $1 million."); NHGRI, *Human Genome Research Project FAQ* (updated Nov. 12, 2018), www.genome.gov/human-genome-project/Completion-FAQ. However, a preliminary rough draft of the sequence was released in 2001. *See generally* 291 SCIENCE 1145 (Feb. 16, 2001) (issue entitled "The Human Genome"); 409 NATURE 745 (Feb. 15, 2001) (issue entitled "Information about the Human Genome Project" dedicated to the release of a preliminary draft map of the human genome). *See generally*, Michael J. Malinowski, *Bartha Maria Knoppers, Claude Bouchard, Symposium: Proceedings of "The Genomics Revolution? Science, Law and Policy,"* 66 LA. L. REV. 1 (2005) (Centennial Issue). *See also* MALINOWSKI, HANDBOOK, *supra* note 28, at xv-xvi, 13–14 (2016); SALLY SMITH HUGHES, GENENTECH: THE BEGINNINGS OF BIOTECH 158–59, 161 (2011). In 2003, Epogen became the first molecule to generate $10 billion annually. *See* Krishon Maggon, *The Ten Billion Dollar Molecule*, PHARM. EXEC. (Nov. 1, 2003), www.pharmexec.com/ten-billion-dollar-molecule. By 2007, Epogen was being administered to virtually every dialysis patient in the US, and it had become the most successful biotech drug in history. *See id*; Editorial Staff, *Opinion, Sacrificing the Cash Cow*, 25 NATURE BIOTECH 363 (2007), www.nature.com/articles/nbt0407-363.

104 In 1996 alone, the FDA approved fifty-three new drugs, many of them truly innovative. *See* CBO, R&D, *supra* note 31. *See also* Michael J. Malinowski, Grant Gautreaux, *Drug Development – Stuck in a State of Puberty?: Regulatory Reform of Human Clinical Research to Raise Responsiveness to the Realities of Human Variability*, 56 ST. LOUIS U. L.J. 363, 393 (2012).

105 ABRAMSON, OVERDOSED, *supra* note 1, at 79.

106 *Id.*

107 *See* STARR, SOCIAL TRANSFORMATION, *supra* note 5, at 420–49 ("The Coming of the Corporation"). *See generally* ABRAMSON, OVERDOSED, *supra* note 1; BRAWLEY, HARM, *supra* note 71; JUAHAR, DOCTORED, *supra* note 58; ROSENTHAL, AMERICAN SICKNESS, *supra* note 43.

108 ROSENTHAL, AMERICAN SICKNESS, *supra* note 43, at 4. *See id* at 1–238. According to Dr. Rosenthal,

> These days our treatment follows not scientific guidelines, but the logic of commerce in an imperfect and poorly regulated market, whose big players spend more on lobbying than defense contractors. Financial incentives to order more and do more—to default to the most expensive treatment for whatever ails you—drive much of our healthcare.

Id. at 5.

109 Jonathan Skinner, Eli Cahan, Victor R. Fuchs, *Perspectives, Stabilizing Health Care's Share of the GDP*, 386(8) N. ENG. J. MED. 709–11, 709 (Feb. 19, 2022), www.nejm.org/doi/full/10.1056/NEJMp2114227?query=WB&cid=NEJM%20Weekend%20Briefing,%20February%2019,%202022%20DM740450_NEJM_Non_Subscriber&bid=837615321.

110 Global interest in HGP inspired a White House ceremony to celebrate completion of a *preliminary* draft map of the human genome in 2000 (the millennial transition year), which President Clinton referred to as "an achievement that represents a pinnacle of human self-knowledge ...." Nicholas Wade, *Genetic Code of Human Life Is Cracked by Scientists*, N.Y. TIMES (June 27, 2000), https://archive.nytimes.com/www.nytimes.com/library/national/science/062700sci-genome.html. The media as well as many experts in medical science probed the potential of HGP to improve medicine and human health. *See* Byjon Heggie, *Genomics: a Revolution in Health Care? Drugs Affect People Differently and we're Increasingly Understanding Why. For Many of us, it's Down to Our Genes*, NAT'L GEO. (Feb. 20, 2019), www.nationalgeographic.com/science/article/partner-content-genomics-health-care; *See* ISAACSON, CODE, *supra* note 34, at 37–41 (2021) (ch. 5, "The Human Genome"). *See generally* 291 SCIENCE 1145 (Feb. 16, 2001) (issue entitled "The Human Genome"); 409 NATURE 745 (Feb. 15, 2001) (issue entitled "Information about the Human Genome Project" dedicated to the release of a preliminary draft map of the human genome).

111 *See* CASTELLS, NETWORK SOCIETY, *supra* note 74, at xxv. *See Chapter 4*, *supra*, at notes 7–16, and accompanying text (addressing ICT and associated social and cultural transformation).

112 *See* ABRAMSON, OVERDOSED, *supra* note 1, at ch. 10, 149–67 ("Direct-to-Consumer: Advertising, Public Relations, and the Medical News"). *See generally* DANIEL CALLAHAN, FALSE HOPES: WHY AMERICA'S QUEST FOR PERFECT HEALTH IS A RECIPE FOR DISASTER (1998). The participatory health movement in clinical care is accompanied by a health freedom movement that challenges orthodox medicine – the latest in a long legacy of such movements. *See generally* GROSSMAN, CHOOSE, *supra* note 78, at 201–24.

113 *See generally*, ABRAMSON, OVERDOSED, *supra* note 1; BRAWLEY, HARM, *supra* note 71; JUAHAR, DOCTORED, *supra* note 58. As observed by Dr. Abramson,

> Largely freed of concerns about out-of-pocket costs, enticed by advertising and media coverage of developments in medicine, and emboldened by a sense of autonomy, patients began requesting, and then demanding, specific tests, drugs, and procedures. Indeed, it became nearly impossible to convince many patients that more medical care was not necessarily better.... To exactly the same extent that a person is seduced by the false hopes and dreams offered by the medical industry's marketing efforts, the ability to trust his or her doctor, especially a primary care doctor, is eroded.

ABRAMSON, OVERDOSED, *supra* note 1, at 80. Unfortunately, in the US health care system, patient decision-making autonomy beyond responsible informed consent during sound (evidentiary science-based) patient-provider decision-making jeopardizes patient health:

> Becoming well informed and reclaiming personal responsibility are the best antidote to a fundamentally flawed system. But there's a hitch. Most of the information available to you (and your doctor) about the diagnosis and treatment of common medical problems comes from the drug and other medical companies themselves. Products that are well marketed DTC sell, even if they do not improve—and actually threaten—consumer health—e.g., hormone replacement therapy (HRT), Celebrex and Vioxx, etc.

Id. at 149. As observed by Dr. Arthur Derse in a 2022 *NEJM* editorial, "Today in the United States, the physician–patient relationship may be more fraught than ever, challenged as it is by greater emphasis on patient autonomy in the context of widespread misinformation and by external forces, constraints, and incentives not aimed at patient benefit." Arthur R. Derse, Perspective, The Physician–Patient Relationship, 387 *New. Eng. J. Med.* 669–672 (Aug. 25, 2022), www.nejm.org/doi/full/10.1056/NEJMp2201630.

114 JUAHAR, DOCTORED, *supra* note 58, at 14.

115 *See* EMANUEL, WHICH COUNTRY, *supra* note 42, at 25 ("A significant portion of the population moves between insurance programs each year and, thus, might have multiple types of insurance during any given year."). Health insurance contracts are negotiated at least a year in advance, and uncertainty about the ACA exacerbated a climate of health care volatility leading into the COVID-19 pandemic. Enactment of the ACA, and then federal and state challenges throughout its implementation with myriad litigation, conjured "a hurricane of uncertainty in the health insurance markets, which translates into higher premiums...." Malinowski, *Triple Threat*, *supra* note 23, at 1037.

116 Michael J. Malinowski, *Capitation*, *supra* note 41, at 342–43. Consider, for example, how advances in the treatment of coronary-artery disease and cancers are juxtaposed with an amassing population of dementia and Alzheimer's patients and R&D efforts to treat them. *See* Cheryl Bond-Nelms, *Alzheimer's is Accelerating Across the US*, AARP (Nov. 17, 2017), www.aarp.org/health/conditions-treatments/info-2017/alzheimers-rates-rise-fd.html. Human genome science is introducing immunotherapies and other gene therapies that may *cure* chronic, seriously debilitating, and life-threatening diseases in some patients, but at enormous cost. *See Chapter 2, supra,* at note 14, and accompanying text. The most expensive medicine in the world is Hemgenix®, a gene therapy approved by the FDA on November 22, 2022, to treat hemophilia B in eligible adults. Hemgenix® is "a one-off [IV] infusion that frees patients from regular treatments but costs $3.5 million a dose, making it the most expensive medicine in the world." Michelle Fay Cortez, *World's Most Expensive Drug Approved to Treat Hemophilia at $3.5 Million a Dose*, BLOOMBERG (Nov. 23, 2022), www.bloomberg.com/news/articles/2022-11-23/world-s-most-expensive-drug-csl-hemgenix-hemophilia-approved-by-fda?leadSource=uverify%20wall. *See also* Brian Park. *FDA Approval*, MPR (Nov. 23,

2022), www.empr.com/home/news/first-gene-therapy-for-hemophilia-b-gets-fda-approval/. For discussion of immunotherapies to treat cancers, see Ezra Cohen, *What is Cancer Immunotherapy?*, CANCER RES. INST. (undated), www.cancerresearch.org/en-us/immunotherapy/what-is-immunotherapy; NIH, *News Release, NCI Study Identifies Essential Genes for Cancer Immunotherapy* (Aug.7, 2017), www.nih.gov/news-events/news-releases/nci-study-identifies-essential-genes-cancer-immunotherapy.

117 *See generally* SACGT, RECOMMENDATIONS, *supra* note 48. *Chapter* 6, *supra*, at notes 43–98, and accompanying text ("The Complexities of Personal Genome Medical Decision-Making").

118 JUAHAR, DOCTORED, *supra* note 58, at 11.

119 *See generally* HHS, *Telehealth: Delivering Care Safely During COVID-19* (reviewed July 15, 2020), www.hhs.gov/coronavirus/telehealth/index.html; Elham Monaghesh, Alireza Hajizadeh, *The Role of Telehealth During COVID-19 Outbreak: a Systematic Review Based on Current Evidence*, 20(1) BMC PUB. HEALTH 1193 (Aug. 1, 2020), www.ncbi.nlm.nih.gov/pmc/articles/PMC7395209/. The related terminology is subject to interpretation, change, and is often used interchangeably. Mobile health/mHealth is utilization of mobile devices, such as cellphones and tablets, to support health care practices, and electronic health/eHealth is a broader term that encompasses the practice of health care supported by electronic processes. *See* Staff Benefits Management/SBMA, *What is the Difference Between mHealth, eHealth, Telehealth, and Telemedicine?* (undated, visited Nov. 13, 2022), www.sbmabenefits.com/2021/03/28/what-is-the-difference-between-mhealth-ehealth-telehealth-and-telemedicine/. Telemedicine refers to remote clinical services, while telehealth encompasses remote clinical and non-clinical services, including medical professional training and CME. *See generally id.*

120 Paul J. Larkin, Marie Fishpaw, Lauen McCarthy, *Telemedicine and Occupational Licensing* 74 ADMIN. L. REV. 747 (2021) (abstract). *Visit* Interstate Medical Licensure Compact Commission/IMLCC, official Site (visited Nov. 11, 2022) (includes thirty-seven states, the District of Columbia and the Territory of Guam, with ongoing legislative initiatives to join in additional states), www.imlcc.org/.

121 *See* Oranicha Jumreornvong, Emmy Yang, Jasmine Race, Jacob Appel, *Telemedicine and Medical Education in the Age of COVID-19*, 95(12) ACAD. MED 1838–43 (2020), www.ncbi.nlm.nih.gov/pmc/articles/PMC7489227/.

122 *See generally* HIPAA, Pub. L. 104–91 (1996); HIPAA Privacy Rule, 45 CFR Part 160, Subparts A and E of Part 164. For discussion of the Privacy Rule and Security Rule, see *Chapter* 4, *supra*, at notes 7, 55, and accompanying text, and *Chapter* 6, *infra*, at notes 180–86, and accompanying text.

123 HHS, OCR, *Notification of Enforcement Discretion for Telehealth Remote Communications During the COVID-19 Nationwide Public Health Emergency* (Mar. 17, 2020), www.hhs.gov/hipaa/for-professionals/special-topics/emergency-preparedness/notification-enforcement-discretion-telehealth/index.html.

124 *See* Tmothy Malouff, Sarvam TerKonda, Dacre Knight et al., *Physician Satisfaction with Telemedicine During the COVID-19 Pandemic: The Mayo Clinic Florida Experience*, 5(4) MAYO CLIN. PROC. INNOV. QUAL. OUTCOMES 771–82 (Aug. 2021), www.ncbi.nlm.nih.gov/pmc/articles/PMC8245346/; Sarah Nies, Shae Patel, Melissa Shafer et al., *Understanding Physicians' Preferences for Telemedicine During the COVID-19 Pandemic: Cross-sectional Study*, 5(8) JMIR FORM RES. (Aug. 13, 2021), https://pubmed.ncbi.nlm.nih.gov/34227993/. See also Monaghesh, Role of Telehealth, supra note 119, at 1193.

125 ABRAMSON, OVERDOSED, *supra* note 1, at 11 ("Increasingly my patients were looking to pills to keep them well instead of making the changes in their lives that evidence showed to be far more beneficial.... Too many visits were turning into nonproductive contests of wills.").

126 Michael J. Malinowski, *A Law-Policy Proposal to Know Where Babies Come from During the Reproduction Revolution*, 9 J. GENDER RACE & JUST. 549, 556 (2006).
127 *See generally Chapter 3, supra.*
128 ABRAMSON, OVERDOSED, *supra* note 1, at 11 (challenges to patient assumptions that medicine is reliably grounded on a bedrock of sound science, is evidence-based, is protected dearly by those entrusted to practice it, and that more is better).
129 WATSON, THE STORY, *supra* note 30, at 216 (illustrating with the example of noninvasive prenatal testing/NIPT, "which takes advantage of the fact that a small amount of fetal DNA can be found circulating in the mother's blood").
130 *See generally Chapter 6, infra.* The delivery-of-care complexities of genetic tests *that meet established evidentiary-science clinical standards* were summarized by SACGT more than two decades ago. *See* SACGT, RECOMMENDATIONS, *supra* note 48. In addition to the subsequent proliferation of clinically sound personal genome testing capabilities, the US market has been inundated with DTC personal genome testing. *See generally* PEW, LAB-DEVELOPED TESTS, *supra* note 47. *See also infra* note 189, and accompanying text (addressing augmentation of the US market presence of personal genome testing in real time as a complement to related R&D).
131 *See generally* ROSENTHAL, AMERICAN SICKNESS, *supra* note 43. *See Chapter 3, supra,* at notes 121–35, and accompanying text (biopharma disease creation, commonly referred to as "disease mongering").
132 *See supra* note 118, and accompanying text (Dr. Juahar quotation and related discussion regarding the impossible time pressures on US physicians to remain informed about medical innovation through the MJE).
133 ABRAMSON, OVERDOSED, *supra* note 1, at 83 ("[T]he boundary between professional responsibilities and personal time is often more blurred in primary care than in other specialties.").
134 *Id.*
135 *See Chapter 1, supra,* at notes 184–89, and accompanying text ("The Resulting Medical Profession-FDA Symbiotic Relationship.").
136 *See infra* notes 259–60, 285, and accompanying test (PDUFA, FDAMA, and PDUFA reauthorizations).
137 *See Chapter 1, supra,* at 184–89 (addressing a shift in the symbiotic relationship between the medical profession and FDA). A notable example: risk evaluation and mitigation strategies/REMS requirements.
138 *See generally* Patricia J. Zettler, Eli Y. Adashi, I. Glenn Cohen, *A Divisive Ruling on Devices – Genus Medical Technologies v. FDA*, 1056 N. ENGL. J. MED. 2409–11 (2021), www.nejm.org/doi/10.1056/NEJMp2117295?url_ver=Z39.88-2003&rfr_id=ori%3Arid%3Acrossref.org&rfr_dat=cr_pub++0pubmed. *See Chapter 3, supra,* at notes 31–70, and accompanying text ("Recognition of Biopharma Marketing as Protected Commercial Speech"). The FDCA defines drugs broadly as "articles … intended for use in the diagnosis, cure, mitigation, treatment, or prevention of disease," and "Device" is a catch-all for myriad products ranging from tongue suppressors to the latest imaging and robotic surgery technologies. *See* 21 U.S.C. § 321. The FDA uses a risk-classification and matching system to regulate devices, which allows device manufacturers to reach the market based upon prior FDA approvals of similar products – a much less invasive rubric than establishing product-specific safety and efficacy, which the agency requires for innovative (versus generic) new drugs and biologics. *See* MALINOWSKI, HANDBOOK, *supra* note 28, at 127–43. The US Court of Appeals for the District of Columbia held that products that meet the FDCA's definition of a device "must be regulated as devices" even when a product meets both device and drug definitions. *See generally Genus*

Medical Technologies v. FDA, 994 F.3d 631 (D.C. Cir. 2021). The dispute at issue in the case was FDA discretion to regulate a line of diagnostic barium sulfate contrast agents as drugs rather than as devices. The FDA had attempted to regulate these contrast agents as drugs in accordance with its regulatory precedents over two decades and a previous judicial mandate to promote consistency: "The FDA has long treated all contrast agents as drugs, without determining whether they work by means of chemical action, at least in part because of a 1997 court decision directing the FDA to regulate contrast agents that are similar to each other in a consistent manner." Zettler, *Divisive Ruling, supra*, at 2410, *citing Bracco Diagnostics v. Shalala*, 963 F. Supp. 20 (D.D.C. 1997).

139 Zettler, *Divisive Ruling, supra* note 138, at 2117297.

140 *See Chapter 1, supra*, at notes 160–62, and accompanying text (physician discretion to prescribe off label).

141 *See generally Chapter 1, supra.*

142 *See Chapter 2, supra*, at notes 32–114, and accompanying text (FDA flexibility in Operation Warp Speed/OWS vaccines and therapeutics R&D); *supra* notes 78–96, and accompanying text (science misinformation during the COVID-19 pandemic); *infra* notes 178–86, and accompanying text (politicization of science).

143 Zettler, *Divisive Ruling, supra* note 138, at 2410–11, *citing* Peter Marks, Scott Gottlieb. *Balancing Safety and Innovation for Cell-based Regenerative Medicine*. 378(10) N. ENGL. J. MED. 954–59 (Mar. 8, 2018).

144 *See* STARR, SOCIAL TRANSFORMATION, *supra* note 5, at 22–23, 117–18; *Chapter 1, supra*, at 35–45, and accompanying text ("US Law-Policy Recognition of Clinical Medicine as the Medical Profession's Domain"), at 160–83, and accompanying text ("Deference to and Reliance on the Medical Profession"). Historically, the US medical profession amassed sovereignty over the practice of medicine by promoting education credentialing and state licensure. "Standardization of training and licensing became the means for realizing both the search for authority and control of the market." STARR, supra, at 22. With encouragement, input, and support from the nationally organized medical profession, states created and then controlled the privilege of practicing medicine within their jurisdictions through enactment of medical practice acts and other legislation. *See Chapter 1, supra*, at 35–45, and accompanying text ("US Law-Policy Recognition of Clinical Medicine as the Medical Profession's Domain"). States entrusted implementation and enforcement to medical licensing and disciplinary boards controlled and administered by their segments of the medical profession. *See id.* at notes 17–18, and accompanying text.

145 *See generally* STARR, SOCIAL TRANSFORMATION, *supra* note 5 (chronicles the medical profession's organization, the formalization of medical education and clinical practice through licensure, and attainment of self-regulation and professional autonomy). *See Chapter 1, supra*, at 35–45, and accompanying text ("US Law-Policy Recognition of Clinical Medicine as the Medical Profession's Domain"), at 160–83, and accompanying text ("Deference to and Reliance on the Medical Profession"). *See* Lars Noah, *Ambivalent Commitments to Federalism in Controlling the Practice of Medicine*, 53 U. KAN. L. REV. 149, 155 (2004) ("Congress repeatedly has announced its intention that federal officials take care not to interfere with the practice of medicine."). Consider that the federal government has shown deference to states regarding what classes of health care professionals may prescribe and dispense pharmaceuticals, including controlled substances. *See id.* at 179–80. *See also* 21 U.S.C. § 802(21) (2000) (defining "practitioner" under the Controlled Substances Act); 21 C.F.R. §§ 1300.01(28), 1304.03(e) (2004) (DEA recognition that a "mid-level practitioner" under state law may be eligible to prescribe or administer controlled

substances). An advanced-practice nurse granted prescribing privileges inclusive of controlled substances may apply for a DEA license. *See* Noah, *supra*, at 180.

146 Noah, *Federalism*, *supra* note 145, at 165 The FDA's authority to make mifepristone market available is being challenged again as this book goes into print.

147 Ronald Welch, *Managed Care and Managed Sentencing – A Tale of Two Systems*, 11 FED. SENT. REP. 139, 140–41 (1998), https://scholarworks.law.ubalt.edu/all_fac/566/.

148 *See* Pub. L. 108–105, 117 Stat. 1201 (enacted Nov. 5, 2003), 18 U.S.C. § 1531. *See generally Gonzales v. Carhart*, 540 US 124 (2007).

149 *See Sternberg v. Carhart*, 530 US 914 (2000). The Nebraska law defined PBA more vaguely, did not include an exception to save the life of the mother, subjected women who procured abortions with the procedure to criminal prosecution, and subjected physicians who performed it to license revocations. *Id*. at 914–15. The Court majority (5–4) struck down the Nebraska law for imposing an undue burden. *Id*. at 920–46.

150 18 US Code 1531. The case record established that PBA was a medical procedure used sparingly in dire circumstances to promote medical safety – to better ensure complete removal of the fetus and thereby lower the risk of toxicity and infection (sepsis). The PBA-Ban does not include an exception to save the life of mother, but provides that:

> A defendant [physician] accused of an offense under this section may seek a hearing before the State Medical Board on whether the physician's conduct was necessary to save the life of the mother whose life was endangered by a physical disorder, physical illness, or physical injury, including a life-endangering physical condition caused by or arising from the pregnancy itself.

Id. In effect, Congress begrudgingly and implicitly acknowledged the possible clinical necessity of using the procedure to protect the life of a pregnant woman.

151 18 US Code 1531. Congress gathered mixed testimony, critical of and supportive of the procedure as one used sparingly when medically necessary, as alluded to in the Supreme Court's acknowledgment of conflicting medical expert testimony. *See infra* note 152, and accompanying text.

152 *See Carhart*, 540 US at 163.

153 *See* Elizabeth Nash, *For the First Time Ever, US States Enacted More Than 100 Abortion Restrictions in a Single Year*, GUTTMACHER INST. (Oct. 4, 2021), www.guttmacher.org/article/2021/10/first-time-ever-us-states-enacted-more-100-abortion-restrictions-single-year. *See generally Planned Parenthood v. Casey*, 505 US 833 (1992) (upholding *Roe v. Wade*, 410 US 113 (1973), but revising jurisprudence). Five abortion clinics and a physician representing himself and a class of doctors who provided abortion services brought the case to challenge five provisions of the Pennsylvania Abortion Control Act of 1982, 18 PA. CONS. STAT. §§ 3203–3220 (1990):

> [A] woman seeking an abortion must be provided specified information at least 24 hours before an abortion is performed, and she must give her informed consent prior to the procedure (§ 3205); a minor may not obtain an abortion without the informed consent of a parent, unless authorized through a judicial bypass procedure (§ 3206); in the absence of specified exceptions, a married woman seeking an abortion must sign a statement indicating that she has notified her husband (§ 3209); "medical emergency" as defined in the act excuses compliance with the preceding requirements (§ 3203); and facilities providing abortion services must satisfy reporting requirements, which keep identities of women served confidential (§§ 3207(b), 3214(a), 3214(f)).

The *Casey* Court held that, before fetal viability, states may not proscribe a woman from making the decision to terminate her pregnancy. However, the Court also held that states may enact regulations to further the health or safety of a woman seeking an abortion – provided they do not impose an undue burden. Under *Casey*, after fetal viability, states could regulate or even proscribe abortion to promote an interest in the potentiality of human life – except when abortion is medically necessary to preserve the life or health of the mother. The Court struck down the spousal notification provision (§ 3209) as an undue burden; the court upheld the others.

154 *See Casey, supra* note 153, 505 US at 874.

155 Many states enacted laws that were "put on hold" pending a Supreme Court deviation from *Casey* limitations. *See* Elizabeth Nash, Lauren Cross, *26 States Are Certain or Likely to Ban Abortion Without Roe: Here's Which Ones and Why*, Guttmacher Inst. (Oct. 28, 2021), www.guttmacher.org/article/2021/10/26-states-are-certain-or-likely-ban-abortion-without-roe-heres-which-ones-and-why.

156 *See* Tex. Health & Safety Code Ann. §171.0031(a) (West Cum. Supp. 2015).

157 *See* La. HB 388 (2014).

158 *See generally Whole Women's Health v. Hellerstedt*, 579 US 582 (2016).

159 Justice Ginsburg underscored this point in her concurring opinion:

> So long as this Court adheres to *Roe v. Wade*, 410 US 113, 93 S.Ct. 705, 35 L.Ed.2d 147 (1973), and *Planned Parenthood of Southeastern Pa. v. Casey*, 505 US 833, 112 S.Ct. 2791, 120 L.Ed.2d 674 (1992), Targeted Regulation of Abortion Providers laws like H.B. 2 that "do little or nothing for health, but rather strew impediments to abortion," *Planned Parenthood of Wis.*, 806 F.3d, at 921, cannot survive judicial inspection.

Whole Woman's Health v. Hellerstedt, 136 S. Ct. 2292, 2321, 195 L. Ed. 2d 665 (2016), *as revised* (June 27, 2016).

160 *See June Med. Serv's v. Russo*, 579 S. Ct. 2103 (2020).

161 *See id.* at 2133–42.

162 *See* Caroline Kelly, *More States are Expected to Pass Anti-abortion Bills Challenging* Roe v. Wade *Ahead of Monumental Supreme Court Case*, CNN (May 18, 2021) (reporting on the Court's decision to consider Mississippi's 15-week ban), www.cnn.com/2021/05/18/politics/mississippi-abortion-case-impact-supreme-court-abortion-bans-activists/index.html.

163 *Heartbeat Bans*, RewireNews (May 30, 2019), https://rewire.news/legislative-tracker/law-topic/heartbeat-bans/. Depending on the equipment used and clinical interpretation, indication of a heartbeat may be detected at approximately twenty-two days after conception, which is 35–42 days (5–6 weeks) after a woman's last period. *See id.*

164 *See* Caroline Kelly, Rebekah Riess, *Federal Judge Blocks Arkansas' Near-Total Abortion Ban*, CNN (July 20, 2021), https://lite.cnn.com/en/article/h_8cef348797653992a2d4649aa26f879a.

165 The Arkansas Unborn Child Protection Act of 2021, Ark. Code § 5-61-304(a), 304(b), bans providers from performing abortions "except to save the life of a pregnant woman in a medical emergency" without exceptions for instances of rape, incest, or fetal anomalies, and those found to violate the law could face fines of up to $100,000 and up to ten years in prison. *See* Kelly, *Near-Total Ban, supra* note 164.

166 *See* Texas Heartbeat Act, Senate Bill 8, 87th Leg., Reg. Sess. (Tex. 2021); Tex. Health & Safety Code Ann. §§171.204(a), 171.205(a) (West Cum. Supp. 2021). *See* Caroline Kelly, Ariane de Vogue, *Supreme Court Takes Up Major Abortion Case Next Term that Could Limit* Roe v. Wade, CNN (updated May 18, 2021 www.cnn.com/2021/05/17/politics/supreme-court-abortion-mississippi/index.html.

167 *See* Senate Bill 8, 87th Leg., Reg. Sess. (Tex. 2021); *United States v. Texas*, No. 1:21-CV-796-RP, 2021 WL 4593319 (W.D. Tex. Oct. 6, 2021), *cert. granted before*

judgment, No. 21-588, 2021 WL 4928618 (US Oct. 22, 2021). The Court heard oral arguments on Nov. 1, 2021. *See* Adriane de Vogue, *Texas 6-week Abortion Ban Takes Effect after Supreme Court Inaction*, CNN (Sept. 1, 2021), www.cnn.com/2021/09/01/politics/texas-abortion-supreme-court-sb8-roe-wade/index.html.

168 *See Whole Women's Health v. Jackson*, 142 S. Ct. 522, 551, 211 L. Ed. 2d 316 (2021).

169 *See id.*

170 *See generally Jackson Women's Health Org. v. Dobbs*, 945 F.3d 265 (5th Cir. 2019), *cert. granted in part*, 141 S. Ct. 2619, 209 L. Ed. 2d 748 (2021). 142 S. Ct. 414, 211 L. Ed. 2d 223 (2021). *See also Roe v. Wade*, 410 US 113 (1973); Ariane de Vogue, *Mississippi Asks US Supreme Court to Overturn* Roe v. Wade, CNN (July 22, 2021), www.cnn.com/2021/07/22/politics/mississippi-roe-v-wade-abortion/index.html.

171 ACOG, Dobbs v. Jackson *Women's Health Organization*, Media Telebriefing (Nov. 30, 2021), www.acog.org/news/news-articles/2021/11/dobbs-v-jackson-womens-health-organization-media-telebriefing. *See generally* Brief of Amici Curiae, American College of Obstetricians and Gynecologists, American Medical Association et al., *Dobbs v. Jackson Women's Health Org.*, No. 19-1392 (S. Ct., Sept. 2021), www.acog.org/-/media/project/acog/acogorg/files/advocacy/amicus-briefs/2021/20210920-dobbs-v-jwho-amicus-brief.pdf?la=en&hash=717DFDD07A03B93A04490E66835BB8C5. The ACOG and AMA were joined on the brief by the American Academy of Family Physicians, American Academy of Nursing, American Academic of Pediatrics, American Association of Public Health Physicians, American College of Medical Genetics and Genomics, American College of Nurse-Midwives, American College of Osteopathic Obstetricians and Gynecologists, American College of Physicians, American Gynecological and Obstetrical Society, American Women's Association, American Psychiatric Association, American Society for Reproductive Medicine, Association of Women's Health, Obstetric and Neonatal Nurses, Council of University Chairs of Obstetrics and Gynecology: Health Professionals Advancing LGBTQ Equality, North American Society for Pediatric and Adolescent Gynecology, National Medical Association, National Association of Nurse Practitioners in Women's Health, Society for Academic Specialists in General Obstetrics and Gynecology, Society of Family Planning, Society of General Internal Medicine, Society of Gynecologic Oncology, and Society of OB/GYN Hospitalists.

172 *See* Josh Gerstein, Alexander Ward, *Supreme Court has Voted to Overturn Abortion Rights, Draft Opinion Shows*, Politico (May 2, 2022), www.politico.com/news/2022/05/02/supreme-court-abortion-draft-opinion-00029473 ("No draft decision in the modern history of the court has been disclosed publicly while a case was still pending. The unprecedented revelation is bound to intensify the debate over what was already the most controversial case on the docket this term.").

173 According to the Guttmacher Institute, of the twenty-six states likely to ban abortion in the absence of *Roe* and *Casey*, "13 have laws in place that are designed to be 'triggered' and take effect automatically or by quick state action if *Roe* no longer applies – Arkansas, Idaho, Kentucky, Louisiana, Mississippi, Missouri, North Dakota, Oklahoma, South Dakota, Tennessee, Texas, Utah, and Wyoming." Guttmacher Institute, *13 States Have Abortion Trigger Bans – Here's What Happens When* Roe *Is Overturned* (June 2022), www.guttmacher.org/article/2022/06/13-states-have-abortion-trigger-bans-heres-what-happens-when-roe-overturned. Also, state "zombie" laws in effect prior to *Roe* may be resurrected. *See generally* Maureen E. Brady, *Zombie State Constitutional Provisions*, 2021 Wisc. L. Rev. 1063 (2021), https://wlr.law.wisc.edu/wp-content/uploads/sites/1263/2021/11/15-Brady-Camera-Ready.pdf.

174 *Dobbs v. Jackson Women's Health Org., et al.*, No. 19-1392, 2022 WL 2276808 (US June 24, 2022).

175 *Whole Women's Health v. Jackson*, 142 S. Ct. 522, 551, 211 L. Ed. 2d 316 (2021) (emphasis added).

176 *See generally* Joanne S. Eglovitch, *FDA, EMA Officials Discuss Impediments to Cell and Gene Therapies*, Reg. Focus (May 2022) (Reg. Affairs Prof. Soc'y publication), www.raps.org/news-and-articles/news-articles/2022/5/fda-ema-officials-discuss-impediments-to-cell-and. Noninvasive prenatal testing/NIPT is addressed in *Chapter 6, infra*, at notes 66–75, and accompanying text.

177 As observed by Prof Lars Noah in 2004,

> In the last decade, a slim but generally reliable majority on the United States Supreme Court has reinvigorated its scrutiny of federal exercises of authority that intrude upon the activities of state governments. At its base, this renewed commitment to federalism seeks to prevent the national government from exceeding its more narrowly construed enumerated powers, and the Court claims thereby to promote a number of valuable purposes.

Noah, *Federalism, supra* note 145, at 154–55. Subsequently, the composition of the Court has shifted to a conservative majority with justices who strongly support federalism jurisprudence and originalist theory regarding interpretation of the US Constitution.

178 For discussion of the dangers of manipulating science for political gain, see generally Michael Gough, Politicizing Science: The Alchemy of Policymaking (2003). *See also* Abramson, Overdosed, *supra* note 1, at xvii, 111, 241–42; Ben Goldacre, Bad Pharma: How Drug Companies Mislead Doctors and Harm Patients ix, 241–42, 287–311 (2012).

179 *See generally* House Oversight Com., Select Sub. on the Coronavirus Crisis, Year-End Staff Report, More Effective, More Equitable: Overseeing an Improving and Ongoing Pandemic Response (Dec. 17, 2021), https://coronavirus.house.gov/sites/democrats.coronavirus.house.gov/files/SSCCInterimReportDec2021V1.pdf.

180 Tom Frieden, Jeffrey Koplan, David Satcher, Richard Besser, *We Ran the CDC. No President Ever Politicized its Science the Way Trump Has*, Wash. Post (July 14, 2020), www.washingtonpost.com/outlook/2020/07/14/cdc-directors-trump-politics/.

181 *See supra* notes 83–84, and accompanying text (public endorsement of hydroxychloroquine and chloroquine for responsiveness to COVID-19).

182 *See Chapter 2, supra*, at notes 32, 58, 75, and accompanying text (discussing BARDA).

183 *See generally* Matt Naham, *Vaccine Expert Files Whistleblower Complaint, Claims Trump Admin Illegally Retaliated Against Him*, Law & Crime (May 5, 2020), https://lawandcrime.com/high-profile/vaccine-expert-files-whistleblower-complaint-claims-trump-admin-illegally-retaliated-against-him/; Dan Mangan, *Coronavirus Whistleblower Rick Bright's Complaint Shows High Likelihood of 'Wrongdoing'*, CNBC (May 14, 2020), www.cnbc.com/2020/05/14/coronavirus-rick-bright-testifies-as-trump-criticizes-him.html. For discussion of OWS, see *Chapter 2, supra*, at notes 32–114, and accompanying text (discussing OWS).

184 *See* Yasmeen Abutale, Damian Paletta, Nightmare Scenario: Inside the Trump Administration's Response to the Pandemic that Changed History 221 (2021) (Alex Azar, Secretary of HHS in the Trump Administration and a lawyer with no medical training, under pressure from President Trump, nearly overruled the FDA to approve hydroxychloroquine and chloroquine for market use in the prevention and treatment of COVID-19). *See generally* FDA, *FDA Cautions Against Use of Hydroxychloroquine or Chloroquine for COVID-19 Outside of the Hospital Setting or a Clinical Trial Due to Risk of Heart Rhythm Problems* (July 1, 2020) (Does

not affect FDA-approved uses for malaria, lupus, and rheumatoid arthritis), www.fda.gov/drugs/fda-drug-safety-podcasts/fda-cautions-against-use-hydroxychloroquine-or-chloroquine-covid-19-outside-hospital-setting-or#:~:text=We%20are%20warning%20the%20public,to%20treat%20or%20prevent%20malaria.

185 *See CBS Sunday Morning, Collins, supra* note 92.

186 *Id.*

187 *See* ABRAMSON, OVERDOSED, *supra* note 1, at vii, 93–110. *See generally* BRAWLEY, HARM, *supra* note 71; JUAHAR, DOCTORED, *supra* note 58; GOLDACRE, BAD PHARMA, *supra* note 178; RAY MOYNIHAN, ALAN CASSELS, SELLING SICKNESS: HOW THE WORLD'S BIGGEST PHARMACEUTICAL COMPANIES ARE TURNING US ALL INTO PATIENTS (2005); ROSENTHAL, AMERICAN SICKNESS, *supra* note 43.

188 INSTITUTE OF MEDICINE/IOM, CONFLICT OF INTEREST IN MEDICAL RESEARCH, EDUCATION, AND PRACTICE 1 (2009) (abstract), https://nap.nationalacademies.org/download/12598.

189 *See supra* note 130, and accompanying text. The DTC personal genome testing sector has a market presence poised for growth with and well beyond 23andMe and its existing corporate contemporaries. *See Chapter 4, supra*, at notes 178–83, and accompanying text. *See generally* CONSUMER GENETIC TECHNOLOGIES (J. Glenn Cohen, Nita A. Farahany, Henry T. Greely, Carmel Schachar eds., 2021); FUTURE OF PRIVACY FORUM, BEST PRACTICES, *supra* note 47. The commercial laboratory sector, an enabler for the DTC personal genome testing sector, has a substantial market presence that too is poised for growth. *See generally* PEW, LAB-DEVELOPED TESTS, supra note 47. DNA sequencing technologies, another fundamental enabler, continue to evolve and proliferate virally – as they did during HGP and by multiples after the draft human genome sequence was completed. *See generally Prologue, supra* (summarizing the dizzying advancement of genome sequencing and testing technologies). Personal genome testing possibilities are being churned by the ongoing identification of biomarkers (potential testing targets) and proteomic research (the study of proteins in the context of an entire set of proteins at a given time, known as a proteome), which are a consequence of robust biopharma R&D with unprecedented access to biobanks – which too are amassing and proliferating. *See generally* CBO, R&D, *supra* note 31; NASEM, PREPARING, *supra* note 31. Moreover, global life science R&D is focused on biotech and genomics, and that focus has been building for some time. The biotech and genomic revolutions transformed the traditional global pharmaceutical sector into a *bio*pharmaceutical sector, as reflected in the US' decision to centralize FDA review of all new drugs, including biologic drugs, in the Center for Drug Evaluation and Research/CDER beginning in 2004. *See* FDA, *Press Release, FDA Completes Final Phase of Planning for Consolidation of Certain Products from CBER to CDER* (Mar. 17, 2003), www3.scienceblog.com/community/older/archives/M/2/fda1387.htm. In 2016, the biotechnology industry's national trade organization, the Biotechnology Industry Organization/BIO, changed its name to the Biotechnology Innovation Organization to reflect its representation of biotech as a shared R&D science platform, rather than representing a distinguishable small and mid-size company sector. *Visit* BIO, official site, www.bio.org (last visited Oct. 13, 2018). In fact, some of the strongest pioneer biotech companies, such as Amgen, Genentech, and Genzyme, have had representation on the board of the global "big pharma" trade organization, the Pharmaceutical Research and Manufacturers of America/PhRMA, since the 1990s. *See also* Malinowski, *Triple Threat, supra* note 23, at 1079, n.172; Malinowski, Gautreaux, *Stuck, supra* note 104, at 389, nn.126, 127.

190 *See infra* notes 199–294, and accompanying text (industry influence on medical journals and their content), notes 295–320, and accompanying text (industry influence on medical profession education about science innovation).

191 *See Chapter 1, supra*, at note 22, and accompanying text; ABRAMSON, OVERDOSED, *supra* note 1, at 96–97.
192 *See* STARR, SOCIAL TRANSFORMATION, *supra* note 5, at 127–34, 198–232.
193 *See id.*; *Chapter 1, supra*, at notes 109–13, and accompanying text (the advent of randomized controlled trials/RCTs, coupled with MJE, pharmaceutical research campuses, and reliable, science and evidence-based regulation to raise trust).
194 ABRAMSON, OVERDOSED, *supra* note 1, at 97.
195 *Id.* at 93.
196 GOLDACRE, BAD PHARMA, *supra* note 178, at 242. "[I]n fact, it's only in the past couple of generations that we have collected good-quality evidence at all, in large amounts, and for all the failures in our current systems, we suddenly now have an overwhelming avalanche of data." *Id.* at 241.
197 *See infra* notes 199–294, and accompanying text (industry influence over the MJE).
198 *See* ANGELL, TRUTH, *supra* note 32, at xviii, 91. *See generally Chapter 6, infra* (addressing the delivery-of-care complexities of clinical genetics and genomics and the potential detrimental impact of personal genome testing on US health care).
199 During its formative years, the AMA campaigned mightily to push corporate influence out of the practice of medicine, and its primary opponent was the patent medicines industry. *See* STARR, SOCIAL TRANSFORMATION, *supra* note 5, at 127–34, 198–232.
200 *See infra* note 239–42, and accompanying text (addressing biophama investment in clinical research and discretion to decide what clinical research is undertaken and disclosed).
201 ABRAMSON, OVERDOSED, *supra* note 1, at 97. Similarly, a 2017 systematic review and empirical study on the association between sponsorship sources and drug research outcomes concluded that industry sponsorship leads to more favorable efficacy results attributable to an industry bias. *See* Andreas Lundh, Joel Lexchin, Barbara Mintzes et al., *Industry sponsorship and research outcome*, 2(2) COCHRANE DATABASE SYST. REV. (Feb. 16, 2017) (updating a previous study), https://pubmed.ncbi.nlm.nih.gov/28207928/.
202 GOLDACRE, BAD PHARMA, *supra* note 178, at 304–05. Dr. Abramson reached the same conclusion:

> In this climate, the editors of the most respected medical journals have warned that they cannot protect their readers from the pro-industry bias sweeping into many of the scientific articles they publish. Nonetheless, publication in respected medical journals still anoints research findings as the scientific evidence upon which good doctors confidently base their clinical decisions. It is not simply due to the "play of chance" that the odds are five times greater that new products will be supported by commercially sponsored studies than by studies with noncommercial sponsorship. The bias is, at best, difficult and often impossible for even the most careful readers to spot, let alone unravel. And simply knowing that it exists is not enough to protect readers from being misled.

ABRAMSON, OVERDOSED, *supra* note 1, at 242.
203 *Id.* at 96.
204 Frank Davidoff, Catherine DeAngelis, Jeffrey Drazen, *Editorial, Sponsorship, Authorship, and Accountability*, 345 N. ENG. J. MED. 825–27, 825 (Sept. 2001), www.nejm.org/doi/full/10.1056/NEJMed010093.
205 *See Chapter 2, supra*, at notes 170–98, and accompanying text (addressing the full implementation of TTLP over decades).
206 *See id. See generally* Michael J. Malinowski, *Keynote, A Law-Policy Proposal to Promote the Public Nature of Research in Contemporary Life Science*, presented at "A Discourse on the Public Nature of Research in Contemporary Life Science," *in* BIENNIAL

Review of Law, Science, and Technology 2–24 (Wen-Tsong Chiou ed., 2010) (hosted by Academia Sinica, Taipei, Taiwan).

207 Unfortunately, subscription rates became prohibitive which limited access to peer-reviewed medical literature for many institutions as well as individuals and gave rise to an open-access movement. *See generally*, Alma Swan, *Policy Guidelines for the Development and Promotion of Open* Access, UNESCO (2012), www.unesco.org/new/en/communication-and-information/resources/publications-and-communication-materials/publications/full-list/policy-guidelines-for-the-development-and-promotion-of-open-access/.

208 Goldacre, Bad Pharma, *supra* note 178, at 304–05.

209 Richard Smith, *The Trouble with Medical Journals*, 99(3) J. R. Soc. Med. 115–19 (Mar. 2006) ("I am proud to have been part of such an energetic, exciting, and, I hope, ultimately useful enterprise as the publishing of journals, but I'm concerned that much of what journals do is ethically weak."), www.ncbi.nlm.nih.gov/pmc/articles/PMC1383755/.

210 *See Chapter 3*, *supra*, at notes 45–66, and accompanying text (discussion of *Washington Legal* and its impact). *See also*, Goldacre, Bad Pharma, *supra* note 178, at 244–45.

211 *See infra* notes 214–94, and accompanying text (risk of industry capture of clinical trial data and journal content).

212 Goldacre, Bad Pharma, *supra* note 178, at 307.

213 *See Chapter 2*, *supra*, at notes 170–98, and accompanying text (TTLP fully implemented over decades).

214 Angell, Truth, *supra* note 32, at xxvi-vi.

215 Defined narrowly, "norm" is "a rule that is neither promulgated by an official source, such as a court or legislature, nor enforced by the threat of legal sanctions, yet is regularly complied with." Jonathan R. Macey, Corporate Governance: Promises Kept, Promises Broken 32–33 (2008), *quoting* Richard A. Posner, *Social Norms and the Law: An Economic Approach*, 87 Am. Econ. Rev. (Papers & Proc.) 365, 365 (1997) (internal quotation marks omitted). Defined more broadly for practical, "real world" purposes consistent with this discussion, the term refers to a reliable predictor of behavior because it has proven to be a dominant behavioral standard over meaningful time. *Cf.* Joan MacLeod Heminway, *Shareholder Wealth Maximization as A Function of Statutes, Decisional Law, and Organic Documents*, 74 Wash. & Lee L. Rev. 939, 972 (2017).

216 *Dodge v. Ford Motor Co.*, 170 N.W. 668, 684 (Mich. 1919). *See also eBay Domestic Holdings, Inc. v. Newmark*, 16 A.3d 1, 34 (2010) ("Having chosen a for-profit corporate form, the craigslist directors are bound by the fiduciary duties and standards that accompany that form. Those standards include acting to promote the value of the corporation for the benefit of its stockholders.").

217 For an excellent discussion of the norm and the ongoing debate, see generally Heminway, *Wealth Maximization*, *supra* note 215.

218 Corporate decisions to deviate from compliance with governing law to maximize profit based on risk and liability calculations are beyond the scope of this discussion.

219 Abramson, Overdosed, *supra* note 1, at 243–45 (discussing "an imbalance between corporate goals and public interest that is no longer self-correcting"). *Id.* at 258.

220 *Id.* at xvii. "Soaring sales have made drug companies the most profitable corporations on the planet during particular years of the past decade [1995–2005]." Moynihan, Cassells, Selling Sickness, *supra* note 187, at xviii.

221 Abramson, Overdosed, *supra* note 1, at 94.

222 *See* Malinowski, Handbook, *supra* note 28, at nn.8–10, pp. xxvi-xxvii; Sy Pretorius, Alberto Grignolo, *Phase III Trial Failures: Costly, But Preventable* 25 Applied Clin. Trials (Aug. 1, 2016), www.appliedclinicaltrialsonline.com/view/

phase-iii-trial-failures-costly-preventable. *See also* N. Nicole Stakleff, *A Drug Life: The Chemistry of Patent and Regulatory Exclusivity for Pharmaceuticals*, 16 FLA. COASTAL. L. REV. 27, 28 (2014).

223 *See generally* Pretorius, Grignolo, *Failures, supra* note 222.

224 CBO, R&D, *supra* note 31 (page numbers unavailable).

225 *See supra* note 195, and accompanying text (persuasive influence of science data published in the medical literature).

226 ABRAMSON, OVERDOSED, *supra* note 1, at 94.

227 *Id.* at 110.

228 *See generally Chapter 2, supra*; NASEM, PREPARING, *supra* note 31; NIH, OFFICE OF TECH. TRANSFER, NIH RESPONSE TO THE CONFERENCE REPORT REQUEST FOR A PLAN TO ENSURE TAXPAYER INTERESTS ARE PROTECTED (2001), www.ott.nih.gov/sites/default/files/documents/policy/wydenrpt.pdf; GOVERNMENT ACCOUNTABILITY OFFICE/GAO, REPORT TO CONGRESSIONAL COMMITTEES, TECHNOLOGY TRANSFER – ADMINISTRATION OF THE BAYH-DOLE ACT BY RESEARCH UNIVERSITIES, *Background*, 2–4 (1998), GAO/RCED 98–126, www.gao.gov/products/rced-98-126.

229 CBO, R&D, *supra* note 31 (page numbers unavailable).

230 For timely discussion of US federal government investment in basic research and regulatory responsiveness to biopharma R&D, see generally *id.* TTLP requires universities and other non-profits to reinvest Bayh-Dole patent revenues in science research and education. *See* 35 U.S.C. § 202(c)(7)(C) (2012). The success of TTP has generated a substantial funding source for new research, and it is discretionary funding (use not specified beyond reinvesting in research). *See* Daniel J. Hemel, Lisa Larrimore Ouellette, *Bayh-Dole Beyond Borders*, 4 J.L. & BIOSCIENCES 282, 285 (2017). The impact of TTLP on basic research correlates with the amount federal basic research grant funding, and Dr. Francis Collins helped to realized substantial increases in NIH's budget during his twelve years acting as director. NIH's budget is now anticipated to reach $50.4 billion. *See CBS Sunday Morning, Collins, supra* note 92. As stated by one observer, "[TTLP] has turned universities into commercial entities, created a multibillion-dollar industry of technology transfer, and subsidized virtually every biotechnology company and discovery of the past twenty-five years." Lorelei Ritchie de Larena, *The Price of Progress: Are Universities Adding to the Cost?*, 43 HOUS. L. REV. 1373, 1375 (2007). For another evaluation of Bayh-Dole, see generally DAVID C. MOWERY, ET AL., IVORY TOWER AND INDUSTRIAL INNOVATION: UNIVERSITY-INDUSTRY TECHNOLOGY TRANSFER AND AFTER THE BAYH-DOLE ACT (2004). *See also* Michael J. Malinowski, *Government Rx-Back to the Future in Science Funding? The Next Era in Drug Development*, 51 U. LOUISVILLE L. REV. 101, 107–109 (2012).

231 CBO, R&D, *supra* note 31.

232 *See supra* notes 31–34, and accompanying text (addressing biopharma investment in clinical research, and its choice to work with CROs). *See generally* TECONOMY, GROWING STATE ECONOMIES, *supra* note 31.

233 *See supra* note 230, and accompanying text (US federal government funding in basic research).

234 *See infra* notes 404–05, and accompanying text (medical profession protection of the integrity and reliability of medical science and the practice of medicine since last century). *See generally Chapter 2, supra.*

235 Dr. Abramson and others have proposed that the NIH and FDA conduct more independent clinical trials. Reminiscent of the AMA establishment of its AMA Council in 1905 with a laboratory to evaluate medicines (*see Chapter 1, supra*, at notes 68–69), Dr. Abramson has proposed the establishment of an independent body to certify the validity

of clinical research as an addition to the peer review process in MJE publication, which also could serve as a check on biopharma marketing:

> Only studies that met these standards would be certified by the new body—thus establishing an effective performance threshold for validation of clinical research. This certification would become part of the peer-review process for medical journals—publication could be restricted to certified research or articles' certification status could be clearly identified for readers. Certification would also be identified in all the scientific evidence presented to doctors in marketing material and continuing education. The public would be similarly informed about the certification status of research referred to in advertising and presented in the media.

ABRAMSON, OVERDOSED, *supra* note 1, at 252. *See also id* at 95.

236 *See supra* notes 31–34 (industry financing and control over clinical research), 42–45 (elevation of industry influence with implementation of TTLP), and accompanying text.

237 ABRAMSON, OVERDOSED, *supra* note 1, at 241.

238 *Id.* at xvii. Dr. Abramson offered the anti-depressant Paxil as an illustrative example:

> The substitution of narrow corporate interests for medical progress has produced some dramatic excesses. When the manufacturer of Paxil performs nine clinical studies on the treatment of adolescents for depression and finds that Paxil is no more effective than placebos and, in fact, significantly increases the frequency of "emotional liability" (including suicidal thoughts and attempts), it's no problem. The company publishes one study that shows a benefit, fails to publish the other eight, and markets away. British drug authorities analyzed all the antidepressant studies involving children and concluded that twice as many children treated with the new [as of 2004] antidepressants became suicidal. The FDA appointed an epidemiologist to do the same, and he reached the same conclusion. The FDA did not allow him to testify at their public hearing on the matter, or to be interviewed by the New York Times.

Id. at 243.

239 Variables such as the scope of trials, comingling industry and other sponsorship, reliance on industry self-reported data, and clinical research not included within the scope of www.ClinicalTrials.gov., a registry of clinical trials before the FDA, complicate analysis. *See Chapter 6, infra*, at note 248, and accompanying text (discussing www.ClinicalTrials.gov). Nevertheless, estimates generally attribute greater than seventy percent of the cost of clinical trials for the US market to biopharma, and that has been the case for some time. For a report on industry investment in clinical research, see generally TECONOMY, GROWING STATE ECONOMIES, *supra* note 31.

240 For discussion of "norm" in the context of the shareholder wealth maximization norm, see *supra* note 215, and accompanying text.

241 *See generally* IRS, *Charities and Nonprofits* (updated Feb. 24, 2022), www.irs.gov/charities-and-nonprofits. Not-for-profit corporate citizens must remain fiscally viable with allegiance to their corporate missions, and they must satisfy requisite standards for transparency and accountability. *Id.*

242 *See* ABRAMSON, OVERDOSED, *supra* note 1, at 95 (referring to CROs as "private research companies"). *See supra* note 34, and accompanying text (addressing industry engagement of CROs).

243 *See* GOLDACRE, BAD PHARMA, *supra* note 178, at 244–45 ("The company can also give money to patient groups, if those groups' views and values help it sell more drugs, and so give them greater prominence, power and platform."); MOYNIHAN, CASSELLS,

SELLING SICKNESS, *supra* note 187, at 122 ("Just as we have seen with the promotion of ADD [attention deficit disorder] and other conditions, advocacy groups earn some of their drug company sponsorship dollars by providing suffering patients to talk to deadline-sensitive journalists.").

244 MOYNIHAN, CASSELLS, SELLING SICKNESS, *supra* note 187, at 62. *See* BRAWLEY, HARM, *supra* note 71, at 230–31.

245 BRAWLEY, HARM, *supra* note 71, at 230–31.

246 Malinowski, *Triple Threat, supra* note 23, at 1048–49.

247 *See Chapter 1, supra*, at notes 160–62, and accompanying text (physician discretion to prescribe off label).

248 *See* Pediatric Research Equity Act/PREA (2003), Pub. L. No. 108–155, 117 Stat. 1936, *codified as amended at* 21 U.S.C. § 355c (2012). PREA is Title IV of the Food and Drug Administration Amendments Act/FDAAA, Pub. L. No. 110–85, 121 Stat. 823 (2007), *codified as amended*, 21 U.S.C. §§ 301-399i (2012). Under PREA, NDA sponsors must satisfy pediatric assessment submission requirements or seek a waiver detailing why a pediatric formulation cannot be developed. The FDA is authorized to require submission of a pediatric assessment if the Secretary of HHS finds that adequate pediatric labeling could benefit pediatric patients or that the absence of adequate pediatric labeling could pose a significant risk to them. Title V of the FDAAA amends BPCA to, among other things, authorize the Secretary to include preclinical studies and to require the studies to be completed using appropriate formulations for each age group in the scope of the study requested. Applicants who do not agree with a pediatric study request must submit to the Secretary the reasons such pediatric formulations cannot be developed. Applicants who agree with a pediatric study request must provide the Secretary with all post-marketing adverse event reports regarding the drug.

249 *See* Common Rule, 45 CFR part 46, subpart D (1991, amended 2017). *See* HHS, *Federal Policy for the Protection of Human Subjects* ("Common Rule") (reviewed Mar. 18, 2016), www.hhs.gov/ohrp/regulations-and-policy/regulations/common-rule/index.html.

250 *See* Lynn Yao, *FDA Takes Steps to Encourage Pediatric Drug Studies*, FDA VOICES (Aug. 26, 2013), https://blogs.fda.gov/fdavoice/index.php/tag/pediatric-research-equity-act-prea/.

251 *See id.*

252 *See* Best Pharmaceuticals for Children Act/BPCA (2007), Pub. L. No. 107–109, 115 Stat. 1408, *codified at* 21 U.S.C. § 355a (2012).

253 *See generally Assoc. Am. Physicians and Surgeons*, 226 F. Supp.2d 204 (DC D. Ct. 2002).

254 *See generally id.*

255 ABRAMSON, OVERDOSED, *supra* note 1, at 103.

256 *Id.* at 104.

257 *See infra* notes 283–86, and accompanying text (discussing negative data publicly available on the FDA site).

258 *See infra* note 286, and accompanying text (addressing MJE publications supportive of Vioxx and Celebrex product sales).

259 *See* FDAMA, 21 U.S.C. § 356b (2006) (presumption of approval with authority to impose follow-on studies); FDA, *Risk Evaluation and Mitigation Strategies* (current Dec. 17, 2021), www.fda.gov/drugs/drug-safety-and-availability/risk-evaluation-and-mitigation-strategies-rems. *See also* PETER BARTON HUTT ET AL., FOOD AND DRUG LAW 734–38 (3d ed. 2007).

260 *See* FDAAA, Pub. L. No. 110–85, 121 Stat. 823 (2007) (codified as amended in scattered sections of 21 U.S.C.). *See* Malinowski, *Popping, supra* note 76, at 1130. *See generally* Barbara J. Evans, *Seven Pillars of a New Evidentiary Paradigm: The Food, Drug, and Cosmetic Act Enters the Genomics Era*, 85 NOTRE DAME L. REV. 419, 460 (2010). Within a decade after passing the FDAAA to instill more FDA scrutiny, Congress

reversed course and passed the 21st Century Cures Act. *See generally* Pub. L. No. 114–255 (Dec. 2016). The Cures Act, supported by large biopharma manufacturers and opposed by many consumer organizations, introduced measures *to accelerate* medical product discovery, development, and delivery – for example, by codifying opportunities for companies to provide "data summaries" and "real world evidence" such as observational studies and insurance claims data rather than full clinical trial results. *Id.* (contains three primary titles that address acceleration of medical product discovery, development, and delivery). *See generally* Sheila Kaplan, *Winners and Losers of the 21st Century Cures Act*, STAT NEWS (Dec. 5, 2016), www.statnews.com/2016/12/05/21st-century-cures-act-winners-losers/.

261 Malinowski, *Triple Threat*, *supra* note 23, at 1052. *See, e.g.*, 60 *Minutes*, *Prescription for Trouble* (Nov. 14, 2004) (CBS television broadcast; interviews with clinical researchers who published negative data about Vioxx in peer-reviewed literature and were subjected to professional attacks from Merck, the drug's manufacturer), www.cbsnews.com/news/prescription-for-trouble/ (print reporting version).

262 *See* Malinowski, *Triple Threat*, *supra* note 23, at 1051–52 (2018); Evans, *Pillars*, *supra* note 260, at 509. *See generally* Barbara J. Evans, *Authority of the Food and Drug Administration to Require Data Access and Control Use Rights in the Sentinel Data Network*, 65 FOOD & DRUG L.J. 67 (2010). HHS charged the FDA to create Sentinel, and the agency launched the initiative in May 2008. Sentinel was in a "Mini-Sentinel pilot" stage as of 2016. *See* Malinowski, *Triple Threat*, *supra* note 23, at 1052.

263 *See* EMANUEL, WHICH COUNTRY, *supra* note 42, at 87, 381–84. *See infra* notes 384–403, and accompanying text ("Health Technology Assessment in US Health Care").

264 *Visit* Swedish MPA, official site, www.lakemedelsverket.se/en.

265 FDA, *The Swedish Medical Product Agency (MPA) – FDA, Confidentiality Commitment* (current July 11, 2019), www.fda.gov/international-programs/confidentiality-commitments/swedish-medical-product-agency-mpa-fda-confidentiality-commitment.

266 *See* ABRAMSON, OVERDOSED, *supra* note 1, at 95. *See* GOLDACRE, BAD PHARMA, *supra* note 178, at 287–303. Corporations "pay professional writers to produce academic papers, following their own commercial specifications, and then get academics to put their names to them." *Id.* at 244–45.

267 Holly Else, Richard Van Noorden, *The Fight Against Fake-Paper Factories that Churn out Sham Science*, NATURE 591, 516–19 (2021), www.nature.com/articles/d41586-021-00733-5.

268 *See id.* In addition to ghost writing and the paper mill industry, as reported in NATURE in October 2022, even the most renowned and trusted researchers may directly engage in image and data manipulation – made much more doable today through artificial intelligence/AI technologies:

> Several research articles co-authored by Nobel-prizewinning geneticist Gregg Semenza are being investigated by publishers after internet sleuths raised concerns about the integrity of images in the papers. Journals have already retracted, corrected or expressed concerns about 17 papers over the past decade, and others are investigating image- and data-integrity issues in further studies.
>
> Semenza, who works at Johns Hopkins University in Baltimore, Maryland, shared the 2019 Nobel prize in physiology or medicine with two other scientists for discovering how cells sense and adapt to oxygen availability in the body. He published his Nobel Prize-winning work in the 1990s; the latest concerns focus on related molecular-biology research published since.

Holly Else, *Dozens of Papers Co-authored by Nobel Laureate Raise Concerns*, NATURE (Oct. 21, 2022), www.nature.com/articles/d41586-022-03032-9. As referenced in the above quote, "Concerns about image integrity have so far led to 17 retractions, corrections or expressions of concern for papers co-authored by geneticist Gregg Semenza." *Id.* The scope of this single Semenza investigation and its potential impact on the integrity of medical research and researchers through co-authorship is expansive:

> Across the 32 papers that have so far drawn publisher scrutiny, all list Semenza as an author, but there are many combinations of different co-authors. Semenza is the corresponding or co-corresponding author on 14 of these papers, which cover research related to the molecular mechanisms of oxygen sensing in different types of cancer, and the function and dysfunction of blood vessels, among other topics. No wrongdoing has been proven, and with a lack of clarity about who contributed what to the papers, it is unclear who might have been responsible for any errors or problems with images. Corresponding authors do, however, carry responsibility for ensuring a paper's overall integrity.

Id.

269 *See* Else, Van Noorden, *Sham Science*, *supra* note 267 (most published within three years of the *Nature* investigation, and from hospitals in China).

270 *Id.*

271 *Id.*

272 *See* Else, van Noorden, *Fake-Paper Factories*, *supra* note 267, at 516–19.

273 *Id.* When too egregious to ignore, there are exceptions. *See, e.g.*, *supra* note 268 (the Nobel Laureate Gregg Semenza controversy reported by *Nature* in October 2022).

274 *See id.*

275 At times, medical professionals engage in ghost writing and readily self-expose – an indication of the normalization of ghost writing. For example, the Vioxx scandal elicited an admission printed in *The New York Times*:

> After a crucial study on the painkiller drug Vioxx was found to have failed adequately to describe the deaths of patients receiving it, the first author told [The] New York Times: "Merck designed the trial, paid for the trial, ran the trial.... Merck came to me after the study was completed and said, 'We want your help to work on the paper.' The initial paper was written at Merck, and then it was sent to me for editing."

GOLDACRE, BAD PHARMA, *supra* note 178, at 287. At times irrefutable proof becomes available when ghostwriting is brazen, as in the following instance:

> Medical writing company STI, for example, wrote a whole physician textbook which appeared with the names of two senior doctors on it. If you follow through the documentation, now in the public domain, a draft of the textbook says it was paid for by GSK, and written by two staff members at the medical writing company they paid. But in the preface to the final published textbook, the doctors whose names appear on the cover merely thank STI for "editorial assistance," and GSK for "an unrestricted educational grant."

Id. at 298.

276 *Id.* at 300.

277 GOLDACRE, BAD PHARMA, *supra* note 178, at 300.

278 *See generally* INTERNATIONAL COMMITTEE OF MEDICAL JOURNAL EDITORS/ICMJE, RECOMMENDATIONS FOR THE CONDUCT, REPORTING, EDITING, AND PUBLICATION OF SCHOLARLY WORK IN MEDICAL JOURNALS 2–3 (updated Dec. 2021), www.icmje.org/icmje-recommendations.pdf.

279 GOLDACRE, BAD PHARMA, *supra* note 178, at 301.

280 ABRAMSON, OVERDOSED, *supra* note 1, at 106 ("Drug companies often keep the results of their studies secret, even from their own researchers, on the grounds that such results are 'proprietary information' of economic value."). *Id.* at 27.

281 *See id.* at 106 ("Readers of medical journals cannot assume that the process of peer review ensures fair and impartial presentation of research results.").

282 ABRAMSON, OVERDOSED, *supra* note 1, at xiii.

283 *See id.* at xxii, 27–28, 38, 259.

284 *See supra* notes 257–58, and accompanying text (FDA awareness of negative data).

285 *See* FDAMA, § 112(a) (FDCA § 506(b)(2)(A)), 111 Stat. at 2309, *codified at* 21 U.S.C. § 356(b)(2)(A) (2012). The FDAMA provision that codified the fast track, 506B, introduced a presumption in favor of market approval, accompanied by FDA enforcement authority under 21 U.S.C. § 356b (2006) to impose phase 4 (follow-on) clinical trial obligations and Risk Evaluation and Mitigation Strategies/REMS. *See* FDA, *Reports on the Status of Postmarketing Studies – Implementation of Section 130 of the Food and Drug Administration Modernization Act of 1997* 1 (2006), www.fda.gov/regulatory-information/search-fda-guidance-documents/reports-status-postmarketing-study-commitments-implementation-section-130-food-and-drug. The purpose of phase 4 studies is to probe lingering questions and to perfect clinical use. *See* HUTT, FOOD AND DRUG, *supra* note 259, at 734–38 (3d ed. 2007).

286 *See supra* notes 257–58, and accompanying text (Vioxx and Celebrex approvals despite negative data). *See* ABRAMSON, OVERDOSED, *supra* note 1, at 28, 259. The Vioxx manufacturer Merck, the FDA, and those who reviewed the data available in 2000 were aware that "Vioxx was significantly more dangerous and no more effective than an older and far less costly anti-inflammatory drug, naproxen (Aleve)." *Id.* at xii.

287 *See id.* at 259.

288 *Id.* at 38.

289 *See id.* at xii.

290 Snigda Prakash, Vikki Valentine, *Timeline: The Rise and Fall of Vioxx*, NPR (Nov. 10, 2007), www.npr.org/2007/11/10/5470430/timeline-the-rise-and-fall-of-vioxx; ABRAMSON, OVERDOSED, *supra* note 1, at 259.

291 *See* ABRAMSON, OVERDOSED, *supra* note 1, at 245 ("However, when all the data from the manufacturer-sponsored study are taken into account, Celebrex offers no significant advantage over much less expensive anti-inflammatory drugs, and may actually cause more GI problems when taken for longer than six months."); Todd Zwillich, *Bextra Taken Off Market; Celebrex Gets Warning Other Anti-Inflammatory Drugs Also to Carry Warnings of Heart, Stomach Risks*, WEBMD (Apr. 7, 2005), www.webmd.com/arthritis/news/20050407/bextra-taken-off-market-celebrex-gets-warning.

292 *See generally* ICMJE, RECOMMENDATIONS, *supra* note 278.

293 *See generally id.*

294 ABRAMSON, OVERDOSED, *supra* note 1, at 106.

295 ANGELL, TRUTH, *supra* note 32, at 135. Dr. Angell felt compelled to publish *The Truth about Drug Companies* (winner of a Polk Award for excellence in journalism) to share her first-hand experiences, both as a practicing physician and with *NEJM*, of growing biopharma company manipulation – through DTP and DTC marketing, and well beyond. *See generally id.*

296 GOLDACRE, BAD PHARMA, *supra* note 178, at 244–45. *See also id.* at 313. "In the US [CME] is now a billion-dollar enterprise, with close to half of that funding flowing directly from the pharmaceutical industry. Doctors are being 'educated' about how to use drugs, and how many of us should take them, in venues sponsored by their makers." MOYNIHAN, CASSELLS, SELLING SICKNESS, *supra* note 187, at 5.

297 *See* GOLDACRE, BAD PHARMA, *supra* note 178, at 244–45 ("All of this is built on the back of a published academic base that drug companies have carefully nurtured, through selective publication of flattering results and judicious use of design flaws, to give a flattering picture of their product.").

298 *Visit* Accreditation Council for Continuing Medical Education/ACCME, official site, www.accme.org/. *See generally* PHRMA, CODE ON INTERACTIONS WITH HEALTH CARE PROFESSIONALS (2009, revised Sept. 2019), www.phrma.org/-/media/Project/PhRMA/PhRMA-Org/PhRMA-Org/PDF/A-C/Code-of-Interaction_FINAL21.pdf.

299 INSTITUTE OF MEDICINE/IOM, CONFLICT OF INTEREST IN MEDICAL RESEARCH, EDUCATION, AND PRACTICE 161 (2009), WWW.NAP.EDU/LOGIN.PHP?RECORD_ID=12598&PAGE=HTTPS%3A%2F%2FWWW.NAP.EDU%2FDOWNLOAD%2F12598. *See generally* Lewis Morris, Julie K Taitsman, *The Agenda for Continuing Medical Education – Limiting Industry's Influence*, 361 N. ENGL. J. MED. 2478–82 (Dec. 2009). *See also* ABRAMSON, OVERDOSED, *supra* note 1, at 118 ("To many senior physicians who have watched the atmosphere at these meetings decline in quality from the sober professionalism of a few decades ago to the trade-show hucksterism of today, it is a dispiriting spectacle.").

300 MOYNIHAN, CASSELLS, SELLING SICKNESS, *supra* note 187, at 7 (internal citations omitted).

301 *See* ABRAMSON, OVERDOSED, *supra* note 1, at 119.

302 *Id.* at 89–90. *See id.* at 249–50. *See also infra* notes 321–83, and accompanying text ("Science, Standard of Care, and the Ineffectiveness of US Practice Guidelines").

303 *See* Morris, Taitsman, *Industry's Influence, supra* note 299, at 2478–82. *See also* ANGELL, TRUTH, *supra* note 32, at 135–55 ("Marketing Masquerading as Education"), 156–72 ("Marketing Masquerading as Research").

304 ABRAMSON, OVERDOSED, *supra* note 1, at 121.

305 *See id.* at 121. *Cf.* Public Citizen, *Comments Advocating a Ban on Commercial Support for Continuing Medical Education* (Sept. 12, 2008), www.citizen.org/article/comments-advocating-a-ban-on-commercial-support-for-continuing-medical-education/.

306 MOYNIHAN, CASSELLS, SELLING SICKNESS, *supra* note 187, at 6.

307 ABRAMSON, OVERDOSED, *supra* note 1, at 118.

308 *Id.* at 112.

309 *Id.* at 123. *See also id.* at 121 ("Clearly, the doctors had been influenced by education sponsored by drug companies, and it was all the more effective because they naively believed themselves impervious to such influence.").

310 *See* MOYNIHAN, CASSELLS, SELLING SICKNESS, *supra* note 187, at 5, 22–40.

311 *Id.* at 23 (internal citation omitted).

312 ABRAMSON, OVERDOSED, *supra* note 1, at 125–26.

313 *See* GOLDACRE, BAD PHARMA, *supra* note 178, at 246 ("So we pay for products, with a huge uplift in price to cover their marketing budget, and that money is then spent on distorting evidence-based practice, which in turn makes our decisions unnecessarily expensive, and less effective.").

314 ABRAMSON, OVERDOSED, *supra* note 1, at 125–26. *See Chapter* 3, *supra*, at notes 21–30, and accompanying text (DTP biopharma marketing).

315 *See generally* Julia B. Berman, Guohua Li, *Characteristics of Criminal Cases Against Physicians Charged with Opioid-related Offenses Reported in the US News Media, 1995–2019*, INJ. EPIDEMIOL. 7, 50 (2020), https://doi.org/10.1186/s40621-020-00277-8 (referencing 372 physician defendants in opioid-related criminal cases between January 1995 and December 2019).

316 *See generally* Malinowski, *Triple Threat*, *supra* note 23.

317 *See* THE PRESIDENT'S COMM'N ON COMBATING DRUG ADDICTION AND THE OPIOID CRISIS, FINAL REP. 28, 117 (2017), https://trumpwhitehouse.archives.gov/sites/whitehouse.gov/files/images/Final_Report_Draft_11-15-2017.pdf.

318 *See* Josh Bloom, *It's The Fentanyl Epidemic, Stupid*, AM. COUNCIL ON SCI. AND HEALTH (Dec. 6, 2021), www.acsh.org/news/2021/12/06/its-fentanyl-epidemic-stupid-15965.

319 *See, e.g.*, Scott E. Hadland, Ariadne Rivera-Aguirre, Brandon D. L. Marshall, Magdalena Cerdá, *Association of Pharmaceutical Industry Marketing of Opioid Products With Mortality From Opioid-Related Overdoses*, 2(1) JAMA NETWORK OPEN (2019), file:///C:/Users/mjmalin/Downloads/hadland_2019_oi_180253.pdf. ("In this study, across US counties, marketing of opioid products to physicians was associated with increased opioid prescribing and, subsequently, with elevated mortality from overdoses. Amid a national opioid overdose crisis, reexamining the influence of the pharmaceutical industry may be warranted.").

320 *See id.*

321 *See* US Department of Energy Office of Science, Office of Biological and Environmental Research, *About the Human Genome Project Information Archive 1990–2003* (last modified Mar. 26, 2019) ("The current consensus predicts about 20,500 genes, but this number has fluctuated a great deal since the project began."), https://web.ornl.gov/sci/techresources/Human_Genome/project/index.shtml.

322 GOLDACRE, BAD PHARMA, *supra* note 178, at ix.

323 As observed by Dr. Goldacre, "Perhaps if all doctors were forced to admit to the uncertainties in our day-to-day management of patients, it might make us a little more humble, and more inclined to improve the evidence base on which we base our decisions." GOLDACRE, BAD PHARMA, *supra* note 178, at 235–36.

324 *See* BRAWLEY, HARM, *supra* note 71, at 282 ("Many physicians are ignorant of some aspects of the field of medicine in which they practice.").

325 *Id.* at 282.

326 *Id.* at 40.

327 ABRAMSON, OVERDOSED, *supra* note 1, at 174–75.

328 RICHARD RETTIG, PETER JACOBSON, CYNTHIA FARQUHAR, WADE AUBREY, FALSE HOPE: BREAST CANCER TRANSPLANTATION FOR BREAST CANCER 3 (2007). *See generally id*; Noah Raizman, Hope Without Evidence, 369 *Lancet* 9580 (June 30, 2007), www.thelancet.com/article/S0140-6736(07)60996-9/fulltext. *See also* BRAWLEY, HARM, *supra* note 71, at 187.

329 *See* Reizman, *Hope*, *supra* note 328, at 9580.

330 *See* BRAWLEY, HARM, *supra* note 71, at 34–35.

331 *See id.* at 34–35.

332 Another published paper reinforced use of ABMT. *See* Werner R. Bezwoda, L. Seymour, R. D. Dansey, *High-Dose Chemotherapy with Hematopoietic Rescue as Primary Treatment for Metastatic Breast Cancer: A Randomized Trial*, 13(10) J. CLIN. ONCOL. 2483–89 (1995), *retracted* 19(11) J. CLIN. ONCOL. 2973 (June 2001), https://pubmed.ncbi.nlm.nih.gov/7595697/#affiliation-1. *See generally* RETTIG ET AL., FALSE HOPE, *supra* note 328.

333 RETTIG ET AL., FALSE HOPE, *supra* note 328. *See* BRAWLEY, HARM, *supra* note 71, at 35. *See generally* Raizman, *Hope Without Evidence*, *supra* note 328.

334 RETTIG ET AL., FALSE HOPE, *supra* note 328, at 3. *See* BRAWLEY, HARM, *supra* note 71, at 187.

335 *See* BRAWLEY, HARM, *supra* note 71, at 34–36, 187.

336 *Id.* at 35. *See* Raizman, *Hope*, *supra* note 328, at 9580 ("some 30 000–40 000 women received the ineffective treatment, at exorbitant cost").

337 *See supra* notes 83–84, 181–86, 337, and accompanying text (discussing hydroxychloroquine and chloroquine). The FDA approved ivermectin for treating some tropical diseases and parasites (worms and lice) in humans, but the drug's primary use is to deworm large animals – so available from your local veterinarian. *See generally Ivermectin may Help Covid-19 Patients – but Only those with Worms*, ECONOMIST (Nov. 27, 2021), www.economist.com/united-states/2021/11/27/ivermectin-may-help-covid-19-patients-but-only-those-with-worms. Physicians (and veterinarians. based on internet chatter) deviated from evidentiary science-based clinical practice and prescribed the drug for COVID-19 patients:

> At last count doctors in America prescribed more than 100,000 tablets of the drug a week, a 30-fold increase since 2019. Ivermectin's advocates insist that there is solid science showing its efficacy. One website lists 67 papers on the subject. Could they all be wrong? Recent analysis suggests ivermectin probably does help one subset of covid patients: those also infected by the worms it was designed to fight.

Id.

338 *See* Michael Hiltzik, *Column: A Warning to Doctors – Spreading COVID Misinformation could Cost you your License*, LA TIMES (Aug. 16, 2021), www.latimes.com/business/story/2021-08-16/doctors-coronavirus-misinformation-license.

339 *See Chapter 2, supra*, at notes 32–114, and accompanying text (discussing OWS as "The Latest US Application of Triple-Threat Science R&D Methodology").

340 *See* Fed'n. State Med. Bds./FSMB, *FSMB: Spreading Covid-19 Vaccine Misinformation May Put Medical License at Risk* (July 29, 2021), www.fsmb.org/advocacy/news-releases/fsmb-spreading-covid-19-vaccine-misinformation-may-put-medical-license-at-risk/.

341 *See generally* Hiltzik, *A Warning to Doctors*, *supra* note 338.

342 Richard J. Baron, Yul D. Ejnes, *Do Right and Wrong Answers Still Exist in Medicine*, N. ENG. J. MED. (May 18, 2022), www.nejm.org/doi/full/10.1056/NEJMp2204813.

343 Ideally, medical practice guidelines, generated from thorough examination of current evidence-based medicine, represent consensus among trusted experts on best practices in health care and represent thoughtful, objective deliberation. *See generally* INSTITUTE OF MEDICINE/IOM, CLINICAL PRACTICE GUIDELINES WE CAN TRUST (2011). *See also* Jako Burgers, Richard Grol, Niek Klazinga, Marjukka Makela, Joost Zatt (for the Agree Collaboration), *Towards Evidence-Based Clinical Practice: An International Survey of 18 Clinical Guideline Programs*, 15 INT. J. QUAL. HEALTH CARE 31–45 (2011), https://academic.oup.com/intqhc/article/15/1/31/1797071.

344 *See* BRAWLEY, HARM, *supra* note 71, at 244, 254.

345 *See id.* at 254. *See* Agency for Healthcare Research and Quality/AHRQ, *US Preventive Services Task Force (USPSTF): An Introduction* (reviewed June 2021), www.ahrq.gov/cpi/about/otherwebsites/uspstf/introduction.html. The USPSTF has sixteen members, most clinicians, drawn from the fields of preventive medicine and primary care, including internal medicine, family medicine, pediatrics, behavioral health, obstetrics/gynecology, and nursing. *Visit* USPSTF, official site, https://uspreventiveservicestaskforce.org/uspstf/home.

346 *See* BRAWLEY, HARM, *supra* note 71, at 244.

347 Congress established AHCPR under the Omnibus Budget Reconciliation Act of 1989, 103 Stat. 2159.

348 AHRQ's earliest predecessor was the National Center for Health Services Research and Development/NCHRD, established in 1968 within the Public Health Service/PHS Health Resources and Services Administration. *See Records of the Agency for Health Care Policy and Research*, NAT'L ARCHIVES (Aug. 15, 2016), www.archives.gov/research/guide-fed-records/groups/510.html. In 1973, NCHRD became the Bureau of Health

Services Research/BHSR within the PHS Health Resources Administration, which was renamed the National Center for Health Services Research/NCHSR in 1975. *See id.* In 1978, NCHSR was transferred to the Office of the Assistant Secretary for Health. In 1985, it was renamed the National Center for Health Services Research and Health Care Technology Assessment/HSRHCTA. *See id.*

349 *See Records*, *supra* note 348.

350 *See id. See also* Ed. Staff, *Opinion, Want Reliable Medical Information? The Trump Administration Doesn't*, N.Y. Times (July 19, 2018), www.nytimes.com/2018/07/19/opinion/trump-medicine-data-hhs-ahrq.html.

351 *See generally* Ed. Staff, *Reliable Medical?*, *supra* note 350.

352 *See AHRQ*, *About NGC and NQMC* (reviewed July 2018), www.ahrq.gov/gam/about/index.html.

353 *See* Healthcare Research and Quality Act of 1999, *amending* Title IX of the Public Health Service Act, 42 U.S.C. 299, *et seq.*

354 *AHRQ*, *About*, *supra* note 352.

355 Ed. Staff, *Reliable Medical?*, *supra* note 350.

356 *See generally AHRQ*, *About*, *supra* note 352; Ed. Staff, *Reliable Medical?*, *supra* note 350.

357 *See* Jerry Avorn, Powerful Medicines: The Benefits, Risks, and Costs of Prescription Drugs 277–88 (2005).

358 AHRQ, *About*, *supra* note 352. *See also* AHRQ, *NQMC Measure Domain Framework* (reviewed July 2018), www.ahrq.gov/gam/summaries/domain-framework/index.html.

359 *See* AHRQ, *About*, *supra* note 352. Although official government reasoning was that the databases were redundant with other programs, AHRG and NGC had reached science and evidence-based conclusions unwelcomed by segments of the medical profession which lobbied against them. *See generally* Ed. Staff, *Reliable Medical?*, *supra* note 350. For example, a late 1990s endorsement of nonsurgical interventions for back pain stirred a back surgeon lobbying attack on AHRQ. *Id.*

360 *See* Abramson, Overdosed, *supra* note 1, at 127.

361 Moynihan, Cassells, Selling Sickness, *supra* note 187, at 4.

362 *See id.* at 5–6 (internal citations omitted). *See also supra* notes 44, 301–02, and accompanying text (thought leaders/key opinion leaders).

363 *See* Niteesh K Choudhry, Henry Thomas Stelfox, Allan S Detsky, *Relationships Between Authors of Clinical Practice Guidelines and the Pharmaceutical Industry*, 287 JAMA 612–17 (2002), https://pubmed.ncbi.nlm.nih.gov/11829700/. *See also* Abramson, Overdosed, *supra* note 1, at xxi, 127–28.

364 *See generally* Jonny Bowden, Stephen Sinatra, The Great Cholesterol Myth, Revised and Expanded: Why Lowering Your Cholesterol Won't Prevent Heart Disease – And the Statin-Free Plan that Will (2020); Barbara H. Roberts, The Truth About Statins: Risks and Alternatives to Cholesterol-Lowering (2012).

365 *See* Moynihan, Cassells, Selling Sickness, *supra* note 187, at 1–3. *Cf. generally* Roberts, Truth About Statins, *supra* note 364.
See generally Bowden, Myth, *supra* note 364; Roberts, Statins, *supra* note 364.

366 Moynihan, Cassells, Selling Sickness, *supra* note 187, at 1 (internal citation omitted).

367 *Id.* at 3–4.

368 Beyond long-standing divisions among states, which license their segments of the medical profession, the profession is divided into specialties, and divided again into subspecialties – and each has a financial and professional stake in controlling what they practice:

> It's not easy to challenge doctors to justify their decisions in the clinic.... [I]t's harder still to challenge a wrongheaded consensus of a medical specialty as it marches in lockstep. This is precisely what happens when professional societies of doctors who perform expansive medical procedures issues "evidence-based guidelines" that are anything but evidence-based guidelines. Instead, the purpose of many of these documents is to protect the specialties' financial stake in the system.

BRAWLEY, HARM, *supra* note 71, at 26.

369 *See supra* note 72, and accompanying text (doctor shortage disproportionate in primary care and family practice).

370 *See* BRAWLEY, HARM, *supra* note 71, at 244.

371 *Id.* at 245

372 *Id.* at 243.

373 *See generally* Roberto Grilli, Nicola Magrini, Angelo Penna et al., *Practice Guidelines Developed by Specialty Societies: The Need for a Critical Appraisal*, 355 LANCET 102–106 (Jan. 8, 2000), www.thelancet.com/journals/lancet/article/PIIS0140-6736(99)02171-6/fulltext. *See also* BRAWLEY, HARM, *supra* note 71, at 243.

374 Physician non-responsiveness to practice guidelines is an explanation for overall physician indifference to the end of the NGC. *See generally* Ed. Staff, *Reliable Medical?*, *supra* note 350. US physicians are vested with clinical discretion, practice medicine with the mindset of individualized patient care, and value their clinical care independence and trust themselves. Many choose to categorically ignore practice guidelines:

> Doctors can no longer blame the lack of clinical information as the reason they need to rely on their personal experience and preferences. The internet has made the best evidenced-based guidelines accessible through nearly all mobile devices.
>
> The problem is not that doctors can't access these evidence based guidelines. They just choose to ignore them.
>
> Let's face it. None of us likes being told what to do, particularly when it comes to our areas of expertise. Doctors are no exception.
>
> In the end, this debate is less about "art" vs. "science." It's about doctors valuing their own intuition over scientific evidence.

Robert Pearl, *Medicine Is An Art, Not A Science: Medical Myth Or Reality?*, FORBES BUS. (June 12, 2014), www.forbes.com/sites/robertpearl/2014/06/12/medicine-is-an-art-not-a-science-medical-myth-or-reality/?sh=64a09ff62071.

375 *See generally*, CDC, *Guideline for Prescribing Opioids for Chronic Pain* (Mar. 16, 2016), www.cdc.gov/mmwr/volumes/65/rr/rr6501e1.htm. *See* Malinowski, *Triple Threat*, *supra* note 23, at 1074.

376 *See generally* Robert M. Califf, Janet Woodcock, Stephen Ostroff, *Special Report: A Proactive Response to Prescription Opioid Abuse*, 374 NEW ENG. J. MED. 1480, 1480 (Apr. 14, 2016) (internal citations omitted), www.nejm.org/doi/pdf/10.1056/NEJMsr1601307. The American Academy of Pain Medicine/AAPM response to the CDC opioid guideline is representative: "We share concerns voiced by patient and professional groups, and other Federal agencies, that the CDC guideline makes disproportionately strong recommendations based upon a narrowly selected portion of the available clinical evidence." AAPM, *Press Release, Statement on CDC Guideline for Prescribing Opioids for Chronic Pain* (Mar. 16, 2016), *quoted in* Malinowski, *Triple Threat*, *supra* note 23, at 1074, n.190. Overall, medical professional associations representing clinical providers and patient groups raised concerns that "one-size-fits-all" limits could impede individual patient care – for treating both chronic pain and opioid use disorder. *See* Malinowski, *Triple Threat*, *supra* note 23, at 1050–51.

377 Califf, Woodcock, Ostroff, *Proactive Response*, *supra* note 376, at 1480.

378 Despite opposition to the CDC 2016 opioid guideline, it "proved immensely influential in shaping policy – fueling a push by insurers, state medical boards, politicians and federal law enforcement to curb prescribing of opioids." Will Stone, Pien Huang, *CDC Issues New Opioid Prescribing Guidance, Giving Doctors more Leeway to Treat Pain*, NPR (updated Nov. 3, 2022), www.npr.org/sections/health-shots/2022/11/03/1133908157/new-opioid-prescribing-guidelines-give-doctors-more-leeway-to-treat-pain. Some of the concerns raised by CDC opioid guideline critics were realized. CDC officials acknowledged in 2022 "that doctors, insurers, pharmacies and regulators sometimes misapplied the [2016] guidelines, causing some patients significant harm, including 'untreated and under-treated pain, serious withdrawal symptoms, worsening pain outcomes, psychological distress, overdose, and [suicide]'...." In November 2022, the CDC introduced a revised *voluntary* guideline with more clarity. "The 100-page document and its topline recommendation serve as a roadmap for prescribers who are navigating the thorny issue of treating pain, including advice on handling pain relief after surgery and managing chronic pain conditions, which are estimated to affect as many as one in every five people in the U.S." *See id. See also* Deborah Dowell, Kathleen R. Ragan, Christopher M. Jones et al., *Perspective, Prescribing Opioids for Pain – The New CDC Clinical Practice Guideline*, New. Eng. J. Med. (Nov. 3, 2022), www.nejm.org/doi/full/10.1056/NEJMp2211040.

379 *See, e.g.*, Maryann Barakso, *The Political Consequences of Internal Dissent in Advocacy Groups: The AMA, Public Opinion and Health Care Reform* (2011) (meeting paper discussing state medical societies' elevation in political influence and the vulnerability of AMA influence as a consequence of internal disagreement), https://cces.gov.harvard.edu/files/cces/files/barakso-_political_consequence_of_internal_dissent.pdf.

380 Rosenthal, American Sickness, *supra* note 43, at 196.

381 *See id.* Some calculate AMA active physician membership much lower and declining, and offset by the AMA inclusion of students, residents, and group practice memberships to inflate the organization's membership numbers:

> So let's break it down further and take a closer look at the AMA's membership numbers ... —there are 1,341,682 physicians/medical students/residents/Fellows in the US today—there are 250,253 AMA members. According to the AMA's own numbers, 22.5% of AMA members are students and 24.7% are residents (this number in 2016 was 235,000 or 1/6th of America's physicians).
>
> Yet students only make up 8.1% and residents, 10.4% in the U.S., so if you remove them from the AMA's published numbers, you get 1,093,472 physicians, and then remove the percentages of students and residents from the previous numbers I quoted, ultimately there are only 132,133 practicing physicians who are AMA members. That's 12.1%. A drop. A decline that has continued for decades.

Kevin Campbell, *Don't Believe AMA's Hype, Membership Still Declining*, MedpageToday (June 19, 2019) (asserting that the AMA's priority is its own commercial and financial interests, not physician interests), www.medpagetoday.com/opinion/campbells-scoop/80583.

382 Rosenthal, American Sickness, *supra* note 43, at 196.

383 *Id.* at 197.

384 Emanuel, Which Country, *supra* note 42, at 6. *See generally Corlette, Monahan, US Health Insurance, supra* note 42.

385 *See generally* Jeffrey Berry, The Interest Group Society (5th ed. 2008) (the work and influence of interest groups within the larger context of the US political, legislative, and regulatory systems). *See* Emanuel, Which Country, *supra* note 42, at 25.

386 *See, e.g.*, Emanuel, Which Country, *supra* note 42, at 381–84 (systematic drug cost evaluation and pricing).

387 *See generally* Clifford Goodman, HTA 101 (3d ed. 2014) (National Information Center on Health Services Research and Health Care Technology/NICHSR), www.nlm.nih.gov/nichsr/hta101/ta10103.html. *See also Chapter* 7, *infra*, at notes 190–202, 287–88, and accompanying text (further discussion of HTA).

388 *See supra* note 57 and accompanying text (HTA in industrialized economy counterparts).

389 *See generally* Emanuel, Which Country, *supra* note 42. For example,

> In a number of European countries, governmental bodies engage in health technology assessments (HTA) that evaluate the cost effectiveness of treatment options and make recommendations about whether they should be paid for by national health systems. These offices consider the estimated number of QALYs [, a quality of life year metric,] that a treatment will create relative to the treatment's cost. Only if the treatment meets a certain threshold (e.g., no more than €50,000/QALY) will it be approved for payment.

Buccafusco, Masur, *Well-Being, supra* note 57 (supporting US adoption of a HTA office or agency to provide valuable data to patients, physicians, insurers, and drug companies about treatment options) (internal footnote omitted). *See* Sorenson, Chalkidou, *Reflections, supra* note 57, at 26 (discussing European HTA mechanisms). For discussion about QALYs, see generally Sarah J. Whitehead, Shehzad Ali, *Health Outcomes in Economic Evaluation: The QALY and Utilities*, 96 Brit. Med. Bul. 5, 13–14 (2010). *See also* Nancy J. Devlin, Paula K. Lorgelly, *QALYs as a Measure of Value in Cancer*, 11 J. Cancer Pol'y 19, 20–21 (2017).

390 *See infra* notes 392–94, and accompanying text (identifying major HTA networks with contact information). The 21st Century Cures Act, Pub.L. 114–255 (2016), encouraged the FDA to consider "real-world evidence" in its regulation of the safety and efficacy of drugs and devices. *See generally* Elizabeth Hall-Lipsy, Leila Barraza, Christopher Roberts, *Practice-Based Research Networks and the Mandate for Real-World Evidence*, 44 Am. J. L. Med. 219–236 (2018), https://pubmed.ncbi.nlm.nih.gov/30106651/. The US FDA established a real-world evidence/RWE framework in 2018, which it has supplemented with guidance documents that address issues such as data standards and registries. *See generally* FDA, *Framework for FDA's Real-World Evidence Program* (Dec. 2018), www.fda.gov/media/120060/download. The FDA also has established a program, RCT Duplicate, to evaluate whether randomized controlled trials/RCTs relied upon for product market approval can be emulated with RWE across a range of therapeutic areas. *Visit* FDA, RCT Duplicate, official site (visited June 14, 2022), www.rctduplicate.org/. *See* Zachary Brennan, *Real World Evidence: Lessons Learned from an FDA Pilot Show the Limits of Emulating RCTs*, Endpointsnews (May 16, 2022), https://endpts.com/real-world-evidence-lessons-learned-from-an-fda-pilot-show-the-limits-of-emulating-rcts/.

391 *See infra* notes 392–94, and accompanying text (identifying HTA networks with citations).

392 *Visit* EC, Health Technology Assessment Network, official site, https://ec.europa.eu/health/technology_assessment/policy/network_en. The HTA Network met for the first time in October 2013. All EU countries appoint a representative, usually from their Ministry of Health or Social Services, and Iceland and Norway participate as observer members. *See id. See* Conference Proceedings (Marino), *Future of Innovation in Medicine: Incentives for New Medical Treatments and Global Health*, 12 Wash. J.L. Tech. & Arts 293, 321 (2017).

393 *Visit* INAHTA, official site, www.inahta.org/.; HTAi, official site, https://htai.org/about-htai/; ISPOR, official site, www.ispor.org/about.
394 *Visit* ISPOR, official site, www.ispor.org/about.
395 A technology assessment mechanism was introduced to better the work of Congress and federal policy, and to potentially improve technology uptake, not to impede it – as reflected in its charge:

> The term "technology assessment" was introduced in 1965 during deliberations of the Committee on Science and Astronautics of the US House of Representatives. Congressman Emilio Daddario emphasized that the purpose of TA was to serve policymaking:
> *[T]echnical information needed by policymakers is frequently not available, or not in the right form. A policymaker cannot judge the merits or consequences of a technological program within a strictly technical context. He has to consider social, economic, and legal implications of any course of action (US Congress, House of Representatives 1967).*
> Congress commissioned independent studies by the National Academy of Sciences, the National Academy of Engineering (NAE), and the Legislative Reference Service of the Library of Congress that significantly influenced the development and application of TA. These studies and further congressional hearings led the National Science Foundation to establish a TA program and, in 1972, Congress to authorize the congressional Office of Technology Assessment (OTA), which was founded in 1973, became operational in 1974, and established its health program in 1975.
> Many observers were concerned that TA would be a means by which government would impede the development and use of technology. However, this was not the intent of Congress or of the agencies that conducted the original TAs. In 1969, a NAE report to Congress emphasized that:
> *Technology assessment would aid the Congress to become more effective in assuring that broad public as well as private interests are fully considered while enabling technology to make the maximum contribution to our society's welfare (National Academy of Engineering 1969).*

Goodman, *Introduction to Health Technology Assessment, in* HTA 101, *supra* note 387 (emphasis in original), www.nlm.nih.gov/nichsr/hta101/ta10103.html.
396 *See id.* (Congress authorized OTA in 1972 and funded it for 1974).
397 See *id. See generally* Bruce Bimber, Politics of Expertise in Congress: The Rise and Fall of the Office of Technology Assessment (1996).
398 Donald Lombardo, a *Washington Times* journalist, declared OTA a duplicative agency that replicated other government work in his popular book, *Fat City: How Washington Wastes Your Taxes (1980).*
399 *See generally* Bimber, Politics of Expertise, *supra* note 397.
400 *See supra* notes 352–59, and accompanying text (NGC and NQMC).
401 *Cf.* Aspen Inst., Health Medicine and Society Program, USC Schaefer Center for Health Policy and Economics, Health Technology Assessment for the US Healthcare System Background Paper 4–7 (2019), https://healthpolicy.usc.edu/wp-content/uploads/2020/02/Health-Technology-Assessment-for-the-U.S.-Healthcare-System_Background-Paper.pdf.
402 *Visit* Centers for Medicare & Medicaid Services/CMS, official site, www.cms.gov/. The "current United States public healthcare system promotes a passive government during

drug pricing negotiations ...." Bryan Willard, *An Easier Pill to Swallow: Subscription Model Agreements as a Solution to the Government's Prescription Drug Pricing Crisis*, 30 S. Cal. Interdisc. L.J. 587, 596 (2021). It must be noted, however, that the Inflation Reduction Act/IRA of 2022, Pub. Law 117–169, which was signed into law by President Biden on Aug. 16, 2022, established precedent (however limited) to override the Medicare Part D noninterference clause, which bars the federal government from using its purchasing power to negotiate lower drug prices. *See Chapter 3, supra, at* notes 85 (noninterference clause), 104 (Inflation Reduction Act/IRA).

403 Abramson, Overdosed, *supra* note 1, at 178. *See generally* Aspen, HTA Background, *supra* note 401.

404 *See Chapter 1, supra*, at notes 35–45, and accompanying text ("US Law-Policy Recognition of Clinical Medicine as the Medical Profession's Domain").

405 *See id.* at notes 160–83, and accompanying text ("Deference to and Reliance on the Medical Profession").

406 *See supra* notes 187–320, and accompanying text (discussing the traditional mechanisms relied upon by the medical profession); *supra* notes 113–77, and accompanying text (discussing contemporary physician decision-making, and distinguishing medical practice throughout much of the twentieth century).

407 Abramson, Overdosed, *supra* note 1, at 258.

408 *Id.* at xviii. For identification and discussion of commercial influences that undermine the science and evidence base of US medicine, see generally Angell, Truth, *supra* note 32; Goldacre, Bad Pharma, *supra* note 178; Moynihan, Cassells, Selling Sickness, *supra* note 187; Rosenthal, American Sickness, *supra* note 43.

409 *See supra* notes 228–38, and accompanying text (addressing TTLP and associated industry influence in medical research and clinical practice).

410 *See supra* notes 384–85, and accompanying text (discussing Professor Emanuel's comparative analysis placement of the US health care system).

411 *See generally Chapter 2, supra*.

412 *See supra* notes 384–403, and accompanying text ("The Absence of Objective, Reliable Health Technology Assessment/HTA in US Health Care").

413 HTA is utilized throughout US healthcare, but by private and government entities in a piecemeal fashion. *See supra* notes 401–02, and accompanying text. Through these entities, the US is engaged in and contributing to the HTA discipline. *Cf.* Thomas J. Parisi, *How Much Did You Pay for Your Heart: Is A Centralized Entity Performing Health Technology Assessment with Cost-Effectiveness Analysis the Answer to the Rising Costs of Health Care?*, 49 Jurimetrics J. 285, 303 (2009).

414 Abramson, Overdosed, *supra* note 1, at 178, and accompanying text.

415 *See generally Chapter* 3, *supra*. *See supra* notes 215–18, and accompanying text (the shareholder wealth maximization norm).

416 *See* Parisi, *How Much*, *supra* note 413, at 303.

417 Emanuel, Which Country, *supra* note 42, at 384.

418 Abramson, Overdosed, *supra* note 1, at 91.

419 *See* Emanuel, Which Country, *supra* note 42, at 385, 403.

420 *Id.* at 10. *See also id.* at 385, 403. *See* Fareed Zakaria, Ten Lessons for a Post-Pandemic World 65 (2020). The US spends eighteen percent of its GDP on health care, which does not account for tax revenue lost to the US by exempting health insurance coverage provided by employers from being taxed as employer and employee income. "In 2019, this tax exemption amounted to nearly $300 billion per year and remains the largest single tax exemption in the United States." Emanuel, Which Country, *supra* note 42, at 21.

421 *See* WORLD HEALTH ORGANIZATION/WHO, WORLD HEALTH REPORT/WHR 2000: HEALTH SYSTEMS: IMPROVING PERFORMANCE 155 (2000), www.who.int/whr/2000/en/whr00_en.pdf?ua=1.

422 "Imagine if you paid for an airplane ticket and then got separate and inscrutable bills from the airline, the pilot, the copilot, and the flight attendants. That's how the health-care market works." ROSENTHAL, AMERICAN SICKNESS, *supra* note 43, at 2.

423 EMANUEL, WHICH COUNTRY, *supra* note 42, at 25.

424 *See id. at* 2.

425 "As the leaders of the Commonwealth Foundation wrote in Health Affairs at the end of 2003, 'The inability of the health care industry to improve care sufficiently on its own and to increase the value that Americans receive for their dollars is an indication of private market failure.'" ABRAMSON, OVERDOSED, *supra* note 1, at 254. In fact, the US does not have a single health care market – far from it. The US has lots of sectors and stakeholders in a decentralized, largely privatized health care system with *lots* of markets. *See supra* notes 410–24, and accompanying text.

426 *See* William Roberts, *Debating the Path Forward on Health Care Reform*, WASH. LAWYER 32–36 (Feb. 2020); ROSENTHAL, AMERICAN SICKNESS, *supra* note 43, at 3.

427 CMS, *Press Release, CMS Office of the Actuary Releases 2021–2030 Projections of National Health Expenditures (Mar. 28, 2022)*, www.cms.gov/newsroom/press-releases/cms-office-actuary-releases-2021-2030-projections-national-health-expenditures

428 Roberts, *Debating the Path*, *supra* note 426, at 36.

429 ROSENTHAL, AMERICAN SICKNESS, *supra* note 43, at 3. *See* ABRAMSON, OVERDOSED, *supra* note 1, at 46 ("The United States spends more than twice as much per person on health care as the other industrialized nations."). As observed by Dr. Abramson,

> Notwithstanding the tremendous progress and the enormous cost of American medicine, over the last 40 years the health of the citizens of the other industrialized countries has been improving at a faster pace. According to researchers from Johns Hopkins, "On most [health] indicators the US relative performance declined since 1960; on none did it improve." .... By 2000, men in the United States were losing 21 percent more years of life before the age of 70 than men in other [Organisation for Economic Co-operation and Development/]OECD countries, and American women were losing 33 percent more.

Id. at 47. However, Americans with excellent health insurance coverage and financial resources enjoy superb health care, care regardless of cost – which explains our overall numbers.

430 ABRAMSON, OVERDOSED, *supra* note 1, at 255.

431 As stated by Dr. Brawley, "We doctors are paid for services we provide, a variant of 'piece-work' that guarantees that we will err on the sale of selling more, sometimes believing that we are helping, sometimes knowing that we are not, and sometimes simply not giving a shit." BRAWLEY, HARM, *supra* note 71, at 24. Dr. Abramson believes that US doctors are predisposed to use the latest technology:

> In my experience, doctors rarely recommend procedures simply to make more money, but like most people, they like to use their special skills to help others; this creates a predisposition to want to use the latest tests, drugs, and procedures.... As the saying goes, "When you have a hammer, the whole world looks like a nail."

ABRAMSON, OVERDOSED, *supra* note 1, at 179.

432 "Care-at-all-costs healthcare norms are deeply embedded. When there is insurance coverage, physicians and patients are reactionary to imminent death and reach broadly

for intervention." Malinowski, *Frankenstein's Grave*, *supra* note 1, at 654. *See also* Malinowski, *Popping*, *supra* note 76, at 1085.

433 BRAWLEY, HARM, *supra* note 71, at 280–81.

434 *See* ABRAMSON, OVERDOSED, *supra* note 1, at 125–26. For discussion of the Trump Administration's efforts to force disclosure of pharmaceutical "sticker" prices, which failed judicial challenges, see *Chapter 3*, *supra*, at notes 34, 67–70, 103–04, and accompanying text (addressing the Trump Administration's Blueprint and Price Rule to lower Rx prices).

435 BRAWLEY, HARM, *supra* note 71, at 87. Defenders of the biopharma pricing reference the enormous cost, risk, and failure rate associated with their R&D. *See generally* CBO, R&D, *supra* note 229. Others, including Dr. Rosenthal, reject this argument:

> [Some] accept the drugmakers' argument that they have to charge twice as much for prescriptions as any other country because lawmakers in nations like Germany and France don't pay them enough to recoup their research costs. But would anyone accept that argument if we replaced the word prescriptions with cars or films? The US is distinguishable in the amount of federal taxpayer dollars we invest in science research and the extent to which we give resulting invention away to industry use through our aggressive technology transfer law and policy.

ROSENTHAL, AMERICAN SICKNESS, *supra* note 43, at 1.

436 Dr. Abramson has proposed that "restoring the integrity of medical science is the best way to finance universal health care and still save hundreds of billions of dollars a year." ABRAMSON, OVERDOSED, *supra* note 1, at xxii. *See also id.* at 241–60 (proposed approach for health care reform).

437 ABRAMSON, OVERDOSED, *supra* note 1, at xiv. *See also supra* notes 257–58, 280–88, 354–67, and accompanying text (discussing Vioxx and cholesterol-lowering drugs).

438 ABRAMSON, OVERDOSED, *supra* note 1, at 15–17.

439 *See generally* Mahnum Shahzad, Huseyin Naci, Anita Wagner, *Estimated Medicare Spending on Cancer Drug Indications With a Confirmed Lack of Clinical Benefit After US Food and Drug Administration Accelerated Approval*, 181(12) JAMA INTERN MED. 1673–75 (2021), https://pubmed.ncbi.nlm.nih.gov/34661616/. *See* Brian Dunleavy, *Study: Medicare Spends Millions on Cancer Treatments Without Clinical Benefit*, UPI: HEALTHNEWS (Oct. 18, 2021), www.upi.com/Health_News/2021/10/18/cancer-drugs-spending-study/1431634568554/. *See also supra* note 102 (addressing over reliance on surrogate endpoints in oncology).

440 *See generally* Shahzad, *Medicare Spending*, supra note 439; Dunleavy, *Without Clinical Benefit*, *supra* note 439.

441 *See* Roberts, *Debating the Path*, *supra* note 426, at 36.

442 "The coronavirus pandemic stripped an estimated 5.4 million American workers of their health insurance between February and May, a stretch in which more adults became uninsured because of job losses than have ever lost coverage in a single year, according to a new analysis." Sheryl Gay Stolberg, *A Record 5.4 Million Americans Have Lost Health Insurance, Study Finds*, N.Y. TIMES SERV. (July 14, 2020), www.boston.com/news/health/2020/07/14/millions-have-lost-health-insurance-in-pandemic-driven-recession.

443 *See supra* notes 86–96, and accompanying text (addressing US COVID-19 vaccine hesitancy). *See generally* Nick Tate, *Vaccine Holdouts Embrace COVID Antibody Treatment, Mystifying Doctors*, WEBMD (Oct. 4, 2021), www.webmd.com/lung/news/20211004/vaccine-holdouts-embrace-covid-antibody-treatment.

444 *See generally Chapter 1*, *supra*.

445 ABRAMSON, OVERDOSED, *supra* note 1, at xviii. *See also supra* note 429, and accompanying text (addressing Dr. Rosenthal's similar conclusion). *See also* ROSENTHAL, AMERICAN SICKNESS, *supra* note 43, at 3.

6

A Warning Label for Direct-to-Consumer/DTC Genetics and Genomics

The US established the medical profession as its trusted gatekeeper of patient access to prescription ("Rx") medicines and clinical testing in the twentieth century, and made clinical medicine the medical profession's domain.[1] Learned and licensed physicians were granted the privileges of writing prescriptions and ordering clinical tests within the scope of their discretion to practice medicine, and US law limited the practice of medicine to them and other learned and credentialed medical professionals.[2] The involvement of licensed physicians as a prerequisite for patient use of Rx products provided assurances of good medicine and consumer protection – to patients, to a medical profession dedicated to evidentiary science-based clinical practice, and to the Food and Drug Administration/FDA.[3] Congress, with American Medical Association/AMA support, charged the FDA with regulatory authority to ensure the safety and efficacy of the Rx medicines and medical devices available on the US market.[4] Congress, the medical profession, and the FDA also limited industry communication about Rx products to the medical profession until the mid-1980s.[5]

The three companies that introduced DTC BRCA genetic testing in 1996 required physician involvement – at minimum, a physician referral – for consumers to access their services.[6] The first, OncorMed, Inc., required customers to have physicians order genetic testing for them, and required physicians ordering the tests to adhere to a thorough and thoughtful protocol the company developed through an independent institutional review board/IRB.[7] Throughout the advancement of genetics and genomics (gene function in the context of an organism's whole genome) in the 1990s into this millennium, the US relied heavily on physicians and board-certified genetic counselors/CGCs to integrate an expanding portfolio of genetic testing, both diagnostic and predictive, into clinical care in accordance with sound science and evidence-based medicine.[8]

DTC genetic health risk/DTCGHR testing services reached the US market in 2007 with media attention and popular culture celebration.[9] *Time* magazine awarded 23andMe the "2008 Invention of the Year" for offering consumers identification of genetic "predispositions for more than 90 traits and conditions ranging from baldness to blindness."[10] The genetic tests 23andMe used to provide these services did not meet established clinical science standards and the company offered consumers direct access to them without medical professional involvement.

The US medical profession responded to the market introduction of DTCGHR testing, though with concern rather than celebration. In 2008, preeminent members of the medical profession co-authored an editorial in *The New England Journal of Medicine/NEJM*, the oldest continuously published, peer-reviewed medical journal and arguably the most prestigious. The authors entitled their editorial "Letting the Genome out of the Bottle – Will We Get Our Wish?"[11] They warned against what they deemed "recreational genetics": "[S]uch premature attempts at popularizing genetic testing seem to neglect key aspects of the established evaluation of genetic tests for clinical applications."[12] Many of the delivery-of-care good medicine concerns these renowned medical profession influencers raised echoed those voiced by other medical professionals, esteemed scientists, bioethicists, and patient advocates in response to the DTC BRCA testing introduced in 1996, which inspired forty-four states to enact genetics legislation by 1999.[13] In 2000, a Secretary's Advisory Committee on Genetic Testing/SACGT, after thoroughly gathering and deliberating expansive, varied stakeholder input, issued recommendations that thoughtfully addressed the delivery-of-care complexities, challenges, and risks of *clinically sound* genetic testing in a report with recommendations to introduce reliable regulatory oversight of medical genetic testing available on the US market.[14]

The science and delivery-of-care complexities of genetics actually had stirred a "quiet revolution" in US medicine a quarter-century before the DTC BRCA testing was introduced in 1996 – and a decade before the US introduced technology transfer law and policy/TTLP in 1980 and incentivized a biotechnology revolution.[15] Sarah Lawrence College established the nation's first master's degree genetic counseling program in 1969, and the National Society of Genetic Counselors/NSGC was founded in 1979.[16] Development of the genetic counseling discipline, recognition of a genetic counseling profession, and uptake of genetic counseling in clinical care beginning in the early 1970s may have been a quiet revolution, but it was visionary, transitional for medicine, and invaluable for the personal genome future of medicine. By 1973, the year the US Supreme Court decided *Roe v. Wade* and checked state law barriers to women's access to abortion medical procedures, several major US universities had introduced additional master's level genetic counseling programs: the University of Denver (1971), the University of Pittsburgh (1971), Rutgers University (1972), the University of California at Berkeley (1973), and the University of California at Irvine (1973).[17]

These programs modeled "genetic counselor" as a medical social worker – the epiphany of Sheldon C. Reed, a renowned American biologist and geneticist, who coined the term "genetic counseling" and advocated for its use in patient care.[18] Professor Reed conceptualized this medical social worker approach to genetic counseling in his 1955 book *Counseling in Human Genetics*.[19] Melissa Richter, the Dean of Graduate Studies at Sarah Lawrence who founded the institution's genetic counseling program, was observant, pragmatic, and visionary regarding the nexus between the ongoing advancement of genetic science and patient care. As she stated in 1971, "Researchers are making new breakthroughs in genetics all the time … but there is nobody to pass these services on to patients. There is a tremendous gap at this point between knowledge and service."[20] Ms. Richter founded her program when the practice of medicine was extremely paternalistic and directive, and when complex genetic testing in the delivery of clinical care was limited to geneticists with MDs or PhDs.[21] Her "objective was to bridge that gap by training smart and caring women who could communicate effectively with patients …"[22]

These early genetic counseling programs were introduced on a legacy of an internationally influential, multidisciplinary US eugenics movement that supported forced sterilization, which was used by the Third Reich to legitimize "Nazi medicine" genocide.[23] Their establishment also "coincided with an extraordinary convergence of phenomena, including second-wave feminism, the decriminalization of abortion, discoveries in medical genetics, the expansion of prenatal services and genetic testing, and changing attitudes toward the patient-physician relationship."[24] Responsive to these influences, the programs instilled appreciation that "the most appropriate way to look at medical genetics was not as large-scale disease prevention but as 'patient care, regardless of its evolutionary effects.'"[25]

The genetic counseling profession developed "nondirectiveness" methodology to guide clinical practice:

> Nondirectiveness is generally understood to mean refraining from providing recommendations or advice to patients, in an effort to provide value-neutral counseling. The original ethical justification for practicing nondirectively was to respect individual patient autonomy. This ethos grew out of a general respect for persons, particularly concerning abortion and disability rights.[26]

Nondirectiveness methodology continues to dominate the genetic counseling discipline. However, the genetic counseling profession is wrestling with and evolving to absorb the impact of human genome science, which the US National Academies of Science, Engineering, and Medicine/NASEM recently surveyed (NASEM issued its findings in a 2017 report), and which The Pew Charitable Trusts recently surveyed with a focus on lab-developed genetic tests/LDTs, including in vitro (noninvasive) diagnostic tests/IVDs that use saliva, blood, and other human biological samples.[27]

Notably, CGCs have been utilized foremost in prenatal care since the profession was recognized in the 1970s, and US prenatal care now is being inundated with use of noninvasive prenatal tests/NIPTs, IVDs run on fetal cells plucked from a few vials of maternal blood – the reliability of which has been called into question.[28] Also, physicians have been drawing CGCs into primary care, family practice, and other areas of medicine increasingly over the last few decades. This trend is likely to increase substantially both to be responsive to more expansive personal genome testing that satisfies clinical standards and to provide responsiveness to patients who bring their

DTC personal genome testing reports to clinical consultations – and perhaps their entire personal genome sequences. In fact, at the 2022 National Society of Genetic Counselors/NSGC Annual Meeting, analysis was presented to suggest whole genome sequencing as first-tier testing for children with suspected genetic disorders and to help diagnose and change clinical management of adult patients with rare diseases.[29] The NSGC recognizes that clinical responsiveness to expansive DTC personal genome testing is a necessary reality. As recently relayed in a *Perspectives* contribution on the NSGC internet site,

> Direct-to-consumer genetic testing (DTC-GT) seems to be a blemish on our practice that just won't go away. Despite attempts to pop, squeeze, and extract the blemish, it is here to stay. As such, the National Society of Genetic Counselors and the American Society of Human Genetics recommend that counseling be offered to consumers of DTC-GT to aid in the interpretation of DTC-GT results.[30]

CGCs are the medical professionals arguably most educated, trained, experienced, and competent to work through the incoming tsunami of DTC personal genome testing in an emerging genomics medicine era.[31] Primary care and family practice physicians without CGCs' specialized education, training, and experience implementing the genetic counseling discipline's medical social worker model also face these challenges, and on a scale spanning the human genome.[32]

Many of the clinical "good medicine" concerns about recreational genetics raised in "Letting the Genome out of the Bottle" were familiar—dating back to the 1996 DTC BRCA testing controversy. However, they were heightened in 2007–2008 by an ongoing and escalating genomic revolution and a US patient self-determination movement charged by information and communication technology/ICT, social media culture, patient suspicion raised by the cost and commercialization of medicine, and patient dissatisfaction with the quality of clinical care.[33] The editorial authors were responding to the tangible beginning of a US medicine future in which patient–consumers demand and have direct access to a swelling, swirling, and dizzying ocean of myriad genetic tests with uncertain clinical validity and utility – the personal genome medicine/PGM era that has just begun.[34] Already, 23andMe has evolved into 23andMe Holding Co., is listed on the NASDAQ stock exchange, and is reaching directly into the clinical practice of medicine through its purchase of Lemonaid Health—a national telemedicine and digital pharmacy company.[35] A DTC personal genome health testing sector has emerged.[36]

Moreover, the US has entered an era of "do-it-yourself biology"/DIY-Bio, also referred to as "biohacking," through increasingly efficient, affordable, and consumer-accessible genome editing technologies – most notably the CRISPR platform of gene editing technologies.[37] The advent of publicly known human germline genetic engineering in reproduction through CRISPR occurred years ago. In November 2018, Chinese scientist He Jiankui announced the birth of twin girls whose genomes were modified using CRISPR technology.[38] "The news of so-called 'CRISPR-babies' prompted a wave of foreboding news headlines and calls for a moratorium on germline editing."[39] Although professionally taboo, the use of CRISPR in human reproduction is "out of the bottle" and the technology is advancing explosively with a cornucopia of potential applications.[40]

The following discussion begins by addressing the complexities of personal genome decision-making with focus on consumer comprehension and medical professional interpretation of personal genome testing. Next, the discussion assesses the impact of consumer genetics, most notably DTCGHR testing, on the US health care system and the risks of muddling patient and physician decision-making, impeding health care, and wasting limited health care resources. SACGT recognized and explained the delivery-of-care complexity of *clinically sound* genetic testing in 2000, which is exacerbated by genetic testing that is not clinically sound and accessible to the public without the involvement of learned, licensed medical professionals.[41]

The discussion then focuses on some paramount ethical, legal, and social implications raised by consumer genetics and genomics. The US' Ethical Legal and Social Implications Research Program/ELSI, which was launched in 1989 to accompany the Human Genome Project/HGP launched in 1990, anticipated and addressed myriad issues regarding genetic testing and resulting information.[42] HGP's founders recognized that genetics is pervasive, powerful, and societal. Today's personal genome consumer reality has made concerns about privacy and associated risks, informed consent and commercialization, and sharing research findings with research participants pressing issues in real time. These issues impact the present and will impact the future of medical science research and the practice of medicine.

THE COMPLEXITIES OF PERSONAL GENOME MEDICAL DECISION-MAKING

US physicians' twentieth-century monopoly on writing prescriptions for medicines and ordering clinical tests has been weakened considerably over the last few decades by states granting some of these privileges to other medical professionals:

> Prescription privileges for non-MD subspecialties have become increasingly common. For example, the Washington State Department of Health (WSDH) lists the following nonphysician professions as having restricted or unrestricted prescriptive authority in the State: Advanced Registered Nurse Practitioners (ARNPs), Physician Assistants (PAs), Certified Registered Nurse Anesthetists (CRNAs), Dentists (DMDs), Naturopathic Doctors (NDs), and Optometrists (ODs).[43]

Also, the FDA has been allowing consumers more direct access to both medications and medical testing. The agency has made in-home testing for pregnancy, HIV, and other medical conditions directly available to consumers for some time.[44] In-home testing for HIV, pregnancy, and other conditions is typically for one health condition and at least meaningfully definitive and reliable.

Genetics, genomics, and proteomics (protein function—proteins turn genes on and off, and genes make proteins—in the context of a complete set of proteins in an organism's genome at a given time, known as a proteome) have introduced expansive DTC *at-home* testing options. This testing is at-home rather than in-home because the testing is performed in a lab, with consumer sample collection through the mail and consumer communication online. Typically, in comparison with FDA approved in-home testing for specific medical conditions, a single at-home self-test purchase offers testing for multiple health associations at marginal cost increases, the tests do not meet FDA diagnostic device standards, do not meet established clinical evidentiary-science standards for validity and utility, and results are not clinically definitive. For example, LetsGetChecked offers an expansive testing portfolio that ranges from general wellness to an "Ovarian Reserve Test … to indicate the number of eggs a woman has left, with online results in 5 days."[45] According to another company, Everlywell, "We make lab tests easy with 30+ at-home kits – from fertility to food sensitivity tests – ordered by you. Our tests offer simple sample collection, free shipping, and physician-reviewed results and insights sent to your device in just days."[46] EveryWell's portfolio of testing options (as of June 2021) includes (as self-labeled by the company): General Wellness Test, Food Sensitivity Test, Heavy Metals Test, Sleep and Stress Test, Cholesterol and Lipids Test, Heart Health Test, HbA1c Test, Omega-3 Basic Test, Omega-3 Plus Test, B Vitamins Test, Folic Acid Test, Lyme Disease Test, Testosterone Test, Men's Health Test, Breast Milk DHA Test, Women's Health Test, Ovarian Reserve Test, Postmenopause Test, Women's Fertility Test, Perimenopause Test, HPV Test–Female, Energy + Weight Test, Thyroid Test, Metabolism Test, Vitamin D and Inflammation Test, Vitamin D Test, Sexual Health Test, STD Test–Male, STD Test–Female, Chlamydia and Gonorrhea Test, Hepatitis C Test, and an HIV Test.[47]

DTC at-home longevity testing, also referred to as "all-cause mortality" testing, has proven extremely appealing to major investors. For example, "A team led by researchers at Amgen subsidiary [deCODE] Genetics [has] used proteomic measurements to develop predictors for short- and long-term risk of all-cause mortality."[48] On June 21, 2022, Human Longevity, a San Diego-based company founded in 2013 by Craig Venter–the former CEO of Celera, HGP's commercial competitor in the race to sequence the human genome–announced a pending $345 million merger to enable the company to go public and to create a combined company valued at approximately $1 billion.[49] Human Longevity, which sells memberships to individuals, self-proclaims to be "the global leader in advancing the Human Longevity Care movement, on a mission to discover and harness the technological and biological unlocks that amplify span of life, health, & high-performance."[50] The company raised $80 million in a Series A financing (the first round of financing after "seed" or start-up funding) in 2014; $220 million in a Series B (second round) financing in 2016 from Illumina, Celgene, GE Ventures, and others; and an additional $30 million in 2019.[51]

In-home at at-home medical testing is a deviation from last-century's consumer and quality-of-care assurance through the traditional involvement and oversight of licensed medical professionals in decisions to undergo medical testing, the selection of which tests to use, and clinical uptake of results. That assurance is introduced later if patients act on the results of in-home and at-home testing by seeking responsive clinical care from medical professionals. To make the regulatory leap in allowing 23andMe's DTCGHR testing services onto the market, the FDA imposed requirements: a disclaimer against clinical use without the involvement of medical professionals and assurance of consumer comprehension. Specifically, the FDA required 23andMe to create a mechanism to accomplish consumer comprehension in its Personal Genome Health Service/PGHS transactions with clients, and to submit data to the FDA to substantiate that sufficient comprehension is reliably achievable in the general population.[52]

The intrinsic public and commercial appeal of DTCGHR and other DTC personal genome testing services is the tangible reality of the medical diseases, health conditions, and health risks they are associated with. Companies that sell DTC personal genome testing services will realize greater consumer demand when they offer testing for health risks associated with diseases, conditions, and wellness traits that the public recognizes and cares about – and more when it fears them. 23andMe's seminal PGHS testing menu included Alzheimer's disease and Parkinson's disease – diseases readily recognized as seriously debilitating and life-threatening. However, these tests do not meet clinical evidentiary-science standards for validity and utility in the general population; they are not clinically definitive for these diseases – if clinically relevant at all for an individual.

In sum, beyond curiosity about one's genetic self and concern about one's overall health, people respond to DTC advertising for personal genome testing services, purchase them, and take them to learn whether they have genetic predispositions for diseases and health conditions they recognize, related to, and at times fear. This is especially so if a testing portfolio includes diseases and health conditions in their family histories and life experiences. 23andMe's commercial success indicates that a lot of people are curious, concerned about their health, or both.[53] The existence of a strong commercial personal genome testing sector echoes the same: "Already in 2018 the global genetic testing and consumer/wellness genomics market was valued at $3.4 billion, with market analysts in 2019 predicting that it will double in value by 2025."[54]

The core contribution of genomics to medicine and human health is understanding at the molecular level that enables science and evidence-based precision medicine (treatments tailored to a person's genome) and personalized medicine (treatments derived from a person's genome) – both utilized in personal genome medicine.[55] While knowledge about genetics has amassed beyond many of the most generous estimates in the early 1990s, the number of genes in the human genome has remained constant. The progress of genomics has just adjusted that number with evidentiary-science accuracy and adjusted perspective about gene interactions and complexity. The enormous observable (phenotypic) variation among individuals also has remained essentially the same. Therefore, although completion of a draft map of the human genome sequence in 2003 was an extraordinary science accomplishment, a proof of principle for the capability of genomic science, the map itself was humbling. Scientists and health care providers realized that a mere 20,500 or so active genes combined with environmental influences are responsible for all readily observable human diversity.[56]

Genes and proteins multitask exponentially more than was anticipated at the outset of HGP, and translating the genome into medical meaning is a dimension, if not dimensions, more complicated.[57] There are relatively few genetic levers, such as the single-gene variations (alleles) responsible for Huntington's disease, Sickle cell disease, and Tay–Sachs disease – Mendelian traits rather than genetic associations with common diseases.[58] Environmental influences matter immensely in an individual's health, and especially over time.[59] "[T]aken together, the relations of genes, organisms, and environments are reciprocal relations in which all three elements are both causes and effects."[60] Even when genes are not identified as decisively causing or otherwise highly influential in causing an individual's particular health condition, genes are ever present and involved, and with the potential to impact an individual's health responsiveness to biopharmaceuticals and biologics, to lifestyle changes, and to other environmental exposures.[61]

The expanding DTC personal genome testing universe already is an extraordinarily varied, dynamic, and rapidly burgeoning blizzard of testing capabilities, which overall are far less definitive and tangible than traditional medical testing – for both patients and other medical professionals. DTC genetic, genomic, and proteomic tests are distinguishable clinically from other categories of medical device diagnostic tests due to the data inconsistencies among them, variation among the genetic influences and health conditions they are associated with, and ambiguity in the information they relay. Most predictive personal genome tests, including those developed to meet FDA clinical use standards, assess susceptibility to medical conditions and the probability of disease onset without definitive precision in the general population – family history and other patient-specific factors matter immensely – and without the capacity to discern the severity of disease.[62]

Consider that "In vitro diagnostic (IVD) tests – which use blood, saliva, and other human samples to detect the presence or risk of certain diseases – are a pillar of modern medicine. Doctors and patients rely on them to guide life-or-death medical decisions, from choosing a cancer treatment to managing a pregnancy."[63] Most recently, IVDs have been invaluable for responsiveness to the COVID-19 pandemic. If these tests are created and used in the same facility, referred to as lab-developed tests/LDTs or "home brew" tests, the Centers for Medicare and Medicaid services/CMS regulates the laboratories performing them under the Clinical Laboratory Improvement Amendments/CLIA.[64] CLIA regulates proficiency – not clinical usefulness.[65] Physicians and other medical professionals are relied on to assure clinical usefulness when they practice sound science and evidence-based medicine. According to an impressive, timely (2021) report by The Pew Charitable Trusts, LDTs frequently are not reviewed by the FDA for safety and efficacy and, "because LDTs are not centrally registered or tracked, no one knows precisely how many of them are on the market, when and why they are used, or how their performance compares with FDA-reviewed diagnostics."[66]

The New York Times recently investigated a category of IVDs, noninvasive prenatal tests/NIPTs, which are run on fetal cells gleaned from a few vials of maternal blood.[67] NIPTs are widely used in pregnancies to detect small missing pieces of chromosomes, called microdeletions, which are associated with rare but potentially severe health conditions. The availability, variety, and use of NIPTs have surged in US prenatal care:

> In just over a decade, the tests have gone from laboratory experiments to an industry that serves more than a third of the pregnant women in America, luring major companies like Labcorp and Quest Diagnostics into the business, alongside many start-ups.
>
> The tests initially looked for Down syndrome and worked very well. But as manufacturers tried to outsell each other, they began offering additional screenings for increasingly rare conditions.[68]

The *Times* investigation analysis of newer NIPTs concluded "that positive results on those tests are incorrect about 85 percent of the time."[69] The investigation reporting suggests that even specialized (medical board certified) physician involvement is not a reliable assurance of good medicine use of NIPTs in the delivery of prenatal care. According to the *Times*:

- "Experts say there is no single threshold for how often a test needs to get positive results right to be worth offering."[70]
- "[T]here are hundreds of microdeletion syndromes, and the most expansive tests look for between five and seven, meaning women shouldn't take a negative result as proof their baby doesn't have a genetic disorder. For patients who are especially worried, obstetricians who study these screenings currently recommend other types of testing, which come with a small risk of miscarriage but are more reliable."[71]
- "Patients who receive a positive result are supposed to pursue follow-up testing, which often requires a drawing of amniotic fluid or a sample of placental tissue. Those tests can cost thousands of dollars, come with a small risk of miscarriage and can't be performed until later in pregnancy – in some states, past the point where abortions are legal."[72]
- "A 2014 study found that 6 percent of patients who screened positive obtained an abortion without getting another test to confirm the result."[73]
- "As companies began looking for ways to differentiate their products, many decided to start screening for more and rarer disorders. All the screenings

could run on the same blood draw, and doctors already order many tests during short prenatal care visits, meaning some probably thought little of tacking on a few more."[74]

- "For the testing company, however, adding microdeletions can double what an insurer pays – from an average of $695 for the basic tests to $1,349 for the expanded panel, according to the health data company Concert Genetics. (Patients whose insurance didn't fully cover the tests describe being billed wildly different figures, ranging from a few hundred to thousands of dollars.)."[75]

State legislative activity to restrict and even ban abortion procedures in response to the Supreme Court decision in *Dobbs v. Jackson Women's Health Org.*, including laws enacted with provisions that impose criminal and other liability on medical providers, will have a profound impact on women in some states – on their access to prenatal testing, and on those who undergo NIPTs and other prenatal testing and receive positive test results.[76]

The completed map of the human genome sequence – the molecular underlay and common denominator for the overall human condition – has drawn a global science research effort to translate the human genome sequence into medical meaning.[77] Personal genome testing must be placed in the context of the complexity and intense dynamism of ongoing global science research and data collection to develop clinical definitiveness for the general population.[78] In sum, the intricacies of genetics, genomics, and proteomics make for extraordinarily complicated medical science, entangled in probabilities and possibilities and subject to the dynamism of expansive, ongoing research across the human genome – biomedical science that, given its reach into human health, is just coming into being in responsible, evidentiary science-based clinical practice.[79]

Human genome science imposes a tremendous burden on clinicians to size up each personal genome test from an academic research perspective removed from the familiar reliability of traditional science and evidence-based medicine.[80] This challenge is exacerbated by inconsistencies among the personal genome tests available and their commercial manufacturers – all in the context of the ongoing, dynamic state of genomics-based medicine. The burden on clinicians to then communicate (translate) bundles of personal genome test results effectively (achieve comprehension) to individual patients who themselves are not learned in biomedical science and medicine is daunting.[81] These health care provider–patient exchanges require individual test specificity and individual patient focus. Imagine the potential burden imposed on physicians when patients present them with their entire personal genome sequence.

According to James Watson, the chief architect of HGP, clinical uptake of whole-genome sequencing is destined: "I think it is inevitable that clinicians will embrace whole-genome sequencing over time, although there are many issues to be confronted, from maintaining IT systems to securing insurance reimbursement to overhauling how modern genetics is taught to medical students."[82] Given the advancement of genomics since completion of HGP in 2003, Mr. Watson and Ms. Wojcicki, co-founder and CEO of 23andMe, appear to be right. DNA sequencing technology already makes whole personal genome sequencing, reliable through multiple runs, possible at a price point feasible for many consumers.[83] Over an undefined stretch of time, and absent some major changes in law-policy, whole-genome sequencing will become cost-effective, accessible, and desirable enough for most patients in the US health care system to obtain their personal genome sequence. When whole genome sequences are accompanied by enough ("critical mass") genomic data that *meets established clinical evidentiary-science standards*, personal genome medicine/PGM will elevate the delivery of care for the general population on an ongoing basis. Whole-genome sequences will need to be revisited in conjunction with ongoing data compilation. Some medical centers with the requisite capabilities already are demonstrating the potential to diagnose "mystery" diseases. "No center has studied more patients' genomes than Baylor College of Medicine in Houston. Christine Eng and colleagues sequenced the DNA of two thousand patients, reaching a positive diagnosis in 25 percent of cases. Similar success rates are observed by most other medical centers...."[84]

Although broad clinical uptake of whole genome sequencing is inevitable, as Mr. Watson and Ms. Wojcicki suggest, it is crucial for the evidentiary-science base of US medicine, for those practicing it and for patients depending on it, that the "meets established clinical standards" variable is satisfied for personal genome testing categorically and with reliability before that milestone is realized. Each individual GHR test determines the presence or absence of a specific allele (genetic variant) or alleles associated with an identified health-related risk or characteristic. There is significant variation among the tests bundled and packaged for purchase in any GHR testing service, such as 23andMe's PGHS. The portfolio of genetic testing capabilities is even more varied and complicated than the genetics and health risks they test for due to variations in the underlying data and how it is compiled, processed, and presented to substantiate each test. Genetic tests for different alleles, or different sets of alleles, associated with the same disease or health condition are intrinsically confusing for the general public, and there already are lots of those on the market.[85] Consider the testing options complexity for BRCA testing in fall 2019, even though enough data had been gathered to develop BRCA testing that meets clinical evidentiary-science standards:

> One big question for patients will be whether they should be getting a different test than the one they choose. For patients who want a BRCA1 or BRCA2 test because they had a family history of breast cancer, the AncestryCore test will only tell them if there is a common "misspelling" in the gene—meaning that many mutations that could cause cancer would be missed. The new AncestryPlus test would be more likely to pick up a problem if it exists. But the patient might be better off with a medical test like the ones made by Myriad Genetics (MYGN) or Color Genomics, which might also be covered by insurance. One of the biggest risks,

experts said, is that patients will wrongly think they are at low risk because of an incomplete genetic test.

"The risk, as with the other consumer genomics, is that patients will think this is somehow a comprehensive and encyclopedic investigation of your entire genomic health," said [Dr. Robert] Green, of the Brigham [and Women's Hospital, Boston, MA]. But he argued: "Discovering some people who are carrying significant and actionable mutations is better than finding none of them."[86]

Proteomic testing generally is at least as clinically complicated as genetic testing, and often more so given its innate level of precision and intricacy in disease pathways and health expression.

First, each test is reflective only of the data it is based upon – meaning the scope and demographics of populations from which the samples were drawn, the information gathered from each subject in each population (each subject's medical profile, family history, lifestyle, and so on), how the data are collected, processed, compiled, analyzed, and presented, and the accuracy and reliability of all of the preceeding.[87] The data and whom they are collected from in relation to the general population varies significantly from test to test and condition to condition, and it is subject to change with ongoing data collection and research.[88] Second, beyond the underlying data, most genetics is about probabilities, possibilities, and variations in human health expression – uncertainties about disease expression and severity. These allele-health associations are deductions derived to establish scientifically sound probabilities, referred to as positive predictive values/PPVs and negative predictive values/NPVs, to establish their clinical validity and utility – the base for interpreting their clinical meaning.[89] In simplest terms, PPV is the probability that subjects with a positive screening test truly have or will get the disease or condition associated. Conversely, NPV is the probability that subjects with a negative screening test truly do not have or will not get the disease or condition associated. When focused on and fully analyzed, the clinical validity and utility of a number of market-available genetic tests, especially for complex traits, have been evaluated and questioned by clinicians with specificity.[90]

Allele associations vary in levels of influence on the conditions they correlate with. Typically, multiple variables impact whether an associated condition materializes and its severity, including a patient's medical profile and family history, environmental exposures, lifestyle choices, and the presence of additional genetic variants – whether presently identified or not. Given the scope of identified and potential variables and the ultimate challenge of application in the life of any individual, clinical interpretation by competent medical professionals is necessary to translate – to clinically assess and interpret each specific test result in the life of each test taker into scientifically sound medical meaning.[91] The responsible medical professional then must achieve patient comprehension and people are often seemingly as complicated interpersonally as their personal genomes. 23andMe and its commercial peers offer consumers portfolios of tests and result bundles with each purchase. The medical meaning of personal genome test results is especially susceptible to misinterpretation when delivered collectively given the variations among tests, genetic influences, associated health conditions, and patient individuality.[92]

A physician's clinical interpretation ability and decisiveness is likely to vary considerably among specific test results depending upon their genomic science acumen, their medical knowledge, their practice areas in relation to the testing, their familiarity with each test, the tests themselves (for example, their established PPV and NPV), the genetic influences tested for, and the associated health conditions – again, all subject to the dynamism of ongoing genomic research and medical science.[93] The GHR information a consumer decides to bring to their physician today may not be scientifically accurate when they and their health care provider attempt to interpret projecting into the future – again, given the ongoing accumulation of data.

The DTCGHR testing 23andMe makes available to consumers does not meet the milestone of general population data that satisfies evidentiary-science clinical standards for each allele tested for, which the company addresses by emphasizing the limits of its testing and clinical use disclaimers. According to the regulatory model established by the FDA and 23andMe, DTCGHR testing service providers must make information available to consumers through the company's internet portal in a tiered (from simplistic to scientific) manner, and consumers must demonstrate a threshold of comprehension about GHR testing prior to use.[94] Arguably, the 23andMe comprehension prerequisite for use, deemed reliably sufficient for the public by the FDA, could be readily satisfied by a middle school student with average intelligence.[95] Consumers are directed to physicians and other medical providers for clinical interpretation and use of their GHR results.[96]

On October 22, 2021, 23andMe announced that it was acquiring Lemonaid Health, a national telemedicine and digital pharmacy company, to overcome client-reported medical profession skepticism and uncertainty about its PGHS reports.[97] The transaction was completed on November 1, 2021, and 23andMe has modified its business plan objectives from DTCGHR personal genome service provider and biopharma R&D company to becoming a full DTC genomic *clinical* service provider.[98] Yes, the genome is out of the bottle and blurring the boundaries of evidentiary science-based US medicine.

US HEALTH CARE SYSTEM AND CONSUMER GENETICS AND GENOMICS MARKET ISSUES

Commercial success draws investors and competitors in the US' highly privatized health care market. 23andMe's business and regulatory successes have been commercially inspirational.[99] "Today, hundreds of companies offer a wide range of genetic testing services directly to consumers without the involvement of a health care provider."[100] Many millions of people already have become DTC personal genome testing consumers, whether for ancestry, health, or both.[101] The cost of genetic sequencing continues to drop, while personal genome testing capabilities soar.[102] US DTC biopharma marketing norms, patient self-determination and autonomy norms in US health care, and the social and cultural familiarity of DNA beckon DTC personal genome testing sector growth.[103]

The current US law-policy environment for DTC personal genome testing is heavy reliance on industry self-regulation with questionable enforcement and impact.[104] The FDA and 23andMe have established a regulatory fast lane to market for DTCGHR testing services *if* providers submit applications to the FDA.[105] Offering testing services with tests performed in a company's own laboratory facility (lab-developed tests/LDTs) that meets CLIA proficiency-centered regulations skirts mandatory FDA regulatory review for clinical safety and efficacy.[106] Medical profession use in the delivery of care, within the clinical practice domain entrusted to the oversight of the medical profession, dissuades FDA intrusion under US law and policy.[107] The Centers for Medicare and Medicaid Services/CMS outsources considerable CLIA certification authority to professional organizations and some state authorities, which decentralizes the CLIA regulation endeavor and market oversight over personal genome testing technologies.[108]

In the early 1990s, when the US had a fraction of the CLIA-certified laboratories it has today, some academic researchers would run patient samples as a courtesy to medical providers they trusted.[109] Today's abundance of CLIA-certified laboratories provides clinical use access, but not with regulatory reliability. The conclusiveness and effectiveness of CLIA enforcement over the entire US market are highly questionable given the number of CLIA-certified labs and the limitations of regulatory enforcement resources, the progress of human genome science, and the ease and cost-effectiveness of running personal genome tests. Genetic testing that escapes both the CMS' CLIA regulations and FDA oversight of diagnostic devices is possible and probable at times – such as in prenatal care.[110] The National Human Genome Research Institute/NHGRI recognized in 2022 that, "As the field of genomics advances, genetic and genomic tests are becoming more common in, and out of, the clinic. Yet most genetic tests today are not regulated, meaning that they go to market without any independent analysis to verify the claims of the seller."[111]

To consumers, more genetic information about susceptibility to more diseases and health conditions for a comparable purchase price equates with more value.[112] Consequently, commercial competition and business growth incentivize offering consumers more GHR testing for the price of their purchases.[113] Increasingly expansive personal genome testing menus with greater variety will become market available. The more testing purchased, the bigger and more varied the results to sort through, and to revisit in an ongoing manner as more data are compiled and clinical interpretations change.[114] The specificity (precision) genomics brings to medicine is contrary to the market scale and revenues realized by traditional "block-buster" pharmaceuticals.[115] The fracture of traditional disease classifications and product market scale is an added incentive for biopharma to market aggressively to achieve clinical uptake at high prices with off-label use, and to disease monger in PGM.[116] More clinical standard personal genome testing and more DTC available without meeting that standard will open a portal to another dimension of disease-mongering opportunity for biopharma:

> The UK health advocacy group GeneWatch has already [in 2005] raised concern that the biotech and pharmaceutical industry may be gearing up to promote widespread genetic testing for common diseases "because it allows them to expand the market for both genetic tests and preventive medication." This group's worry is that mass gene screening may spark a new level of inappropriate medications, as we have already seen with osteoporosis. "Because the predictive value of most genetic tests is very low, many children could end up taking medicines that they do not need," says the report.[117]

The FDA's regulatory model for DTCGHR testing theoretically offsets the absence of medical provider involvement and the absence of data sufficient to meet clinical testing standards with (1) emphasis to purchasers that the tests are for defining health risks, not for diagnoses, (2) disclaimers about the medical decisiveness of the tests, and (3) strong direction to seek medical provider input for clinical interpretation and use.[118] The FDA requires DTGHR testing service providers to explicitly warn against clinical use other than by a sufficiently learned and credentialed medical professional.[119] However, the FDA's authority when authorizing products for market use, which includes control over label content, product insert requirements, and the imposition of special conditions, has limited reach into provider discretion to practice medicine.[120]

In the US privatized, free-market, patient/consumer-driven health care system, the DTCGHR information individuals purchase is theirs to act upon and to use to pressure health care providers. Just as US physicians routinely stray from labels and product inserts to engage in substantial off-label use, many layperson consumers of GHR reports are likely to disregard comprehension mechanisms and special controls—perhaps ignore them as readily as the generally expansive and often serious (frequently life-threatening) adverse event warnings narrated during captivating biopharma Rx television commercials. They risk arriving at false assurances and acting on those to their health care detriment.[121] Patients may act on false positives, as has been documented with prenatal testing.[122] Although warned not to, patients may, inspired by the genetic, genomic, and proteomic science-based information, stray from existing doctor orders – including how and whether they take the medications prescribed to them.[123] Many will be inspired by their DTCGHR reports to seek out medical providers for consultations– as 23andMe cautions and advises them to do in compliance with the special conditions the FDA has required.[124] DTCGHR consumers, especially if they interpret one or more of their test results as a reason for concern, will bring their reports, amalgamations of GHR test results, to their physicians and ask them to provide learned medical interpretation. Patients will expect their physicians to be responsive, and with clinical accuracy and decisiveness.[125] Those with health insurance are likely to pressure physicians for follow-on testing, clinical examinations, and prescriptions – perhaps for medications they have become aware of through television advertisements and other DTC biopharma marketing.[126] In the litigious US, medical providers practice defensive medicine; they are sensitive to the very real possibility of legal liability. When patients present them with DTCGHR testing results and their personal genome sequences, medical providers must consider the potential liability consequences of not being responsive – which are valid concerns.[127] Practicing defensive medicine in the US incentivizes more clinical testing:

> Three-fifths of doctors in the United States admit that they do more diagnostic testing than is necessary because of the threat of litigation. And why not? The risk of ordering an extra test is nil, but the threat of a lawsuit because of a test not ordered is ever present—even when the likelihood of serious disease is very low and reasonable professional judgment would say the test was not necessary.[128]

US medical training and delivery of care center on individualized patient care.[129] When there is payer coverage for health care, care often is rendered regardless of, and even without awareness of, cost.[130] Medical screening in the US "is a big business that's easy to get into because of the prejudice that screening must be beneficial."[131] Over-consultation and over-testing have become US health care norms:

> The culture today is to grab patients and generate volume.... The probability that a visit to a physician results in a referral to another physician has nearly doubled in the past ten [2005–2015] years, from 5 percent to more than 9 percent. Referral rates to specialists in the United States are estimated to be at least twice as high as in Great Britain. The rates reflect several aspects of American medicine: increasing specialization, the lack of time for any doctor to give to complex cases, and fear of lawsuits over not consulting an expert. At the same time, referrals are also a way for cash-strapped doctors to generate business.[132]

The US medical profession, recipient of genomic innovation that meets evidentiary-science clinical standards and biopharma DTP marketing, is likely more prone to be responsive to patient demands for testing delivered with human genome science:

> Ever since Louis Pasteur discovered that bacteria cause disease, doctors have been committed to the biomedical approach to medicine: the idea that the cause and cure of every symptom and every disease can, with enough research, be understood and successfully treated at its most basic biological level. Modern scientists and doctors find this idea enormously appealing—identify the biological process that has gone awry, and fix it.[133]

Medical testing often has a multiplication effect: "These extra tests can and often do set off a cascade effect, requiring even more tests to follow up on abnormal results, many of which then turn out to be normal."[134] As observed by Dr. Brawley,

"Consumers – and even many doctors – just don't understand the science and why screening can be a very bad thing. Some chose to stay uninformed. Many actually believe in screening and have no doubts – contrary to the science. Screening is like a religion to them."[135] Extensive screening programs in the US for prostate cancer,[136] breast cancer,[137] and lung cancer[138] arguably have harmed more patients than they have helped, and they certainly have been – and continue to be – costly. According to Dr. Brawley, the US medical screening culture has extended to screening for the clinically unknown: "Recently, I heard an interesting word for people diagnosed with cancers of unknown significance: previvor, as opposed to survivor. We have to accept the fact that we are harming many of these people."[139]

US physicians do not have the education, training, and experience in human genome science and genetic counseling necessary to receive an expansive increase in personal genome testing capabilities that meet FDA clinical diagnostic standards, and certainly not the patient demands likely generated by widely available DTC personal genome testing services. The educational and experiential prerequisites to practice medicine, including residencies, fellowships, and other post-graduate education, already are expansive and expensive in the US. Physician specialization has been the governing trend for decades.[140] Responsible physicians will draw more upon certified genetic counselors/CGCs. CGCs professionally trained, board-certified, and learned of evolving genetic science were in short supply at the launch of HGP in 1990.[141] An ominous deficit amassed during the 1990s with the dizzying advancement of genetics and genomics and increased appreciation and demand for sound genetic counseling in the practice of medicine.[142] Subsequently, many graduate programs have been introduced and, according to recent assessments, the CGCs supply is projected by the profession to meet demand.[143] However, these assessments are based on scientifically sound clinical genetic testing in consultation with physicians delivering responsible patient care. They do not account for the market availability of DTC personal genome testing services and the additional demands on health care providers they are likely to generate.

The genetic counseling profession has recognized DTC personal genome testing as a global health care systems problem:

> Direct-to-consumer genetic testing for disease ranges from well-validated diagnostic and predictive tests to "research" results conferring increased risks. While being targeted at public curious about their health, they are also marketed for use in reproductive decision-making or management of disease. By virtue of being "direct-to-consumer" much of this testing bypasses traditional healthcare systems. We argue that direct-to-consumer genetic testing companies should make genetic counseling available, pre as well as post-test. While we do not advocate that mandatory genetic counseling should gate-keep access to direct-to-consumer genetic testing, if the testing process has the potential to cause psychological distress, then companies have a responsibility to provide support and should not rely on traditional healthcare systems to pick up the pieces.[144]

Consider that, while 23andMe's DTCGHR testing was under a FDA cease and desist order (from 2013 until market approval in 2017), the company "opened in the United Kingdom and elsewhere subsidiaries that are not subject to FDA restrictions."[145] The UK's Medicines and Healthcare Products Regulatory Agency approved DTC genetic testing in 2014, and 23andMe's DNA kits were "openly sold by one British high street pharmacy chain."[146] Canada's single-payer universal health care system typically approves genome sequencing and testing when health care providers show that it will lead to a diagnosis and elevate the management of patient care.[147] However, according to a recent study, Canadian clinicians sometimes feel restricted by these clinical standards and seek alternatives to their health care system ("cheat the system") to obtain personal genome testing for their patients.[148]

Moreover, in the US' largely privatized health care system, health insurers frequently challenge paying for clinical genetic tests and genetic counseling by CGCs – as they have done for decades.[149] CGCs often spend time with and for patients beyond what is billable and reimbursable at the risk of burnout. "Burnout is not only more common in genetic counselors than doctors and nurses, it is the most frequent reason cited for leaving the profession."[150] Health insurers, providers, and other stakeholders throughout the US health care system share a fundamental dilemma – sorting through a constantly amassing entanglement of market available genetic tests of widely varying clinical validity and utility. The NHGRI recognized this dilemma in 2019:

> Genomic medicine has the capacity to revolutionize clinical practice. The mapping of the human genome has created new opportunities for genetic tests to predict, prevent, and treat disease. Tests for breast cancer and for hereditary forms of colorectal cancer can assess disease risk and guide screening and preventive measures. Other tests can predict optimal chemotherapy regimens or predict the likelihood of drug response or toxicities and avoid exposing patients to ineffective or overly toxic regimens.
>
> There are many other examples of clinically useful information available through newly developed genetic tests. In order for patients to have full access to the benefits of genetic testing, payers such as insurance companies and Medicare need systematic ways of evaluating genetic tests for reimbursement. Currently, there are barriers that make it difficult for payers to do so. Without this information, insurers cannot properly assess how to reimburse for genetic tests.
>
> One challenge insurers face is the difficulty of deciding when to reimburse for genetic tests that health care providers have offered their patients. The reason this is difficult is that insurers may not be able to easily evaluate what type of genetic test was performed, whether the test was appropriate to perform and whether the test is scientifically valid. This is in part because procedures are billed according to a standardized system of Current Procedural Terminology (CPT) codes developed by the American Medical Association, and fewer than 200 CPT codes exist for about 70,000 genetic tests. This means that there is no straightforward way to bill for many tests or for payers to identify what genetic tests were given.

> Moreover, payers are having trouble keeping up with the volume of new genetic and next-generation sequencing tests that are coming onto the market. Additionally, there is a lack of extensive data evaluating the economics of genetic testing. This makes it even more difficult to evaluate which tests should be covered and under what circumstances they should be covered. NHGRI hopes to serve as a resource for advancing genomic medicine by assisting all types of payers in their efforts to evaluate emerging genetic tests for reimbursement, and by promoting research into the health benefit and cost-effectiveness of genetic testing.[151]

Even James Watson, a proponent of DTC personal genome testing, was critical of premature genetic testing in 1991.[152] The ongoing firehose infusion of extensive DTC personal genome testing without established clinical validity and utility for the general population in an era of patient self-determination will exacerbate existing tensions between providers and patients, disputes with health insurers, and pressures on CGCs and physicians. It will create more medical practice dilemmas. Practicing PGM in the US without adherence to science and evidence-based clinical practice standards for personal genome testing will cause confusion when there should be more certainty and direction through human genome science, waste valuable health care resources, and muddle both the practice of medicine and patient care.

CONSUMER GENETICS AND GENOMICS ETHICAL, LEGAL, AND SOCIAL IMPLICATIONS

FDA market approval of DTCGHR testing in April 2017 renewed many concerns and criticisms addressed in the 1990s by the Ethical Legal and Social Implications Research Program/ELSI, which was launched in 1989 to complement HGP.[153] During the early to mid-1990s, when progress mapping the human genome was laboriously incremental, and consumer genetics and PGM were largely speculative, the ELSI program favored interdisciplinary, often academic approaches to concerns about individuals' rights over information derived from their DNA, informed consent, and commercial exploitation.[154] Much of the ELSI work drew heavily from regulations to protect human subjects and placed genetic testing primarily in a research law-policy context, rather than addressing genetic testing principally in a US commercial medical product regulation context.[155] When Michael Yesley, who coordinated the Department of Energy's involvement in ELSI (HGP was a joint NIH-DOE initiative), reflected on the program in 2008, he stated "ELSI has produced a large portfolio of academic and professional literature, but little impact on public policymaking."[156]

The DTC BRCA predictive genetic testing introduced to the US market in 1996 made many of the issues addressed by ELSI much more tangible, and the related debate much more pragmatic. The most illustrative example is the work of SACGT, which built upon the work of the ELSI Genetic Testing Task Force that came before and culminated in a 2000 report with recommendations.[157] The subsequent advancement of DNA sequencing technologies and human genome science, expansion of *clinical* genetic testing capabilities, and the advent of FDA-sanctioned nonclinical DTC personal genome testing without requisite medical provider involvement have renewed concerns, controversies, and debate over privacy, informed consent, and commercialization with heightened pragmatism and immediacy.[158]

PRIVACY AND ASSOCIATED RISKS

By 2019, over 126 million people had submitted their DNA to companies to trace their lineage.[159] As observed by Mark Rasch, a cybersecurity and privacy expert, "One of the things about DNA is it is almost always unique. Therefore, while you can change your ID, you can change your password, it is really difficult to change your DNA."[160] Even James Watson—an impassioned advocate of personal genome access, DNA autonomy, and personal genome self-determination—has acknowledged that, "As more and more people acquire access to their genomic information, it is not surprising that some should worry about the privacy and security of that information."[161] The US Pentagon is concerned. In December 2019, the Pentagon issued a warning to military enlistees to not use popular home DNA testing kits after determining that they "could expose personal and genetic information" and "potentially create unintended security consequences and risk."[162] Leading DTC genetic testing companies have recognized privacy concerns as well:

> In the summer of 2018, leading DTC-GT companies partnered with the Future of Privacy Forum (FPF) to develop *Privacy Best Practices for Consumer Genetic Testing Services*, nonbinding guidelines for the collection, use, and sharing of consumer genetic data. The FPF is a Washington think tank that "brings together industry, academics, consumer advocates, and other thought leaders to explore the challenges posed by technological innovation and develop privacy protections, ethical norms, and workable business practices." In drafting the guidelines, the "FFP and privacy leaders at the companies incorporated input from the FTC, a wide variety of genetics experts, and privacy and consumer advocates."[163]

However, these industry self-regulation guidelines are voluntary and are not accompanied by a reliable enforcement mechanism.[164] According to a recent assessment of DTC genetic testing business practices, "not only do the *Best Practices* have several limitations and shortcomings, but none of the eight companies examined appeared to be in full compliance with the guidelines."[165]

1990s history could repeat itself. Just as state legislatures responded to the commercial DTC BRCA testing introduced in 1996, state legislatures could introduce consumer protections targeted to DTC personal genome testing and population genetic/genomics data.[166] New York has considered such legislation, the New York Privacy Act, and California enacted the California Consumer Privacy Act/CCPA of 2018, which took effect on January 1, 2020.[167] However, the internet and markets transcend state borders, and states have limited enforcement resources. Industry, much of the general public, and many commentators not appreciative of the implications for science and evidence-based medicine favor industry self-regulation of DTC personal genome testing to promote individual access, autonomy, and patient self-determination.[168]

DNA sequencing capabilities, DNA samples, and accompanying medical information are the means to rapidly translate the human genome into more medical meaning.[169] As explained by Eric Lander, a trailblazer in the DNA sequencing world who joined forces with Francis Collins in the US government effort to map the human genome sequence, "You have to compare genomes to learn anything … maybe between dozens or hundreds or thousands of people with a disease or without a disease."[170] The US has recognized as much in its update to the regulations to protect human subjects, known as the Common Rule, which governs clinical research involving human subjects conducted or sponsored by some sixteen Federal departments and agencies that have adopted it.[171] On January 19, 2017, the US Department of Health and Human Services/HHS finalized long-awaited revisions to the Common Rule – the first comprehensive set of changes since the Common Rule was officially recognized in 1991, and after more than a decade of exhaustive dialogue, debate, and deliberation complementing expansive biotech and genomic R&D.[172] The revisions relaxed regulations for population genetic and genomic research, though coupled with reinforcement of privacy accountability in accordance with US federal medical privacy law.[173] Important for the advancement of population genomics, the Common Rule now unambiguously permits researchers to obtain broad consent from participants to use their health information and biospecimens in *yet-to-be-identified* research studies, often referred to as "secondary studies" or "follow-on studies."[174]

Biobanking initiatives, from the US' All of Us Research Program ("AllUs") to 23andMe's customer data compilation, appeal to potential research participants' faith in science research, medicine, and the potential of human genome science to improve health care and human health overall.[175] The AllUs recruitment message is particularly direct and clear: "The future of health begins with you."[176] DTC personal genome testing service customers are asked to contribute to the human health cause by simply sharing the saliva (DNA) and accompanying information they submit to perform the testing services they purchase to discover more about their genetic selves.[177] These companies typically ask their consumers to contribute to research at the outset and, subsequently, they periodically request greater research participation and more information.[178] 23andMe initiates an ongoing relationship: periodic notice of and access to PGHS updates as research progresses, and intermittent email requests to participate further in the company's research.[179]

The US' primary federal medical privacy law, the Health Insurance Portability and Accountability Act/HIPAA, makes medical information the patient's property for practical purposes under its Privacy Rule.[180] HIPAA's scope encompasses "covered entities" and their business associates.[181] HIPAA's definition of covered entities includes health plans, clearinghouses that process health information, and health care providers.[182] Even if not deemed covered entities under HIPAA, commercial DTC personal genome testing companies and their associates may be deemed "business associates" and drawn into HIPAA compliance through their interactions (even if through a business associates chain) with covered entities, including health care providers. Informed consent is a HIPAA staple, and HIPAA promotes the flow of medical information to better the quality of care (for example, consultations among medical professionals), to advance medical education, for public health administration and research, and to administer health care – such as the billing necessary to provide access to health care in the US.[183] Routine notice to patients and consent are important function-enabling features of the law, as is the responsibility of covered entities and the business associates of covered entities to track and trace the flow of medical information to be accountable custodians of it.[184]

HIPAA, itself reliant on notice, consent, and tracking accountability to enable routine health care while protecting patients' medical privacy, is heavily deferential to consent and the flow of protected health information/PHI in research use.[185] In fact, HIPAA promotes medical education and research, including public health research and use: "Public health authorities and others responsible for ensuring public health and safety may access protected health information that is necessary to carry out their public health mission, and as such, individual authorization by patients is not required in a number of circumstances …"[186] Similarly, the Genetic Information and Nondiscrimination Act/GINA of 2008, which prohibits certain employers and health insurers from discriminating based on genetic information, works with institutional review board/IRB implementation of the Common Rule for research purposes.[187] GINA also has a research exemption to its general prohibition against health insurers and group health plans from requesting individuals to undergo a genetic test. "This exception allows health insurers and group health plans engaged in research to request (but not require) that an individual undergo a genetic test."[188] Moreover, even when GINA's prohibition against genetic discrimination is applicable, the burden is on the victims of discrimination to recognize and then to prove that they have been discriminated against in violation of the law protecting them.[189]

Contributing to the noble quest to translate the human genome sequence into medical meaning for the benefit of human health is compelling, as is contributing to improve medical treatments for health conditions that resonate in one's own life experience. However, donors must fully appreciate that DNA is who we are on the molecular DNA level and beyond. As coined by Professor George Annas decades ago, our DNA is our "present and future medical diaries" – as well as, to some extent, those of our biological relatives.[190] The capability to make medical sense out of the human genome, enhanced by our individual DNA profiles and medical information contributions to human genome research, makes each of our personal DNA samples a widening portal to us individually, and increasingly so as the genomic mission to translate the human genome sequence into medical meaning advances.[191]

Our DNA and accompanying information, if added to a reliable and research-enabling biobank, will become part of a sought-after, valuable commodity given investment in genomic R&D and the insatiable need for DNA samples and accompanying information to move genomics forward into clinical care.[192] 23andMe and many other biobankers give donors an option to withdraw from future research at any time.[193] Ancestry's terms and conditions allow customers to have their DNA data deleted and genetic sample destroyed by making the request and going through a two-step process.[194] However, for the sanctity of ongoing research, even under the Common Rule, there is limited if any opportunity to erase research involvement already in motion up to that point – meaning no opportunity to remove oneself from research use already underway even if in a nascent stage. Inclusion in an established set of data put into research use is likely involvement in perpetuity – by the biobank's owner or owners if that has shifted, collaborators, and licensees. DNA data banks are a valuable commercial commodity, and ownership of all involved is highly subject to change given the dynamism within the biopharma sectors.[195] Donation of one's DNA and medical information to a capable and reputable research entity creates the likelihood that a multitude of researchers will seek access and churn the resulting data into myriad uses – all as unpredictable as research itself. Unless a condition in the consent for original participation, which likely would be an obligation contractually limited to the recipient biobanker, today's biobank donor will not have an entitlement to any financial return on use or any access to resulting medical treatments, even when access to such treatments could be a matter of life and death.[196]

23andMe, Ancestry, and many of their DTC personal genome testing corporate counterparts have adopted consumer privacy policies and practices fundamentally consistent with the regulations to protect human subjects under the Common Rule, even if they are not recipients of federal funding – which is the regulatory trigger for Common Rule applicability.[197] These market-successful companies recognize that trust is a prerequisite for consumers to purchase their services, and certainly for consumers to volunteer to participate in research with blanket consent to unidentified future uses by unidentified future users.[198] Both 23andMe and Ancestry have vowed to never disclose an individual's data to insurance providers, employers, or law enforcement unless compelled by a valid legal process.[199]

Valid legal process is evolving rapidly. The DNA databases of DTC companies that provide services for genetic genealogy and ancestry are innately accessible to their customers – the purpose of purchase is to discover biological connections to others – and especially publicly accessible when they allow third-party use. Law enforcement is accessing them to identify suspects, as in the heavily media covered "Lavender Doe" case[200] and the even more media covered prosecution of Joseph James DeAngelo Jr., the "Golden State Killer."[201] The databases of GEDMatch and FamilyTreeDNA are notable in that GEDMatch compiles DNA data files from multiple testing companies, and FamilyTreeDNA, through a network of partnerships, has enormous global reach.[202] Other such databases exist and are commercially accessible. Investigative genetic genealogy is evolving pandemically through extraordinary use successes, which is fueling law enforcement uptake and validation – an extension of the long-validated use of forensic DNA analysis.[203] Successful identification of some 150 suspects of murder and sexual assault as of September 2021 – just the cases prosecuted and brought to fruition, and many of them extraordinary cold cases profiled in the media – is a remarkable accomplishment for such a new field.[204]

Courts are setting precedent in which investigative genetic genealogy results are accepted as evidence, as in the Golden State Killer case. Even if that were to change, cracking cases though investigative genetic genealogy enables law enforcement to hone in on suspects and build their evidence directly – such as by shadow collecting sources of DNA from suspects' discarded drink containers and other personal debris. The only potential roadblocks are DNA database access and the need for more professionals with the requisite expertise in genetics and investigation – such as the exceptional CeCe Moore, the Chief Genetic Genealogist of Parabon Nanolabs, Inc.[205] Building genetic genealogy trees is often incredibly laborious, technical, and intensively unforgiving: There is no room for speculation, much confirmation is essential, and the work must be done with precision through perseverance. Mistakes have been made.[206]

Especially with judicial validation of investigative genetic genealogy, DNA testing companies could be court-ordered to disclose customer information.[207] Also, companies license use and engage in collaborations, and they change policies and ownership. Ancestry is a case in point.[208] In 2014, after briefly becoming a publicly traded company, Ancestry was acquired by a private equity group and decided to shut down its MyFamily.com site.[209] Although the company gave customers a few months to download photos, it did not back up data and many users lost conversations, exchanges, and other family data.[210] Then, in 2015, Ancestry abruptly decided to put a publicly available DNA database it had acquired in 2012 behind a firewall after Idaho law enforcement used it to identify a suspect in a 1996 cold-case murder, made a false match, and aggressively questioned an innocent New Orleans man.[211] Ancestry had purchased the database from the Sorenson Molecular Genealogical Foundation and, according to Sorenson's former executive director, had entered into a contract stipulating that it would continue to make the database public.[212]

Consistent with DNA sequencing technology, information and communication technology/ICT continues to advance explosively and carries the risk of cyber theft with its progress. Again, biobanks and DNA databases are an invaluable commercial commodity in our genomics era.[213] Cybersecurity vulnerability is underscored when owners of the information are in the business of licensing and collaborating with it, and in technology sectors where licensing and collaborating are frenetic and corporate ownership itself is dynamic.[214] Due to a 2017 hacking incident, Ancestry had to shut down its RootsWeb site, which provided online forums that enabled people to research their family histories, and professed to notify customers whose sign-on information may have been stolen.[215] After purchasing RootsWeb in 2000, some seventeen years prior to the incident, Ancestry had not fully upgraded its security protocols.[216]

In 2018, journalists engaged in a three-month investigation that included visits to Ancestry's headquarters and one of its main testing labs.[217] Their investigation determined "a pattern of breached promises to customers, security concerns and inflated marketing pledges that could give consumers some pause."[218] According to the investigation, in addition to the MyFamily.com, Sorenson, and RootsWeb incidents, there are wide gaps in Ancestry's ethnic markers for Asia and other sections of the world. According to independent geneticists and anthropologists, "Ancestry and other companies are making misleading claims about the accuracy of their ethnic analyses."[219] Also, Ancestry obtains consent from most of its customers to share de-identified DNA with science research partners to advance human health, but its main research partner is a secretive Google subsidiary called Calico Life Sciences.[220] Calico's mission is to extend human longevity through biotechnology, and critics allege that it is a vanity project financed by several Silicon Valley billionaires.[221]

A May–June 2022 incident involving Illumina, Inc. vividly illuminates cybersecurity vulnerability in the context of DNA databases. Illumina, Inc. reduced the cost of sequencing a human genome from approximately $1 million in 2007 to $1,000 in 2014 and became a (by many accounts *the*) market leader in sequencing, genotyping, gene expression, and proteomics enabling technologies.[222] Illumina's expansive client base encompasses biopharma companies, contract research organizations/CROs, genomic research centers, and academic institutions. 23andMe and Ancestry use Illumina sequencing technology to provide DTC genetic testing services, as do many of their DTC personal genome testing contemporaries.[223] On June 2, 2022, the FDA informed laboratories and health care providers about a cybersecurity vulnerability in some Illumina sequencing instruments:

> These instruments are medical devices that may be specified either for clinical diagnostic use in sequencing a person's DNA or testing for various genetic conditions, or for research use only (RUO). Some of these instruments have a dual boot mode that allows a user to operate them in either clinical diagnostic mode or RUO mode. Devices intended for RUO are typically in a development stage and must be labeled "For Research Use Only. Not for use in diagnostic procedures." – though many laboratories may be using them with tests for clinical diagnostic use.[224]

Though no actual breaches have been reported yet (as of June 23, 2022), the incident has made cybersecurity and privacy vulnerability in human genome science a tangible, potentially pervasive, and immediate reality.

INFORMED CONSENT AND COMMERCIALIZATION

Voluntary, informed consent is the central tenet of researcher obligations to people who participate in research and, when properly applied, it guides interactions to ensure respect for individual choice and human subject dignity. "Respect for Persons" is the first of the three core principles in the Belmont Report – the bedrock for US law-policy to protect human subjects in research created by the National Commission for the Protection of Human Subjects of Biomedical and Behavioral Research, which the Commission issued in 1978 and published in the Federal Register in 1979.[225] As stated in the Belmont Report, "In most cases of research involving human subjects, respect for persons demands that subjects enter into the research voluntarily and with adequate information."[226] The Belmont Report was implemented and codified to become the Common Rule, the US baseline regulations to protect human subjects in research.[227] The ongoing human genome science research undertaken to develop biopharma products and to improve health care and human health is dependent upon population genetics and genomics. Much of the pace of progress in genomics is driven by access to collections of individual DNA samples and accompanying medical information.[228] Responsiveness to this research need is evident in the 2017 update to the Common Rule, which makes consent compliance easier for population genetics and genomics – such as NIH's own ambitious AllUs.[229]

Voluntary, informed consent also is a cornerstone in the US medical provider–patient relationship.[230] Development of the discipline of bioethics last century created a bridge between clinical research and clinical care – acknowledgement of patient rights and medical professionals' responsibility to respect those rights and patient autonomy.[231] Professor Susan Wolf observed in 1999 that "Ours has been the century of informed consent. Justice Cardozo's revolutionary pronouncement in 1914 that every competent adult 'has a right to determine what shall be done with his own body' kicked off a struggle to end millennia of physician nondisclosure and decisions for their patients."[232] The US legacy of physician paternalism during the twentieth century has been tempered considerably since the 1980s by heightened recognition of patient autonomy and self-determination, and by a robust participatory health movement in this millennium.[233] As applied in US medicine, "The classic informed-consent paradigm presumes the sovereignty of patients' preferences, variously assessed, when clinical needs arise. It disregards the influence of insurance coverage, and of economic incentives and pressures more generally, on sick patients' choices."[234]

Achieving informed consent with competent adults requires that an individual has sufficient information and the capacity to comprehend that information, and that the individual does comprehend with reasonable reliability. Also, the consent must be voluntary, meaning individual vulnerabilities and other influences must be assessed and addressed – often through more information and communication. As stated by the NIH, "Informed consent refers to the process by which a volunteer confirms his or her willingness to participate in the research after having been informed of all aspects of the trial that are relevant to the volunteer's decision to participate."[235] As recognized by the AMA, "Informed consent to medical treatment is fundamental in both ethics and law. It helps patients make well-considered decisions about their care and treatment."[236]

The challenge of science and evidence-based clinical practice uptake of medical innovation in the US is met by a dual government-medical profession regulatory rubric.[237] The FDA requires that the medicinal products on the US market it is charged to oversee satisfy safety and efficacy standards. A sufficiently learned and licensed medical profession, guided by the MJE and peer review, uses FDA-approved products in the delivery of care with adherence to medical ethics and evidentiary science-based clinical practice.[238] The integrity and reliability of the base of US medicine depend on this infrastructure working, especially so during times of extraordinary medical innovation. Ultimately, the practice of medicine in the US is largely self-regulated by the medical profession, which is shown deference in clinical care decision-making under US law and policy.[239]

In the seminal FDA market approval of DTCGHR testing, the FDA found that 23andMe achieved sufficient layperson comprehension through the company's terms and conditions, disclaimers of clinical use unless with the consultation of learned and licensed medical professionals, and customer internet portal access to tiered layers of information culminating with the scientific data each test is based upon.[240] However, consumer completion of question-and-answer exercises to confirm comprehension of a very simplistic baseline (first tier) of information is enough for individuals to access 23andMe's DTCGHR testing service – its Personal Genome Health Service/PGHS.[241] This company–customer communication prerequisite for PGHS use raises disturbing questions about layperson information uptake and comprehension of DNA and genetics, GHR testing distinguished from clinical-standard personal genome testing, distinctions among GHR tests bundled in a single PGHS service, the commercial R&D the company is engaged in with the DNA and health care information it collects from customers, and the medical meaning of resulting personal genome "health risk" information.

As observed by Peter Pitts, a former associate commissioner for the FDA and now director of the Center for Medicine in the Public Interest, few consumers read the details of DTC personal genetic testing companies' terms and conditions: "People need to be aware there are risks and benefits … Right now they see the benefit as being able to have cocktail-party conversation about their genetic makeup. They aren't thinking about the risks of giving up their personal information, and the long-term implications."[242] Primary concerns about voluntary, informed consent in DTC personal genome testing company interactions with their customers include insufficient consumer comprehension regarding: (1) the risks and implications of sharing DNA and medical information with a corporate biopharma entity that may change policies and procedures, ownership, and corporate form over time, (2) the implications of consenting to undefined follow-on (secondary, tertiary, and so on) uses, (3) the same regarding third-party users (the company's licensees and collaborators, and their licensees and collaborators, and so on) and their uses, and (4) the potential impact on their privacy, the privacy of close biological relatives, and the privacy of members of their larger genetic genealogical family.[243]

Over time, corporations change terms and conditions, policies and procedures, engagements, and collaborators – and even ownership through buyouts, mergers, acquisitions, and bankruptcies. All occur frequently in dynamic technology sectors. Corporate entrepreneurialism and dynamism, reflective of the innovation commodities that is the business of technology sectors, tends to fuel their commercial success. Technology sector companies also frequently engage in corporate dynamism out of necessity and for survival. Even if a DTC personal genome testing company adheres to the terms, conditions, policies, and procedures in place at the time of a consumer purchase of service, the company must impose the same consistently on multiple third-party users *and police their compliance over time* to realize any reliability.[244]

For reliability, the terms, conditions, policies, and procedures would have to be imposed absolutely in future transactions contractually, and consent and use extinguished when major events occur that invite high-deviation potential – at least for major corporate ownership and control events such as merger, acquisition, and bankruptcy. Even when original terms and conditions stand as a binding legal contract with the consumer, law pragmatism places the burden on consumers to know that they have been breached, to establish any damages, and to prove both in legal proceedings. Plaintiffs must do so entirely at their expense unless through a class action or contingency-fee arrangement with legal counsel.[245] Even when a company assures that it does not share or sell consumer data or only does so in an aggregated and anonymized form as is common, the company may engage with collaborators or make acquisitions that fail to comply – as was realized with Ancestry.[246]

A consumer who consents to share their DNA and accompanying medical information or, as in the case with Ancestry, fails to opt out of doing so, also introduces the risk of consenting to share on behalf of their biologically close relatives, and potentially beyond – as when used in investigative genetic genealogy.[247] Even if not officially added to a consumer's medical record, the personal genome information created is *family* information shared to some extent among biological relatives. One person is opting to generate personal genome health information shared among biologically close relatives who did not go through their own deliberation and consent to generate it, and who did not make the choice to create it. In these exchanges, one person's personal genome autonomy and choice trumps that of their close biological relatives and members of their extended genetic geological family. Such a loss of choice and autonomy due to the personal genome choice exercised by one person undermines 23andMe's vision for a full transformation of health care – a society in which *each* individual has the *opportunity to choose* to be enlightened about their personal genome and then to choose exercising heightened direct control over their health and health care.[248]

Without reliable assurance of personal genome autonomy for all, which human genome science innately makes a daunting challenge, DTC personal genome testing shifts vision of the not-too-distant future away from Ms. Wojcicki's (23andMe) personal genome autonomy and toward the society depicted in the 1997 movie GATTACA.[249] In the GATTACA society, personal genome sequences are readily available, realizing and using them is the societal norm and expectation, and individuals are pressured into generating and disclosing their personal genome sequences for professional opportunities and other societal advantages, and to avoid disadvantages.[250] Ms. Wojcicki was directly questioned about GATTACA implications in a number of interviews over the years, and she has consistently either failed to understand this connection or she simply has chosen to disregard it.

A very tangible reality is that 23andMe successfully patented a method for genetically designing a baby, from eye color to disease risk – a patent awarded on September 24, 2013, for "Gamete donor selection based on genetic calculations."[251] When questioned about this patent, Ms. Wojcicki again dismissed the connection to GATTACA's "not-too-distant future" (Perhaps she has avoided actually viewing the movie?) with assurance that 23andMe's intended use is simply *recreational* genetics for prospective parents to explore the likelihood of their child inheriting any given trait, such as red hair or lactose intolerance, using the company's Family Traits Inheritance Calculator.[252] Again, technology and corporate policies and procedures change – frantically so in human genome science and technology sectors.

Ms. Wojcicki's recreational-use-only assurance about the company's baby-making patent is analogous to the "non-clinical" lane designation for its PGHS and the "recreational genetics" addressed in "Letting the Genome out of the Bottle." Another reality is that the company aggressively markets its PGHS (lately in a major national television advertising campaign) to consumers as medically meaningful – as a tool to improve one's health. In a television commercial 23andMe began running nationally and frequently in January 2022, a narrator declares "eighty percent of users get genetically meaningful health info from their DNA reports."[253] 23andMe's Traits Inheritance Calculator is less innately recreational than its PGHS if used by prospective parents for making choices in assisted reproduction clinical treatment.[254] Arguably, beyond its genetic tests approved by the FDA for *clinical* use, 23andMe should be allowed to only market its PGHS as recreational, and be compelled to explicitly declare it recreational in marketing communications. Incidentally, since September 24, 2013 (the date of patent issuance), 23andMe's gamete donor selection patent and Family Traits Inheritance Calculator have been complemented by the advent of CRISPR technologies – gene-editing tools that enable genetic engineering with very tangible "do-it-yourself biology"/DIY-Bio possibilities.[255]

All concerns about the sufficiency of consumer consent are augmented when the consent encompasses broad (at times blanket), *undefined* follow-on uses, third-party users, and third-party uses. 23andMe and Ancestry, seminal DTC personal genome companies, engage in these forms of consent – as do most of their DTC personal genome testing contemporaries.[256] Concerns about open consents are augmented when the collectors of DNA samples and medical information are for-profit biopharma companies. The shareholder wealth maximization norm, whether wholly or partially determinative of for-profit corporate behavior, is a reality in capitalism – and thankfully so, at least for the most part, when corporations act in compliance with governing law and that is sufficient.[257] For-profit corporations are created under US law with a purpose, and that has served the US economy well over a long period of time. For-profit corporations typically engage in research activity removed from federal funding and the obligations imposed under the Common Rule.[258] Moreover, they engage in R&D under corporate guidance not restricted by the obligations imposed for the privilege of Internal Revenue Service/IRS non-profit status.[259] Biotech and genomic R&D is the embodiment of US technology transfer, collaborations even among competitors, and creative licensing both to access research-enabling technologies and to generate revenue streams – meaning multiples more of unpredictability, third-party engagement, and follow-on uses and users.[260] DNA and related health information is a precious and pricey commodity in our age of genomics. "For DNA testing companies, the genetic code that customers pay to have analyzed is a gift that keeps on giving. Not only do these companies profit from DNA analysis, but they stand to make money for decades more marketing people's data to the highest bidders."[261]

Consumers of commercial DTC personal genome testing services who also agree to contribute to companies' research endeavors do so, whether in whole or in part, to advance R&D for medical treatments for health conditions that resonate in their lives, to advance medical science, and to improve human health overall. Their decisions are laudable and speak well for humanity. For pragmatic purposes, there is full integration of government, academia, and industry in the human genome science R&D enterprise, and the incentive of commercial success in an entrepreneurial culture coupled with innovation in medical science has proven potent – to the benefit of medical science and human health. The COVID-19 vaccines and therapeutics are illustrative.[262] "COVID vaccines reduced the potential global death toll during the pandemic by almost two-thirds in their first year, saving an estimated 19.8 million lives, according to a mathematical modeling study … in *The Lancet Infectious Diseases*."[263] The connection between R&D success and financial returns is evident in the legislative intent of US technology transfer law and policy/TTLP, its methodology of harnessing commercial incentives to advance research and to build the US science-technology innovation economy, and the vibrant and substantial biotech sector it spawned within just a decade from the enactment of its foundational legislation.[264]

The research uses, users, and *financial profits* realized by these DTC personal genome testing companies over time is a likely indicator of their R&D contributions to the advancement of genomics and the realization of personal genome medicine. However, to maintain trust and participation in research during societal progress towards some version of the 23andMe vision of responsible, science and evidence-based personal genome medicine, the consent standard must be elevated. The consent standard for personal genome testing must include sufficient consumer comprehension of the scope of potential financial returns the research they participate in might generate, and *especially if it proves successful*. They must truly appreciate and accept potentially enormous financial returns to a DTC personal genome testing company that they are paying to take their sample and personal health information at the outset, followed by subsequent requests for more of their information, time, and trust. Consumers also must comprehend the potential harsh reality of contributing directly to research that achieves innovative medical interventions for seriously debilitating and life-threatening conditions that prove inaccessible to them personally and to others they care about – regardless of how dire the health care need.

The current US law-policy environment for DTC personal genome testing is supported by many learned in human genome science, medicine, and both – including those responsible for the FDA's decisions to approve 23andMe's DTCGHR testing and to create a regulatory express lane to market for this technology.[265] One justifying libertarian rationale is that, if individuals want to access their personal genomes now and without the intrusion of medical professionals, companies are offering them affordable opportunities to do so, and resulting genetic, genomic, and proteomic information *might* enable some of them to improve their health and health care. Individual choice should be respected and determinative. After all, DTCGHR testing is classified as nonclinical for FDA regulatory purposes, and US clinical medicine is the domain of the US medical profession. Learned and licensed medical professionals would have to decide to uptake the resulting information for it to be used in clinical care, and licensed and learned medical providers are deferred to under US law-policy as reliable sentinels for evidentiary science-based medicine.

Another supportive rationale is that, given the potential of human genome science to improve individual health care and human health, this phase of risk to privacy and medical use uncertainty is justifiable. The proliferation of DTC personal genome testing is a means to gather the DNA samples and accompanying health information necessary to translate the human genome sequence into clinical meaning as quickly as possible. The biobanks these companies are building in conjunction with selling their DTC personal genome testing services are a means to realize the health care and human health potential of genomics, to achieve science and evidence-based personal genome medicine, as soon as possible. This rationale influenced modification of the Common Rule to be more friendly to population genetics and genomics by condoning informed consent for unspecified secondary uses.[266]

Adherence to evidentiary science-based medicine and to the fundamental tenets of informed consent during the transition to personal genome medicine as standard of care is essential to protect that transition, trust and research participation, patient health care, and the clinical reliability of US medicine. Deviation from either threatens to ultimately elongate the transition, and to undermine evidentiary science-based personal genome medicine. For example, more DNA samples and accompanying medical information is only better if there is quality data collection. Research is the pursuit of objective science truth. Substandard data pollute the rest and cause distraction and confusion in science R&D, which impedes progress and consumes time and resources. The integrity of science and resulting medical innovation is jeopardized, along with trust and clinical use outcomes. 23andMe collects information self-reported by PGHS consumers who make their purchases and later volunteer to respond to periodic questionnaires with shallow queries that offer yes/no response options. Presumably, 23andMe is being as noninvasive as possible to maximize consumer responsiveness, so quantity trumps specificity and quality. Some scientists question the soundness of 23andMe's data:

> Neurogeneticist Ashley Winslow, for instance, who led a high-profile collaboration with Pfizer to identify genetic markers associated with depression, says that peer reviewers of the resulting paper were concerned about the veracity of 23andme's customer data. They argued that people who said that they had been diagnosed with clinical depression might just have been feeling low on the day that they took the company's survey.[267]

Deviation from voluntary, informed consent threatens baseline research participant understanding. Without achieving voluntary, informed consent and associated participant understanding at the outset, trust is unreliable over time. The research endeavor is ill prepared for future issues – such as litigation challenges, cybersecurity breaches, and commercial exploitation controversies investigated and reported by the media. Such controversies jeopardize the willingness of the public to participate in research overall. Moreover, deviation from voluntary, informed consent shifts norms and invites more substantial deviations over time.

In sum, the fundamental tenets of voluntary, informed consent in research and clinical care mandate considerable consumer communication and comprehension in DTC personal genome testing commercial transactions. At the very least, the innate recreational nature of nonclinical testing, risks to personal and biological relatives' medical privacy, and the uncertainty of ownership and use of DNA and medical information over time must be communicated with and comprehended by consumers for valid informed consent to be realized. Such communication and consumer comprehension are a prerequisite for DTC personal genome testing purchases and research participation to be truly informed and voluntary.

RESEARCH FINDINGS AND PARTICIPANTS: WHETHER TO SHARE

When I introduce coverage of protection of participants in research involving human subjects in my Bioethics and Biotechnology courses, we discuss HeLa cell lines and the story of Henrietta Lacks. Author Rebecca Skloot brought HeLa cells and Mrs. Lacks story to the public's attention in 2011 in her widely acclaimed book, *The Immortal Life of Henrietta Lacks*.[268]

Mrs. Lacks was a young mother of five, just thirty years of age, when she went to Johns Hopkins Hospital in Baltimore, Maryland in 1951 for a routine treatment, was diagnosed to have cervical cancer, and was admitted. She was an impoverished

Black woman, a tobacco farmer, and Hopkins was an excellent hospital dedicated to serving the underserved. At the time, researchers were struggling to establish human cell lines for research without much success. Mrs. Lacks did not survive (she died eight months later), but her cells did – immortally. Cells from a tumor biopsied during Mrs. Lacks' treatment and cultured without her knowledge proved miraculously virulent due to the presence of an enzyme that repairs the ends of chromosomes. They became the HeLa (for Henriette Lacks) cell line – the first immortalized human cell line. HeLa cells proved an extraordinary enabler in research, including expansive commercial research that produced the profound human health medicinal products introduced during the second half of the twentieth century. Medical supply companies made fortunes commercializing HeLa cells. As summarized by Ms. Skloot, "HeLa cells were vital for developing the polio vaccine; uncovered secrets of cancer, viruses, and the atom bomb's effects; helped lead to important advances like in vitro fertilization, cloning, and gene mapping; and have been bought and sold by the billions."[269] HeLa cells are utilized in research today.

Scientists investigating HeLa cells began involving Mrs. Lacks' husband and children in research; family medical records were published in the 1980s without informed consent. In fact, the Lacks family had no idea of HeLa cells and their enormity in biomedical research until they were approached by author Rebecca Skloot. Ms. Skloot, who had studied biology as an undergraduate and became fascinated by HeLa cells, undertook the mission to research and write the HeLa cells human story, and she reached out to the Lacks family. One of the most stunning aspects of the HeLa human story is that Mrs. Lacks was buried in an unmarked grave on the slave-worked land that is her family's legacy. Another is that, in addition to growing up in poverty and without their mother, her surviving children struggled with health care issues without the health insurance necessary to access the care they needed. Mrs. Lacks' middle child, Sonny, was $100,000 in debt after bypass surgery.

Surprisingly, given the media coverage after the publication of *The Immortal Life of Henrietta Lacks*, many of my students have not heard the story – or just vaguely remember it. Many are outraged that an individual could make such a contribution to research and be so entirely forgotten. I then explain that, between then and now, the US enacted regulations to protect human subjects, and I begin the lecture. Over the years I have been working on this book project, I have been asking students if they are customers of 23andMe, Ancestry, and I name a few other popular commercial DTC personal genome testing service companies. To those who respond yes, I ask if they consented to be included in research. The number is smaller, but usually not by much. My final questions: "What, if anything, do you expect to get back? What, if anything, do you think you should get back?"

As individuals join the millions who already have contributed to biobanks organized by government and academia and who have sent their DNA samples and information to DTC personal genome testing service providers, the genomic revolution will continue to expand and advance at a quickening pace. More alleles (gene variations) associated with seriously debilitating and life-threatening health conditions will be identified, along with the means to select the most beneficial treatments for patients – the best therapeutic option and the best dosage. Clinical evidentiary-science standards will be met and adhered to in clinical practice. Assessments of health risks that are reliable and clinically useful will bolster health care rather than complicate, confuse, and muddle it. We will realize the science and evidence-based personal genome medicine that is the shared mission of the research community engaged in the genomic revolution, human genome science overall, the medical profession's vocation, and the stated mission of Ms. Wojcicki and 23andMe.

Researchers engaged in human genome science (excluding researchers who work with wholly autonomized DNA samples) have the means to share research findings with those who participate in their research even in primary (commonly referred to as "bench or basic") research. Tremendous population genetics and genomics research is underway, and much more is needed to realize personal genome medicine as standard of care across clinical practice. Under what circumstances could and should the holders of one's DNA and medical information make personal genome medical information available to the individuals who make their research possible? The opportunity to receive personal genome information has incentivized many individuals to pay for it, as DTC personal genome testing providers have demonstrated.

The genomic research community not collecting samples and data from individuals through DTC sales of personal genome testing services to them for commercial gain has been grappling with and debating "whether and to what extent results should be returned to participants of genomic research" for many years.[270] The debate has been enriched by the conclusions reached in a recent systematic review of the empirical literature exploring the perspectives of stakeholders in primary genomic research on returning individual research results/IRR:

> We found overwhelming evidence of high interest in return of IRR from potential and actual genomic research participants. There is also a general willingness to provide such results by researchers and health professionals, although they tend to adopt a more cautious stance. While all results are desired to some degree, those that have the potential to change clinical management are generally prioritized by all stakeholders. Professional stakeholders appear more willing to return results that are reliable and clinically relevant than those that are less reliable and lack clinical relevance. *The lack of evidence for significant enduring psychological harm and the clear benefits to some research participants suggest that researchers should be returning actionable IRRs to participants.*[271]

Most responsible researchers sensitive about the clinical complexities of personal genome testing would not even contemplate sharing speculative genetic health information with participants other than in unique circumstances. Delivering clinically sound (established PPV, NPV, validity, and utility) genetic information responsibly often is complicated and problematic.[272] To what extent exactly is genetic information with strong predictive value for diseases that are preventable and treatable distinguishable from fatal, presently non-treatable diseases such as Huntington's? The tension among public health ethics, medical ethics, and bioethics is tangible.

Some biobanking trailblazers have much application experience grappling with these questions, including Iceland – the home of deCODE Genetics:

> Sometime in the future, US researchers will be able to press a button and reliably identify the thousands of people who carry cancer-causing genes, including those that trigger breast cancer. In Iceland, that day is already here. With a relatively uniform population and extensive DNA databases, Iceland could easily pinpoint which of its people are predisposed to certain diseases, and notify them immediately. So far, the government has refused to do so. Why? Iceland confronts legal and ethical obstacles that have divided the nation and foreshadow what larger countries may soon face.[273]

NIH, which to some extent is competing with DTC personal genome testing service providers for research participation, has been grappling with this dilemma in its administration of AllUs.[274] As of July 2019, more than 70,000 people had consented to participate in AllUs, and some with the expectation that they would be able to access select personal genome health risk information from the study if they decided they wanted it.[275] NIH deliberated sharing some personal genome health risk information with research participants through a separate consent process, accompanied by genetic counseling services, and began doing so in December 2022. According to Anastasia Wise, director of scientific return to participants and impact at AllUs:

> Returning health-related genetic results to participants was a significant undertaking.... It included working with the program's institutional review board on protocols for returning results, seeking guidance from community partners to ensure information is shared in a way that's easy to understand and returned with an eye toward diversity and inclusivity, and obtaining an investigational device exemption (IDE) from the US Food and Drug Administration. All of Us received the long-awaited IDE from the FDA in 2020; at the time, All of Us officials had estimated the program would start returning health-related genetic results in late 2021.[276]

AllUs research participants are not purchasers of DTC personal genome testing services and reports, and NIH is not commercially selling anything directly to the public. There is no company-consumer quid pro quo. As explained by Dr. Francis Collins, the former Director of NIH, the mission of the project is to build a resource to provide health care information, not to provide individual care, and "Feedback can cause more harm than good."[277] Dr. Collins' assessment was likely influenced by, and is certainly supported by, an experiment the UK Biobank conducted:

> The accumulation of tremendous caches of medical data is raising troubling questions about what participants should be told. The UK Biobank, for instance, considered returning results to participants, but decided against it after an experiment. It

> involved participants getting whole-body scans for the program. For some subjects, a radiologist systematically assessed the scans to see if anything seemed abnormal. If it did, the patient and the patient's doctor were informed.
>
> As it turned out, 20 percent of participants had abnormalities. They often went on to have other tests, some of which were invasive and involved major surgery, like removal of a lobe of the lung. Yet in the end, only one in eight with abnormal scans actually had a medical problem, and even then there was nothing they could do about it most of the time, said Dr. Rory Collins, chief executive of the UK project. Other experts disagree with the British approach. At Geisinger [Health System, a US regional health care provider], participants are told if they have a genetic variant that might affect their disease risk.
>
> They are offered genetic counseling if they want it—and so far, about two-thirds do. The medical system has sufficient counselors to handle the demand, said Adam H. Buchanan, co-director of the [Geisinger] counseling program.[278]

The now defunct Ancestry Health grappled with many of these same information-sharing questions in determining what information to make available to its paying customers who were also its research participants.[279] Rather than grappling similarly, the very viable and thriving 23andMe negotiated a lane through the FDA regulatory process to make nonclinical standard GHR information directly available to customers at a price by disclaiming clinical use.[280] Specifically, the FDA approved 23andMe's wholly DTCGHR testing services (its PGHS) conditioned on denouncing clinical use without physician or other appropriately learned and credentialed (notably CGCs) medical professional involvement.[281] Moreover, based upon this approval, the FDA announced a "genetic health risk assessment system devices" *category* eligible for exemption from premarket review and even PMN once a manufacturer has submitted a PMN for their first DTCGHR test(s).[282] The resulting DTCGHR regulatory fast lane to the US market is paved and open for traffic.[283]

The FDA's regulation of medical devices, which includes clinical diagnostics, relies considerably on precedent and familiarity.[284] With DTC market use and familiarity, will the FDA widen the regulatory express lane for DTC personal genome testing? The advancement of human genome science, competition among DTC personal genome testing service providers, growth projections in their business plans, and public demand for DTC personal genome testing services will create pressure on the FDA to not impede that lane and, instead, to widen it. As we have witnessed with the FDA's approval of 23andMe's portfolio of DTCGHR testing in 2017, the FDA is a government entity subject to political forces and public demand for access to the products it is charged to regulate, and the public wants access to DTC personal genome testing services.[285] 23andMe is amassing enormous data from its millions of PGHS customers, which it is checked by the FDA from sharing with customers as clinically useful without the involvement of medical professionals – even for instances of strong but not yet clinical standard predictability, validity, and utility for seriously debilitating and life-threatening conditions. Will the FDA relax its current conditions – requisite clinical use disclaimers – on the information DTCGHR testing service providers are able to offer their customers in the not-so-distant future? Is 23andMe's DTC marketing of its PGHS as medically useful – "80% receive a report with a meaningful genetic variant. Will you be part of the 80%?" – okay?[286] May 23andMe simply "involve" its own medical providers through its acquisition of Lemonaid Health and expansion into providing comprehensive genomic clinical services, and may other companies follow that model?[287]

The biggest questions are foundational and demand immediate attention. Will societal familiarity with DTC personal genome testing services change norms in research? Will it quiet, maybe even end, the debate over "whether and to what extent results should be returned to participants of genomic research" that has raged for years?[288] Will competition for research participants, societal norms, and popular cultural pressure researchers not engaged in providing DTC personal genome testing services for a fee, even government endeavors such as AllUs, to provide GHR and other personal genome testing "feedback" to individuals as well?[289] The biggest question of all: What impact will this have on the evidentiary-science base of US medicine, the practice of medicine, and patient health?

NOTES

1 *See Chapter 1, supra*, at notes 35–45 ("US Law-Policy Recognition of Clinical Medicine as the Medical Profession's Domain"), 160–83 ("Deference to and Reliance on the Medical Profession"), and accompanying text.

2 *See id.* at notes 35–45, and accompanying text ("US Law-Policy Recognition of Clinical Medicine as the Medical Profession's Domain").

3 *See id.* at notes 105–08, and accompanying text (establishment of a prescription-only or "Rx" category of drugs).

4 *See Chapter 1, supra*, at notes 81–101 ("National Regulation to Require *Premarket* Proof of Safety"), 109–44 ("National Regulation to Require *Premarket* Proof of Efficacy"), and accompanying text. For discussion of FDA regulation of medical devices, see *id.* at notes 140, 166–69, and accompanying text.

5 *See Chapter 1, supra*, at notes 102–03, 106 (AMA Council's professional regulation that limited drug-maker marketing communication to physicians), 107–08 (prescription-only category of drugs established under US law).

6 *See Chapter 4, supra*, at notes 25–34, and accompanying text (DTC BRCA testing introduced in 1996). *See* Michael J. Malinowski, Robin J.R. Blatt, *Commercialization of Genetic Testing Services: The FDA, Market Forces, and Biological Tarot Cards*, 71 TUL. L. REV. 1211, 1212 (1997) (addressing BRCA testing introduced to the US market in 1996, with citations to sources responsive at the time).

7 *See* Malinowski, *Tarot Cards*, *supra* note 6, at 1254–55 (discussing Oncormed, Inc.'s consumer intake protocol developed with independent IRB involvement).

8 *See generally* GENETIC COUNSELING PRACTICE: ADVANCED CONCEPTS AND SKILLS (Patricia M. Veach, Bonnie S. LeRoy, Nancy P. Callanan eds., 2nd ed. 2020); A GUIDE TO GENETIC COUNSELING (Jane L. Schuette, Beverly M. Yashar, Wendy R. Uhlmann eds., 2nd ed. 2009). CGCs are health professionals with specialized graduate-level training in medical genetics *and psychosocial counseling*. They are trained in accredited

Master's degree programs and individually certified via examinations administered by the American Board of Genetic Counseling/ABGC, which was established in 1973. *Visit* ABGC, official site, www.abgc.net/; National Society of Genetic Counselors/NSGC (established in 1979), official site, www.nsgc.org/. Licensing requirements vary by state, and statutes that do not require licensure typically require certification. *Visit id.*

9 deCODE Genetics and 23andMe, Inc. introduced DTC personal genome testing services for genetic health risk factors without any requisite medical professional involvement to the US market in 2007. *See Chapter 4, supra*, at notes 81–86, and accompanying text (addressing the initial market introduction of DTCGHR testing services).

10 Anita Hamilton, *Best Invention of 2008, 1. The Retail DNA Test*, TIME (Oct 29, 2008), http://content.time.com/time/specials/packages/article/0,28804,1852747_1854493_1854113,00.html. *See also* James W. Hazel, *Privacy Best Practices for Direct-to-Consumer Genetic Testing Services: Are Industry Efforts at Self-Regulation Sufficient?*, *in* CONSUMER GENETIC TECHNOLOGIES 260 (J. Glenn Cohen, Nita A. Farahany, Henry T. Greely, Carmel Schachar eds., 2021).

11 *See generally* David J. Hunter, Muin J. Khoury, Jeffrey M. Drazen, *Letting the Genome out of the Bottle – Will We Get Our Wish?*, 358 N. ENG. J. MED. 2184–85 (May 15, 2008), www.nejm.org/doi/full/10.1056/nejmp0708162. For more discussion of this editorial, see *Chapter 4, supra*, at notes 184–85, and accompanying text.

12 Hunter et al., *Bottle, supra note* 11, at 2185.

13 *See generally* William F. Mulholland, II, Ami S. Jaeger, *Genetic Privacy and Discrimination: A Survey of State Legislation*, 39 JURIMETRICS J. 317, 318 (1999). *See* Michael J. Malinowski, *Separating Predictive Genetic Testing from Snake Oil: Regulation, Liabilities, and Lost Opportunities*, 41 JURIMETIRCS 21 (2001) (live and published symposium).

14 *See generally* SECRETARY'S ADVISORY COMMITTEE ON GENETIC TESTING/SACGT, ENHANCING THE OVERSIGHT OF GENETIC TESTS: RECOMMENDATIONS OF THE SACGT (July 2000), https://osp.od.nih.gov/sagct_document_archi/enhancing-the-oversight-of-genetic-tests-recommendations-of-the-sacgt/. *See also* Neil A. Holtzman, *FDA and the Regulation of Genetic Tests*, 41 JURIMETRICS J. 53, 54–56 (2000).

15 *See Chapter 2, supra*, at notes 30, 170–83, and accompanying text (addressing US enactment and implementation of TTLP).

16 *See generally* Audrey Heimler, *An Oral History of the National Society of Genetic Counselors*, 6(3) J. GENET. COUNSEL 315–36 (1997), https://onlinelibrary.wiley.com/doi/epdf/10.1023/A%3A1025680306348; Alexandra Minna Stern, *A Quiet Revolution: The Birth of the Genetic Counselor at Sarah Lawrence College, 1969*, 18 J GENET. COUNSEL 1–11, 1 (2009).

17 *See Roe v. Wade*, 410 US 113 (1973); Stern, *Quiet Revolution, supra* note 16, at 8. North America had fifty-five accredited graduate programs in genetic counseling as of 2020 according to the Accreditation Council for Genetic Counseling/ACGC. *See* ACGC ANNUAL ACCREDITATION REPORT JULY 1, 2019 – JUNE 30, 2020 2 (Dec. 2020), www.gceducation.org/wp-content/uploads/2020/12/ACGC19-20_AnnualReport_v4_FINAL.pdf. According to the American Board of Genetic Counselors/ABGC, the US had 5,629 CGCs as of 2021. *See also* National Society of Genetic Counselors/NSGC, *Genetic Counselor Workforce* (Apr. 21, 2021, data), www.nsgc.org/Policy-Research-and-Publications/Genetic-Counselor-Workforce.

18 *See* Stern, *Quiet Revolution, supra* note 16, at 5. *See generally* SHELDON C. REED, COUNSELING IN MEDICAL Genetics (1955).

19 *See id.* (Stern; REED).

20 Stern, *Quiet Revolution*, *supra* note 16, at 3 (internal citation omitted).

21 *See generally* JAY KATZ, THE SILENT WORLD OF DOCTOR AND PATIENT (1984) (addressing paternalism in twentieth century US medicine). Stern, *Quiet Revolution*, *supra* note 16, at 3.

22 Stern, *Quiet Revolution*, *supra* note 16, at 3.

23 *See generally* NAZI MEDICINE: IN THE SHADOW OF THE REICH (First Run Features, 1997) (documentary written and directed by John J. Michalczyk); DANIEL JONAH GOLDHAGEN, HITLER'S WILLING EXECUTIONERS 456 (1997) (explaining that the German people "willingly acquiesced" to the Nazi German revolution, including the German medical profession, the involvement of which proved invaluable to the Third Reich). *See also* Michael J. Malinowski, *Choosing the Genes of Children: Our Eugenics Past – Present and Future?*, 36 CONN. L. REV. 125, 134–60 (2003).

24 Stern, *Quiet Revolution*, *supra* note 16, at 9–10.

25 *Id*. at 9 (quoting Richter lecture in 1970).

26 Leila Jamal, Will Schupmann, Benjamin E. Berkman, *An Ethical Framework for Genetic Counseling in the Genomic Era*, *in* CONSUMER GENETIC TECHNOLOGIES, *supra* note 10, at 233–45.

27 *See generally* THE PEW CHARITABLE TRUSTS, REPORT, THE ROLE OF LAB-DEVELOPED TESTS IN THE IN VITRO DIAGNOSTICS MARKET 1 (Oct. 2021), www.pewtrusts.org/-/. *See infra* notes 63–66, and accompanying text (discussion of LDTs and the Pew report findings). Soon after the US enacted the cornerstone legislation for its technology transfer law and policy/TTLP in 1980, the Reagan Administration worked with the agencies most destined to be recipients of biotech products to determine a systemic regulatory approach. The agencies were asked whether their existing regulatory infrastructure prepared them to receive the forthcoming generation of biotech products. The result was the Coordinated Framework for the Regulation of Biotechnology/CF, 51 FED. REG. 23302 (June 26, 1986). The overall methodology adopted was to regulate biotech products as products and not to center regulation on the use of biotechnology to make them—a "products over process" approach. The CF also mandates coordination among involved federal agencies to avoid duplicative regulation. *See* MICHAEL J. MALINOWSKI, HANDBOOK ON BIOTECHNOLOGY LAW, BUSINESS, AND POLICY 12–13 (2016). In 2015, the Obama Administration undertook an evaluation and update of the US' overall regulatory approach to biotechnology. The resulting study surveyed the present landscape and approaching wave of biotech innovation in medicine and commerce overall. *See generally* US NATIONAL ACADEMIES OF SCIENCE, ENGINEERING, AND MEDICINE/NASEM, PREPARING FOR THE FUTURE PRODUCTS OF BIOTECHNOLOGY (2017), www.nap.edu/catalog/24605/preparing-for-future-products-of-biotechnology. NASEM concluded that adherence to the CF is necessary because any substantial departure would consume too much time given the biotech innovation present and fast approaching, and the winding and time-consuming nature of the US legislative and regulatory processes. *See generally* Barbara J. Evans, *Programming Our Genomes, Programming Ourselves: The Moral and Regulatory Challenge of Regulating Do-It-Yourself Gene Editing*, *in* CONSUMER GENETIC TECHNOLOGIES, *supra* note 10, at 129–144. *See also* Jamal, *Ethical Framework*, *supra* note 26; Stern, *Quiet Revolution*, *supra* note 16, at 7–9.

28 *See generally* PEW, ROLE, *supra* note 27. *See infra* notes 67–75, and accompanying text (also discussing the *New York Times* investigation of noninvasive prenatal tests/NIPTs).

29 *See generally* Ciara Curtin, *Whole-Genome Sequencing Can Help Diagnose Adults with Rare Disease, Study Presented at NSGC Finds*, GENOMEWEB (Nov 21, 2022) (addressing the results of research that utilized the Undiagnosed Diseases Network, a US NIH

Common Fund-backed effort that aims to improve the diagnosis rate of individuals with rare diseases), www.genomeweb.com/sequencing/whole-genome-sequencing-can-help-diagnose-adults-rare-disease-study-presented-nsgc-finds#.Y36So3bMK3A. Whole personal genome sequencing through next-generation sequencing/NGS technologies is price-point accessible for many (the $1,000 whole genome sequencing price point was reached in 2014), with an ongoing trajectory of declining cost coupled with rising capability. *See Prologue, supra,* at notes 6–13, and accompanying text. In December 2022, Genomics England and the UK Department of Health and Social Care, National Health Service/NHS announced that £105 million of its £175 million (about $215 million) investment in genomic research will fund a study to sequence the whole genomes of 100,000 Newborns:

> Genomics England will lead the newborn screening study in partnership with the UK's National Health Service. The investigators' aim is to assess the effectiveness of using whole-genome sequencing to find and treat rare conditions in infants. As part of the Newborn Genomes Program, which will commence next year, about 100,000 newborns will be sequenced. Based on the outcome of the study, UK policymakers will then decide if it makes sense to introduce whole-genome sequencing of newborns across the country as part of routine care for infants.

Justine Petrone, *Genomics England, NHS to Lead £105M UK Study with Aim to Sequence 100K Newborns*, GenomeWeb (Dec 13, 2022), www.genomeweb.com/research-funding/genomics-england-nhs-lead-ps105m-uk-study-aim-sequence-100k-newborns#.Y5jpynbMK3A. For further discussion of the UK NHS's uptake and prioritization of genomics and related infrastructure and undertakings, see *Chapter 7, infra,* at notes 203-5, 282-86, and accompanying text. Beyond the UK, the European Union/EU has introduced an Integrated and Standardized [Next-Generation Sequencing/]NGS Workflows for Personalised Therapy project ("Instand-NGS4P") to standardize NGS workflows and advance making precision medicine through genomics a standard of care in oncology. Instand-NGS4P is "intended to develop workflows for integrating, standardizing, and analyzing data from cancer gene testing, pharmacogenomics testing, and medication databases to support clinical decision support at the bedside." Neil Versel, *EU Awards €4.8M to Support Transition of NGS Workflows to Clinical Settings*, GenomeWeb (Dec 16, 2022), www.genomeweb.com/cancer/eu-awards-eu48m-support-transition-ngs-workflows-clinical-settings#.Y6ClnbMK3A. In December 2022, the EU moved this project into its second phase by awarding eleven contracts collectively worth nearly €4.8 million ($5.1 million). *See id.*

30 Sara Spencer, *Perspectives: Providing Counseling to Patients Using Direct-to-Consumer Testing* (Apr. 29, 2021) (page nos. unavailable), https://perspectives.nsgc.org/Article/TitleLink/Providing-Counseling-to-Patients-Using-Direct-to-Consumer-Testing. For the international genetic counseling profession's perspective regarding the impact of DTC genetic testing on health care systems globally, see *infra* notes 144–48, and accompanying text.

31 *See generally* Mulholland, *Survey, supra* note 13. *See* Malinowski, *Snake Oil, supra* note 13, at 21. In a recently released (Oct. 2022) study to assess "manifestations and navigations of uncertainty in the practice of diagnostic next-generation sequencing (NGS) testing," the researchers concluded that, "By not only minimising but also sustaining or inviting uncertainty, genetic healthcare professionals are able to advance the practices around NGS in a way that matches their multidisciplinary understandings, considerations and more normative stances." *See generally* Janneke M. L. Kuiper, Pascal Borry, Danya F. Vears et al., *Navigating the uncertainties of next-generation sequencing in the genetics clinic*, Soc. Health Ill. (Oct. 3, 2022) (quote from abstract), https://pubmed.ncbi.nlm.nih.gov/36189958/.

32 *See Chapter* 5, *supra*, at notes 72, 133–34, 324, 369, and accompanying text (addressing the specialization trend in US medicine). Personal genome sequencing capabilities and the results they generate, especially with the emergence of market available and price-point accessible whole personal genome sequencing, are already overwhelming both primary care physicians and subspecialty physicians:

> [A] survey by the eMERGE network of primary care physicians and subspecialty physicians found such providers often felt unprepared to handle sequencing results, especially if they had not ordered the test themselves.... [T]he physicians highlighted the need for clinical decision support tools, including consultants and patient materials.... [T]his finding was in line from what a survey of investigators in the IGNITE network found, namely that provider education and clinical decision support are barriers to the adoption of genomic medicine.

Ciara Curtin, *Whole-Genome Sequencing*, *supra* note 29.

33 *See Chapter* 5, *supra*, at notes 78–79, 97–99, and accompanying text (addressing the US patient self-determination movement in health care, stirred in the late 1980s by AIDS activism). The US patient self-determination movement has gained momentum since 2008. and it continues to build with dissatisfaction regarding US health care. According to the results of a Gallup poll released in January 2023:

> Most adults in the US consider the quality of the country's health care to be unfavorable, according to a new survey. This is the first time in a 20-year trend from Gallup polls that the share of adults who rated the quality of the nation's health care to be "excellent" or "good" dipped below 50%. The share of adults who rated it as "poor" jumped above 20%, also for the first time.
>
> Nearly half of adults said that the system has "major problems." Another one in five adults said that US health care is in a "state of crisis," the largest share in about a decade

Deidre McPhillips, *New Poll Shows Jump in Adults who Rate the Quality of US Health Care as* 'Poor', CNN (Jan. 19, 2023), www.cnn.com/2023/01/19/health/us-health-care-poll-gallup/index.html.

34 In fact, the FDA requires DTCGHR service providers to expressly denounce their clinical value in the absence of qualified medical professional involvement. *See Chapter* 4, *supra*, at notes 120, 128–29, 134, 161–62, and accompanying text (addressing FDA-imposed special conditions).

35 *See Chapter* 4, *supra*, at notes 116–83, and accompanying text (discussion that profiles 23andMe as the seminal US DTCGHR testing service company); *infra* notes 97–98, 286, and accompanying text (addressing 23andMe's purchase of Lemonaid Health and the company's new personal genomic clinical services business plan priority). *See generally* Neil Versel, *23andMe Pins Future on 'Genomic Health Service,' Therapeutic Development*, GenomeWeb (Aug. 9, 2022), www.genomeweb.com/business-news/23andme-pins-future-genomic-health-service-therapeutic-development#.Y1MLmnbMK3A; 23andMe, *A Letter from Anne: Making Personalized Healthcare a Reality* (October 22, 2021), https://you.23andme.com/p/28ba69b793a2c6ff/article/a-letter-from-anne-making-personalized-healthcare-a-reality-3ebee7dfb59a/.

36 *See generally* Future of Privacy Forum, Best Practices for Consumer Genetic Testing Services (July 31, 2018), www.geneticdataprotection.com/wp-content/uploads/2019/05/Future-of-Privacy-Forum-Privacy-Best-Practices-July-2018.pdf.; Hazel, *Best Practices*, *supra* note 10.

37 *See* Scott J. Schweikart, *Governance in the Era of CRISPR and DIY-BIO: Regulatory Guidance of Human Genome Editing at the National and Global Levels*, *in* CONSUMER GENETIC TECHNOLOGIES, *supra* note 10, at 66–67. For excellent discussion about CRISPR, see generally WALTER ISAACSON, THE CODE BREAKER (2021). CRISPR technologies are gene editing tools – "DNA scissors" that enable cutting and replacing DNA to "change the code of life itself." *Id.* at xvii (crediting CRISPR with "hasten[ing] our transition to the third great revolution of modern times" – a "life science revolution"). CRISPR already has been used to seemingly cure (in an observational, very limited study) Sickle Cell anemia, which is caused by a single nucleotide variation in a single gene, and an international consortium is developing CRISPR technologies. *See Fareed Zakaria, Global Public Square, GPS* (CNN Nov. 29, 2020). CRISPR and advanced messenger RNA/mRNA technologies (next-generation mRNA technologies), are enabling the realization of several long-awaited gene therapies as this book goes into print. *See generally* Jim Daley, *Four Success Stories in Gene Therapy*, Nature (Oct. 26, 2021) ("After numerous setbacks at the turn of the century, gene therapy is treating diseases ranging from neuromuscular disorders to cancer to blindness."), www.nature.com/articles/d41586-021-02737-7. On Nov. 22, 2022, the FDA approved Hemgenix, "an adeno-associated virus vector-based gene therapy for the treatment of adults with Hemophilia B (congenital Factor IX deficiency) who currently use Factor IX prophylaxis therapy, or have current or historical life-threatening hemorrhage, or have repeated, serious spontaneous bleeding episodes." FDA, *Press Release, FDA Approves First Gene Therapy to Treat Adults with Hemophilia B* (Nov. 22, 2022), www.fda.gov/news-events/press-announcements/fda-approves-first-gene-therapy-treat-adults-hemophilia-b. Hemgenix is a one-time gene therapy product given as a single dose by IV infusion, but at a cost of $3.5 million – making it the world's most expensive drug, with more similarly priced gene therapies to come. *See* Miryam Naddaf, *Researchers Welcome $3.5-million Haemophilia Gene Therapy – But Questions Remain*, NATURE (Dec. 6, 2022), www.nature.com/articles/d41586-022-04327-7.

38 *See* R. Alta Charo, *Rogues and Regulation of Germline Editing*, 380 N. ENG. J. MED. 976, 976 (2019), www.nejm.org/doi/10.1056/NEJMms1817528?url_ver=Z39.88-2003&rfr_id=ori:rid:crossref.org&rfr_dat=cr_pub%20%20pubmed.

39 Schweikart, *Governance*, *supra* note 37, at 65.

40 *See generally* ISAACSON, *supra* note 37.

41 *See generally* SACGT, RECOMMENDATIONS, *supra* note 14.

42 The HGP founders, notably James Watson who was its chief architect, championed the necessity of accompanying genetics research with the social science disciplines to probe ethical, legal, and social implications of the underlying research. *See* Michael J. Malinowski, *Dealing with the Realities of Race and Ethnicity: A Bioethics-Centered Argument in Favor of Race-Based Genetics Research*, 45 HOUS. L. REV. 1415, 1473 (2009) (presented at "One Origin, One Race, One Earth: Genetics, Human Rights and the Next Phase of Human Evolution," Nov. 15–17, 2007, Calgary, Alberta, Canada, sponsored by the University of Calgary, Alberta Law Foundation, and Alberta Civil Liberties Research Centre). NIH and the Department of Energy/DOE, the funding agencies for HGP, dedicated 3–5% of their annual HGP budgets toward ELSI research. *See* US DOE, *HGP Research Area: Ethical, Legal, and Social Issues Research* (Apr. 23, 2019) (Human Genome Project Information Archive 1990–2003), https://web.ornl.gov/sci/techresources/Human_Genome/research/elsi.shtml. ELSI proved an essential complement to HGP and, today, there are ELSI counterparts to virtually all major genetics and genomics research undertakings. *Visit* NHGRI, *Ethical, Legal and Social Implications Research Program* (updated Apr. 6, 2021), www.genome.gov/Funded-Programs-Projects/ELSI-Research-Program-ethical-legal-social-implications. *Visit also* NHGRI, *Coverage*

and Reimbursement of Genetic Tests (updated Aug. 15, 2019), www.genome.gov/about-genomics/policy-issues/Coverage-Reimbursement-of-Genetic-Tests. For further discussion of ELSI and its impact, see *infra* notes 153–56, and accompanying text.

43 David S. Shearer, S. Cory Harmon, Brian M. Seavey, Alvin Y. Tiu, *The Primary Care Prescribing Psychologist Model: Medical Provider Ratings of the Safety, Impact and Utility of Prescribing Psychology in a Primary Care Setting*, 19 J. Clin. Psychol. Med. Settings 420–29, 420 (2012), www.nebpsych.org/Resources/Documents/Shearer%20et%20al.%202012.RxP.pdf#:~:text=The%20practice%20of%20medicine%20continues%20to%20evolve%20as,service%20delivery%20model%20for%20the%20past%202%20years.

44 *See generally* Iman Eikram, *How Technology Is Shifting Agency from Doctors to Patients: The Cost and Impact of Medical Technologies to Traditional Liability and Malpractice*, 44 J. Corp. L. 609 (2019); Tuan C. Nguyen, *Home Medical Tests: Which Can You Trust?*, Berkeley Wellness (May 4, 2016) (listing devices that the FDA trusts, as well as an assortment of unreliable home tests that have not met FDA standards for accuracy or safety). *Cf.* Mobolaji Ibitoye, Timothy Frasca, Rebecca Giguere, Alex Carballo-Diéguez, *Home Testing Past, Present and Future: Lessons Learned and Implications for HIV Home Tests*, 18 AIDS Behav. 933–49 (2014).

45 LetsGetChecked, official site, *Home Female Fertility Testing* (visited June 21, 2022), www.letsgetchecked.com/home-female-fertility-test/.

46 Everlywell, official site (visited June 21, 2022), www.everlywell.com/. The company is a "Shark Tank" (an extremely popular US television show) commercial success story:

> When was Everlywell on Shark Tank?
> Everlywell founder and CEO Julia Cheek appeared on Shark Tank in November 2017 to acquire additional funding for the Austin-based startup. After Lori Greiner joined Everlywell as an investor on season 9 of Shark Tank, Everlywell was able to make incredible strides to grow the company. This growth included expanding to new retailers like Target and CVS, leading a major rebrand, and launching new mail-in lab tests like the Indoor & Outdoor Allergy Test and the COVID-19 Test Home Collection Kit DTC*.
> Where is Everlywell now?
> In March 2021, Everlywell acquired PWNHealth and Home Access Health Corporation and formed parent company Everly Health. With a user-first digital experience, easy-to-use, self-collected mail-in lab tests, and providing access to telehealth options with a national clinician network working to improve early detection and prevention of disease, Everly Health is committed to transforming lives through high-quality diagnostic care.

The Everlywell Story: from Shark Tank to Now, Everlywell Blog (2023) (visited Jan. 21, 2023, 12:12 PM), www.everlywell.com/blog/news-and-info/everlywell-shark-tank/.

47 *Visit* Everlywell, official site, *supra* note 46 (visited June 21, 2022).

48 Staff reporter, *[deCODE] Study Identifies Proteomic Predictors of All-Cause Mortality*, GenomeWeb (Jun 18, 2021) (page no. unavailable), www.genomeweb.com/proteomics-protein-research/decode-study-identifies-proteomic-predictors-all-cause-mortality.

49 *See* Staff Reporter, *Human Longevity to Go Public through $345M SPAC Merger*, GenomeWeb (June 21, 2022) (page nos. unavailable), www.genomeweb.com/business-news/human-longevity-go-public-through-345m-spac-merger#.YtxgHXbMK3A. For discussion of Celera's competition with HGP and related controversies, see generally Georgina Ferry, John Sulston, The Common Thread: A Story of Science, Politics, Ethics and the Human Genome (2002).

50 Human Longevity, official site (visited June 21, 2022), https://humanlongevity.com/.

51 *See* Staff Reporter, *Human Longevity*, *supra* note 49.

52 *See infra* notes 94–6, 240–43, and accompanying text (discussing 23andMe consumer comprehension).*See also Chapter 4, supra*, at notes 120, 134, 161–62, and accompanying text (discussing FDA-imposed special conditions, which address clinical use and consumer comprehension).

53 *See Chapter 4, supra*, at notes 116–83, and accompanying text (discussion that profiles 23andMe as the seminal US DTCGHR testing service company.

54 *See* Carmel Shachar, I Glen Cohen, Nita A. Farahany, Henry T. Greely, *Introduction*, *in* CONSUMER GENETIC TECHNOLOGIES, *supra* note 10, at 1, *citing* GRAND VIEW RESEARCH, PREDICTIVE GENETIC TESTING AND CONSUMER GENETICS MARKET SIZE, SHARE & TRENDS ANALYSIS REPORT BY TEST TYPE (POPULATION SCREENING, SUSCEPTIBILITY), BY APPLICATION, BY SETTING TYPE, AND SEGMENT FORECASTS, 2019–25 (2019). *Cf. generally* FUTURE, BEST PRACTICES, *supra* note 36; PEW, ROLE, *supra* note 27. *See generally* NASEM, PREPARING, *supra* note 27.

55 *See generally* Byjon Heggie, *Genomics: A Revolution in Health Care? Drugs Affect People Differently and We're Increasingly Understanding Why. For Many of Us, It's Down to Our Genes*, NAT'L GEO. (Feb. 20, 2019), www.nationalgeographic.com/science/article/partner-content-genomics-health-care. *See also* ISAACSON, *supra* note 37, at 37–41 ("The Human Genome").

56 *See generally* Malinowski, *Realities of Race*, *supra* note 42; Michael J. Malinowski, Commentary, *Respecting, Rather than Reacting to, Race in Basic Biomedical Research: A Response to Professors Caulfield and Mwara*, 45 HOUSTON L. REV. 1475 (2009). *Cf.* Michael J. Malinowski, *Could Biobanking Be a Means to Give Health Care "Have-Nots" a Presence in the Genomics Revolution?*, 9 DEPAUL J. HEALTH CARE L. 1005 (2005).

57 *See generally* US Department of Energy Office of Science, Office of Biological and Environmental Research, *About the Human Genome Project Information Archive* 1990–2003 (last modified Mar. 26, 2019) ("The current consensus predicts about 20,500 genes, but this number has fluctuated a great deal since the project began."), https://web.ornl.gov/sci/techresources/Human_Genome/project/index.shtml; NHGRI, *Human Genome Project FAQ* (last updated Feb. 24, 2020), www.genome.gov/human-genome-project/Completion-FAQ.

58 For discussion regarding Mendelian traits versus common diseases, see *Chapter 2, supra*, at notes 3–8, and accompanying text. *Visit* National Human Genome Research Institute/NHGRI, Centers for Mendelian Genomics (visited May 2, 2022), www.genome.gov/Funded-Programs-Projects/NHGRI-Genome-Sequencing-Program/Centers-for-Mendelian-Genomics-CMG. A variation (allele) in the HTT gene causes Huntington disease, in the HBB gene causes sickle cell disease, and in the HEXA gene causes Tay-Sachs disease. While scientist discovered these genetic levers decades ago, the quests for medical cures continue. *See* NIH, *Huntington Disease*, GEN. HOME REF. (July 28, 2020), https://ghr.nlm.nih.gov/condition/huntington-disease; NIH, *Sickle Cell Disease*, GEN. HOME REF. (1uly 28, 2020), https://ghr.nlm.nih.gov/condition/sickle-cell-disease#genes; NIH, *Tay Sachs Disease*, GEN. HOME REF. (July 28, 2020), https://ghr.nlm.nih.gov/condition/tay-sachs-disease#genes. At this time, an experimental gene therapy for sickle cell disease administered in a small number of patients has demonstrated cure potential. *See 60 Minutes, Overtime, More on the Trial Aiming to Cure Sickle Cell* (July 26, 2020) (profiling clinical research headed by Dr. Francis Collins, former Director of NIH), www.cbsnews.com/news/more-on-the-trial-aiming-to-cure-sickle-cell-60-minutes-2020-07-26/.

59 Epigenetics is the study of changes in organisms caused by modification of gene expression due to environmental influences, rather than alteration of the genetic code itself. *See*

generally NESSA CAREY, THE EPIGENETICS REVOLUTION: HOW MODERN BIOLOGY IS REWRITING OUR UNDERSTANDING OF GENETICS, DISEASE, AND INHERITANCE (2013); Richard C. Francis, EPIGENETICS: HOW ENVIRONMENT SHAPES OUR GENES (2012).

60 JOHN ABRAMSON, OVERDOSED AMERICA: THE BROKEN PROMISE OF AMERICAN MEDICINE 206 (2005) (quoting Richard Lewontin).

61 The promise of personal genome medicine, the realization of which is the self-stated driving mission of Ms. Anne Wojcicki and 23andMe, centers on this understanding. *See Chapter 4, supra,* at notes 95–7, and accompanying text.

62 *See generally* SACGT, RECOMMENDATIONS, *supra* note 14.

63 PEW, ROLE, *supra* note 27, at 1.

64 *See id. See Chapter 4, supra,* at notes 34–37, 121–24, and accompanying text (discussing CLIA regulations).

65 *See Chapter 4, supra,* at notes 34–37, 121–24, and accompanying text (discussing CLIA regulations).

66 PEW, ROLE, *supra* note 27, at 1.

67 *See* Sarah Kliff, Aatish Bhatta, *Prenatal Tests for Rare Defects Often Produce False Positives*, N.Y. TIMES (Jan. 2, 2022), www.nytimes.com/2022/01/01/upshot/pregnancy-birth-genetic-testing.html.

68 *Id.* (page no. unavailable online). "One large test maker, Natera, said that in 2020 it performed more than 400,000 screenings for one microdeletion – the equivalent of testing roughly 10 percent of pregnant women in America." *Id.*

69 *Id.* (page nos. unavailable online).

70 *Id.* (page nos. unavailable online).

71 *Id.* (page nos. unavailable online).

72 *Id.* (page nos. unavailable online).

73 *Id.* (page nos. unavailable online), *citing* Pe'er Dar, Kirsten J. Curnow, Susan J. Gross et al., *Clinical Experience and Follow-up with Large Scale Single-nucleotide Polymorphism-based Noninvasive Prenatal Aneuploidy Testing*, 211(5) AM. J. OBSTET. GYNECOL. P527.e1–17 (2014).

74 Kliff, Bhatta, *False Positives*, *supra* note 67 (page nos. unavailable online).

75 *Id.* (page nos. unavailable online).

76 *See Dobbs v. Jackson Women's Health Org. et al.*, No. 19-1392, 2022 WL 2276808 (US June 24, 2022); *Chapter 5, supra,* at notes 170–77, and accompanying text. *See generally* Sabrina Weiss, Roe's *Fall Will Limit Screening for Fatal Congenital Conditions*, SCIENCE (May 18, 2022) ("Many life-limiting conditions can only be detected 12 weeks into pregnancy – but some US states are planning to set to the abortion limit much earlier."), www.wired.com/story/roe-fall-limit-screening-fatal-congenital-co.

77 *Visit* NHGRI, official site, www.genome.gov/about-genomics.

78 *See* Martina C. Cornel, Carla G. van El, Pascal Borry, *The Challenge of Implementing Genetic Tests with Clinical Utility while Avoiding Unsound Applications*, 5(1). J. COMM. GENET. 7–12 (2014), www.ncbi.nlm.nih.gov/pmc/articles/PMC3890066/. *See generally* CARL ZIMMER, SHE HAS HER MOTHER'S LAUGH: THE POWERS, PERVERSIONS, AND POTENTIAL OF HEREDITARY (2018).

79 *Visit* NHGRI, official site, www.genome.gov/about-genomics. *See generally* JAMES D. WATSON, DNA: THE STORY OF THE GENETIC REVOLUTION (2nd ed. 2017) (with Andrew Berry, Kevin Davies) (updated to commemorate the fiftieth anniversary of the discovery of the double helix); ISAACSON, CODE, *supra* note 37.

80 This clinical complexity holds true even for *clinically sound* genetic testing that meets FDA evidentiary-science standards. *See generally* SACGT, RECOMMENDATIONS, *supra* note 14.

81 *See generally id.* According to the authors of a study published in 2022 based on multi-site fieldwork conducted at a large Centre for Human Genetics in Belgium, which addressed uncertainties regarding next-generation sequencing/NGS in clinical care and the commingling of genomic research and clinical care:

> Patients were at times kept in the genetic framework, even if it was not supported by 'the data'. As in the work of Skinner et al. (2016), this was done by offering 'not yet diagnoses' to patients with class 3 or negative results. Additionally, we showed how clinical intuition was used as complementary evidence to break the certainty of a negative result.... Although, with the intention to provide good care, one could wonder if the patient is sufficiently central in this care practice.

Janneke M.L. Kuiper, Pascal Borry, Danya F. Vears et al., *Navigating the Uncertainties of Next-generation Sequencing in the Genetics Clinic*, SOC. HEALTH & ILLNESS (Oct. 2022), https://pubmed.ncbi.nlm.nih.gov/36189958/. *See also infra* notes 268-89, and accompanying text (addressing whether and when medical providers should share unsolicited genetic testing findings with patients).

82 WATSON, STORY, *supra* note 79, at 214.

83 *See Prologue, supra*, at 1–13, and accompanying text (progress from the $1,000 to the $100 whole genome sequencing goal).

84 WATSON, STORY, *supra* note 79, at 213. At its 2022 annual meeting, the National Society of Genetic Counselors/NSGC discussed research to assess whole genome sequencing as first-tier testing for children with suspected genetic disorders and to help diagnose and change clinical management of adult patients with rare diseases. *See supra* note 29, and accompanying text. *See generally* Curtin, *Whole-Genome Sequencing, supra* note 29. The UK has undertaken a £105M study to sequence the whole genomes of 100,000 Newborns. *See supra* note 29.

85 *See* Matthew Herper, *Ancestry Launches Consumer Genetics Tests for Health, Intensifying Rivalry with 23andMe*, STAT NEWS (Oct. 15, 2019), www.statnews.com/2019/10/15/ancestry-health-launch/.

86 *Id.* (page nos. unavailable).

87 The clinical complexities of sound (meeting FDA evidentiary-science standards) genetic testing were thoughtfully addressed by the SACGT. *See generally* SACGT, RECOMMENDATIONS, *supra* note 14.

88 Consider NIH's AllUs effort to draw data reflective of diversity in the US population. *Visit* AllUs, official site, https://allofus.nih.gov/. *See Prologue, supra*, at notes 26–28, and accompanying text (discussing AllUs). *See also infra* notes 175–76, 229, 274-77, and accompanying text. In January 2023, NIH announced that it earmarked nearly $4.8 million in grant funding for FY2023 to support the analysis of data from AllUs and the development of new data analysis tools and methods. *See* Staff Reporter, *NIH Commits $4.8M in Grant Funding for All of Us Data Analysis, Related Tools*, GENOMEWEB (Jan 03, 2023), www.genomeweb.com/sequencing/nih-commits-48m-grant-funding-all-us-data-analysis-related-tools#.Y7S9FHbMK3A.

89 SACGT thoughtfully explained PPV, NPV, clinical validity, and clinical utility in its report and recommendations. *See generally* SACGT, RECOMMENDATIONS, *supra* note 14.

90 *See, e.g.*, Cornel, *Challenge of Implementing, supra* note 78, at 7–12; Monica A. Giovanni, Matthew R. Fickie, Lisa S. Lehmann et al., *Health-care Referrals from Direct-to-Consumer Genetic Testing*, 14(6) GENET. TEST. MOL. BIOMARKERS 817–19 (2010), www.ncbi.nlm.nih.gov/pmc/articles/PMC3001829/pdf/gtmb.2010.0051.pdf; Christine Patch, Jorge Sequeiro, Martina C. Cornel, *Direct to Consumer Genetic Tests*, 17(9) EUR. J. HUM. GENET. 1204 (2009), www.nature.com/articles/ejhg200966.

91 *Cf.* Hunter, *Bottle, supra* note 11 (*NEJM* editorial).

92 Inconsistencies among allele tests include the scope of the population data upon which they are based (the DNA samples and the information collected from those individuals), the genetic influences of each allele on the health conditions they are associated with (variations in risk of onset), and the health conditions themselves (variance in life impact, symptom severity, and available treatment options) – all subject to the dynamism of an ongoing, swirling deluge of emerging human genome science and personal genome medicine. *See generally* Cornel, *Challenge of Implementing, supra* note 78.

93 As many consumers have experienced with ancestry testing, DNA test results change over time as the sets of data they are based on expand and evolve – through added consumer use of personal genome services, inclusion of data from other sources such as other biobanks and data set acquisitions, and the progress of related human genome research. The alleles they test for and health impact interpretations are modified in accordance with scientific progress and capabilities introduced by research discovery and access to additional samples and data. The same individual's DNA tested for the same heredity traits, health risks, conditions, or diseases by different testing providers or the same provider using a different test typically produces results that vary in medical meaning. *See supra* note 86, and accompanying text (addressing the now defunct AncestryHealth's attempt to address the dynamism of ongoing genomic tests and research by offering consumers two distinct products, AncestryCore and AncestryPlus).

94 *See supra* note 52, and accompanying text (addressing the FDA-imposed consumer comprehension requirement). *See Chapter 4, supra*, at notes 120, 134, 161–62, and accompanying text (discussing the FDA-imposed special conditions, which address clinical use and consumer comprehension).

95 I purchased and used 23andMe's Personal Genome Health Service/PGHS to have the 23andMe customer experience in conjunction with researching and writing this book – and, admittedly, with a good amount of curiosity about my genetic self. I also authored a children's book to introduce very young children, approximately 7–10 years of age, to the meaning of DNA and genetics. *See generally* MICHAEL J. MALINOWSKI, WHY AM I ME? (2019). I engaged in a solid amount of comprehension research for that project. I found the 23andMe comprehension prerequisite for use to be disturbingly minimal – perhaps at the level of a middle school student with average intelligence as stated in the text.

96 *See Chapter 4, supra*, at notes 120, 134, 161–62, and accompanying text (discussing FDA-imposed special conditions, which address clinical use and consumer comprehension).

97 23andMe, *A Letter from Anne: Making Personalized Healthcare a Reality* (Oct. 22, 2021), https://you.23andme.com/p/28ba69b793a2c6ff/article/a-letter-from-anne-making-personalized-healthcare-a-reality-3ebee7dfb59a/.

98 *See* 23andMe Holding Co., *Current Report (Form 8-K)*, GENOMEWEB (NOV. 1, 2021), https://investors.23andme.com/static-files/8a43d3a5-2529-422c-937b-db40a7eeb875. On August 9, 2022, the company declared "expan[sion] beyond its core consumer genetic testing into a new business line called its genomic health service." Neil Versel, *23andMe Pins Future on 'Genomic Health Service,' Therapeutic Development*, (Aug. 9, 2022), www.genomeweb.com/business-news/23andme-pins-future-genomic-health-service-therapeutic-development#.Y1MLmnbMK3A. *See 23andMe,* A *Letter from Anne, supra* note 97.

99 *See Chapter 4, supra*, at notes 116–83, and accompanying text (23andMe profiled as the seminal DTCGHR testing services company).

100 Hazel, *Best Practices, supra* note 10, at 260. *See generally* FUTURE, BEST PRACTICES, *supra* note 36. *Cf.* CBO, RESEARCH AND DEVELOPMENT IN THE PHARMACEUTICAL INDUSTRY (2021), www.cbo.gov/publication/57126; NASEM, PREPARING, *supra* note 27.

101 23andMe alone amassed more than a million DNA profiles and related health information by 2015, and over five million globally by 2018. *See Chapter 4, supra*, at note 103, and accompanying text (citations provided).
102 *See Prologue, supra*, at notes 1–13, and accompanying text.
103 *See* NHGRI, *Regulation of Genetic Tests* (Feb. 2, 2022), www.genome.gov/about-genomics/policy-issues/Regulation-of-Genetic-Tests; *Chapter 4, supra*, at notes 171–83, and accompanying text. *See also* Carmel Shachar, I Glen Cohen, Nita A. Farahany, Henry T. Greely, *Introduction, in* CONSUMER GENETIC TECHNOLOGIES, *supra* note 10, at 1, *citing* GRAND VIEW RESEARCH, PREDICTIVE GENETIC TESTING AND CONSUMER GENETICS MARKET SIZE, SHARE & TRENDS ANALYSIS REPORT BY TEST TYPE (POPULATION SCREENING, SUSCEPTIBILITY), BY APPLICATION, BY SETTING TYPE, AND SEGMENT FORECASTS, 2019–25 (2019) (projecting the global genetic testing and consumer wellness genomic market, valued at $2.24 billion in 2015, to double by 2025). *Cf.* FUTURE OF PRIVACY FORUM, BEST PRACTICES, *supra* note 36; PEW, ROLE, *supra* note 27. *See generally* NASEM, PREPARING, *supra* note 27.
104 *See* FUTURE, BEST PRACTICES, *supra* note 36. *See generally* Hazel, *Best Practices*, *supra* note 10 (addressing the self-regulation environment, industry's *Best Practices for Consumer Genetic Testing Services*, and the disappointing implementation of those practices). *Cf.* PEW, ROLE, *supra* note 27.
105 *See Chapter 4, supra*, at notes 125–36, and accompanying text (FDA recognition of a DTCGHR testing category).
106 *See generally* PEW, ROLE, *supra* note 27.
107 *See Chapter 1, supra*, at notes 160–83, and accompanying text ("Deference to and Reliance on the Medical Profession").
108 *See* MALINOWSKI, HANDBOOK, *supra* note 27, at 179–82. *See generally* PEW, ROLE, *supra* note 27.
109 *See generally* Michael J. Malinowski, *Coming into Being: Law, Ethics, and the Practice of Prenatal Genetic Screening*, 45 HASTINGS L. J. 1435 (1994) (providing examples, drawing from field work in the Houston-area in the early 1990s).
110 *See generally* PEW, ROLE, *supra* note 27. *See supra* notes 67–75, and accompanying text (*NY Times* investigation).
111 NHGRI, *Regulation, supra* note 103.
112 *See supra* notes 28, 63–76, and accompanying text (addressing non-invasive prenatal tests/NIPTs).
113 *See supra* notes 66–76, and accompanying text (commercial desire to differentiate from competitors by offering more expansive testing, and no established threshold).
114 As a 23andMe Personal Genome Health Service/PGHS purchaser, I periodically receive updates, as well as options to purchase enhanced services.
115 *See generally* Michael J. Malinowski, Grant G. Gautreaux, *Drug Development – Stuck in a State of Puberty? Regulatory Reform of Human Clinical Research to Raise Responsiveness to the Reality of Human Variability*, 56 ST. LOUIS U. L.J. 363 (2012) (advocating for more use of single subject study design and less reliance on group design in biopharma clinical R&D); Michael J. Malinowski, Grant G. Gautreaux, *All that is Gold Does Not Glitter in Human Clinical Research: A Law-Policy Proposal to Brighten the Global "Gold Standard" for Drug Research and Development*, 45 CORNELL J. INT'L LAW 185 (2012) (advocating for more single subject study design in Rx clinical R&D, consistent with delivery of care in personal genome medicine).
116 *See Chapter 3, supra*, at notes 121–35, and accompanying text (addressing Rx disease mongering).

117 RAY MOYNIHAN, ALAN CASSELS, SELLING SICKNESS: HOW THE WORLD'S BIGGEST PHARMACEUTICAL COMPANIES ARE TURNING US ALL INTO PATIENTS 154–55 (2005). *See Chapter* 3, *supra*, at notes 121–35, and accompanying text (discussing biopharma disease mongering). *But see generally* STEPHEN LANDSMAN, MICHAEL J. SACKS, CLOSING DEATH'S DOOR: LEGAL INNOVATIONS TO STEM THE EPIDEMIC OF HEALTHCARE HARM (2020) (proposing that the US medical profession resists uptake of technology that would enable patients to make medical decisions and to check the safety of medical interventions).

118 *See Chapter* 4, *supra*, at notes 125–29, and accompanying text (discussing the FDA's terms, conditions, and warning). *See id* at notes 118–20, and accompanying text (FDA imposed consumer comprehension requirement). I have worked in the field of biotechnology law-policy for approximately thirty years, and I am a purchaser and user of 23andMe's PGHS. I also am the author of a children's book to introduce very young children – approximately 7–9 years of age – to the meaning of DNA and genetics. *See generally* MICHAEL J. MALINOWSKI, WHY AM I ME? (2019). I found the 23andMe comprehension prerequisite for purchase to be frighteningly minimal. *See supra* note 95.

119 *See Chapter* 4, *supra*, at notes 120, 125–29, 134, 160–63, and accompanying text (discussing the FDA-imposed special conditions, which address clinical use and consumer comprehension).

120 *See* OTIS WEBB BRAWLEY, HOW WE DO HARM: A DOCTOR BREAKS RANK ABOUT BEING SICK IN AMERICA 83–84 (2011). *See also Chapter* 1, *supra*, at notes 184–89, and accompanying text (discussing the FDA-medical profession symbiotic relationship to protect and promote evidentiary science-based medicine). The FDA must not unduly infringe on the practice of medicine and doctor-patient decision making. FDA approvals put medicinal products on the market for physicians to utilize in the delivery of care at their professional discretion, provided they do not use them in a manner that a licensed, competent, and reasonable medical professional would know to cause harm. *See id*. at note 162, and accompanying text; BRAWLEY, *supra*, at 83–84. Consequently, physician off-label uses of FDA-approved medicinal products – at times uses far removed from the clinical data market authorization was based upon – is routine and substantial. *See Chapter* 3, *supra*, at notes 48–70, and accompanying text (physician discretion to prescribe off label, and biopharma's free speech right to disseminate article reprints to physicians to promote off-label uses).

121 *See, e.g., supra* notes 28, 66–76, and accompanying text (addressing noninvasive prenatal tests/NIPTs).

122 *See id.*

123 Many patients are acting on nonconclusive NIPTs administered in prenatal care by terminating their pregnancies. *See supra* notes 28, 66–75, and accompanying text.

124 In competition for research participants, NIH deliberated sharing AllUs research findings with subjects over several years, and AllUS has begun doing so. *See infra* notes 268–89, and accompanying text ("Research Findings and Participants: Whether to Share").

125 Studies support that many DTC personal genome testing companies do not directly involve clinically trained and regulated health care professionals in a sufficient manner, and customers often need help to interpret their reported disease risks correctly. *See generally* Scott McGrath, Jason Coleman, Lotfollah Najjar et al., *Comprehension and Data-Sharing Behavior of Direct-To-Consumer Genetic Test Customers*, 19(2) PUB. H. GENOMICS 116–24 (Mar. 2016), www.researchgate.net/publication/297595794_Comprehension_and_Data-Sharing_Behavior_of_Direct-To-Consumer_Genetic_Test_Customers;

Adrian Burton, *Are We Ready for Direct-to-consumer Genetic Testing?*, 14(2) LANCET NEUROL. 138–39 (2015), www.thelancet.com/journals/laneur/article/PIIS1474-4422(15)70003-7/fulltext. Research also confirms that DTC personal genome testing customers turn to health care providers for results interpretation. *See generally* Gemma R Brett, Sylvia A Metcalfe, David J Amor, Jane L Halliday, *An Exploration of Genetic Health Professionals' Experience with Direct-to-consumer Genetic Testing in Their Clinical Practice*, 20(8) EUR. J. HUM. GENET. 825–30 (2012), https://pubmed.ncbi.nlm.nih.gov/22317975/.

126 "When wealthy patients demand irrational care, it's not hard to find a doctor willing to provide it. If you have more money, doctors sell you more of what they sell, and they just might kill you." BRAWLEY, HARM, *supra* note 120, at 23. Expansive use of clinical standard personal genome testing is being endorsed by some medical professional organizations. For example, in September 2022, the National Comprehensive Cancer Network/NCCN updated its guidelines "to recommend genetic testing of patients diagnosed with breast cancer at the age of 50 or younger, no matter their family history or triple-negative disease status. They also recommend testing when it could guide [pharmacological inhibitors of the enzyme poly ADP ribose polymerase/]PARP inhibitor treatment." Staff reporter, *Universal Genetic Testing in Breast Cancer Further Supported in New Invitae-Led Study*, GENOMEWEB (Sept. 22, 2022), www.genomeweb.com/cancer/universal-genetic-testing-breast-cancer-further-supported-new-invitae-led-study#.Y4Tpn3bMK3A. The NCCN decision was heavily influenced by a study led by Invitae Corp., a genetic diagnostic testing company, that found "Limiting germline genetic testing to only a subset of breast cancer patients may lead other patients to miss out on data that could inform their clinical management …." *Id.* The American Society of Breast Surgeons/ASBrS has gone even furth and recommended universal germline genetic testing. *See id. See also supra* note 29, and accompanying text (discussing NSGC consideration of whole genome sequencing as first-tier testing for children with suspected genetic disorders, and to help diagnose and clinically manage adult patients with rare diseases).

127 *See* Gary E. Marchant, Mark Barnes, Ellen W. Clayton, Susan M. Wolf, *Liability Implications of Direct-to-Consumer Genetic Testing*, *in* CONSUMER GENETIC TECHNOLOGIES, *supra* note 10, at 21–4.

128 ABRAMSON, OVERDOSED, *supra* note 60, at 84. *See also* Marchant et al., *Liability*, *supra* note 127, at 21–4.

129 The US medical profession's opposition to definitive practice guidelines, including the CDC's recommended guideline for prescribing opioids for pain management after at least a decade of excessive prescribing that fed a public health opioid addiction crisis, is illustrative. *See Chapter* 5, *supra*, at notes 375–78, and accompanying text. *See also* Deborah Dowell, Kathleen R. Ragan, Christopher M. Jones et al., *Perspective, Prescribing Opioids for Pain – The New CDC Clinical Practice Guideline*, NEW. ENG. J. MED. (Nov. 3, 2022), www.nejm.org/doi/full/10.1056/NEJMp2211040.

130 *See* ABRAMSON, OVERDOSED, *supra* note 60, at 125–26.

131 BRAWLEY, HARM, *supra* note 120, at 229.

132 SANDEEP JUAHAR, DOCTORED: THE DISILLUSIONMENT OF AN AMERICAN PHYSICIAN 97 (2015).

133 ABRAMSON, OVERDOSED, *supra* note 60, at 189.

134 *Id.* at 84.

135 BRAWLEY, HARM, *supra* note 120, at 229. Consider that, with limited COVID-19 testing availability during the first wave of the pandemic, the US market was flooded with questionable COVID-19 antibody tests used to determine COVID-19-positive status even

though antibody-associated immunity was undefined. These tests were able to reach the market through the FDA's Self-Validation and Voluntary Compliance System. *See 60 Minutes, The Wild West of Testing* (first aired June 28, 2020).

136 As observed by Dr. Brawley,

> When money is to be made, the system can be proactive, again to the detriment of the patient. Call it "disease mongering" or call it the marketing of disease, but as I write this, a fleet of aquamarine, white, and blue mobile homes is bringing prostate cancer screening to a shopping mall near you… The blood test is free, but the cascade of follow-up services will ring up considerable sales for treatments that leave guys impotent and incontinent. Treatment that may have a miniscule chance of saving them from cancer, but have a much larger chance of treating a cancer that never would have harmed them, or may not even have been there in the first place.

BRAWLEY, HARM, *supra* note 120, at 25.

137 The medical profession has debated the age trigger for and frequency of mammogram screening for years, and both have shifted. Physicians have discretion to provide individualized patient care and are likely to stray from any thin majority consensus. According to Dr. Brawley, "Many people are lost in this national debate because it turns on statistics, which are hard for even a statistician to comprehend …. We need a better test, but satisfaction with and the belief in mammography causes complacency. What we need is more support for research aimed at finding a better test." BRAWLEY, HARM, *supra* note 120, at 267–68.

138 Pervasive population screening risks impeding the compilation of evidentiary science-based data to establish clinical effectiveness with reliability. Dr. Brawley has identified lung-cancer screening with chest X-rays (prior to the advent of immunotherapy and other treatments for some cases) as an example:

> A number of organizations encouraged it because it found disease at an earlier, more treatable stage. These organizations used false logic to justify screening. This led to increased survival times among those who got screen-detected and still died of lung cancer. These endorsements actually discouraged the completion of the randomized prospective trials that showed that chest X-ray screening at best did not save lives and may well have increased risk of death.

BRAWLEY, HARM, *supra* note 120, at 229–30.

139 *Id.* at 255.

140 *See Chapter* 5, *supra*, at notes 72, 133–34, and accompanying text (addressing specialization in US medicine).

141 *See* Malinowski, *Coming into Being*, *supra* note 109, at notes 41–43, and accompanying text (citations provided); Benjamin P. Sachs, Bruce Korf, *The Human Genome Project: Implications for the Practicing Obstetrician*, 81 OB. & GYN. 458, 459 (1993), https://pubmed.ncbi.nlm.nih.gov/8437805/.

142 As I published in 1997:

> Although adequate genetic counseling could, perhaps, enable people to cope better with genetic information, genetic counseling is expensive and not necessarily covered by insurance; the United States does not have enough certified, practicing genetic counselors; and health care providers are not knowledgeable enough about genetics to help stretch these limited resources.

Malinowski, *Tarot Cards*, *supra* note 6, at 1249–50 (1997) (providing citations).

143 The National Society of Genetic Counselors/NSGC accredited its 50th genetic counseling program in fall 2020. *See* Kate Reed, *Perspectives: The Creation of Genetic Counseling Training Programs – 55 and Counting!*, NSGC (May 3, 2021), https://perspectives.nsgc.org/Article/TitleLink/The-Creation-of-Genetic-Counseling-Training-Programs-55-and-Counting. According to the NSGC, "discussion of a shortage likely originated 30 years ago, and focused on genetic specialists – not genetic counselors, specifically. While medical geneticists have contracted as a profession, the opposite is true of certified genetic counselors (CGCs)." NSGC, *Genetic Counselor Workforce* (visited Jan. 17, 2022), www.nsgc.org/Policy-Research-and-Publications/Genetic-Counselor-Workforce. A study published in 2017 concluded that "it is reasonable to expect that the number of new programs may be higher than anticipated by 2026. If true, and assuming that growth in programs is matched by equivalent growth in clinical training slots, the supply of CGCs in direct patient care would meet demand earlier than these models predict." Jennifer M Hoskovec, Robin L Bennett, Megan E. Carey et al., *Projecting the Supply and Demand for Certified Genetic Counselors: a Workforce Study*, 27(1) J. GENET COUNS. 16–20, 16 (Oct. 2017), https://pubmed.ncbi.nlm.nih.gov/29052810/.

144 Anna Middleton, Alvaro Mendes, Caroline M. Benjamin, Heidi Carmen Howard, *Direct-to-consumer Genetic Testing: Where and How Does Genetic Counseling Fit?*, 14 PER MED. 249–57 (2017) (abstract), https://pubmed.ncbi.nlm.nih.gov/29767582/.

145 WATSON, STORY, *supra* note 79, at 211. The global personal genome testing sector's access to and presence in European markets is amassing rapidly. For example, in September 2022, the Indian genetic testing company Genes2Me named Axonlab, a Swiss company, as a distribution partner in nine European markets. "Under the terms of the deal, Axonlab will offer Genes2Me's next-generation sequencing and point-of-care testing products in Switzerland, Liechtenstein, Austria, Germany, Slovenia, Croatia, Belgium, Luxembourg, and the Netherlands." Staff Reporter, *Genes2Me Signs European Distribution Deal With Axonlab*, GENOMEWEB (Sept. 6, 2022), www.genomeweb.com/molecular-diagnostics/genes2me-signs-european-distribution-deal-axonlab#.Yxe25XbMK3A. Earlier in 2022, Genes2Me obtained CE marking – confirmation of conformity with European health, safety, and environmental protection standards – for more than twenty-five next-generation sequencing-based panels for oncology, pharmacogenomics, and hereditary diseases. *See id.*

146 *Id. See* Catherine M. Sharkey, *Direct-to-Consumer Genetic Testing: The FDA's Dual Role As Safety and Health Information Regulator*, 68 DEPAUL L. REV. 343, 344–45 (2019) (addressing UK approval of DTC genetic testing). It is important to note that European Medicines Agency/EMA market approval is not synonyms with uptake by universal health care systems. Clinical utility and cost are evaluated by individual countries through health technology assessment/HTA mechanisms, and prices are negotiated. *See Chapter* 5, *supra*, at notes 384–403, and accompanying text ("The Absence of Centralized, Objective, Reliable Health Technology Assessment/HTA in US Health Care"). The UK has a universal health care system (a nationalized medicine system, as opposed to a socialized medicine system like Germany's or a national/single-payer health insurance system like Canada's) that controls health care system clinical uptake and distinguishes health care products market available to consumers for their use but at their own expense, independent of system clinical care. *See* EZEKIEL J. EMANUEL, WHICH COUNTRY HAS THE WORLD'S BEST HEALTH CARE? 83–114 (2020) (explaining factually, though using the terminology differently).

147 See Salma Shickh, Chloe Mighton, Marc Clausen et al., *Doctors Shouldn't have to "Cheat the System": Clinicians' Real-World Experiences of the Utility of Genomic*

Sequencing, GENETICS IN MED. (May 25, 2022), www.gimjournal.org/article/S1098-3600(22)00754-7/fulltext; Staff Reporter, *Canadian Healthcare Providers, Policymakers Value Different Aspects of Clinical Genomic Sequencing*, GENOMEWEB (May 27, 2022), www.genomeweb.com/sequencing/canadian-healthcare-providers-policymakers-value-different-aspects-clinical-genomic#.Y5PognbMK3A.

148 *See generally* Shick, Mighton, *Cheat the System*, *supra* note 147.

149 *See, e.g.*, Francesca Spinosi, Shama Khan, Christine Seymour, Elena Ashkinadze, *Trends in Coverage and Reimbursement for Reproductive Genetic Counseling in New Jersey by Multiple Payers from 2010 to 2018*, 30(6) J. GENET. COUNS. 1748–56 (Dec. 2021) ("Commercial insurance covered 65% of encounters billed but this varied between payers."), https://pubmed.ncbi.nlm.nih.gov/34223664/. State licensure of CGCs improves reimbursement (twenty-seven states have introduced licensure of CGCs), and pending federal legislation, the Access to Genetic Counselor Services Act, would provide Medicare recognition of CGCs and help overall with reimbursement from the Centers for Medicare and Medicaid Services/CMS. *See* John Richardson, *Perspectives, Update: State Licensure and CMS Recognition*, NSGC (Apr. 24, 2019), https://perspectives.nsgc.org/Article/TitleLink/State-Licensure-and-CMS-Recognition. *See* Malinowski, *Tarot Cards*, *supra* note 6, at 1212.

150 Staff, *Perspectives, Genetic Counselor Burnout Often Related to Stress, Depression*, NSGC (Nov. 18, 2020) (reporting baseline data from study, and quoting Colleen Caleshu, co-lead investigator), https://perspectives.nsgc.org/Article/genetic-counselor-burnout-often-related-to-stress-depression.

151 NHGRI, *Coverage and Reimbursement of Genetic Tests* (Aug. 15, 2019), www.genome.gov/about-genomics/policy-issues/Coverage-Reimbursement-of-Genetic-Tests. The *CPT Manual* and codes are addressed in *Chapter* 5, *supra*, at notes 62–68, and accompanying text.

152 *See* Malinowski, *Coming into Being*, *supra* note 109, at 1471 (James Watson's criticism of the premature market availability of genetic tests in the early 1990s, with reference to Japan as particularly problematic).

153 *See generally* Michael S. Yesley, *What's ELSI got to do with it? Bioethics and the Human Genome Project*, 27 NEW GENETICS & SOC'Y 1–6 (2008), www.tandfonline.com/doi/full/10.1080/14636770701843527; Kathi E. Hanna, *The Ethical, Legal, and Social Implications Program of the National Center for Human Genome Research: A Missed Opportunity?* (1992) (page nos. unavailable online), www.ncbi.nlm.nih.gov/books/NBK231976/#:~:text=This%20belief%20led%20to%20the%20creation%20of%20the,support%20for%20the%20project%20went%20on%20%28Watson%2C%201988%29. The HGP founders, and foremost James Watson, championed the necessity of accompanying genetic research with the social science disciplines to probe ethical, legal, and social implications of the underlying research. *See* Malinowski, *Realities of Race*, *supra* note 42, at 1473. A percentage of the HGP budget was slated to address ELSI issues – for 1992, three percent of the overall HGP budget and five percent of the NIH share (HGP was a joint NIH-DOE initiative). *See* Hanna, *Missed Opportunity?*, *supra*.

154 The ELSI program was questioned and criticized during its formative years, and even after. *See generally* Hanna, *Missed Opportunity?*, *supra* note 153; INSTITUTE OF MEDICINE /IOM, SOCIETY'S CHOICES, SOCIAL AND ETHICAL DECISION MAKING IN BIOMEDICINE (Ruth Ellen Bulger, Elizabeth Meyer Bobby, Harvey V. Fineberg eds., 1995) (includes Ms. Hanna's essay), https://nap.nationalacademies.org/catalog/4771/societys-choices-social-and-ethical-decision-making-in-biomedicine. *See*

also Malinowski, *Snake Oil, supra* note 13, at 39 (providing explanation with citations). Regardless of the additional contributions ELSI could have made, the program proved an important complement to HGP. Today, there are ELSI counterparts to virtually all major genetics and genomics research undertakings. *Visit* NHGRI, *Coverage and Reimbursement of Genetic Tests* (updated Aug. 15, 2019), www.genome.gov/about-genomics/policy-issues/Coverage-Reimbursement-of-Genetic-Tests; NHGRI, *Ethical, Legal and Social Implications Research Program* (updated Apr. 6, 2021), www.genome.gov/Funded-Programs-Projects/ELSI-Research-Program-ethical-legal-social-implications.

155 *Cf.* Hanna, *Missed Opportunity?, supra* note 153.

156 Yesley, *ELSI, supra* note 153, at 4.

157 *See generally* SACGT, RECOMMENDATIONS, *supra* note 14; Malinowski, *Snake Oil, supra* note 13; Malinowski, *Tarot Cards, supra* note 6. *See also* Santa Slokenberga, *Direct-to-Consumer Genetic Testing: Changes in the EU Regulatory Landscape*, 22(5) EUR. J. HEALTH L. 463–480 (2015), https://pubmed.ncbi.nlm.nih.gov/26665691/; Stuart Hogarth, Gail Javitt, David Melzer., *The Current Landscape for Direct-to-Consumer Genetic Testing: Legal, Ethical, and Policy Issues*. ANNU. REV. GENOMICS HUM. GENET. 9, 161–82 (2008), www.annualreviews.org/doi/10.1146/annurev.genom.9.081307.164319.

158 *See generally* CONSUMER GENETIC TECHNOLOGIES, *supra* note 10 (anthology of contributions complementing the Petrie-Flom Center for Health Law Policy, Biotechnology, and Bioethics at Harvard Law School's "Annual Conference, Consuming Genetics: The Ethical and Legal Considerations of Consumer Genetic Technologies," held May 17, 2019).

159 *See NBC Nightly News, Mark Rasch, Cybersecurity & Privacy Expert* (Dec. 23, 2019) (reporting on Pentagon warning to military enlistees).

160 *Id.* One's set of DNA instructions is activated differently in specific cells to produce ears and toes, hearts and lungs (cellular differentiation), but all of a person's cells, with the exception of gametes (sperm and ova), contain the same complete base set of DNA instructions.

161 WATSON, STORY, *supra* note 79, at 217.

162 *NBC, Cybersecurity, supra* note 159.

163 Hazel, *Best Practices, supra* note 10, at 261 (internal citations omitted). *See generally* FUTURE, BEST PRACTICES, *supra* note 36.

164 *See* Hazel, *Best Practices, supra* note 10, at 272.

165 *Id.* at 262.

166 *See* Mulholland, *Survey, supra* note 13, at 318. *See Chapter 4, supra*, at notes 38–54, and accompanying text (reactions and responses to the DTC BRCA testing introduced in 1996).

167 *See* California Consumer Privacy Act/CCPA, Cal. Civ. Code §§ 1798.100-199 (2018); New York Privacy Act, S.B. 5462, 2019 Leg. Reg. Sess. (NY 2019). *See* Cal. Dep. Just., *Fact Sheet, California Consumer Privacy Act (CCPA)*, https://oag.ca.gov/system/files/attachments/press_releases/CCPA%20Fact%20Sheet%20%2800000002%29.pdf. The CCPA restricts the collection, use, and sharing of biometrics data, which the law defines as "an individual's physiological, biological or behavioral characteristics, including an individual's deoxyribonucleic acid (DNA), that can be used, singly or in combination with each other identifying data, to establish individual identity." *Id.* at § 1798.140(b). *See* Hazel, *Best Practices, supra* note 10, at 275–76.

168 *See generally* CONSUMER GENETIC TECHNOLOGIES, *supra* note 10. The editors of this anthology recognized the many "calls for self-regulation found throughout this volume." *Id.* at 9.

169 *See Prologue, supra*, at notes 17–19, and accompanying text (the necessity of having the DNA samples and information needed to engage in comparisons).

170 Meg Tirrell, *Genome Sequencing: A Glimpse of the Future CNBC* (Dec. 10, 2015) (page nos unavailable online), www.cnbc.com/2015/12/10/unlocking-my-genome-was-it-worth-it.html.

171 *See* 45 CFR part 46. *See* HHS, Federal Policy for the Protection of Human Subjects ("Common Rule") (last reviewed Mar. 18, 2016), www.hhs.gov/ohrp/regulations-and-policy/regulations/common-rule/index.html.

172 *See generally* HHS, Revised Common Rule (content last reviewed Jan. 19, 2017), www.hhs.gov/ohrp/regulations-and-policy/regulations/finalized-revisions-common-rule/index.html; *Council on Gov. Rel's, Common Rule Overview* (Feb. 1, 2017), www.cogr.edu/sites/default/files/Summary%20of%20Changes%20to%20the%20Common%20Rule_COGR.pdf. The revised Common Rule permits researchers to obtain broad consent from participants to use their encrypted but identifiable biospecimens and private information in yet-to-be specified research studies. *See* Jerry Menikoff, Julie Kaneshiro, Ivor Pritchard, *The Common Rule, Updated*, 376 N. Eng. J. Med. 613, 614 (2017), www.proquest.com/docview/1869528360.

173 *See generally* Health Insurance Portability and Accountability Act/HIPAA, HIPAA Privacy Rule, 45 CFR Part 160, Subparts A and E of Part 164.

174 "The final rule allows for the optional use of broad consent for storage and secondary research use of identifiable private information or identifiable biospecimens in lieu of obtaining study-specific informed consent." *Council on Gov. Rel's, Overview, supra* note 172. *See* Menikoff, *Updated, supra* note 72, at 614. *See also infra* notes 229, 274–77, and accompanying text (also discussing AllUs).

175 Through AllUs, NIH is attempting to recruit a cohort of a million or more residents in the US representative of the nation's population diversity. *Visit* AllUs, official site, https://allofus.nih.gov/. *See Prologue, supra*, at notes 24–6, and accompanying text (discussing AllUs). *See also infra* notes 229, 274–77, and accompanying text (discussing AllUs).

176 AllUs, official site, home page, https://allofus.nih.gov/.

177 *See generally*, Stuart Leavenworth, *Ancestry Wants your Spit, Your DNA and your Trust. Should you Give them All Three?*, McClatchy Newspapers (May 29, 2018) (page nos. unavailable), www.mcclatchydc.com/news/nation-world/article210692689.html#cardLink=row1_card1. As explained by science writer Carl Zimmer,

> So you can choose sort of different levels of privacy with a lot of these services. And so for example, some people will say, I want you to look at my DNA. I want you to tell me about my ancestry. I want you to tell me about – you know, for 23andMe, they'll give you a few bits of information about your medical conditions. And that's it. But they will try to get you to opt in to sharing your data for their own basic research. So at 23andMe, for example, there's a whole team of researchers who are studying all sorts of things, all sorts of diseases, sleep patterns, and so on. And then they will also go into partnerships with drug development companies, who will take their data looking at, say, 50,000 people with lupus and 50,000 people who don't have lupus and try to look for the genetic differences. Those could point the way towards possible drugs.

Carl Zimmer, *A Science Writer Explores the 'Perversions And Potential' Of Genetic Tests*, NPR Fresh Air (June 11, 2018), www.npr.org/sections/health-shots/2018/06/11/618870881/a-science-writer-explores-the-perversions-and-potential-of-genetic-tests.

178 *See* Leavenworth, *Ancestry Wants, supra* note 177. 23andMe had amassed some 5,000,000 customer research participants as of 2019. AncestryHealth had the same in 2018, and approximately seventy percent of its customer contributors agreed to participate in research. *See* Stuart Leavenworth, *DNA for Sale: Who is the Secretive Google Subsidiary that has Access to Ancestry's DNA Database?*, CHIC. TRIB. (June 6, 2018), www.chicagotribune.com/news/nationworld/sns-tns-bc-dna-data-20180606-story.html. I purchased 23andMe's Personal Genome Health Service/PGHS in conjunction with this project, and I participated in subsequent requests for information until I became concerned about the quality (shallowness) of information collected and the possibility that 23andMe data through its licenses and collaborations would poison the broader well of research data. For example, I was asked if I am either nearsighted or farsighted, but there was no opportunity for me to qualify my answer – in my case, by indicating that I had LASIK eye surgery. *See Chapter 4, supra*, at note 102, and accompanying text (my "garbage in, garbage out" concern regarding data used in research, and the use of resulting innovation in medical decision making).

179 This is my experience as a 23andMe PGHS customer over approximately four years (2019 to the present). *See also* MISHA ANGRIST, HERE IS A HUMAN BEING 262 (2011).

180 *See* HIPAA Privacy Rule, 45 CFR Part 160, Subparts A and E of Part 164. *Visit* US Dep. of Health and Human Services/HHS, *Health Information Privacy* (visited Jan. 24, 2022), www.hhs.gov/hipaa/index.html. *See* HHS, *Summary of the HIPAA Security Rule* (reviewed July 26, 2013), www.hhs.gov/hipaa/for-professionals/security/laws-regulations/index.html; HHS, *Your Rights under HIPAA* (reviewed Jan 19, 2022), www.hhs.gov/hipaa/for-individuals/guidance-materials-for-consumers/index.html.

181 *See* 45 CFR 160.103.

182 *See* CMS, *Are You a Covered Entity?* (modified Dec. 1, 2021), www.cms.gov/Regulations-and-Guidance/Administrative-Simplification/HIPAA-ACA/AreYouaCoveredEntity.

183 *See generally* HHS, *HIPAA, Understanding Some of HIPAA's Permitted Uses and Disclosures* (reviewed Feb. 12, 2016), www.hhs.gov/hipaa/for-professionals/privacy/guidance/permitted-uses/index.html.

184 HHS promoted and expanded adoption of health information technology responsive to the Health Information Technology for Economic and Clinical Health Act/HITECH of 2009, which was enacted under Title XIII of the American Recovery and Reinvestment Act/ARRA of 2009, Pub. L. 111–5. HIPAA strongly promotes implementation of secured health information technology systems for security, accountability, and tracking health information – which encompasses the ability to correct inevitable errors under the HIPAA Privacy Rule, and to maintain overall HIPAA compliance. For a HIPAA covered entity or business associate even modest in size, satisfying compliance necessitates use of secured electronic medical information systems. Requisite HIPAA Supplemental Security Training ("Security Rule"), with its focus on security, is responsive to HITECH and addresses electronic protected health information (e-PHI, or ePHI) for administrative and systematic purposes. "Essentially, the Security Rule operationalizes the protections contained in the Privacy Rule by addressing the technical and nontechnical safeguards that covered entities must implement to secure ePHI." AMA, *HIPAA Security Rule and Risk Analysis* (undated), www.ama-assn.org/practice-management/hipaa/hipaa-security-rule-risk-analysis.

185 *See* 45 CFR 164.501, 164.508, 164.512(i). *See also* 45 CFR 164.514(e), 164.528, 164.532. Deidentified data may:

be shared without patient permission and do not have to be stored according to the Security Rule's standards. The Privacy Rule considers health information to be deidentified if a qualified expert determines that there is a "very small" risk that it could be reidentified (i.e., connected to the patient). Alternatively, users can deidentify data by removing 18 specific items, including the patient's name, certain geographic details, dates (except the year), facial images, and telephone, fax, account, and social security numbers.

Sharona Hoffman, *Perspective, Privacy and Security* – Protecting Patients' Health Information, 1056(10) N. Eng. J. Med. 1913–16, 1915 (Nov. 24, 2022), www.nejm.org/doi/full/10.1056/NEJMp2201676. Moreover,

> The Privacy Rule relaxes the data-deidentification requirements for circumstances in which having additional patient details might be necessary, such as in research contexts. It allows covered entities to share "limited data sets" for such uses without patient consent if recipients sign data-use agreements outlining specific restrictions and protections. Limited data sets have been stripped of most identifiers, but they retain information on dates and locations, though not patients' addresses.

Id. As summarized by HHS,

> In the course of conducting research, researchers may obtain, create, use, and/or disclose individually identifiable health information. Under the Privacy Rule, covered entities are permitted to use and disclose protected health information[/PHI] for research with individual authorization, or without individual authorization under limited circumstances set forth in the Privacy Rule.

HHS, HIPAA, *Research* (reviewed June 13, 2018), www.hhs.gov/hipaa/for-professionals/special-topics/research/index.html.

186 Heather F. Delgado, Lara D. Seng, Alexandra D. Dumezich, *Relaxing of HIPAA Laws During COVID-19 Pandemic, XII (3)*, Nat'l L. J. (Mar.18, 2020), www.natlawreview.com/article/relaxing-hipaa-laws-during-covid-19-pandemic. In spring 2020, HHS waived provisions of the HIPAA Privacy Rule 2020 to better enable a coordinated public health response to the COVID-19 pandemic. *See id. Visit*, HHS, *HIPAA and COVID-19* (reviewed Sept. 30, 2021), www.hhs.gov/hipaa/for-professionals/special-topics/hipaa-covid19/index.html.

187 *See generally* GINA, Pub. L. No. 110–233, 122 Stat. 881 (2008) (codified as amended in scattered sections of 29 U.S.C. and 42 U.S.C.); NHGRI, *Genetic Discrimination* (updated Jan. 6, 2022), www.genome.gov/about-genomics/policy-issues/Genetic-Discrimination#gina; Office for Human Research Protections/OHRP, *Guidance on the Genetic Information Nondiscrimination Act: Implications for Investigators and Institutional Review Boards* (Mar. 24, 2009), www.hhs.gov/ohrp/regulations-and-policy/guidance/guidance-on-genetic-information-nondiscrimination-act/index.html#:~:text=GINA%20includes%20a%20%22research%20exception%22%20to%20the%20general,require%29%20that%20an%20individual%20undergo%20a%20genetic%20test.

188 HHS, *Guidance for Investigators, supra* note 187.

189 *See* Leavenworth, *DNA for Sale, supra* note 178.

190 *See generally* George J. Annas, *The Patient Rights Advocate: Redefining the Doctor-Patient Relationship in the Hospital Context*, 27 Vand. L. Rev. 243 (1974).

191 The Personal Genome Project/PGP offers to sequence entire personal genomes for donors willing to share:

> In 2005, Harvard Medical School geneticist George Church established the Personal Genome Project (PGP), aiming to flip this problem on its head. The PGP is building a data repository where all information is open to the public. Church offers volunteers the possibility of having their complete genome decoded; in return, they agree to deposit their genetic and medical records into the public domain.

WATSON, STORY, *supra* note 79, at 218. *Visit* Harvard Personal Genome Project/PGP, official site, https://pgp.med.harvard.edu/.

192 *See Prologue, supra*, at notes 17–19, and accompanying text. *See also supra* notes 169–70, and accompanying text (quoting Eric Lander). *See Chapter 4, supra*, at notes 50, 87, 139–42, 151, and accompanying text (identifying major biobank undertakings, including 23andMe's).

193 *See* Hazel, *Best Practices, supra* note 10.

194 *See* Leavenworth, *DNA for Sale, supra* note 178.

195 For example, consider the research participants in the deCODE, Ancestry, and 23andMe endeavors. *See generally Chapter 4, supra*, at notes 87–90 (deCODE began amassing a biobank of the population of Iceland in the 1990s), 112 (23andMe had amassed over 5 million DNA profiles and related health information globally by summer 2018), 167 (Ancestry had amassed more than 3.6 million subscribers and 18 million people in its DNA network by 2019), and accompanying text.

196 Consider Mrs. Henrietta Lacks' seismic though involuntary contribution to twentieth century science research – a platform contribution spanning the forefront of Rx R&D – and her family's difficulties affording and accessing US health care. *See infra* notes 268–69, and accompanying text.

197 *See* 45 CFR part 46. *See also Council on Gov. Rel's, Overview, supra* note 172; HHS, *Federal Policy for the Protection of Human Subjects ("Common Rule")* (last reviewed Mar. 18, 2016), www.hhs.gov/ohrp/regulations-and-policy/regulations/common-rule/index.html.

198 As explained by Eric Heath, Ancestry's Chief Privacy Officer,

> Privacy is basically our top priority here … In terms of security, you know, we are very cognizant that without our customers' trust, we do not have a business … To prevent disclosure of customer identities, the kits and spit tubes that Ancestry sends to Illumina are marked only with bar codes, not people's names and addresses. After Illumina finishes its analysis, the results are sent back to Ancestry, which, according to Heath, is the only entity that can reconnect the results with individual customers. After Ancestry generates an ethnicity estimate for a customer, it is forwarded onto that person's email.

Leavenworth, *Ancestry wants, supra* note 177.

199 *See generally* ERIN MURPHY, INSIDE THE CELL: THE DARK SIDE OF FORENSIC DNA (2015).

200 "Lavender Doe" was a DNA Doe Project case. The DNA Doe Project uses genetic genealogy to identify John and Jane Does. *Visit* DNA Doe Project, official site (visited Feb. 4, 2022), https://dnadoeproject.org/; *Success Stories, Lavender* Doe, https://dnadoeproject.org/case/lavender-doe/. The body of Dana Lynn Dodd (also known as "Lavender Doe") was found in 2006 in Kilgore, Texas. Efforts to identify her through dental records, DNA comparisons with the DNA of missing persons, and renderings from clay reconstructions (her body was exhumed for this) disseminated to the public were unsuccessful. *See id.* The DNA Doe Project took the case in 2018, announced they had identified Lavender Doe in January 2019, and released her identity the following month. *See id.*

201 *See generally* Heather Murphy, Tim Arango, *Joseph DeAngelo Pleads Guilty in Golden State Killer Cases*, N.Y. Times (June 29, 2020), www.nytimes.com/2020/06/29/us/golden-state-killer-joseph-deangelo.html. Mr. DeAngelo, a former police officer, pled guilty to multiple counts of murder and kidnapping on June 29, 2020, and, as part of his plea bargain, admitted to numerous crimes he had not been formally charged with. *See id.* He committed at least thirteen murders, more than fifty rapes, and over 100 burglaries in California between 1973 and 1986, but Mr. DeAngelo was not prosecuted until 2018. *See id.* Law enforcement, with the expertise of CeCe Moore, the Chief Genetic Genealogist of Parabon Nanolabs, Inc, uploaded his DNA profile from a rape kit to the personal genomics website GEDmatch, constructed his family tree through biological relatives who were consumers of DTC personal genome testing services (ancestry and/or health), and identified him. *See* Susan Scutti, *What the Golden State Killer Case Means for your Genetic Privacy*, CNN (May 1, 2018), https://edition.cnn.com/2018/04/27/health/golden-state-killer-genetic-privacy/index.html. *See also* Michael Levenson, *A Half-Century Later, DNA Helps Police Identify a Murder Suspect and His Victim*, N.Y. Times (July 26, 2020), at 20 (genetic genealogy utilized to identify both a 1968 murder victim and her killer). *See generally* Murphy, Cell, *supra* note 199. Law enforcement recently used investigative genetic genealogy to link Bryan Christopher Kohberger to the murders of University of Idaho students Ethan Chapin, Kaylee Goncalves, Xana Kernodle, and Madison Mogen, *See* Aaron Katersky, Luke Barr, Josh Margolin, Mary Kekatos, *Idaho Murders: Suspect was Identified through DNA using Genealogy Databases*, Police Say, ABC News (Jan. 2, 2023), https://abcnews.go.com/US/idaho-murders-suspect-identified-dna-genealogy-databases-police/story?id=96088596.

202 *Visit* GEDMatch, official site (visited Feb. 4, 2022), www.gedmatch.com/; FamilyTreeDNA, official site (visited Feb. 4, 2022), www.familytreedna.com/.

203 *See generally* Suzanne Bell, John M. Butler, Understanding Forensic DNA (Understanding Life) (2022).

204 *See* Christi J. Guerrini, Ray A. Wickenheiser, Blaine Bettinger et al., *Four Misconceptions about Investigative Genetic Genealogy*, 8 (1) J. Law Biosciences (Apr. 2021), www.ncbi.nlm.nih.gov/pmc/articles/PMC8043143/.

205 *Visit* Parabon Nanolabs, Inc., official site (visited Feb. 4, 2022), www.parabon-nanolabs.com/. Parabon provides DNA phenotyping (matching DNA to persons) services for law enforcement organizations through its Parabon Snapshot. *Visit* Snapshot Home (visited Feb. 4, 2022), https://snapshot.parabon-nanolabs.com/. The US Department of Defense/DOD provided some $2,000,000 for the development of Snapshot. *See* Clive Cookson, *DNA: the Next Frontier in Forensics*, Fin. Times (Jan. 30, 2015), www.ft.com/content/012b2b9c-a742-11e4-8a71-00144feab7de.

206 *See, e.g., infra* note 211, and accompanying text (discussing a New Orleans man wrongfully accused). DNA *itself* may cause confusion and mistakes, such as through the occurrence of human "chimeras" – people with DNA from more than one embryo. *See generally* Dan Vergano, *DNA Showed a Mother was Also her Daughter's Uncle – How Scientists Solved this Medical Mystery*, Science (Nov. 25, 2022) (explaining human chimeras and the possibility that they could be more common than researchers previously thought), www.grid.news/story/science/2022/11/25/dna-showed-a-mother-was-also-her-daughters-uncle-how-scientists-solved-this-medical-mystery/.

207 See Murphy, Cell, *supra* note 199.

208 "But over the last five years [2013–18], the company has reneged on promises to customers and partners .... [F]ormer employees say this backtracking raises questions about whether the company will follow through on consumer privacy pledges as it develops the world's largest DNA database." Leavenworth, *Ancestry Wants, supra* note 177.

209 *See* Stuart Leavenworth, *Ancestry Has a History of Backtracking on Promises to Customers* (May 30, 2018; updated July 10, 2018), www.mcclatchydc.com/news/nation-world/article210969549.html.
210 According to the former CEO of MyFamily.com, "With impunity, corporations can change the terms of engagement even after publicly stating: 'Here is our plan, here is our agreement ....'" *Id.*
211 *See* Stuart Leavenworth, *History, supra* note 209.
212 *See id.*
213 *See Prologue, supra*, at notes 17–19, and accompanying text (the necessity of having DNA samples and related information to engage in comparisons). For discussion of biobanking, see *Prologue, supra*, at notes 23–32, and accompanying text.
214 Incidents of expansive breaches of personal information in recent years abound, from Facebook allowing the political data firm Cambridge Analytica to access data from fifty million customers to the US Office of Personnel Management exposing more than a million personnel records and security clearances to hackers. *See* Leavenworth, *Ancestry wants, supra* note 177. Notably, in July 2020, a 19-year-old from the UK, a 22-year-old from Florida, and a US minor used social engineering (they used the account of a Twitter employee who had access to the company's master controls) to hack the Twitter accounts of former President Obama, presidential candidate Joe Biden, and a slew of major celebrities and companies including Microsoft. *See* Donie O'Sullivan, Josh Campbell, Three *People Charged in Twitter Hack that Hit Biden and Obama*, CNN BUSINESS (July 31, 2020), www.cnn.com/2020/07/31/tech/alleged-twitter-hacker-arrested/index.html.
215 *See* Leavenworth, *Ancestry wants, supra* note 177.
216 *See id.*
217 *See id.*
218 *Id.* (page nos. unavailable).
219 *Id.* (page nos. unavailable).
220 *See id.*
221 *See id.* "Ancestry's DNA database includes more than 5 million records, and ... anywhere from half to 70 percent of customers consent to have their data used for research." *Id.* Calico, founded by Google in 2013 with $1 billion in funding, has been highly secretive. *See* Leavenworth, *DNA for Sale, supra* note 178. Craig Venter, a former NIH scientist who built a commercial challenger to HGP in a race to complete a draft map of the human genome sequence, has a new company, Human Longevity, which shares Calico's mission. Human Longevity seeks to identify key DNA variants that underlie longevity and health through analysis of the sequenced genomes of patients with Alzheimer's and other terminal illnesses associated with advanced age. *See* WATSON, STORY, *supra* note 79, at 229. In 2020, the company anticipated sequencing a million human genomes, and Mr. Venter "predicts that some of the information might prove commercially valuable to pharmaceutical companies." *Id.*
222 *See* KEVIN DAVIES, $1,000 GENOME: THE REVOLUTION IN DNA SEQUENCING AND THE NEW ERA OF PERSONALIZED MEDICINE 29 (2010); WATSON, STORY, *supra* note 79, at 218, 224. *Visit* Illumina, Inc., official site (visited June 22, 2022), www.illumina.com/.
223 *See* Christina Farr, *Consumer DNA Testing Hits a Rough Patch: Here's How Companies like Ancestry and 23andMe Can Survive*, CNBC EVOLVE (Feb. 9, 2020), www.cnbc.com/2020/02/07/how-dna-testing-companies-like-ancestry-and-23andme-can-survive.html.

224 FDA, *Illumina Cybersecurity Vulnerability May Present Risks for Patient Results and Customer Networks: Letter to Health Care Providers* (June 2, 2022), www.fda.gov/medical-devices/letters-health-care-providers/illumina-cybersecurity-vulnerability-may-present-risks-patient-results-and-customer-networks-letter.

225 *See generally* NAT'L COMM'N FOR THE PROT. OF HUM. SUBJECTS OF BIOM. AND BEHAV. RSCH., US DEP'T OF HEALTH, ED., & WELFARE, THE BELMONT REP. (1979), www.hhs.gov/ohrp/sites/default/files/the-belmont-report-508c_FINAL.pdf.; US Dep. Health, Ed., and Welfare/HEW, Protection of Human Subjects; Notice of Report for Public Comment, 44 Fed. Reg. no. 76, 23191-7 (Apr. 18, 1979).

226 *Id.* (page nos. unavailable online). *See generally* RUTH R. FADEN, TOM L. BEAUCHAMP, A HISTORY AND THEORY OF INFORMED CONSENT (1986).

227 *See* MALINOWSKI, HANDBOOK, *supra* note 27, at 84–89 (discussing mandate for federal agencies to implement the Belmont Report, HHS's leading initiative to do so, and adoption of HHS's regulatory work by other federal agencies, resulting in the Common Rule). *See also supra* notes 171–74, 195–99, and accompanying text (addressing the Common Rule and its application in DTCGHR testing service company research).

228 *See Prologue, supra*, at notes 17–19 (the necessity of having DNA samples and related information to engage in comparisons), 23–32 (biobank enablers), and accompanying text. *See also supra* notes 169–70, and accompanying text (quoting Eric Lander).

229 *See supra* notes 172–74, and accompanying text (discussing revisions to the Common Rule to allow broad consent for inclusion in future, unidentified research studies). *See supra* notes 175–76, and accompanying text (discussing AllUs). NIH earmarked nearly $4.8 million in FY2023 grant funding to support the analysis of data from AllUs and to develop new data analysis tools and methods. *See* Staff Reporter, *NIH Commits, supra* note 88.

230 "The medical community has long considered informed consent to be a fundamental component of the doctor-patient relationship." J. Aidan Lang, *The Right to Remain Silent: Abortion and Compelled Physician Speech*, 62 B.C. L. REV. 2091, 2125 (2021). According to the AMA's Code of Medical Ethics, "Informed consent to medical treatment is fundamental in both ethics and law. Patients have the right to receive information and ask questions about recommended treatments so that they can make well-considered decisions about care." AMA, Code Med. Ethics Op.2.1.1 (visited Feb. 4, 2022), www.ama-assn.org/delivering-care/ethics/informed-consent.

231 *See* FADEN, BEAUCHAMP, HISTORY, *supra* note 226, at 23.

232 Susan M. Wolf, *Toward A Systemic Theory of Informed Consent in Managed Care*, 35 HOUS. L. REV. 1631, 1631–32 (1999), *quoting Schloendorff v. Society of New York Hosp.*, 105 N.E. 92, 93 (N.Y. 1914).

233 *See generally* JAY KATZ, SILENT WORLD, *supra* note 21 (addressing paternalism in twentieth century US medicine). *See Chapter 5, supra*, at notes 113–77, and accompanying text (subsection entitled "Today's US Physician-Patient Relationship, and the State of Physician Decision Making").

234 M. Gregg Bloche, *The Invention of Health Law*, 91 CAL. L. REV. 247, 271 (2003).

235 NIH, *Protocols and Informed Consent* (reviewed July 30, 2019), www.niaid.nih.gov/research/dmid-protocols-informed-consent.

236 AMA, *Ethics: Code of Medical Ethics: Consent, Communication & Decision-Making* (visited Feb. 5, 2020), www.ama-assn.org/delivering-care/ethics/code-medical-ethics-consent-communication-decision-making.

237 *See Chapter 1, supra*, at notes 184–89, and accompanying text ("The Resulting Medical Profession-FDA Symbiotic Relationship").

238 *See Chapter* 5, *supra*, at notes 178–206, and accompanying text ("Stewardship of the Evidentiary-Science Base of Medicine").

239 *See Chapter* 1, *supra*, at notes 35–45, and accompanying text ("US Law-Policy Recognition of Clinical Medicine as the Medical Profession's Domain").

240 *See Chapter* 4, *supra*, at notes 125–29, and accompanying text (addressing FDA approval of 23andMe's DTCGHR tests and service).

241 I purchased and used a 23andMe kit for this project and found the comprehension prerequisite for use to be disturbingly insufficient. *See supra* note 95, and accompanying text.

242 Leavenworth, *Ancestry wants*, *supra* note 177.

243 *See id.* (quoting Ms. Marcy Darnovsky, Director of the Center for Genetics and Society, a biotech watchdog group based in Berkeley, California, as stating "You are not just taking the test for you. You are taking it for the whole family ...."); Leavenworth, *DNA for Sale*, *supra* note 178. *See generally* Emilia Niemiec, Heidi Carmen Howard, *Ethical Issues in Consumer Genome Sequencing: Use of Consumers' Samples and Data*, 8 Appl. Transl. Genom. 23–30 (2016), www.ncbi.nlm.nih.gov/pmc/articles/PMC4796706/; Anna Middleton, *Communication about DTC Testing: Commentary on a Family Experience of Personal Genomics*, 21 J. Genet. Couns. 392–98 (2012), https://pubmed.ncbi.nlm.nih.gov/22223062/; Heidi Carmen Howard, Bartha Maria Knoppers, Pascal Borry, *The Research Activities of Direct-to-Consumer Genetic Testing Companies Raise Questions about Consumers as Research Subjects*, 11 EMBO Rep. 579–82 (2010). Such open consent with the option to later opt out is is reminiscent of the presumed consent deCODE used to build a biobank of the people of Iceland, which later was deemed unconstitutional. *See* Stuart Leavenworth, *This Nation Faces a DNA Dilemma: Whether to Notify People Carrying Cancer Genes*, McClatchy Newspapers (June 14, 2018), www.mcclatchydc.com/news/nation-world/article213014904.html. The company's representatives persuaded Iceland's parliament to pass the Health Sector Database Act to create a vast database of Icelanders' genetic information and medical records for scientific research through *presumed* consent and allowed deCODE to license and control access to the data. *Id.* However, in 2003, an Icelandic woman challenged the inclusion of her father's medical records in the database, and Iceland's Supreme Court found the presumed consent unconstitutional and ruled in her favor. *Id.* For discussion of privacy implications and considerations, see *supra* notes 159–224, and accompanying text ("Privacy and Associated Risks").

244 *See* Leavenworth, *DNA for Sale*, *supra* note 178. Ancestry disclosed in its 2016 Securities and Exchange Commission/SEC filing that its research collaborations pose privacy risks: "If our third-party DNA testing or research providers fail to comply with privacy and security standards, as required pursuant to the terms of our agreements with such providers, this could have a material adverse effect[/MAC] on our business, financial condition and results of operations." *Id.*

245 As stated by Joel Winston, a privacy lawyer who has examined the legal rights of DNA-testing customers, "Consumers, for example, have no way of knowing if Ancestry actually destroys their DNA samples, and the company won't say where it stores them." Leavenworth, *DNA for Sale*, *supra* note 178. After outsides labs (Ancestry and 23andMe both heavily utilize Illumina for DNA sequencing) extract a small amount of saliva from a customer submission, the remainder is returned to the DTC company's custody, and "Where that DNA is stored, and how long it will be stored, is unknown. Company officials won't say." Leavenworth, *Ancestry wants*, *supra* note 177.

246 *See* Herper, *Ancestry, supra* note 85 (addressed in the discussion *infra*). *See supra* notes 208–21, and accompanying text (discussing Ancestry).
247 *See supra* notes 200–12, and accompanying text (discussing investigative genetic genealogy). *See also* Leavenworth, *Ancestry Wants, supra* note 177 ("Unless customers request otherwise, Ancestry adds people's DNA data to its proprietary database, the largest of its kind. In a mere six years, the database has grown to include DNA from more than 5 million people, up from 2 million in mid-2016, according to company figures.). *See generally* ZIMMER, MOTHER'S LAUGH, *supra* note 78.
248 Investigative genetic genealogy, already very tangible, underscores this point. *See supra* notes 200–12, and accompanying text (addressing familial DNA and personal genome autonomy).
249 *See* GATTACA (Columbia Pictures 1997).
250 As stated by James Watson, "Few, if any, of us would wish to imagine our descendants living under the sort of genetic tyranny suggested by Gattaca. Setting aside the question of whether the scenario foreseen is technologically feasible, we must address the central issue raised by the film: Does DNA knowledge make a genetic caste system inevitable? A world of congenital haves and have-nots?" WATSON, STORY, *supra* note 79, at 431.
251 Michelle Starr, *Gattaca Designer Baby Patent: Scientists Respond*, CNET (Oct. 3, 2013), www.cnet.com/news/gattaca-designer-baby-patent-scientists-respond/.
252 *See id.* For discussion of the substantial uptake of NIPTs in an era of demand for and supply of in vitro tests/IVTs and assisted reproduction technologies, see generally PEW, ROLE, *supra* note 27. *See infra* notes 28, 67–75, and accompanying text (discussing *New York Times* investigation of NIPTs).
253 *23andMe TV Spot, 'DNA Reports: 80%: $129'*, ISPOTTV (Jan. 2, 2022), www.ispot.tv/ad/qeaX/23andme-dna-reports-80-129; 23andMe, *80% receive a report with a meaningful genetic variant. Will you be part of the 80%?*, official site (visited Apr. 9, 2022), www.23andme .com/?evr=epv.
254 Noninvasive prenatal testing has a large and growing presence in US prenatal care. *See supra* notes 28, 63–76, and accompanying text.
255 *See supra* notes 37–40, and accompanying text (DIY-Bio). For discussion of CRISPR, see *id.*
256 *See generally* Hazel, *Best Practices, supra* note 10.
257 *See Chapter* 5, *supra*, at notes 215–24, and accompanying text (addressing the shareholder wealth maximization norm in the context of Rx drugs).
258 *See Council on Gov. Rel's, Overview, supra* note 172.
259 *See generally* IRS, *Exemption Requirements – 501(c)(3) Organizations* (reviewed Feb. 17, 2022), www.irs.gov/charities-non-profits/charitable-organizations/exemption-requirements-501c3-organizations.
260 *See generally* MALINOWSKI, HANDBOOK, *supra* note 27.
261 *See* Leavenworth, *DNA for Sale, supra* note 178.
262 *See generally Chapter* 2, *supra*, at notes 32–114, and accompanying text (discussing Operation Warp Speed/OWS).
263 *See* Jim Wappers, *COVID-19 Vaccines Saved an Estimated 20 Million Lives in 1 Year*, Center for Infectious Disease Research and Policy/CIDRAP (June 24, 2022) (page nos. unavailable online), www.cidrap.umn.edu/news-perspective/2022/06/covid-19-vaccines-saved-estimated-20-million-lives-1-year. *See generally* Oliver J. Watson, Gregory Barnsley, Jaspreet Toor et al., *Global Impact of the First Year of COVID-19 Vaccination: A Mathematical Modelling Study*, LANCET INFEC. DIS. (June 23, 2022) (page nos, unavailable online), www.thelancet.com/action/showPdf?pii=S1473-3099%2822%2900320-6.

264 *See generally Chapter 2, supra*.
265 *See Chapter 4, supra*, at notes 124–29, and accompanying text (discussing the FDA's 2017 decision to approve 23andMe's DTCGHR testing); *infra* notes 282–83, and accompanying text (discussing the FDA's recognition of a DTCGHR testing category).
266 *See supra* notes 171–74, and accompanying test (discussing updates to the Common Rule).
267 Hayden, *The Rise and Fall and Rise Again of 23andMe*, 550 NATURE 174–77 (Oct. 11, 2017), www.nature.com/news/the-rise-and-fall-and-rise-again-of-23andme-1.22801. I participated in 23andMe's consumer research, and I found the company's data collection to be extremely shallow, as discussed *supra*, in note 178.
268 Subsequently, this powerful story has been covered extensively in the popular press and other media, at academic conferences, and beyond. *See, e.g., CBS Sunday Morning, The Gift of Immortal Cells* (2011), www.youtube.com/watch?v=joAkJXI2Yxk (a brief, excellent summary). HBO relayed the story in a movie starring Oprah Winfrey as Deborah Lacks, Henrietta's daughter who was responsive to Rebecca Skloot and worked with her to learn more about her mother. *See generally* THE IMMORTAL LIFE OF HENRIETTA LACKS (HBO, 2017). In October 2021, the 70th anniversary of Mrs. Lacks' death, Henrietta Lacks' estate, represented by civil rights Attorney Benjamin Lloyd Crump, filed a lawsuit against Thermo Fisher Scientific for profiting from the HeLa cell line without consent, and requested the defendant's full net profits as damages. *See The Estate of Henrietta Lacks v. Thermo Fisher Scientific Inc.*, No. 1:2021cv02524 (U.S. D. Md.), https://dockets.justia.com/docket/maryland/mddce/1:2021cv02524/500650 (docket).
269 REBECCA SKLOOT, THE IMMORTAL LIFE OF HENRIETTA LACKS (2011) (from the book synopsis).
270 Danya F. Vears, Joel T. Minion, Stephanie J. Roberts et al., *Return of Individual Research Results from Genomic Research: A Systematic Review of Stakeholder Perspectives*, 16(11) PLoS ONE e0258646 (2021), https://doi.org/10.1371/journal.pone.0258646. A related issue is the extent to which certified genetic counselors/CGCs should share unsolicited findings/UFs with patients during clinical care – the discovery of pathogenic variants that cause disease but are not related to why the patient underwent testing in the first place. In this situation, a provider-patient relationship and duty of care has been established, but the discovery is beyond the provider-patient expressly intended scope of testing. According to researchers who conducted an interview-based study of genetic counselors published in the *Journal of Genetic Counseling*, "an expert panel [should] be established to help support clinical geneticists determine which UFs are medically actionable." Editorial Staff, *Analysis of How Geneticists Discuss Unsolicited Findings With Patients*, GENOMEWEB (Nov 14, 2022), www.genomeweb.com/scan/analysis-how-geneticists-discuss-unsolicited-findings-patients#.Y3KZkHbMK3A.
271 *Id.* (page nos. unavailable online) (emphasis added). According to the authors, the study "spanned at least 22 different countries with most [research participants] (144/65%) being from the USA. Most (76%) discussed clinical research projects, rather than biobanks. More than half (58%) gauged views that were hypothetical." *Id.*
272 *See generally* SACGT, RECOMMENDATIONS, *supra* note 14.
273 Stuart Leavenworth, *DNA Dilemma, supra* note 243. The DNA and medical information of the population of Iceland was organized into a biobank by deCODE Genetics beginning in the 1990s. *See Chapter 4, supra*, at notes 87–90, and accompanying text.
274 *See supra* notes 175–76, and accompanying text (discussing AllUs).
275 *See* Stuart Leavenworth, *Dilemma, supra* note 243.

276 Jessica Kim Cohen, *NIH All of Us Program Returns First Health-Related Genetic Results to Participants*, GenomeWeb (Dec. 13, 2022), www.genomeweb.com/sequencing/nih-all-us-program-returns-first-health-related-genetic-results-participants#.Y5js6XbMK3A. *See also* Stuart Leavenworth, *Dilemma, supra* note 243 (discussing AllUs original plan to return some research results questioned and deliberated).

277 Gina Kolata, *The Struggle to Build a Massive 'Biobank' of Patient Data*, N.Y. Times (Mar. 19, 2018), at D1, www.nytimes.com/2018/03/19/health/nih-biobank-genes.html.

278 *Id.* The UK Biobank is discussed in the *Prologue, supra*, at notes 15, 23, 31.

279 *See* Herper, *Ancestry, supra* note 85. Technically, AncestryHealth Plus was slated to sequence a patients' exome – all genes identified as coding for proteins in the body. However, Ancestry then decided to release only a small amount of information to users:

> Dr. Eric Topol, director and founder of the Scripps Research Translational Institute, said the American College of Medical Genetics recommends that harmful mutations in 58 genes should be disclosed to people after sequencing is conducted. He noted that Geisinger Health, in its exome sequencing efforts, does this. "It's minimal," he wrote of the AncestryHealth Plus test. He called it "a step in the right direction, but not in keeping with consensus and practice in the medical community." Catherine Ball, Ancestry's chief scientific officer, said that the decision to focus on highly actionable diseases results from Ancestry's efforts to understand the needs of its customers and the primary care physicians who will need to help them react to their test results. The key, she said, was to include only tests that can "improve outcomes for our customers and for their families."

Id.

280 *See* Chapter 4, *supra*, at notes 120, 128–29, 134, 161–62, and accompanying text (discussing the FDA-imposed special conditions, which address clinical use and consumer comprehension).

281 *See* FDA, DEN160026, EVALUATION OF AUTOMATIC CLASS III DESIGNATION FOR The 23andMe Personal Genome Service (PGS) Genetic Health Risk Test for Hereditary Thrombophilia, Alpha-1 Antitrypsin Deficiency, Alzheimer's Disease, Parkinson's Disease, Gaucher Disease Type 1, Factor XI Deficiency, Celiac Disease, G6PD Deficiency, Hereditary Hemochromatosis and Early-Onset Primary Dystonia, DECISION SUMMARY (Apr. 6, 2017, revised May 2, 2017, correction Nov. 2, 2017), www.accessdata.fda.gov/cdrh_docs/reviews/DEN160026.pdf. *See also*, FDA, *Press Release, FDA Allows Marketing of First Direct-to-Consumer Tests That Provide Genetic Risk Information for Certain Conditions* (Apr. 6, 2017), www.fda.gov/NewsEvents/Newsroom/PressAnnouncements/ucm551185.htm.

282 Section 866.5950 (Genetic health risk assessment system) of Title 21 provides, in part:

> The genetic health risk assessment system device, when it has previously received a first-time FDA marketing authorization (e.g., 510(k) clearance) for the genetic health risk assessment system (a "one-time FDA reviewed genetic health risk assessment system"), is exempt from the premarket notification procedures in part 807, subpart E, of this chapter subject to the limitations in 866.9. The device must comply with the following special controls ....

21 CFR 866.5950 (revised Apr. 1, 2020), www.accessdata.fda.gov/scripts/cdrh/cfdocs/cfcfr/cfrsearch.cfm?fr=866.5950.

283 *See Chapter 4, supra*, at notes 126–29, and accompanying text (discussing the FDA's recognition of a DTCGHR category).

284 *See id.* at notes 121–24, and accompanying text (discussing the Center for Devices and Radiological Health/CDRH matching system).

285 The FDA was influenced by public demand for access to DTCGHR testing services, as it acknowledged when it granted 23andMe market approval and established a DTCGHR category for expedited review and approval. In its communication with patients and physicians, the FDA stated "Consumers are increasingly embracing direct-to-consumer genetic testing to better understand their ancestry or individual risk for developing diseases." Jeffrey Shuren, Janet Woodcock, *Jeffrey Shuren, M.D., J.D., Director of the FDA's Center for Devices and Radiological Health, and Janet Woodcock, M.D., Director of the FDA's Center for Drug Evaluation and Research on Agency's Warning to Consumers About Genetic Tests That Claim to Predict Patients' Responses to Specific Medications*, FDA (Nov. 1, 2018), www.fda.gov/NewsEvents/Newsroom/PressAnnouncements/ucm624794.htm.

286 *See supra* note 253, and accompanying text (addressing 23andMe's national television advertising campaign and quoting marketing on the company's official site).

287 *See supra* notes 35, 97–8, and accompanying text (discussing 23andMe's Lemonaid acquisition and expansion into full DTC genomic clinical services).

288 Vears et al., *Return*, *supra* note 270, and accompanying text.

289 The demand and competition for research participants in genomic research is immense and international, and especially so for the extremes – namely population genetics and genomics that depends on the number of participants, and research on rare diseases with limited populations to draw from. Unfortunately, uncertainty in US law-policy impedes responsible federally funded (Common Rule applicable) and otherwise government supported initiatives:

> Direct-to-participant (DTP) recruitment and enrollment via the internet has proven to be an effective way of conducting genomic research, especially research on rare diseases. Although this novel manner for researchers to interact with prospective and enrolled participants has been approved by institutional review boards (IRBs) and research ethics committees (RECs) for domestic research, some IRBs and RECs have been reluctant to approve it for international research because of concerns about its legality in other countries.

Mark A. Rothstein, Ma'n H. Zawati, Laura M. Besko et al., *Legal and Ethical Challenges of International Direct-to Participant Genomic Research: Conclusions and Recommendations*, 47 J. Law Med. Ethics 705–731, 705 (2019). For discussion of US government initiatives to advance research for rare disorders, see *Chapter 2*, *supra*, at notes 5-8, 189-90, and accompanying text.

7

Protecting and Promoting the Evidentiary-Science Base of Personal Genome Medicine/PGM

Compassion, integrity, and trust often prove outcome determinative in medicine – even in an age of genomics.[1] Applying these essentials, responsible, evidentiary science-based clinical medicine integrates science with experience, knowledge, and acumen. "Ancient medicine was the mother of science."[2] Progress in medicine is synonymous with advancing responsible, repeatable (verifiable), and objective medical science. The advancement of medical science during the twentieth century and over the last few decades elevated certainty in the practice of medicine:

> Make no mistake, medical practice is a skilled profession. And there is art to that skill, particularly in building good doctor-patient relationships and eliciting a clear patient history. But today's doctors simply have more certainty than they did in the past in how best to diagnose and treat specific medical problems.
>
> Even with highly complex problems like cancer–where a person's unique genetic makeup requires a "personalized medicine" solution–the best course of care has a scientific basis.[3]

The precision of clinically sound genetics, genomics, and proteomics will elevate certainty in medicine to spectacular new heights through personal genome medicine/PGM.[4] However, science and evidence-based PGM as standard of care throughout US medicine is just coming into being.[5] Mendelian traits, single genetic variations (alleles) that are inheritable and cause diseases such as sickle-cell anemia, Tay-Sachs disease, and Huntington's chorea – inheritable genetic "levers" for disease – are the exception, not the norm.[6] For Mendelian diseases, the positive predictive value/PPV, negative predictive value/NPV, penetrance (the likelihood that an associated disease or health condition will become symptomatic), and sensitivity of genetic tests approach one hundred percent.[7] In contrast, the genetic complexity of most common diseases and conditions is reflected in the personal genome testing associated with them and in the clinical complexities those genetic tests introduce.[8] Overall, genes multitask and interface feverishly, environment influences genes substantially, and genomic science – science on the molecular level to identify gene and protein function in the context of whole genomes – is transporting medicine into a new dimension of precision *and complexity*.[9]

The complexity of human genome science and clinical-standard (satisfying established evidentiary-science standards) personal genome testing in human health was emphasized at the outset of this millennium in an impressive report issued by the Secretary's Advisory Committee on Genetic Testing/SACGT after exhaustive investigation, stakeholder input, public commentary, and deliberation.[10] The committee's information intake encompassed the solicitation of multidisciplinary input from a broad portfolio of experts and stakeholders and substantial public commentary.[11] As experienced thus far, and especially since completion of the first draft map of the human genome sequence in 2003, clinical certainty through genetics, genomics, proteomics, and next-generation sequencing will be realized at an accelerating pace, but incrementally, sporadically, and often unpredictably.[12] The advancement of the human genome sciences will continue to reveal layer-upon-layer of clinical complexity for common diseases and health conditions.

The medical profession's ability to understand and practice responsible PGM will rise with the progress of the human genome sciences, as will the ability of medical providers to communicate personal genome health information effectively to patients. Also, instances when the influence of genes is significant and well defined clinically – with definitive, scientifically-sound PPV, NPV, penetrance, and sensitivity to establish clinical validity and to shape clinical utility – will become more frequent and prevalent.[13] In those instances, many individuals will be able to comprehend the health care significance of their related personal genome health information, at times independent from learned medical professionals, in a manner that enables them to better understand and improve their health and health care decision-making.[14]

Human genome science innovation already has touched, and at times reached into, clinical care, individuals' lives, and personal health care decision-making.[15] Personal genome information has become socially and culturally familiar, commercially available, price-point accessible, and desirable for millions of consumers.[16] Health-related direct-to-consumer/DTC personal genome testing is a burgeoning business.[17] The proliferation of clinically sound – reliable accuracy, clinical validity, and defined clinical utility – and medically beneficial personal genome testing is inevitable and welcomed by responsible medical providers and consumers alike. The accomplished progress of biotech research and development/R&D over the last several decades and the scale of ongoing human genome science R&D make the PGM future of US health care a certainty.[18] Over time, the precedent of the clinical development of BRCA genetic testing from the testing Oncormed, Inc. offered to consumers in 1996 to the clinically sound testing celebrity Angelina Jolie underwent, utilized in her health care decision-making and shared publicly in 2013, will permeate throughout health care.[19] Waves of clinically sound human genome science innovation will deluge medicine with capabilities that elevate the discipline and practice of medicine to heights not even fully ascertainable today.

The transformation of US health care to clinically sound PGM, the aspiration of James Watson and other forefathers of the genomic revolution and the stated business mission of 23andMe and other companies in the DTC personal genome testing sector, *will be realized*.[20] However, there are profound uncertainties separating then and now – most notably, how quickly the two join, and whether the evidentiary-science base of US medicine will be adhered to and sustained with reliability throughout the ongoing transition to our PGM future. The evidentiary-science base of PGM must be protected and promoted during this transition – consistent with the formative ethos of the US medical profession and the base of US medicine established and reinforced throughout the twentieth century.[21]

The following discussion first addresses how the US responded to a buyer-beware patent medicines marketplace in the early twentieth century by introducing professional and government regulation centered on protecting consumers and building the evidentiary-science base of medicine. The discussion then addresses how the US has resurrected buyer beware with DTC personal genome testing, and the importance of introducing increased regulatory oversight of health-related personal genome testing – the cornerstone of evidentiary science-based PGM.

TWENTIETH-CENTURY REGULATION OF PATENT MEDICINE MANUFACTURERS TO PROTECT CONSUMERS AND ESTABLISH THE EVIDENTIARY-SCIENCE BASE OF MEDICINE

The profound progress of medical science and US medicine during the twentieth century—and especially during the second half of the twentieth century—was made possible by an organized, centralized US medical profession that collaborated with the Food and Drug Administration/FDA, and their joint authority, prowess, resources, and shared commitment to protecting and promoting the evidentiary-science base of medicine.[22] The AMA established and exercised considerable control over individual physicians through the formalization of medical education, promotion of state licensure, and overall imposition of evidentiary-science standards in clinical medicine.[23] The association wielded its influence over physicians and physician influence over patients to generate voluntary medicine manufacturer participation in science scrutiny of their products through the Council on Pharmacy and Chemistry ("AMA Council") decades before Congress empowered the FDA to do the same under the rule of law.[24] The AMA, which made medicine manufacturers choose to communicate *either* with physicians or directly with the public, lobbied for government regulation to limit consumer self-medication.[25] In 1951, Congress codified a prescription-only ("Rx") category of drugs into law.[26] By 1954, the FDA was devoting at least a third of its budget earmarked for drug regulation to ensuring physician control over Rx drugs – to prevent medicine manufacturer fraud and to prohibit manufacturer direct sales of Rx products to consumers.[27]

The organized US medical profession, Congress, and the FDA recognized a need to channel patients into decision-making with learned and licensed physicians at a time when medical science was much simpler and the medical profession was much smaller, centralized, and unified.[28] The medical profession supported the FDA's role as market gatekeeper and sentinel to ensure the safety and efficacy of medicinal products, and the FDA deferred to the medical profession's sovereignty over the practice of medicine – physician discretion in the clinical use of FDA-approved medicinal products to provide individualized patient care – as did the US judiciary.[29]

Commercial Rx drug and vaccine crises enlightened industry to the benefits of consumer safety and confidence through regulation.[30] Together, the US medical profession and the FDA squelched direct interaction between manufacturers and consumers to ensure the safety and efficacy of Rx products on the US market, to protect patient consumers, to bolster confidence in commercial medicinal products, to counter and prevent commercial exploitation, to identify and reward sound commercial clinical Rx product innovation, to protect and promote the base of US medicine, and to improve US health care.[31]

TWENTY-FIRST-CENTURY RESURRECTION OF BUYER BEWARE IN DTC GENETICS AND GENOMICS

Today, at the outset of our PGM era, the US has resurrected the early twentieth-century buyer-beware health care market environment. DTC personal genome testing is a contemporary counterpart to the patent medicines, elixirs, and manufacturer self-proclaimed miracle cures prevalent in the early twentieth century.[32] Clinically questionable DTC personal genome tests are directly available to the public through manufacturer-consumer communication and transactions, with the involvement of licensed and learned medical providers optional and incidental.[33]

The integration of government, academia, and industry, the core methodology for US technology transfer law and policy/TTLP, a potent catalyst for the biotech and genomic revolutions, has elevated industry influence throughout US science R&D (laboratory bench and clinical research), health care, and clinical medicine.[34] Biopharma's influence over consumers, physicians, and the practice of medicine is profound.[35] Aggressive DTC and direct-to-physician/DTP biopharma marketing became socially and culturally familiar in the US and a normalcy some time ago.[36] Biopharma influence permeates US medical education and the medical journal establishment/MJE relied upon by the medical profession for clinical scrutiny and uptake of Rx product innovation.[37]

The FDA's decision in 2017 to pave a regulatory express lane to market for DTC genetic health risk/GHR testing that does not meet clinical standards incentivized a burgeoning and largely self-regulated DTC personal genome testing sector.[38] The FDA strayed from clinical standards and condoned the expansion of recreational genetics (culturally and socially popular for ancestry since the 1990s) to encompass genetic health risk testing without requisite medical professional involvement. The agency was influenced by consumer demand for access to their personal genomes and gave into that demand – albeit with a consumer warning against clinical medicine use without the involvement of medical professionals.[39] As acknowledged by the FDA when issuing its warning, "Consumers are increasingly embracing direct-to-consumer genetic testing to better understand their ancestry or individual risk for developing diseases."[40]

Today's human genome science is sophisticated and dizzyingly complicated overall, even for learned and licensed medical professionals.[41] Personal genome tests that are scientifically and clinically sound enough to improve human health meaningfully, reliably, and in definitive ways are just the edge of an amassing, churning ocean of health-related testing capabilities that are evolving (changing in real time) scientifically and clinically, including testing directly available to US consumers.[42] Contemporary genetic, genomic, and proteomic science, generations more sophisticated than mid-twentieth century medical science, is charged by TTLP and likely to overwhelm the US practice of medicine.[43] The symbiotic relationship between the medical profession and the FDA that protected the evidentiary-science base of US medicine effectively during the twentieth century has shifted and no longer is as reliable.[44] Much more of that responsibility is on the medical profession with reliance on its ability to police and maintain science and evidence-based clinical practice in a DTC personal genome testing era.

Since Congress enacted the Food and Drug Modernization Act/FDAMA in 1997, the FDA has made the US health care markets and consumers much more accessible to the manufacturers of medicinal products – as reflected in the FDA's allowance of biopharma DTC television advertising in 1997 (not coincidentally, the same year Congress enacted FDAMA and renewed the Prescription Drug User Fee Act/ PDUFA of 1992) and its creation of a regulatory fast lane to market for DTC genetic health risk/DTCGHR testing services in 2017.[45] This fundamental change was not FDA self-determination. Congress, the branch of government that enacted PDUFA, FDAMA, the Food and Drug Administration Safety and Innovation Act/FDASIA of 2012, and the 21st Century Cures Act of 2016 has not meaningfully increased the FDA's authority to control industry direct communication with the public and physicians.[46] Quite the contrary. These laws have heightened industry influence consistent with TTLP, and the public in our "business of medicine" and information and communication technology/ICT age is more confident in health care self-determination and less deferential to learned and licensed medical providers.[47]

Today's medical profession is far less centralized, unified, and capable of containing industry influence in the practice of medicine than the mid-twentieth-century version of itself.[48] AMA membership dropped from nearly 278,000 to 217,000 between 2002 and 2011, and today only about twenty-five percent of eligible physicians join.[49] The US medical profession cannot be relied upon to clinically evaluate and responsibly absorb an ongoing deluge of personal genome testing capabilities from myriad sources, including the bundles of genetic test results brought to them by the purchasers of DTC personal genome health services/PGHSs.[50] Sweeping clinical uptake of questionable noninvasive prenatal tests/NIPTs to detect microdeletions in prenatal care, as documented by a Pew Charitable Trusts assessment and a related *New York Times* investigation, attests to the medical profession's unreliability as sentinel of the science and evidence base of PGM.[51] "In just over a decade, [NIPTs] have gone from laboratory experiments to an industry that serves more than a third of the pregnant women in America, luring major companies like Labcorp and Quest Diagnostics into the business, alongside many start-ups."[52] According to the *Times* investigation and analysis, approximately eighty-five percent of the positive results from newer NIPTs are false positives.[53]

23andMe, the seminal US DTCGHR testing company and regulatory precedent setter, now is the publicly traded 23andMe Holding Co ("23andMe Holding") and engaged in full biopharma R&D.[54] The company, beyond its DTC marketing and PGHS, also has ventured directly into the practice of medicine to facilitate medical professional responsiveness to its non-clinical standard personal genome tests.[55] On October 22, 2021, 23andMe Holding announced its acquisition of Lemonaid Health, a national telemedicine and digital pharmacy company, to overcome physician skepticism and uncertainty about its PGHS reports.[56] The transaction was completed on November 1, 2021, and the company declared in 2022 that its business plan for the future centers on providing DTC genomic health services—becoming a full-service PGM medical provider.[57]

The precedent of the seminal DTCGHR testing company purchasing a national conglomeration of telehealth medical providers in the US' highly privatized, decentralized, and commerce-driven health care system to complement and sell its PGHS turns the US medicine legacy and accompanying law-policy on its head. For more than a century, the US has protected the evidentiary-science base of medicine by shielding it from undue corporate financial influences. This legacy is profound, beginning with judicial recognition and state legislative codification of the Corporate Practice of Medicine Doctrine in the early twentieth century to prohibit corporate citizens and unlicensed individuals from practicing medicine.[58] In the mid-twentieth century, the US introduced prescription-only access to medicinal products, restricted Rx medicinal product manufacturers' direct communication with consumers about Rx drugs, and imposed safety and efficacy pre-market requirements on industry.[59] With the managed care and commercialization of US medicine movement in the 1980s, Congress mandated physician control over hospital medical staff bylaws and the practice of medicine within hospitals under the Health Care Quality Improvement Act/HQIA of 1986.[60] Congress also restricted health care provider referrals to laboratories and other health care services in which they have a financial interest under the Anti-Kickback Statute and Stark Law.[61]

REGULATORY OVERSIGHT OF THE PERSONAL GENOME TESTING CORNERSTONE OF PGM

The US TTLP introduced in 1980 and complemented by subsequent regulatory responsiveness to biotech R&D has proven a potent catalyst for biotech innovation beneficial to US medicine, the US economy, and human health.[62] The sufficiency of existing US regulatory infrastructure to uptake foreseeable biotech innovation has been called into questioned well beyond US health care. In 2015, the Obama Administration charged the Environmental Protection Agency/EPA, the FDA, and the US Department of Agriculture/USDA to commission "an external, independent analysis of the future landscape of biotechnology products with a primary focus on potential new risks and risk-assessment frameworks."[63] These agencies charged the National Academies of Science, Engineering, and Medicine/NASEM to survey novel biotech products expected to enter the market within five-to-ten years, and to assess the sufficiency of the nation's regulatory infrastructure.[64] NASEM established a multidisciplinary committee that considered changes to the foundational regulatory policy the US established in 1986 for the regulation of biotech products, the Coordinated Framework for Regulation of Biotechnology Products ("Coordinated Framework").[65] The US last updated the Coordinated Framework meaningfully in 1992 – two years after it launched the Human Genome Project/HGP.[66] Under the Coordinated Framework, the US adopted a product-over-process approach to regulating biotech innovation: Products made with biotechnology are regulated consistent with the regulation of products overall, rather than with focus on the use of biotech to make them. The Coordinated Framework also charges federal agencies to coordinate their regulatory efforts to avoid duplicative regulation of biotech products.[67]

The NASEM committee released its report in 2017, *Preparing for Future Products of Biotechnology*, in which it assessed the approaching generation of biotech products, confirmed the scope and complexity of forthcoming biotech innovation, and identified associated regulatory challenges.[68] The committee concluded that the US should prepare by strategically modifying regulatory infrastructure while adhering to the Coordinated Framework foundation, rather than attempting to significantly modify it.[69] The committee assessed that biotech innovation is approaching too expansively and too quickly to effectuate substantial foundational changes.[70] According to Professor Barbara Evans, who served on the committee, "The landscape study assumed that major legal reforms take longer than ten years to complete by the time Congress enacts new legislation, courts hear legal challenges, and federal agencies promulgate regulations implementing the new statutes."[71]

DTC genetics and genomics are present, thriving, and propagating.[72] The regulatory baseline for US medicine, established in the twentieth century, is medical profession self-regulation of the practice of medicine and FDA regulation of medicinal products in a symbiotic relationship. The two regulate with the shared objective of protecting and promoting science and evidence-based clinical practice and patient care.[73] Under existing US law and policy, DTC genetics and genomics threaten to elevate the role of individuals in medical decision-making to their health care detriment and to the detriment of US medicine by undermining the role of medical professionals, science and evidence-based clinical practice, and the progress of responsible, clinically-sound PGM.[74] PGM must evolve in tandem with continued, reliable assurances of good medicine, patient protection, and the advancement of human health – meaning in a manner consistent with the astounding progress of US medicine last century through the advancement of medical science with dependable oversight by the medical profession and the FDA.[75]

Personal genome sequencing and testing is the cornerstone of the emerging PGM future. There is tremendous US consumer demand for access to personal genome testing,[76] and US law-policy is protective of the rights of biopharma corporate citizens in the business of meeting that demand.[77] The NASEM committee's sweeping assessment of and suggested strategic regulatory approach to forthcoming biotech innovation provides guidance. The regulatory infrastructure built over the last several decades on the Coordinated Framework foundation and responsive to biotech innovation is immense, entrenched, and relied upon.[78] It is familiar and expected, and perhaps taken for granted. The same is true regarding the regulatory foundation for US medicine – its evidentiary-science base established and reinforced last century.[79]

The US medical profession and FDA must continue their symbiotic mission with reliability. However, a decisive addition to the established regulatory infrastructure is essential to support science and evidence-based PGM – to support the medical profession and the FDA in their ongoing mission. Given the PGM cornerstone significance of personal genome testing, the US must prioritize and modify its regulatory infrastructure for health-related personal genome tests and testing. It must do so with focus on reinforcing US medicine legacy norms and mechanisms to continue what the US medical profession and FDA accomplished in the twentieth century – to protect and promote the evidentiary-science base of medicine in our genomic era. The proposed increase in national regulatory oversight of personal genome tests and testing is consistent with SACGT's recommendations and promotes the sanctity of physician–patient decision-making, individualized patient care, and an evidentiary science-based standard of care in clinical medicine—unlike the Supreme Court's recent decision in *Dobbs v. Jackson Women's Health Org.* In *Dobbs*, the Court recognized state discretion to intervene in clinical care and the doctor-patient relationship to ban abortion procedures.[80] Notably, although subject to litigation challenges, HHS Secretary Xavier Becerra informed health care providers on July 11, 2022, that physicians must provide abortions in medical emergencies under federal law and will face penalties if they do not.[81]

Many commentators have proposed enhancing FDA regulation of genetic *tests* (distinguishable from laboratory *testing services*) beginning in the 1990s in response to the 1996 DTC BRCA testing and continuing into the present.[82] The following discussion assesses this approach. The discussion concludes that it would be inconsistent with the FDA's enabling legislation, the agency's interactive relationship with industry in the genomic era under TTLP, PDUFA, FDAMA, FDASIA, and the Cures Act, the US patient self-determination movement and public demand for access to personal genome testing, and the medical profession's sovereignty over the practice of medicine with a premium on individualized patient care established early last century and recognized extensively in US law-policy since then.[83]

Commentators also have proposed introducing greater regulatory oversight of genetic *testing* by modifying US regulations of laboratories that perform diagnostic testing under the Clinical Laboratory Improvement Amendments/CLIA of 1988.[84] The Clinical Laboratory Improvement Advisory Committee/CLIAC explored this possibility in the 1990s, and SACGT recognized the option in its 2000 report and recommendations.[85] The following discussion assesses this approach and concludes that reliance on CLIA modifications to introduce the regulatory oversight of personal genome testing necessary to shore up the evidentiary-science base of PGM would be misplaced. The reliability of ongoing CLIA implementation and enforcement is questionable, and CLIA regulates laboratory testing *proficiency* with deference to the medical profession to assess clinical utility and to determine clinical use.[86]

PROPOSALS TO ENHANCE FDA REGULATION OF PERSONAL GENOME TESTS

In June 1998, approximately two and one-half years after Oncormed, Inc. introduced the first DTC genetic testing for BRCA alleles (January 1996), the Clinton Administration chartered the Secretary's Advisory Committee on Genetic Testing/SACGT:

> Among the general issues that the Committee took up included: the development of guidelines, including criteria regarding the risks and benefits of genetic testing, to assist Institutional Review Boards in reviewing genetic testing protocols in both academic and commercial settings; the adequacy of regulatory oversight of genetic tests; provisions for assuring the quality of genetic testing laboratories; the need for mechanisms to track the introduction of genetic tests to enable accuracy and clinical effectiveness over time to be evaluated; and safeguarding the privacy and confidentiality of genetic information and preventing discrimination and stigmatization based on genetic information.[87]

Donna Shalala, Secretary of HHS at the time, established SACGT in response to recommendations from two HGP-related working groups – the Task Force on Genetic Testing ("Task Force") and the joint National Institutes of Health/NIH and Department of Energy/DOE Committee to Evaluate the Ethical, Legal, and Social Implications/ELSI Program of the Human Genome Project ("Joint Committee").[88]

SACGT was charged "to assess, in consultation with the public, the adequacy of current oversight of genetic tests and, if warranted, to recommend options for additional oversight."[89]

The three companies that introduced DTC BRCA testing to the US market in 1996 did not first submit their genetic tests to the FDA for review and approval and, in fact, they declared that they did not have to.[90] The FDA countered with a proclamation that it had authority but was choosing not to exercise it at that time. More precisely, the FDA's stated position was "that it has authority, by law, to regulate such tests, but the agency has elected as a matter of enforcement discretion to not exercise that authority, in part because the number of such tests is estimated to exceed the agency's current review capacity."[91] However, the Task Force, which contemplated establishment of a governing body dedicated to genetic testing, concluded in 1997 that "developers of genetic tests who do not rely on federal funds are *under no legal obligation* to submit protocols to the proposed [national governing body] and have not always obtained [institutional review board/]IRB approval for validation protocols of tests they plan to market as laboratory services."[92]

In 2000, SACGT concluded that existing regulatory oversight of genetic testing was not sufficient to assure their clinical accuracy and effectiveness.[93] The committee identified regulatory options:

> SACGT identified a number of possible directions that could be taken to improve oversight of genetic tests, including 1) strengthening and expanding current [Clinical Laboratory Improvement Amendments/CLIA of 1988 regulations for commercial laboratories performing diagnostic tests, which are implemented and enforced by the Centers for Medicare and Medicaid Services/CMS in partnership with CDC and FDA,] or FDA regulations or voluntary standards and guidelines; 2) forming interagency review boards; or 3) forming a consortium of representatives from government, industry, and professional organizations. SACGT also recognized that there are many areas beyond test development, use, and marketing, such as training and educating health care providers and enhancing public understanding of genetics, that might have an equally important impact on assuring the safety and effectiveness of a genetic test.[94]

SACGT also made thoughtful, well-substantiated recommendations by applying long-established clinical standards to the complexity of genetic testing in human health.[95] When the committee made its regulatory recommendations to assure the clinical accuracy and effectiveness of genetic tests, it acknowledged opposition, including strong opposition to augmentation of FDA regulation:

> During the second round of public comments received on the preliminary conclusions and recommendations, a number of individuals from industry and professional organizations expressed concerns about the impact that additional oversight may have on the development, availability, and accessibility of genetic tests and expressed strong opposition to an increased role for FDA.[96]

SACGT's work was done under the Clinton Administration, and its report and recommendations were released on the eve of its end. President George W. Bush took office on January 20, 2001, after defeating Al Gore in a legally contested election, which ended with a controversial Supreme Court ruling that settled a recount dispute over "hanging chads" (partially punched holes in paper ballots) in Florida.[97] A US regulatory response to commercial genetic testing reflective of SACGT's exhaustive effort did not materialize. SACGT's recommendations were essentially shelved as a biotech revolution raged and a robust genomic revolution emerged.

The FDA did not take any definitive regulatory action to directly confront DTC health-related genetic testing until November 2013 when 23andMe launched a television campaign to market its DTCGHR testing service without any requisite medical professional involvement in its transactions with consumers.[98] 2013 also was the year the "Angelia effect" – celebrity Angelina Jolie shared her decision to undergo surgeries after BRCA genetic testing – popularized genetic testing in health care.[99] The FDA issued 23andMe a cease-and-desist letter to enjoined the company from reporting any health-relevant genetic findings to customers.[100] 23andMe and the agency then engaged in involved negotiations. The result was FDA market approval in April 2017 of 23andMe's DTCGHR tests for ten diseases, including Alzheimer's and Parkinson's – unquestionably seriously debilitating and life-threatening diseases without sufficiently effective treatment options.[101] The FDA also established a "genetic health risk assessment system devices" *category* eligible for exemption from premarket review and even premarket notification/PMN once a manufacturer has submitted a PMN for their first DTCGHR test(s).[102]

The FDA's decision to approve 23andMe's DTCGHR testing through its PGHS reinvigorated 1990s debate about regulation of DTC genetic testing. SACGT's report and recommendations, based on an expansive intake of information, were a culmination of the 1990s debate. SACGT concluded that "the roles of [laboratory regulation under CLIA] and FDA in oversight should be strengthened and expanded" and that the "FDA should be the federal agency responsible for the review, approval, and labeling of all new genetic tests that have moved beyond the basic research phase."[103] Then and now, the FDA is the agency that embodies distinguishable expertise and experience evaluating the safety and efficacy of both medical devices and therapeutics, and many commentators have proposed increasing the FDA's oversight of genetic tests. For example, Dr. Neil ("Tony") Holtzman, who chaired the NIH-DOE Joint Committee Working Group charged with studying regulation of genetic tests and testing in the 1990s before SACGT was established, wrote in 2000 that the "FDA could readily implement the [SACGT's] recommendation, assuring that data on clinical validity are available to assist decision making."[104] According to Dr. Holtzman, "expanding FDA's coverage to include all genetic tests is the most workable option for assuring safe and effective testing."[105]

In the same live and published symposium in which Dr. Holtzman shared his assessments, I likewise concluded that "the FDA is the best regulatory authority."[106]

The US generally recognized genetic tests as patentable at the time, and I assumed that there would be increased regulatory oversight – whether by government, the medical profession, or both. I also thought a government regulatory framework for genetic testing—whether direct, by harnessing the medical profession, or in combination—was a prerequisite for commercial certainty and the R&D investment necessary for increased, timely market access to clinically sound genetic testing capabilities.[107] I was wrong. Full implementation of the Health Insurance Portability and Accountability Act/HIPAA of 1996, with finalization of the Privacy Rule in 2002 and the Security Rule in 2003, and enactment of GINA in 2008 provided meaningful national medical privacy assurances.[108] Enactment of the Affordable Care Act (ACA) in 2010 introduced meaningful assurance of access to health insurance without consideration of preexisting conditions, including identified genetic predispositions to health conditions.[109] The advancement of genomics reduced the price point of DNA sequencing dramatically and expanded personal genome testing possibilities exponentially.[110] The US Supreme Court significantly curtailed the patentability of genetic tests in 2012 and 2013 decisions, which invited commercial and clinical uptake of existing testing capabilities; many became available for research, commercial use, and clinical use.[111]

Perhaps even more important, US culture and society changed immensely. DNA became ever-present and familiar, ICT and social media became pervasive, and the commercialization of medicine jolted the doctor-patient relationship in US medicine towards patient self-determination and autonomy.[112] I never anticipated lingering government and professional regulatory non-responsiveness to DTC genetic testing until the advent of FDA approval of *non-clinical standard* DTCGHR testing *without requisite medical professional involvement* seventeen years later. When I suggested increased regulation of genetic testing in 2000, I also wrote that:

> [R]egulatory deference must be shown to professional medical community standards. Professional societies should develop professional guidelines that make their way into licensing and other requirements. Many relevant organizations exist. Although predictive genetic testing is just starting to affect the delivery of health care, much work has been done. There is no panacea that can proactively resolve the complicated delivery of care issues predictive genetic testing will raise in the clinic. However, the evolving expertise of the medical community hopefully will be enriched through increased market access as a result of implementation of the needed regulatory framework.[113]

I did not anticipate that the US medical profession would fail to exercise political persuasion and self-regulation to realize at least some effective responsiveness to the SACGT's report and recommendations. Similarly, I did not anticipate that the US opioid epidemic under the watch of the US medical professional would escalate and amass as it did without an intervention, and the role the US medical profession would play in feeding the nation's addiction over 10-15 years through often egregious (even "pill mill") physician opioid over prescribing.[114] In hindsight, the twenty-first century US medical profession and FDA are not their mid-twentieth-century counterparts, though each has continued to rely on the other to fulfill their joint mission to protect and promote the evidentiary-science base of medicine in our genomic era.

Debate about DTC genetic testing today is in the context of a much more expansive debate about the regulation of DTC genomics, which includes proteomic testing and do-it-yourself/DIY genomics ("DIY-Bio").[115] Some commentators have resurrected the notion that the FDA should regulate DTC personal genome testing much more meaningfully, and they have introduced proposals for the agency to do so. For example, largely echoing fundamentals in SACGT's 2000 report and recommendations, Catherine Sharkey, Xiahan Wu, Michael Walsh, and Kenneth Offit recently wrote that "Different genetic tests can pose unique risks to consumers, and the FDA is in an advantageous position to mitigate those risks through regulation. Risk-based classification gives the FDA precise tools such as special controls to customize its regulatory oversight."[116]

Professor Sharkey has told her version of 23andMe's story with a focus on the company's interactions with the FDA and the agency's market approval of its DTCGHR testing through its PGHS.[117] Professor Sharkey has interpreted the basis for a proposed change in the FDA's role from reviewer and regulator of the products under its watch to "dual role as safety and health information regulator."[118] According to Professor Sharkey:

> The FDA has traditionally served an information production function (albeit one not as readily appreciated as its safety function). In the era of "big data," the FDA is poised to play an enhanced role as health information regulator. The FDA can leverage its regulatory authority to coordinate the production, dissemination, and use of genomic information. Given its expertise, the FDA is primed to serve this gatekeeping role. Moreover, the FDA's medical device center has experience regulating software incorporated into medical devices.[119]

My interpretation is that the FDA decisively avoided this role in any meaningful manner other than mandating "consumer comprehension" communication and warnings to emphasize that these tests do not meet evidentiary science-based clinical standards.[120] The FDA *declared DTCGHR tests nonclinical* and, with that distinction in place, proceeded to condone them with regulatory market approval. The agency distinguished DTCGHR tests from medical devices used in the practice of clinical medicine to avoid expansion of its regulatory role – consistent with the FDA's twenty-first century relationship with industry and the agency's deference to the practice of medicine from the time it was established and empowered to regulate Rx products.[121] The FDA made a deliberate decision to allow DTCGHR testing to go forward as *nonclinical* to remove the technology categorically from its bulky charge to regulate clinical products, to meet consumer demand for access, and to avoid potential legal actions for allegedly imposing on the rights of corporate citizens, with the ultimate impact on individual patient care and the practice of medicine to be sorted out by the medical profession.

I share the position taken by Professor Barbara Evans, who recently assessed potential FDA regulation of DIY genomics overall. After explaining that "The FDA regulates manufacturers and distributors, not consumers," Professor Evans reached a conclusion reflective of our genomic era culture and regulatory norms: "The FDA is not the right agency to regulate DIY genomics. If I, an adult of sound mind, choose to edit my genome to grow rabbit ears on top of my head, is it legitimately the FDA's role to stop me? The agency's role is to protect me from harms inflicted by others – not to protect me from myself."[122]

Recognizing the limitations of FDA regulation in the twenty-first century should shift the focus of FDA reform proposals to improving the agency's effectiveness enforcing standards for safety and efficacy and ensuring the evidentiary-science soundness of clinical products under its charge. For example, Congress could charge and fund the FDA to conduct independent clinical research to spot-check the clinical research undertaken and financed by biopharma – as the agency did with pediatric studies prior to being granted the authority to mandate them[123] For decades, preeminent physicians have proposed that the FDA and NIH fund more clinical trials, including to parallel or replace industry trials, as an assurance of research integrity and fundamental, objective clinical understanding, and to reduce reliance on a medical journal establishment/MJE too susceptible to industry influence.[124]

Now that the FDA has approved market access for DTCGHR testing, the agency is highly unlikely to close it in any meaningful manner. In fact, the opposite is true. The FDA builds upon its decision precedents, and an express lane for DTCGHR testing approvals has been paved.[125] New medical devices are able to enter the market by literally piggybacking on previous FDA approvals ("510(k) application devices"), and the vast majority of new medical devices have been reaching the US market this way for some time.[126] "Between 95 and 98 percent of medical devices on sale in the US were cleared by the FDA through the 510(k) process, meaning the vast majority of medical devices used on patients have received little government scrutiny."[127]

The FDA has been making these decisions in advance for whole categories of products – including DTCGHR tests marketed and sold directly to consumers without any requisite medical professional involvement – with increasing frequency.[128] The FDA has done so consistent with the US medical profession's sovereignty over the practice of medicine and ultimate responsibility for protecting and promoting the evidentiary-science base of medicine in the delivery of clinical care.[129] Public demand for access to DTCGHR testing, which was strong enough to influence the FDA to approve market access in the first place, has continued to build with DTC marketing and the multiplication effect created through consumer use and popularity.[130] The public appeal of genetic consumerism, consumer demand for DTC personal genome testing services, Supreme Court decisions that significantly limit the patentability of genetic tests and impediments to DTC personal genome testing providers, a vibrant DTC personal genome testing sector, the FDA's welcoming regulatory stance for what is familiar, and the ongoing advancement of genomic science indicate that the lane for market entry will widen and be heavily trafficked.[131]

The FDA is a vulnerable institution politically, financially, and legally. It is a government entity dependent on industry user fee revenue and susceptible to annual budgeting, the political decisions and demands of whoever happens to be the current US President, a Congress with shifting majorities and volatile divisiveness, myriad sectors and stakeholders in the US "interest group society," public sentiment and demands influenced significantly by biopharma marketing, increased judicial recognition of the rights of biopharma corporate citizens, the medical profession's sovereignty over the practice of medicine, and the premium placed on individualized patient care in a patient self-determination era.[132] The accumulated regulatory responsibilities placed on the FDA since it was established are beyond vast and constantly increasing. In addition to its charge to evaluate and make market approval determinations, the agency is responsible for ongoing oversight of the products it makes market available and those accumulate. The FDA has long been "understaffed, underfunded, and under pressure, according to its own employees."[133]

The spring 2022 US infant formula shortage forced some public awareness that the FDA is charged with overwhelming regulatory responsibilities.[134] The FDA is responsible for the product safety of: foods, including dietary supplements, bottled water, food additives, infant formulas, and other food products (though the US Department of Agriculture/USDA is primarily responsible for regulating meat, poultry, and egg products); drugs, including both brand-name and generic Rx drugs, and non-prescription (over-the-counter/OTC) drugs; biologics, including vaccines, blood, blood products, cellular and gene therapies, tissue and tissue products, and allergenics; myriad medical devices spanning from tongue depressors to surgical implants for vital organs and surgical robotics; electronic products that emit radiation, including microwave ovens, x-ray equipment, laser products, ultrasonic therapy equipment, mercury vapor lamps, and sunlamps; cosmetics ranging from color additives in makeup to nail polishes, hair dyes and other chemical treatments, perfumes, and cosmeceuticals (cosmetics with medicinal properties); veterinary products, from pet food to veterinary drugs and devices; and tobacco products, from cigarettes to e-cigarettes.[135]

The FDA struggles to stretch limited resources to regulate reliably during explosive science innovation ongoing in real time with immediate, expansive human health consequences in a decentralized, highly privatized, and commerce-driven health care system.[136] The agency is in a chronic state of fending off allegations from myriad industry sectors, patient advocates, the public, and the medical profession – voices often joined in chorus – that it is holding back medical innovation to the detriment of patient lives and human health.[137] The FDA regulates with constant prodding that time is of the essence, and that the cost of regulatory time is lost opportunities to alleviate sickness and to save lives.

Legally, the FDA is restrained from intruding on the practice of medicine and US corporate citizens' market freedoms, which include commercial free speech.[138] As an organization, the FDA suffers internally from existence schizophrenia. The agency is the market sentinel for ensuring the safety and efficacy of Rx products with ongoing oversight through a regulatory methodology that is product and patient-centric. The FDA often is referred to as a quasi-independent agency. However, as made vivid during the COVID-19 pandemic, administratively and ultimately, the FDA is an agency that operates from within the Department of Health and Human Services/HHS.[139] HHS's overriding perspective and agenda, reflective of its charge under US law, is the overall US health care system and the nation's health. The FDA must meet its charged mission of ensuring the safety and efficacy of human medicinal products while coexisting within HHS's systemic mission of administering and advancing US health care and that nation's health.[140] Also, the FDA and HHS share a legacy, codified under US law-policy, of promotion and uptake of medical innovation with deference to and reliance on the US medical profession as the ultimate delivery-of-care decision-maker and patient protector.[141]

There is a misconception among many industry representatives, patient advocates, members of Congress, other stakeholders, and the general public that the FDA imposes a paternalistic standard for new Rx product approvals and chokes market entry to the detriment of health care innovation and patient health.[142] Some influential scholars and other commentators from multiple disciplines have legitimized and promoted this position.[143] For example, according to renowned law professor Richard Epstein in 2006, the pharmaceutical industry picked the Rx "low-hanging fruit" in the mid-to-late twentieth century, a subsequent slump in R&D harvest was inevitable,[144] the slump was exacerbated by FDA overregulation, and FDA overregulation impedes industry from reaching higher Rx fruit through innovation.[145] This position is not grounded in factual reality.

Low-hanging Rx fruit may have been harvested during the twentieth century, but the US introduced TTLP in 1980 and stirred a biotech revolution, from which emerged a genomic revolution that rages on.[146] Astonishing advances in science on the molecular level have created unprecedented biopharma R&D opportunity for more than three decades. Genomics and related disciplines (proteomics, bioinformatics, next-generation sequencing/NGS, pharmacogenomics, and pharmacogenetics, to name just a few) seeded new orchards of opportunity long ago and those are producing an abundance of low and high-hanging fruit.[147] The genomic Rx orchard acreage melds into the distant horizon and beyond view.

For biopharma R&D, there is a chasmic divide – a definitive before and after TTLP was introduced in 1980.[148] Traditional pharma needed to transition to biopharma and modify its R&D methodology to reflect the precision of genetics, genomics, and proteomics, and it did.[149] As reported by the GAO in 2021, "The number of new drugs approved each year has also grown over the past decade. On average, the Food and Drug Administration (FDA) approved 38 new drugs per year from 2010 through 2019 (with a peak of 59 in 2018), which is 60 percent more than the yearly average over the previous decade."[150] Post enactment of FDAMA in 1997 and certainly today, undermining the FDA categorically with allegations that FDA overregulation chokes the market entry of biopharma innovation is factually inaccurate, misinformed, detrimental to the FDA's effectiveness, inimical to science R&D and the advancement of US medicine, and dangerous to both the practice of medicine and patient health.

FDAMA was the product of government-industry negotiations that began with enactment of PDUFA in 1992.[151] PDUFA, negotiated by industry through its PhRMA and BIO trade organizations and stakeholders, introduced industry user fees to finance (a quid pro quo with much industry-negotiated specificity) operational resources to elevate agency responsiveness, performance, and timeliness according to indicators and with agency self-reporting transparency. Industry's negotiation leverage was made ongoing through five-year sunset provisions; PDUFA must be renewed every five years, as it has been since its original enactment.[152] In fact, industry leverage has increased over time with FDA's financial dependence on the user fee revenue stream. At least since FDAMA, the FDA is heavily dependent on user fee revenue to finance its operations, including the salaries of its application reviewers. "In FY 2021, FDA had net collections of $1.153 billion in prescription drug user fees, spent $1.109 billion in user fees for the human drug review process, and carried $245 million forward for future fiscal years."[153] The Agency is accountable to industry to maintain that revenue because, ultimately, industry agrees to the user fee renewals. As observed by Dr. Abramson early in this millennium (2005), "How absurd to have more than half the budget of the FDA division that approves new drugs (the Center for Drug Evaluation and Research, CDER) paid directly by the drug companies' user fees because the federal government is unwilling to provide adequate funding."[154] Beginning in 2002, medical device manufacturers pay the agency user fees too, and the manufacturers of generics and biosimilars began to pay them as well in 2012.[155]

As affirmed by two post-FDAMA surveys of FDA staff, agency officers are under pressure to approve new medicinal products unless they have sound reason not to well beyond the influence of agency dependence on user fee revenue.[156] According to a 2005 survey run outside of the agency by Public Citizen, "many officers felt under pressure to approve new drugs, received inappropriate phone calls from drug companies, and too often FDA senior officials intervened on a company's behalf in drug approval."[157] A 2001 survey run inside the agency by its staff reached consistent conclusions. "Summarizing the responses of more than 130 officers, that survey found that people reviewing drugs reported feeling pressure to 'favor the desires of sponsors over science and the public health.' One-third reported that they did not feel comfortable expressing their differing scientific opinion."[158] FDAMA, itself a product of industry-government user fee negotiations ongoing after the enactment of PDUFA I in 1992, and PDUFA II added efficiency to the FDA's mission of ensuring product safety and efficacy, and section 506(b) created a presumption in favor of market approval with follow-on studies and market observation.[159] The FDA's culture was changed by law.

These "modernizations" to the agency, which directly increased industry influence beyond nearly two decades of TTLP implementation, necessarily increased reliance on the medical profession to protect the evidentiary-science base of US medicine. When biopharma manufacturers apply for limited market approval with supportive data meeting or exceeding FDA base standards for safety and efficacy (outperforming a placebo control, meaning better than nothing, with acceptable safety data), the FDA must approve with awareness that physicians may ignore product labels, inserts, and warnings and use the medicinal products off label. The FDA also is aware that US physicians *often* do.[160]

The FDA also is susceptible to patient demands for access. Consider the drug Lotronex introduced by GlaxoSmithKline/GSK to treat irritable bowel syndrome/IBS. GSK pulled the popular drug from the market in 2000, less than ten months after market approval, when it was linked to severe gastrointestinal effects that resulted in hospitalizations and deaths:

> About 300,000 people had taken it. It was withdrawn because about 70 patients had developed severe constipation or ischemic colitis, a lack of blood flow to the colon. Some needed surgery, including one woman who had to have her entire colon removed. There were five deaths, including three possibly linked to the drug. Nonetheless, several thousand patients have contacted the F.D.A. since the recall, wanting Lotronex back.[161]

The FDA then allowed the drug to be reintroduced in 2002 with availability and use restrictions based on data that Lotronex is beneficial to people with *severe* forms of IBS.[162] "Banning drugs that might be valuable to a few who are genuinely ill certainly seems an unattractive option. But approving drugs likely to harm many healthy people is surely also undesirable."[163] The FDA does so with reliance on the US medical profession to abide by agency restrictions, to watch and report, and to adhere to evidence-based science even when biopharma DTC marketing creates consumer demand and biopharma DTP marketing and "education" generate physician responsiveness to that demand.[164]

The actual performances of the FDA and the biopharma sectors at the outset of this millennium – notably, the Vioxx and Celebrex (Cox 2 inhibitors) controversy, several other major innovative new drug recalls, reports by the Institute of Medicine/IOM and the Government Accountability Office/GAO generated by these recalls, and Congress's FDAAA response – make categorical arguments of FDA over-regulation of biopharma contrary to factual reality, irresponsible, and arguably absurd.[165] The US' early twenty-first-century biopharma-FDA experience also underscores the need for a regulatory mechanism for personal genome testing, the cornerstone of PGM, beyond the FDA – a regulatory mechanism to enable members of the US medical profession, individual physicians, to practice responsible, evidentiary science-based PGM with reliability.

PROPOSALS TO ENHANCE CLIA REGULATION OF PERSONAL GENOME TESTING

As stated by the Centers for Disease Control and Prevention/CDC, "Facilities in the United States that perform laboratory testing on human specimens for health assessment or disease diagnosis, prevention, or treatment are regulated under the Clinical Laboratory Improvement Amendments of 1988 (CLIA)."[166] The Centers for Medicare and Medicaid Services/CMS, in partnership with CDC, sets standards and issues certificates for clinical laboratory testing, and CDC conducts studies and convenes conferences in an ongoing manner to assess when regulatory changes are necessary.[167] Laboratories that are within the scope of CLIA must be registered, inspected, and certified CLIA-compliant, which CMS does directly and also outsources to several national professional organizations and a few states that have assumed this responsibility. CLIA imposes facility, operational, and administrative requirements, such as for laboratory personnel and batch testing, and laboratory testing must meet proficiency requirements assigned according to test complexity.[168] Once CLIA-certified, laboratories are subject to inspection at least every two years.[169]

As of January 2021, the US had 323,086 CLIA-registered laboratories – a surge from 286,396 in 2020, and a ninety-one percent increase from the 169,531 CLIA-registered laboratories in 2000 when SACGT issued its recommendations for regulation of clinical genetic testing that meets established evidentiary-science standards.[170] CLIA laboratories pay user fees, so regulatory resources increase with the number of CLIA laboratories provided fee rates at least meet certification and inspection expenses. However, when regulatory requirements are met and sustained, CLIA labs are not limited in the number of tests they may perform. Popular US DTC personal genome service providers and most of the DTC genetic and proteomic testing companies perform lab-developed tests/LDTs in their own facilities (literally or contractually), also referred to as home brew tests.[171] Manufacturers may contractually engage a CLIA-certified lab to perform the genetic tests they sell, meaning one CLIA-certified lab with capacity may service multiple LDT testing service providers.[172] Moreover, under CLIA, tests and systems that satisfy risk, error, and complexity requirements are issued certificates of waiver/CWs. Tests FDA-approved for home use automatically qualify for CWs.[173] Manufacturers of in vitro diagnostic tests/IVDs – tests performed with a sample of blood, saliva, or other bodily substance – that the FDA categorizes as "moderate complexity" may submit a CW application to the FDA.[174] CMS, directly and through outsourced authority, issued 246,358 CWs in 2021.[175]

CLIA regulations also recognize provider-performed microscopy/PPM procedures – tests that do not meet the criteria for waiver because they are not simple procedures and require training and specific skills for reliable test performance.[176] A CLIA certificate for PPM procedures permits physicians and midlevel practitioners to perform a list of moderate complexity microscopic tests and waived tests in conjunction with a patient's visit. In 2021, CLIA regulators issued 29,759 PPM certificates.[177] Although sites performing PPMs are held to CLIA quality standards for moderate complexity testing, the complete testing process for these procedures, typically done patient-by-patient or for small numbers of patients, escapes laboratory-scale controls and monitoring. Also, PPM certificate sites are not subject to routine biennial inspections.

SACGT acknowledged in its 2020 report and recommendations that, overall, the sweeping and inclusive input it gathered from myriad stakeholders favored increasing regulatory oversight of genetic testing by strengthening and expanding the CLIA program.[178] Predecessors to SACGT and contemporaries of SACGT also charged in the 1990s with assessing the regulation of clinical genetic tests – namely the ELSI Task Force, the NIH-DOE Working Group, and the CLIA Advisory Committee/CLIAC – explored the CLIA program approach and made related recommendations.[179] Although the CLIA program may be drawn from to enhance some aspects of regulatory oversight of genetic testing in our genomic era, the program's overall regulatory methodology is misplaced for medical use regulation of DTC personal genome testing. CLIA was created to regulate commercial laboratories and their testing proficiency. In simplest terms, CLIA is form and function (laboratory administration and testing proficiency) over clinical use substance. Even when CLIA is applicable, CLIA waivers and PPMs abound.[180] Beyond FDA regulation of medicinal products and their manufacturers and Federal Trade Commission/FTC and state regulation of relevant health care markets to protect consumers from fraud, consistent with US regulation of the practice of medicine overall, assessment of the clinical utility of commercial genetic tests is left to the medical profession.[181] With DTCGHR testing, consumers decide their medical use of them and whether and how they wish to involve learned and licensed medical providers.

CLIA implementation is largely outsourced and decentralized, and CLIA is not even a reliable regulatory mechanism for awareness of the personal genome testing available on the US' highly privatized, decentralized, commerce-driven, and dynamic national and state health care markets.[182] The effectiveness of CLIA in regulating the facility and proficiency standards imposed by CLIA depends upon compliance, implementation, and enforcement, there is an abundance of US CLIA-certified laboratories, many CWs and PPMs are issued, tests may be paid for out-of-pocket and without a payor check on use, and the US health care system is fragmented.[183] Although all manufacturers of medical devices within the scope of FDA-charged oversight theoretically must be on the FDA's radar, the FDA has increasingly diluted its regulation of medical devices by approving new devices based on matching with and piggybacking on devices it already has approved.[184] Moreover, the FDA has expressly recognized DTCGHR tests as *nonclinical use* tests – meaning nondiagnostic. For regulatory (certainly not marketing) purposes, DTC personal genome test providers are encouraged to self-classify as recreational genetics companies. 23andMe vividly demonstrated long ago that genetic testing has reached a consumer pay-out-of-pocket price point.[185] Dealing directly with consumers and without the involvement of health insurers was one of the company's founding principles, along with making medical provider involvement consumer-optional.

When SACGT issued its report and recommendations in 2000, the committee observed that,

> [a]t present, genetic testing is clinically available for more than 300 diseases or conditions in more than 200 laboratories in the United States, and investigators are exploring the development of tests for an additional 325 diseases or conditions. A recent survey of genetic testing laboratories found that over a three-year period, the total number of genetic tests performed increased by at least 30 percent each year, rising from nearly 100,000 in 1994 to more than 175,000 in 1996.[186]

A completed draft sequence of the human genome was released three years later.[187] With advances in next-generation sequencing/NGS technologies, the cost of personal genome testing has come down considerably since 23andMe was founded in 2006 and testing capabilities have soared.[188] The Pew Charitable Trusts, in an impressive, timely (2021) report, documented that, "because LDTs [,also known as home brew tests,] are not centrally registered or tracked, no one knows precisely how many of them are on the market, when and why they are used, or how their performance compares with FDA-reviewed diagnostics."[189]

CENTRALIZED, RELIABLE, ONGOING AWARENESS AND CLINICAL ASSESSMENT OF US MARKET-AVAILABLE PERSONAL GENOME TESTS

The US is distinguishable among industrialized nations in not having a centralized, universal health care system with strong government stewardship, the comprehensive, reliable information gathering and awareness that universal health care systems enable, and the extent to which the nation defers to and relies on an independent, self-regulating medical profession to govern the practice of medicine.[190] In biotech R&D, provided science integrity is coveted and maintained and corporate citizens act in compliance with governing law-policy, the incentive force of commercial drive generates innovation riches that benefit both human health and the economy. US TTLP has proven to be a potent catalyst for medical science innovation, but TTLP also has deliberately infused industry influence throughout the R&D continuum – from the laboratory bench to the pharmacy shelf – and in the delivery of clinical care.[191] In biotech R&D, provided science integrity is coveted and maintained and US law is complied with, the incentive force of commercial drive is desirable. Consequently, when resulting innovation reaches clinical medical practice, the US must be all that more protective of the evidentiary-science base of medicine. Evidence-based science research, repeatable and verifiable, is an ongoing quest for objective truth.[192] US law and policy have not evolved in sync with TTLP implementation to reinforce evidence science-based clinical practice – to fortify evidentiary-science truth in medicine:

> The production and implementation of medical knowledge in the United States is by now [as of 2005] so riddled with conflict of interest at virtually every level and every stage that nothing less than a new independent national public body is needed to protect the public's interest in medical science. Such a body must have the independence and expertise of the Institute of Medicine (part of the National Academies of Science), which would be well suited to accept responsibility for evaluating the scientific evidence. Lessons from the past show that this public body would require maximum insulation from political and commercial influence, on the model of the Federal Reserve Board—long and staggered terms, no financial ties to industry, and secure funding from Congress—to avoid evisceration when its findings were not to the liking of powerful interest groups. Surely the health of the American people and almost $2 trillion in annual expenditures are important enough to warrant such rigorous oversight.[193]

Centralized, objective health technology assessment/HTA is a means to reliably distinguish and commercially reward medical science innovation that meaningfully improves human health and US health care.[194] The US distinguishes itself among industrialized nations again by not formalizing, centralizing, and utilizing HTA – even though the US first introduced comprehensive government HTA in 1975 by establishing the Office of Technology Assessment/OTA.[195] The US dismantled OTA in 1995, five years after the launch of HGP and decades into the biotech revolution stirred by TTLP.[196] There have been recent political movements to restore OTA.[197] The US could benefit from centralized, reliable HTA beyond its industrialized counterparts given that its health care system is decentralized, fragmented (with myriad national, state, and national-state markets, sectors, and stakeholders, private and public), largely privatized, commerce-driven, and distinctively expensive.[198] Overall, the complicated US health care system has not fared well in comparison with those of its industrialized counterparts despite much more per capita spending for some time:

> The failure of the market to serve Americans' medical needs is certainly demonstrated by the combination of our poor health status compared with that of other industrialized countries, the low quality of our medical care (barely half of the standards for basic medical care are being met, according to a study done by the Rand Corporation and published in the NEJM [*The New England Journal of Medicine*] in December 2003), and the singularly high cost of our medical care.[199]

The US relies heavily on its self-regulating medical profession (independent compared with industrialized counterparts) and market forces to sort out HTA in a fragmented, decentralized, and unreliable fashion. This approach, which may have proved effective in much of the twentieth century, is not practicable and reliable in this one. In contrast, the US' industrialized counterparts have utilized HTA increasingly over the last several decades.[200] They incorporate the medical profession fundamentally in government stewarded health care decision-making with HTA to promote and protect the evidentiary-science base of medicine, to assess technologies for their overall clinical value, and to contain costs and spend health care dollars responsibly.[201] Moreover, they collaborate in HTA and share.[202]

For example, Britain established a General Practice Research Database/GPRD in 1987 to collect anonymized data from patient records, which it has done continuously since then.[203] The GPRD, a computerized database owned and run by the Medicines and Healthcare products Regulatory Agency/MHRA, now contains information on approximately 3.6 million patients in the UK – approximately six percent of the UK population – with ongoing data collection from more than 480 general practices nationwide.[204] Participating family practice physicians simply submit anonymized health records that they would generate in clinical practice regardless of the GPRD. The GPRD complements the limited clinical trial data that makes products market-available with real-world data/RWD on patient progress, side effects, and overall use experience. It is a resource for monitoring, spotting patterns, assessing, and making decisions about health technologies.[205]

The GPRD represents government-medical profession collaboration that is the foundation for health care decision-making success in universal health care systems. Consistent with the US, other industrialized nations empower their medical profession to regulate medicine, and they fully utilize their medical profession's education, training, experience, and expertise directly in national government health care decision-making. The medical profession is part of, and the driving delivery-of-care component of, universal health care systems. However, governments are the ultimate health system decision-makers and, as such, they are accountable to their citizens for the health care they make available within their borders.[206]

The US opioid addiction crisis, present and undeniable in the practice of medicine at the outset of this millennium, illustrates the US medical profession's self-regulation unreliability all too vividly. The crisis amassed patient-by-patient, prescription-by-prescription, for over a decade before CDC data defined it with numbers damning enough for the US to officially acknowledge that opioid addiction had become a public health emergency.[207] The medical profession resisted responsive self-regulation even after this health emergency declaration. Notably, the AMA's Opioid Task Force challenged the CDC's 2017 proposed *Guideline for Prescribing Opioids for Chronic Pain* on the grounds that a guideline might interfere with individualized patient care and necessary physician prescribing discretion.[208] That same year, the President's National Commission on Combating Drug Addiction and the Opioid Crisis reported that four out of every five new heroin users first used prescription opioids, and the CDC reported that "20 percent of patients who receive an initial 10-day prescription for opioids will still be using" (or at least receiving) them after a year.[209]

The US is the primary global epicenter for biotech R&D due largely to aggressive TTLP implementation over four decades, the effectiveness of which was demonstrated recently through the application of its methodology in Operation Warp Speed/OWS.[210] The astonishing advancement of genomic innovation is undeniable and increasingly tangible in clinical care.[211] The clinical complexities of the human genome sciences and the US market availability of DTC genetic and genomic technologies, including DTC personal genome testing services and emerging DIY genomics, are tangible and undeniable.[212] Centralized, reliable, and transparent assessment of the clinical soundness of health-related personal genome testing, the cornerstone of PGM, should be a regulatory priority – for the US government, medical profession, and patients. Industry too could benefit, as responsible twentieth-century patent medicine manufacturers discovered through their AMA Council and early FDA experiences.[213] Rx product regulation by the medical profession and the US government protected consumers, elevated patient and physician confidence in patent medicines, distinguished and commercially rewarded sound science innovation, and improved the practice of medicine and patient health.[214]

Today's US medical profession needs a regulatory mechanism to enable it to continue its twentieth-century accomplishment – to protect and promote the evidentiary-science base of PGM. Although libertarian and non-intrusive government sentiments resonate strongly in the US at this time, especially after government mandates debate triggered by the COVID-19 pandemic, regulation has the potential to benefit biopharma significantly as TTLP, PDUFA and its renewals, FDAMA, FDASIA, and the Cures Act have demonstrated.[215] The US has bountiful experience integrating government, industry, and academia to overcome daunting challenges through science innovation – from the Manhattan Project during WWII to OWS, with TTLP a potent catalyst for biotech and genomic revolutions in between.[216] As recognized by President Roosevelt at the outset of the twentieth century,

> It is no limitation upon property rights or freedom of contract to require that when men receive from government the privilege of doing business under corporate form ... they shall do so upon absolutely truthful representations .... Great corporations exist only because they are created and safeguarded by our institutions; and it is therefore our right and duty to see that they work in harmony with these institutions.[217]

Monetary returns are an intoxicating incentive, especially in a capitalist economy and culture. Thoughtful regulatory infrastructure to police truthfulness in medical science and corporate citizen compliance with US law-policy are essential to prevent market impediments in a largely privatized, commerce-driven, free market system. This is especially so when directly integrating government and academia with industry, when medical science R&D is commercially driven (incentivized) from the laboratory bench to market products, when medicine is business, and when the integrity of medical science and patient health care are at risk.

SACGT surveyed clinical genetic testing exhaustively and made recommendations to establish reliable US regulatory oversight of clinical genetic testing more than two decades ago. SACGT delivered its 2000 report and recommendations three years prior to the completion of a draft map of the human genome sequence, before seismic progress in genome sequencing technologies and personal genome testing capabilities, and seventeen years prior to the advent of FDA-approved DTCGHR testing that does not meet clinical standards and is market available to consumers without the involvement of medical professionals. SACGT concluded that "The oversight of genetic testing must be accomplished through new and innovative oversight mechanisms that will not limit the development of new tests or inordinately delay their availability."[218] SACGT recommended "multiple agencies in collaboration with the private sector ... to develop and implement a new multi-step process of evaluation for genetic tests."[219] SACGT's call for government-private sector integration is consistent with TTLP and its call for coordination among federal agencies is consistent with the Coordinated Framework – the US' regulatory foundation for biotech innovation, which the nation has been implementing since 1986.[220] SACGT, addressing private sector involvement, noted that professional organizations frequently serve as agents for the government, such as by performing CLIA accreditation in partnership with CMS and CDC.[221] The committee recognized that "[o]ther organizations, such as the American Academy of Pediatrics[/AAP], the American College of Obstetrics and Gynecology[/ACOG], the American Society of Human Genetics[/ASHG], and the National Society of Genetic Counselors[/NSGC], are also involved in the development of guidelines and recommendations regarding the appropriate use of genetic tests."[222]

Overall, SACGT recommended establishing comprehensive, reliable regulatory oversight of *clinical* genetic testing with registration and regulation of the labs performing them through CLIA modifications, and genetic test developer responsibility for collecting data to establish analytical validity.[223] SACGT proposed a test classification methodology and criteria to evaluate the analytical validity, clinical validity, and clinical utility of genetic tests, and application of these criteria to assess the clinical benefits and risks of genetic tests with evidentiary science.[224] SACGT acknowledged that data compilation and evaluation had to be an ongoing process with public transparency:

> Regardless of the option chosen for data collection, once the data have been collected and evaluated, they must be disseminated in an appropriate manner to health care practitioners and the public. One public commenter stated that "the public needs to be informed about general information that evolves from the data about genetic tests, at the same time as the practitioners are informed." Others suggested that information should be easily accessible by all and recommended an Internet-based database system.[225]

SACGT did not anticipate today's genetic testing reality – certainly not DTCGHR testing services market aggressively (and effectively) to the public with claims that the information generated is worthy of purchase because of its potential medical (health care decision-making) use, though with FDA-required clinical use disclaimers, and purchased directly by consumers with any learned medical professional involvement wholly consumer optional and incidental. Quite the contrary. SACGT was definitive: "No test should be introduced in the market before it is established that it can be used to diagnose and/or predict a health-related condition in an appropriate way."[226]

Health-related DTC personal genome testing that does not meet established clinical standards is a very present and burgeoning US market reality, with strong public consumption, consumer demand for access, and aggressive manufacturer DTC marketing to facilitate more.[227] The genome is very much out of the bottle, as suggested in a 2008 *NEJM* editorial, and the public wants direct access to it.[228] In fact, strong public demand persuaded the FDA to officially pop the cork on that bottle in 2017.[229] NASEM's 2017 study of forthcoming biotechnology innovation and its assessment of US regulatory infrastructure provides guidance for introducing reliable regulatory oversight of personal genome tests.[230]

Well-established US government regulatory infrastructure, such as CLIA and the FDA, must be utilized and *complemented* rather than fundamentally changed. The FDA's opioid intervention strategy, reflective of how the agency has evolved to regulate in the twenty-first century, is consistent with NASEM's guidance. In 2016, the FDA's *physician* leadership (Dr. Robert Califf, Dr. Janet Woodcock, and Dr. Stephen Ostroff) expressly recognized the very real limits of the agency's regulatory reach – limits that have been codified by Congress and clarified by the judiciary over the last several decades.[231] They did so when explaining the FDA's methodology of collaborating with and complementing other government agencies, the medical profession, and other stakeholders in their summary of the agency's opioid response strategy in *The New England Journal of Medicine*:

> We are launching renewed effort in the context of a broad national campaign that includes a major initiative led by the Department of Health and Human Services (HHS) designed to attack the problem from every angle.... [S]imply reinforcing opioid-related activities that are within the FDA's traditional regulatory scope will not suffice to stem the tide. Instead, we must work more closely with key federal agencies (including many within HHS), the clinical and prescriber communities, and other stakeholders to ensure that all available effective tools are brought to bear on this epidemic and that the evidence base for proper pain management and appropriate opioid use is optimized and translated into practice.[232]

The US should introduce centralized, reliable, and clinically meaningful regulatory oversight of the health-related personal genome tests available on the US market *as a means for the US medical profession* to continue what it accomplished in US medicine last century jointly with the FDA – protection and promotion of the evidentiary-science base of PGM. The driving objective should be to enable the US medical profession to succeed in meeting its foundational mission and responsibility as sentinel over clinical medicine and individualized patient care.[233] Today, much more than in the twentieth century when the US medical profession was more unified, capable of regulating the behavior of its members, and able to check undue influences on responsible clinical decision-making, individual physicians must be provided with the means to practice evidentiary science-based PGM and held accountable to do so. In fact, the oversight mechanism should provide clinical guidance for individual physicians, health insurers, health care institutions, health care managers, federal and state regulators, and the public to sort through an incoming firehose of market-available personal genome testing.

The mechanism must be comprehensive, coordinated, meaningful, and sustainable because the human genome sciences are dynamic and prolific, and the need will intensify with the forthcoming infusion of DTC personal genome testing and results generated through company-consumer transactions without medical professional involvement. The mechanism must provide a means to realize reliable *medical profession self-governance* over PGM by enabling the medical profession to adhere to evidentiary science-based *clinical standards* for personal genome testing in clinical practice. The mechanism must enable individual physicians to distinguish and utilize clinically sound personal genome testing capabilities and provide ready access to evidentiary science-based explanations to offset and stand firm against contrary patient self-determination demands. The introduction of such a mechanism would incentivize physicians to do so beyond practicing good medicine by today's standards because the standard of care for practing respsonible, clinically sound PGM would be elevated and they would be held accountable to that standard.[234] The resulting clinical clarity also would provide guidance for health insurer reimbursement and government health care program inclusion.[235]

The New England Journal of Medicine published an editorial in April 2022, entitled "Governance of Emerging Technologies in Health and Medicine – Creating a New Framework," in which the authors addressed the formation of a Committee on Emerging Science, Technology, and Innovation/CESTI in health and medicine.[236] The National Academy of Medicine/NAM formed CESTI "to serve as a platform for convening diverse stakeholders who have insights into the different aspects of emerging technology in order to assess governance in health and medicine and drive collective action."[237] According to the authors,

> Our current laws, regulatory bodies, and other governance structures — both "hard" (such as legally binding laws and regulations) and "soft" (such as voluntary guidelines, standards, and norms) — were largely built for a research, development, and market landscape that has changed substantially over recent years. As a result, our current approach to governance is no longer fit for purpose. Part of the challenge to our current system is encapsulated in the so-called Collingridge dilemma: early in a new technology's development, uncertainty and minimal evidence about its impact impede policymaking, but once the technology has diffused and harmful effects have become clear, it may be too late to act.

* * *

> We need a more comprehensive or coordinated approach to ensure that we have a broad view of the development and evolution of technology across sectors (government, private, nonprofit, academic, consumer, or volunteer), applications, and stakeholders.[238]

CESTI shares fundamentals with SACT and ELSI – diverse expertise and perspectives from a range of disciplines and multiple public and private sectors, a broad agenda and commitment to both clinical and ethics considerations, solicitation of ample stakeholder input, and overall coordination with inclusiveness.[239] ELSI and SACT made meaningful contributions to the advancement of genetic testing and genomics, ELSI continues to do so, and CESTI is poised to make important contributions as well, and at a juncture when crucially needed. However, neither ELSI nor SACGT made a significant, tangible, direct impact on comprehensive national genetic testing law and policy, other than perhaps by influencing enactment of the Genetic Information and Nondiscrimination Act/GINA.[240] SACG's thoughtful, pragmatic application of clinical standards and recommendations were shelved due to a political shift and the outcome of a national election.[241] Michael Yesley, who coordinated the Department of Energy's involvement in ELSI, provided a reflective summation of the program's contributions in 2008: "ELSI has produced a large portfolio of academic and professional literature, but little impact on public policymaking."[242]

Genomics, proteomics, and DNA sequencing technologies have made astounding progress since SACGT issued its genetic testing report with recommendations in 2000, and a draft map of the human genome sequence was completed a generation ago.[243] Astounding progress continues in real time.[244] Lab-developed genetic tests/LDTs, in vitro diagnostic tests/IVDs including noninvasive prenatal tests/NIPTs, and DTCGHR testing are very present realities in the US market and health care, and they have been for some time.[245] While CESTI undertakes its ambitious agenda of exploration, fact gathering, and deliberation, the US should take pragmatic, decisive, and immediate action with implementation. The regulatory approach undertaken should integrate government, academia (in medicine and science), and industry consistent with the US TTLP methodology – the potent catalyst for genetics and genomics innovation, including personal genome testing, which has changed and will continue to shape prevailing norms in medical science research, biopharma, and US medicine. Most importantly, consistent with US medicine legacy and related law-policy, the primary objective should be to enable medical providers to practice and protect evidentiary science-based PGM in an ongoing manner as the human genome sciences advance and to enable the medical profession to hold its members accountable for doing so.

The following discussion proposes that the US establish a comprehensive, transparent registry for *all* health-related personal genome tests available on the US market. This proposal draws from FDA regulation of medical devices and use of transparency in other areas, such as the comprehensive, transparent registry of clinical trials ongoing with FDA oversight, www.ClinicalTrials.gov.[246] The discussion proposes that the comprehensive registry be implemented in three cumulative phases to accelerate implementation while making the transaction costs manageable. Each of the phases is addressed individually. Phase I is to define the US health-related personal genome testing landscape by establishing a comprehensive registry for all health-related personal genome tests available on the US market. Phase II is to add a clinical data repository component inclusive of all scientifically reliable data submitted (inclusive beyond data submitted by test manufacturers/service providers) regarding a registered test. Phase III is to add a clinical use assessment component based on established, evidentiary science-based clinical criteria.

The discussion then addresses the importance of public transparency and user-friendly access consistent with www.ClinicalTrials.gov. and the portal to tiers of information approach utilized in 23andMe's PGHS – which was developed through company-FDA negotiations and interface for market approval of the company's DTGHR testing. The remaining discussion identifies existing US government means to implement the proposed comprehensive registry and clinical clearinghouse. The discussion also explores the potential for international collaboration consistent with HGP and COVID-19 responsiveness, and numerous other human genome sciences-related undertakings.

The proposed comprehensive registry and clinical use assessment clearinghouse, the result of implementing all three proposed phases, would be a means to maintain twentieth-century commitment to the evidentiary-science base of US medicine and to elevate personal genome autonomy throughout the US health care transformation to PGM. The US would continue its legacy of reliance on and deference to the medical profession in the practice of medicine, but with a government-academia-industry integrated regulatory mechanism to enable the medical profession to satisfy that awesome, challenging responsibility in our emerging PGM era.

The US has changed socially and culturally – profoundly so – since the advent of the ICT era and DTC BRCA genetic testing introduced in the 1990s. DNA is conceptually familiar and popular, federal medical privacy laws and the Affordable Care Act/ACA prohibition against health insurer consideration of preexisting conditions have infused consumer comfort with use of personal genome testing services, and patient autonomy and self-determination are social and cultural mantras that impact patient–medical provider interactions.[247] If the US establishes the proposed regulatory oversight means for the medical profession to protect and promote evidentiary science-based PGM, it does not have to impose on existing consumer personal genome testing access. The US could shore up the evidentiary-science base of PGM without denying consumer demand for personal genome autonomy and access to health-related DTC personal genome testing. In fact, with sufficient professional regulatory oversight of clinical uptake and responsiveness to DTC personal genome testing, direct consumer access to it might even contribute to the transformation of US health care to PGM with adherence to the evidentiary-science base of medicine.

PHASE I: A COMPREHENSIVE REGISTRY FOR ALL HEALTH-RELATED PERSONAL GENOME TESTS AVAILABLE ON THE US MARKET

The US should define its genetic, genomic, and proteomic testing market landscape by establishing a comprehensive registry for all health-related personal genome tests available on the US market – a counterpart to the clinical trials registry www.ClinicalTrials.gov. ClinicalTrials.gov, which is administered by the US National Library of Medicine and NIH, has been available to the public through the internet since February 29, 2000.[248] FDAMA required NIH to create and operate this registry, which tracks Rx clinical trials authorized by FDA-approved Investigational New Drug/IND applications. A primarily objective was to increase public awareness of and access to experimental Rx therapeutics. As of March 2022, the registry included 408,395 research studies in all fifty states and in 220 countries.[249]

All manufacturers/testing service providers of human health-related personal genome tests presently market available should be required to register their tests as a condition for continued market access. Once the registry is established, registration should be a precondition for US market access and manufacturers should be required to update their registrations at least once annually for their personal genome tests to remain market available. The registry should require manufacturers to self-identify and to individually profile each personal genome test for which they seek market access. Each test profile should identify manufacturer/testing service provider self-proclaimed health associations based on the manufacturer's supportive data and provide that data. This data transparency requirement is consistent with the consumer comprehension element of the FDA's approval of 23andMe's DTCGHR testing through its PGHS. 23andMe's consumers already have access to supportive science data through the company's internet portal to tiers of information.

The directors of laboratories that run these tests should be personally accountable for confirming the requisite manufacturer and test registration before performing health-related personal genome tests given that CLIA-certified labs often perform multiple tests from multiple sources. Closing the loop for regulatory oversight through extended compliance responsibility is familiar under US medical privacy law, HIPAA, which imposes compliance responsibility on both covered entities *and their business associates*.[250] This base registry, limited to comprehensively and reliably defining the US health-related personal genome testing market landscape, should be established and publicly available without delay, and then maintained in an ongoing manner with endowment funding to insure sufficient resources and to provide assurance of continuity without disruption. A user fee could be introduced for entities that register their tests to make the registry at least somewhat self-funding, consistent with PDUFA, other FDA user fees, and the US Patent and Trademark Office/USPTO user fees, though without a sunset provision that triggers chronic biopharma negotiation and intrusion with FDA resource allocations and operations.

PHASE II: A CLINICAL DATA REPOSITORY COMPONENT

The FDA requires 23andMe to disclaim clinical use of its DTCGHR tests without the involvement of medical professionals, though the company directly markets medical relevance and utility to consumers – lately aggressively so in a national television campaign in which a narrator professes that "Eighty percent of users get genetically meaningful health info from their DNA reports."[251] Medical relevance and alleged medical benefits from use are the intrinsic consumer market appeal and value of health-related personal genome testing, and companies competing in the DTC sector market these to the public – not the joys of genetic health risk recreation.[252]

As soon as practicable, the proposed comprehensive registry should include a clinical data repository/CDR open to evidentiary science-reliable submissions beyond the data submissions of registered manufacturers in support of their self-identified health-related associations. The CDR should apply a peer review mechanism for intake analogous to MJE peer review, including requisite disclosure of conflicts of interest, but one relaxed to welcome *incremental* clinical data supportive of *defined health care uses for some individuals in specified circumstances*. The base standard for health use data inclusion should be evidentiary-science integrity, verifiability, and reporting accuracy; research study and other data limitations should be directly addressed and identified with clarity for each inclusion. In addition to data supportive of health care uses from testing service providers and others, the CDR should invite challenges to those submissions and conflicting or otherwise negative data and interpretations. Registered manufacturers of tests with sound base clinical data should welcome third-party contributions as a resource to accelerate development of their tests to realize evidentiary science-based clinical standards.

The CDR would add an element of science objectivity and scrutiny to the registry's manufacturer-provided data. The objective of the CDR should be to establish a resource for medical providers and the public (for medical providers to explain to the public as necessary) to better assess *health care uses* of personal genome tests on a case-by-case basis – distinguished from full clinical use assessments in accordance with established evidentiary-science standards for clinical genetic tests.[253] Through centralized clinical data transparency with direct, efficient, and friendly user access, the CDR would enable heightened consumer and medical provider awareness for individual medical use interpretation. Consumers and their medical providers would be better able to evaluate and communicate potential clinical responsiveness and nonresponsiveness to personal genome test results on a patient-by-patient basis.

PHASE III: A CLINICAL USE ASSESSMENT COMPONENT

As soon as practicable, the comprehensive registry should be expanded to include a *clinical use assessment* component that applies established evidentiary-science clinical standards. Mainstreaming health-related personal genome testing in the general population in a manner that maintains and enhances the base of US medicine necessitates a reliable clinical evidentiary-science filter. Such a resource would better enable learned medical professionals to efficiently and reliably discern clinical soundness and use on a patient-by-patient basis. It would enable them to sort through a continuously expanding and burgeoning portfolio of clinically dynamic predictive and diagnostic personal genome testing capabilities and to deliver emerging PGM to patients responsibly. As demonstrated by 23andMe, mainstreaming health-related personal genome testing otherwise could advance data collection and human genome science research through consumer use volume, while generating commercial profit that incentivizes more data collection. However, continuing with this approach risks muddling the evidentiary-science base of medicine during the US health care transition to PGM with personal genome autonomy and control as Ms. Wojcicki envisions and 23andMe persues.[254]

To introduce this clinical assessment component, the US should draw from and develop the base work done by SACGT for clinical genetic testing assessment and related follow-on work done by other entities.[255] CESTI should be expressly charged with complementing and advancing SACGT's work moving forward. Such a pragmatic charge would anchor CESTI and significantly improve the committee's likelihood of making tangible, timely, and needed US health care law-policy contributions. Possibly orchestrated and coordinated by CESTI, the US government, medical profession, science community, and other stakeholders should collaborate to establish this clinical use assessment component of the registry – essentially a clinical use assessment clearinghouse component that applies evidentiary science-based clinical standards. Consistent with the ongoing progress of genomic science, clinical data should be updated on an ongoing basis and assessment entries updated periodically.

Such a clinical use assessment resource would protect and advance the clinical evidentiary-science base of PGM analogous to the advancement of basic human genome sciences research through the public dissemination of data in conjunction with HGP and as planned for the All of Us Research Program.[256] Beyond the draft human genome sequence map completed in 2003 with similar collaboration and transparency, a corrected, gapless map of the human genome sequence was released in 2022, and the UK Biobank has undertaken an initiative to assemble a proteomics complement to the human genome sequence with sharing transparency.[257]

PUBLIC TRANSPARENCY AND USER-FRIENDLY ACCESS

The comprehensive registry should be a public common for health-related personal genome tests on par with www.ClinicalTrials.gov for ongoing clinical research. Users and uses will vary considerably. The registry should apply a tiered approach to information for user-friendly access based upon purpose and choice – essentially the approach taken by 23andMe in its PGHS.[258] Tests identified through universal searches in the base registry should provide users with the option of selecting and accessing tiers of related information about them.

The registry must clearly distinguish test uses determined to meet established clinical standards from all other health-related and recreational uses, but with access to test-associated data to enable patient-specific application assessments. The registry should classify tests categorically according to a rubric of base sorting criteria, such as clinical diagnostic versus screening and predictive uses, complexity, and other criteria drawn from those identified by SACGT in its recommendations and proposed test classification methodology.[259] SACGT even developed the base for an algorithm for the classification of genetic tests. SACGT's work and any related follow-on work by other entities would provide a foundation for developing clinical assessment content and overall information organization. Although human genome science has advanced seismically since 2000, core clinical use standards are a constant. As addressed and deliberated by SACGT, the registry should provide a test-specific application of a rubric of established clinical standard criteria for evaluation of analytical validity, clinical validity, and clinical utility.[260]

EXISTING MEANS TO IMPLEMENT THE PROPOSED COMPREHENSIVE REGISTRY AND CLINICAL USE ASSESSMENT CLEARINGHOUSE

The site www.ClinicalTrials.gov. has been managing expansive clinical data with public accessibility since 2000, and the US government has additional existing technology, experience, and infrastructure to draw upon. For example, post completion of the draft human genome sequence in 2003, NIH and its international counterparts, notably the international consortium GENCODE, have continuously analyzed and revised the sequence and gene tally.[261] NIH has had a data-sharing policy since 2003, though the agency has required compliance only for large studies. On March 30, 2022, NIH announced:

> Beginning in January 2023, researchers funded by the National Institutes of Health will be required to submit a data management and sharing plan. Both the Federation of American Societies for Experimental Biology and the Association of Biomolecular Resources Facilities are working to ease challenges to their adoption. FASEB has launched an initiative called DataWorks to help researchers meet this requirement, while an ABRF working group plans to develop templates for core laboratories to provide to their users while also developing best practices for data-sharing policies.[262]

The US already has established and maintains several national registries at least loosely analogous to the proposed personal genome test registry in terms of national access and use, which demonstrate existing science data management technologies and capabilities. For example, the Combined DNA Index System/CODIS and

National DNA Index System/NDIS, which is part of CODIS, are long-established forensic DNA databases managed in an ongoing manner and used routinely by law enforcement across the nation.[263] The National Practitioner Data Bank/NPDB, established under the Health Care Quality Improvement Act/HCQIA of 1986, is a national staple for collecting and disseminating information throughout the medical profession and health care system.[264] Although still in a pilot stage, Sentinel, a national electronic oversight system for medical product safety surveillance charged under the Food and Drug Administration Amendments Act/FDAAA of 2007, is another government resource that could be drawn from.[265]

On point with the proposed personal genome test registry and clinical use clearinghouse, CDC was leading an interagency effort more than twenty years ago "to explore how voluntary, public/private partnerships might help encourage and facilitate the gathering, review, and dissemination of data on the clinical validity of genetic tests" and included pilot data collection efforts for cystic fibrosis and hereditary hemochromatosis.[266] Similarly, during the same timeframe, HHS was engaged in an interagency effort to assess ways to establish systematic national data collection on the validity and utility of genetic tests inclusive of genetic counselors, patient advocates, health care providers, industry representatives, and academics.[267]

The CDC recently demonstrated and elevated clinical research data collection and dissemination capabilities during the COVID-19 pandemic.[268] COVID-19 necessitated collaborative global clinical data collection and management in real time through Operation Warp Speed/OWS to research and develop responsive vaccines and therapeutics, and to monitor general population use – which is ongoing, Dr. Francis Collins, former director of NIH, announced a cross-continent pathogen surveillance network in October 2022.[269] The FDA, well versed in collecting and managing expansive clinical data, recently issued guidance for using registries as sources of real-world data/RWD for agency decision-making.[270]

Over the last several years, NIH has launched major genomic research initiatives to advance clinical care through public-private networks that depend on ICT capabilities to coordinate expansive research data and to engage in public interface. For example, NIH launched the Accelerating Medicines Partnership/AMP in 2014 – a public–private partnership among the NIH, FDA, multiple biopharma and other life science companies, and non-profit organizations "to transform the current model for developing new diagnostics and treatments."[271] The AMP program challenge is to utilize genomics, proteomics, and imaging technologies to identify changes in genes, proteins, and other molecules that cause disease and influence disease progression and to develop clinical testing and therapeutic applications.[272] NIH launched the Precision Medicine Initiative/PMI in 2015, recast as the All of Us Research Program in 2016, to build a research network that directly "taps into converging trends of increased connectivity, through social media and mobile devices, and Americans' growing desire to be active partners in medical research."[273] In October 2021, NIH launched the AMP Bespoke Gene Therapy

Consortium/BGTC, the sixth AMP initiative, "to develop platforms and standards that will speed the development and delivery of customized or 'bespoke' gene therapies that could treat the millions of people affected by rare diseases."[274] NIH also is engaged in a global Somatic Cell Genome Editing/SCGE Consortium that "aims to accelerate the development of safer and more-effective [CRISPR] methods to edit the genomes of disease-relevant somatic cells in patients, even in tissues that are difficult to reach."[275]

The US private sector has developed and applied much of the ICT needed to establish the proposed registry, and especially the existing DTC personal genome testing sector. A notable example is 23andMe's consumer-friendly Personal Genome Health Service/PGHS, which the FDA provided input for during its negotiations with the company and which it evaluated when granting market approval of 23andMe's DTCGHR testing through its PGHS in 2017.[276] If commercial DTC genetic test service providers are mandated to register their tests and provide data to access the US market and then update data periodically to maintain market access, they will be incentivized to provide registry and site creation input, drawing from the technologies they have already developed and have use experience with. In the event industry resists or needs arise that industry cannot readily meet, US agencies have decades of experience engaging with the private and public sectors to realize science and technology R&D – such as through cooperative research and development agreements/CRADAS. Under long-established and heavily implemented US law,

> Each Federal agency may permit the director of any of its Government-operated Federal laboratories, and, to the extent provided in an agency-approved joint work statement or, if permitted by the agency, in an agency-approved annual strategic plan, the director of any of its Government-owned, contractor-operated laboratories—
>
> (1) to enter into cooperative research and development agreements on behalf of such agency (subject to subsection (c) of this section) with other Federal agencies; units of State or local government; industrial organizations (including corporations, partnerships, and limited partnerships, and industrial development organizations); public and private foundations; nonprofit organizations (including universities); or other persons (including licensees of inventions owned by the Federal agency); and
>
> (2) to negotiate licensing agreements under section 207 of title 35, or under other authorities (in the case of a Government-owned, contractor-operated laboratory, subject to subsection (c) of this section) for inventions made or other intellectual property developed at the laboratory and other inventions or other intellectual property that may be voluntarily assigned to the Government.[277]

HHS's Biomedical Advanced Research and Development Authority/BARDA is an established and experienced intermediary between government and industry in science-technology R&D – as BARDA demonstrated impressively in OWS.[278]

GLOBAL COLLABORATION CONSISTENT WITH THE HUMAN GENOME PROJECT/HGP, COVID-19 RESPONSIVENESS, AND OTHER INITIATIVES

The human genome science and PGM medicine transcend US borders and invite international collaboration, as experienced some three decades ago with the orchestration of scientists globally to map the human genome DNA sequence through the International Human Genome Sequencing Consortium/IHGSC.[279] An ongoing Personal Genome Project/PGP, initiated in 2005, embodies a "coalition of projects across the world dedicated to creating public genome, health, and trait data."[280] As Francis Collins and Harold Varmos wrote in 2015 in *The New England Journal of Medicine* regarding US research initiatives to advance clinical medicine through genomics, proteomics, and imaging technologies, "The efforts should ideally extend beyond our borders, through collaborations with related projects around the world. Worldwide interest in the initiative's goals should motivate and attract visionary scientists from many disciplines."[281]

The UK is an ideal potential US collaborator for establishing the proposed health-related personal genome testing and clinical use assessment clearinghouse with much to contribute. The UK already has established a National Genomic Test Directory, which specifies which genomic tests are commissioned by the National Health Service/NHS, the technology through which they are available, and the patients eligible to access them.[282] The UK's NHS has a Genome UK national genomic health care strategy, and "has been increasingly turning to genomics to alleviate burdens on the British healthcare system."[283] In March 2022, the British Pharmacological Society and the Royal College of Physicians jointly issued a report, *Personalised Prescribing: Using Pharmacogenomics to Improve Patient Outcomes*, which recommends that the NHS uptake pharmacogenomic testing fully, fairly, and quickly, and provides guidance for doing so.[284] The report recommends utilization of pharmacogenomics and pharmacogenetics in primary care, secondary care settings, and in specialized centers throughout the UK (England, Northern Ireland, Scotland, and Wales) to avoid "a postcode lottery of care."[285] As acknowledged in the report's executive summary, "Although we focus on the UK, many of the issues discussed in the report are also relevant to other global healthcare systems, and learning from each other will be important in optimising medicines use around the world."[286]

The US' industrialized counterparts are collaborating in clinical genomic initiatives, such as a European research project to deliver a cancer genome interpretation/CGI platform that can be implemented clinically across Europe in CGI Clinics, and they collaborate in HTA routinely and meaningfully.[287] Well-established organizations such as the ECRI Institute (founded as the Emergency Care Research Institute), an independent nonprofit organization that serves over 10,000 healthcare organizations worldwide, and the Institute for Safe Medication Practices/ISMP, an ECRI affiliate, exist to utilize HTA to improve the safety, quality, and cost-effectiveness of care across all health care settings worldwide.[288] The COVID-19 pandemic forced unprecedented global collaboration and *science data sharing* among governments, private sector corporations, academic institutions, and the science and medical communities, which proved essential and remarkably successful.[289]

The US could engage in collaboration, in whole or in part, to establish and maintain the proposed personal genome testing registry and clinical use clearinghouse. Thoughtfully orchestrated collaboration would promote timeliness, technology sharing, data sharing, cost sharing and, most importantly, objectivity and reliability. International collaboration also could help synchronize US and European markets and registry collaboration could better enable the US to enforce a registry mandate to prevent manufacturers from simply selling to US consumers from abroad to skirt scientifically sound clinical use assessment, as has been threatened:

> Genomics has no local component, no intimate relationship with a physician for the first step. All things being equal, [Stanley Lapidus, a prolific bioscience entrepreneur], says he'd rather have his test run by an appropriately regulated domestic laboratory, but if the FDA should ever clamp down on direct-to-consumer testing, Lapidus said the industry will simply move offshore. "If consumers think this is valuable, guys in India will open up All India Genetics Testing—you get you're A's, C's, G's, and T's on the Web. The government will be able to regulate American labs, but it won't be able to regulate personal genomics.[290]

European nations regulate corporate speech in cyberspace much more meaningfully than the US, where corporate citizen and individual free speech are higher priorities in the overall debate over regulation of the internet.[291] At least from a European perspective, "The Internet is remarkably susceptible to traditional methods of regulation, to traditional models of political pressure and traditional policy-making, none of which should be underestimated."[292] European nations and Europe collectively have developed and employ related law-policy and enforcement technology, some of which may prove adaptable for the proposed registry.[293]

Although the proposed comprehensive registry is for personal genome testing, the registration, data collection, and clinical use assessment elements invite possibly drawing from another established international collaborative resource for operational insight. The International Council for Harmonisation of Technical Requirements for Pharmaceuticals for Human Use/ICH has evolved immensely since it was founded in 1990 to bring together regulatory authorities and pharmaceutical executives to address scientific and technical aspects of drug registration.[294] "ICH's mission is to achieve greater harmonisation worldwide to ensure that safe, effective, and high quality medicines are developed and registered in the most resource-efficient manner."[295] With active, expansive participation, "Harmonisation is achieved through the development of ICH Guidelines via a process of scientific consensus with regulatory and industry experts working side-by-side. Key to the success of this process is the commitment of the ICH regulators to implement the final Guidelines."[296] ICH has proven a potent catalyst for global collaboration in quality standard setting, technical requirements development, and sharing, while promoting worldwide harmonization and efficiency – well beyond good clinical practices/GCPs and good manufacturing practices practices/GMPs, which were foundational focus areas.

International collaboration to establish and build the proposed comprehensive registry and clinical use assessment clearinghouse resource for personal genome tests, the type of collaboration that achieved a draft sequence of the human genome ahead of schedule and under budget and multiple truly innovative and effective vaccines for COVID-19 within a year, should at least be considered and explored by CESTI. Even realizing just some meaningful international collaboration could make accomplishing the proposed personal genome test registry and clinical use assessment clearinghouse more doable, affordable, reliably objective scientifically, and enforceable, and would shore up the personal genome testing cornerstone of PGM beyond US borders.

TRANSITION AND TRANSFORMATION: PERSONAL GENOME AUTONOMY AND RESPONSIBLE PGM

The transition of US health care to PGM with personal genome autonomy and control is underway. Personal genome testing is the cornerstone of PGM. Health-related DTC personal genome testing without requisite medical provider involvement is a US market reality. The potential scope of market-available DTC personal genome testing that does not meet evidentiary-science clinical standards spans the human genome and human health. The US must introduce the regulatory oversight necessary to assess and sort through the clinical validity and utility of personal genome tests to enable physicians and other medical providers to practice clinically sound, responsible PGM on an individualized patient care basis.

The proposed comprehensive registry and clinical use assessment clearinghouse has the potential to elevate clinical decision-making throughout the US health care system. This added regulatory oversight is necessary for the transformation of US medicine to clinically sound, responsible PGM with adherence to the evidentiary-science base of US medicine during the transition. US consumers will bring DTC personal genome testing into US health care. Many already have. Providers, insurers, and other stakeholders throughout the US health care system will share a fundamental dilemma – sorting through a constantly amassing entanglement of market-available personal genome tests that encompasses a spectrum of reliability, analytical validity, clinical validity, and clinical utility with individual patient variation.[297]

Payer reimbursement is a prerequisite staple for reliable access in the US' decentralized, largely privatized, and commerce-driven health care system. Health insurers frequently challenge paying for clinical genetic, genomic, and proteomic tests.[298] They also often resist reimbursement for genetic counseling by CGCs, at times categorically and often in scope, as they have done for decades – with the need and demand for CGC services directly proportional to the market availability and clinical complexity of personal genome tests churned from the genomic revolution.[299] Predictable payer reimbursement is essential to make clinically sound, medically useful personal genome tests and accompanying medical professional expertise and services available in US health care, as recognized by the NHGRI in 2019:

> Genomic medicine has the capacity to revolutionize clinical practice. The mapping of the human genome has created new opportunities for genetic tests to predict, prevent and treat disease. Tests for breast cancer and for hereditary forms of colorectal cancer can assess disease risk and guide screening and preventive measures. Other tests can predict optimal chemotherapy regimens, or predict the likelihood of drug response or toxicities and avoid exposing patients to ineffective or overly toxic regimens.
>
> There are many other examples of clinically useful information available through newly developed genetic tests. In order for patients to have full access to the benefits of genetic testing, payers such as insurance companies and Medicare need systematic ways of evaluating genetic tests for reimbursement. Currently, there are barriers that make it difficult for payers to do so. Without this information, insurers cannot properly assess how to reimburse for genetic tests.
>
> One challenge insurers face is the difficulty of deciding when to reimburse for genetic tests that health care providers have offered their patients. The reason this is difficult is that insurers may not be able to easily evaluate what type of genetic test was performed, whether the test was appropriate to perform and whether the test is scientifically valid. This is in part because procedures are billed according to a standardized system of Current Procedural Terminology (CPT) codes developed by the American Medical Association, and fewer than 200 CPT codes exist for about 70,000 genetic tests. This means that there is no straightforward way to bill for many tests or for payers to identify what genetic tests were given.
>
> Moreover, payers are having trouble keeping up with the volume of new genetic and next-generation sequencing tests that are coming onto the market. Additionally, there is a lack of extensive data evaluating the economics of genetic testing. This makes it even more difficult to evaluate which tests should be covered and under what circumstances they should be covered. NHGRI hopes to serve as a resource for advancing genomic medicine by assisting all types of payers in their efforts to evaluate emerging genetic tests for reimbursement, and by promoting research into the health benefit and cost-effectiveness of genetic testing.[300]

HHS and NASEM have recognized this challenge and introduced reports to provide some guidance and structure for decision-making.[301] The proposed health-related personal genome test registry and clinical use assessment clearinghouse would introduce a reliable mechanism to sort through the clinical use confusion, gauge and negotiate reimbursement, and regulate health insurers and testing service providers. It also would elevate information in the US market about the scientific validity and clinical utility of personal genome tests to influence consumer demand

and medical provider use and responsiveness to DTC personal genome testing results. This information would better enable the US' commerce-driven health care system to capitalize on the impact of market forces – to better align demand for personal genome tests with medical use value.

Effective regulatory oversight, whether it be regulation of health insurers or health-related personal genome testing service providers, is strategic, thoughtful, decisive, and maximizes implementation, compliance, and enforcement clarity to minimize transaction costs. Although the FDA and FTC share concurrent jurisdiction to regulate the marketing of medicinal products, medical providers are the ultimate consumer protectors in US medicine.[302] Under the 23andMe precedent, medical provider involvement is wholly optional in DTC personal genome test transactions, and incidental to consumer demand and use.[303] Learned medical professional involvement in company-consumer transactions is marginalized, if not eliminated. The present US law-policy environment for health-related DTC personal genome testing undermines the medical profession's legacy role of sentinel over the practice of medicine and accompanying US jurisprudence.[304]

In a television commercial 23andMe began running nationally in January 2022, a narrator relays that "Eighty percent of users get genetically meaningful health info from their DNA reports."[305] The company entices potential PGHS consumers on its internet site with the same message: "80% receive a report with a meaningful genetic variant. Will you be part of the 80%?"[306] Although the intrinsic consumer appeal of health-related DTC personal genome testing is personal health care relevance and use, not recreation, the FDA has declared DTCGHR tests "nonclinical" and has established a regulatory express lane to market without regulatory assessment of clinical utility.[307]

Thoughtful, clinically sound – consistent with established, evidentiary science-based clinical standards – medical professional responsiveness to DTC personal genome testing is essential to realize evidentiary science-based PGM. Medical professionals must not allow manufacturer marketing and patient DTC personal genome test results that generate patient demands to trigger related clinical services unless the information is scientifically and clinically sound. The clinical complexity of health-related DTC personal genome testing market available in the US encompasses the decisiveness and reliability of tests for individual patients, the labs performing them, how they are performed, and use of the results they generate in individual patient care. These complexities undermine the reliability of consumer protection through medical providers even when consumers decide to involve them. Ultimately, in terms of clinical and other medical uses beyond recreation, personal genome testing technology is test and patient specific.[308] A genetic test with questionable clinical validity and utility for the general population may hold clinical utility for a particular individual – a direly ill patient who, in light of their medical history and profile particularities, is able to hone in on a treatment option.[309] The US must prioritize and protect patient care over consumer demand by establishing the regulatory infrastructure necessary to filter and discern health-related personal genome tests that achieve clinical standards for PGM uptake – meaning those likely, based on sufficient evidentiary science, to improve health care diagnosis, treatment, and disease prevention in the lives of individual patients.

The FDA's 2017 regulatory stance on DTCGHR testing, following essentially regulatory nonresponsiveness to DTC genetic testing for over a quarter-century, underscores that the agency cannot be relied upon to protect DTC personal genome testing customers. According to some commentators, the Federal Trade Commission/FTC is the US federal agency with the most potential to, in conjunction with state authorities, meaningfully protect those consumers and regulate the sector's market presence. In addition to expertise and experience policing consumer fraud, "The FTC appears to be the agency best positioned to achieve the right balance between oversight and industry self-regulation so that consumer privacy can be protected without unduly inhibiting the personal, commercial, and research benefits that come from the flow of genetic information."[310] The FTC also has considerable internet commerce expertise, which the FDA defers to and draws upon for matters within their concurrent FDA-FTC jurisdiction.[311] The FTC's authority could be utilized to better define the need for increased regulatory oversight and prompt federal, state, professional, and even industry action:

> The FTC has the ability to shape the debate surrounding best practices for DTC-GT[/direct-to-consumer genetic testing] through its authority to generate reports and recommendations for Congress and the public. The FTC should use this authority to conduct, in coordination with other relevant government agencies (for example, the FDA and CMS), a systematic assessment of whether ongoing self-regulatory efforts and the existing regulatory framework afford sufficient protection to consumers of DTC-GT services. These efforts should incorporate feedback from a wide variety of stakeholders, including consumer and industry advocacy groups, science and technology experts, DTC-GT companies, and the public.[312]

The proposed comprehensive health-related personal genome test registry and clinical use assessment clearinghouse would introduce a means for the FTC to meet this potential in our ongoing genomic revolution era. The registry and clinical use clearinghouse also would be a resource for Congress and other government regulators, federal and state, and for the US medical profession entrusted with oversight of the practice of medicine. The registry and clinical use clearinghouse would make the personal genome testing available on the US market transparent and incentivize meaningful industry self-regulation – as opposed to industry's recent attempt at self-regulation to address concerns about consumer privacy. This industry effort resulted in *Privacy Best Practices for Consumer Genetic Testing Services* – nonbinding guidelines issued in 2018 for the collection, use, and sharing of consumer genetic data not accompanied by a reliable enforcement mechanism.[313] The industry attempt at meaningful self-regulation in DTC personal genome testing to promote consumer privacy has not proven effective.[314]

The establishment of a comprehensive, reliable source of information about the personal genome tests available on the US market, updated in an ongoing manner, and accessible to medical providers, regulators, and consumers has the potential to overcome an existing, chronic, and pervasive US health care market impediment. "The problem is not with the market itself, but with the inadequate information and flawed incentives that currently shape our health care market. Drug companies earn higher profits when more people use expensive drugs, not when more people achieve better health."[315]

In a highly decentralized, privatized, commerce-driven, and complex US health care system, market forces cannot work without regulation to ensure that the information necessary to make sound consumption and clinical decisions is available. The biopharma influence throughout US medical science innovation R&D and clinical health care incentivized over decades of TTLP implementation with DTC and DTP biopharma marketing freedom must be checked by a sound evidentiary-science baseline of information. The need is underscored when the public drives consumption decision-making in medicine and the product is personal genome testing during an ongoing genomic revolution. The proposed health-related personal genome test registry and clinical use clearinghouse could provide this sound information baseline to better enable medical providers to adhere to the practice of evidentiary science-based medicine even when inundated by DTC personal genome testing reports with accompanying patient demands for clinical responsiveness.

The genome has been freed from the bottle and is market-available for direct consumer consumption, as anticipated in the 2008 *NEJM* editorial.[316] The US public, stakeholders, and politically persuasive interest groups that support patient self-determination and personal genome autonomy will resist regulatory proposals that significantly limit existing access to DTC personal genome testing. In 2000, I wrote:

> Presumably, commercial life science, delivery of health care, public health politics, patient advocacy, and bioethics are united by the shared objective of improving human health. The individual-centered genetic testing debate must rage on, for society will reap the benefits when genetic testing technologies become plentiful, commercially accessible, and heavily used.[317]

The day has come but without the regulatory oversight essential to protect and promote evidentiary science-based PGM. The proposed health-related personal genome test registry and clinical use assessment clearinghouse would provide comprehensive awareness of all genetic tests available on the US market and centralized, reliable, ongoing clinical data and use assessment of them.

With such a mechanism in place, public access to health-related DTC personal genome testing could become copasetic with adherence to responsible, evidence-based clinical practice in a PGM era. The medical profession, insurers, regulators, and the public simply need this means to sort, filter, and make informed clinical use decisions. As demonstrated by 23andMe, mainstreaming DTC personal genome testing has the potential to advance data collection and genomic science with commercial profit through use volume. Consumer consumption of DTCGHR testing builds personal genome testing familiarity which, to some extent, prepares the public and medical providers for PGM. However, the same might be accomplished without the expense of muddling US medicine and opportunities to incrementally realize clinically sound PGM and enhanced individual patient care.

The expression "garbage in, garbage out' is very applicable to the uptake of data in science research and to the uptake of medical science innovation in clinical care. Failing to adhere to the evidentiary-science base of US medicine will confuse and likely lengthen the transition journey to the personal genome autonomy in US health care envisioned by Anne Wojcicki, CEO and co-founder of 23andMe:

> I think that there's a huge opportunity for the consumer to have a voice. People want to engage. People want to learn about themselves. They want to be healthier. They want to know more [about] what they can do. I feel like I now have this responsibility to tell you, "I told you you're high risk for Alzheimer's, you're high risk for Parkinson's, you're high risk for a stroke. I told you really meaningful information about yourself. Now I need to help you execute on your life." I think that's where, when I think about the potential of raising this capital, ... we want to expand, and I think that there's a real opportunity to think about an affordable consumer-centric health care system.[318]

The progress of genetics, genomics, proteomics, and next-generation sequencing and their infusion into clinical medicine in recent years makes the transformation of standard of care to personal genome medicine a foreseeable future probability, if not a certainty. Personal genome autonomy is a lofty and desirable goal, provided it is accomplished in sync with evidentiary science-based medicine. The future of US medicine must be one in which human genome science technologies enable rather than replace learned and licensed medical professionals. Protecting the science and evidence base of PGM along the journey to the health care future is essential to realize PGM with adherence to evidentiary science-based clinical practice – the US medical profession's most profound twentieth-century accomplishment.[319]

During the ongoing transition to evidentiary science-based PGM as standard of care, the US' governing regulatory goal should be to accompany individuals' direct access to their personal genomes and use in health care decisions with the means for learned medical professionals to practice better medicine, to reach more patients and patient needs, and to improve overall human health. While the health-related DTC personal genome testing commercial sector empowers individuals through access to their personal genomes, the US must protect and elevate the practice of medicine and patient care.

The US must introduce increased regulatory oversight to protect the base of medicine in the present and future commensurate with how the medical profession did so last century through self-regulation sovereignty over the practice of medicine.

Shoring up the evidentiary-science base of PGM is a prerequisite to fully realize the potential gifted through human genome science innovation. As science research translates the human genome sequence into medical meaning and compiles the pages in our "present and future medical diaries" with increasing clarity, US law and policy must be modified to reinforce and at times move beyond twentieth-century norms.[320] Individual access to personal genomes is desirable in US health care, but only if on the evidentiary-science bedrock of clinically sound PGM.

NOTES

1 *See* Gavin Francis. *Medicine: Art or Science?*, 395(10217) LANCET 24–5 (Jan. 4, 2020) ("No matter how much technology there is, when you're ill, you're still going to have to find someone you can trust."), www.thelancet.com/journals/lancet/article/PIIS0140-6736(19)33145-9/fulltext.

2 Panda Sadhu Charan, *Medicine: Science or Art?*, *in* WHAT MEDICINE MEANS TO ME 127 (Ajai R. Singh, Shakuntala A. Singh eds., 2006), www.ncbi.nlm.nih.gov/pmc/articles/PMC3190445/.

3 Robert Pearl, *Medicine Is An Art, Not A Science: Medical Myth Or Reality?*, FORBES BUS. (June 12, 2014), www.forbes.com/sites/robertpearl/2014/06/12/medicine-is-an-art-not-a-science-medical-myth-or-reality/?sh=64a09ff62071.

4 Clinical PGM is advancing through ongoing innovation culled from genetics, genomics, proteomics, DNA sequencing capabilities (next-generation sequencing/NGS), and imaging technologies. *See* Francis S. Collins, Harold Varmos, *Perspective*, *A New Initiative on Precision Medicine*, 372 N. ENG. J. MED. 793–95, 95 (Feb. 26, 2015) (addressing the US' Precision Medicine Initiative/PMI, which was recast as the All of Us Research Program/AllUs), www.nejm.org/doi/full/10.1056/NEJMp1500523. *See generally* FRANCIS S. COLLINS, THE LANGUAGE OF LIFE: DNA AND THE REVOLUTION IN PERSONALIZED MEDICINE (illustrated ed. 2011); MISHA ANGRIST, HERE IS A HUMAN BEING: AT THE DAWN OF PERSONAL GENOMICS (2010); KEVIN DAVIES, THE $1,000 GENOME: THE REVOLUTION IN DNA SEQUENCING AND THE NEW ERA OF PERSONALIZED MEDICINE (2010). Genes make proteins, and proteins impact gene expression and cellular differentiation. *See generally* Sagar Aryal, *Genomics Vs. Proteomics- Definition And 10 Major Differences*, THE BIOLOGY NOTES (Feb. 16, 2021), https://thebiologynotes.com/difference-between-genomics-and-proteomics/#:~:text=Genomics%20is%20the%20study%20of%20genomes%20which%20refers%20to%20the,the%20genome%20of%20an%20organism. An organism's genome is the complete set of genes in the nucleus of each of the organism's cells – the organism's set of DNA instructions. An organism's genome is a constant; the organism's cells all carry the same set of genes and DNA instructions. Nevertheless, cells differentiate to become specific cell and tissue types. *See id.* The set of proteins produced through gene expression in each of an organism's cells varies in accordance with cell and tissue type, and it is dynamic. *See id.* A proteome is the complete set of proteins that is or can be expressed by a genome, cell, tissue, or organism at a given time, under defined conditions. *See id.* Proteomics is the study of the proteome. *See generally* NATIONAL RESEARCH COUNCIL/NRC, DEFINING THE MANDATE OF PROTEOMICS IN THE POST-GENOMICS ERA: WORKSHOP REPORT (2002), www.ncbi.nlm.nih.gov/books/NBK95348/pdf/Bookshelf_NBK95348.pdf. Genetics is the study of gene expression and function, and genomics is the study of gene expression,

function, and interactions in the context of an organism's entire genome. "The main difference between genomics and genetics is that genetics scrutinizes the functioning and composition of the single gene whereas genomics addresses all genes and their inter relationships in order to identify their combined influence on the growth and development of the organism." World Health Organization/WHO, *Genomics* (Nov. 12, 2020), www.who.int/news-room/questions-and-answers/item/genomics#:~:text=The%20 main%20difference%20between%20genomics,and%20development%20of%20the%20 organism.

5 *See generally* COLLINS, LANGUAGE OF LIFE, *supra* note 4; ANGRIST, DAWN, *supra* note 4. *Cf.* SECRETARY'S ADVISORY COMMITTEE ON GENETIC TESTING/SACGT, ENHANCING THE OVERSIGHT OF GENETIC TESTS: RECOMMENDATIONS OF THE SACGT (July 2000) (addressing the complexities of utilizing genetic testing in clinical care), https://osp.od.nih.gov/sagct_document_archi/enhancing-the-oversight-of-genetic-tests-recommendations-of-the-sacgt/. *See also Chapter* 6, *supra*, at notes 43–98, and accompanying text ("The Complexities of Personal Genome Medical Decision-Making").

6 Worldwide, some 400 million people have been diagnosed with one of about 7,000 Mendelian diseases, which make them rare diseases with immense potential to treat through human genome science theoretically given strong genetic influences, but they represent relatively small commercial markets. *See* National Human Genome Research Institute/NHGRI, *NIH Funds New Effort to Discover Genetic Causes of Single-Gene Disorders* (July 15, 2021), www.genome.gov/news/news-release/NIH-funds-new-effort-to-discover-genetic-causes-of-single-gene-disorders. In 2021, the US National Institutes of Health/NIH established the Mendelian Genomics Research Consortium responsive to this situation. *See id.* NIH also launched the AMP Bespoke Gene Therapy Consortium/BGTC focused on developing gene therapies for rare diseases. *See infra* note 274, and accompanying text.

7 *See* Neil A. Holtzman, *FDA and the Regulation of Genetic Tests*, 41 JURIMETRICS J. 53, 55 (2000).

8 *See id.* at 54–56. *See generally* SACGT, RECOMMENDATIONS, *supra* note 5.

9 *See Chapter* 6, *supra*, at notes 43–98, and accompanying text ("The Complexities of Personal Genome Medical Decision-Making").

10 *See generally* SACGT, RECOMMENDATIONS, *supra* note 5.

11 *See id.* at iii (stating that contributors included "more than 400 individuals and groups who provided input into the report and commented on the recommendations as they were being developed"), 4–5 (charge to the committee and public consultation process), App. B. ("Public Comments on Preliminary Conclusions and Recommendations on Oversight"), https://osp.od.nih.gov/sagct_document_archi/enhancing-the-oversight-of-genetic-tests-recommendations-of-the-sacgt-appendix-b/. *See also* National Advisory Council for Human Genome Research, *Summary of Meeting, Bethesda, Md, May 22, 2000*, www.genome.gov/10001361/may-2000-nachgr-meeting-summary.

12 *Visit* NHGRI, *Genomics and Medicine* (visited Sept. 22, 2021), www.genome.gov/health/Genomics-and-Medicine. *See generally* COLLINS, LANGUAGE OF LIFE, *supra* note 4; ANGRIST, DAWN, *supra* note 4; DAVIES, $1,000 GENOME, *supra* note 4.

13 SACGT discussed and applied these terms in the context of genetic testing, clinical validity, and clinical utility when presenting its recommendations. *See generally* SACGT, RECOMMENDATIONS, *supra* note 5, at 15–19.

14 *Cf.* National Human Genome Research Institute/NHGRI, *Coverage and Reimbursement of Genetic Tests* (Aug. 15, 2019), www.genome.gov/about-genomics/policy-issues/-Reimbursement-of-Genetic-Tests.

15 *See generally Chapter 4, supra* (discussing market uptake and regulation of DTCGHR testing with consumer data); James W. Hazel, *Privacy Best Practices for Direct-to-Consumer Genetic Testing Services: Are Industry Efforts at Self-Regulation Sufficient?, in* CONSUMER GENETIC TECHNOLOGIES 260–76 (J. Glenn Cohen, Nita A. Farahany, Henry T. Greely, and Carmel Schachar eds., 2021). *See also* THE PEW CHARITABLE TRUSTS, REPORT, THE ROLE OF LAB-DEVELOPED TESTS IN THE IN VITRO DIAGNOSTICS MARKET 1 (Oct. 2021), www.pewtrusts.org/-/; FUTURE OF PRIVACY FORUM, BEST PRACTICES FOR CONSUMER GENETIC TESTING SERVICES (July 31, 2018), www.geneticdataprotection.com/wp-content/uploads/2019/05/Future-of-Privacy-Forum-Privacy-Best-Practices-July-2018.pdf.

16 *See generally Chapter 4, supra* (discussing market uptake of DTCGHR testing with consumer and sector information).

17 *See generally* Hazel, *Best Practices, supra* note 15. *See also* Carmel Shachar, I Glen Cohen, Nita A. Farahany, Henry T. Greely, *Introduction, in* CONSUMER GENETIC TECHNOLOGIES, *supra* note 15, at 1, *citing* GRAND VIEW RESEARCH, PREDICTIVE GENETIC TESTING AND CONSUMER GENETICS MARKET SIZE, SHARE & TRENDS ANALYSIS REPORT BY TEST TYPE (POPULATION SCREENING, SUSCEPTIBILITY), BY APPLICATION, BY SETTING TYPE, AND SEGMENT FORECASTS, 2019–2025 (2019) (projecting the global genetic testing and consumer wellness genomic market, valued at $2.24 billion in 2015, to double by 2025). *Cf.* FORUM, BEST PRACTICES, *supra* note 15; PEW, REPORT, *supra* note 15.

18 *See generally* CONGRESSIONAL BUDGET OFFICE/CBO, RESEARCH AND DEVELOPMENT IN THE PHARMACEUTICAL INDUSTRY (2021), www.cbo.gov/publication/57126; *Prologue, supra* (summarizing the advancement of genome sequencing and personal genome testing technologies); OFFICE OF TECH. TRANSFER, NAT'L INSTS. OF HEALTH, NIH RESPONSE TO THE CONFERENCE REPORT REQUEST FOR A PLAN TO ENSURE TAXPAYER INTERESTS ARE PROTECTED (2001) (confirming the effectiveness of US technology transfer law and policy/TTLP); US GOV'T ACCOUNTABILITY OFFICE/GAO, GAO-98-126, TECHNOLOGY TRANSFER: ADMINISTRATION OF THE Bayh-DOLE ACT BY RESEARCH UNIVERSITIES (1998) (TTLP background, methodology, and effectiveness). *Cf.* US NATIONAL ACADEMIES OF SCIENCE, ENGINEERING, AND MEDICINE/NASEM, PREPARING FOR THE FUTURE PRODUCTS OF BIOTECHNOLOGY (2017) (assessment of the landscape of forthcoming biotech innovation), www.nap.edu/catalog/24605/preparing-for-future-products-of-biotechnology.

19 *See Chapter 4, supra,* at notes 66–68, and accompanying text (clinical development of BRCA testing from 1996 to 2013).

20 *See Chapter 4, supra,* at notes 95–97, and accompanying text (Ms. Wojcicki's vision and 23andMe's mission regarding personal genome medicine). Mr. Watson, after acknowledging that "the medical establishment has every right to be cautious about the scientific accuracy and clinical validity of retail DNA testing," has declared, "I for one wholeheartedly endorse consumers' right to know their personal genetic information and to take what measures seem appropriate." JAMES D. WATSON, DNA: THE STORY OF THE GENETIC REVOLUTION 208 (2nd ed. 2017) (with Andrew Berry, Kevin Davies, updated commemoration of the fiftieth anniversary of the discovery of the double helix). In addition to the expansive biotech innovation realized over the last several decades and visible on the forthcoming US biotech products landscape, the exponential advancement of DNA sequencing technologies over the last few decades and projected moving forward, the DTC personal genome testing already available on the US market with substantial consumer uptake, and the personal genome testing sector's projected growth, human genome science is progressing with intensity and resource infusion globally from public and private sectors. *See generally Prologue, supra* (DNA sequencing technologies); CBO, R&D, *supra* note 18 (biopharma investment and success trends); NASEM, PREPARING, *supra* note 18 (2017 assessment of the forthcoming biotech innovation landscape). Several US NIH

undertakings are addressed *infra* at notes 261–62, 269, 271–75, and in the accompanying text, and genomics and proteomics are global endeavors. For example, the UK Biobank has undertaken a project to assemble a proteomics complement to the HGP human genome sequence map. *See* Adam Bonislawski, *UK Biobank Proteomics Project Produces Large-Scale Map of Human Gene-Protein Linkages*, GenomeWeb (July 29, 2022), www.genomeweb.com/proteomics-protein-research/uk-biobank-proteomics-project-produces-large-scale-map-human-gene?utm_source=Sailthru&utm_medium=email&utm_campaign=GWDN%20Wed%20PM%202022-06-29&utm_term=GW%20Daily%20News%20Bulletin#.YrywoXbMK3A. The UK has adopted a national genomic health care strategy, "Genome UK." *See infra* notes 282-86, and accompanying text.

21 *See generally Chapter 1, supra.*

22 *See generally id.*

23 *See* Paul Starr, The Social Transformation of American Medicine: The Rise of a Sovereign Profession and the Making of a Vast Industry 102–27 (1984) (winner of the 1984 Pulitzer Prize for general nonfiction).

24 *See Chapter 1, supra*, at notes 68-69, 102-03, 106, 115, and accompanying text (introduction of the AMA Counsel and its work and impact on the US medicines market and US medicine overall).

25 *See id. See also* James G. Burrow, The Prescription-Drug Policies of the American Medical Association in the Progressive Era, *in* Safeguarding the Public: Historical Aspects of Medicinal Drug Control 112, 112–22 (John B. Blake ed. 1970).

26 *See* Pub. L. No. 82–215, § 1, 65 Stat. 648 (1951), *codified as amended*, 21 U.S.C. § 353(b). *See also* Lars Noah, *Reversal of Fortune: Moving Pharmaceuticals from Over-the-Counter to Prescription Status?*, 63 Vill. L. Rev. 355, 393 (2018).

27 *See* Peter Temin, Taking Your Medicine: Drug Regulation in the United States 121 (1980).

28 *See id.*

29 *See* Starr, Social Transformation, *supra* note 23, at 132–34.

30 *See Chapter 1, supra*, at notes 53–135, and accompanying text (addressing deaths in 1901 from a contaminated diphtheria antitoxin, at least 107 deaths in 1937 from a sulfanilamide elixir, children contracting polio in 1955 from bad batches of vaccine distributed in a long-anticipated vaccination campaign, and congenital damage to and loss of pregnancies during an international thalidomide crisis in the late 1950s and early 1960s).

31 *See Chapter 1, supra*, notes 102–08, and accompanying text ("The Medical Profession's Role as Sentinel Over Clinical Use").

32 *See id.* at notes 46–52, and accompanying text. *See also* Starr, Social Transformation, *supra* note 6, at 128–29; Steven Johnson, Extra Life: A Short History of Living Longer 127 (2021); Nathan A. Brown, Eli Tomar, *Could State Regulations Be the Next Frontier for Preemption Jurisprudence? Drug Compounding as A Case Study*, 71 Food & Drug L.J. 271, 273 (2016).

33 *See Chapter 4, supra*, at notes 125–29, and accompanying text (addressing the FDA's 2017 market approval of 23andMe's DTCGHR tests provided to consumers through its Personal Genome Health Service/PGHS, and establishment of a DTCGHR tests category for express approval moving forward).

34 *See generally Chapter 5, supra.*

35 *See generally id.*

36 *See* Elisabeth Rosenthal, An American Sickness: How Healthcare Became Big Business and How You Can Take It Back 100 (2017) ("drug advertising is now a constant in our lives"); John Abramson, Overdosed America: The Broken Promise of American Medicine 150–52 (2005). FDA rules were relaxed to allow biopharma

television advertising in sync with the passage of FDAMA in 1997. *See Chapter 3, supra*, at note 11, and accompanying text.

37 *See Chapter 5, supra*, at pages 222–41.

38 *See Chapter 4, supra*, at notes 125–29, and accompanying text. *See generally* Consumer Genetic Technologies, *supra* note 15. *Cf.* Forum, Best Practices, *supra* note 15; Pew, Report, *supra* note 15.

39 Consider that 23andMe amassed more than a million DNA profiles and related health information by 2015, and over 5 million globally by 2018. *See Chapter 4, supra*, at note 103, and accompanying text.

40 Jeffrey Shuren, Janet Woodcock, *Jeffrey Shuren, M.D., J.D., Director of the FDA's* Center *for Devices and Radiological Health, and Janet Woodcock, M.D., Director of the FDA's Center for Drug Evaluation and Research on Agency's Warning to Consumers About Genetic Tests That Claim to Predict Patients' Responses to Specific Medications* (Nov. 1, 2018), www.fda.gov/NewsEvents/Newsroom/PressAnnouncements/ucm624794.htm.

41 *See Chapter 6, supra*, at notes 43–98, and accompanying text ("The Complexities of Personal Genome Medical Decision-Making").

42 *See Chapter 4, supra*, at notes 178-83. See *generally* CBO, R&D in Pharma, *supra* note 18; *Prologue, supra* (summarizing the advancement of genome sequencing and testing technologies); Nasem, Preparing for the Future, *supra* note 18.

43 *See Chapter 6, supra*, at notes 43–98, and accompanying text ("The Complexities of Personal Genome Medical Decision-Making").

44 *See Chapter 1, supra*, at notes 184–89, and accompanying text ("The Resulting Medical Profession-FDA Symbiotic Relationship").

45 *See Chapter 4, supra*, at notes 125–29, and accompanying text (seminal FDA approval of DTCGHR testing).

46 *See* Food and Drug Administration Safety and Innovation Act/FDASIA of 2012, P.L. 107–250. Congress questioned FDA reliability after Vioxx, Celebrex, and other Rx recalls and controversies at the outset of the millennium, and it directed the agency to scrutinize new drug applications more closely under the Food and Drug Administration Amendments Act/FDAAA of 2007, Pub. L. No. 110–85, 121 Stat. 823 (2007), *codified as amended*, 21 U.S.C. §§ 301–399i (2012). However, support for heightened regulatory scrutiny and caution at the expense of time in innovator drug review and approval waned. The Food and Drug Administration Safety and Innovation Act/FDASIA, signed into law on July 9, 2012, affirmed PDUFA V and expanded the FDA's authority to collect user fees from industry to fund review of innovator new drugs with increased stakeholder involvement in FDA processes. *See* FDA, *FDASIA* (current Mar. 28, 2018), www.fda.gov/regulatory-information/selected-amendments-fdc-act/food-and-drug-administration-safety-and-innovation-act-fdasia. The mantra of FDASIA was to increase FDA authority to promote innovation and to advance public health by *accelerating access* to innovator drugs, medical devices, generic drugs, and biosimilar biologic products with increased FDA surveillance – an updated FDAMA legislative intent. *See id*. Congress did not effectively impede biopharma DTC and DTP marketing practices in the FDAAA, nor between enactment of the FDAAA and FDASIA, and it has not since. *See generally Chapter 3, supra*. In fact, within a decade after passing the FDAAA to instill more FDA scrutiny and caution, Congress reversed course and passed the twenty-first Century Cures Act, Pub. L. No. 114–255 (Dec. 2016). The Cures Act, supported by large biopharma manufacturers and opposed by many consumer organizations, introduced measures *to accelerate* medical product discovery, development, and delivery beyond FDAMA – notably by codifying opportunities for companies to provide "data summaries" and "real world evidence" such as observational studies and insurance claims data rather than full

clinical trial results. *Id.* (contains three primary titles that address acceleration of medical product discovery, development, and delivery). *See generally* Sheila Kaplan, *Winners and losers of the 21st Century Cures Act*, STAT NEWS (Dec. 5, 2016), www.statnews.com/2016/12/05/21st-century-cures-act-winners-losers/.

47 *See generally* JAY KATZ, THE SILENT WORLD OF DOCTOR AND PATIENT (1984) (addressing paternalism in US health care during the twentieth century). *See* Sara Spencer, *Perspectives: Providing Counseling to Patients Using Direct-to-Consumer Testing* (Apr. 29, 2021) (addressing contemporary challenges to certified genetic counselors/CGCs), https://perspectives.nsgc.org/Article/TitleLink/Providing-Counseling-to-Patients-Using-Direct-to-Consumer-Testing. *See Chapter* 3, at pages 136-39 ("Impact of Biopharma Marketing on the Practice of Medicine"); 139–40 ("Twentieth-Century Marketing Norms in a PGM Era").

48 *See* ROSENTHAL, AMERICAN SICKNESS, supra note 36, at 196. *Cf. The American Medical Association: Power, Purpose, and Politics in Organized Medicine*, 63 YALE L.J. 938, 948 (1954) (the AMA's mid-century status).

49 *See* ROSENTHAL, AMERICAN SICKNESS, *supra* note 36, at 196. Some calculate AMA active physician membership much lower and declining. The AMA includes students, residents, and group practice memberships, which inflates numbers:

> So let's break it down further and take a closer look at the AMA's membership numbers … —there are 1,341,682 physicians/medical students/residents/Fellows in the US today—there are 250,253 AMA members. According to the AMA's own numbers, 22.5% of AMA members are students and 24.7% are residents (this number in 2016 was 235,000 or 1/6th of America's physicians).
>
> Yet students only make up 8.1% and residents, 10.4% in the U.S., so if you remove them from the AMA's published numbers, you get 1,093,472 physicians, and then remove the percentages of students and residents from the previous numbers I quoted, ultimately there are only 132,133 practicing physicians who are AMA members. That's 12.1%. A drop. A decline that has continued for decades.

Kevin Campbell, *Don't Believe AMA's Hype, Membership Still Declining*, MEDPAGETODAY (June 19, 2019) (asserting that the AMA's priority is its own commercial and financial interests, not physician interests), www.medpagetoday.com/opinion/campbells-scoop/80583.

50 *See Chapter* 6, *supra*, at notes 43–98, and accompanying text ("The Complexities of Personal Genome Medical Decision-Making").

51 *See* Sarah Kliff, Aatish Bhatta, *Prenatal Tests for Rare Defects Often Produce False Positives*, N.Y. TIMES (Jan. 2, 2022) (reporting the findings of a NY *Times* investigation"), www.nytimes.com/2022/01/01/upshot/pregnancy-birth-genetic-testing.html. *See generally* PEW, REPORT, *supra* note 15. *See also Chapter* 6, *supra*, at notes 66–75, and accompanying text (Pew report and NY *Times* investigation of lab-developed tests and noninvasive prenatal tests/NIPTs).

52 *See* Kliff, Bhatta, *Prenatal*, *supra* note 51.

53 *Id.*

54 *See Chapter* 4, *supra*, at notes 116–83, and accompanying text ("23andMe: The Seminal DTCGHR Testing Services Company"). *See also* Kristen V. Brown, *23andMe Goes Public as $3.5 Billion Company With Branson Aid*, BLOOMBERG (Feb. 4, 2021), www.bloomberg.com/news/articles/2021-02-04/23andme-to-go-public-as-3-5-billion-company-via-branson-merger. The combined company was renamed 23andMe Holding Co. and became publicly traded on NASDAQ on June 17, 2021. *See* Natalie Clarkson, *23andMe and Virgin Group's VG Acquisition Corp. successfully close business combination*, VIRGIN (June 16, 2021)

(Virgin journalist reporting), www.virgin.com/about-virgin/virgin-group/news/23andme-and-virgin-groups-vg-acquisition-corp-successfully-close-business; Staff Reporter, *23andMe Stock Soars 22 Percent on Closing of Merger With VG Acquisition Corp.*, GENOMEWEB (June 17, 2021) (anonymous staff reporter), www.genomeweb.com/business-news/23andme-stock-soars-22-percent-closing-merger-vg-acquisition-corp#.YtLJ5XbMK3A.

55 *See 23andMe, A Letter from Anne: Making Personalized Healthcare a Reality* (Oct. 22, 2021), https://you.23andme.com/p/28ba69b793a2c6ff/article/a-letter-from-anne-making-personalized-healthcare-a-reality-3ebee7dfb59a/.

56 *See id.*

57 23andMe Holding Co., *Current Report (Form 8-K)* (Nov. 1, 2021), https://investors.23andme.com/static-files/8a43d3a5-2529-422c-937b-db40a7eeb875. *See Chapter 4, supra*, at notes 175-76, and accompanying text (quoting the company's October 2022 email declaration to its Personal Genome Health Service/PGHS customers); Neil Versel, *23andMe Pins Future on 'Genomic Health Service,' Therapeutic Development*, GENOMEWEB (Aug. 9, 2022), www.genomeweb.com/business-news/23andme-pins-future-genomic-health-service-therapeutic-development#.Y1MLmnbMK3A.

58 *See Chapter 1, supra*, at notes 36–37, and accompanying text.

59 *See* Pub. L. No. 82–215, § 1, 65 Stat. 648 (1951), *codified as amended* 21 U.S.C. § 353(b).

60 Health Care Quality and Improvement Act/HCQIA of 1986, 42 U.S.C. § 11101, *et seq.*

61 Anti-Kickback Statute, 42 U.S.C. § 1320a-7b(b); Stark Law, 42 U.S.C. § 1395nn.

62 *See* MICHAEL J. MALINOWSKI, HANDBOOK ON BIOTECHNOLOGY LAW, BUSINESS, AND POLICY 1–20 (2016) (US regulatory responsiveness to biotech and the resulting success story). *See generally* CBO, R&D, *supra* note 18; TECONOMY PARTNERS LLC, BIOPHARMACEUTICAL INDUSTRY-SPONSORED CLINICAL TRIALS: GROWING STATE ECONOMIES (2019), www.phrma.org/-/media/TEConomy_PhRMA-Clinical-Trials-Impacts.pdf%EF%BB%BF. In 2001, the NIH assessed TTLP and deemed it a success – a solid return on taxpayer investment despite US Rx pricing. *See generally* HHS, NIH RESPONSE TO THE CONFERENCE REPORT REQUEST FOR A PLAN TO ENSURE TAXPAYER INTERESTS ARE PROTECTED (2001), www.techtransfer.nih.gov/sites/default/files/documents/policy/wydenrpt.pdf. The NIH report was consistent with a GAO full and positive assessment in 1998. *See generally* US GOV'T ACCOUNTABILITY OFFICE, GAO-98-126, TECHNOLOGY TRANSFER: ADMINISTRATION OF THE BAYH-DOLE ACT BY RESEARCH UNIVERSITIES (1998), www.gao.gov/assets/rced-98-126.pdf.

63 NASEM, PREPARING, *supra* note 18, at 1 ("Summary").

64 *Id.*

65 *See* Coordinated Framework for Regulation of Biotechnology, 51 FED. REG. 23302 (June 26, 1986). As stated in the preface to NASEM's resulting report,

> In light of some of the recent advances in biotechnology, including in genome editing, gene drives, and synthetic biology, the federal government is in the process of making much needed updates to the Coordinated Framework, which had its last major revision in 1992. The task of this committee was to look into the future and describe the possible products of biotechnology that will arise over the next 5–10 years, as well as provide some insights that can help shape the capabilities within the agencies as they move forward

NASEM, PREPARING, *supra* note 18, at ix.

66 *See id.*

67 *See id.* at 6. *See also* MALINOWSKI, HANDBOOK, *supra* note 62, at 12–13.

68 *See generally* NASEM, PREPARING, *supra* note 18.

69 *See generally id.*; Barbara J. Evans, *Programming Our Genomes, Programming Ourselves: The Moral and Regulatory Challenge of Regulating Do-It-Yourself Gene Editing*, *in* CONSUMER GENETIC TECHNOLOGIES, *supra* note 15, at 129–44.
70 *See generally* NASEM, PREPARING, *supra* note 18.
71 Evans, *Programming Our Genomes*, *supra note* 69, at 129.
72 *See generally* CONSUMER GENETIC TECHNOLOGIES, *supra* note 15; FUTURE OF PRIVACY, *supra* note 15; PEW, REPORT, *supra* note 15. *Cf.* CBO, R&D, *supra* note 18; NASEM, PREPARING, *supra* note 18.
73 *See Chapter 1, supra. Cf.* at notes 184–89, and accompanying text ("The Resulting Medical Profession-FDA Symbiotic Relationship").
74 *See Chapter* 5, *supra*, at notes 113–77, and accompanying text ("Today's US Physician-Patient Relationship, and the State of Physician Decision Making"); *Chapter* 6, *supra*, at notes 43–152, and accompanying text ("The Complexities of Personal Genome Medical Decision-Making" and "US Health Care System and Consumer Genetics Market Issues").
75 *See generally Chapter 1, supra. Cf.* SACGT, RECOMMENDATIONS, *supra* note 5.
76 *See supra* notes 39–40, and accompanying text (FDA acknowledgement of consumer demand). *See* Carmel Shachar, I Glen Cohen, Nita A. Farahany, Henry T. Greely, *Introduction*, *in* CONSUMER GENETIC TECHNOLOGIES, *supra* note 15, at 1, *citing* GRAND VIEW RESEARCH, PREDICTIVE GENETIC TESTING AND CONSUMER GENETICS MARKET SIZE, SHARE & TRENDS ANALYSIS REPORT BY TEST TYPE (POPULATION SCREENING, SUSCEPTIBILITY), BY APPLICATION, BY SETTING TYPE, AND SEGMENT FORECASTS, 2019–25 (2019) (projecting the global genetic testing and consumer wellness genomic market, valued at $2.24 billion in 2015, to double by 2025). *See generally* FUTURE OF PRIVACY, *supra* note 15; PEW, REPORT, *supra* note 15.
77 For example, DTC and DTP biopharma marketing have been recognized by the courts as constitutional free speech rights. *See Chapter* 3, *supra*, at notes 31–70, and accompanying text ("Recognition of Biopharma Marketing as Protected Commercial Speech").
78 *See* MALINOWSKI, HANDBOOK, *supra* note 62, at notes 1–20, and accompanying text (the US biotech success story through regulatory responsiveness to R&D and other commercialization needs).
79 *See generally Chapter 1, supra.*
80 *See Dobbs v. Jackson Women's Health Org., et al.*, No. 19–1392, 2022 WL 2276808 (US June 24, 2022); *Chapter* 5, *supra*, at notes 170–77, and accompanying text. *See also Editorial, How the Biden Administration Could Protect Abortion Rights*, N.Y. TIMES (July 10, 2022) (identifying potential federal government interventions to protect rights to access abortion procedures post *Dobbs*), www.nytimes.com/2022/07/08/opinion/abortion-pills-policy.html.
81 *See* Kimball, *Doctors Must Provide Abortions in Medical Emergencies, Regardless of State Law, HHS says*, CNBC (July 11, 2022), www.cnbc.com/2022/07/11/roe-v-wade-hhs-says-physicians-must-provide-abortions-in-medical-emergencies-regardless-of-state-law.html.
82 *See, e.g.*, Catherine M. Sharkey, Xiaohan Wu, Michael F. Walsh, Kenneth Offit, *Regulatory and Medical Aspects of DTC Genetic Tests*, *in* CONSUMER GENETIC TECHNOLOGIES, *supra* note 15; Catherine M. Sharkey, *Direct-to-Consumer Genetic Testing: The FDA's Dual Role as Safety and Health Information Regulator*, 68 DEPAUL L. REV. 343, 375–76 (2019). *See generally* SACGT, RECOMMENDATIONS, *supra* note 5.
83 *See generally Chapter 1, supra*, and accompanying text.
84 These laboratory regulations, collectively referred to as CLIA, encompass the Clinical Laboratory Improvement Act/CLIA of 1967, 42 U.S.C. § 263(a) and Clinical Laboratory

Improvement Amendments of 1988, Pub. L. No. 100–578, 102 Stat. 2903, *codified as amended at* 42 U.S.C. § 263a (2000). *See* MALINOWSKI, HANDBOOK, *supra* note 62, at 141–43, 171–82. *See also* Michael J. Malinowski, *Separating Predictive Genetic Testing from Snake Oil: Regulation, Liabilities, and Lost Opportunities*, 41 JURIMETIRCS 23, 23–52 (2001) (live and published symposium); Malinowski, Blatt, *Biological Tarot*, *supra* note 25, at 1229–33.

85 *See generally* SACGT, RECOMMENDATIONS, *supra* note 5. CLIAC, which is managed by the CDC and has a diverse membership across laboratory specialties, professional roles, and practice settings, provides scientific and technical advice and guidance to HHS and responds to specific charges through working groups – as it did regarding genetic testing in the 1990s. *Visit* CDC, CLIAC, official site, *About CLIAC* (reviewed Feb. 23, 2022), www.cdc.gov/cliac/about.html. Relevant examples include the CLIAC Genetic Workgroup and the CLIAC Next Generation Sequencing/NGS Workgroup. *See generally* BIN CHEN, MARIBETH GAGNON, SHAHRAM SHAHANGIAN ET AL., GOOD LABORATORY PRACTICES FOR MOLECULAR GENETIC TESTING FOR HERITABLE DISEASES AND CONDITIONS, CDC MMWR RECOMMENDATIONS AND REPORTS (June 12, 2009), www.cdc.gov/mmwr/preview/mmwrhtml/rr5806a1.htm; Carole Green, Workgroup Chair, Presentation, *CLIAC Genetics Workgroup Good Laboratory Practices for Molecular Genetic Testing* (Sept. 2008), www.cdc.gov/cliac/docs/addenda/cliac0908/addendum-g.pdf; CLIAC NGS WORKGROUP, SUMMARY REPORT (undated, visited July 7, 2022), www.cdc.gov/cliac/docs/addenda/cliac0419/10a_ngs_workgroup_report.pdf.

86 *See infra* notes 166–89, and accompanying text ("Proposals to Enhance CLIA Regulation of Personal Genome Testing").

87 National Institutes of Health/NIH, Office of Science Policy, *Secretary's Advisory Committee on Genetic Testing Archives* (Apr. 26, 2017, visited Mar. 2, 2002), https://osp.od.nih.gov/scientific-sharing/secretarys-advisory-committee-on-genetic-testing-archives/

88 *See id.*

89 SACGT, RECOMMENDATIONS, *supra* note 5, at 1.

90 *See* Michael J. Malinowski, Robin J.R. Blatt, *Commercialization of Genetic Testing Services: The FDA, Market Forces, and Biological Tarot Cards* (1997), 71 TULANE L. REV. 1212, 1214–15; *OncorMed BRCA1 Testing Service Commercialization Enters Second Phase Through New IRB Protocol*, 39 BLUE SHEET 6, 6–7 (1996). *See Chapter 4, supra*, at notes 25–33, and accompanying text.

91 SACGT, Recommendations, *supra* note 5, at 10.

92 Joint Working Group, *Proposed Recommendations of the Task Force on Genetic Testing, Meeting Notice*, 62 FED. REG. 4539, 4544 (1997) (emphasis added). The former NIH-DOE Joint Working Group on the Ethical, Legal and Social Implications of Human Genome Research/ELSI ("Joint Working Group") launched the Task Force in 1994 to make recommendations to the Secretary of HHS. *See id. See* SACGT, RECOMMENDATIONS, *supra* note 5, at vi-vii ("Executive Summary"). *See also* NHGRI, *National Human Genome Research Institute Task Force Makes Final Recommendations on US Genetic Testing* 1 (Oct. 1997), www.genome.gov/10000667/1997-release-task-force-makes-final-recommendations-on-us-genetic-testing (last visited Nov. 28, 2019). The Joint Working Group charged the Task Force, which was comprised of a diverse group of scientists, health care professionals, business executives, regulators, health insurers, and consumers, to comprehensively evaluate genetic testing in the US, and to recommend "policies that will reduce the likelihood of damaging effects so the benefits of testing can be fully realized." Joint Working Group, *Proposed Recommendations*, *supra*, at 1. Federal funding in research triggers the Common Rule – the US' law and policy base for the protection of human subjects when federal funding is involved. *See* 45 CFR part 46. *See*

also HHS, *Federal Policy for the Protection of Human Subjects* ("Common Rule") (last reviewed Mar. 18, 2016), www.hhs.gov/ohrp/regulations-and-policy/regulations/common-rule/index.html.

93 *See generally* SACGT, Recommendations, *supra* note 5.

94 *Id.* at 25.

95 *See generally id.*

96 *Id.* at 26.

97 *See Bush v. Gore*, 531 US 98 (2000).

98 *See Chapter 4, supra*, at notes 113–15, and accompanying text.

99 *See id* at 70–71; Jeffrey Kluger, Alice Park, *The Angelina Effect*, Time (May 27, 2013), at 28, http://healthland.time.com/2013/05/15/the-angelina-effect-times-new-cover-image-revealed/.

100 *See* Watson, The Story, *supra* note 20, at 210.

101 *See* FDA, DEN160026, EVALUATION OF AUTOMATIC CLASS III DESIGNATION FOR The 23andMe Personal Genome Service (PGS) Genetic Health Risk Test for Hereditary Thrombophilia, Alpha-1 Antitrypsin Deficiency, Alzheimer's Disease, Parkinson's Disease, Gaucher Disease Type 1, Factor XI Deficiency, Celiac Disease, G6PD Deficiency, Hereditary Hemochromatosis and Early-Onset Primary Dystonia, DECISION SUMMARY (Apr. 6, 2017, revised May 2, 2017, correction Nov. 2, 2017), www.accessdata.fda.gov/cdrh_docs/reviews/DEN160026.pdf. *See also* FDA, *Press Release, FDA Allows Marketing of First Direct-to-Consumer Tests That Provide Genetic Risk Information for Certain Conditions* (Apr. 6, 2017), www.fda.gov/NewsEvents/Newsroom/PressAnnouncements/ucm551185.htm.

102 Section 866.5950 (genetic health risk assessment system) of Title 21 provides, in part:

> The genetic health risk assessment system device, when it has previously received a first-time FDA marketing authorization (e.g., 510(k) clearance) for the genetic health risk assessment system (a "one-time FDA reviewed genetic health risk assessment system"), is exempt from the premarket notification procedures in part 807, subpart E, of this chapter subject to the limitations in 866.9. The device must comply with the following special controls ....

21 CFR 866.5950 (revised Apr. 1, 2020), www.accessdata.fda.gov/scripts/cdrh/cfdocs/cfcfr/cfrsearch.cfm?fr=866.5950.

103 SACGT, Recommendations, *supra* note 5, at 27.

104 Holtzman, *Regulation*, *supra* note 7, at 53. At the time, Dr. Holtzman was a Professor of Pediatrics, Professor of Epidemiology, Professor of Health Policy & Management, and Director of Genetics and Public Policy Studies at Johns Hopkins.

105 *Id.* at 54.

106 Malinowski, *Snake Oil*, *supra* note 84, at 43.

107 *See id.* at 45.

108 *See Chapter 4, supra*, at notes 7–10, and accompanying text (addressing enactment of HIPAA and GINA, and their impact on genetic privacy concerns). *See generally* HHS, *Summary of the HIPAA Privacy Rule* (undated, visited July 8, 2022), www.hhs.gov/hipaa/for-professionals/privacy/laws-regulations/index.html; HHS, *Summary of the HIPAA Security Rule* (undated, visited July 8, 2022), www.hhs.gov/hipaa/for-professionals/security/laws-regulations/index.html.

109 *See Chapter 4, supra*, at note 10, and accompanying text.

110 *See Prologue, supra*, at notes 1–13, and accompanying text (the advancement of DNA sequencing and next-generation sequencing/NGS technologies).

111 *See generally Association for Molecular Pathology v. Myriad Genetics, Inc.*, 133 S. Ct. 2107, 569 US 12 (2013) (holding that patent protection does not extend to the isolation of natural forms of DNA); *Mayo Collaborative Servs. v. Prometheus Labs., Inc.*, 132 S. Ct. 1289, 182 L. Ed. 2d 321 (2012) (holding unanimously that claims directed to adjusting the dosage of a drug based upon the measurement of properties naturally produced by patients, determined by genetic testing in this case, are not patentable subject matter). Prior jurisprudence was receptive to recognizing genetic testing with defined uses as patentable (inventive) processes consistent with other precedent. *See also Gottschalk v. Benson*, 409 US 63, 70 (1972) ("A process is a mode of treatment of certain materials to produce a given result. It is an act, or a series of acts, performed upon the subject-matter to be transformed and reduced to a different state or thing."); In re *Kollar*, 286 F.3d 1326, 1332 (Fed. Cir. 2002) ("[A] process…consists of a series of acts or steps…. It consists of doing something, and therefore has to be carried out or performed."). *See Chapter* 4, *supra*, at notes 72–78, and accompanying text (addressing the Supreme Court's decisions and their impact). *Cf.* Anna B. Laakmann, *The Meaning of Myriad*, 5 UC Irvine L. Rev. 1001 (2015).

112 *See Chapter* 4, *supra*, at notes 11–24, and accompanying text (addressing social and cultural change, and the accompanying public perception shift regarding genetic testing).

113 Malinowski, *Snake Oil*, at 45.

114 *See generally* Michael J. Malinowski, *The US Science and Technology "Triple Threat": A Regulatory Treatment Plan for the Nation's Addiction to Prescription Opioids*, 48 U. Mem. L. Rev. 1027 (2018).

115 *See generally* Consumer Genetic Technologies, *supra* note 15.

116 Sharkey, Wu, Walsh, Offit, *DTC Genetic Tests*, *supra* note 82, at 289.

117 *See generally* Sharkey, *Dual Role*, *supra* note 82.

118 *Id*. at 349–58.

119 *Id*. at 375–76.

120 *See Chapter* 4, *supra*, at notes 118, 128, and accompanying text (FDA approval with special controls and assurance of consumer comprehension).

121 Congress amended the FDCA in 1976 to also regulate medical devices for safety and efficacy. For discussion of the FDA's regulation of medical devices, see generally Judith Johnson, *FDA* Regulation of Medical Devices, Cong. Res. Serv. (2016), http://med.a51.nl/sites/default/files/pdf/R42130.pdf. *Visit* FDA, *Medical Devices*, www.fda.gov/medical-device. For a very brief, user-friendly summary, see Malinowski, Handbook, *supra* note 62, at 138–43.

122 Evans, *Programming Our Genomes*, *supra note* 69, at 144.

123 Under the Best Pharmaceuticals for Children Act/BPCA, 42 U.S.C. § 284m(b), (c)(7) (2006), the FDA could not force pediatric testing on a commercial sponsor, but it could surpass sponsor resistance by independently conducting pediatric trials under the agency's oversight, either through the NIH or through third parties, with funding from a federal trust. *See* Malinowski, Handbook, *supra* note 62, at 55–56. Congress granted the FDA some authority to mandate sponsors to conduct pediatric studies under the Pediatric Research Equity Act/PREA of 2003, and 2007 amendments to the PREA and to the BPCA. *See* PREA (2003), Pub. L. No. 108–155, 117 Stat. 1936, *codified as amended at* 21 U.S.C. § 355c (2012). The PREA is Title IV of the Food and Drug Administration Amendments Act/FDAAA, Pub. L. No. 110–85, 121 Stat. 823 (2007), *codified as amended at* 21 U.S.C. §§ 301–399i (2012). Under the PREA, new drug application/NDA sponsors must satisfy pediatric assessment submission requirements or seek a waiver detailing why a pediatric formulation cannot be developed. *See id*. The FDA is authorized to require submission of a pediatric assessment if the Secretary of HHS finds that adequate pediatric

labeling could benefit pediatric patients or that the absence of adequate pediatric labeling could pose a significant risk to them. Title V of the FDAAA amends the BPCA to, among other things, authorize the Secretary to include preclinical studies and to require the studies be completed using appropriate formulations for each age group for which such a study is requested. *See id*. Applicants who do not agree with a pediatric study request must submit to the Secretary the reasons such pediatric formulations cannot be developed, and applicants who agree with a pediatric study request must provide the Secretary with all post-marketing adverse event reports regarding the drug. *See id*.

Commentators have called for clinical trials independent from new medical product sponsors beyond pediatric studies. For example, Dr. Marcia Angell has proposed that clinical trials be administered by an independent government entity "To ensure that clinical trials serve a genuine medical need and see that they are properly designed, conducted, and reported, I propose that an Institute for Prescription Drug Trials be stablished within the NIH to administer clinical trials of prescription drugs." MARCIA ANGELL, THE TRUTH ABOUT DRUG COMPANIES 245 (2004) (emphasis in original eliminated) (winner of a Polk Award for excellence in journalism) (proposing establishment of an independent Institute for Prescription Drug Trials within NIH to administer clinical trials of prescription drugs). Dr. Abramson also has proposed independent clinical trial oversight by a regulatory body: "[T]he new body would need authority to require that all clinical trials were registered at the outset, with a clearly identified research design ('protocol'), including the duration of the study, the outcomes, and adverse effects to be measured." ABRAMSON, OVERDOSED, *supra* note 36, at 251. According to Dr. Abramson,

> Probably the single most important change that the fully empowered regulatory body could implement would be requiring transparency in medical research—making all research data available for external audit and public scrutiny.... Medical researchers must have access to all the results of their studies, perform their own analyses of the data, write up their own conclusions, and submit the report for publication to peer-reviewed medical journals. Research data must also be made available to peer reviewers for medical journals and to the new oversight body for independent evaluation.

Id. at 251–52

124 *See, e.g.*, ANGELL, TRUTH, *supra* note 123, at 244–46. *Cf*. ABRAMSON, OVERDOSED, *supra* note 36, at 95, 209.

125 *See Chapter 4, supra*, at notes 125–29, and accompanying text (FDA's April 2017 approval of 23andMe's DTCGHR testing through its PGHS, and establishment of a DTGHR testing category for express approval).

126 Elaine Silvestrini, *FDA 510(k) Clearance Process*, DRUGWATCH (Mar. 15, 2021), www.drugwatch.com/fda/510k-clearance/.

127 *Id*.

128 *See generally* JUDITH A. JOHNSON, THE FDA MEDICAL DEVICE USER FEE PROGRAM, CONG. RES. SERV. (June 25, 2012). *Visit* FDA, *Medical Devices*, www.fda.gov/medical-device. For a very brief, user-friendly summary, see also MALINOWSKI, HANDBOOK, *supra* note 62, at 138–43. *See Chapter 4, supra*, at notes 122–24, and accompanying text (matching and precedents approach to device regulation).

129 *See Chapter 1, supra*, at notes 184–89, and accompanying text ("The Resulting Medical Profession-FDA Symbiotic Relationship").

130 *See* Shuren, Woodcock, *FDA Statement*, *supra* note 40. *See also Chapter* 4, *supra*, at note 137, and accompanying text (quoting FDA acknowledgement of consumer demand with warning).

131 *See* Carmel Shachar, I Glen Cohen, Nita A. Farahany, Henry T. Greely, *Introduction*, *in* CONSUMER GENETIC TECHNOLOGIES, *supra* note 15, at 1, *citing* GRAND VIEW RESEARCH, PREDICTIVE GENETIC TESTING AND CONSUMER GENETICS MARKET SIZE, SHARE & TRENDS ANALYSIS REPORT BY TEST TYPE (POPULATION SCREENING, SUSCEPTIBILITY), BY APPLICATION, BY SETTING TYPE, AND SEGMENT FORECASTS, 2019–25 (2019) (projecting the global genetic testing and consumer wellness genomic market, valued at $2.24 billion in 2015, to double by 2025). *See generally* FUTURE OF PRIVACY, *supra* note 15; PEW, REPORT, *supra* note 15. *Cf.* CBO, R&D, *supra* note 18; NASEM, PREPARING, *supra* note 18.

132 *Cf. generally* JEFFREY BERRY, THE INTEREST GROUP SOCIETY (5th ed. 2008) (the workings of interest groups within the larger context of the US political-legislative system). As observed by Dr. Abramson early in this millennium, "The drug industry hires 625 lobbyists, more than one for each member of the House and Senate[, which have 535 voting members total]." ABRAMSON, OVERDOSED, *supra* note 36, at 90.

133 ABRAMSON, OVERDOSED, *supra* note 36, at 85. *Visit* FDA, official site, *What We Do* (current Mar. 28, 2018), www.fda.gov/about-fda/what-we-do.

134 *See* Ximena Bustillo, *The FDA Is Facing an Investigation into Its Handling of the Baby Formula Shortage* (June 3, 2022), www.npr.org/2022/06/03/1103025750/fda-investigation-baby-formula-shortage.

135 *See* FDA, *What Does FDA Regulate* (current Jan. 18, 2022), www.fda.gov./about-fda/fda-basics/what-does-fda-regulate.

136 *See* EZEKIEL J. EMANUEL, WHICH COUNTRY HAS THE WORLD'S BEST HEALTH CARE? 6, 25, 30 (2020). *See Chapter* 5, *supra*, at notes 384–403, and accompanying text ("The Absence of Centralized, Objective, Reliable Health Technology Assessment/HTA in US Health Care"). *See generally* Sabrina Corlette, Christine H. Monahan, *Perspectives, US Health Insurance Coverage and Financing*, 387 (25) NEW. ENG. J. MED. 2297-300 (Dec. 2, 2022), www.nejm.org/doi/full/10.1056/NEJMp2206049?af=R&rss=currentIssue.

137 In contrast, when biopharmaceutical products reach market, stakeholders often turn against biopharma over product pricing. *Cf.* Benjamin N. Rome, Alexander C. Egilman, Aaron S. Kesselheim, *Opinion, Prices for New Drugs Are Rising 20 Percent a Year. Congress Needs to Act* (June 8, 2022), www.nytimes.com/2022/06/08/opinion/us-drug-prices-congress.html. The "Right-to-Try" movement also has provoked hostility from patients and their advocates against both the FDA and industry. *See generally* Rebecca Dresser, *The "Right to Try" Investigational Drugs: Science and Stories in the Access Debate*, 93 TEX. L. REV. 1631 (2015). The FDA, which expanded its compassionate use (patient-specific) and investigational use (groups of patients) tracks for patient access to experimental treatments during their clinical research stage prior to the Right-to-Try movement, is challenged as a regulatory impediment to a chance for life. Yet, "The FDA approval rate for compassionate use therapy is ninety-nine percent." *See* Roseann B. Termini, *The Latest "Federal Movement" in the Food and Drug Law Arena: The Federal Right-to-Try or Rather Right-to-Know and Thus Request Investigational Therapies for Individuals with a Life-Threatening Disease or Condition*, 16 IND. HEALTH L. REV. 101, 108 (2018). Industry sponsors are pressured to make limited product supply needed for clinical trials available outside of them and at a nominal cost (they may only recoup the manufacturing cost under US law) or for free – especially since insurance coverage often does not encompass experimental treatments. Industry is pressured to scale-up manufacturing prematurely and assume that cost and risk. Also, though separate from the clinical trials carried out under FDA oversight to generate data for market

review and approval, independent patient uses also raise the possibility of adverse reactions that spill into and impede clinical trial progress. Of course, there also is the possibility of favorable outcomes that complement clinical trial progress, but the risk element for sponsors is unavoidable.

138 *See Chapter* 3, *supra*, at notes 31–70, and accompanying text ("Recognition of Biopharma Marketing as Protected Commercial Speech"). Even when biopharmaceutical companies make unfounded claims about medicinal products that reach the market through the FDA, without delivery of care evidence of harm from physicians, "the armamentarium of penalties that the FDA can impose … doesn't include the removal of indication. The agency may send warning letters or, at worst, impose fines." Otis Webb Brawley, How We Do Harm: A Doctor Breaks Rank about Being Sick in America 83–84 (2011).

139 *See generally* Kirti Datla, Richard L. Revesz, *Deconstructing Independent Agencies (and Executive Agencies)*, 98 Cornell L. Rev. 769 (2013) ("all agencies should be regarded as executive and seen as falling on a spectrum from more independent to less independent"), https://scholarship.law.cornell.edu/cgi/viewcontent.cgi?article=3270&context=clr. Although the Office of the Secretary of HHS delegates considerable authority to the FDA, HHS must meet its charge and the Office of the Secretary retains power to meet that responsibility – for example, authority to override the FDA and CDC in the event of a public health emergency. President Trump's Secretary of HHS, Alex Azar, a lawyer with no medical or science formal education, clinical training, or delivery-of-care expertise, nearly exercised that power to force market approval of hydroxychloroquine and chloroquine to prevent and treat COVID-19 despite a dearth of supportive evidentiary-science data and FDA opposition supported by the agency's established standards for safety and efficacy, existing evidentiary science, and the expertise of its officials and advisory committee members. *See Chapter 1, supra*, at notes 179–83, and accompanying text. *See also* Yasmeen Abutaleb, Damian Paletta, Nightmare Scenario: Inside the Trump Administration's Response to the Pandemic that Changed History 221 (2021).

140 *See generally* Datla, *Deconstructing*, *supra* note 139.

141 *See Chapter* 1, *supra*, at notes 160–83, and accompanying text ("Deference to and Reliance on the Medical Profession").

142 *See* Michael J. Malinowski, *Throwing Dirt on Doctor Frankenstein's Grave: Access to Experimental Treatments at the End of Life*, 65 Hastings L.J. 615, 642–43 (2014). As observed by attorney Linda Katherine Leibfarth, "Historically, the American public clamored for increased FDA regulation of new drugs; however, more recent criticism has focused on how the FDA's 'gold standard' impedes consumer access to new, potentially lifesaving, treatments." Linda Katherine Leibfarth, *Giving the Terminally Ill Their Due (Process): A Case for Expanded Access to Experimental Drugs Through the Political Process*, 61 Vand. L. Rev. 1281, 1286 (2008). *See also supra* note 137, and accompanying text (addressing the Right-to-Try movement).

143 *See, e.g.*, Richard A. Epstein, Overdose: How Excessive Government Regulation Stifles Pharmaceutical Innovation (2006); David Gratzer, The Cure: How Capitalism Can Save American Health Care (2006).

144 According to Professor Epstein,

> I stated at the outset of this book that it is hard to return the pharmaceutical industry to its glory days of fifty or sixty years ago. In the interim we have gathered all the low-hanging fruit. But the current challenge is not whether we can recreate the heady optimism of Vannevar Bush's 1945 praise of The Endless Frontier, any more than it is whether we can make the California gold rush last forever.

EPSTEIN, OVERDOSE, *supra* note 143, at 239–40.

145 *See generally id.*

146 *See generally Chapter 2, supra*; CBO, R&D, *supra* note 18; NASEM, PREPARING, *supra* note 18.

147 US TTLP introduced in 1980 marks a chasmic before-and-after divide. *See* Malinowski, *Throwing Dirt, supra* note 142, at 642.

148 *See generally Chapter 2, supra.*

149 *See generally* Michael J. Malinowski, Grant G. Gautreaux, *Drug Development – Stuck in a State of Puberty? Regulatory Reform of Human Clinical Research to Raise Responsiveness to the Reality of Human Variability*, 56 ST. LOUIS U. L.J. 363 (2012) (advocating for more use of single subject study design and less reliance on group design in biopharma product development); Michael J. Malinowski, Grant G. Gautreaux, *All that is Gold Does Not Glitter in Human Clinical Research: A Law-Policy Proposal to Brighten the Global "Gold Standard" for Drug Research and Development*, 45 CORNELL J. INT'L LAW 185 (2012) (advocating for more single subject study design in Rx development, consistent with individualized clinical care and emerging personal genome medicine).

150 CBO, R&D, *supra* note 18.

151 *See Chapter 3, supra*, at notes 11–15, 72, 141–43, and accompanying text (discussing the impact of PDUFA and FDAMA on the FDA/FDA regulation).

152 *See id.*

153 FDA, FY 2021: FINANCIAL REPORT TO CONGRESS FOR THE PRESCRIPTION DRUG USER FEE ACT OF 1992 3 (2022).

154 ABRAMSON, OVERDOSED, *supra* note 36, at 249. "Even worse, the FDA has fallen under the influence of the drug and medical-device industries, so much so that it was labeled 'a servant of industry' by Dr. Richard Horton, the editor of the British journal *The Lancet*." *Id.* at 85.

155 *See* Food and Drug Administration Safety and Innovation Act/FDASIA of 2012, P.L. 107–250. *See generally* JUDITH A. JOHNSON, THE FDA MEDICAL DEVICE USER FEE PROGRAM, CONG. RES. SERV. (June 25, 2012). Congress introduced user fees for medical device manufacturers under the Medical Device User Fee and Modernization Act of 2002 ("MDUFA I"), which was reauthorized subsequently, including as MDUFA III under FDASIA, P.L. 112–44. Congress enacted the Generic Drug User Fee Act/GDUFA in 2012 under FDASIA. *See* FDA, *Generic Drug User Fee Amendments* (current Feb. 15, 2022), www.fda.gov/industry/fda-user-fee-programs/generic-drug-user-fee-amendments. The FDA Reauthorization Act/FDARA of 2017 revised and extended the user-fee programs for drugs, medical devices, generic drugs, and biosimilars. *See* FDARA, Pub. L. 115–52, 131 Stat. 1005 (Aug. 18, 2017). *See also* FDA, *FDA Reauthorization Act of 2017 (FDARA)* (current June 21, 2018), www.fda.gov/regulatory-information/selected-amendments-fdc-act/fda-reauthorization-act-2017-fdara.

156 *See* MOYNIHAN, ALAN CASSELS, SELLING SICKNESS: HOW THE WORLD'S BIGGEST PHARMACEUTICAL COMPANIES ARE TURNING US ALL INTO PATIENTS 167 (2005).

157 *Id.* at 167.

158 MOYNIHAN, SICKNESS, *supra* note 156, at 167.

159 *See* FDAMA, § 112(a) (FDCA § 506(b)(2)(A)), 111 Stat. at 2309 (codified at 21 U.S.C. § 356(b)(2)(A) (2012)). The FDAMA provision that codified the fast track, 506B, introduced a presumption in favor of market approval, accompanied by FDA enforcement authority under 21 U.S.C. § 356b (2006) to impose phase 4 (follow-on trials for targeted surveillance after market approval) clinical trial obligations. *See* FDA, *Reports on the*

Status of Postmarketing Studies – Implementation of Section 130 of the Food and Drug Administration Modernization Act of 1997 1 (2006), www.fda.gov/regulatory-information/search-fda-guidance-documents/reports-status-postmarketing-study-commitments-implementation-section-130-food-and-drug. The purpose of phase 4 studies is to probe lingering questions and to perfect clinical use. *See id. See also* PETER BARTON HUTT ET AL., FOOD AND DRUG LAW 734–38 (3d ed. 2007). Technically, the FDA's central mission was directly changed in PDUFA II (renewal of PDUFA I) with complementary provisions in FDAMA. While the FDA mission to ensure safety and efficacy was affirmed in both FDAMA and PDUFA II, section 406 of PDUFA II expanded the agency's mission to include efficiency and required the agency to balance safety and efficacy with timeliness. Specifically, section 406 requires the FDA to "promote the public health by promptly and efficiently reviewing clinical research and taking appropriate action … in a timely manner." 21 U.S.C. § 393(b)(1), as amended.

160 *See Chapter 3*, *supra*, at notes 45–66, and accompanying text (discussing *Washington Legal* and subsequent off-label prescribing).

161 Denise Grady, *F.D.A. Pulls a Drug, And Patients* Despair, N.Y. TIMES (Jan 30, 2021), www.nytimes.com/2001/01/30/health/fda-pulls-a-drug-and-patients-despair.html.

162 *See* Denise Grady, *US Lets Drug Tied to Deaths Back on Market*, N.Y. TIMES (June 8, 2002), www.nytimes.com/2002/06/08/us/us-lets-drug-tied-to-deaths-back-on-market.html.

163 MOYNIHAN, SICKNESS, *supra* note 156, at 165 (2005). *See id.* at 166–67 (discussing the Lotronex controversy and associated allegations of industry influence over the FDA).

164 *See generally Chapter 3*, *supra*.

165 *See Chapter 5*, *supra*, at notes 257–60, 283–91. Vioxx and Celebrex were two of the Rx drugs most heavily marketed to both patients and doctors at the beginning of this millennium and they generated $5.3 billion in sales in 2003. *See id.*; ABRAMSON, OVERDOSED, *supra* note 36, at 259. The FDA knew of the health risks and issued warning letters to their manufacturers about false and misleading marketing in February 2001. The FDA did not "effectively [correct] doctors' and the public's erroneous beliefs about the true clinical value of these drugs …." ABRAMSON, *supra*, at 259.

166 CDC, *Provider-Performed Microscopy (PPM) Procedures* (reviewed Sept. 29, 2021), www.cdc.gov/Improvement Act of 1967/CLIA67; 42 U.S.C. § 263(a); Clinical Laboratory Improvement Amendments of 1988/CLIA88, Pub. L. No. 100–578, 102 Stat. 2903, *codified as amended*, 42 U.S.C. § 263a (2000). *See* MALINOWSKI, HANDBOOK, *supra* note 62, at 141–43, 171–82.

167 *See* SACGT, RECOMMENDATIONS, *supra* note 5, at 9.

168 *See* MALINOWSKI, HANDBOOK, *supra* note 62, at 171–82.

169 *See* SACGT, RECOMMENDATIONS, *supra* note 5, at 9.

170 *See* CMS, *CLIA Historical Numbers – January 2022*, www.cms.gov/regulations-and-guidance/legislation/clia/clia_statistical_tables_graphs.

171 *See generally* PEW, REPORT, *supra* note 15 (addressing in vitro tests performed with bodily fluids).

172 *See generally id.* For example, Illumina, Inc. provides sequencing services to 23andMe, Ancestry, and many other personal genome testing service providers. *See Prologue*, *supra*, at notes 11–13, and accompanying text.

173 *See* FDA, *CLIA Waiver by Application* (current Feb. 25, 2020), www.fda.gov/medical-devices/ivd-regulatory-assistance/clia-waiver-application.

174 *See id.*

175 *See* CMS, *Numbers*, *supra* note 170.

176 *See* CDC, *PPM*, *supra* note 166.
177 *See* CMS, *Numbers*, *supra* note 170.
178 *See* SACGT, Recommendations, *supra* note 5, at 28.
179 *See id*. at 3–4.
180 *See supra* notes 173–78, and accompanying text.
181 *See generally Chapter 1, supra*.
182 *See generally* Future of Privacy, *supra* note 15; Pew, Report, *supra* note 15.
183 *Cf*. Pew, Report, *supra* note 15.
184 *See Chapter 4, supra*, at notes 34–37, 160–63, and accompanying text (matching and precedents approach to device regulation with DTGHR testing application); *Chapter 6, supra*, at notes 63-66, 106–111 (CLIA regulation, including in the context of personal genome testing).
185 *See Chapter 4, supra*, at notes 116–83, and accompanying text ("23andMe: The Seminal DTCGHR Testing Services Company").
186 SACGT, Recommendations, *supra* note 5, at 3, *citing* Margaret M. McGovern, Marta O. Benach, Sylvan Wallenstein *et al*., *Quality Assurance in Molecular Genetic Testing Laboratories*, 281(9) JAMA 835–40 (1999), https://jamanetwork.com/journals/jama/fullarticle/188962.
187 Subsequently, scientists focused on finding and correcting errors, often attributed to the "shot gunning" methodology employed by Human Genome Sciences, a commercial competitor to the government effort founded by Craig Venter in 1992, and filling gaps in the sequence generally deemed "inactive" in 2003. The NHGRI announced completion of the first *gapless* sequence of the human genome on March 31, 2022. *See* Prabarna Ganguly, *Researchers Generate the First Complete, Gapless Sequence of a Human Genome* (Mar. 31, 2022), www.genome.gov/news/news-release/researchers-generate-the-first-complete-gapless-sequence-of-a-human-genome. "According to researchers, having a complete, gap-free sequence of the roughly 3 billion bases (or 'letters') in our DNA is critical for understanding the full spectrum of human genomic variation and for understanding the genetic contributions to certain diseases." *Id*. The difference has been analogized to introducing a new pair of glasses for scientists that enables markedly clearer vision. *See id*.
188 *See Prologue, supra*, at notes 1–13, and accompanying text (the advancement of DNA sequencing technologies).
189 Pew, Report, *supra* note 15, at 1 (Oct. 2021).
190 *See* Emanuel, Which Country?, *supra* note 136, at 6, 25, 30. *See Chapter 5, supra*, at notes 384–403, and accompanying text ("The Absence of Centralized, Objective, Reliable Health Technology Assessment/HTA in US Health Care"). *See generally Corlette, Monahan, US Health Insurance Coverage, supra* note 136, and accompanying text.
191 *See generally Chapter 5, supra* (discussing TTLP, PDUFA, FDAMA, FDASIA, and the Cures Act, and resulting biopharma influence); CBO, R&D, *supra* note 18; Nasem, Preparing, *supra* note 18.
192 *See* Fareed Zakaria, Ten Lessons for a Post-Pandemic World 79 (2020).
193 Abramson, Overdosed, *supra* note 36, at 250.
194 *See Chapter 5, supra*, at notes 384–403, and accompanying text ("The Absence of Centralized, Objective, Reliable Health Technology Assessment/HTA in US Health Care").
195 *See id*.
196 As stated by Dr. Abramson,

> The United States was actually the first country to implement just such a program, known as health technology assessment, in 1975. Since then, most of the other industrialized nations have established formal mechanisms to determine the optimal use of new medical technologies and to protect their citizens from unproven or wasteful innovations.... As the influence of technology assessment programs has grown abroad, the United States has virtually dismantled its own.

ABRAMSON, OVERDOSED, *supra* note 36, at 178.

197 *See generally* Darrell M. West, *It Is Time to Restore the US Office of Technology Assessment*, BROOKINGS INST. (February 10, 2021), www.brookings.edu/research/it-is-time-to-restore-the-us-office-of-technology-assessment/. *See, e.g., House Bill Would Revive Office of Technology Assessment after Two Decades* (May 2, 2019), 2019 WL 1950227.

198 *See* EMANUEL, WHICH COUNTRY?, *supra* note 136, at 6, 25, 30. *See generally Corlette, Monahan, US Health Insurance Coverage, supra* note 136, and accompanying text.

199 ABRAMSON, OVERDOSED, *supra* note 36, at 254–55. *See generally* EMANUEL, WHICH COUNTRY?, *supra* note 136.

200 *See Chapter* 5, *supra*, at notes 384–403, and accompanying text ("The Absence of Centralized, Objective, Reliable Health Technology Assessment/HTA in US Health Care").

201 *See generally* EMANUEL, WHICH COUNTRY?, *supra* note 136. As stated by Dr. Abramson,

> Without a formal mechanism of health technology assessment, new medical services can be brought into use without strong scientific evidence of benefits. And without limits on spending, new services can be brought into use without evidence that they provide more health value than the services they would be replacing. The absence of both of these constraints on growth of medical technology allows the US health care system to be uniquely shaped by financial incentives.

ABRAMSON, OVERDOSED, *supra* note 36, at 178.

202 *See Chapter* 5, *supra*, at notes 391–94, and accompanying text (collaboration among national HTA mechanisms).

203 *Visit* The General Practice Research Database/GPRD, official site, (visited July 16, 2022), https://cprd.com/; Medicines & Healthcare Products Regulatory Agency/MHRA, official site (visited Apr. 2, 2022), www.gov.uk/government/organisations/medicines-and-healthcare-products-regulatory-agency. The UK also has established a Clinical Practice Research Datalink/CPRD, jointly sponsored by the MHRA and the National Institute for Health Research/NIHR, as part of the Department of Health and Social Care, with the same methodology. CPRD acts as a real-world data research service to support retrospective and prospective public health and clinical studies. *See id.*

204 *Visit* CPRD, official site (visited Apr. 2, 2022), https://cprd.com/.

205 *See* BEN GOLDACRE, BAD PHARMA: HOW DRUG COMPANIES MISLEAD DOCTORS AND HARM PATIENTS 227 (2012).

206 *See generally* EMANUEL, WHICH COUNTRY?, *supra* note 136; READINGS IN COMPARATIVE HEALTH LAW AND BIOETHICS (eds. Nathan Cortez, I. Glenn Cohen, Timothy Stoltzfus Jost, 3rd ed. 2020). *See also* Timothy Jost, *Why Can't We Do What They Do? Health Care Reform Abroad* (published prior to the Affordable Care Act/ACT), AM. J. L., MED. & ETHICS 433–41 (fall 2004). *See generally Corlette, Monahan, US Health Insurance Coverage, supra* note 136, and accompanying text.

207 *See generally* Malinowski, *Triple Threat, supra* note 114.

208 *See id.* at 1050–51.

209 The President's Comm'n on Combating Drug Addiction and the Opioid Crisis, Final Report, 28, 117 (2017), www.whitehouse.gov/sites/whitehouse.gov/files/images/Final_Report_Draft_11-1-2017.pdf. *See also* The President's Comm'n on Combating Drug Addiction and the Opioid Crisis, Draft Interim Report 3 (2017), www.whitehouse.gov/sites/whitehouse.gov/files/ondcp/commission-interim-report.pdf.; President's Commission on Combating Drug Addiction and the Opioid Crisis, 82 Fed. Reg. 16,283 (Mar. 29, 2017); Malinowski, *Triple Threat*, *supra* note 114, at 1030–34. *See generally* Katie Thomas, Charles Ornstein, *Amid Opioid Crisis, Insurers Restrict Pricey, Less Addictive Painkillers*, N.Y. TIMES (Sept. 17, 2017), www.nytimes.com/2017/09/17/health/opioid-painkillers-insurance-companies.html.

210 *See generally Chapter 2, supra.*

211 *See generally* CBO, R&D, *supra* note 18; Nasem, Preparing, *supra* note 18.

212 *See generally* Consumer Genetic Technologies, *supra* note 15; Pew, Report, *supra* note 15.

213 *See Chapter 1, supra*, at notes 53–135, and accompanying text (national crises that prompted regulation for safety, trust, and confidence in commercial Rx).

214 *See generally Chapter 1, supra.*

215 *See Chapter 5, supra*, at notes 79–96, and accompanying text (politicization of science during the COVID-19 pandemic). *See also supra* notes 45–47, and accompanying text (addressing PDUFA, FDAMA, FDASIA, and Cures Act regulatory responsiveness to biopharma); *supra* notes 62–71, 210–14, and accompanying text (addressing TTLP and regulatory responsiveness impact on biopharma R&D and commercialization); *supra* note 150, and accompanying text (CBO documentation of a significant increase in FDA Rx drug approvals over the previous decade).

216 *See generally Chapter 2, supra.*

217 President Theodore Roosevelt, *quoted in* Abramson, Overdosed, *supra* note 36, at vii.

218 SACGT, Recommendations, *supra* note 5, at ix–x.

219 *Id.* at x.

220 *See supra* notes 65–67, and accompanying text (addressing the Coordinated Framework).

221 *See* SACGT, Recommendations, *supra* note 5, at 12.

222 *Id.* The US, and notably the US medical profession, had much infrastructure to draw from at the time SACGT prepared and released its report. The College of American Pathologists/CAP was conducting proficiency testing programs and developing standards for its members; the National Committee on Clinical Laboratory Standards/NCCLS was developing consensus recommendations for standardization of test methodologies; the American College of Medical Genetics/ACMG was working with CAP to provide proficiency tests and developing test-specific guidelines and methodologies for clinical use; the American Academy of Pediatrics/AAP was engaged in developing test-specific guidelines and recommendations for appropriate clinical use; the American College of Obstetrics and Gynecology/ACOG was developing test-specific guidelines and recommendations for appropriate clinical use; and the American Society of Human Genetics/ASHG and the National Society of Genetic Counselors/NSGC were engaged in developing test-specific guidelines and recommendations for appropriate use. *See* Notice of Intent; Genetic Testing Under the Clinical Laboratory Improvement Amendments, 65 Fed. Reg. 25,928 (May 4, 2000), www.govinfo.gov/content/pkg/FR-2000-05-04/html/00-11093.htm. *See also* Malinowski, *Snake Oil*, *supra* note 84, at 45.

223 *See* SACGT, Recommendations, *supra* note 5, at 23–25.

224 *See generally id.*

225 SACGT, Recommendations, *supra* note 5, at 23.

226 *Id.* at 14.
227 *See generally Chapter 4, supra* (discussing the personal genome testing sector, US regulation of it, and US regulation of the tests and services it sells). *See* Carmel Shachar, I Glen Cohen, Nita A. Farahany, Henry T. Greely, *Introduction, in* CONSUMER GENETIC TECHNOLOGIES, *supra* note 15, at 1, *citing* GRAND VIEW RESEARCH, PREDICTIVE GENETIC TESTING AND CONSUMER GENETICS MARKET SIZE, SHARE & TRENDS ANALYSIS REPORT BY TEST TYPE (POPULATION SCREENING, SUSCEPTIBILITY), BY APPLICATION, BY SETTING TYPE, AND SEGMENT FORECASTS, 2019–25 (2019) (projecting the global genetic testing and consumer wellness genomic market, valued at $2.24 billion in 2015, to double by 2025). *See generally* FUTURE OF PRIVACY, *supra* note 15; PEW, REPORT, *supra* note 15. For discussion of biopharma marketing, see generally *Chapter 3, supra.*
228 *See* David J. Hunter, Muin, J. Khoury, Jeffrey M. Drazen, *Letting the Genome out of the Bottle – Will We Get Our Wish?*, 358 N. ENG. J. MED. 2008 105 (Jan. 10, 2008), www.nejm.org/doi/full/10.1056/nejmp0708162.
229 *See supra* note 130; Shuren, Woodcock, *FDA Statement, supra* note 40.
230 *See generally* NASEM, PREPARING, *supra* note 18; Evans, *Programming Our Genomes, supra note* 69.
231 *See* Robert M. Califf, Janet Woodcock, Stephen Ostroff, *Special Report: A Proactive Response to Prescription Opioid Abuse*, 374 NEW ENG. J. MED. 1480 (Apr. 14, 2016), www.nejm.org/doi/pdf/10.1056/NEJMsr1601307.
232 *Id.* at 1480–81 (internal citations omitted). Frankly the FDA, a government agency with increasingly overwhelming responsibilities and limited resources, has demonstrated that it does not want to assume the medical profession's responsibilities, and Congress and the courts have prohibited the agency from doing so should it be tempted. *See Chapter 1, supra*, at notes 102–08, and accompanying text ("The Medical Profession's Role as Sentinel Over Clinical Use"); Malinowski, *Triple Threat, supra* note 114, at 1043–50 (footnotes and internal citations omitted).
233 *See generally* Chapter 1, *supra*.
234 *See* Gary E. Marchant, Mark Barnes, Ellen W. Clayton, Susan M. Wolf, *Liability Implications of Direct-to-Consumer Genetic Testing, in* CONSUMER GENETIC TECHNOLOGIES, *supra* note 15, at 21–24.
235 *See generally* NHGRI, *Reimbursement, supra* note 14. *See also infra* notes 298–301, and accompanying text.
236 *See generally* Debra J.H. Mathews, Celynne A. Balatbat, Victor J. Dzau, *Governance of Emerging Technologies in Health and Medicine – Creating a New Framework*, 386 N. ENG. J. MED. 2239–42 (Apr. 17, 2022), www.nejm.org/doi/full/10.1056/NEJMms2200907. Visit NAM, CESTI, official site, https://nam.edu/programs/committee-on-emerging-science-technology-and-innovation-in-health-and-medicine/#:~:text=CESTI%20brings%20together%20experts%20in,a%20cross%2Dsectoral%20governance%20framework.
237 Mathews, *Governance, supra* note 236, at 2242.
238 *Id.* at 2239.
239 *See generally id.*
240 GINA, Pub. L. No. 110–233, 122 Stat. 881 (2008) (codified as amended in scattered sections of 29 U.S.C., 42 U.S.C.).
241 *See Bush v. Gore*, 531 US 98 (2000). *See supra* note 97, and accompanying text (addressing the case).
242 Michael S. Yesley, *What's ELSI Got to Do with It? Bioethics and the Human Genome Project*, 27 NEW GENETICS & SOC'Y 1–6, 4 (2008), www.tandfonline.com/doi/full/10.1080/14636770701843527.

243 *See generally* CBO, R&D, *supra* note 18; NASEM, PREPARING, *supra* note 18; WATSON, THE STORY, *supra* note 20; *Prologue, supra* (addressing the advancement of DNA sequencing technologies).

244 *See generally* CBO, R&D, *supra* note 18; NASEM, PREPARING, *supra* note 18 (addressing the approaching biotech innovation landscape). For example, an ongoing Personal Genome Project/PGP, initiated in 2005, embodies a "coalition of projects across the world dedicated to creating public genome, health, and trait data." *Visit* Personal Genome Project, official site (visited July 5, 2022), www.personalgenomes.org/ (providing links to global network of participants). The UK Biobank has undertaken a project to assemble a proteomics complement to the HGP sequence. *See* Bonislawski, *Proteomics Project, supra* note 20.

245 *See generally* PEW, REPORT, *supra* note 15; FUTURE OF PRIVACY, *supra* note 15. *See also* Carmel Shachar, I Glen Cohen, Nita A. Farahany, Henry T. Greely, *Introduction, in* CONSUMER GENETIC TECHNOLOGIES, *supra* note 15, at 1, *citing* GRAND VIEW RESEARCH, PREDICTIVE GENETIC TESTING AND CONSUMER GENETICS MARKET SIZE, SHARE & TRENDS ANALYSIS REPORT BY TEST TYPE (POPULATION SCREENING, SUSCEPTIBILITY), BY APPLICATION, BY SETTING TYPE, AND SEGMENT FORECASTS, 2019–25 (2019) (projecting the global genetic testing and consumer wellness genomic market, valued at $2.24 billion in 2015, to double by 2025).

246 *Visit* www.ClinicalTrials.gov.

247 *See Chapter 4, supra,* at notes 11–20, and accompanying text (addressing the advent of ICT, internet access, and DNA familiarity, and their social and cultural impact).

248 US Nat'l Library of Med., *Fact Sheet, ClinicalTrials.gov* (May 3, 2011).

249 *Visit* www.ClinicalTrials.gov (ongoing updates, retrieved Mar. 21, 2002), https://clinicaltrials.gov/. The site has been modernized to the ClinicalTrials.gov beta website, https://beta.clinicaltrials.gov/. *See* US Nat'l Library of Med., *ClinicalTrials.gov Modernization* (reviewed Mar. 2022), www.clinicaltrials.gov/ct2/about-site/modernization.

250 As explained by HHS,

> The Privacy Rule allows covered providers and health plans to disclose protected health information to these "business associates" if the providers or plans obtain satisfactory assurances that the business associate will use the information only for the purposes for which it was engaged by the covered entity, will safeguard the information from misuse, and will help the covered entity comply with some of the covered entity's duties under the Privacy Rule.

HHS, *Business Associates* (reviewed May 24, 2019), www.hhs.gov/hipaa/for-professionals/privacy/guidance/business-associates/index.html.

251 *23andMe TV Spot, 'DNA Reports: 80%: $129'*, ISPOTTV (Jan. 2, 2022), www.ispot.tv/ad/qeaX/23andme-dna-reports-80-129. *See infra* notes 305–06, and accompanying text.

252 *See Chapter 4, supra,* at notes 120, 134, 161–62, and accompanying text (discussing the medical relevance of genetic health risk testing and FDA-imposed special conditions, which address clinical use and consumer comprehension).

253 For discussion of clinical assessment of genetic testing in accordance with established science and evidence standards, see generally SACGT, RECOMMENDATIONS, *supra* note 5.

254 *See Chapter 6, supra,* at notes 43–152, and accompanying text ("The Complexities of Personal Genome Medical Decision-Making" and "US Health Care System and Consumer Genetics Market Issues").

255 *See generally* SACGT, RECOMMENDATIONS, *supra* note 5.

256 *See infra* notes 273–76, and accompanying text (discussing the All of Us Research Program), 279, and accompanying text (discussing the International Human Genome Sequencing Consortium).
257 *See supra* note 187 (discussing subsequent work to correct errors and fill gaps in the draft sequence and announcement of the completion of the full human genome sequence). *See* Ganguly, *Complete, Gapless Sequence, supra* note 187. The UK Biobank has undertaken a proteomic exome initiative – a proteomic complement to HGP. *See generally* Bonislawski, *Proteomics Project, supra* note 20.
258 *See Chapter 4, supra*, at note 128, and accompanying text (relaying author's experience using 23andMe PGHS and portal). *Visit* 23andMe, official site (visited July 17, 2022), www.23andme.com/?utm_source=google&utm_medium=search_brand&utm_campaign=US_evergreen_sales_prs_alpha&gclid=EAIaIQobChMInJia1Y-A-QIVbwutBh34vA33EAAYAiAAEgKbZ_D_BwE&gclsrc=aw.ds.
259 *See* SACGT, RECOMMENDATIONS, *supra* note 5, at viii–ix.
260 *See generally* SACGT, RECOMMENDATIONS, *supra* note 5.
261 *See* WATSON, THE STORY, *supra* note 20, at 229, 223 (includes genes tally comparisons table). Scientists also have corrected errors and filled gaps in the sequence. *See supra* notes 187, 257, and accompanying text.
262 Ciara Curtin, *FASEB, ABRF Preparing for NIH Data Management, Sharing Plan*, GENOMEWEB (Mar 30, 2022), www.genomeweb.com/policy-legislation/faseb-abrf-preparing-nih-data-management-sharing-plan?utm_source=Sailthru&utm_medium=email&utm_campaign=GWDN%20Wed%20PM%202022-03-30&utm_term=GW%20Daily%20News%20Bulletin#.YkWk3S3MK3A.
263 The DNA Identification Act of 1994, 42 U.S.C. §14132, authorized the establishment of NDIS, in which all fifty states, the District of Columbia, the federal government, the US Army Criminal Investigation Laboratory, and Puerto Rico participate. *See* Criminal Justice Information Services/CJIS, *Frequently Asked Questions on CODIS and NDIS* (undated), www.fbi.gov/services/laboratory/biometric-analysis/codis/codis-and-ndis-fact-sheet; Catherine Shaffer, *Cold Cases Heat Up with New Forensic DNA Methods*, GEN. ENG. & BIOTECH. NEWS (Sept. 1, 2020), www.genengnews.com/insights/cold-cases-heat-up-with-new-forensic-dna-methods/.
264 *Visit* HHS, National Practitioner Databank/NPDB, official site (ongoing updates, visited Mar. 22, 2022), www.npdb.hrsa.gov/index.jsp.
265 *See* D. Tyler Coyle, FDA (CDER) Presentation, *Sentinel System Overview* (Feb. 5, 2018), www.fda.gov/media/110795/download. HHS directed the FDA to create Sentinel, and the agency launched the initiative in May 2008. Sentinel was in a "Mini-Sentinel pilot" stage as of 2016, evolving with a stringent budget considering the task and practicality realizations and adjustments, but producing experiential, technological, and data management capabilities through application. *See* Malinowski, *Triple Threat, supra* note 114, at 1052; Barbara J. Evans, *Seven Pillars of a New Evidentiary Paradigm: The Food, Drug, and Cosmetic Act Enters the Genomics Era*, 85 NOTRE DAME L. REV. 419, 509 (2010). *See generally* Barbara J. Evans, *Authority of the Food and Drug Administration to Require Data Access and Control Use Rights in the Sentinel Data Network*, 65 FOOD & DRUG L.J. 67 (2010).
266 SACGT, RECOMMENDATIONS, *supra* note 5, at 9.
267 *See* Malinowski, *Snake Oil, supra* note 84, at 50.
268 *See Chapter 2, supra*, at notes 92–112, and accompanying text (from "OWS Implementation of Triple-Threat R&D Methodology").
269 *See id.*, and accompanying text. NIH announced in May 2022 that it will license eleven COVID-19 research tools and early-stage diagnostic and vaccine candidates through the

World Health Organization's Technology Access Pool ("C-TAP"), via the United Nation's backed Medicines Patent Pool/MPP, to allow manufacturers worldwide to use these technologies to engage in R&D to produce vaccines, therapeutics, and diagnostics accessible in low and middle-income economy countries. *See* Tyler Patchen, *Global License Program to Receive Covid-19 Support from the NIH*, EndPoints News (May 12, 2022), https://endpts.com/global-license-program-to-receive-covid-19-support-from-the-nih/. In October 2022, Dr. Collins called for an "African Moonshot" in the form of a network for Genomic Centers of Excellence/GenCoE and the establishment of a pathogen surveillance network:

> Speaking at the American Society of Human Genetics[/ASHG] annual meeting, the former director of the National Institutes of Health proposed a cross-continent network of eight to 10 centers based on a "hub-and-spoke" model focusing on genomics applications such as pathogen surveillance and advancing genomics for precision medicine.
>
> A pathogen surveillance network, Collins explained, could prove instrumental in future pandemic preparedness, vaccine development, and vector control, while genomic initiatives aimed at precision medicine could bring advances in newborn screening, as well as tackling longstanding African health challenges such as HIV and sickle cell anemia.

Staff reporter, *Francis Collins Calls for African Genomics 'Moonshot'*, GenomeWeb (Oct. 27, 2022), www.genomeweb.com/genetic-research/francis-collins-calls-african-genomics-moonshot#.Y5yZoXbMK3A.

270 *See* Ellen Schneider, *FDA Offers Draft Guidance for Registries as RWD*, Reg. Affairs Prof. Soc'ty (RAPS), (posted Nov. 29, 2021), www.raps.org/news-and-articles/news-articles/2021/11/fda-offers-draft-guidance-for-registries-as-rwd. This guidance provided transparency regarding how the agency will receive RWD when considering a new drug indication or assessing post-approval requirements. *See id.*

271 NIH, *Accelerating Medicines Partnership® (AMP®)* (undated), www.nih.gov/research-training/accelerating-medicines-partnership-amp.

272 *Id.* at *The Challenge*.

273 Collins, Varmos, *Perspective, supra* note 4, at 793. Precision medicine (treatments tailored to a person's genome) and personalized medicine (treatments derived from a person's genome) are both utilized in personal genome medicine. *See id.* For discussion of AllUs, see *Prologue, supra*, at notes 26–28, and accompanying text.

274 *See* NIH, *Accelerating Medicines Partnership® (AMP®): Bespoke Gene Therapy* Consortium (reviewed Apr. 20, 2022), www.nih.gov/research-training/accelerating-medicines-partnership-amp/bespoke-gene-therapy-consortium. In 2022, "The US Food and Drug Administration's (FDA) top biologics regulator said the use of a 'playbook' or platform approach for developing multiple cell and gene therapy products and a globally harmonized template would facilitate the development of such products at a 17 May meeting of the American Society of Gene and Cell Therapy (ASGCT)." Joanne S. Eglovitch, *FDA, EMA [European Medicines Agency] Officials Discuss Impediments to Cell and Gene Therapies*, Reg. Focus (May 2022) (Reg. Affairs Prof. Soc'y publication), www.raps.org/news-and-articles/news-articles/2022/5/fda-ema-officials-discuss-impediments-to-cell-and.

275 Krishanu Saha, Erik J. Sontheimer et al., *The NIH Somatic Cell Genome Editing Program*, 592 Nature 195–204 (Apr. 7, 2021), www.nature.com/articles/s41586-021-03191-1.

276 *See Chapter 4, supra*, at notes 116–37, and accompanying text (FDA approvals of 23andMe's DTCGHR and other genetic testing, beginning with FDA approval of

the company's DTCGHR *carrier* screening test for Bloom Syndrome in 2015). *Visit* 23andMe, official site, 23andme.com/?utm_source=google&utm_medium=search_brand&utm_campaign=US_evergreen_sales_prs_alpha&gclid=EAIaIQobChMI_c2Zn5yA-QIVMRXUAR0yhAp2EAAYAiAAEgJAz_D_BwE&gclsrc=aw.ds.

277 15 U.S.C. § 3710a.

278 *See Chapter 2, supra*, at notes 58, 75, and accompanying text (discussing BARDA).

279 *See* NHGRI, *What is the Human Genome Project?* (updated Oct. 28, 2018), www.genome.gov/human-genome-project/What.

280 *Visit* Personal Genome Project, official site (visited July 5, 2022) (providing guidelines and links to global network of participants), www.personalgenomes.org/.

281 Collins, Varmos, *Perspective*, *supra* note 4, at 95 (regarding the US' Precision Medicine Initiative/PMI, which was recast as AllUs), www.nejm.org/doi/full/10.1056/NEJMp1500523.

282 *Visit* NHS, National Genomic Test Directory (visited Apr. 1, 2022), www.england.nhs.uk/publication/national-genomic-test-directories/.

283 Staff Reporter, *UK Report Urges Widespread NHS Uptake of Pharmacogenomics*, GenomeWeb (Mar 29, 2022), www.genomeweb.com/policy-legislation/uk-report-urges-widespread-nhs-uptake-pharmacogenomics#.YtQyonbMK3A. *See also* Justine Petrone, *Genomics England, NHS to Lead £105M UK Study with Aim to Sequence 100K Newborns* GenomeWeb (Dec 13, 2022) ("The UK Department of Health and Social Care announced this week that it will invest £175 million (about $215 million) in genomic research…."), www.genomeweb.com/research-funding/genomics-england-nhs-lead-ps105m-uk-study-aim-sequence-100k-newborns#.Y5jpynbMK3A.

284 Royal College of Physicians, British Pharmacological Society, Personalised prescribing: using pharmacogenomics to improve patient outcomes (2022), www.rcp.ac.uk/projects/outputs/personalised-prescribing-using-pharmacogenomics-improve-patient-outcomes.

285 *Id.* at 6 (*Foreword*). "Pharmacogenetics is the study of genetic causes of individual variations in drug response whereas pharmacogenomics deals with the simultaneous impact of multiple mutations in the genome that may determine the patient's response to drug therapy." Willard H. Dere, Tamas S. Suto, *The Role of Pharmacogenetics and Pharmacogenomics in Improving Translational Medicine*, 6(1) Clin. Cases Miner Bone Metab. 13–16, 13 (Jan. 2009), www.ncbi.nlm.nih.gov/pmc/articles/PMC2781217/#:~:text=Pharmacogenetics%20is%20the%20study%20of,patient's%20response%20to%20drug%20therapy.

286 Royal College, *supra* note 284, at 7. Global healthcare systems share many of the personal genome medicine issues addressed throughout this book. For example, the sufficiency of consent in population genetics and genomics and the impact of such research on groups under study who self-identify by ancestry and related variables such as culture and legacy is an issue shared among global health care systems – especially with the global reach of human genome science research. The issue was litigated in the US in a case brought by the Havasupai Tribe against Arizona State University/ASU after researchers used blood-DNA samples for a migration study and later published the results. *See generally Havasupai Tribe of Havasupai Reservation v. Ariz. Bd. of Regents*, 204 P.3d 1063 (Ariz. Ct. App. 2008), *review denied* (April 20, 2009). The Havasupai Tribe's DNA was put to many research uses:

> Although the project ended for the purposes allegedly consented to by the Havasupai, researchers at ASU and elsewhere, including the University of Arizona, continued to perform research and publish articles based on data from tribal members' blood samples. Among the publications were at least four doctoral dissertations

> and various academic papers, some of which concerned evolutionary genetics, rather than medical genetics. Some of the papers generated from the blood samples dealt with schizophrenia, inbreeding and theories about ancient human population migrations from Asia to North America. The latter body of work is contrary to the Havasupai belief that, as a people, they originated in the Grand Canyon

Id. at 1067. In 2010, the tribe was given $700,000 in compensation, and their blood samples were returned. *See* Amy Harmon, *Indian Tribe Wins Fight to Limit Research of Its DNA*, N.Y. TIMES (Apr. 21, 2010), www.nytimes.com/2010/04/22/us/22dna.html.

287 *See* Petrone, *Clinical Validation of Cancer Genome Interpretation Platform at Heart of New €10M European Project*, GENOMEWEB (Dec 02, 2022), www.genomeweb.com/informatics/clinical-validation-cancer-genome-interpretation-platform-heart-new-eu10m-european#.Y5dSYnbMK3A; *Chapter* 5, *supra*, at notes 384–403, and accompanying text ("The Absence of Centralized, Objective, Reliable Health Technology Assessment/HTA in US Health Care"). The European Union/EU introduced an Integrated and Standardized Workflows for Personalised Therapy ("Instand-NGS4P") project to standardize next-generation DNA sequencing/NGS workflows to advance making precision medicine a standard of care in oncology. Instand-NGS4P is "intended to develop workflows for integrating, standardizing, and analyzing data from cancer gene testing, pharmacogenomics testing, and medication databases to support clinical decision support at the bedside." Neil Versel, *EU Awards €4.8M to Support Transition of NGS Workflows to Clinical Settings*, GENOMEWEB (Dec 16, 2022), www.genomeweb.com/cancer/eu-awards-eu48m-support-transition-ngs-workflows-clinical-settings#.Y6ClnbMK3A. In December 2022, the EU moved the project into its second phase by awarding eleven contracts worth nearly €4.8 million ($5.1 million)." *See id.*

288 *Visit* ECRI Institute, official site (visited Apr. 2, 2022), www.ecri.org/.

289 *See generally Fareed Zakaria, Global Public Square*, GPS (CNN, aired Nov. 22, 2020).

290 DAVIES, $1,000 GENOME, *supra* note 4, at 262–63. *Cf.* William DuBois, Note, *New Drug Research, The Extraterritorial Application of FDA Regulations, and the Need for International Cooperation*, 36(1) VAND. J. TRANSNAT'L LAW 161 (2003) ("Regardless of whether US courts allow the FDA to bring actions against companies for violations abroad, international cooperation is needed to control drug testing.").

291 *See generally* ANDREJ SAVIN, US INTERNET LAW (2017) (monograph), www.elgaronline.com/view/9781784717957/10_chapter1.xhtml.

292 *Id.* at *Chapter 1: Internet regulation in the European Union.*

293 *See generally id.*

294 *Visit* ICH, official site, www.ich.org/.

295 ICH, *Mission: Harmonisation for Better Health* (visited Mar. 28, 2020), www.ich.org/page/mission. *Visit* ICH, official site (visited Apr. 3, 2022), www.ich.org/.

296 ICH, *Mission*, *supra* note 295.

297 *See generally* NASEM, AN EVIDENCE FRAMEWORK FOR GENETIC TESTING (2017), https://nap.nationalacademies.org/catalog/24632/an-evidence-framework-for-genetic-testing.

298 *See generally* NHGRI, *Reimbursement*, *supra* note 14.

299 *See, e.g.*, Francesca Spinosi, Shama Khan, Christine Seymour, Elena Ashkinadze, *Trends in Coverage and Reimbursement for Reproductive Genetic Counseling in New Jersey by Multiple Payers from 2010 to 2018*, 30(6) J. GENET. COUNS. 1748–56 (Dec. 2021) ("Commercial insurance covered 65% of encounters billed but this varied between payers."), https://pubmed.ncbi.nlm.nih.gov/34223664/. State licensure improves reimbursement (twenty-seven states have introduced licensure of CGCs), and pending

federal legislation, the Access to Genetic Counselor Services Act/AGCSA, would provide Medicare recognition of CGCs and help with reimbursement from the Centers for Medicare and Medicaid Services/CMS overall – namely with Medicaid coverage and reimbursement. *See* John Richardson, *Perspectives, Update: State Licensure and CMS Recognition* (Apr. 24, 2019), https://perspectives.nsgc.org/Article/TitleLink/State-Licensure-and-CMS-Recognition. *See* Malinowski, Blatt, *Tarot Cards, supra* note 90, at 1212.

300 NHGRI, *Reimbursement, supra* note 14 (page nos. unavailable).

301 *See generally* NASEM, FRAMEWORK, *supra* note 297; HHS, REPORT OF THE SECRETARY'S ADVISORY COMMITTEE ON GENETICS, HEALTH, AND SOCIETY, COVERAGE AND REIMBURSEMENT OF GENETIC TESTS AND SERVICES (2006), https://osp.od.nih.gov/sacghsdocs/coverage-and-reimbursement-of-genetic-tests-and-services/.

302 Under a long-standing agreement between the agencies, the FDA has primary regulatory responsibility for Rx products. *See* Memorandum of Understanding Between FTC and the FDA, 36 FED. REG. 18,539 (Sept. 15, 1971), https://fda.report/media/99834/Memorandum-of-Understanding-Between-Federal-Trade-Commission-and-the-Food-and-Drug-Administration.pdf. *See Chapter* 3, *supra*, at note 76, and accompanying text (addressing FDA-FTC coordination and collaboration). The agencies collaborate at times, such as to advance competition in the biologics marketplace given their extreme cost. *See Joint FDA-FTC Statement Regarding Collaboration to Advance Competition in the Biologic Marketplace* (February 3, 2020) ("Public and private insurers in the US spent $125.5 billion on biologics in 2018 alone."), www.ftc.gov/public-statements/2020/02/joint-fda-ftc-statement-regarding-collaboration-advance-competition.

303 *See generally* CONSUMER GENETIC TECHNOLOGIES, *supra* note 15, at 144.

304 *See generally Chapter* 1, *supra*.

305 *23andMe TV Spot, 'DNA Reports:* 80%: $129', ISPOTTV (Jan. 2, 2022), www.ispot.tv/ad/qeaX/23andme-dna-reports-80-129.

306 23andMe, official site (visited Apr. 9, 2022), www.23andme.com/?evr=epv.

307 *See Chapter* 4, *supra*, at notes 125–29, and accompanying text.

308 *See* SACGT, RECOMMENDATIONS, *supra* note 5, at 6–8 (providing explanation with examples).

309 *See* Malinowski, *Snake Oil, supra* note 84, at 514.

310 Hazel, *Best Practices, supra* note 15, at 276.

311 *See Chapter* 3, *supra*, at note 76, and accompanying text (discussing FDA-FTC collaboration with examples). *See, e.g.*, FTC, *Press Release, FTC Staff Provides FDA with Comments on Direct-To-Consumer Prescription Drug Advertising* (Dec. 2, 2003), www.ftc.gov/news-events/press-releases/2003/12/ftc-staff-provides-fda-comments-direct-consumer-prescription-drug; FTC, *Press Release, FTC Testifies on the Internet Sale of Prescription Drugs From Domestic Web Sites* (Mar. 27, 2003), www.ftc.gov/news-events/press-releases/2003/03/ftc-testifies-internet-sale-prescription-drugs-domestic-web-sites.

312 Hazel, *Best Practices, supra* note 15, at 274–75.

313 *See id.* at 261, 272. *See generally* FUTURE OF PRIVACY, *supra* note 15. *See also Chapter* 6, *supra*, at notes 163–65, and accompanying text (addressing industry summer of 2018 self-regulation effort in partnership with the Future of Privacy Forum/FPF).

314 *See* Hazel, *Best Practices, supra* note 15, at 261, 272.

315 ABRAMSON, OVERDOSED, *supra* note 36, at 255.

316 *See generally* Hunter, Khoury, Drazen, *Bottle, supra* note 228, and accompanying text.

317 Malinowski, *Snake Oil, supra* note 84, at 40.

318 Recode, *Full Transcript: 23andMe CEO Anne Wojcicki Answers Genetics and Privacy Questions on Too Embarrased to Ask* (Sept. 29, 2017), www.vox.com/2017/9/29/16385320/transcript-23andme-ceo-anne-wojcicki-genetics-privacy-health-questions-too-embarrassed-to-ask. *See also NBC Nightly News with Lester Holt, High-Tech Heritage* (aired July 14, 2018) (interview with Anne Wojcicki, in which she explains, "We're big believers in that the more I can educate you earlier in life, the more you're actually going to have information to try to prevent the condition.").

319 *See generally Chapter 1, supra.*

320 Professor George Annas had the foresight to recognize our DNA as our "present and future medical diaries" nearly a half-century ago. *See generally* George J. Annas, *The Patient Rights Advocate: Redefining the Doctor-Patient Relationship in the Hospital Context*, 27 VAND. L. REV. 243 (1974).

Epilogue

The Personal Genome Future of US Medicine

In Nikki Erlick's novel *The Measure*, every person twenty-one years of age and older awakes on an early spring morning to find a small box with their name inscribed on the cover:

> The boxes appeared on finely mowed lawns in the suburbs, nestled between hedges and the first blooms of the hyacinth. They sat atop well-trampled doormats in the cities, where decades of tenants had passed through the threshold. They sank into the warm sands outside tents in the desert and waited near lonely lakeside cabins, gathering dew in the breeze off the water. In San Francisco and Sao Paulo, in Johannesburg and Jaipur, in the Andes and the Amazon, there wasn't anywhere, or anyone, that the boxes couldn't find.[1]

From that day onward, every individual receives their box on the morning of their twenty-second birthday just as mysteriously. "There was something both comforting and unsettling about the fact that every adult on earth suddenly seemed to be sharing the same surreal experience, the ubiquity of the boxes both a terror and a relief."[2]

In addition to the person's name, "inscribed on every box was a simple, yet cryptic message, written in the native tongue of its recipient: *The measure of your life lies within.*"[3] Each box contains a single string of varying lengths. Within weeks, the US Department of Health and Human Services/HHS and international task forces determine that the strings are accurate, absolute measures of the duration of one's life. With six months of global data collection for comparative analysis, reminiscent of the global COVID-19 pandemic data collection and sharing in real time, people may access a string measurement site – a simplistic counterpart to the personal genome testing registry and clinical use assessment clearinghouse proposed in this book – to calculate the extent of their lives down to the very month.

Governments and societies respond differently to the "new normal." As reasoned by one of the characters, "Had the strings arrived in any other century, … nobody would have dared ask what was inside your box, leaving each household to quietly mourn or celebrate on their own, behind closed doors and drawn curtains. But not now, not in this modern era when feuds and flirtations [are] played out online, when family milestones, professional achievements, and personal tragedies [are] all on display."[4] The US becomes a divided society of short-stringers and long-stringers, with short-stringers subjected to discrimination in everything from college admissions to employment, loans, and adoption. "Once the truth of the strings had been acknowledged by all but the final few holdouts, the new world came into focus: a garden in which many inhabitants had eaten the apple, while the rest remained too scared to bite."[5]

Fiction resonates most with me when it compels me to confront, contemplate, and wrestle with reality. *The Measure* speaks directly to a very present DTC personal genome testing reality. Some "hot" DTC personal genome testing companies are on a business plan mission to provide each of us with our personal genome "strings" – longevity testing, also referred to as "all-cause mortality testing." Major investors are confident that we will want and pay for these testing services, or at least that we will not be able to resist the temptation to purchase and to "know" – especially if we have opportunity to lengthen our strings with the information. For example, "A team led by researchers at Amgen subsidiary [deCODE] Genetics [has] used proteomic measurements to develop predictors for short and long-term risk of all-cause mortality."[6] Ancestry.com LLC, the holder of millions of customers' personal genome information, has partnered with an Alphabet Inc. (the parent company of Google) subsidiary called Calico Life Sciences, which is reported to be financed by several Silicon Valley billionaires on a quest to beat their mortality (and presumably ours too, if we share their desire and can afford to join their quest beyond the cost of their longevity testing and the limits of our health insurance coverage).[7] Calico's stated mission is to extend human longevity through genomics.[8] On June 21, 2022, Human Longevity, a San Diego company that raised $80 million in 2014, $220 million in 2016, and $30 million in 2019, announced a pending $345 million merger to enable the company to go public and to create a combined company valued at approximately $1 billion.[9] Human Longevity, which sells memberships to individuals, self-proclaims to be "the global leader in advancing the Human Longevity Care movement, on a mission to discover and harness the technological and biological unlocks that amplify span of life, health, & high-performance."[10] Provided this DTC personal genome longevity testing meets evidentiary-science clinical standards and is affordable, some (maybe most) individuals will be able to use test results from their DNA sequences to improve their health and to extend their productive lives – unlike the string absolutes in *The Measure*.

My objective undertaking this project was to draw from US medicine's past and present, with focus on its evidentiary-science base and its personal genome medicine/PGM future. When I first engaged professionally in biotech-related health law-policy in the early-mid 1990s after graduating from law school (I published my first full law review article in 1994, which addressed prenatal genetic testing with field work interviewing genetic counselors and their patients who terminated wanted pregnancies based on prenatal genetic testing results), I sought advice from leading medical and public health professionals, and especially from established health law professors and practitioners. Almost uniformly, they warned me (several kindly dismissed me) that I should temper my enthusiasm for the forthcoming impact of biotech innovation on health care. The message was variations of "Trends in medical science come and go, I have experienced many, and you are caught up in one." I was advised to not be overly influenced by Wall Street hype, and it was obvious they thought I was.

This well-intentioned advice raised concerns and triggered the second-guessing chatter that has been "part of my DNA" for as long as I can remember. Yet, even though my interest was grounded in health law-policy rather than lucrative biotech Wall Street opportunities, I stayed the course – at the risk of wasting the professional opportunities bestowed by a Yale Law School degree. The chatter was loud, at times incessant and deafening, given that neither of my parents had graduated from high school and, in fact, only two of their siblings had achieved that milestone (a deviation from employment and an academic luxury for that blue-collar generation). Why did I do it and make everything so difficult for myself? Biotechnology had become tangible, real medicine to me in the early 1970s when I was a child (six to seven years of age) due to unusual personal circumstances – which, as a young adult facing major career choices, I understood to be anecdotal and an undue influence (more than justifiable second-guessing chatter). I quieted the self-doubt chatter by reassuring myself that I had made a valiant attempt at self-policing due diligence by following biotech science, its reported accomplishments and critiques, and major events in related US law-policy since the mid-1980s, at least to the best of my abilities, and I continued to do so with acquired skills and knowledge. I still do.

What were the unusual circumstances? My father was diagnosed with extremely advanced hairy cell leukemia in 1973 – a death sentence at the time.[11] After suffering severe illness with hospitalizations for over a year, he was rushed from Worcester, Massachusetts to Boston with a fatal prognosis and no diagnosis – literally a last-ditch effort to extend his life, even though he did not have health insurance (not so uncommon then, and unacceptably true today for many US citizens and legal residents). A treating physician accurately diagnosed him without delay and immediately referred him to a Harvard-affiliated specialist who took over his care and put him on an ongoing experimental clinical trial protocol. My father was perfect for the study because he was young and, though direly ill, he and his organs were still physically strong from a lifetime of manual labor in construction. The clinical trial he joined contributed to the development of Biogen Inc.'s Interferon Alpha (IFN-α). My father experienced fourteen additional years of productive life.[12] Thanks to that clinical study and others, many hairy cell leukemia patients subsequently experienced the same. "The introduction of alpha interferon in 1984 initiated a new and exciting turnaround in the treatment of hairy-cell leukemia."[13]

Now, some three decades later, the pace of progress in biotech and genomics has exceeded my 1990s expectations – however lofty they may have been. Over that span of time, research and development/R&D momentum has built exponentially.[14] Creative US law-policy responsive to biotech R&D, most notably technology transfer law and policy/TTLP with a methodology of harnessing commercial incentives and application ingenuity, has enabled the realization of remarkable, cumulative progress over decades.[15] Now, a barrage of human genome sciences innovation is reaching clinical care more quickly than I imagined in the 1990s.[16] I continue to embrace the creative and responsive US law-policy in R&D that has proven a potent catalyst for enormous opportunity to improve the practice of medicine and human health. However, I also fully appreciate that the US must shore up the evidentiary-science base of medicine to prepare for PGM and to fully realize that opportunity.

The recommendations the Secretary's Advisory Committee on Genetic Testing/SACGT issued in 2000 were shelved in part because many feared impeding the progress of clinical genetic testing:

> During the second round of public comments received on the preliminary conclusions and recommendations, a number of individuals from industry and professional organizations expressed concerns about the impact that additional oversight may have on the development, availability, and accessibility of genetic tests and expressed strong opposition to an increased role for FDA.[17]

The SACGT recommendations, reflective of the committee's exhaustive collection and analysis of stakeholder input and public commentary from more than 400 individuals and groups, embody a presumption that medical professionals would be involved in personal genome testing and would apply established evidentiary-science clinical practice standards.[18] In fact, one of SACGT's overarching principles was that "No test should be introduced in the market before it is established that it can be used to diagnose and/or predict a health-related condition in an appropriate way."[19] Assessing the personal genome testing landscape in 2000 with this presumption, it is understandable that some would conclude that the regulatory intervention recommended by SACGT was premature – that there was time before expansive US public access to and uptake of personal genome testing, especially with a medical profession filter on public access. As addressed throughout this book, widespread DTC personal genome testing that does not meet evidentiary-science clinical standards and that is available to consumers without medical professional involvement is a very present and amassing US market and medicine reality.[20] The global health-related personal genome testing market was valued at $2.24 billion in 2015 and projected to double by 2025 to nearly $5 billion.[21] The luxury of time before meaningful law-policy responsiveness to DTC personal genome testing has been spent.[22]

The shareholder wealth maximization norm is an indicator of corporate behavior in the US' free market and capitalism-culture regulatory environment. Overall, the norm has and continues to serve the US well.[23] Corporations exist to reward their investors and shareholders – even in the business of life science. For-profit companies are driven by profit, not philanthropy, and not-for-profts must remain profitable to sustain themselves unless otherwise endowed. Many of the most esteemed US academic institutions, such as the Massachusetts Institute of Technology/MIT and Harvard University, seek profit voraciously through TTLP even with enormously vast endowments. Raw, aggressive biopharma capitalism has fueled innovation, bolstered the US economy, and advanced medical science remarkably.[24] US TTLP, implemented for over four decades, has embraced that incentivizing force and channeled it into both basic and clinical research. The very purpose of TTLP is commercial application of invention to create product innovation and economic returns through the integration of government, academia, and industry.[25]

TTLP, the Prescription Drug User Fee Act/PDUFA of 1992 and its renewals, the Food and Drug Administration Modernization Act/FDAMA of 1997, the Food and Drug Administration Safety and Innovation Act/FDASIA of 2012, and the 21st Century Cures Act of 2016 are notable examples of how government regulation is not innately hostile to biopharma. In fact, it has established R&D infrastructure that is a (arguably *the*) primary catalyst for the commercial sector's present and future progress.[26] Regulation, like science, is neither innately good nor bad. It is law-policy power – to use to do good or bad, or to waste when there is opportunity to address salient, tangible regulatory needs. Predictable, workable, and enforceable regulatory checks by the US medical profession and government to ensure medical science integrity and to protect the evidentiary-science base of clinical medicine create a sound parameter, and capitalism may be embraced and market forces harnessed to their fullest. Without sound regulatory parameters to protect the base of US medicine, that commercial drive threatens the integrity of medical science and evidentiary science-based clinical practice. Industry may be perversely incentivized to be less entrepreneurial, innovative, dynamic, and prolific – so long as it is profitable and meets, better yet exceeds, its financial and fiduciary obligations to investors and shareholders.

Regulatory parameters to protect the base of US medicine also must be sound enough in the US' decentralized, fragmented (an entanglement of markets and myriad sectors – operating on the state, national, and state-national levels), and largely privatized health care system to endure public consumerism in medicine – both to protect the evidentiary-science base of medicine and to avoid waste.[27] Physicians and other medical professionals are required to satisfy rigorous education and training prerequisites and to obtain and maintain licenses and certifications to practice medicine for sound reason: to protect the evidentiary-science base of medicine, for assurance of ongoing medical practice competency given its complexity and dynamism, and because of the human health implications – literally life and death. The public overall is not learned in the human genome sciences and is certainly not competent at translating medical meaning from it. In fact, neither is most of the medical profession given the human health expanse of the human genome sciences, their dynamic nature with explosive progress in real time, and the clinical complexities of personal genome testing.[28]

I believe in the personal genome future of medicine and in the US medical profession. My belief is not blind faith – quite the contrary. It is based on what the US medical profession accomplished last century, what has been accomplished in biotech and genomic R&D during my professional lifetime, and how those accomplishments were realized.[29] The contemporary US medical profession, as did its mid-twentieth century predecessor, must muster and exercise commitment to its professional mission to protect and promote the evidentiary-science base of PGM. Today's US medical profession, with the last-century precedent of the AMA Council on Pharmacy and Chemistry ("AMA Council") and a medical profession-FDA symbiotic relationship, must work with the US government, industry, and other stakeholders to repeat its twentieth century US medicine accomplishment at the outset of this PGM millennium.

Yes, the genome is very much out of the bottle – largely because the public demanded access with enough industry and other stakeholder political pressure to pop the cork.[30] The US public, with a mindset of self-determination and health care autonomy in our age of genomics, wants access to DTC personal genome testing and industry is providing it – increasingly so. Ms. Anne Wojcicki co-founded 23andMe, the seminal health-related DTC personal genome testing company, to offer individuals direct internet access to their personal genomes through the company's Personal Genome Health Service/PGHS unimpeded by physician permissions.[31] She envisions a full transformation of US health care to personal genome-enabled, consumer-centric medicine: Individuals who choose to be enlightened about their personal genomes do so affordably, and then utilize that information to take more control of their health and preventative care with medical provider involvement subject to their discretion and direction.[32] The 23andMe business plan and corporate mission now encompass becoming a provider of full DTC genomic *clinical* services. Ms. Wojcicki's vision presupposes individuals' capacity to exercise autonomy in medical decision-making in a manner that achieves and does not detract from obtainable, medically sound results. It assumes access to responsive, sufficiently learned, and responsible/scientifically objective medical professionals with the needed personal genome test assessment and patient communication capabilities to realize patient comprehension essential for their medical decision making. Ms. Wojcicki's vision also presupposes solid evidentiary science-based personal genome medicine that enables consumers and providers to realize clinically accurate and meaningful medical interpretations on an individual patient basis, patient-by-patient, in the context of a full medical practice.[33]

The human genome sciences are voluminous in scope, volcanic, dynamic, and enmeshed in dimensions of complexity.[34] Evidentiary science-based PGM is coming into being in a sporadic and varied manner, and it will be for some time. Genetics, genomics, and proteomics are generating a tsunami of swirling data and delivery-of-care capabilities across human health, and responsible medical providers are treading water as they attempt to keep their sight on the evidentiary-science base of medicine. Medical personal genome tests that are scientifically and clinically sound enough to improve human health meaningfully and in definitive ways are but the edge of a vast ocean of testing capabilities removed from this standard – including DTC genetic health risk/DTCGHR testing available on the US market. DTC personal genome testing could improve individual patient clinical care and US medicine if medical providers have a pragmatic, reliable, evidentiary-science means to assess the clinical utility and validity of personal genome tests in a patient-specific manner. Patients could be made more aware of health problems that might (at times will) affect them or their children and be better able to take proactive steps in disease management and prevention. Medical provider and patient experience with personal genome testing with adherence to evidentiary-science clinical practice standards could advance responsible PGM through use familiarity.

The proposed comprehensive and publicly accessible health-related personal genome test registry for the US market would introduce a medical provider means for assessing personal genome tests without challenging the public's demand for direct access to DTC personal genome testing services.[35] Fully implemented, the registry would introduce a clinical use assessment clearinghouse for personal genome tests – a contemporary counterpart to the AMA Council, which was created by the US medical profession at the outset of the twentieth century to asses patent medicines.[36] The proposed registry and clinical use clearinghouse is consistent with the US legacy of learned and licensed medical providers having control over the practice of US medicine and physician discretion in individualized patient clinical care.[37]

In the event the AMA is unwilling or unable to orchestrate establishment of the registry in collaboration with US government agencies and stakeholders, there are medical profession alternatives. Notably, much medical profession influence regarding the evidentiary-science base of clinical practice has shifted over the years to the National Academy of Medicine/NAM.[38] This shift has been vividly illustrated in recent years by the FDA's interaction with NAM for responsiveness to the opioid epidemic and NAM's formation in 2022 of a Committee on Emerging Science, Technology, and Innovation/CESTI in health and medicine.[39] Pragmatically, the proposed registry and clearinghouse is consistent with www.ClinicalTrials.gov, ongoing US government genomic data sharing initiatives, evidentiary-science clinical practice standards, and other delivery-of-care norms established by the medical profession long ago.[40] The proposal draws heavily from existing technology infrastructure, and includes a best practices opportunity for the DTC personal genome testing companies that have developed much of the needed user-friendly internet interface and genomic data management technology.[41]

The proposed registry and clinical use assessment clearinghouse would better enable medical providers and health insurers to uptake personal genome testing in clinical care with adherence to evidentiary-science clinical practice standards and to resist contrary US consumer-patient demands with explanation that elevates both patient comprehension and trust through a reliable public resource they share access to – similar to www.ClinicalTrials.gov.[42] Rushing medical uptake and skewing the incremental clinical soundness of PGM as it comes into being risks muddling patient health care choices and patient–provider decision making.[43] It threatens to delay the transformation of US health care to sound, responsible PGM – to the detriment of patient care, US medicine, and responsible allocation of limited health care resources while that transition to PGM is underway.[44]

In sum, the existing US regulatory rubric for DTC personal genome testing incentivizes premature and irresponsible clinical and consumer medical uptake of PGM. The regulatory status quo jeopardizes the realization of PGM's potential to improve human health during the transformation of US health care envisioned by Ms. Wojcicki and pursued by 23andMe and its commercial sector contemporaries.[45] PGM must not be rushed beyond evidentiary science-based clinical practice. PGM must evolve and be realized in clinical care in tandem with reliable assurances of adherence to evidentiary science, responsible clinical practice, patient protection with elevated patient access to scientifically sound information and comprehension in our patient self-determination era, and the advancement of human health – just as US medicine evolved and earned trust last century.[46]

NOTES

1 Nikki Erlick, The Measure 2 (2022).
2 *Id.*
3 *Id.*
4 *Id.* at 44.
5 *Id.* at 69.
6 Staff Reporter, *[deCODE] Study Identifies Proteomic Predictors of All-Cause Mortality*, GenomeWeb (Jun 18, 2021) (page numbers unavailable), www.genomeweb.com/proteomics-protein-research/decode-study-identifies-proteomic-predictors-all-cause-mortality.
7 *Visit* Calico Life Sciences, official site (visited July 30, 2022), www.calicolabs.com/. Alphabet Inc. is a US multinational technology conglomerate holding company created through a restructuring of Google on October 2, 2015, and the parent company of Google and several former Google subsidiaries. *Visit* Alphabet Inc., official site (visited July 30, 2022), https://abc.xyz/. Fortune 500 ranked Alphabet 8 in 2022 and declared it "the top-performing Big Tech stock of 2021 as its shares soared by more than 65%, nearly three times the Nasdaq's 22% gain." *Fortune* 500, Fortune (2022), https://fortune.com/company/alphabet/fortune500/. *See generally* Stuart Leavenworth, *Ancestry wants your spit, Your DNA and your trust. Should you give them all three?*, McClatchy Newspapers (May 29, 2018) (page numbers unavailable), www.mcclatchydc.com/news/nation-world/article210692689.html#cardLink=row1_card1. "Ancestry's DNA database includes more than 5 million records, and … anywhere from half to 70 percent of customers consent to have their data used for research." *Id.* Calico, founded by Google in 2013 with $1 billion in funding, has been highly secretive. *See* Stuart Leavenworth, *DNA for Sale: Who Is the Secretive Google Subsidiary That Has Access to Ancestry's DNA Database?*, Chic. Trib. (June 6, 2018), www.chicagotribune.com/news/nationworld/sns-tns-bc-dna-data-20180606-story.html.
8 *See id.*

9 *See* Staff Reporter, *Human Longevity to Go Public through $345M SPAC Merger*, GenomeWeb (June 21, 2022) (page numbers unavailable online), www.genomeweb.com/business-news/human-longevity-go-public-through-345m-spac-merger?utm_source=Sailthru&utm_medium=email&utm_campaign=GWDN%20Tues%20AM%202022-06-21&utm_term=GW%20Daily%20News%20Bulletin#.YrHoynbMK3A. Human Longevity seeks to identify key DNA variants that underlie longevity and health through analysis of the sequenced genomes of patients with Alzheimer's and other terminal illnesses associated with advanced age. *See* James D. Watson, DNA: The Story of the Genetic Revolution 229 (2nd ed., 2017) (with Andrew Berry, Kevin Davies) (updated commemoration of the fiftieth anniversary of the discovery of the double helix). In 2020, the company anticipated sequencing a million human genomes, and Mr. Craig Venter, co-founder of Human Longevity, "predicts that some of the information might prove commercially valuable to pharmaceutical companies." *Id.*

10 Human Longevity, official site (visited June 21, 2022), https://humanlongevity.com/.

11 *See* Michael J. Malinowski, *Throwing Dirt on Doctor Frankenstein's Grave: Access to Experimental Treatments at the End of Life*, 65 Hastings L.J. 615, 616–17 (2014).

12 *See id.*

13 Shahid Ahmed, Kanti R Rai, *Interferon in the Treatment of Hairy-cell Leukemia*, 16(1) Best Pract. Res. Clin. Haematol. 69, 69–81 (2003) (abstract), https://pubmed.ncbi.nlm.nih.gov/12670466/. *See also* Harvey M. Golomb, *Hairy Cell Leukemia: Treatment Successes in the Past 25 Years*, 26 J. Clin. Oncol. 2607, 2607–09 (2008), https://ascopubs.org/doi/full/10.1200/JCO.2007.15.7420.

14 *See generally* US National Academies of Science, Engineering, and Medicine/NASEM, Preparing for the Future Products of Biotechnology 28 (2017) (study surveying the present and approaching wave of genomic innovation in medicine and commerce), www.nap.edu/catalog/24605/preparing-for-future-products-of-biotechnology; Congressional Budget Office/CBO, Research and Development in the Pharmaceutical Industry (2021), www.cbo.gov/publication/57126.

15 *See generally Chapter 2, supra.*

16 *See generally* NASEM, Preparing, *supra* note 14; CBO, R&D, *supra* note 14; Watson, The Story, *supra* note 9; *Prologue, supra* (addressing the advancement of DNA sequencing technologies).

17 Secretary's Advisory Committee on Genetic Testing/SACGT, Enhancing the Oversight of Genetic Tests: Recommendations of the SACGT 26 (July 2000). https://osp.od.nih.gov/sagct_document_archi/enhancing-the-oversight-of-genetic-tests-recommendations-of-the-sacgt/. The work of SACGT is discussed in *Chapter 6, supra*, at notes 14, 41, 157, and accompanying text, and *Chapter 7, supra*, at notes 10, 85, 87–89, 93–97, 103–04, 218–26, 259–60, and accompanying text.

18 *See generally* SACGT, Recommendations, *supra* note 17.

19 *Id.* at 14.

20 *See* The Pew Charitable Trusts, Report, The Role of Lab-Developed Tests in the In Vitro Diagnostics Market 1 (Oct. 2021), www.pewtrusts.org/-/. *See also Chapter 6, supra*, at notes 63–75, and accompanying text (discussion of lab developed tests/LDTs, the Pew Report findings, and a *New York Times* investigation of noninvasive prenatal tests/NIPTs). *See generally* James W. Hazel, *Privacy Best Practices for Direct-to-Consumer Genetic Testing Services: Are Industry Efforts at Self-Regulation Sufficient?*, *in* Consumer Genetic Technologies 260–76 (J. Glenn Cohen, Nita A. Farahany, Henry T. Greely, Carmel Schachar eds., 2021); Future of Privacy Forum, Best Practices for Consumer Genetic Testing Services (July 31, 2018), www.geneticdataprotection.com/

wp-content/uploads/2019/05/Future-of-Privacy-Forum-Privacy-Best-Practices-July-2018 .pdf. *Cf.* NASEM, PREPARING, *supra* note 14; Byjon Heggie, *Genomics: A Revolution in Health Care? Drugs Affect People Differently and We're Increasingly Understanding Why. For Many of Us, It's Down to Our Genes*, NAT'L GEO. (Feb. 20, 2019), www.nationalgeo graphic.com/science/article/partner-content-genomics-health-care.

21 Carmel Shachar, I Glen Cohen, Nita A. Farahany, Henry T. Greely, *Introduction*, *in* CONSUMER GENETIC TECHNOLOGIES, *supra* note 20, at 1, *citing* GRAND VIEW RESEARCH, PREDICTIVE GENETIC TESTING AND CONSUMER GENETICS MARKET SIZE, SHARE & TRENDS ANALYSIS REPORT BY TEST TYPE (POPULATION SCREENING, SUSCEPTIBILITY), BY APPLICATION, BY SETTING TYPE, AND SEGMENT FORECASTS, 2019–25 (2019).

22 *See supra* notes 20–21, and accompanying text.

23 *See Chapter* 5, *supra*, at notes 215–18, and accompanying text (addressing the norm in the context of Rx drugs).

24 *See generally* NASEM, PREPARING, *supra* note 14; CBO, R&D, *supra* note 14.

25 *See Chapter* 2, *supra*, at notes 30, 170–83, 187–98, and accompanying text (US enactment and implementation of TTLP and complementary legislation). *See generally id.*

26 *See Chapter* 3, *supra*, at notes 11–15, 72, 141–43, and accompanying text (discussing PDUFA and FDAMA); *Chapter* 7, *supra*, at notes 62-71, and accompanying text (addressing TTLP regulatory responsiveness and the impact on biopharma R&D); *id.* at notes 45–47, 83, 215, 245–47, and accompanying text (addressing PDUFA, FDAMA, FDASIA, and Cures Act regulatory responsiveness to biopharma); *id.*

27 *See Chapter* 5, *supra*, at notes 404–45, and accompanying text ("The Cost and Waste Consequences of Weakening the Evidentiary-Science Base of US Medicine").

28 *See generally* SACGT, RECOMMENDATIONS, *supra* note 17. *See also Chapter* 6, *supra*, at notes 43–98, and accompanying text ("The Complexities of Personal Genome Medical Decision-Making").

29 *See generally* PAUL STARR, THE SOCIAL TRANSFORMATION OF AMERICAN MEDICINE: THE RISE OF A SOVEREIGN PROFESSION AND THE MAKING OF A VAST INDUSTRY (1984) (winner of the 1984 Pulitzer Prize for general nonfiction); NASEM, PREPARING, *supra* note 14. *See generally also Chapter* 2, *supra* (addressing the biotech and genomic accomplishments of the US' triple-threat R&D methodology). *Cf. generally* STEVEN JOHNSON. EXTRA LIFE: A SHORT HISTORY OF LIVING LONGER (2021); SIDDHARTHA MUKHERJEE, THE SONG OF THE CELL (2022).

30 *See generally* David J. Hunter, Muin, J. Khoury, Jeffrey M. Drazen, *Letting the Genome out of the Bottle – Will We Get Our Wish?*, 358 N. ENG. J. MED. 105 (Jan. 10, 2008), www .nejm.org/doi/full/10.1056/nejmp0708162; Jeffrey Shuren, Janet Woodcock, *Jeffrey Shuren, M.D., J.D., Director of the FDA's* Center *for Devices and Radiological Health, and Janet Woodcock, M.D., Director of the FDA's Center for Drug Evaluation and Research on Agency's Warning to Consumers About Genetic Tests That Claim to Predict Patients' Responses to Specific Medications* (Nov. 1, 2018), www.fda.gov/NewsEvents/Newsroom/ PressAnnouncements/ucm624794.htm. *See also Chapter* 4, *supra*, at note 137, and accompanying text (quoting FDA acknowledgement of consumer demand in its warning).

31 *See* Recode, *Full Transcript: 23andMe CEO Anne Wojcicki Answers Genetics and Privacy Questions on Too Embarrassed to Ask* (Sept. 29, 2017), www.vox.com/2017/9/29/16385320/ transcript-23andme-ceo-anne-wojcicki-genetics-privacy-health-questions-too-embarrassed-to-ask. *See also Chapter* 4, *supra*, at notes 23–24, and accompanying text (quoting Ms. Wocjicki); KEVIN DAVIES, THE $1,000 GENOME: THE REVOLUTION IN DNA SEQUENCING AND THE NEW ERA OF PERSONALIZED MEDICINE 32 (2010).

Although 23andMe's DTCGHR tests are removed from medical insurance when consumers pay out-of-pocket and the FDA has declared most of them non-clinical, the US Internal Revenue Service/IRS has determined that their cost constitutes "medical care" for tax purposes and, therefore, is tax deductible. *See* Richard Rubin, Amy Dockser Marcus, *IRS Greenlights Tax Breaks for Buyers of 23andMe Genetic*, WALL ST. J. (July 22, 2019), www.wsj.com/articles/irs-greenlights-tax-breaks-for-buyers-of-23andme-genetic-tests-11563800520 (last visited July 25, 2019).

32 23andMe was founded with governing principles that include:

- Individuals should have the right to search for their own genetic information;
- Individuals should control their own information but can share it with others if they so choose;
- The value of a person's genetic information will increase over time; and
- Privacy is paramount.

DAVIES, $1,000, *supra* note 31, at 32. For discussion of Ms. Wojcicki's driving health care and PGM influences, see *id.* at 35–37.

33 For discussion of the complexities of patient-specific clinical use of personal genome testing that meets evidentiary-science clinical standards, see generally SACGT, RECOMMENDATIONS, *supra* note 17. *See also Chapter 6, supra*, at notes 43–98, and accompanying text ("The Complexities of Personal Genome Medical Decision-Making").

34 *See generally* SACGT, RECOMMENDATIONS, *supra* note 17. *See also Chapter 6, supra*, at notes 43–98, and accompanying text ("The Complexities of Personal Genome Medical Decision-Making").

35 *See Chapter 7, supra*, at notes 233–96, and accompanying text (proposing the establishment of a comprehensive health-related personal genome test registry with a clinical use clearinghouse, and addressing implementation).

36 *See Chapter 1, supra*, at notes 68–69, 102–03, 106, 115, and accompanying text (introduction of the AMA Council on Pharmacy and Chemistry, its work, and its impact on the US medicines market and US medicine overall).

37 *See Chapter 1, supra*, at notes 35–45, and accompanying text ("US Law-Policy Recognition of Clinical Medicine as the Medical Profession's Domain"), at notes 160–83, and accompanying text ("Deference to and Reliance on the Medical Profession").

38 *Visit* National Academy of Medicine/NAM, official site (visited July 31, 2022), https://nam.edu/.

39 *See generally* Debra J.H. Mathews, Celynne A. Balatbat, Victor J. Dzau, *Governance of Emerging Technologies in Health and Medicine – Creating a New Framework*, 386 N. ENG. J. MED. 2239–42 (Apr. 17, 2022), www.nejm.org/doi/full/10.1056/NEJMms2200907. *See Chapter 7, supra*, at notes 236–38 (addressing establishment of CESTI and its charged role). *See also* Michael J. Malinowski, *The US Science and Technology "Triple Threat": A Regulatory Treatment Plan for the Nation's Addiction to Prescription Opioids*, 48 U. MEM. L. REV. 1027, 1044 (2018) ("[T]he FDA reached out to the National Academy of Medicine to draw upon evidence-based medicine to improve its' regulatory framework for opioid review, approval, and monitoring.'").

40 www.ClinicalTrials.gov is discussed in *Chapter 7, supra*, at notes 246, 248–49, and accompanying text. *See also Chapter 7, supra*, at notes 261–78, and accompanying text ("Existing Means to Implement the Proposed Comprehensive Registry").

41 *See Chapter 7, supra*, at notes 261–78, and accompanying text ("Existing Means to Implement the Proposed Comprehensive Registry and Clinical Use Clearinghouse").

42 *See id.* at notes 258–60, and accompanying text ("Public Transparency and User-Friendly Access.").
43 *See generally Chapter 6, supra.*
44 *See Chapter* 5, *supra*, at notes 404–45, and accompanying text ("The Cost and Waste Consequences of Weakening the Evidentiary-Science Base of US Medicine").
45 *See supra* notes 31–32, and accompanying text.
46 *See generally Chapter* 1, *supra*; STARR, SOCIAL TRANSFORMATION, *supra* note 29.

Index

Printed in the USA
CPSIA information can be obtained
at www.ICGtesting.com
LVHW011732240823
756138LV00003B/240